RELIGION AND GLOBALIZATION

RELIGION & Globalization

WORLD RELIGIONS IN HISTORICAL PERSPECTIVE

John L. Esposito   •   Darrell J. Fasching   •   Todd Lewis

New York   •   Oxford

OXFORD UNIVERSITY PRESS

2008

Oxford University Press Inc., publishes works that further Oxford University's
objective of excellence in research, scholarship, and education.

Oxford New York
Auckland   Cape Town   Dar es Salaam   Hong Kong   Karachi
Kuala Lumpur   Madrid   Melbourne   Mexico City   Nairobi
New Delhi   Shanghai   Taipei   Toronto
With offices in
Argentina   Austria   Brazil   Chile   Czech Republic   France   Greece
Guatemala   Hungary   Italy   Japan   Poland   Portugal   Singapore
South Korea   Switzerland   Thailand   Turkey   Ukraine   Vietnam

Published by Oxford University Press, Inc.
198 Madison Avenue, New York, New York 10016
http://www.oup.com

Oxford is a registered trademark of Oxford University Press

Library of Congress Cataloging-in-Publication Data
Esposito, John L.
  Religion & globalization : world religions in historical perspective / John L. Esposito,
Darrell J. Fasching, Todd Lewis New.
    p. cm.
  Includes bibliographical references and index.
  ISBN–13: 978–0–19–517695–7 (pbk. : alk. paper) 1. Religions. 2. Globalization—Religious
aspects. I. Title: Religion and globalization. II. Fasching, Darrell J., 1944– III. Lewis, Todd
Vernon, 1949– IV. Title.
  BL80.3.E87 2008
  200—dc22   2007032125

Printed in the United States of America on acid-free paper

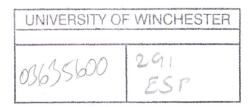

Dedicated to three scholars who inspired us to study the past in order to comprehend the future of the world's religious traditions:

Ismail and Lamya al-Faruqi (JE)
John S. Dunne (DF)
Theodore Riccardi, Jr. (TL)

CONTENTS

PREFACE

In 2002 Oxford University Press published the first edition of *World Religions Today*. Our goal was to introduce a new type of textbook on world religions, not just one that focused on the origins and classical expressions of the great world religions in their premodern "purity," but one that would help students understand the roles that the world's religions play in shaping current social and political events. Achieving this goal requires a better understanding of the role of religions in history, especially their social and political impacts and how these contributed to an emerging postmodern age of globalization.

We sought to provide chapters on the different religions that not only illuminated the origins and classical expressions of the world's religions but also placed a major emphasis on their journey through the modern era and into the postmodern era. Evaluations from professors who used the first edition of *World Religions Today* in colleges and universities across the nation indicated that we had produced a very helpful book for advanced courses on religion and politics and also on religion and globalization. However, we were told, it was too advanced for many students in introductory courses. So we returned to the drawing board and produced a thoroughly revised second edition of *World Religions Today* (2006), which has made the subject more approachable for the introductory student.

Having completed that project we responded to the suggestion of reviewers who had used the first edition of *World Religions Today*. And so we have revised and updated the original text and added three new chapters to create *Religion and Globalization* for advanced undergraduate and graduate courses in the fields of religion and politics, and religion and globalization.

Although this is a multiauthored text with each of us taking primary authorship of different chapters (John Esposito: Islam; Darrell Fasching: Judaism, Christianity, and New Religions; and Todd Lewis: Asian traditions and Primal Religions), it has truly been a collaborative project from start to finish. We have worked out our overall vision, which is articulated in the first chapter, and implemented it in the chapters on the religious traditions. Throughout the entire process we shared and commented on each other's material. Oxford colleagues and outside reviewers provided feedback at every stage.

We wish to thank Robert Miller, Executive Editor in Oxford's Higher Education Group, and Sarah Calabi and Lisa Grzan for their support in producing both *World Religions Today* and this new volume, *Religion and Globalization.*

John L. Esposito
Darrell J. Fasching
Todd Lewis

RELIGION AND GLOBALIZATION

CHAPTER ONE

INTRODUCTION

Religion and Globalization

No matter where we live today, it is more and more likely that our next-door neighbors are ethnically, politically, and, yes, even religiously diverse—coming from many parts of the globe (see Map 1.1). In an emerging global economy, most neighborhoods, work places, and schools reflect this diversity as well.

"This book opens with a city that was, symbolically, a world: it closes with a world that has become, in many practical aspects, a city."[1] These opening words of Lewis Mumford's *The City in History* are appropriate for this book, *Religion and Globalization*, as well. For in the ancient world cities were founded in sacred places that were believed to mark the center of the world. Every city saw itself in religious and mythological terms as "the cosmos writ small." From the earliest times religious visions have been cosmic in scope even when parochial in fact.

In our time the ancient vision and contemporary reality are merging. In an age of globalization, the world "in many practical aspects" has become a city. "Today it seems that almost everyone is everywhere," says Mark Jeurgensmeyer.[2] So Los Angeles is simultaneously the second largest Filipino, Iranian, and Mexican city in the world. And the Chinese city of Beijing finds itself having to deal with "dissident Chinese Muslims and Christians." Islam is now the third largest religion in North America and second largest in Europe. Homogeneous cultures sharing one religion are disappearing as one's neighbors come from various parts of the world, bringing diverse cultural and religious traditions with them. In America mosques and Buddhist and Hindu temples stand alongside Christian churches and Jewish synagogues. Today our

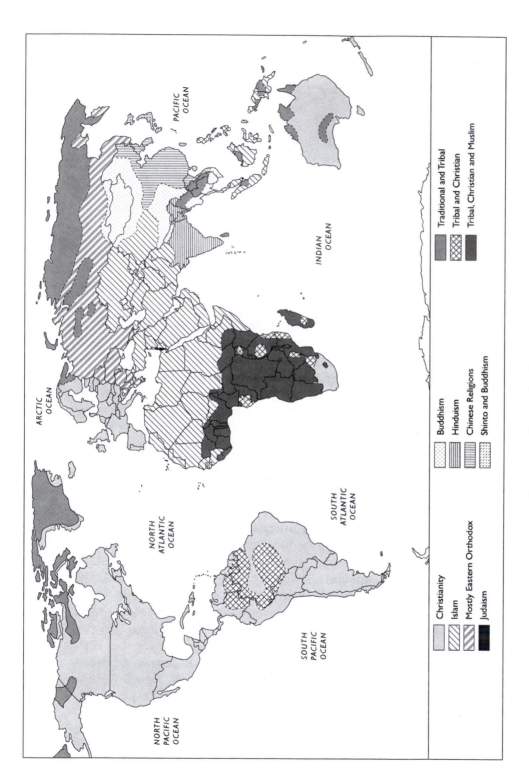

Map 1.1 Distribution of world religions today.

Legend:

Christianity
Islam
Mostly Eastern Orthodox
Judaism

Buddhism
Hinduism
Chinese Religions
Shinto and Buddhism

Traditional and Tribal
Tribal and Christian
Tribal, Christian and Muslim

ARCTIC OCEAN
PACIFIC OCEAN
INDIAN OCEAN
NORTH ATLANTIC OCEAN
SOUTH ATLANTIC OCEAN
SOUTH PACIFIC OCEAN
NORTH PACIFIC OCEAN

cities have no single sacred center but rather many centers. The center, we could say, is found everywhere, reflecting the many sacred stories and practices that diversity brings. Perhaps there is no more apt description of the postmodern world produced by globalization than "a circle whose circumference is nowhere and whose center is every where." This definition, borrowed from the Renaissance geometrician and mystic Nicholas of Cusa (c. 1400–1450 CE), who used it to describe God, is equally apt as a way of describing the diverse paths to God that comingle in the postmodern global village.

Globalization is the product of the growing interdependence of cultures through emerging global techno-economic and sociocultural networks. These networks transcend national boundaries and in the process tend to challenge previous forms of authority and identity. In a world of instant global communication and jet travel, time and space shrink and force a new awareness upon all the inhabitants of the earth. In a world integrated by global transportation, mass markets, the Internet and other such forces, human thought and action increasingly are shaped by a conscious awareness that (whether one likes it or not) one's actions are increasingly responses to global events and realities that transcend local and national frames of reference. The first cities of the ancient world, despite their grand cosmological visions, were parochial. Today this parochialism is giving way to a new world order that fulfills the dream of the ancient Stoic philosophers, who even then hoped for something more—a "cosmopolitan" world, where all are global citizens sharing a common earth.

Mass media have played an important role in bringing about this transition by generating profound alterations in human consciousness. For instance, the role of the media played a powerful role in the sixteenth century, at the beginning of the modern period, when Martin Luther was able to utilize the newly invented printing press to mass produce a German translation of the Bible credited with helping to create German national consciousness. He also used the press to mass produce pamphlets against the papacy that drew popular support and elicited protection from the German nobility, making it impossible for Rome (the papacy) to extradite him to stand trial for heresy.

Four centuries later Mohandas K. Gandhi was able to tap advances in technology that created the first international media (radio, telegraph, and the international press) to garner international support for his campaign against British colonialism as a form of Western domination. At the same time, he also used the media to promote global interdependence and religious harmony. A generation later, Osama bin Laden depends on a new international medium that travels around the globe almost instantaneously—cable television (e.g., CNN, Al-Jazeera, etc.) to promote religious and cultural disharmony, engaging in global terrorism against what he perceives as Western domination and the profanation of Islamic lands.

These illustrations of the interdependence of religions and the media suggest that globalization represents an important shift in human consciousness, one already anticipated at the end of the eighteenth century by Immanuel

Kant. In his "Idea for a Universal History from a Cosmopolitan Point of View," Kant argued that, living on a round earth, we cannot escape from each other and are forced to recognize our equality and interdependence with each other as human beings.3 Critiquing the immorality of Western colonialism, Kant called for a "league of nations" to be created to promote our common human rights and bring an end to all war. By integrating the Stoic dream of cosmopolitan citizenship with Christian millennial hopes for the coming of a new city in which all tribes of the earth would live in perpetual peace, Kant anticipated the ideals that led to the experiment with the League of Nations from 1920 to 1946 and the birth of the United Nations in 1945.

Religions have played a formative role both in promoting and in resisting the emergence of globalization. Globalization, we might imagine, began when the first human beings in tribal communities welcomed strangers and began to expand their understanding of what it means to be human to include the beliefs and practices of those from beyond the boundaries of their own community and tradition. Emerging from the misty recesses of time, as we have suggested, the earliest tribes, villages, city-states, and even empires expressed their respective understandings of their identities in cosmic-mythological terms. One's community lived at the center of the cosmic world, as a mirror image of the cosmos, *the cosmos writ small.* Such mythic visions expressed an understanding that one's way of life reflected the true sacred order of the cosmos and consequently what it means to be human and how one ought to live.

The long journey, from symbolic globalization in the ancient world to globalization in practice today, begins with the meeting of sacred cosmic orders. Such meetings lead to the discovery that the stranger's "strange ways" do not seem strange to them, for they too believe that their way of life reflects the sacred order of the cosmos. This discovery can elicit a variety of responses, such as violence (persecution and conquest of those who are understood as "delusional and in error"), syncretistic adaptation (your gods and rituals are really the same as mine but under other names), unconscious borrowing (as with prayer beads traveling from Hinduism to Buddhism to Catholic Christianity and Islam), and finally mutual transformation, such as when, for example, in the second half of the twentieth century, the Christian monk Thomas Merton and the Buddhist monk Thich Nhat Hanh each sought to adapt elements of the other's belief and practice.

Globalization, Mark Jeurgensmeyer has argued, is a process as old as religious practice itself because religions have permeable boundaries that absorb "foreign" influences as they move around the globe, carried by their peripatetic practitioners. Indeed, he identifies three forms of religious globalization: (1) the *diaspora religious patterns* of those disbursed in self-contained communities around the world, of which Judaism is the archetypal example, (2) *transnational religious patterns* found in missionary religions such as Buddhism, Christianity, and Islam, oriented to converting whole cultures, and (3) the *pattern of religious pluralism*, as modeled, for instance, in Ghandi's global movement. In this book we shall explore how all three models emerged and spread in the history of the world's religions.

As we shall see, there is an intrinsic link between globalization and postmodern forms of society. Jean-Francois Lyotard, in his book *The Postmodern Condition: A Report on Knowledge* (1984), defined postmodern society as a society characterized by the collapse of its "grand narratives" or "metanarratives."[4] Such narratives could be the religious narratives that have shaped whole civilizations (Hindu or Buddhist, Islamic or Christian civilizations, etc.) or they could be the secular grand narratives of modern "scientific" society, the great stories of evolution and the progress of history.

Metanarratives are those "grand stories," those great cosmic-mythological narratives that give each civilizational order a defining normative center and a sense of cosmic meaning. There is no substantive difference between a grand narrative and what Lyotard calls a "collapsed" or "small" narrative. It is the same narrative but its function in society is changed by pluralism. Instead of providing a normative center for public order in society as a whole, it is relativized. It now functions normatively only for a particular religious community as one among many.

In traditional societies, where the overwhelming majority of people share common religious stories and rituals, the veracity of their way of life is taken for granted. Convictions and practices, widely shared, take on a kind of self-evident authority. The intermingling of religions and cultures, brought on by globalization, however, makes the authority of all such narratives problematic. Convictions and practices that differ tend to erode confidence and require defense. The threat of relativism emerges. The diverse stories remain powerful for their individual adherents, but, in a pluralistic world, deciding which of the many narratives will be authoritative for the public order of society can readily feed conflict if modes of compromise and cooperation are not discovered.

Sociologically, relativism manifests itself as the erosion of taken-for-granted confidence in one's world view, given a pluralism of worldviews. Intellectually, relativism manifests itself as the inability to appeal to common rational premises widely shared so as to resolve disputes through reason, given that the rational premises of diverse worldviews seem to be diverse. If modes of compromise cannot be found for relativism in either form, the response will be what Nietzsche called "the will to power"—conflict and attempted conquest.

Postmodernity, therefore, is in large part defined by the "loss of a center," a normative center. Consequently, postmodern societies appear to be normless and without commonly shared meaning. Thus, under the impact of globalization, postmodern societies, like postmodern cities, present themselves as an eclectic mélange, rich in diversity but seemingly superficial, having no overarching standards.

Insofar as religions have been the main source of normative or sacred cosmic stories, the emergence of postmodernity challenges all traditional religious

worldviews, threatening to desacralize human life. In return, adherents of traditional worldviews, especially those who champion fundamentalist responses,
tend to view the postmodern world as shallow and profane, and as threatening
to those who wish to maintain the purity of past ways of life, ways that keep life
sacred. It is especially the global power of mass media and mass marketing
that promote a postmodern view of society by offering eclectic, seductive, and
(to traditionalists) hedonistic ways of life that erode the authority of the grand
stories that have kept human life sacred. As Bryan S. Turner argues in
Orientalism, Postmodernism and Globalism:

> What makes religious faith or religious commitment problematic in a
> globalized postmodern society is that everyday life has become part of a
> global system of exchange of commodities which are not easily influ-
> enced by political leaders, intellectuals or religious leaders. The corrup-
> tion of pristine faith is going to be brought about by Tina Turner and
> Coca-Cola and not by rational arguments and rational inspection of pre-
> suppositions and the understanding of Western secularism. . . . Modern
> fundamentalism is a two pronged movement to secure control within
> the global system and also to maintain a local regulation of the life-
> world.5

In interpreting religion and globalization, distinguishing between "postmodernity" and "postmodernism" is important. Postmodernity or postmodern
society is a term that describes how globalization has transformed society into
a pluralistic, multicentered reality subject to global influences that raise difficult questions about public norms and public order—questions that can easily
lead to conflict.

"Postmodernism," by contrast, is a philosophy or ideology that affirms,
among other things, that pluralism and relativism are good. They are good
because, as Lyotard argues, they undermine the totalism or totalitarian authoritarianism of both traditional and modernist societies. The unfolding conun-
drum among the world's religions in an age of globalization is whether, living
in a postmodern society, one ought to reject or embrace postmodernism. The
question is whether to reject the changes brought about by globalization and
return to one's traditional sacred way of life, as fundamentalists argue, or
embrace postmodern pluralism as good and somehow compatible with one's
sacred way of life, as some religious postmodernists argue.

In this book we focus on the diverse ways in which we humans have been
religious in the past and are religious today. Indeed, the end of the twentieth
century seems to have brought with it a period of religious resurgence, a
development that defies countless theorists who predicted that the irresistible
secularization of civilization by the forces of modern science would lead to the
disappearance of religion. Religions, it was thought, are tied to ancient premodern world views that have been replaced by a modern scientific world

view. Indeed, the clash of traditional religions with modern scientific and secular society is a major concern of this textbook. This is essential if we are to understand the interactions between religions and cultures in the world today. Thus we will begin each chapter (starting with Chapter 2) not with the origins and early history of religious communities but with examples of the encounter of each religion with the "modern" world that illustrate the tension between premodern ways of looking at the world and new ways introduced by modernity.

We describe our present time as one in transition between "modernity" and a new postmodern era that seems to be emerging as we begin the twenty-first century. To understand what is "new" about our emerging situation, we will have to understand the premodern period of each tradition and how the premodern world view of each relates and contrasts with the modern period. In particular we will have to compare the premodern period in each tradition with the changes brought about by an era that began with the rise of science after 1500 and declined after World War II, giving way to postmodernity. In surveying the great world religions we shall not be able to cover everything that could be said about them. Our selection will be governed primarily by the question: "What do we need to know about the past to understand the role of religion in the world we live in today?" To begin, we will need to understand core concepts. To that task we now turn.

UNDERSTANDING RELIGIOUS EXPERIENCE AND ITS EXPRESSIONS

The first thing we need is a working definition of the term "religion." To help explain how we are using the term, we need to return to the first century in Rome. Why are we interested in that time and place? Because the word "religion" has its roots in the language of the Romans, understanding how the Romans used that term should help us understand our topic. Imagine yourself now walking down a street in Rome in the first century. When you approach a small group of Romans on a street corner and you ask them: "What religion are you?" they look at you strangely as if you are speaking a foreign language (which of course you are—Latin). They understand the individual words used but the phrasing is awkward. People don't normally use the words the way you are using them. Some give you blank stares, while others just look puzzled. Frustrated, you try rephrasing your question and ask: "Are you religious?" Suddenly their faces light up and they smile and say, "Of course, isn't everyone?"

The first question assumes that religion is a noun describing distinct social bodies in the world, such that you can be a member of one only if you are not a member of another. So the question seeks to find out to which one you belong. This way of understanding religion naturally arises among monotheists, for monotheism asks individuals to choose one god and exclude all others.

However, such an exclusiveness is foreign to antiquity and is not appropriate for understanding religious traditions among many Africans and Asians, for example.

When you rephrased the question, you shifted from treating "religion" as a noun, describing something you join, to treating it as an adjective, describing an attitude toward the human condition—a way of seeing, acting, and experiencing all things. In most times and places throughout history, religion and culture were like two sides of the same coin. Therefore people did not think of what they did as "a religion"—a separate reality one had to choose over and against another. Today, in Japan for instance, it is possible to follow Buddhism, Daoism, Confucianism, and Shintoism at the same time. This seems odd from the monotheistic perspective of Western religion where one can be, for instance, either a Muslim or a Jew but not both at the same time. And yet, paradoxically, both Jews and Muslims claim to worship the same God.

In first-century Rome, with very few exceptions, people didn't belong to a religion in any exclusive sense. They were, however, religious. Our first-century respondents would probably continue their answer to your question something like this: "Am I religious? Of course I am. Isn't everyone? It's simply a matter of common sense. I respect all those powers of nature that govern my destiny. Therefore I worship all the gods and goddesses. It would be stupid not to. If I am going to war I want the god of war on my side. So I perform the correct ritual sacrifices before going into battle. And needless to say if I am planting my crops I certainly want to insure that the goddess of fertility and the gods of the wind and rain are on my side. I am not a complete idiot. Anything else would be stupid."

What does this tell us? For the ancient Romans, and nearly all other human beings in all places and all times throughout history, religion has been about power and the meaning of power for human destiny. Although its exact root is uncertain, the word "religion" is probably derived from the Latin *religare*, which literally means "to tie or bind" and the root *ligere* which has the connotation of "acting with care." It expresses our sense of being "tied and bound" by relations of obligation to whatever powers we believe govern our destiny—whether these powers be natural or supernatural, personal or impersonal, one or many. Ancient peoples everywhere believed that the powers governing their destiny were the forces of nature. Why? Because nature was experienced as that awesome collection of powers that surround and, at times, overwhelm human beings: providing them with life and all the good things of life (food, clothing, shelter, etc.) on the one hand but, on the other hand, turning on them and destroying them quite capriciously through earthquakes, storms, floods, and so on. Therefore the forces of nature evoke in human beings the ambivalent feelings of fascination and dread. Rudolf Otto, the great twentieth-century pioneer of comparative religions, argued that the presence of these two ambivalent emotions is a sure sign that one is in the presence of the sacred. They are a defining mark of religious experience across cultures. They are the emotions that are elicited by the uncanny experience of being in the presence of that power or powers one believes have the ability to determine whether one lives or dies, and beyond that how well one lives.

Religion as a form of human experience and behavior, therefore, is not just about purely "spiritual" things. Religion is not just about gods or God. People's religiousness is as diverse as the forms of power they believe govern their destiny, whether it be the gods as forces of nature, or wealth, or political power, or the forces of history. Religious attitudes in the modern world can be discerned in what many people would consider purely secular and very "unspiritual" attitudes and behaviors in relation to power. Hence, whatever powers they believe govern their destiny will elicit a religious response from them and inspire them to wish "to tie or bind" themselves to these powers in relations of ritual obligation, so that they act with respect and care toward them and can be sure these powers will be on their side. How do they know what their obligations to these powers are? Throughout history this knowledge has been communicated through myth and ritual.

Myth and Ritual

Our word "myth" comes from the Greek *mythos* which means "story." Myth, we could say, is a symbolic story about the origins and destiny of human beings and their world; myth relates human beings to whatever powers they believe ultimately govern their destiny and explains to them what these powers expect of them. Unlike the contemporary English use of "myth" to indicate something untrue or misunderstood, from within every religious tradition "myth" is what conveys the essential truths of life as conveyed in grand stories of origin and destiny rather than abstract theoretical and scientific theories. The world's major religions have preserved these accounts in the most durable material of the times, first on stone, parchment, and tree bark, later on paper, and today on CD-ROM disks.

Ritual actions connect the individual and the community to the sacred reality. Such actions often involve the symbolic reenactment of the stories that are passed on from one generation to the next. Myth and ritual are closely tied to the major festivals or holy days of a religious tradition. By celebrating a cycle of festivals spread throughout the year, people come to dwell in the stories that tell them who they are, where they came from, and where they are going. For example, Passover is one of the most important holy days in Judaism. At Passover, Jewish families gather for a meal at which they hear the retold story of the Exodus, the liberation of the Jews from slavery in Egypt. As the story is retold, participants eat certain foods to remind themselves of what was important in the past. The Passover Seder is not a literal reenactment of the Exodus but a symbolic reenactment. Nevertheless, this symbolic reenactment is experienced as having the power to make one an actual participant in the original event. The distance between past and present is felt to dissolve and the events of the Exodus are "happening now." Through participation in the Passover

Seder, Jews experience who they are—a chosen people, called by the God of all creation to live justly and be a light (that is, example) to the nations. This celebration reminds Jews that God acts in history and will one day overcome all suffering and death. In this way each Jew knows that his or her life is not trivial. On the contrary, each life has cosmic significance, helping to bring about the fulfillment of all things. The myth and ritual thus perform a religious function—that is, they "tie or bind" the life of the individual into a great cosmic drama, serving the highest power that gives life meaning and purpose. What we said of Judaism is also true of the myths and rituals of all religions.

Naturally the leaders of religious communities over the many generations have sought to make myth and ritual, world view and ethos, belief and practice, idea and emotion, mutually reinforcing. Yet some of the great schisms within the faiths of the world have been based more on practice than on belief. Sometimes it is difficult to discern which comes first—the myth or the ritual. We should not assume that rituals communicate only ideas or beliefs. Religions are not confined merely to doctrines regarding the sacred but include many *careful acts* that, in their own right, *tie and bind* people to each other and to cosmic meaning. Being religious thus entails taking decisive action at times, abstaining from certain acts at others—offering, for instance, precious gifts to supernatural beings, making pilgrimages to sacred places, or following a discipline of spiritual practices (such as meditation). For devout believers of many faiths, acting in the prescribed manner, called *orthopraxy*, is more important than *orthodoxy*—conforming to the often intricate doctrines set forth in texts and formulated by scholars. A Muslim performing the five daily prayers, a Buddhist or Hindu visiting a temple to offer flowers on the full moon day, a Chinese person cleaning the family's ancestral grave during the spring festival, or a Christian being baptized—all of these acts are as central to "being religious" as is adopting orthodox beliefs.

Carefully choreographed religious rituals recall important events in the history of each faith: the "Night Journey" of the Prophet Muhammad, the enlightenment of the Buddha, the birthday of Krishna. Other rituals have been designed to have the faithful donate gifts to the supernatural beings who can profoundly affect their lives. Still other rituals require mutilation of the body (circumcision, tattoos, burn marks) to set the believers off from nonbelievers, fostering group solidarity. The consumption of certain foods as part of some rituals suggests that the believer can acquire the "same essence" as the divine through ingestion, as in the Christian communion, Hindu pûjâ, or tribal eating of a totemic animal to affirm common identity.

The great annual festivals in the world's religions give devotees a break from the profane time of normal working life, times for special rituals, for fasts or feasting, periods of rest and reflection on life's most fundamental truths. These events also reinforce life's most important ties with family and fellow devotees. The need to orchestrate such crucial religious actions also leads followers to create institutions that occupy central places in their societies.

Pivotal figures of each world religion are the priests who mediate between the deity and the community, with each tradition that relies on them designating specific qualities (e.g., purity of birth, intense training, possession by the god) that legitimate the members of the priesthood. The world's oldest religious specialist is the shaman, a man or woman who goes into a trance to communicate with supernatural beings (gods, demons, ghosts). Practitioners of this art (also called "mediums" or "oracles") have been found depicted on cave walls across Eurasia from the Neolithic period twenty-five thousand years ago, and shamans still exist in many parts of the world, not only among the remaining tribal peoples but also even where populations have "converted" to one of the great world religions.

Since all the world religions have relied on written records, there have always been scholars who have learned to write and read and thereby interpret the sacred texts, translating them for the great majority of rank-and-file followers, most of whom, until the modern era, were illiterate. Among this group were those who specialized in being spiritual teachers (e.g., the Hindu guru, the Jewish rabbi, the Sufi Muslim shaykh). Although we can point to interesting comparative patterns among religious rituals and between those who serve as "technicians of the sacred," it is also true to say that each tradition can be known by its own unique set of religious practitioners and institutions. To understand the great world religions thus entails not only knowing what believers believe but also how they are expected to act, what rituals are essential, what distinctive institutions have supported the community and in what unique architectural settings (mosque, church, synagogue) individuals practice meditation, pray, venerate their ancestors, and praise or please their gods (or God).

Seeing every "religion" as equally involving belief and practice can make us aware that all of the fundamental changes introduced with the modern era are grounded in a social context and carried forward through institutions. Reformers and traditionalists, "fundamentalists" and "modernists" (and "postmodernists" too) have all survived through the institutions that made their distinctive religious and social practices possible and united people to express and propagate their respective beliefs.

Morality

In most religious traditions, ritual and morality have been closely intertwined. "Right" is often defined by "Rite"—the ritual patterns of behavior that keep life sacred. Morality is an inherent dimension of religious experience, for religion is not only about sacred powers but also about the sacred way of life they require and make possible.

The religious experience of sacredness—what matters most to a given community—provides the ground for the moral experience of the virtuous life. Whatever is sacred provides a yardstick for measuring rightness of human actions. The blueprint for the parameters of right action is expressed in myth and ritual. For Muslims, the teachings of the Quran (Islam's sacred book) and *Hadith* (stories or traditions about the Prophet Muhammad) exemplify the moral way of life that God expects of human beings. These requirements will be communicated from one generation to the next through the ritual reenactment and recitation of Islam's sacred stories of origin and destiny.

This is just one example of how a religious tradition shapes morality. It is important to recognize that even the most secular and seemingly nonreligious morality, insofar as it treats anything as sacred, can be understood as having a religious dimension. In the former Soviet Union, May Day was a great national festival celebrating the Russian revolution and the founding of a secular state that was atheistic. At this celebration, the values of the way of life in the USSR were held up as sacred—worth living for and worth dying for. Although atheistic, this festival served a profound religious purpose: it told Soviet citizens that their individual lives were important, a part of the great cosmic and historical drama that would inevitably lead to a pure and egalitarian communist society. Once we realize that religion is about what people hold sacred and the way of life that is required, then it makes sense to say that all religion requires morality and every morality (no matter how secular it appears) is grounded in religious experience, namely in the experience of what matters most (i.e., what is held sacred) to a given community. Such an observation leaves open the philosophical question as to what degree the sacred morality of a tradition is truly ethical. For ethics, as Socrates taught, is the questioning of our sacred moralities, asking whether what people customarily say is good or virtuous really is good or virtuous.

Thus, we can see that myth and ritual not only tie and bind individuals to whatever power(s) they believe govern their destiny but also tie and bind each person to others in a community of identity and to the cosmos in which they live. This is accomplished through a complex of stories and ritual obligations that express a morality or sacred way of life.

Religious Language

One of the most challenging tasks facing anyone trying to understand the diversity of religious experience is to grasp the nature of religious language. To understand religious language literally will cause you to misunderstand it. Religious language is inherently symbolic. For example, in Western religious experience, especially in the biblical tradition of the Psalms, people often say things such as "God is my shepherd" or "God is my rock." We know this is not meant literally. God is literally neither a rock nor a shepherd. When we speak like this we are speaking metaphorically. A metaphor uses things that are more familiar to help us understand what is less familiar. Shepherds and rocks we know something about, God is a little more mysterious. So we use the familiar to help us understand the mysterious. A person who says "God is our shepherd" simply means that God is like a shepherd, in the sense that God watches over and cares for persons in the same way that a shepherd does his sheep.

Similarly, "God is our rock" simply means that God is a reality as firm, solid, real, and dependable as a rock—a reality that can always be relied upon.

Where do these metaphors and symbolic expressions come from? To answer this question requires a little sympathetic imagination. Suppose that it is a beautiful warm summer evening, the sky is clear, and millions of stars are shining brightly. The evening is so breathtaking that you decide to go for a walk in the rolling hills just outside the city. While you are on this walk you are suddenly overcome by an experience so overwhelming that it cannot be expressed in words. After a short time, which seems like an eternity, you return to your normal consciousness and wander back to the city, where you run into some friends at the local cafe. You order a cola and then you say to them: "You will never guess what happened to me tonight. I had the most incredible experience, so incredible it defies description." Well, as you can imagine, the very first question you will be asked is: "What was it like?" As soon as that question is asked, we have entered the realm of metaphor and symbolic language.

What your friends are asking you to do is to describe what you have just said is indescribable by drawing analogies to things with which they are already familiar. So you might say that it was like being in the presence of a shepherd who really cares for his flock. At least you might say that if you and your friends were nomads familiar with raising sheep. Once the people of ancient Israel, for example, stopped being nomads and settled into a fixed territory under the rule of a king, they started speaking of God as a king who protects his subjects. Today some people seem unsure how to speak of God. Many women point out that most images of God have been male. Some seek to shock their hearers into an awareness of the metaphorical nature of religious language by referring to God as "our Mother."

Nor are religious experiences limited to theistic language. For example, Theravada Buddhists in ancient India refused to use the word *Brahman* (a Hindu word roughly equivalent to the English word "God") to describe their religious experiences. Instead they spoke of "emptiness" and "the void" and the inadequacy of all spoken metaphors to explain their goal, the transcendent experience of *nirvana*. And yet they too used metaphors to try to help people understand what they had experienced as "the blissful," as "having suchness," or as "true awakening." In fact, the word "God," which is so central to Western religious experience, is just one of a class of diverse terms used in different religions and cultures across the world to express that which is ultimate in value and meaning for them. This class of terms includes not only the God of Western theism but also the impersonal Brahman of Hinduism, the transpersonal nirvana of Buddhism, and the impersonal power of the *Dao* at work in all things that is central to Chinese religions. At the same time one can find some parallels to Western monotheism in Asia, too: T'ien, the Lord of Heaven, in China; incarnations of Brahman such as Shiva or Krishna in devotional schools of Hinduism; and the cosmic Buddhas and bodhisattvas to which Mahâyâna Buddhists pray.

All these expressions for what is truly ultimate and meaningful may in fact refer to different forms of religious experience—or perhaps different people use language unique to their own cultures and times to point to what may ultimately be the same reality. Here lies the challenge, mystery, and fascination of studying the religions of the world: do differences in religious terminology reflect experiences of different realities, or are they different expressions of the same reality? Because religious metaphors come out of particular cultural times and places and because they are symbolic forms of expression, it is necessary to put ourselves, at least imaginatively, in the time and place of their origins to begin to understand the religious languages and messages of different religious traditions.

Religious language, as symbolic language, can take one of two forms: the way of analogy and the way of negation. The examples just used (e.g., "God is my shepherd," "God is my rock") were examples of the way of analogy (*via analogia*). We used something familiar to create an analogy to something less familiar. However, there is another form of religious language, the way of negation (*via negativa*). This way of speaking religiously proceeds not by asserting what God or ultimate reality is (or, is like) but by saying what it is not. This approach is very typical of the mystical traditions. The mystic declares that God is "nothing," God is beyond (i.e., transcends) or is different from anything in our material universe and experience. God is not this thing and not that thing, God is in fact no "thing" at all. God is beyond all finite things and hence is no-thing. In general, Western theism has emphasized the way of analogy by saying God is like humans, able to "know "and to "love," but in a superior fashion. Thus, God is described as all-knowing, all-loving, or all-powerful. By contrast, Buddhism, of all the religions, has emphasized most strongly the way of negation, insisting that what is most valuable cannot be either named or imaged. Yet both ways are found in all traditions. Some Jewish, Christian, and Muslim mystics have referred to God as a "Nothingness," even as some Hindus have referred to the ultimate reality as a cosmic person (*purusha*) rather than an impersonal power (Brahman). Moreover, we should note that these two ways are not really in conflict, for the way of analogy includes the way of negation within it. That is, every time we say God is *like* some thing, we are at the same time saying God is *not* literally that thing. Every analogy implies a negation.

Our discussion of religious language should help us to appreciate just how confusing it can be to study and compare various religious traditions. Just as religious communities and religious traditions from different parts of the world use different metaphors and symbols, they also mix the way of analogy and the way of negation in varying degrees. Therefore, it is possible that two different traditions may sometimes talk about the same human experience in two different ways that seem to be in total contradiction with each other. For example, it may seem that a Jewish theist and a Theravada Buddhist hold diametrically opposed religious beliefs. For Jews believe in a personal God and

Theravada Buddhists do not. Yet, when we look more closely at Jewish beliefs we discover that Jews believe that God can neither be named nor imaged, even as Theravada Buddhists believe that ultimate truth is beyond all names and images. And yet, for both, experiencing the nameless is said to make one more human or compassionate, not less.

Perhaps theistic and nontheistic experiences are really not that far apart. However, it is also possible that they are truly different. To pursue this great human question, we must begin by withholding judgment and simply try to understand how stories and rituals shape people's lives—their views, values, and behavior. Perhaps the real measure of comparison should be how people live their lives rather than the apparently diverse images and concepts they hold. If both Jews and Buddhists, for example, are led by their religious experiences and beliefs to express compassion for those who suffer or are in need, then perhaps there is more similarity than difference between them.

THE GREAT RELIGIOUS STORIES OF THE WORLD

Since the beginning of historical time people have told stories. We human beings are not just storytellers, we are "storydwellers." We live in our stories and see and understand the world through them. Even our understanding of what is good and evil, right and wrong, is shaped by the kind of story we see ourselves in and the role we see ourselves playing in that story. Although religious stories need not only be about gods and other spiritual beings, most of the earliest stories that have shaped human religious life have been.

While specific religious stories are indeed unique and diverse, we can group religious stories into four main types, each of which presents a symbolic story of the origins and destiny of human beings and the challenges they face in striving to realize their sacred destiny. These four main types of sacred story are: the myths of nature, the myths of harmony, the myths of liberation, and the myths of history.

The Myths of Nature

If one goes back far enough into the history of any society, the earliest religious stories you will find everywhere are versions of the myths of nature. These are stories about the forces of nature that govern human destiny, which portray them as either personal forces (gods, spirits, and ancestors) or impersonal magical forces (what anthropologists call "mana" religions). Such religions tend to see time as cyclical. Time always returns to its origins as sure as winter and death are followed by spring and new life, starting the cycle of seasons all over again. Myth and ritual are the means to erase the distance between "now" and the time of origins "in the beginning" when the gods and ancestors first created the world fresh and new. In such stories the problem of life is time. Time is the enemy. Time brings decay. It brings old age, sickness, and death. The ideal of life is to return to the newness of life at the beginning of creation before time began. Hence a return to the beginning renews the earth, erasing time and making all things new. The means for bringing about this return is the recitation of myths and the performance of rituals reenacting the stories of creation. In these societies, it is the shaman who masters these and who makes trance journeys to bargain with ancestral spirits and restore harmony between human community and the forces of nature. Hunter-gatherer stories emphasize the fertility of the earth, the need for the ritual renewal of life in harmony with the seasons, and the eternal place of the tribe in the cosmic order.

Few groups survive in the contemporary world who have maintained such primal traditions. Between such forms of religion found in ancient cultures and the great world religions lies an important cultural and societal transition—the transition from tribal hunting and gathering cultures to complex urban life sustained by agriculture. Out of this transition emerged the great world religions, communicated through three new types of stories.

The Great Transition: From Tribal Life to Urban Life and the Emergence of World Religions

From about 8000 BCE the domestication of plants and animals made village life possible. Dating from approximately 3000 BCE, this agricultural skill allowed the development of cities, and this brought about a great transformation in human experience. Urban life drew human beings together out of different tribal cultures, an important step in the history of globalization. In the tribe everyone lived in close harmony with the rhythms of nature, in extended families or clans that shared a common set of stories and rituals. Now in the cities human beings came together from different tribes, bringing with them different stories, different rituals, and different family identities.

Urban life also brought with it the specialization of labor. Whereas in tribal societies everyone shared the same tasks of hunting and gathering, in the cities the agricultural surplus created by the peasant farmers made it possible for others to engage in diverse occupations such as carpentry, blacksmithing, and record-keeping. Society became more complex and differentiated into classes (e.g., peasants, craftsmen, noblemen, priests, etc.). Also, whereas in cultures that lack a written language knowledge is limited to the simple formulaic patterns of thought that people can hold in their memory, the emergence of writing in the new urban centers made possible the storage and retrieval of information in great detail. All of this fundamentally transformed human identity. In the tribe, identity was collective because everybody shared the same stories and actions. The cities, by contrast, were communities of strangers. People did not share a collective consciousness. Tribal persons were confronted with differences that forced them to individuate their identities. Urban life enhanced awareness of how one person differs from another.

The loss of tribal collective life and the emergence of large, impersonal, and often brutal urban city-states in Egypt, India, China, and Mesopotamia was like a change from paradise to a world of suffering and cruelty. Life in these new city-states, ruled by absolute monarchs who were either considered gods or representatives of the gods, and where every person was a stranger to the other, led to a threefold crisis of mortality, morality, and meaning. In the tribe identity was collective. The tribe was experienced as eternal; it never dies. Individual death was not so much a rupture or removal as it was a change of position in the community. The dead did not disappear, never to be heard from again, but took their place among the sacred ancestors who were believed to continue to dwell with the living in a single community. Under the impact of urban individuation, however, persons began to think of themselves as individuals, and death suddenly emerged as a personal problem even as life seemed more cruel and uncertain. With the development of individual self-awareness, death presented people with a new and unsettling problem—the loss of self.

Urban individuation also created the new problems of law and morality. In the tribe the right thing to do was prescribed by ritual, and everyone shared the same rituals. In the cities people from a variety of mythic and ritual traditions lived together as individualistic strangers, each looking out for his or her own good, if necessary at the expense of others. Thus in the cities law emerged to set the minimum order necessary to sustain human life, and a need for ethics emerged to raise up the highest ideals of what human life could be. In the cities, once human identity was individuated, individuals experienced themselves as living in a world without morality, the pawns of "divine kings" who ruled arbitrarily and waged wars of conquest at their expense. Such a situation evoked a crisis of meaning. Can life really have any meaning if it is filled with injustice and ends in death? These are the great questions that are asked by the Epic of Gilgamesh in the Ancient Near East at the beginning of the Urban period (c. 3000–1500 BCE)—an epic that expresses the anguish of the new urban individual.

It is to answer these questions that the great world religions emerged. Once city dwellers were individuated in their identities, the old tribal answers to the problems of mortality, morality, and meaning no longer worked. Individuation is a kind of loss of innocence. Once people became individuals they could not deliberately return to a collective sense of identity. The only possible answer was to move forward and discover deeper wells of religious experience that could provide a new sense of human identity. This new identity had to resolve the new urban problems of mortality, morality, and meaning, and do so in a way that transcended local tribal and city identity so as to account for the common humanity of diverse peoples. That is the challenge the great world religions faced as they emerged in the three great centers of civilization in the ancient world—China, India, the Middle East. Between 1000 BCE and 1000 CE all the great world religions developed their classical expressions, dividing much of the world among them (see Map 1.2).

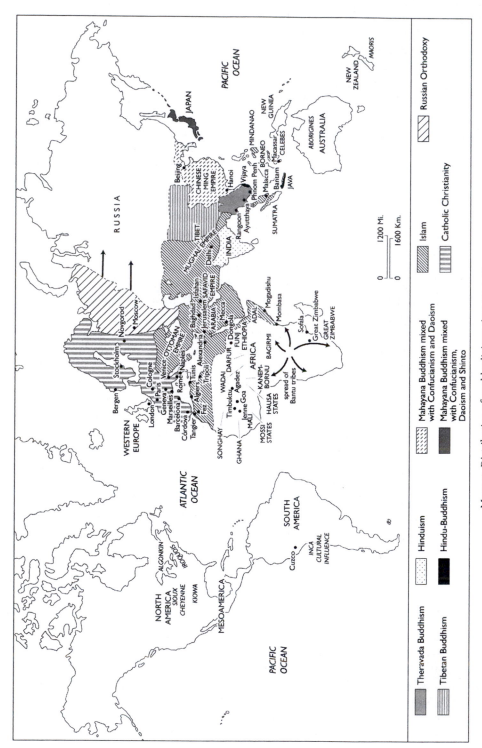

Map 1.2 Distribution of world religions circa 1500 CE.

Legend:

- Theravada Buddhism
- Tibetan Buddhism
- Hinduism
- Hindu-Buddhism
- Mahayana Buddhism mixed with Confucianism and Daoism
- Mahayana Buddhism mixed with Confucianism, Daoism and Shinto
- Islam
- Catholic Christianity
- Russian Orthodoxy

Map labels:

RUSSIA

PACIFIC OCEAN

JAPAN

CHINESE MING EMPIRE

Beijing

TIBET

MUGHAL EMPIRE

INDIA

Delhi

Hanoi

Vijaya

Phnom Penh

Ayutthaya

Rangoon

MINDANAO

BORNEO

NEW GUINEA

Malacca

Macassar

CELEBES

Bantam

JAVA

SUMATRA

AUSTRALIA

ABORIGINES

NEW ZEALAND

MAORIS

Novgorod

Moscow

Stockholm

Bergen

WESTERN EUROPE

London

Cologne

Paris

Geneva

Venice

Marseilles

Barcelona

Córdoba

Tanger

Fez

Algiers

Tunis

Rome

Naples

Tripoli

OTTOMAN EMPIRE

Alexandria

Jerusalem

Baghdad

Isfahan

SAFAVID EMPIRE

Mecca

ARABIA

Mogadishu

Mombasa

ADAL

ETHIOPIA

Dongola

FUNJ

DARFUR

WADAI

KANEM-BORNU

BAGIRMI

Agadez

Timbuktu

Jenne

Gao

SONGHAY

GHANA

MALI

MOSSI STATES

HAUSA STATES

AFRICA

Sofala

Great Zimbabwe

GREAT ZIMBABWE

spread of Bantu tribes

ATLANTIC OCEAN

NORTH AMERICA

ALGONKIN

IROQUOIS

SIOUX

CHEYENNE

KIOWA

MESOAMERICA

SOUTH AMERICA

INCA CULTURAL INFLUENCE

Cuzco

PACIFIC OCEAN

Scale:

0 _____ 1200 Mi.

0 _____ 1600 Km.

The world religions emerged in conjunction with the formation of great empires that united peoples of various tribes and city-states into larger political unities. Such new political orders created a need for a new understanding of what it means to be human. They redefined the meaning of being human in terms beyond the boundaries of the tribe and the city-state, seeing a higher unity to reality beyond the many local gods and spirits. In China, all humans were said to share in common the *Dao* (the hidden power of harmony that governs the universe); in India, for Hindus, it was the reality of *Brahman* (the universal, impersonal, eternal spirit that is the source of all things), and for Buddhists, the *Buddha nature* (understood as the interdependent becoming of all things); in the Middle East it was that all were children of the *one God* (the source and creator of all things). These answers were serviceable until globalization occurred in the modern and postmodern periods.

China and the Myths of Harmony

In China there emerged the great cosmic story of the Dao (sometimes rendered Tao). One's true self is knowable only in relation to the universal Dao, which all beings share. It is the hidden harmony of the universe at work in all the forces of nature. All of creation works via the opposites of *yin* and *yang*, of dark and light, of earth and heaven, of female and male. Yin and Yang are never polar opposites but rather each flows into the other with no absolute division, the way day flows into night and night into day, so that nothing is ever the total opposite of anything else. There is always a little day in every night, a little male in every female (and vice versa). The ideal of life then is balance and harmony. The great problem of existence is the disharmony that occurs when the elements of society and /or the universe are out of balance. To restore balance, the two different religions of Daoism and Confucianism that emerged in China sought to bring harmony between heaven and earth, self and society. These two traditions offered different means to overcome the problem and realize the ideal. Daoist sages urged humans to seek harmony with the rhythms of nature through cultivating simplicity through *wu-wei* (i.e., the art of "not doing" or "not interfering" with the natural flow of life) first, and out of that harmony the harmony of society would flow spontaneously. Confucian sages urged humans to seek to establish harmony in society through the practice of *li* (i.e., ritual observance of obligations attached to one's station in society), and when social harmony is achieved, people will spontaneously be in harmony with the rhythms of the universe.

India and the Myths of Liberation

In India, like China, life was seen through the metaphors of natural cycles and rhythms of nature, but in India the rhythms were to be escaped from rather than affirmed. That is, human lives were thought to recapitulate the seasons and cycles of nature in an endless round of death and rebirth. Life was seen as suffering, not because there is nothing good about life but because no matter how good it is, it always ends in old age, sickness, and death. The problem of life is that we humans are caught in an endless cycle of suffering, death, and rebirth because of ignorance of our true identity. The goal of religion is to destroy the illusions fostered by our selfish desires, for only when these are mastered can humans be freed from the wheel of death and rebirth (samsara). In that moment of liberation or enlightenment we will come to realize the ultimate reality and find union with it. For Hindus, the true self (*atman*) is merged with the eternal Brahman in either the personal or impersonal form. For Buddhism it is the imminent possibility of removing selfish attachments and realizing enlightenment (*sambodhi*) within the suffering and impermanence of life, achieving the indescribable and transpersonal reality called nirvana. Hinduism and Buddhism, as two versions of the myth of liberation, offer a variety of means for achieving this liberation, including meditation, the selfless performance of one's duties, spiritual knowledge and insight, and selfless love or devotion toward a divine incarnation of the ultimate truth or reality.

The Middle East and the Myths of History

The myths of nature, of harmony, and of liberation use the human experience of the rhythms and cycles of nature as the basis for religious metaphors and symbolic language expressed in their sacred stories. In the myths of history, by contrast, it is not nature but history that comprises the realm of human experience from which the metaphors for religious experience are primarily drawn. While all religions communicate their traditions by telling stories, only the religions of the Middle East, beginning with Judaism, make "story" itself the central metaphor of religious expression. Unlike the rhythms of nature that are eternally cyclical, stories have a beginning and an end. Ancient Judaism conceived of the cosmos as a great unfolding story told by a great divine storyteller (God): in the beginning God spoke, the world was created, and the story began. The story is the story of the God who acts in time and leads his people through time toward a final fulfillment. The story begins with an initial harmony between God and humans, proceeds through a long period in which that harmony is disrupted by human idolatry and selfishness or sin, and looks toward a hopeful end of time in the future when all injustice, suffering, and death will be overcome and those wronged will be compensated—a time when the dead shall be raised and the whole of creation transformed.

There emerged three versions of this story in the Middle East—first the Judaic, then the Christian, and finally the Islamic. For each of these, we all are human by virtue of being children of the one God who created all things. All three traditions trace themselves back to the Patriarch Abraham, whom each considers to be the true model of faith and to Adam and Eve as the first human beings. In all three, the problem of life is viewed as "sin"—a combination of idolatry and human selfishness that leads to injustice. The ideal goal of life is the restoration of human wills to harmony with the will of God so that peace and justice reign and death is overcome. The means for bringing this about vary but include obedience to the will of God, but also dialog and debate with God in the case of Judaism, the acceptance of divine grace or aid and the incarnation of God in the case of Christianity, and submission to the will of God in Islam. Thus, although the story of the cosmos has many ups and downs, many trials and tragedies, it is seen as the story of a journey that is headed for a happy ending. Unlike in the myths of nature, harmony, and liberation, in the myths of history time is not the enemy but rather the vehicle for encountering the ultimate reality, which is God. The goal is not to escape time by returning to the beginning through myth and ritual, nor rising above time in mystical ecstasy, but of meeting God in time and making a journey with God through time. Time is promising, and the future ultimately hopeful.

Conclusion

Each of the great narrative traditions sought to answer the problem of mortality by going beyond the answer of collective eternal identity provided by tribal religions. In China and India the answer was essentially mystical: all selves find their true identity through inner transformation, achieving union or harmony with the same ultimate reality (whether Brahman or the Dao) or in the case of Buddhism, experiencing the same ultimate destiny of nirvana. In the Middle East, the answer was not primarily mystical but apocalyptic—the end of time, which leads to the final resurrection of the dead.

Each of these traditions answers the problem of morality as well by helping the individual get beyond self-centeredness and grasp the essential unity and interdependence of all human beings. And each sought to provide human life with meaning by seeing individuals and communities as participating in a great cosmic story that gives drama and purpose to human life. These were stories that were not interrupted and made absurd by death but rather reveal to individuals a way to transcend death.

Finally, it is necessary to make a qualifying statement about the unity and diversity of religions. When we stand back at a great distance we can group religions under the four types of myth or story—those of nature, harmony, liberation, and history. As we get closer we discover that each of these stories has diverse versions that express the differences in different doctrines and practices. And as we draw even closer to any one of these religions we will discover even more diversity. Those familiar with Christianity need only recall how many different kinds of Christianity there are. There is such a great difference between a simple Quaker service, an enthusiastic Southern Baptist service, and a formal high-church Episcopalian service that it is hard to believe they are all examples of the same religion. This range of diversity is true of every religious tradition. So by discovering some forms of unity in the diversity of religions we must not be fooled into thinking that we have gotten rid of the diversity. The diversity is as important as the unity, and no form of human religiousness can be understood unless we take both into account. As we will see, part of the postmodern predicament for every faith is to make sense of this very fact of the enduring, seeming irreducible, multiplicity of paths by which humanity seeks ultimate meaning, value, and salvation.

In the chapters to come we will be examining how human beings struggle to continue the religiousness of their ancestors in a new and radically different modern world. We will be examining how Western civilization gave birth to modernity and through its colonial expansion spread its religious and cultural influence (politics, economics, etc.) around the world, disrupting the premodern religious worlds it encountered. By colonialism we mean the political, social, cultural, and economic domination of one society by another. Colonialism is as old as civilization and is part of the story of virtually all religions and civilizations, East and West. But modern Western colonialism came closest to achieving global dominion. With this, Christianity became the first faith to spread globally, forcing every religion to reckon with its beliefs, practices, and its critiques of non-Christians. The Protestant criticisms of Catholicism were particularly influential on Hindu and Buddhist reformers. We will see how this colonialism, in turn, provoked a postcolonial reaction that has tended to divide those within each religious and cultural tradition into fundamentalists, who reject the failures of modernity and want to go back to what they perceive as the purity of an "authentic" social/political order governed by God's law, and those who, while rejecting the dominance of Western modernity, seek to go forward into a new postmodern situation that affirms both global diversity and change in their religious tradition. Still others, perhaps most, as we shall see, seek to find a middle ground between these extremes by trying to selectively choose to include some aspects of modernity while rejecting others. At the fundamentalist end of the spectrum, a few purist religious movements seek to reject everything modern but most accept those aspects they believe do not threaten the purity of their religious tradition. Thus many fundamentalists embrace modern technology while rejecting those aspects of science (especially the social sciences) that would call into question their religious worldview. At the modernist end of the spectrum, a few movements reject everything in their religious tradition that is not consistent with their understanding of the "modern world view" but most pick and choose, arguing that some parts of the religious tradition must change while some must not. What is distinctive about the modernist end of the spectrum is the view that the human understanding of religious truth and practice is subject to historical change and development, a notion that the fundamentalist end of the spectrum rejects.

Beginning with Chapter 2 you can expect each chapter to address these issues using the following format:

- Overview
- Encounter with Modernity

- Premodern
- Modern
- Postmodern
- Conclusion

The *Overview* that begins each chapter will introduce you to the basic world view and statistics concerning the religious tradition under discussion. The following section, *Encounter with Modernity*, describes a particular moment in which the premodern religious tradition clashed with the modern world view and explains the diverse responses that emerged from that encounter. Next, each chapter will leap back to the *premodern* period and begin to trace the origins and development of the tradition so one can better understand why modernity represents a challenge to it. This history will be accounted for in two phases—a "formative period," which traces the origins of the traditions, and a "classical period," which explains its fully developed premodern world view (both myth and ritual). Then the section on *modernity* will trace the diverse fundamentalist and modernist responses that occurred in each tradition as it was typically overwhelmed by the emergence of Western colonialism and its modern scientific/technological world view. This will be followed by a *postmodern* section that will survey the most recent reactions to the adaptations each tradition has made to globalization in the emerging postmodern world. These reactions tend to be postcolonial attempts (in most regions, after 1945) to reclaim the religious and cultural identities that existed before the advent of modern Western colonialism. In this way we hope to be able to better understand why the world, with all its possibilities for conflict and for cooperation, is the way it is today. Finally, in the *conclusion* to each chapter, some of the implications of this history for the future of each tradition will be addressed.

MODERNIZATION IN GLOBAL PERSPECTIVE

Before we can move on to explore the struggle of peoples everywhere to continue the religiousness of their ancestors in a new and radically different world, we need to be clear about what we mean by the terms "premodern" "modern," and "postmodern" in relation to modern colonialism and postcolonial reactions. In general, premodern history around the globe describes a wide range of cultures in which religion played the decisive role in explaining and ordering life. In premodern societies religion provided the most certain knowledge one could have of the world, and consequently religious authority played a central role in the political and economic ordering of public life in society. In this respect, all premodern cultures have more in common with each other than with modern "secular" (i.e., nonreligious) culture.

With the coming of modernization, modern science replaced religion as the most certain form of knowledge, religion coming to be viewed by many as a matter of personal opinion rather than objective knowledge. Gradually every area of life was secularized, that is, religion no longer played a governing role in such areas as politics, economics, and public education. Instead, religion was privatized (i.e., restricted to personal and family life). The most dramatic institutional expression of this change in the West was the emergence of the secular state that enforced a separation of church and state. This was the "modern" solution to the relation of religion and politics—politics ruled the public life and religion was a private matter.

Every premodern culture saw its universe through explicitly religious eyes and pronounced its vision of life sacred. Since all premodern societies were dominated by the influence of religious authority, they all understood and ordered their worlds through ancient myths and rituals. Modern culture, by contrast, understands its world through the myths and rituals of rational and empirical science. And, as we shall see in the chapter on Christianity, the scientific world view brought with it certain distinctive features, especially (1) the tendency to reject the premodern past, its beliefs and traditions regarded as irrational and superstitious (especially religious beliefs) (2) a view of history as inevitable progress toward an ideal future and (3) the insistence that only science with its "objective view" of the world had access to the knowledge that could bring about this glorious future, finally ending the centuries of human hatred, oppression, and bloodshed caused by religions.

While much more can and will be said in the next chapter about the premodern/modern contrast, enough has been said here to suggest that the contrast between premodern and modern is dramatic and clear. But a word needs to be said about our use of "postmodern." As we have already noted, our postmodern situation, according to Jean-Francois Lyotard, is characterized by the collapse of all metanarratives, those grand all-encompassing stories through which human beings interpreted their lives in their respective cultures as if they were true for all times and places. In ancient cultures those metanarratives were typically religious myths of the four types we have described. In modern culture the primary metanarrative has been the story of history as progress driven by science and technology. But the globalization of religious and cultural interaction in the modern period has tended to relativize all such stories, including the modern one. In the premodern world a single grand narrative was typically experienced as true, valuable, and meaningful by the overwhelming majority of people in a given culture. Our postmodern situation is that we are forced to live in a world of religious and cultural diversity which is explained by a new metanarrative of pluralism. In this metanarrative, no single story can possibly be all encompassing for all people in a given culture—especially as global culture emerges and the world's religions are found in everyone's home town. Diversity relativizes all stories. The grand stories of the world religions have thereby become miniaturized. Everyone is left with his or her own stories, knowing full well that others live by other stories. In fact, the very creation of textbooks on world religions encourages just such a postmodern awareness of the relativity of all our stories. In this situation the adherents of each religious tradition have to deal with the conflicting and often bewildering diversity within their own traditions, as well as the diversity among traditions. All, but especially those who follow the great missionary faiths—Christianity, Islam, Buddhism—must explain how it is that the world continues in this ever-multiplying religious pluralism and why their own ultimate reality (God, Allah, Brahman, Buddha nature, Dao) has not led all the world into their own path.

We suggest that there is a strong correlation between the postmodern challenge to modernity and the postcolonial challenge to colonialism. The emergence of a postcolonial era in global history is typified by a rejection of the modern Western historical metanarrative of scientific-technological progress and in this way opens the door to a postmodern awareness. However, that door swings two ways, for faced with the diversity of cultural and religious narratives, some argue for a return to premodern fundamental truth and practice, insisting that there is only one true narrative and way of life, while others embrace the postmodern situation and welcome diversity. What fundamentalisms and postmodern pluralisms have in common is a rejection of the modern strategy of privatizing religion. Both insist that religion ought to play a role in influencing public life. But fundamentalists advocate accomplishing this by returning to an absolute religious metanarrative that should shape public life for everyone, whereas postmodernists, at least as we will use the term, reject such "totalisms" and embrace the acceptance of a plurality of narratives, recognizing the public benefits of pluralism in contemporary society.

There are today a wide variety of philosophical movements seeking to claim the title "postmodern" for their particular way of seeing and explaining the world. Our task is not to settle this argument in favor of any particular school. As we use the term, the contrast between "modern" and "postmodern" does not describe either a philosophy or an existing historical period but rather what many see as trends leading to a newly emerging historical era that will someday be as different from modernity as modernity is from premodernity. So we are really talking about postmodern trends within the modern world. A postmodern trend is one that challenges the assumptions of modernity without simply reverting to premodern views of reality, and thus represents something new. In particular, we might expect postmodern pluralism to challenge modern "science" as the single form of objective knowledge about the world and also the modern practice of privatizing religion. Today, virtually all the world's religions are caught up in the struggle between their premodern, modern, and possible postmodern, postcolonial, forms.

The history of global modernization and reactions to it is complicated by the fact that modernization was largely a product of the spread of modern science and technology (the industrial revolution) via European economic and political colonialism around the globe, especially from the eighteenth through the twentieth centuries. Understanding world religions today entails studying the impact of modern science, technology, and economics (i.e., capitalism) on societies that had been shaped by premodern sacred stories and rituals. The story of world religions and modernization, then, is the story of the conflicts and compromises between diverse world views, sacred and secular, in the struggle to determine what stories (religious/mythological or secular/scientific) will shape the public life of societies.

Some have asked whether modernization is a form of Western cultural and perhaps even religious imperialism that has been forced on other cultures. The answer is probably both yes and no. Yes, insofar as modernization began in the West; no, insofar as Western modernization brings about such a profound transformation in humanity's understanding of itself that it really represents a crisis for all traditional religions and cultures. If, as we will argue in the course of this book, Judaism and Christianity helped to secularize and therefore modernize the world, it remains true that secularization by its very nature implies an autonomy from religion that permitted the "secular world" to turn against religion—including Judaism and Christianity. Modernization and secularization challenge all sacred traditions and identities. The patterns of impact on and response of diverse religions and cultures are quite variable and will be explored in the remaining chapters of this book.

Our discussion of the great world religions begins with Christianity, not because it is the largest of the world's religions but because it is the dominant religion of the civilization that produced modernization. In some aspects, Christianity facilitated the emergence of modernity. At the same time it went through the trauma of accommodation to modernity first, and in slower stages than those religions that first encountered modernization in a later more developed form. Therefore, the chapter on the history of Christianity and modernization in Western civilization will set the explanatory context for understanding the reactions of other religions to modernization. Modernization did not have an impact on all religions simultaneously, nor did all react in exactly the same way, although there are striking similarities. Therefore, we should not expect that all religions and cultures will exhibit exactly the same patterns and responses.

MODERN COLONIALISM, THE SOCIALIST CHALLENGE, AND THE END OF MODERNITY

In the nineteenth century the synergy of Western science, economics (capitalism), and technology fostered among the dominant European nations, especially England and France, a thirst for building colonial empires. Their colonial ambitions were paralleled in the modern period by those of only one Asian nation—Japan. By 1914 most of the world was under the domination of Western culture. Geographically the Russians and the British controlled about a third of the globe. In terms of population, the British Empire controlled about a fifth of the human race—nearly 400 million people, while France controlled over 50 million colonial subjects. (See Map 1.3.)

The spread of science, technology, and capitalism along with colonial politics was accompanied by a strong sense of paternalism that was traumatic to indigenous cultures and their religious traditions. The impressive achievements of Western civilization often elicited an initial phase of emulation of Western ways, leading indigenous populations to embrace modernization, including the privatization of religion. This was typically followed, however, by a religious and political backlash, manifested in a struggle for national liberation and independence as indigenous peoples sought to reclaim their autonomy and to reaffirm the value of their own ways of life. This backlash brought with it the deprivatizing of religion, that is, a resurgence of religious influence over society and politics often as a force in anti-colonial struggles. This signals the beginning of the postmodern situation in which religious and political movements emerge committed to either returning to premodern unity of religion and society (fundamentalism) or to experimenting with new forms of cooperative pluralistic interactions between religion and society (postmodernist trends). However, in so doing, all embraced and adopted a key element of Western civilization—nationalism—as an unavoidable necessity in the struggle to resist occupation as well as exploitation and to protect their religious and cultural identities.

Many of these movements paradoxically struck an alliance with a Western philosophical and political movement—socialism. Socialism arose in the nineteenth century in Europe among the new urban working class as a protest against the poverty and social dislocation created by early capitalism and the industrial revolution. Socialism was itself a modernist movement, sustained by a vision of scientific progress, and yet it also championed premodern values of community against the rampant individualism of modern capitalism. In Karl Marx's formulation of "scientific socialism," it became an international movement that had as profound an impact on world history as that of any world religion. Indeed, as religious societies around the globe revolted against Western colonial imperialism, most inevitably experimented with socialism as a modern way of protesting and changing modernity. In the twentieth century we see examples around the world in Jewish, Christian, Islamic, Hindu, Buddhist, and Neo-Confucian forms of socialism. In its secular form socialism became the dominant element in Russian culture, spreading throughout Eastern Europe. And it swept across China, the largest country of Asia, as well.

Marx secularized the biblical myth of history by replacing the will of God as the directing force of history with the "scientific" laws of social development, which guide the progressive unfolding of history. He argued that the very laws of social development that created complex class societies (culminating in modern capitalist society in which most of the wealth is in the hands of a few) would also inevitably undo this stage. In time, it would bring about

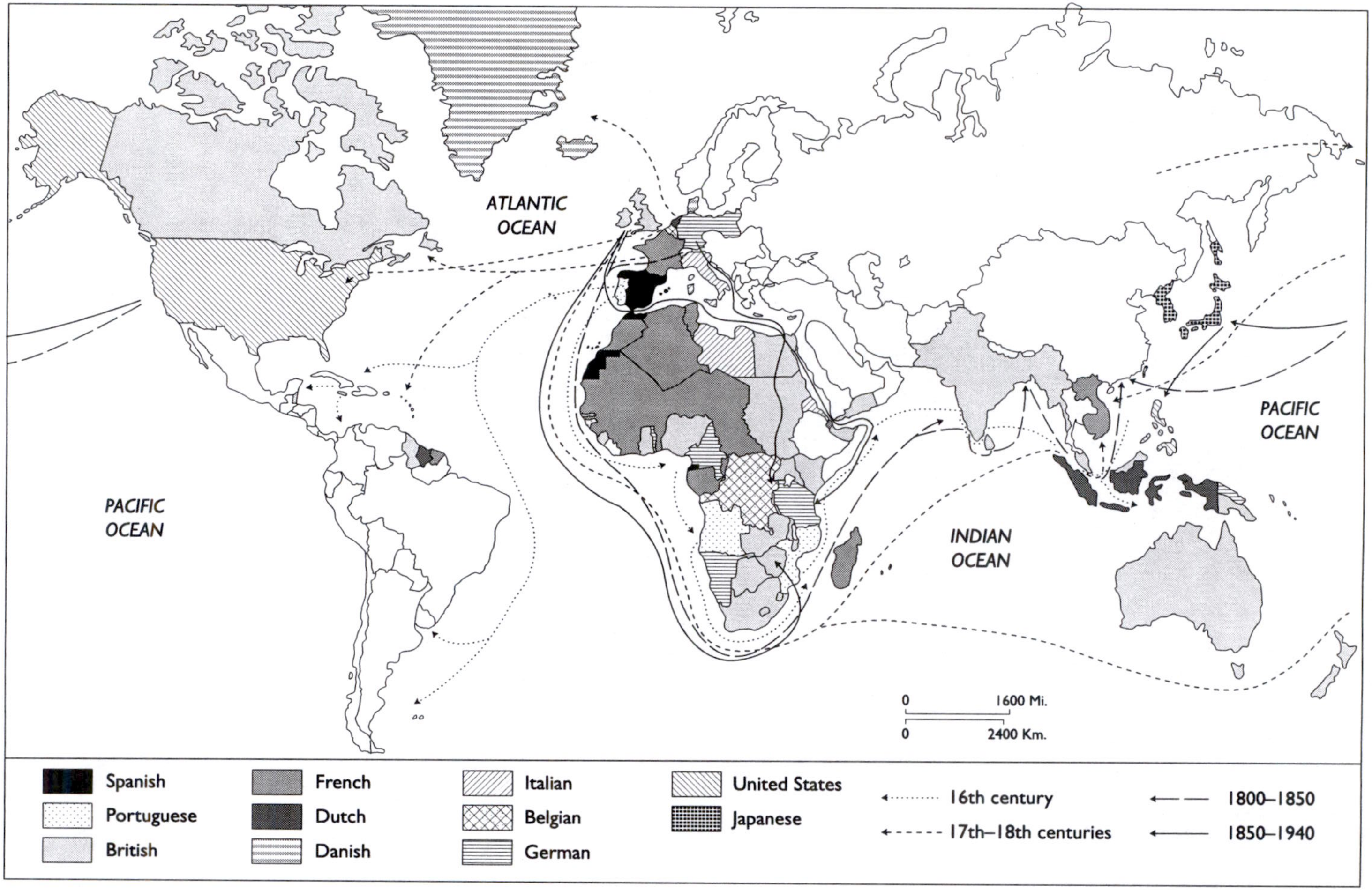

Map 1.3 Missions and colonialism.

THE POWER OF MODERN MYTH: KARL MARX'S VIEW OF HISTORY

Consistent with the myth of modernity, Karl Marx saw history as progressively unfolding in three stages. He defined these stages in terms of a class theory of society that went from (1) primitive communism (tribal societies) in which all were equal, through (2) the rise of complex urban civilizations, which gave birth to bureaucratic societies of stratified classes pitted against each other, to (3) a final stage of history in which society will once more be communistic. In this last age all will again be equal—for all complex class-defined institutions will wither away so that people will live in spontaneous harmony with each other. As many who have studied Marx and Marxist adherents have suggested, this vision is a secularized version of the biblical myth of history culminating in the appearance of the messianic age, but recast as the coming to earth of a classless society in a secular earthly kingdom.

a final age of freedom and justice where all human beings treat each other as equals. Marx believed that this would come about because capitalism depended on creating a large class of urban workers, who, once they were gathered together in the industrial cities of the modern world, would organize, creating an international workers union that would lead to a worldwide revolution. This revolution would result in the replacement of class-based capitalist societies with a new classless society in which freedom, equality, and social justice for all would be guaranteed. Socialism emerged as an ambivalent rejection of the modern scientific world dominated by a capitalism—a capitalism that seemed to make the rich richer and the poor poorer. Yet it promoted itself as "modern," "secular," and "scientific." However, unlike capitalism, it retained much of the religious and ethical power of biblical tradition with its emphasis on justice for the poor, the widow, the orphan, and the stranger as the final outcome of history. For many, Marxist communism became their new "religious" compass.

While socialism provided a vehicle to protest the impact of modernity on human life, two world wars decisively undermined belief in inevitable progress toward greater scientific understanding, prosperity, and benevolent coexistence. World War I (1914–1918) and World War II (1939–1945) were the great wars of modern technology that shattered this myth. Science and technology, which had been viewed as the engines of progress, had become the means of unprecedented destruction. The utopian dream of technological progress ended in the nightmare of a future of global mass death when newly invented atomic bombs were dropped on Japan in August of 1945.

The atomic bomb brought World War II to an end, only to usher in a "cold war" between Russia and the United States. Throughout the second half of the twentieth century, an armed standoff between the Soviet Union and the United States threatened to bring an end to the whole human race in a third and final war of thermonuclear annihilation. The makers of the modern myth of progress had failed to foresee that a technology that increases efficiency can be used not only to create less expensive consumer goods more efficiently but also weapons of mass destruction. Indeed, since World War II progress in the means of mass death has developed at a staggering rate. It took the Nazis six years to kill six million Jews in their death camps. Today, nuclear powers can destroy virtually the whole human race in a few days.

World War I and World War II not only called into question the "scientific age of progress" but also brought an end to the modern age of empires. The twentieth century saw the withdrawal of European powers from the Middle East, Southeast Asia, East Asia, Indonesia, and Africa. European colonial powers left behind independent nation-states, many of which had arbitrarily and illogically drawn boundaries, their peoples often divided without regard to ethnic identity or religious communities, their economies underdeveloped due to the legacy of exploitative colonial practices.

POSTMODERN TRENDS IN A POSTCOLONIAL WORLD

Postmodern trends begin in the nineteenth century. The emergence of the social sciences (especially ethnography/anthropology, sociology, and critical historiography) turned critical empirical modes of inquiry that had been invented to understand nature (i.e., the natural sciences) back upon human beings themselves, especially upon human history and human society. Comparative cross-cultural studies revealed that although human beings in every premodern culture had thought they existed within *the* sacred natural order, tremendous diversity existed. Consequently, all forms of human knowledge were seen not as mirrors of reality but as imaginative human creations.

This awareness produced another loss of innocence. Just as Copernicus (1473–1540) showed humanity that it did not live at the center of the universe, and as the biologist Charles Darwin in the nineteenth century seemed to argue that scientific evidence showed that human beings were descended from apes, so historians and social scientists argued that all religions and cultures could be seen as human creations and hence as biased interpretations of reality, with no one interpretation inherently more true than another. This awareness of the *plurality* of world views tended to *relativize, individualize,* and *privatize* every world view (except of course, the scientific one). That is, it invalidated assumptions that any given world view constituted an objective description of reality and so caused people to begin to see their religious standpoints either as arbitrary, collective, culturally relative social constructs or as private personal acts, and subjective convictions.

In the modern period the social authority of religion was undermined by the new scientific rationalists whose descriptions of reality they themselves believed explained how the world "really is," in contrast to the fanciful myths of religions. What we are calling "postmodernity" had its origins in the late nineteenth century, although its impact was not realized until the last quarter of the twentieth century. During this period, the same techniques of sociological and historical criticism that had been directed against religion were used to critique scientific knowledge, leading to the suggestion that it too offered relative, not absolute, interpretations of the world.

The postmodern world begins with the further loss of innocence that occurred as many human beings maintained that not only religious knowledge but also scientific knowledge was relative in important ways, that it too was an imaginative interpretation of the world based on faith (in the intelligibility of the world) and did not offer the final truth about reality either. Of course, many today dispute this understanding of science in arguments that remind one of the arguments between premodern religious philosophers (defending religion) and the new secular scientists (challenging religion) at the beginning of the modern period. However, no matter who is right, the very existence of such a dispute suggests that we are in a postmodern situation in which the unquestioning faith humans had in science during the modern era has been broken.

From a postmodern perspective, all knowledge is relative, including religious and scientific knowledge. Postmodern trends seem to promote a radical cultural and ethical relativism. Some rejoice in this, arguing that it means the end of all absolutisms that people have used to justify violence against each other. Others are afraid that such a total relativism means the end of civilization and the beginning of a new barbarism—that once we relativize the distinction between good and evil, we will plunge into an ethical void in which any atrocity can be justified.

With the relativizing of scientific knowledge in the postmodern period, religious knowledge no longer suffers from the disadvantage that had allowed modern critics to dismiss its validity. Now both science and religion come to be seen as equal, if only because, from a postmodern perspective, they are equally relative. Therefore the position that scientific secularism should be viewed as providing public and certain knowledge while religious knowledge should be viewed as mere private opinion no longer seems valid to many. Consequently, with the emergence of postmodern trends there has been a resurgence of religion in the public realm—a resurgence whose diverse forms are responses to both the threat and the promise of postmodernity.

In many ways, as we enter the twenty-first century we live in a time of transition that has overtaken the modern world. Although we still live in a world of nation-states, the nineteenth and twentieth centuries have created a world that is more economically and technologically interconnected on a global scale. The industrial revolution has been transformed into a global technological revolution, where electricity and metal alloys have replaced the steam engine and iron. Electronic communications and the mass media are uniting the world, and genetic and social engineering are transforming human life. Many see in this the beginning of a new global civilization. We now live in a world increasingly dominated by multinational corporations and ever more linked by international travel. Today, one's neighbors are likely to have been born not in one's own town or village but in another part of the country or even the globe. Even for those who never leave home, the world comes to them if not through new neighbors then through mass communications via television, film, radio, telephone, the printed word, and the Internet. Knowledge of history and of other cultures is no longer restricted to the educated class but is available to all through these media. As a result, awareness of world religions and the pluralism of human world views has come to touch virtually all human beings. Many find these changes alluring, even liberating, but others find them alarming.

The emergence of a global postmodern civilization seems to be eliciting another stage in the history of religions, namely the meeting of world religions and the globalization of world religions. Until the modern period the great world religions had largely divided the globe between them with some modest overlap. But in the postmodern world, more and more, all the world's religions have members in every society, so that, for example, we find Hindus, Buddhists, and Muslims in significant numbers in virtually all large American cities and increasingly in smaller ones. Anyone using the Internet can view the major temples, shrines, churches, mosques, or monasteries from around the world, not to mention offer ritual prayers or make monetary offerings to them. This is an example of what we mean by globalization.

The Postmodern Situation: We Are All Heretics

In the premodern period, people, for the most part, acquired their religious identities because of where they were born on the globe. In the postmodern world, however, every individual is faced with what sociologist Peter Berger, calls "the heretical imperative." Berger notes that the word "heretic" comes from an ancient Greek word that means "to choose." In our postmodern world every religious person becomes a heretic, that is, one who is not just born into his or her identity but is forced to choose it, even if it is the identity offered by the circumstances of one's birth. According to Peter Berger, this modern task of self-consciously choosing one's religious adherence in the face of diversity was first worked out with the emergence of modernity during the Protestant Reformation when Catholic universality was shattered and Christianity splintered into a myriad of diverse denominations. As modernity spread around the world with Western colonialism and its Christian missionary movements, the whole world became more and more Protestant, not in the sense of becoming doctrinally Christian but in the sense of becoming organizationally denominational. The situation, says Berger, "becomes ... ironic as one observes that Hinduism, along with other non-Western religions, is now energetically returning the compliment of the Protestant missionary outreach—evangelizing Christians and Jews, from California's icy mountains to Long Island's not-so-coral strands. The Protestant disease has become a planetary epidemic."[2]

Because of our awareness of both the relativity and the plurality of ways of viewing the world, we cannot avoid choosing. This is what we believe places us irrevocably in a postmodern situation, whether we affirm this situation or refuse to acknowledge it. In this sense the various fundamentalisms and orthodoxies that thrive today are just as much postmodern "heresies" as some of the more innovative expressions of religions. This leads to the paradox that the absolutisms of fundamentalist religious movements that reject all postmodern relativism can assert themselves only by embracing a relativist stance of "choosing" to be against the modern and postmodern. Thus today's ultrafundamentalists are postmodern—urging people to "choose" to return to the ancient premodern truths and practices. But in having to make that choice people have lost their innocence—they have to act in such a way as to respond to the fact that the present situation is postmodern, not premodern. Before the advent of modernization, this was not a challenge individuals faced.

In this world of "heretics," all the world's religions, each of which originated to provide a universal answer to the question of human identity, have been forced to take account of the others. They have come face to face with their own particularism in a world of diverse faiths. Until postmodern trends set in, other people's religions could be readily dismissed in a series of negative stereotypes. When people of diverse religions are neighbors, this option gets both more difficult and more dangerous. To the degree that stereotyping and discrimination persist, they promote prejudice, conflict, and violence. The alternative is to develop a new understanding of the relation between world religions and global cultures—one that allows the peoples of the earth to share their wisdom with each other with mutual respect and understanding. Gandhi is the great pioneer of this postmodern option. We know that this alternative—to appreciate what they have in common as well as to acknowledge their distinctive differences—is possible because of the example of great religious figures of the twentieth century such as Gandhi and, later, Martin Luther King, Jr. As we shall see in the final chapter, each leader "passed over" from his own religion and culture to that of the other's and came back enriched by that second tradition without abandoning his own. You are invited to embark on a similar journey through the world's religions today.

DISCUSSION QUESTIONS

1. Define religion, myth, and ritual and explain the possible relations among them.

2. How do the authors understand the relationship between religion and morality?

3. In what ways does religious language complicate the question of whether there is agreement or disagreement between religions on various issues? Describe in terms of the via analogia and the via negativa, giving examples of each.

4. Explain the four types of religious story and give an historical example of each.

5. Why did urbanization lead to the emergence of the great world religions? That is, what new urban problems did these religions address?

6. What is colonialism and what is its significance for the religions and cultures in the modern period?

7. How are the terms "premodern," "modern," and "postmodern" being used in this text and how are they related to modern colonialism?

8. How do the authors define "fundamentalism" and understand its relation to postmodern relativism?

9. According to the authors, modernization privatizes religion whereas in premodern and postmodern religious movements religion plays a public role in society but in different ways. Explain.

10. Explain Marxist socialism and why it was an attractive option to those religious movements protesting modernity.

11. According to the authors, why are both postmodernist and fundamentalist religious movements examples of Peter Berger's "heretical imperative"?

KEY TERMS

cosmopolitan	postmodern	ritual
globalization	premodern	sacred
metanarrative	privatization	via analogia
modern	relativism	via negativa
myth	religion	
pluralism	religious	

SUGGESTED READINGS

Peter Berger, *The Heretical Imperative* (New York: Anchor Press, Doubleday, 1979).

Peter Beyer, *Religion and Globalization* (London: Sage Publications, 1994).

Mark Juergensmeyer, editor, *Global Religions: An Introduction* (Oxford: Oxford University Press, 2003).

Bryan S. Turner, *Orientalism, Posmodernism and Globalism* (London: Routledge, 1994).

NOTES

1. Lewis Mumford, *The City in History*, (Harcourt, Brace & World, Inc.: 1961), p. xi.

2. Mark Jeurgensmeyer, *Global Religions: An Introduction* (Oxford University Press, 2003), p.4.

3. Immanuel Kant, "Idea for a Universal History from a Cosmopolitan Point of View" (1784) and also on "Perpetual Peace" (1795) found in *On History, Kant*, edited by Lewis White Beck (Indianapolis: Bobbs-Merrill Co., 1957, 1963).

4. Jean-Francois Lyotard, *The Postmodern Condition: A Report on Knowledge* (Minneapolis: University of Minnesota Press, 1984).

5. Bryan S. Turner, *Orientalism, Postmodernism and Globalism* (London & New York: Routledge, 1994), p. 10 and p. 78.

CHAPTER TWO

CHRISTIANITY AND THE ROAD TO GLOBALIZATION

Overview

In a storefront church in the midwest of the United States, Christians—male and female, black and white—gather and raise their arms above their heads, their hands extended as if in a plea toward heaven, the eyes of many closed and some with an earnest rapture on their faces. Soon many begin to speak in an unknown language. These Christians are "charismatics" and they are engaged in "speaking in tongues," believing that the Holy Spirit of God has descended upon them and speaks through them, even as this Spirit guides their daily walk with *Christ*. Meanwhile in Rome, the pope (leader of the largest Christian denomination in the world, the Roman *Catholic* Church) processes into the great Cathedral of St. Peter escorted by a long line of men in flowing robes. They make their way between the majestic rows of stone pillars led by one carrying a processional cross, followed by incense bearers swinging pots of rich aromatic incense whose smoke wafts through the air as if carrying the sounds of organ music and Gregorian-style chants up to heaven. Soon the Pope will arrive at the altar to begin a solemn high mass.

Meanwhile, somewhere in Africa, villagers gather to dance and sing their tribal chants in praise of the risen Christ, even as somewhere in England, in a small unadorned room, a dozen Quakers sit quietly in wordless prayer until such time as the Holy Spirit inspires one of them to speak a message to the rest. Back in the United States, at an inner-city Episcopal church in the northeast, a woman priest consecrates bread and wine as the body and blood of Christ. Elsewhere, in a small village in Latin America, a group of poor peasants, in preparation for sharing bread and wine as the body and blood of

Christ, sit in a circle on a hillside under the morning sun and study the Gospel of Luke, and Jesus' words that call for the liberation of the poor and the downtrodden. And in a village in India, a small group of Christians, virtually indistinguishable from the Hindus of their village, gather to offer flower petals before a statue of Jesus. At the same time, an international television broadcast of the Billy Graham crusade beams Graham's call for the thousands who fill a sports stadium to come forward and declare themselves for Christ with the whole world watching.

Despite their incredible diversity, all of the foregoing are Christians engaged in Christian prayer and worship. The challenge before us is to understand the unity and diversity among Christians, especially in the contemporary world.

As we shall see, like Jews and Muslims, Christians believe that there is but one God, the God who made all things and rules over history. This God is the highest reality, and to act in harmony with the will of this God is the highest goal of life. Christians are unique, however, in believing that God is one God yet three persons (Father, Son, and Holy Spirit) and that the reality of this God is uniquely revealed in the life and person of Jesus of Nazareth. For Christians believe the eternal Word of God was united to humanity through the person of Jesus who suffered and died on the cross for the sins of the world, only to be raised from the dead three days later, and to ascend to heaven after forty days. There he reigns until he comes again at the end of time to judge the living and the dead at the final resurrection.

Like Jews and Muslims, Christians also believe that the gravest problem in human life is sin—the failure to live in harmony with the will of God. Sin has two dimensions: idolatry and injustice. Idolatry is more than worshiping the images of false and foreign deities. It is treating anything that is not God as if it were as important as God—such as wealth or power. When that occurs injustice follows, for if nothing is more important than satisfying one's selfish desires for wealth and power, then other human beings are less important and can be mistreated, if that is necessary to acquire these desired "goods."

However, Christians differ from Jews and Muslims in their view of sin and how it is to be overcome. For most Christians define "sin" in terms of the concept of *Original Sin*, which says that the will to do the good in all human beings has been corrupted by the sin of disobedience to God's will by the first human beings—Adam and Eve—and through this disobedience sin and death came into the world. Thus most Christians believe that while human beings were created good, their good will (the desire to do what is good) was corrupted by the inherited consequences of the sin of Adam and Eve, so that humans feel compelled to act selfishly. Humans are enslaved to the power of sin and not fully capable of obeying the will of God. Out of compassion for human beings, God chose to send a savior, Jesus Christ, to redeem them by dying in reparation for their past sins and restoring human nature (recreating a good will in them) in order for obedience to the will of God to be possible and in order to restore human destiny to its true goal of eternal life with God.

God sent his only son, the eternal Word of God, to become incarnate in the world—that is, fully embodied—in the life and person of Jesus of Nazareth. In doing so, God united his divine nature to human nature, healing its flaws. The primary means for Christians to overcome sin and live in harmony with the will of God is for them to die spiritually and to rise with Jesus Christ. By dying to self and being raised up through faith in Christ, the Christian believes he or she has become a new creature and part of a new creation in which all sin and death will be overcome. Only as a new creature is a Christian finally free to obey the word of God as revealed in the scriptures. In so doing Christians believe they are called to help bring about the Kingdom of God—the beginning of a new creation of love, compassion, and justice in which death will finally be overcome, even as Jesus overcame his death on the cross with his bodily resurrection.

In century after century, as Christians have sought to foster this "Kingdom of God," they have puzzled over how this kingdom is to be accomplished. This goal has forced Christians to try to understand the relationship between the church and the world, and how their faith and way of life should be related to the larger non-Christian world around them. Christians have struggled with this question in all ages, including the present one.

Despite the explanation of Christianity just given, it would be misleading to think that all Christians in all times and places would agree with it. Like all religions, Christianity is more than one thing. It has taken many forms and been many things to many people. In the remainder of this chapter we shall try to understand both the unity and diversity of Christianity.

Today Christianity is the largest religion in the world. With over 1,870 million adherents, of which a little over 1,000 million are Catholics, Christians represent approximately one-third of the world's population. This 33 percent of the world's population breaks down roughly into Catholics, 19 percent; Protestants, 8%; Orthodox, 3 percent; and other forms of Christianity, 3 percent. *Our primary task in this chapter is not just to understand Christianity but also to understand the role that Christianity has played in the development of modern society and the various Christian responses to that society.* Some have argued that the alliance of Christianity with modernization is a mistake that can be corrected by returning to the "fundamentals" of the faith, as they believe these fundamentals were understood and practiced before the emergence of the modern scientific and secular view of the world. Others have argued that modernization is itself evidence of the power of the Christian *Gospel* to transform the world and therefore should be embraced as the path to human dignity and liberation. Some today have opted to maintain a premodern faith (fundamentalism), others maintain a modern faith (modernism), and yet others seek a third postmodern way.

The Christianity of yesterday helped give birth to the modern world in all its diversity; and to understand the latter we need also to understand the former. We shall begin with the *Protestant* encounter with modernity and then look at Catholicism's struggle with the modern world. Then we shall return to the beginning in the first century and journey forward so as to understand how things came to be the way they are today.

ENCOUNTER WITH MODERNITY: THE FUNDAMENTALIST–MODERNIST CONTROVERSY

The Protestant Confrontation with Modernity

The nineteenth century marked a critical turning point in the history of Christianity as it sought to find a way to coexist with an increasingly "modern" secular and scientific world whose views challenged many of the fundamental truths and practices of Christians. The central issue in modern Christianity has been the struggle between modernism and fundamentalism. Indeed, we get the term "fundamentalism" from the American Protestant experience and its confrontation with "modernism"—a confrontation it shared with Catholicism.

Modernization in nineteenth-century America was profoundly shaped by the growth of industrialization, which, in turn, fueled urbanization, drawing people away from agrarian life to seek jobs in the cities in large numbers. This brought not only tremendous changes but tremendous problems—unfair wages and resulting strikes, poverty, alcoholism, racial and ethnic tensions, child and female labor abuses, and so on. At the same time the churches were growing dramatically. Between 1860 and 1900, Protestant churches tripled in numbers to about sixteen million. But Catholicism was growing even faster, especially due to emigration from Europe.

At the same time the United States was becoming more secular, especially in the areas of science and higher education. At the middle of the century most colleges were under *evangelical* Protestant leadership and interpreted knowledge in relation to the Bible and the Christian world view. By the end of the century higher education was more and more in the hands of universities modeled on the German scientific ideal of scholarship in which each discipline has its own rational and empirical standards that make no direct appeal to the Bible or Christian beliefs. In this context, Charles Darwin's theories of biological evolution had caught the popular imagination and had given rise to a Social Darwinism that came to view not only nature but also modern capitalist society as evolutionary and driven by a competition that allowed for only the "survival of the fittest." Less popularly known but very much on the minds of evangelical preachers was the new "biblical criticism" that had come out of Germany, which looked upon the Bible as an historical, humanly created document and challenged many pious beliefs about its teachings.

The challenges stemming from Darwinism and biblical criticism were a double blow to Christian beliefs and elicited two opposing responses: the modernism of liberal Christian evangelicals, on the one hand, and the fundamentalism of conservative Christian evangelicals on the other. Liberal evangelicals responded by developing a new theology that could show how modernism and Christianity were compatible. They saw God at work in evolution and in history. Christians, they argued, have an ethical calling to cooperate with God's will operative in evolution and history to transform this world into the kingdom of God. Out of this new theology the Social Gospel movement emerged, seeking to reconcile science, Christian faith, and Christian ethics by calling for a new Christian sociology and a new Christian socialism. It drew on the social sciences to understand the social problems that came from modernization and to solve them by changing the structures of society. It saw both sin and salvation primarily as having to do with life in this world. The Gospel was about transforming a sinful society into the Kingdom of God.

By the end of World War I, liberal evangelical Christianity dominated the mainline northern denominations. However, in the eyes of many other evangelical Protestants, the attempt to adapt Christianity to the modern world was doomed to failure. What one ended up with was a Christianity emptied of everything that made it Christian and filled with everything that was secular and modern.

It was modernization that split evangelical theology in two: opposing the Social Gospel was Protestant Fundamentalism. Whereas the theologians of the Social Gospel believed they represented the next logical stage in the historical development of Christianity, those evangelicals who responded in a *fundamentalist* mode were convinced that there could be no historical development with respect to the Gospel. If there was a conflict between the scriptures and modern science then it must be modern science, not the Bible, that was in error.

In a series of twelve paperback books entitled *The Fundamentals*, published between 1910 and 1915, various champions of the fundamentalist movement spoke in defense of Bible-based religion and against the apostasy, as they perceived it, of modernism. Convinced that liberal theology and Darwinism were undermining American civilization, they took their stand on the inerrancy of the Bible. By the 1920s the movement had been dubbed by the popular press as "Fundamentalism" and was understood to refer to militantly antimodernist evangelical Protestants. The Fundamentalist movement succeeded in banning the teaching of evolution in many public schools in the South. The legal case that decisively formed the public image of fundamentalism was the Scopes trial held in Dayton, Tennessee, in 1925. Three-time candidate for president of the United States William Jennings Bryan squared off against Clarence Darrow in a trial that dominated the newspapers nationally. John Scopes, a high school teacher, was accused of breaking the law by teaching evolution. Bryan was no match for the wit of Clarence Darrow, and although he won the case in court he lost the case in the media. He, and Fundamentalism in general, were portrayed as the philosophy of ignorant backwood hicks. After that, fundamentalism lost all popular support and Protestant liberalism, which sought to embrace modernity, held sway largely unchallenged until the surprising resurgence of fundamentalism in the last quarter of the twentieth century.

The Catholic Confrontation with Modernity

In 1864 Pope Pius IX issued a Syllabus of Errors listing eighty "modern" teachings that Catholics must reject because they challenged the control of all knowledge and all politics by the church. Pius IX thought that such ideas could only lead to a godless society that would no longer heed the eternal and unchanging fundamental truths of the one true church. Thus in 1869 Pius IX called the First Vatican Council of all cardinals and bishops to shore up the teachings of the church against the threat of modernism. The papacy was under siege not only by modern ideas but by modern secular politics. In 1870 the new secular Kingdom of Italy seized the papal estates from Pope Pius IX and the Vatican lost the political power it had enjoyed for centuries. Precisely at that moment in time when the intellectual and political authority of the papacy was at its weakest and was most threatened, Vatican I, at the insistence of Pius IX, declared the pope to be infallible, such that his declarations on faith and morals could not be altered, not even with the consent of the church, including any future council.

There is a striking similarity-in-contrast between Protestant and Catholic antimodernist responses. Both attempted to prevent modernization and historical change from entering the church by an appeal to an infallible or inerrant authority that they believed was higher than scientific and secular authority. For Protestants it was the Bible, for Roman Catholics it was the pope as the final authority on how the Bible was to be interpreted.

It is all the more remarkable therefore, that almost a century later a new pope would seek to reverse many of the decisions of Vatican I and embrace the modern world. When Angelo Roncalli chose the name "John XXIII" in 1958 and called the Catholic church to the Second Vatican Council in 1962, in one dramatic gesture he sought to reverse the more than four centuries of the church's rejection of the emerging modern world that had culminated in Vatican I. And he sought to heal the religious divisions of Christianity going back to the Protestant Reformation and even earlier. Moreover, in its *Declaration on the Relationship of the Church to Non-Christian Religions*, the council expressed a new openness to the teachings of non-Christian religions around the world. Indeed, it declared: "The Catholic Church rejects nothing which is true and holy in these religions." Therefore, whereas Vatican I and earlier councils had sought to close the door on modernization and pluralism, Vatican II threw open the doors and announced a spirit of *aggiornamento*—the updating or modernizing of the church in order to speak more effectively to the modern world. Neither Christianity nor the world has been the same since.

The Second Vatican Council's meetings lasted from 1962 to 1965. John XXIII, who died in 1963, did not live to see them completed, but in his brief papacy (1958–1963) he unleashed a spirit that transformed the Catholic church from a world-shunning church into one that was open to the modern world. In the decades since Vatican II, Catholicism has continued its ambivalent journey, with some wanting to return to the fundamentals of the Catholicism of Vatican

I, before Vatican II changed everything, and others wanting to follow the road of *aggiornamento*.

The Nineteenth-Century Historical and Social-Scientific Revolution

In the situations we have just described, both Catholics and Protestants were responding to a fundamental revolution in human thought that had occurred in the nineteenth century. This revolution was precipitated by the emergence of the social and historical sciences. The social sciences represented the final shock wave of modern consciousness. The first wave was created by the natural sciences. Copernicus had shocked the European world when he suggested in 1543 CE that the earth was not the center of the universe. Later, geologists concluded that the earth was far older than anyone had ever calculated who used the Bible as a guide. Then Charles Darwin came along to suggest in *The Origin of Species* (1859) that human beings did not appear on the earth suddenly on the seventh day of creation but had evolved gradually from lower species over thousands of years. Moreover, he claimed that the operative force in this evolution was not divine providence but a struggle between species that resulted in the "survival of the fittest."

POPE JOHN XXIII

The name Cardinal Roncalli chose for himself when he was elected pope, John XXIII, was highly significant and offered an important clue to the kind of pope he intended to be. For this name had been used before by a man who claimed to be pope during a period in the history of the papacy known as "the Babylonian Captivity." This was a period, during the fourteenth and early fifteenth centuries, in which the papacy moved from Rome to Avignon in France and was largely under the control of the French kings. It was also a period of great decadence in the history of the papacy, in which three different men claimed to be the pope. One of these was John XXIII. The confusion was finally settled when bishops of the church met at the Council of Constance in 1414 and deposed all three popes and elected a new one, Martin V. In so doing the council made a dramatic statement: "The ecumenical council assembled at Constance represents the whole church. It derives its authority immediately from Christ. Everyone, even the pope, owes obedience to it in all that concerns the faith, the unity of the Church and the reform of both head and members." It went on to decree that only another council could change the decree of a council, no one else, not even the pope. In embracing the name of John XXIII, Angelo Roncalli was telling the world that he recognized both the authority of that council and its vision of the church as governed by shared conciliar authority.

The social sciences delivered the second shock wave, especially critical histo-riography, which showed that popular legends about the past did not accurately portray what "really happened." At first the tools of history and archaeology were applied to ancient civilizations and their religions and cultures. But even-tually the same methods began to be applied to European history and Christianity. For many, as we have already seen, the use of modern historical methods on the Bible was too much. Many turned to fundamentalism out of a desire to preserve "the fundamentals" of Christianity from the incursion of both evolution and history.

The other social sciences did little to ease the shock. Sociologists and anthro-pologists who studied societies comparatively created an awareness that, con-trary to many traditional teachings, societies were not created by the gods and sacred ancestors. On the contrary, they suggested, humanity invented the gods to make their various ways of life seem sacred. This view was reinforced by Sigmund Freud's suggestion that God was a projection or wish fulfillment—a necessary illusion that human beings needed to create to give them a feeling of security in an unstable world. Now human beings were asked to think of both society and human identity as created by human choices rather than by the actions and decisions of gods.

This new awareness created a profound problem. The question that came to divide modern Christianity was whether to reject these developments of modernity, as did Protestant Fundamentalism and Vatican I Catholicism, or accept them, as did Protestant evangelical liberalism and Vatican II Catholicism—or strike some kind of compromise in between. The paradox of the situation was that although modernity appeared to be a threat to Christianity, it was also a development that had been nurtured, in significant part, by Christianity itself. Our task now is to return to the beginning of Christianity so that we can better understand the historical circumstances that led it to contribute to the development of the modern world it feels so ambiva-lent about.

PREMODERN CHRISTIANITY: THE FORMATIVE ERA

Ancient and Modern: Contrasting World Views

When the first followers of Jesus of Nazareth looked up into the night sky in the first century, they did not see what modernists did when they looked upward in the nineteenth century. For modernists saw a cosmos with stars and planets scattered in infinite space. They knew that the earth was not at the center of the universe but was just one of the planets circumnavigating a star (the sun) in one of many galaxies. And the stars and planets they saw, they knew were made up of inert matter, to be accounted for in terms of physics and chemistry. When the first-century Christians looked up they saw a world shaped not by the modern imagination but by the imagination of the ancient Greeks. They understood from the Greeks that the earth was at the center of seven spheres. The higher spheres of the stars and the planets embodied spiritual beings (Paul of Tarsus called them the "principalities and powers") that governed the universe. Everything above the moon, they believed, belonged to the realm of the spiritual and eternal. Everything below the moon belonged to the realm of the physical and temporal. The souls of all humans had their origin in the spiritual realm and had descended into the material or bodily realm. But their spiritual goal, their hope of salvation, was to return to the eternal realm above, beyond time, decay, and death.

In addition to the legacy of the Greeks, the way the first Christians saw the world owed a debt to the Hebraic tradition of ancient Israel. In this world view, creation is a story unfolding in time. In the beginning God spoke and the story began. As it unfolds the story has many dramatic ups and downs, but at its end, God will bring the present world to an end, judge it, and transform it into a new creation. Today "modern" Christians wrestle with the question of whether being a Christian requires adherence to the ancient world view or can accommodate changing world views, including the modern scientific one.

The New Testament

The journey of Christianity from the ancient to the modern world begins in the first century with the life and teachings of Jesus of Nazareth as communicated in the Gospels of the New Testament. Being a Jew, Jesus participated in a religious tradition that went back another two thousand years before his time. This is acknowledged in the Christian Bible, which is made up of two parts. What Christians call the "Old Testament" is basically an adoption of the Pharisaic and Hellenistic Jewish collections of sacred writings that had become the official scriptures of Judaism at the end of the first century of the common era (CE). The sacred scriptures of Christianity found in the New Testament did not assume the form of the twenty-seven books we have now until the year 367 CE—more than three hundred years after the death of Jesus. During that time frame there were in circulation many stories of the life and sayings of Jesus, most of which were finally not included in the New Testament. What is striking is that the tradition did not settle on a single story of Jesus for its Bible but actually included four different stories—the Gospels of Matthew, Mark, Luke, and John. To these were appended many letters by the Apostle Paul and others, a short history of the early church (the Acts of the Apostles), and a vision of the end of time (the Book of Revelation). These scriptures were written to show that Jesus of Nazareth is the messiah to come, in accordance with the prophesies recounted in the older testament.

According to tradition, the order in which the Gospels were written is the order in which they are found at the beginning of the New Testament: Matthew, Mark, Luke, and John. After careful scrutiny of the literary structure and probable historical context of each Gospel, many modern scholars, using historical-critical methods, have come to the conclusion that Mark's Gospel is probably the first (written at the time of the fall of the temple in 70), and that Matthew and Luke both used Mark's Gospel as a model in writing their own (sometime between 80 and 90). The Gospel of John (written after 90) is so different in literary tone, content, and structure that it seems to have been a largely independent creation.

Also, according to tradition, the Gospels were written by disciples (or disciples of disciples) of Jesus. Taking advantage of archaeological findings that shed additional light on the biblical period, modern scholars doubt that any of the Gospels actually had a single author. Rather, each Gospel probably began in shared oral traditions about Jesus as told in different communities of believers after his death on the cross and attested resurrection. These traditions were eventually written down and edited so as to place the sayings within the context of different remembered events from Jesus' life.

As we have noted, the sacred scriptures of Christianity were first examined through the eyes of the critical historian in the nineteenth century. Within Christianity the validity of this modern approach is in dispute. Fundamentalists reject it, while other Christians see it as helpful for understanding the development of faith in the early church. And yet for all their differences, and quite apart from the historical question of "what really happened," all forms of Christianity share a common reverence for the stories of Jesus as they are found in the New Testament as the basis for Christian faith.

The Stories of Jesus

The power of the Christian message is revealed in the stories of Jesus, especially the Sermon on the Mount (Matthew 5–7), with its message of loving your neighbor and doing good even to your enemy. It is that message of compassion and forgiveness that has moved millions. What the stories of Jesus tell is that God has manifested God's true being in the life of a human being, Jesus. Therefore, contrary to some Gnostic Christians, who taught that the human body was evil, emerging "orthodox" christianities taught that being human was nothing to be belittled, for God embraced and affirmed the embodied humanity of every human being in the life of Jesus.

Jesus was born at the beginning of the first century, possibly in either Bethlehem or Nazareth. In any case he was raised in Nazareth in ancient Palestine, then under Roman rule (see Map 2.1). Little is known of his youth, but according to the scriptures he was the son of a carpenter, Joseph, and his wife, Mary. The birth of Jesus was said to have been miraculous, for Mary became pregnant through the power of God as announced by an angel rather than through her relationship to Joseph.

Around the age of 30, Jesus had a traumatic experience. Someone he knew, admired, and was related to—the very one who baptized him, John the Baptist—was arrested on orders from King Herod and eventually beheaded. To everyone's surprise, soon after John's arrest Jesus began teaching the very

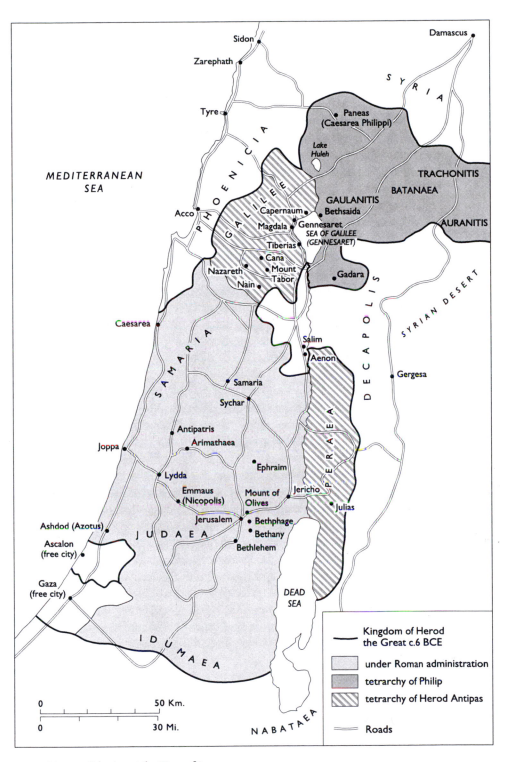

Map 2.1 Palestine at the Time of Jesus.

message that had gotten John the Baptist in trouble with Herod—"Repent, for the Kingdom of God is at hand" (Matt. 4:17).

While his family and friends thought he had gone mad, he soon attracted followers who thought otherwise and called him *rabbi*, which means "teacher." Jesus' message is exemplified in a passage from the Sermon on the Mount.

> You have heard that it was said, "An eye for an eye and a tooth for a tooth." But I say to you, offer no resistance to one who is evil. When someone strikes you on (your) right cheek, turn the other one to him as well. If anyone wants to go to law with you over your tunic, hand him your cloak as well. Should anyone press you into service for one mile, go with him for two miles. Give to the one who asks of you, and do not turn your back on one who wants to borrow. You have heard that it was said, "You shall love your neighbor and hate your enemy." But I say to you, love your enemies, and pray for those who persecute you, that you may be children of your heavenly Father, for he makes his sun rise on the bad and the good, and causes rain to fall on the just and the unjust. For if you love those who love you, what recompense will you have? Do not the tax collectors do the same? And if you greet your brothers only, what is unusual about that? Do not the pagans do the same? So be perfect, just as your heavenly Father is perfect.
> —*(Matthew 5:38–48)*

In addition to preaching repentance and love, according to the scriptures, Jesus began working miracles—healing the sick (Mark 1:40–45, Matthew 9:27–31), walking on water (Mark 6:45–52; John 6:16–21), casting out evil spirits (Mark 1:23–28; Matthew 8:28–34), miraculously multiplying a few loaves and fishes to feed a multitude (Mark 6:30–44; Matthew 14:13–21). Some from among the Sadducees and Pharisees, according to the stories, grew jealous of him and began to plot his demise. They had him handed over to the Romans who had heard some call him "messiah." While the Gospels typically make it appear as if the Jews, not the Romans, are the cause of Jesus' crucifixion, historians have pointed out that only the Romans had that power. Moreover, for the Romans the term "messiah" was associated with the Zealots, a militaristic sect of Judaism that engaged in guerrilla warfare against the Roman legions, for whom a messiah was a political revolutionary sent by God to overthrow the Roman Empire. Historically, the reason the Romans condemned Jesus to die nailed to a wooden cross was that they thought of him as such a political enemy of the state.

Despite this, the followers of Jesus came to find deep spiritual meaning in the crucifixion. What is striking about Mark's account of the crucifixion (found in Matthew 27:46 also) is the bleakness of Jesus' final words: "My God, my God, why have you forsaken me?" This is very different from the final words of Jesus reported in other Gospels: "Into your hands I commend my spirit"

(Luke 23:46) and "It is finished" (John 19:30). Mark's account presents a Jesus with whom even a hearer in the depths of despair can identify.

And yet the Gospels do not allow despair to be the final word. For they offer hope to the one in despair. Just as Jesus was lifted out of death and despair, so may the believer be who in faith embraces the life of the one who knew despair and death, yet was raised up. So according to the Gospel of John (20:1–10), the disciples of Jesus came to the grave on Sunday morning, the first day of the week, only to find an empty tomb: the stone over the opening was rolled back and the burial cloth was discarded.

Soon the disciples, who had been afraid, began to be filled with a new and bold spirit—the Holy Spirit of the God who had raised Jesus from the dead (Acts 2). Emboldened by this spirit they began to proclaim the message of the risen Lord who had conquered death and would return very soon to raise the dead, judge the heavens and the earth, and inaugurate the kingdom of God. This would be a kingdom in which all injustice would be overcome, as well as all suffering and death.

In a world filled with injustice, suffering, and death under the rule of the Roman oppressors, such a message inspired hope and joy. In a world of tragedy it offered people a sense of having a destiny that transcended tragedy and death. In a world where everything seemed to be governed by chance and fate it suggested that a personal God guided the lives of individuals toward ultimate meaning and fulfillment. The world was not a cold and uncaring place, for the love of God fell like the gentle rain from heaven, nourishing every creature. The life of Jesus presented people with a story of suffering and tragedy that was real yet not final, for suffering and death were overcome in the resurrection. In the life of Jesus, people saw a mirror image of their own lives, giving them hope that their own tragedies would not be final and that they too would be resurrected. In the life of Jesus people discovered a God who cared about them personally and was personally involved in their own destiny. To understand these things is to understand why Christianity has become the religion of one-third of the world's population.

Christianity's Emergence from Judaism

If one is to understand the religious, social, and political tensions that have existed between Jews and Christians throughout the centuries, into the modern period, it is important to note a paradox contained in the stories told about Jesus in the New Testament. On the one hand, the message of Jesus is one of love and forgiveness, not only of one's neighbor but even of one's enemies. On the other hand, the way the stories of Jesus are told tend to portray the Jews as the enemies of Jesus: enemies who commit what later Christians consider the unforgivable sin of betraying Jesus and handing him over to death on the cross.

Jesus was born a Jew, lived as a Jew, and died as a Jew. Many of his followers, however, came to believe that the Jews did not understand his message and that his gentile (i.e., non-Jewish) followers did. As a consequence, what began as a form of Jewish faith came to be embraced almost exclusively by those who thought of themselves as practicing a new and improved form of faith—Christianity. And these gentile Christians came to teach what some scholars have called the myth or story of supersession—that God had rejected the Jews and chosen gentiles instead.

Christianity, in fact, began as a Jewish sectarian movement. After two thousand years of biblical history, especially after the Babylonian exile (586–538 BCE), a variety of movements (such as those of the Sadducees, Pharisees, Hellenists, Zealots, Samaritans, Essenes, and Nazarenes—see the next chapter) developed in Judaism. One needs to realize that there was no agreement among these movements on a common set of sacred writings. Only at the end of the first century did the Hebrew bible as we know it come into existence, largely due to the influence of the Pharisees. At the beginning of the century, however, these groups and others were engaged in an ongoing argument about the right way of life for the people of Israel. At least some of the more sectarian groups, for example the Essenes, practiced baptismal rites, that is, rites of ritual immersion and purification. Such a ritual immersion was already a requirement for any gentile convert to Judaism (along with circumcision for males). What was new about the use of this practice was insisting that not only gentile converts but also Jews must undergo this rite if they had strayed from the true path of Israel. What path was that? Naturally, each movement saw itself as the model and all others as deviant. When you put all these factors together, what emerges is a picture of diverse sectarian movements, each proclaiming a message something like this: "We are the true Israel (i.e., the true Jews) you are not. The end of the world is at hand. God will come soon to judge the heaven and the earth, therefore it is important to repent, be ritually immersed (since Jews who have strayed are no better than the pagans), and become true Israel again—a true Jew; namely, one who lives the way we do." The "we" here of course was a different "we" depending on who was preaching the message. Of course any Jews who were not part of that "we" were likely to find the message an insult.

The Fall of the Temple

This whole picture of diversity changed dramatically in the year 70 CE when the Romans did just what the Sadducees (members of the Jewish upper class who tried to keep peace with the Romans) had feared; namely, lost their temper because of constant guerrilla attacks coming from the Zealots, marched into Jerusalem with thousands of troops, burned down the temple, and drove the Jews out of Jerusalem. In the aftermath of the fall of the temple two movements emerged to shape Western religious history: the Pharisaic movement, which became Rabbinic Judaism, and the Nazarene movement, which became gentile Christianity.

The Pharisees survived because they were able to provide a flexible leadership under dramatically new conditions. We shall discuss their important role in the formation of Rabbinic Judaism in the next chapter. Unlike Pharisaic Judaism, the Nazarene movement did not win a large following among Jews. Its greatest success was as a missionary movement for the conversion of Gentiles. The Nazarenes were an apocalyptic movement, believing that the end of time was at hand and that their special mission was to convert the Gentiles before the final judgment. In this they were inspired by the prophecies of Isaiah that at the end of time all nations would be gathered into Jerusalem (Isaiah 66:18–20).

A critical issue for the Nazarenes was the status of new gentile converts. This was taken up in the year 48 in a meeting in Jerusalem. The conservatives from Jerusalem argued that Gentiles had to be circumcised and obey the whole Mosaic law as was required of other Jews. Paul of Tarsus came to this meeting from Antioch where he and other Hellenistic Jews were converting large numbers of Gentiles. Hellenistic Jews were the great missionaries of first-century Judaism, who believed in adopting Greek culture and language in order to make Judaism attractive to Gentiles. Paul and others sympathetic to the Hellenistic mission argued that Gentiles should be exempt from the requirement of circumcision and should be required to keep mainly the moral commandments of the Mosaic covenant while being exempted from most of the ritual obligations. The faction led by Paul won the argument and a letter urging these changes went out to all the mission communities (Acts 15:19–21).

This ruling was decisive for the growth of the Nazarene movement among Gentiles. The message to the Gentiles now went something like this: "Would you Gentiles like to be full members of the house of Israel? For a short time only, between now and the end of time, God is offering Gentiles a special deal. You can be a part of Israel without having to be circumcised and without having to obey the whole Mosaic law, as long as you declare faith in Jesus, the rabbi from Nazareth who was raised from the dead and will be returning soon as the Messiah, to judge the heavens and the earth."

Gentiles flooded into the movement. By the second century Jewish members made up a smaller and smaller proportion of the total membership compared with Gentiles. And as the leadership fell more and more into the hands of Gentiles, the movement lost its sense of identity as a Jewish movement and began to think of itself as a separate new religion—Christianity.

The Origins of Christian Anti-Jewish Sentiment

We are now in a position to understand how the problem emerged that has plagued the relationship between Jews and Christians throughout the history of Western civilization. For the New Testament reflects the context of the Jewish sectarian arguments that had been going on in the first century, in which groups like the Zealots and the Essenes and others were saying to each other: "We, not you, are the true Israel, the true Jews. Therefore repent and be baptized (ritually immersed) and become Jews the way we are, for the end of time and God's judgment are at hand."

These first-century Jewish sectarian arguments were incorporated into the sacred writings of Christianity found in the New Testament. However, when these statements were read and repeated by the leaders of the "Christian" movement in the second and later centuries, they were no longer seen as exhortations from one Jewish group to another; now gentiles who had developed a separate identity for themselves as Christians took up the refrain: "We are the true Israel, you are not." And thus were born the Christian myths of supersession and divine rejection. Christians now argued: "We Christians have replaced you Jews as God's chosen people. God has rejected you and chosen us to supersede you, because you did not recognize Jesus as messiah and had him crucified instead."

Soon this logic was disastrously extended to the position that since "the Jews" had brought about the death of the very son of God who was sent to save them, not only had God rejected the Jews for all time, but it was the Christians' duty to punish them. It was a view that played a tragic role in the persecution of Jews throughout much of Western history. It was not until the time of Vatican II (1962–1965) that a commission created by Pope John XXIII condemned the teachings of supersession and divine rejection of the Jews and affirmed Paul's view, namely, that gentiles are like a wild olive branch grafted onto the tree of Judaism (Rom. 11:17–24) to share in God's promises to Abraham. By the end of the twentieth century, most Protestant churches had come to affirm this view as well.

Jesus Christ as Son of God

In the first four centuries after the time of Jesus, as gentile Christianity separated itself from Judaism, Christians struggled to formulate an understanding (dogma) of who Jesus is and what his significance is. The essential problem that faced the early followers of Jesus who, like the Apostle Paul, believed that they had a special mission to convert the gentiles (non-Jews), was how to translate an essentially Jewish message into terms non-Jews could understand. That is, if you stood on a corner in first-century Jerusalem and announced that the messiah was coming, you might get an audience who had some idea what you were talking about, but if, like Paul himself, you stood on a corner in first-century Corinth (in Greece), people would have no idea what you were talking about.

The task of the early Christians was to express the unique relationship they believed existed between Jesus and God in such a way that it did not violate their own sensibilities concerning idolatry—that is, making any creature equal to God. Coming out of a Jewish frame of reference, they did not want pagans to confuse their claims about Jesus being *Son of God* with the various pagan mythologies about divine beings coming down to earth in humanlike bodies. So the issue was how to speak correctly and clearly about the being and meaning of Jesus of Nazareth without claiming either too little (that Jesus was just a good man) or too much (that Jesus was not really human but rather a divine being like the gods of pagan mythology). For about three hundred years, Christians debated the various possible ways of thinking and speaking about

Jesus and held several church councils. By the time the argument was settled, both of these extremes came to be considered heresy.

The most important councils were those of Nicea in 325 and Chalcedon in 450. Some bishops and theologians argued that Jesus was a divine being with neither a mortal mind nor body. Some argued that Jesus had a human body and a divine mind, others that although his mind too was human and mortal he had a divine will, and so on. Such views made Jesus a kind of half-man and half-god, not unlike other such beings found in pagan mythology. The Council of Chalcedon rejected all such views, insisting that Jesus had a human body, a human mind. He was fully and completely human with a birth and a death like all others. Jesus' humanity differed from that of others in only one way—he was without sin. And yet the paradox is that in this man Jesus, God was wholly present, without confusion and without mixture. The formula arrived at to express this was that there were "two natures" (divine and human) *united yet completely distinct* (that is, without confusion or mixture) in the person of Jesus. The formula rejected the idolatry of claiming Jesus was "God" (i.e., a divine being and therefore not human), while at the same time it claimed that Jesus

THE NICENE CREED

Out of the doctrinal struggles of the early church came the following definitive creed of Christian belief:

We believe in one God the Father All-Sovereign, maker of all things visible and invisible;

And in one Lord Jesus Christ, the only begotten Son of God, begotten of the Father before all ages, Light of Light, true God of true God, begotten not made, of one substance with the Father, through whom all things were made; who for us men and for our salvation came down from the heavens, and was made flesh of the Holy Spirit and the Virgin Mary, and became man, and was crucified for us under Pontius Pilate, and suffered and was buried, and rose again on the third day according to the Scriptures, and ascended into the heavens, and sitteth on the right hand of the Father, and cometh again with glory to judge [the] living and dead, of whose kingdom there shall be no end:

And in the Holy Spirit, the Lord and the Life-Giver, that proceedeth from the Father, who with Father and Son is worshiped together and glorified together, who spake through the prophets:

In one holy Catholic and Apostolic Church:

We acknowledge one baptism unto remission of sins. We look for a resurrection of the dead, and the life of the age to come.

was unique and like no other human being in having the fullness of divinity present in him and united to his human nature.

Two beliefs had to be held together in this formula, that of Nicea—that the eternal Word through which all things were created was the "same as" (*homoousios*) God (i.e., eternal)—and that of Chalcedon—that the man Jesus was a mortal human being to whom that eternal Word (that preexisted Jesus) was united. If the Word was not eternal it could not confer eternity, and if Jesus was not mortal his resurrection offered no hope to all other mortals. This formula was meant to combat the views of the Christian Gnostics, who were declared heretics. They held that Jesus was a divine (i.e., purely spiritual) being—a god who only appeared to be human (i.e., only appeared to have a physical body), and therefore Jesus never really died, and so never really arose from the dead.

The formula of *two natures in one person* developed at Chalcedon was complemented by another unique doctrine or belief of Christians—the belief in God as a *Trinity*, affirmed earlier at the Council of Constantinople in 381. This doctrine asserted that God is one essence but three persons. The formula "three persons in one God, Father, Son, and Holy Spirit" is not really about mathematics but rather an affirmation that God can be creator of the universe yet be immanently present in the life of Jesus and in all things in the world through God's Word and Spirit—without ceasing to be transcendent. The doctrine of the Trinity affirmed that God is *in* all things (pan-en-theism) without accepting the pantheistic notion that God *is* all things.

Jews and Muslims, who embrace a prophetic monotheism, insisting that God is one and not three, have typically misunderstood the meaning of the doctrine of the Trinity. But then so have many Christians, so this should not be surprising. Nevertheless, the intent of both the "two natures in one person" doctrine concerning Jesus and the doctrine of the trinity concerning God is meant to affirm the uniqueness of a God who is both transcendent and immanent and who has no equals—the God of Abraham—the very same God affirmed by Jews and Muslims.

Constantinianism: The Marriage of Christianity and Empire

Perhaps the single most important political event in the history of Christianity was the conversion of the Roman emperor Constantine, who was the first emperor to champion the rights of Christianity by issuing the Edict of Toleration (also known as the Edict of Milan) in 313, and who was baptized on his deathbed. With this declaration Christianity went from being a persecuted religion to a permitted (and eventually the favored) religion in the empire. Constantine defeated his enemies for the control of the Roman Empire after seeing a vision of the cross in the sky. For the first time a Roman emperor saw Christianity not as the enemy of the empire but as conferring a divine blessing on the empire under his rule. Until this time Christians had tended to see Roman civilization, with its imperialism and colonial domination of foreign territories, as the work of the devil. That is how it is portrayed in the Book of

ORTHODOX CHRISTIANITY

While our main emphasis is on Latin Christianity, because that is the form of Christianity that fostered the emergence of modernity, we need to say something about the Greek churches. Although subject to the emperor, internally these churches were conciliar, placing ultimate authority not in a single bishop (a pope) but in church councils as meetings of all the bishops. The four great centers of Orthodoxy, Constantinople, Alexandria, Antioch, and Jerusalem, were each ruled by a patriarch who saw himself as equal to the others and to the bishop of the Latin church in Rome. The bishops of Rome and Constantinople were held in especially high esteem, but all the bishops together were seen as sharing authority.

Orthodox Christianity was distinctive for its mystical emphasis: Christ became human, it is said, so that humans could become divinized and share mystically in the eternal life of God. Orthodoxy is also distinctive for its understanding of sin as ignorance rather than corruption of the will through Original Sin as put forward in Latin-*Augustinian* Christianity. For the Orthodox churches, Christ is the great teacher who comes to dispel human ignorance of oneness with God and to restore humans to mystical unity with God. The emphasis is not on Christ as the Lord of History but on the cosmic Christ through whom all things are created, held together, and brought to fulfillment. From the beginning there was tension between the Eastern and Western churches, but a formal split did not occur until 1054.

Revelation, for instance. After Constantine, Christians began to see imperialism as a good thing, as a way of spreading the Gospel throughout the world. This was a decisive step in shaping the Western religious vision of a Christian civilization. The Constantinian vision achieved the status of official political policy when Christianity finally became the official religion of the Roman Empire under Emperor Theodosius in 381. By 391 all pagan worship was declared illegal and all pagan temples were closed. Only Judaism was permitted as an alternative to Christianity, and it existed under severe legal restrictions, Jews losing many of the freedoms they had had under the Romans.

The Greek-speaking churches of the East took Constantine's relationship to the church as a model of how things should be. There were four great centers of Greek Orthodoxy, in Constantinople, Alexandria (Egypt), Antioch (Syria), and Jerusalem, each ruled by a patriarch. Church and state existed in a symbiotic unity of a society that was to be both politically and religiously Christian. The emperor called church councils and even appointed the patriarchal bishops to rule over the church. The emperor ruled over both church and state in the name of Christ.

However, the pattern of the Western civilization that shaped the road to modernity was not that of Eastern Christianity but an important modification of it that put church and empire in a precarious relationship of both cooperation and antagonism. The Constantinian model thrived in Byzantium until the fifteenth century, but in the West, Roman political rule collapsed after the time of Theodosius, and the Latin-speaking world was no longer under the rule of an emperor. The political vacuum created by the absence of an emperor in the West allowed the bishops of the Latin-speaking churches to develop a different model of church and state relations. Since they were not directly answerable to political authority, they assumed much greater independence with respect to the state. This was especially true of the bishop of Rome, whose power and authority grew as secular political power and authority collapsed, leading gradually to the idea of the primacy of the bishop of Rome as "pope" over all other bishops. In the Latin church the idea of a separation between church and state developed. The idea that the bishop should have power and authority independent of the state led to a model of church and state where each had its own autonomy in a shared division of labor for the building of a Christian civilization. The chief architect of this alternate vision was Augustine of Hippo.

Augustine, Architect of Western Christianity

From the first of the medieval Popes, Gregory I, on through the Protestant Reformation and the emergence of modernity, the West has been deeply influenced by the theological thought of Augustine of Hippo, whom Christians typically refer to as "St. Augustine." After Jesus and the Apostle Paul, probably no other individual in history is more responsible for the shape of Western Christianity. Augustine's vision deeply shaped the development of Roman Catholicism from the fifth through the twelfth centuries. Then he was eclipsed by Thomas Aquinas, only to be recovered by the Protestant reformers Luther and Calvin in the sixteenth century. If Christians, in century after century, have assumed that one's nation should be a Christian nation, it is largely due to the way in which Augustine and others of his time understood the relation between history and biblical history—and that understanding was deeply influenced by the rule of Constantine.

Constantine died in 337; Augustine was born in 354 and died in 430. Consequently he lived through the time of Theodosius and witnessed firsthand the transformation of the Roman Empire from a pagan empire into a Christian one. The stunning reversal this represented could not fail to impress him and his contemporaries. They could not believe it was just chance or good luck that the pagan Roman Empire had become Christian. They concluded instead that it was the will of God—God had made the Roman Empire possible in order to provide the political unity and stability needed to spread the Gospel to the ends of the earth. They could not help but see the hand of God in these events, and they searched the scriptures for a vision to confirm their faith.

Between 397 and 423 Augustine wrote the three most important and influential books of his career. His famous autobiography *The Confessions*, was completed about 400. Then he began work on *The Trinity*, and concurrently (from 410) *The City of God*. *The Confessions* recounted his life story, which he saw as a miniature version of the cosmic drama of the history of salvation as outlined in the scriptures—a history he elaborated in *The City of God*. In *The Confessions* Augustine tells the story of the intellectual and emotional struggles that defined his quest for wisdom and led to his conversion. This story of conversion provided a model of the relation of faith and reason, just as *The City of God* told the story of history as an ongoing relationship between two cities (the city of God and the city of man). Although inspired by Constantine's actions, Augustine provided a different model for the relationship between church and state than that envisioned by Constantine.

In century after century, Christians turned to *The Confessions* as a model of conversion and spiritual piety. And in century after century the rulers of the church and of the state turned to *The City of God* as a model for the political order. Indeed, the first great medieval pope, Gregory I, used Augustine's vision to justify his exercise of power over the political order, and Charlemagne (c. 800), the first Holy Roman Emperor, is said to have slept with a copy of *The City of God* under his pillow. The influence of the vision of personal life embodied in *The Confessions* and the vision of history embodied in *The City of God* on the history of European Christianity is so vast and profound that it is almost impossible to calculate.

Faith, Reason, and the Quest for Wisdom

A key turning point in Augustine's life, as he relates it, was the awakening of his mind and heart to a passion for wisdom when he was 19 years old. Before that event Augustine's life was dominated by one passion—the selfish desire for wealth, fame, power, and sexual pleasure. About the time Augustine was completing his studies in Carthage, he came across a book by the pagan author Cicero entitled *Hortensius*. It was, he says, a book on wisdom. This book set him on fire with a new kind of desire—the desire for wisdom. "I was not encouraged by this work of Cicero's to join this or that sect; instead I was urged on and inflamed with a passionate zeal to love and seek and obtain and embrace and hold fast wisdom itself, whatever it might be" (*Confessions*, III,4,57). Augustine doesn't say that *Hortensius* changed his thinking but rather that it "altered my way of feeling…and gave me different ambitions and desires" (III,4,56). Augustine's wording here is very important. His experience changed his feelings and desires, which in turn eventually changed his thinking also. Christianity is a religion of the transformation of the heart as the seat of the emotions. Christianity began with the call of Jesus to his hearers for a change of heart, and virtually every great reform and renewal movement in Christian history has returned to this theme.

Between the age of 19 and his conversion to Catholic Christianity at age 31, a great contest of cosmic significance went on in Augustine's soul. Throughout he followed the questions wherever they led him—through Gnosticism, Skepticism, and Platonism—until his intellect was satisfied of the truth of

Catholic Christian beliefs. But still he could not embrace the Gospel. Why? Because, he said, his will was divided by conflicting emotions. He both wanted to "turn" to the Lord (*conversio*) and at the same time wanted wealth, fame, and sensual pleasures. His final conversion came about when God seduced him "in the bedroom" of his heart and "turned him around"—a conversion in which his will was no longer divided but united with that of God's. This, said Augustine, is the meaning of *grace*—God making possible what one cannot do oneself.

Augustine's story of his conversion became a model for understanding the relationship between faith and reason. Theology is "faith seeking understanding." For Augustine faith is the ground of reason because one's first act of faith is to trust that doubt and questioning can lead one to God. This was the lesson he learned when at 19 he began his quest for wisdom with the book of a pagan author, Cicero. In his *Confessions* he says that only later did he come to realize that the wisdom at work in his doubt was actually Christ, the wisdom of God. Therefore, when he had the faith to doubt he already had an implicit faith in Christ.

As he grew older, Augustine seemed to forget the adventurousness of his own quest for wisdom and insisted that church and state must work together to compel those he perceived as heretics to accept his point of view as a bishop of the church. It is this later Augustine who no doubt was the inspiration behind the views of those like Pope Pius IX and the First Vatican Council, who fought modernity by denying individual conscience and affirming the right of the church to demand special protection from all *heresy*, using the power of the state. And it was no doubt the earlier Augustine whose spirit lies behind those who championed Pope John XXIII's vision at the Second Vatican Council and opened themselves to the pluralistic world around them, on the chance that they too might find some of the wisdom of God among nonbelievers even as Augustine had from Cicero.

Augustine's Tale of Two Cities

In the same way that *The Confessions* provided an ambivalent model of faith and reason, *The City of God* provided an ambivalent model of church and state. The meaning of history is unraveled for Augustine by a symbolic reading of the biblical stories as a history of two cities—the human city and the city of God. These two cities lived in the world guided by two different loves, *cupiditas* (selfish love) and *caritas* (selfless love), respectively. These, of course, are the same two loves Augustine saw at war in his own life in *The Confessions*. Augustine's theory about the relationship of these cities set the model between the church and the state, religion and politics, and the sacred and the secular for most of Western history.

Augustine's story of the human city was the history of civilizations going through endless cycles of progress and decline—a story without any clear purpose or meaning. But hidden within that history was another history—that of the city of God. Its story, which is revealed in the Bible, has a clear direction—a beginning, middle, and end. And it has a clear purpose, for it is the story of a journey with God through time toward a final resurrection and eternal life for all who belong to the city of God. It is a story of the relationship between this city and the human city made up of the pagan nations. The city of God, however, was not identical with the church. For the church is a "mixed body," since not all who belong to the visible church are true members, and some who do not belong (for example, some Greek philosophers), are. Only at the final judgment will human beings come to know who truly belongs to the city of God.

In defining the religious and political relationship between these two cities Augustine set up a fundamental reciprocal tension between church and state. For he argues that God created the state to provide order against the chaos of sin, and that its authority comes from God in order to establish the peace necessary for the spread of the Gospel. Both state and church exist through God's will to serve God's purposes. In the journey through history each should serve the other. The state should be subject to the church in spiritual matters, and the church should be subject to the state in earthly matters. Neither should seek to dominate the other. However, in actual history neither side could fully agree with the other as to where to draw the line between earthly matters and spiritual matters. And too often each side forgot the part about not dominating the other. Indeed, throughout most of Western history both popes and emperors sought to upset the balance between the two by trying to dictate to the other. Unlike the pure Constantinian vision, Augustine separates church and state (e.g., pope and emperor). Yet Augustine's vision is not yet the modern one that insists on a secular or nonreligious state, for he assumes that both powers must work together to transform the world into a Christian civilization. This was a fundamental assumption of medieval Catholicism.

Since the time of Augustine, most Christians have assumed that the task of Christianity is to transform every society into a "Christian nation" constituted by two kingdoms: church and empire (or church and state). This pattern continued even after the "Holy Roman Empire" collapsed and the Protestant Reformation helped usher in the modern era. In that era the spread of modern European culture came to replace Roman civilization as the political order, which Christians believed God willed for the spread of Christianity around the world. Only gradually, after the religious wars the Protestant Reformation provoked, did Christians begin to explore an alternative—the fully modern idea of a secular (i.e., nonreligious) state as the guarantor of religious freedom in a religiously pluralistic world. We will return to this observation when we discuss modernization.

PREMODERN CHRISTIANITY: THE CLASSICAL ERA

In 476 the last Roman emperor in the West was deposed. Less than a century after the time of Augustine of Hippo, the Roman Empire and its civilization collapsed in the West. Most commerce ceased, for example, and the Roman money economy was replaced by a barter economy. The only institution to survive and carry civilization forward into Europe was the church, primarily through the spread of Christian monasteries. It was monasticism that provided the bridge of civilization between the ancient world and the modern world, bringing technological development and the light of learning to a European period that has been otherwise described as "the dark ages."

Over several centuries Europe was invaded by tribes from the north. Eventually a melange of feudal kingdoms developed as tribal leaders turned into feudal lords. The feudal system was a network of loyalties established between a landholder (king or a nobleman) and those who served him and his estates. It was a hierarchical network extending from the nobility through vassals to serfs and slaves at the bottom. This hierarchy was anchored in land grants or "fiefs" to vassals in exchange for loyalty and service. The nobility at the top of this system was a combination of a secular warrior aristocracy and religious aristocracy, for bishops and abbots (the heads of monasteries) too could be feudal lords, and the church was a major landholder.

The Middle Ages roughly spans the time from the sixth to the fourteenth centuries. Christians lived in a world where only the elite among the clergy and the nobility were educated and could read. Moreover, it was a world without printing presses, so that the few existing books were handwritten. The average Christian got his or her religious view of life from the sermons of the priest and from the artwork inscribed in the windows and walls of the churches and cathedrals of Europe. Scripture came through the mediation of the clergy. The later development of Protestant Christianity was not even a possibility at this time, for people had no Bibles of their own and could not have read them if they did. Consequently, a Christianity based on the later Protestant principle of "scripture alone" was unimaginable.

The Medieval World View: Sacraments and Festivals

Sacraments

Life in this world was a testing place and a place of waiting to enter one's true home in heaven, if one passed the test. Before that day of final judgment, Christians believed that when they died their souls would be separated from their bodies and come before God for individual judgment. In the future (at an unknown time) this age would come to an end and Jesus Christ would return to raise the bodies of the dead and unite them to their souls. Those who had been faithful and good would be rewarded for all eternity in heaven, enjoying the "beatific vision" or presence of God; the rest would be consigned to eternal punishment in hell.

The church was God's gift to this world to help Christians prepare for their final judgment. The church was founded by Jesus Christ, the Son of God, who had passed on leadership of the church to his chief apostle, Peter

THE SEVEN SACRAMENTS AND THE LIFE CYCLE

The seven sacraments, which developed by the late Middle Ages, were a system of seven rituals that provided assistance to the Christian at every stage of life, from birth to death. The word "sacrament" comes from the Latin term for the Greek word for "mystery." Sacraments stood apart from other rituals in their power to unite humans to God and eternal life, thus guaranteeing salvation from sin and death. With the coming of the Protestant Reformation in the sixteenth century, only baptism and communion were retained. The remaining five sacraments were rejected on the ground that they could not be found in the New Testament and therefore were not biblical. However, many of these "rejected" practices are continued in some Protestant denominations as rituals but not sacraments in the full sense.

Baptism   In the New Testament period there were many pagan "mystery" religions. These religions offered rituals by which one could be united to one's god and achieve eternal life. The early converts to Christianity followed the Jewish practice of ritual immersion for new converts. (Remember, Jesus himself was baptized by John the Baptist.) A new twist was added to this ritual, however, in that Christians interpreted their immersion as a spiritual dying and a rising with Christ. The convert's whole body was ritually submersed in water (a river, a lake, or a special pool, for instance). The full submersion of the body was seen as participation in Christ's death in the tomb; the emergence of the body from the water was equated with Christ's resurrection and departure from the tomb. The immersion was accompanied by the words, "I baptize you in the name of the Father, the Son, and the Holy Spirit."

This was a powerful experience for the adult. However, as the practice of infant baptism developed in later generations, the ritual was transformed. Instead of ritual immersion, it was determined that the pouring of water over the forehead was more practical and suitable. At baptism, a newborn infant had water poured over him or her in the sign of a cross and in the name of the Trinity. This ritual was believed to flood the soul with divine grace (divine love, forgiveness, and assistance), erasing all stain of original sin, the sin of Adam and Eve that was believed to mark every newborn child. Baptism was believed to change the destiny of the child from death to eternal life. The child, now removed from the power of sin, was provided with additional grace along life's journey.

Communion   Equal in importance as a sacrament was the holy eucharist, or communion. This practice seems to have been an adaptation of the Jewish blessing of the bread and wine at meals, especially as it was practiced at Passover (i.e., the Jewish remembrance of their deliverance by God from slavery in Egypt). In the Gospels Jesus is portrayed as having used the occasion of his last Passover meal to create a ritual by which his followers could spiritually share his body and blood by eating the bread and wine he blessed and in this way participate in his coming death and resurrection. At this last Passover he took the bread and said, "This is my body," and the wine and said, "This is the cup of my blood shed for you and for many for the forgiveness of sins." So by eating the bread and drinking the wine consecrated by a priest who represents Jesus, Christians believe they are partaking of the very body and blood of Jesus who died for their sins on the cross and brought them to eternal life. Both baptism and communion were established well before the Middle Ages. However, to these, five other sacraments were added.

Confirmation   In the beginning of Christianity the baptized were adult converts who made a conscious decision to follow Christ. As the practice of infant baptism developed, so did a controversy over whether this was appropriate, since the infant was too young to make such a choice. But since baptism was thought to be essential for eternal life, many believed it was too risky to delay it to adulthood. Moreover, it was argued that baptism was about God's choice of the infant, not vice versa. It was, however, clear that at some point the child needed to make a conscious choice to live for Christ. The practice of confirmation was a ritual by which the young person at about the age of 13 (the onset of adulthood in the ancient world, especially in Judaism) demonstrated his or her knowledge of the faith, was anointed on the forehead with oil, and made a public declaration of commitment to Christ. In this way, as the infant became a young adult he or she was *confirmed* in the faith, freely accepting responsibility for that faith.

Marriage   During the Middle Ages, marriage was also transformed into a sacrament. The union between a man and a woman came to be compared to the union between Christ and the church. As such it became more than a union between and man and woman for the purpose of raising a family. It became a ritual for uniting the man and the woman to each other in Christ, which conferred God's grace and eternal life. The husband and wife promised to love and care for each other as Christ loved and cared for his church.

Ordination   In the Middle Ages, a ritual also developed for ordaining men to the priesthood. According to Catholic teachings that developed in the early church, the apostles appointed their successors, who in turn appointed their successors, the bishops, for the next generation in an unbroken chain of authority from Christ into the far distant future. This chain of succession was believed to guarantee the Catholic Church as the preserver of the true teachings. The bishops were Christ's representatives in the community of the faithful. Bishops, in turn, ordained others, priests, to assist them in representing Christ in every worshiping community. Priests were ordained by bishops in ritual ceremonies in which their hands were anointed with oil as an expression of their sacred role in conferring the grace of God upon Christians through the administration of the sacraments.

Until the late Middle Ages, ordained priests could also be married. Later reforms established the requirement that priests remain unmarried or celibate. From this point on a man had to choose between the sacrament of marriage and that of ordination. (Ordination was not available to women. The fact that Christ and all the first apostles were male was interpreted as an expression of God's will that all priests be male. In the modern period, many Protestant denominations have discarded this rule.)

Confession and Extreme Unction Finally, two additional sacraments were developed during the Middle Ages, the first, confession, to mediate God's forgiveness for sin, and the second, extreme unction (anointing with oil) to confer God's power of healing in times of illness. In the early church it was common for people to put off baptism until near death for fear that if one sinned after baptism there was no further means to have one's sins washed away. Such a practice was a gamble, since it is usually difficult to know just when death will come. To encourage baptism in infancy, the church developed a sacrament for the forgiveness of sins. This ritual required the penitent to confess his or her sins and express true sorrow for them to a priest who would then "absolve" or forgive the sins in the name of Christ. This forgiveness restored the sinner to his or her original baptismal destiny of eternal life with God. The priest would also give the sinner an appropriate "penance" to complete in "reparation" for his or her sins. Such a penance varied depending on the seriousness of the sin but most frequently required the penitent to repeat certain prayers or make a pilgrimage to a sacred place and resolve not to fall into sin again.

Closely associated with the practice of confession in times of serious illness was the practice of extreme unction, or anointing with oil. In cases of extreme illness, a priest would be sought to anoint the Christian with oil on the extremities of the body (the forehead, lips, hands, and feet) in hopes of mediating God's grace to heal the person. Because this ritual of healing often occurred when the person was near death, it often included the sacrament of confession as well, and over time the sacrament of extreme unction came to be thought of as the sacrament of the dying.

(Matthew 16:8). This apostolic succession was continued by the popes, who were seen as the direct successors of Peter, guaranteeing that the church would be divinely guided because the pope speaks with the authority of Christ on earth. The Catholic Church claimed that apostolic succession proved that it alone was the one true church.

Through the descending hierarchy of the pope, the bishops, and the clergy, as Christ's priesthood, the grace of God was conferred on humankind, mediated to every Christian through seven *sacraments*: baptism, confirmation, holy eucharist (i.e., communion), marriage, ordination, confession, and extreme unction. These sacraments were believed to mediate the grace (forgiveness and divine assistance) of God to Christians, helping them grow spiritually and morally toward holiness or saintliness. Such grace was considered an undeserved gift from God. However, it was also seen as an invitation to a renewed spiritual life that required human cooperation, accepting the aid offered by God, and adding one's own effort to use that aid for spiritual and moral improvement. Because the sacraments could be administered only by ordained clergy, every Christian was dependent on the priests and bishops of the church under the rule of the Pope to be in a right relationship to God. Outside the church there was no salvation.

Festivals

If the sacraments carried Christians from cradle to grave, the annual cycle of religious festivals carried them through the seasons of the year and created for them a world of stories in which to dwell. The early church saw itself as living in the time between Easter and the "advent" or "coming" of Christ to raise the dead and judge the heavens and the earth. By the Middle Ages the times of the year became more detailed. The church year began with Advent, whose stories evoked hope for the *Second Coming*. Gradually a concurrent theme of Advent as preparation for Christmas developed, overshadowing its theme of hope for the final resurrection. Then Christmas and Epiphany were developed as festival seasons to celebrate the stories of the birth of Jesus and the visits of the wise men from the East and the baptism of Jesus. No one knew the date on which Jesus was born; December 25 was chosen to compete with the popular pagan festival honoring the sun god. The season of Christmas/Epiphany is followed by that of Lent. This is a time of fasting and prayer in preparation for Easter. Its stories recall the temptations, healings, and teachings of Jesus. Lent culminated in Holy Week, in which the stories of Jesus' trial and death are recalled. The Easter season begins with the celebration of the stories of the resurrection and is followed by the final season of the church year, Pentecost. This season recalls the descent of the Holy Spirit upon the apostles and the birth and growth of the church. After Pentecost, of course, comes Advent and a new year of hope and expectation. Thus, through the cycle of festivals, Christians dwelt in a world of stories that tied and bound them into the great cosmic drama in which God was bringing salvation to the whole world through the church, its stories, and its sacraments.

Medieval Christians grounded in the sacraments and oriented by the festivals and their stories also sought divine aid through the help of the saints and angels in heaven. That is, they believed that exemplary Christians (saints) who had died, and other spiritual beings, known as angels, had the ear of God in heaven. This was, after all, how things got done on earth in medieval feudal

HOLY WEEK

Although Christmas has become the most culturally popular festival of the Christian calendar in Western civilization, the most important, religiously, is Easter and the week that precedes it, known as Holy Week. While not all forms of Christianity observe this week in exactly the same way, those churches that emphasize ritual (for example, Catholic, Eastern Orthodox, Episcopal, some forms of Lutheranism) typically engage in the following practices:

During the week Christians recall the arrest, trial, crucifixion, death, and resurrection of Jesus, which is the cornerstone of their faith. The week begins on Palm Sunday, which recalls the triumphant entry of Jesus into Jerusalem riding on a donkey and acclaimed by the crowds, one week before his death. On this Sunday many churches pass out palms during the service to remind Christians of the story, and the entire "passion story" of one of the Gospels is read, recounting all the events from the arrest of Jesus through his crucifixion.

Next, on Holy Thursday Christians typically celebrate a communion service that recalls the events of Jesus' "last supper." This was his last Passover meal during which he blessed bread and wine, declaring it to be his body and blood—a ritual Christians have repeated ever since. On this night another of the passion stories will be read, and in some churches a ritual foot washing of representative members of the congregation will occur, recalling how Jesus washed the feet of his disciples before the last supper began. Typically, the altar is stripped bare of all candles, flowers, and altar cloths at the end of this service and will remain so until Easter Sunday. Then on Good Friday it is customary to have a prayer service, which will recount another Gospel's passion story and/or recall the seven last words of Jesus on the cross. The altar remains bare and the tone of the service is somber. On Saturday of Holy Week there is no activity at all, recalling the period that Jesus was in the grave. In some churches there may be a midnight Easter vigil of prayers and devotions in anticipation of Easter morning.

On Easter morning many churches offer a sunrise service. Whatever the time of the services, all are communion services of great festivity. The altar will be decorated in white cloths, candles, and flowers; there will be joyous hymns and choir anthems; and the scripture readings for the day will announce the resurrection of Jesus Christ from the dead. The service is typically followed by families and friends gathering for festive meals in their homes. The participation of the Christian in this week of events is often preceded by forty days of fasting and prayer (Lent). Holy Week itself can be a rather intense experience that leads the Christian through a kind of spiritual death and resurrection and deepens and renews his or her faith.

society. If you wanted a favor from a member of the nobility or the king, it was best to go through someone at court who could intercede for you. Similar hierarchies of saints and angels were believed to exist in heaven and to work in a similar fashion. On the other hand, it was believed that some angels who rebelled against God, the devil and his minions, exercised an evil influence over human beings that must be resisted through the power of prayer and the sacraments.

This medieval world view represented the full integration of the biblical world view of life, death, and resurrection of the body with the Greek metaphysical world view of the cosmos as a hierarchical order. It forms the essence of the Catholic world view. Lacking the historical consciousness that came after the Renaissance, medieval Christians thought this amalgamated world view was exactly what Jesus Christ proclaimed in the Gospels. It was the one true doctrine of the one true church.

The Two Cities Revisited

Throughout the Middle Ages there was an ongoing struggle between the two cities that Augustine had described. From the time of the first Holy Roman Emperor, Charlemagne (800), the Holy Roman emperors sought to dominate the church and the popes sought to dominate the state. This is well illustrated by Charlemagne's coronation. He was crowned as the first Holy Roman Emperor on Christmas day in the year 800. Charlemagne had intended to crown himself, but Pope Leo III, in a surprise move, seized the crown and placed it on Charlemagne's head before he could object. This move attempted to say that the church had the power to appoint state leaders; it was symbolic of the struggle between popes and emperors (church and state) throughout the Middle Ages.

A turning point in the development of the power of the papacy was its emulation of the monastic model of church discipline that was established with the Cluny reforms. Because Benedictine monasticism had a strong work ethic that treated work done for God as a form of prayer, even while the monks led simple lives, the monasteries eventually became great centers of wealth, which in turn led to abuses. In 910 a new reform movement swept through monasticism, and a new monastery was founded at Cluny in France in 910. The Cluny reforms sought spiritual renewal and reorganization.

Organizationally, before this reform each monastery was an autonomous world unto itself under an abbot. The Cluniac monasteries provided an important model for the development of colonialism, first adopted by the church and later emulated by the secular institutions of modernity. These monasteries provided the first models for an international corporation, with subsidiaries spread throughout the world but answerable to a central command—in this case the monastic headquarters in Cluny. Under Pope Gregory VII (1073–1085), the Cluniac reforms in turn became the model adopted by the papacy for centralizing its authority over all the bishops in the church. Just as the abbot demanded obedience from all his monks, the pope came to expect obedience from all his bishops.

The height of papal power occurred under Pope Innocent III (1198–1216), who forced the kings of England and France into submission, authorized the Fourth Crusade, and carried forward the Inquisition against all heretics with impunity. Innocent actually had the spiritual and temporal power the papacy aspired to have, as no pope has had before or since. The weakest moment of papal power, by contrast, occurred (as we have noted) under Pius IX in the late nineteenth century.

The Promise and Threat of Christian Mysticism

Like every great religion, Christianity has a long tradition of mysticism—meaning, in this context, those beliefs and practices that are thought to lead to a direct experience of God in Christ. The heart of Christian mysticism is rooted in the biblical claim that human beings are created in the image and likeness of a God who is without image. The closer one comes to being like God, the more empty of all self-identity one has to become to be in the image of one who is without image. Christian mysticism expresses itself in two dramatically different forms—the mysticism of love and union (the divine-human marriage) and the mysticism of identity. The former is exemplified by Spanish mystics of the sixteenth century, St. Theresa of Avila and her student, St. John of the Cross; the latter by the German mystic, Meister Eckhart. Unlike Christian theology, Christian mysticism is rich in the names of women: Theresa of Avila, Catherine of Siena, Theresa of Liseaux, Julian of Norwich, to name a few. In part this is because mystical experience is viewed as a gift from God that cannot be institutionally controlled.

The place of the Christian mystic in the tradition has always been an ambivalent one, more so for the mystics of identity than for those of unity. This is because mystics often speak not of the difference between God and the person but of their oneness. God and the self, they sometimes say, are so close that the two seem indistinguishable. Whenever mystics speak in this way they are in danger of being accused of blasphemy and heresy—of confusing themselves with God and claiming to be God. This is a problem not just for Christianity but also for the great prophetic religions of Judaism and Islam. And yet, despite this seemingly ever-present danger, each of these traditions has chosen to maintain an uneasy peace with its mystics rather than deny the importance or validity of mysticism.

Christianity, Judaism, Islam: The Crusades and the Inquisition

One cannot leave the Middle Ages without discussing the Crusades and the Inquisition. The Crusades brought dramatic changes, for while they were an attempt to rid Christendom of all "false religion" by conducting war against both Jews and Muslims, they ended up exposing Europeans to heretofore unexperienced religious and cultural diversity as the crusaders traveled to the Middle

East, to liberate Jerusalem and drive back the "infidel." The Crusades also opened up new trade and interactions between cultures and stimulated economies. As a result of their exposure to new ideas and attitudes and new religious beliefs and practices, some Europeans embraced new forms of ancient Christian Gnosticism. Groups known as the Cathari or Albigensians believed in reincarnation, and their goal was to liberate the spirit from the evil of a fleshly body. This led Pope Lucius III (1184) to inaugurate the infamous Inquisition. The Inquisition began as a crusade to stamp out heresy. The Fourth Lateran Council in 1215 authorized the punishment of all heretics by the state and also prescribed distinctive dress for Jews and Muslims (e.g., pointed hats or yellow badges) and restricted Jews to living in ghettos.

There were other more constructive consequences of the Crusades as well, ones that opened the door to modernity, for contact with the Muslim world led to the rediscovery of Aristotle, Greek metaphysics, and science. Most of Aristotle's work had been lost to the West but was preserved in Islamic civilization. The rediscovery of Aristotle led to new and controversial ways of thinking in the new universities of Europe in the twelfth and thirteenth centuries. And for a brief time Jewish, Muslim, and Christian philosophers, like Maimonides (1135–1204), Averroes (Ibn Rushd, 1126-1198), and Thomas Aqunas (1224–1274), respectively, all used a common philosophical language to learn from each other's traditions, even if only, in the end, so that each could argue for the superiority of his own.

There were four main Crusades, in 1095, 1147, 1189, and 1201. Armies were organized to march to the Holy Land (the modern state of Israel) and free it from the Muslim infidels. But as the crusading armies marched through Europe they unleashed devastating violence on the Jewish communities they encountered along the way, fed by ancient Christian stereotypes of Jews as a "rejected people" because they were "Christ killers." The result was an unbelievable amount of suffering and death. In 1096, as the armies of the First Crusade passed through the Rhine valley in Germany, an estimated ten thousand Jews were slain—somewhere between a third and a fourth of the Jewish population of Germany. These mob actions became a typical pattern restricted not just to the period of the Crusades but extending into the centuries that followed. These "pogroms," as they were called in later centuries, eventually led to the expulsion of Jews from countries like France and Spain and their resettlement mostly in Eastern Europe, where they remained until the Nazi Holocaust killed two-thirds of East European Jews in the twentieth century.

While the Jews were the "incidental" targets of the Crusaders, the Muslims were the direct targets. For the Muslims held the Holy Land in their possession and threatened the Eastern church, whose main center was Constantinople. Thus the Crusades were ostensibly for the purpose of driving back the Muslims, reclaiming Jerusalem, and reuniting the Eastern and Western church. Pope Urban II, who preached the First Crusade, promised its soldiers that all who fought the infidel would have their sins forgiven and enter heaven. In addition,

Crusaders were promised that they could keep the lands they conquered. The Crusaders reached Jerusalem in June of 1099 and laid siege to the city, which fell on July 15. Men, women, and children lost their lives in a bloody massacre.

Islam, which seemed to appear abruptly in the Arabian desert in the early seventh century, had grown within the span of a century into a civilization larger than the Roman Empire had been. Jews were a known quantity to Christians, but Muslims were something new. Yet Muslims claimed to be as old as Abraham and to have maintained the faith of Abraham while both Jews and Christians strayed. Christians did not know whether to brand Islam pure paganism or a new form of Christian heresy. In the end they made both types of claims. Moreover, they found the spread of Islam intimidating. Indeed, for a time it looked as if Muslims might proceed beyond Spain to conquer most of Europe. But Charles Martel, whose initiative led to the formation of the Carolingian dynasty and the Holy Roman Empire, turned the Muslims back at Tours in 732, and Europe remained Christian.

To medieval Christians, Jews and Muslims represented a threat to the oneness and truth of Christianity—a threat from within (Jews) and from without

WOMEN IN PREMODERN CHRISTIANITY

Christianity (like Judaism, Islam, and the religions of Asia) created patriarchal (male-dominated) societies. Historically, women have played the greatest roles in those forms of Christianity that emphasized direct and immediate religious experience as more authoritative than the institutional authority of the bishops. Thus in the early church women played a greater role in Gnostic (mystical and otherworldly) and Montanist (apocalyptic and ecstatic) Christianity than in Catholic (institutionally hierarchical) Christianity. And yet there were always some women who were exceptions to the rule. Women had leadership roles in some of the early Christian communities, but as the early church became institutionalized, prevailing assumptions of male dominance from the surrounding culture seemed to reassert themselves, and the pattern of excluding women from roles as priests and bishops took hold. During the Middle Ages women found ways to exercise autonomy and independence by founding monastic orders for women. With the Protestant Reformation, however, even that option was taken from them, and women were largely confined to the home and child rearing until nineteenth-century missionary movements offered women new opportunities for leadership. The role of women in these missions played an important part in the political development of the woman's suffrage movement for independence and the right to vote.

(Muslims). Rather than seeing them as sharing a common heritage, since all three claimed to be children of Abraham, Christians tended to see both Jews and Muslims as "children of the devil" who willfully refused to see the truth of Christianity. And of course Jews and Muslims were equally mistrustful of Christians. The fear and mistrust that grew out of this history has colored relations between these three communities throughout the modern period. It is an open question whether that will change in the future, for in all three traditions some want to return to the fundamentals that divide them while others want to seek a new path of harmony and cooperation.

CHRISTIANITY AND MODERNITY

The Emergence of Modernity

Protestantism and modernity are like two sides of the same coin, arising out of the *via moderna* and *devotio moderna* of the late medieval theology to flourish in the Renaissance and Reformation. Therefore, unlike all other religious traditions, Protestantism did not, at first, experience modernization as the intrusion of an outside force but rather as a form of experience nurtured from within. It was only as modernization and secularization took on lives of their own, independent of the Protestant Reformation, that they began to appear threatening.

The Renaissance and Reformation fostered a new modern way of thinking (*via moderna*) and feeling (*devotio moderna*) that valued the autonomy of individual experience and individual conscience and saw the authority to rule coming from the bottom up. This was brought about by their separating Christian belief from the ancient and medieval hierarchical world view embodied in Greek metaphysics and encouraging the gradual and ambivalent development of democracy, equality, and human rights in both the religious and secular political life of the West.

Nevertheless, the ancient dream of empire and colonial rule did not die. Rather it was transformed into a desire to spread this new "modern" Western culture (science, technology, politics, and economics) and the Christian Gospel around the world in a new mission of global colonization. As we will see, the colonial sense of cultural superiority often was at odds with the message of equality fostered by modernity.

By the year 1500, Europe had been transformed from a primitive and undeveloped land into a network of significant urban centers. In these cities individualism, an independent money economy, and democratic self-governance began to emerge through a process of incorporation, a legal agreement with the nobility that gave citizens the right of self-governance in exchange for taxes. With increased craftsmanship and trade, corporate charters were also granted to the new craft guilds known as "universities." These corporations mark the beginnings of the secularization of institutions that is one of the defining characteristics of modernization, that is, self-governing institutions that operate independently of direct religious authority and also of traditional medieval political authority (kings and lords). Education, too, declared its independence from the monasteries and cathedral schools, as scholars banded together to form their own guilds or universities. It was in these universities, then, that a second level of secularization began to be achieved, as scholars for the first time began to think about their subject matters with a sense of independence from direct church authority. In this way the social and intellectual differentiation and institutional complexity characteristic of modern secular societies began to develop. And in this environment three trends converged to shape the modern West: (1) the millennialism of historical progress, (2) the via moderna of autonomous reason, and (3) the devotio moderna of emotional transformation.

Millennialism: History as Progress

One strand of modernity had its roots in the apocalyptic visions of the twelfth-century Cistercian monk and abbot from southern Italy, Joachim of Fiore (1132-1202) who looked forward to the coming of the third and final age of history, known as the "millennium," which he believed was predicted in the Book of Revelation. Joachim's vision of history deeply influenced the modern age. In his *Everlasting Gospel*, Joachim suggested that history can be divided into three ages corresponding to the three persons of the Trinity in Christianity—the age of the Father (beginning with Abraham), which was superseded by the age of the Son (beginning with Christ), which would in turn be replaced by a third and final age, that of the Holy Spirit. Joachim thought of himself as living the final age of the Spirit in which there would no longer be any need for the institutional church and its clergy—nor for any other institutions, including the state. The direct infusion of the Spirit in mystical piety, which Joachim expected, would create a natural spontaneous harmony between all individuals and render all institutions superfluous. The third age would be an age of perfect freedom and harmony, and was destined to last a millennium (that is, one thousand years).

Joachim's version of the myth of history as proceeding through three ages profoundly shaped the modern view of history as a story of progress—history moves forward from the ancient period through the medieval and culminates in the modern age. For Joachim the third age was identified with the triumph of mysticism over the institutional church. But his three ages became increasingly secularized during the Enlightenment in Western Europe, so that while the three-age model persisted it was no longer identified with the Trinity. For instance, Gotthold Lessing, the great Enlightenment scholar, held that the education of the human race passed through three phases: childhood, adolescence, and adulthood. The last or third age he identified with the Age of Enlightenment in which the autonomy of reason (instead of the Holy Spirit) would lead to a natural and rational harmony among human beings. This vision of three ages was carried forward into the nineteenth century, when

Auguste Comte, the founding father of sociology, divided history into the ages of myth, philosophy, and science. One can find further parallels in the visions of other nineteenth-century philosophers such as Hegel and Marx.

The Via Moderna

According to the great medieval theologian Thomas Aquinas, faith complements and completes reason. Rightly used, the two can never contradict each other. However, the generation of schoolmen or scholars that followed Aquinas took a more radical stand. These theologians, who were called "nominalists," argued that not only were faith and reason independent from each other, but also that reason was of little help in discerning the will of God. The nominalists rejected the idea that the God of the Bible was the same as the God of Greek metaphysics. For the nominalists, the only way to know what God wills is through faith and scriptures, and the only way to know the world God has created is through rational empirical investigation of the world God has actually created. The roots of the split between faith and science begin here.

The nominalist William of Ockham (1285–1349), for instance, rejected the ancient metaphysical way of thinking (*via antiqua*) and advocated a new *via moderna* or "modern way" of thinking. The new way secularized the world by separating faith and reason. Greek metaphysics emphasized the continuity between God and the world, but the new modern way emphasized the discontinuity: God alone was holy and so the world was secular rather than sacred. The new way of thinking shifted the focus of reason away from Greek metaphysics and toward empirical inquiry, for if the world is radically contingent on God's will as the Bible seems to suggest, then the structure of reality cannot be logically deduced through Greek metaphysics but only empirically investigated. And if one wants to know the will of God one either has to consult the actual world God created (in regard to secular or "worldly" matters) or the scriptures God revealed (in matters of faith). In either case, what is required is individual empirical inquiry, not deductive metaphysics.

The Renaissance and the Protestant Reformation are siblings that grew up together. The Renaissance began as a literary movement in the south of Europe, especially Italy, in the fourteenth century. It did not reach northern Europe (France, Germany, and England) much before the sixteenth century and the time of the Protestant Reformation. It began as a movement to recover the pre-Christian wisdom of the ancient world of Greece and Rome. The Reformation, in a parallel fashion, sought to reach back into antiquity and recover the original New Testament Christian vision before it had been integrated with Greek metaphysics by the medieval theologians. So a modern way of thinking was used to recover a lost past in order to throw off the recent past (the medieval world) and create a new modern world. This process was greatly facilitated by a new technological invention, the printing press (1454) and with it a growing popular literacy that made possible the rapid and wide dissemination of new ideas. It has been estimated that by 1500 some nine million copies of thirty thousand different works were already in existence. The press also greatly facilitated the development of national identities by promoting a common language and shared ideas within a geographic area.

The initiator of the Protestant Reformation was Martin Luther (1483–1546), an Augustinian monk who embraced the new modern way of thinking. Thus, Luther declared reason a "whore" that could not be trusted to lead one to God—knowledge of God rather comes through *faith alone* and *scripture alone*. This, in fact, became the central doctrine of the Protestant Reformation, as we shall see. This modern way was embraced by the second major figure of the Protestant Reformation, John Calvin (1509–1564), who created the first and only European model of a pure Protestant social order in the Swiss city of Geneva.

This new way of thinking not only separated faith and reason but fostered a new individualism. In medieval philosophical traditions, for example, individual trees are real only by participation in the universal essence of "treeness" that resides in the mind of God. This way of thinking was metaphysical and hierarchical. That which was universal and higher not only gave reality to that which was lower but consequently had authority over the lower. Thus all authority was thought to come from the top down—from God to the pope (church) and the Holy Roman Emperor (state) through the bishops and nobility to the peasants at the bottom of the ladder. But the new modern way of thinking reversed this. The nominalists argued that only individual things are real while all universals are simply *names* (hence, "nominalism") for abstractions in the mind. Therefore, individual trees are real and "treeness" is simply an abstraction.

This way of thinking had a powerful impact on the way of life that was emerging in the new free cities. The Renaissance and Reformation gave birth to people who cherished their own individuality and had a sense of their individual dignity and equality with all others. At the same time, this new sense of equality was put in jeopardy by the emergence of nationalism, as people more and more began to define their identity not in terms of religion but of nationality—an identity based on shared language, customs, and geography. Within nation-states equality might reign; between them inequality and conflict tended to be emphasized.

The new nation-states were no longer shaped by the ancient social patterns of sacred hierarchical order. Now, instead of seeing authority as coming from the top down, scholars like Marsilio Ficino (1433–1499) saw it as coming from the bottom up. This meant a shift from a hierarchical view of authority to a democratic view—rulers get their authority from the consent of the governed. Knowledge through empirical inquiry and political power through democratic representation lie at the heart of the revolution called "modernization." It is the encounter with the modern notions of knowledge and power, throughout the nineteenth and twentieth centuries, that has placed anxiety in the hearts of traditional or premodern societies around the globe, societies that typically shared with premodern Europe a sense of sacred, cosmic (metpahysical), hierarchical order mirrored in the hierarchical order of society. In this sense, Protestantism was unique in that from the beginning it was part of the revolutionary shift away from sacred hierarchy toward individuality, equality, and dignity.

Devotio Moderna and the Protestant Reformation

If the via moderna split faith and reason apart and confined reason largely to the secular parts of life, the devotio moderna of mystical piety played a parallel role, making faith the domain of emotion. By the fourteenth and fifteenth centuries, a new kind of "this worldly" mysticism—the devotio moderna— was creating popular pietistic movements for spiritual renewal that grew up spontaneously and without official church approval. These "grass-roots" movements focused on personal piety founded on intense emotionally transforming religious experiences that emphasized the equality of all before God and the spiritual importance of living simply. They were often critical of the medieval Catholic church, its wealth and its hierarchical order. By their critique these movements contributed to the democratization of society. This devotio moderna is exemplified in Martin Luther's powerful emotional experience of being born again.

The Reformation was the product of a double drama: the inner drama of Luther's quest for the experience of God's immediate forgiving presence and the outer drama of Luther's protest against the decadence and corruption of the Catholic church.

Martin Luther's inner drama grew out of the struggle to find spiritual reassurance. Luther was born into a medieval Catholic world in transition toward the modern world of the Renaissance. He was the son of a peasant who had turned to mining. At the insistence of his father he began to train in law as a young man, but after nearly getting hit by lightning in a rainstorm, he abandoned that path and became an Augustinian monk and Catholic priest. His quest for moral and spiritual perfection drove him into feelings of great anxiety and hopelessness, for he felt that he could never live up to what was expected of him by God. Then, somewhere between 1511 and 1516, he had a powerful spiritual experience. While studying the letter of the Apostle Paul to the Romans he suddenly came to see the meaning of Romans 1:17, "the just shall live by faith." What he came to realize, he said, was that he was acceptable before God with all his imperfections, so long as he had faith in Christ who died for his sins. There is nothing one can do to be saved. God has done everything. Faith alone is sufficient. All sinners must do is have faith and because of that faith, God will treat sinners as if they were saints, as if they were without sin. As this realization came over him, Luther said: "Thereupon I felt myself to be reborn and to have gone through open doors into paradise. The whole of scripture took on a new meaning." In this moment Luther was overcome by a powerful liberating and exhilarating experience of his immediate presence before a forgiving and compassionate God. And he now knew that *justification* before this God was not by his works but by his faith alone, through scripture alone. Not through reason, not through the church and its hierarchy, and not through the tradition of the Catholic church.

Luther's outer drama focused on the problem of how to reform a church tradition gone corrupt. His solution was to criticize the tradition by raising faith and scriptures to a level higher than church tradition as a norm by which to judge and reform tradition. This was an option open to him that was not available to the Catholic tradition as it developed in the first five centuries, for at that time there was not yet an agreed upon set of writings called the New Testament. It was the Catholic tradition that picked the scriptures and created the Christian Bible, as Catholics would say, "under the guidance of the Holy Spirit." Without the success of Catholicism, Protestantism's "faith alone, scriptures alone" would not have been possible, and without the failures of Catholicism, Protestant reform would not have been necessary.

In 1516, Pope Leo X authorized the selling of indulgences to raise funds to rebuild the Cathedral of St. Peter in Rome. This meant that if someone gave a generous donation to the church, the pope promised that all the punishment due that person after death for his or her sins would be wiped away. For Luther, this was the last straw. Salvation was not something one could purchase. On the contrary, it comes by grace and faith alone. On October 31, 1517, Luther posted *Ninety-five Theses Against the Sale of Indulgences* on the church door of Wittenberg Castle, calling for public debate. That event marks the symbolic beginning of the Reformation. Luther started out protesting abuses in the church but he quickly moved on to challenge the entire mediating role of the church, the sacraments, and the papacy, as we have already noted. Luther did not start out to create a new form of Christianity, only to reform the Catholic tradition. But events took on a life of their own that very quickly turned a reformation into a revolution, and Protestant Christianity was born in a radical break with the ancient medieval way. It was no longer to be the ancient Catholic way of faith *and* reason, scripture *and* tradition, guided by papal authority but rather the new modern way of faith alone, scripture alone, the individual alone before his or her God.

The Reformation: Luther and Calvin on Church and State, and the Protestant Ethic

Protestantism was unique in that from the beginning it was part of the revolutionary shift away from sacred hierarchy toward not only secular rationality but also individuality and equality. In this, Protestantism, in conjunction with Renaissance humanism, laid the groundwork for the emergence of the idea of human dignity and human rights in the West. And yet, in the relation of Christianity to the state and to society, the basic assumptions operative in the Constantinian/Augustinian vision of a Christian civilization remained intact, at least for the major strands of the Reformation shaped by Martin Luther, John Calvin, and Ulrich Zwingli (1484–1531). Having criticized the Catholic church on the grounds of scripture, Luther used the power of the state to protect himself from retribution by the Roman Catholic church by seeking the protection of a German prince, Frederick, who hid him in Wartburg castle for two years. After that the Reformation had become so widespread that the papacy was no longer able to touch Luther.

Next to Luther, John Calvin was the greatest of the reformers. Luther was a peasant at heart, who knew how to enjoy life. Although Luther had been a monk, it was Calvin who exhibited a kind of monastic self-discipline and severity. He has been described as a self-disciplined, self-contained workaholic. He was in many ways the model for the entrepreneurs of the new capitalist era he helped to create. Calvin was very much a Renaissance humanist. He held a degree in law, and his genius seems to have been for social organization.

Geneva was an island of opportunity for the great Protestant experiment in creating a Christian civilization. Just before calling Calvin to be their pastor, the citizens of Geneva had won their independence from both the nobility and the Catholic church. Geneva was the one city in Europe where a compromise with the old Catholic hierarchical order of things did not have to be made. Calvin spent his life transforming Geneva into a model for Protestant civilization. He drew up both the civil and the church constitutions of Geneva. Arguing that human sinfulness requires that all power be limited, he created a democratic republic with a division of powers among its representative bodies. This institutional strategy served as a model to later secular democracies.

The Protestant work ethic associated with Calvinism really represents the secularization of the Benedictine monastic tradition's belief that "to work is to pray." Indeed, a major teaching of Luther and Calvin is the idea that work in the world (whether as a shoemaker or doctor, etc.) is as holy a task as praying in a monastery somewhere—indeed, a holier task. What makes work holy is not where it is done but doing it as a result of God's call. The *Protestant ethic* demanded that one live simply and work hard. One was to "earn all you can, save all you can" in order to "give all you can" for the greater glory of God. The sociologist Max Weber argued that this ethic helped to fuel the emergence of capitalism in Europe by encouraging the hard work needed to prosper and the savings needed for investment.

This ethic was linked to the belief that God predestined some to salvation and some to eternal damnation. The paradox was that belief in predestination seemed not to discourage human activity but rather encourage it, since no one knew if he or she was or was not among the elect. In Weber's view, what drove Calvinists to work so hard was the belief that prospering was a sign of divine favor, reinforcing the hope that the prosperous were among those predestined to salvation. Calvin's views are important to note here because in Europe and North America, it was Calvin's rather than Luther's vision of Protestant civilization that most influenced the future course of events, through its merging with the new modern spirit that gave rise to democracy on the one hand and colonialism on the other.

Other Reform Movements

The Anabaptist Rebellion Against Both Church and State

What we have described so far is the Lutheran and Calvinist center of the Protestant Reformation. However, there were wings to the left and right of this center as well. On the left were the radical reformers and on the right the Anglicans. The radical reformers have deep roots in the mystical and millennial movements of the late Middle Ages that we have already mentioned. The Anabaptists argued that there should be no practice of infant baptism, because there was none in the New Testament and because only those who freely choose to believe should be baptized. In this they were deeply influenced by the Renaissance return to the pre-Augustinian and pre-Christian classical view of human nature that affirmed freedom of the will and denied predestination. Thus for them faith had to be a matter of conscious choice, which only an adult could make. This emphasis on "making a decision for Christ" was to become an important theme in the later evangelical Christianity. It points to one of the paradoxes of the fundamentalist forms of evangelical Christian challenge to modernity, namely, that it is rooted in a notion of individual autonomy that came not from the Bible but from Renaissance modernism. The views of the Anabaptists alienated them from both the center of Protestantism and from Catholicism and led to their severe persecution by both. By 1535 over fifty thousand Anabaptists had been martyred.

Interestingly, the pacifist strands of this movement sought to break with the Constantinian vision of a Christian civilization, rejecting both the authority of the hierarchical church and the authority of the state. This meant that pacifist Anabaptists refused any role in public service, since the state condones killing and since they must refuse to take any oaths because one cannot serve two masters. The Hutterites, the Mennonites, and the Amish are all products of the Anabaptist wing of the Reformation. The most pious of their twentieth-century descendants are distinctive for their sectarian refusal to compromise with the emergence of modernity, even to the extent of refusing to utilize modern electricity and motor vehicle transportation.

The Anglican Reformation

At the other extreme, the English Reformation was initiated by the state rather than by the church. Initially the English political establishment championed Catholicism against Luther's "heretical" views. Indeed, Pope Leo X actually conferred the title "Defender of the Faith" on King Henry VIII. Problems arose, however, when Henry, who had no male heir to the throne, wanted to divorce and remarry in hopes of producing a male child. The pope refused to give his permission. So in 1534 Henry nationalized the church, making it the Church of England, and he had Parliament declare his marriage invalid. Nevertheless, apart from breaking with the papacy, the English church remained essentially Catholic. Only after Henry's death were Protestant reformers allowed into England.

Subsequently, Protestantism and Catholicism rose and fell with the rise and fall of the religious preferences of the monarchs of England. Life became precarious for its citizens, who were expected to change their religion to match that of their ruler. In 1563, the thirty-nine Articles of the Anglican church were formulated as its creed, revealing a church whose original Catholicism was now strongly influenced by Calvinist Protestantism. But its Calvinism was not pure enough for the Puritans, who were radicals intent on returning to a New Testament Christianity purified of all Catholic "popery." After a short period of dominance under Oliver Cromwell (1646–1658), Puritans became the object of persecution. Puritanism was a diverse and fragmented movement that had splintered into Congregationalists, Presbyterians (who prevailed in Scotland), Separatists, and Nonconformists, including Baptists—all refusing to conform to the thirty-nine articles. In 1620 101 Pilgrims sailed for North America. Over 40,000 Pilgrims fled England in the next twenty years, bringing to the new colonies their propensity for sectarian diversity.

The Catholic Counter-Reformation

The Council of Trent (1545–1563) met to respond to the reformers. It denied conciliarism of the Council of Constance (as we have already noted) and reinforced the absolute power of the pope and made the theology of Thomas Aquinas normative for the church. Trent froze Catholicism in its late medieval form. It affirmed that the Catholic tradition stood on a par with scripture, that Latin should remain the language of the Bible and of worship. It also retained the seven sacraments (which Protestantism had reduced to two, baptism and communion), and the importance of the saints, relics, and indulgences. Indeed, the buying and selling of indulgences was not even discussed. The pope followed the conference with a declaration that there is "no salvation outside the Catholic faith." In this way Roman Catholicism responded to the Reformation, first by trying to suppress it, then later by trying to respond to its legitimate criticisms through reform and, in Vatican I, by building a wall around itself so as to keep modernizing influences out. Finally, in Vatican II, it took Reformation criticisms seriously and created an ecumenical movement for Christian unity.

Religious Diversity: Church and State—War and Peace

The Reformation led to political divisions and open warfare between Catholics and Protestants throughout Europe. For, as we have seen, with the exception of the Anabaptists, Protestants, like Catholics, assumed that the goal of Christianity was a Christian civilization. The problem was that for the most part neither side considered the other side Christian. Each tended to think the other was doing the work of the devil. Consequently Christians resorted to warfare to settle whose religion would shape the public order. In Germany, a series of wars between Protestants and Catholics ended in the Peace of Augsburg in 1555, where the compromise *"cuius regio, eius religio"* was reached—"the religion of the ruler shall be the religion of the land." As a consequence, the splintering of the church tended to match the splintering of Europe into nation-states. Another series of wars, known as the Thirty Years War, broke out. This conflict was brought to a conclusion with the Peace of Westphalia in 1648, which reestablished the conditions of the Peace of Augsburg with additional protections for minorities and encouragement of religious toleration (see Map 2.2). The price of conflict was high. For example, between the fourteenth and seventeenth centuries, deaths from plagues and wars reduced Germany's population from sixteen million to six million.

The Protestant Reformation and the religious wars that followed relativized and privatized religion. The Protestant Reformation did not create a new and purer unity but a new and chaotic diversity. The more people learned to read the Bible for themselves, the more a diversity of interpretations emerged, leading in turn to more and more diverse forms of Christianity. This pluralism made the interpretations of the Bible seem more and more private and subjective. The Reformation helped to create a key element in modern consciousness, the awareness of the relativity of one's understanding of the world and the need to choose one's identity. The result was the transformation of both Protestantism and Catholicism into denominational religions expressing the private views of their adherents, unlike medieval Catholicism that claimed to be the sole repository of cosmic truth.

Once this privatization of faith occurred, Christianity was on a path leading to a new relationship to the public and political order of society. In Europe, and especially in North America, largely in response to the religious wars that followed the Reformation, a new understanding of the state emerged—the state as a secular and neutral political institution that favored no religion so as to be the neutral arbiter among them all. Hence, especially from the time of the French and American revolutions, the secular, democratic nation-state that functioned by privatizing religion (restricting it to peoples' personal lives) became the normative model for the modern world. Paradoxically, this development coexisted with the continued assumption by many Christians that the task of Christianity was to Christianize the world. Consequently, as Europe's public order was becoming more and more secular in the eighteenth and nineteenth centuries, European Christians were setting out to Christianize the world in concert with Western colonialism's political and economic attempts at global conquest.

Enlightenment Rationalism and Christian Pietism

Two responses to the doctrinal, social, and political divisions created by the Reformation emerged—rationalism and pietism. These were rooted in the split between faith and reason (the devotio moderna and via moderna) that we have already described. And both contributed to the development of Western notions of universal human rights.

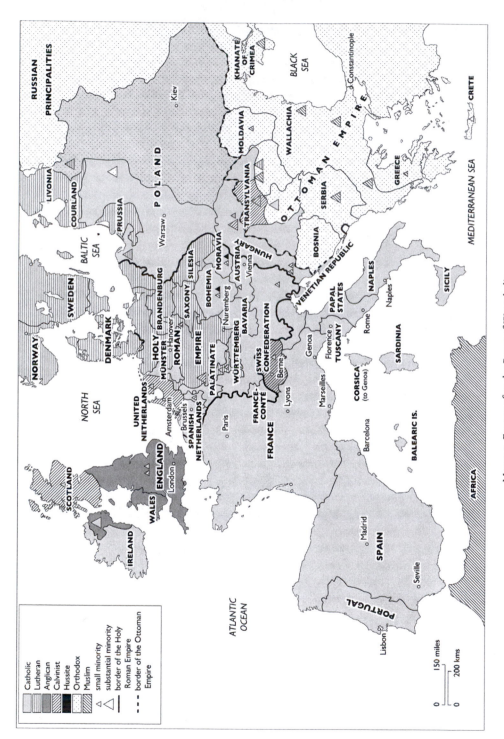

Map 2.2 Europe after the Peace of Westphalia.

Rationalism

The rise of modern science and technology was dramatic and impressive. Science came to express the most public and certain knowledge that people believed they had about their world. And the more public and certain scientific knowledge appeared to be, the more personal and uncertain religious knowledge seemed to be. The certainty of empirical observation came to be contrasted with the uncertainty of faith and religious belief. Scientists like Isaac Newton, the founding father of modern (pre-Einsteinian) physics, believed that science disclosed the wondrous intelligence of the divine Creator. However, as science developed, scientists came to believe that they had less and less need to bring God into their explanations. In the nineteenth century, the French astronomer Pierre Laplace announced that he had no need of the "God hypothesis" to explain the world.

Enlightenment rationalism became the foundation of all scientific and public knowledge. The Enlightenment was built on four key concepts: (1) the courage to use one's own reason, (2) the freedom from tradition through the rational critique of the past, (3) a view of nature as a finely tuned machine whose mechanisms can be understood, and (4) a view of history as being guided by hidden laws of progress. The power of reason was thought capable of freeing human beings from the irrationality of the past (including the irrationality of much of religion), of discovering how the universe really works, and of leading humanity into a golden age of progress. Indeed, according to the great Enlightenment philosopher Gotthold Lessing (1729–1781), the story of history is a story of progress toward rational autonomy. The childhood (the ancient world) and adolescence (the medieval world) of history were finally over; with the coming of the Enlightenment, adulthood was at hand. No longer did human beings have to be told what to believe. Now they were adults, encouraged to "think for themselves."

Enlightenment rationalism fostered the emergence of *Deism*, which thought of the world as a clock and of God as the divine clockmaker. Just as the clockmaker makes a perfect machine that runs on its own without interference from its maker, so God, as creator, has no need to interfere in the world. And the scientist, who knows that God created the world machine, does not need to refer to the maker to explain how the machine runs. The God of Deism was a God designed to accommodate the new modern world view of Newtonian science and technology. He was a God conceived of within the limits of the new scientific reason, a God who had no need of irrational acts like miracles, which would be both unnecessary and disruptive of the smooth operation of the mechanisms of creation.

Enlightenment rationalism promised to overcome the divisions among human beings expressed in the religious wars by stripping religion of its past superstitions and reducing it to its rational elements. Such rationality, it was believed, would create a more tolerant world. Enlightenment rationalists believed that reason was the one universal that all humanity shared and therefore that the exercise of universal reason would lead people of every religion and culture into greater tolerance and harmony. They hoped that as people became more enlightened and rational they would abandon the irrational religious beliefs that divided them and come to be united under the one God of reason. In the process they would come to share a common morality, which was the essence of enlightened theism. This rationalism was embodied in religious denominations like the Unitarians and the Universalists, who played an important role in championing universal rights for all human beings. Enlightenment morality contributed to the emergence of a modern ethic of human dignity and human rights by stressing the fundamental unity of the human race. And indeed, in England and elsewhere laws of toleration began to be passed.

Pietism

What was missing in Deism was any warmth or emotion. It was too cold, mechanical, and rational. Ironically, the same thing had become true of Protestant orthodoxy. The alternative to the cold rationality of both Enlightenment rationalism and Protestant rationalism was supplied by the new pietism that gave rise to evangelical Christianity. In their search for a way of uniting people across the divide of dogma and religious conflict that had been created by the Protestant Reformation, the Pietists explored the other side of the split between faith and reason. Indeed, it was a movement to recover the mystical piety of the Reformation.

Pietists sought to transcend religious differences by minimizing the role of rational dogma, which seemed to divide Christians, and maximizing the role of religious emotion, which they hoped would unite them. The true test of Christian faith, Pietists argued, is not found so much in right belief or dogmas as in a changed heart. Thus the goal of evangelical piety was from the beginning transdenominational. One of its greatest representatives, John Wesley (1703–1791), saw such deep emotions as the way to unity among Christians. So he argued that doctrinal differences should not separate Christians. "If thou lovest God and all mankind, I ask no more: 'give me thine hand.'"

The first wave of Pietism came in the seventeenth century. It included such groups as the Moravians and the Quakers. The greatest and most far-reaching expression of Pietism in the eighteenth century was the Methodist movement begun by Wesley, who was deeply influenced by the Moravians as well as by Catholic and Anglican mystics. As a student at Oxford he was drawn into a devotional group whose "methodical" schedule of prayer gave them the name "Methodists." The turning point in his life occurred at Aldersgate on May 24, 1738, when his own spiritual doubts and anxieties were overcome in a powerful conversion experience that he described by saying that his heart was "strangely warmed." Wesley was deeply influenced by Calvinism and its stress on community discipline and sanctification as a process of spiritual and moral improvement. His preaching and teaching took this Calvinist theme to a new level by insisting that the goal of the Christian life is growth in "perfection." At the same time, he rejected the Calvinist teaching of predestination, siding with the Anabaptist emphasis on the freedom of the will and the importance of freely choosing faith in Christ.

Wesley's message was primarily aimed at the new working class of the industrial revolution. As people left the rural areas and flooded the cities to work in the new factories, overcrowding, poverty, disease, and crime became commonplace. Moreover, factory owners did not always pay just wages and working conditions and hours were often inhumane. The Methodist movement was one of the first constructive responses of Christianity to these changing conditions. Methodist communities were committed to morality and simplicity—seeking to perfect both self and society. Methodism's most striking accomplishments include playing a leading role in the abolition of slavery in England (1833) and in introducing women into the ministry. Both exemplify the important role that evangelical piety played in the development of the modern commitment to human dignity, equality, and rights.

The tremendous power of the Methodist movement, with its emphasis on the equality and dignity of all persons before God drawn from the devotio moderna, lay in its tapping a long tradition in the history of Christianity. This is the tradition of combining the simple life of prayer and devotion with life in small communities of discipline and mutual encouragement oriented toward improving the world. This formula fueled the monastic movement that missionized the tribes of Europe and brought learning and civilization to Europe. This same spirit was then carried forward in Calvinism and was transferred to evangelical Christianity primarily (but not exclusively) through Methodism and carried around the world in the global missions of the nineteenth century. Thus, paradoxically, the Augustinian vision of a mission to Christianize the world that fueled the Inquisition and the Crusades carried within it the seeds of an alternate vision of human dignity and equality. The arrogant side of Western colonialism brought with it the seeds of its own demise as it spread around the world. Today (as we shall soon see) this alternate vision is taking on new postcolonial forms in the base communities of liberation theology and the communities of indigenous (non-European) spiritual renewal among African and Asian Christians touched by the evangelical missionary message.

The Nineteenth-Century Romantic Reaction

The French Revolution
What both the rationalism and pietism of the Enlightenment shared in common was a faith in the progress of the human race. Drawing on the myth of the three ages as formulated by Joachim of Fiore in the thirteenth century, both Pietists and Rationalists shared a millennial faith that they lived in the final age of history—the modern age—when human beings would finally throw off the authoritarianism of past tradition and institutions and live instead guided by

a direct inner light that would bring with it progress and harmony. For the Rationalists this inner light was the light of reason. For the Pietists it was the light of spiritual illumination, which comes from being born again. Thus both share the millennial mysticism (of Joachim of Fiore) that has driven the modern spirit of progress. However by the eighteenth and nineteenth centuries history was no longer understood to be guided by the hand of divine providence so much as by its secular equivalent—what Adam Smith called "the invisible hand" of the marketplace wherein economic competition was said to mysteriously transform private acts of self-interest into goods for the benefit of all.

Another secular version of this myth of progress was espoused by the French intellectual Jean Jacques Rousseau (1712–1778), who argued in *The Social Contract* (1762) that the distortions of past tradition and its social order must be swept away. This is necessary so that humanity, once freed from the artificialities of tradition (in this case medieval tradition), might be able to be in touch with the natural harmony that was typical of the "noble savage" in primitive communistic societies, which Rousseau thought were exemplified by the then recent discovery of South Sea island cultures. On the one hand, Rousseau affirmed the Enlightenment myth—culture and historical tradition corrupt and the liberation from them brings progress. On the other hand, he introduced a new twist that made him an initiator of the Romantic period, whose dominant theme was rejection of the mechanical order of modernity to return to a primal past of the "noble savage" untouched by "history," who lived in a more organic harmony with nature.

Rousseau stood at the transition point in European history between the eighteenth-century Enlightenment and the nineteenth-century Romantic reaction to the Enlightenment. The political event that facilitated that reaction was the French Revolution.

At the end of the eighteenth century economic conditions grew very bad in France, and they were not helped by the extravagance of the court of King Louis XIV. This led to a massive revolt. In the place of Christianity the new leaders created a "Cult of Reason" and later a "Cult of the Supreme Being (Deism)." The churches were transformed into "Temples of Reason" and filled with statues of "nature goddesses" and "the goddess of reason." In the Reign of Terror thousands of clergy and nobility were arrested and beheaded.

The French Revolution, which began July 14, 1789, brought about a considerable disillusionment with reason. Reason had been embraced at the beginning of the Enlightenment as the way out of fanaticism, dogmatism, violence, and intolerance. And yet in the French Revolution reason had shown itself to be fanatical, dogmatic, violent, and intolerant. People grew weary of the violence and of the complexity of civilization and longed for the simplicity of nature uncorrupted by civilization. With the failure of reason, many people turned to emotion as the foundation for the renewal of life. If the Enlightenment was rationalistic and mechanistic, the Romantic period was emotional and organic. If the Enlightenment had sought to escape the history and tradition of the past into a bright new mechanistic future, Romanticism sought to return to the organic and familial connections of traditional society. An ambivalent struggle between these alternative visions remains very much a part of contemporary culture.

Protestantism, Philosophy, Theology, and Modernity

Kant Along with Rousseau, the German philosopher Immanuel Kant (1724–1804) is a key transitional figure between the Enlightenment and the Romantic period. Kant set out to resolve a fundamental conflict in the modern world view: On the one hand, science seemed to require a mechanistic world view in which everything is causally determined, while on the other hand, morality seemed to require a world view in which freedom of choice is possible. Scientific determinism and human moral freedom can coexist for Kant because determinism is an abstraction based in the structures of the mind for organizing sense data "as if the 'phenomenal world'" (the world "out there") was completely determined, whereas the subjective or inner realm of freedom (which Kant called the "noumenal world") is verified in our immediate experience of moral choice and moral responsibility.

We are now in a position to see why Kant is known as the Protestant philosopher. For the foundational principle of the Protestant view of the world was the split between faith and reason, in which reason cannot grasp the reality of God and is limited to operating on the empirical world of finite secular concerns that belong to what Augustine called the "city of man." Kant's noumenal (inner) and phenomenal (outer) worlds of experience correspond directly to the division of reality into the "kingdom of God" (inner/emotional) and the "kingdom of this world" (outer/rational-empirical), as articulated in Protestantism. This division in turn came to be reduced to the "modern" secular categories of private (subjective) and public (objective) life, in which religion and morality are supposed to be privatized and kept separate from the secular and public activities of politics and science. That model is the backbone of the world view that shaped modern societies and that is only collapsing with the emergence of postcolonial movements of protest against modernity.

Kant's philosophy was the culmination of the Enlightenment and yet it opened the door to Romanticism by focusing on the inner life of self-consciousness as a distinct realm of experience to be taken seriously, apart from that of scientific experience of the external world. If the Protestant Pietist movement represented a rebellion against the rationalism of Protestant Orthodoxy, Romanticism represented the parallel rebellion against the secular rationalism of the Enlightenment. Both opposed cold abstract rationality with intense personally transformative experience—whether the experience is one of being born again in the Spirit or of having an equally transformative encounter with the beauty of nature.

Schleiermacher If the Enlightenment sought to identify religion with universal rationality, the Romantic reaction deliberately sought to celebrate the

nonrational and even irrational aspects of human experience, including religious experience. Kant (following the nominalist tradition) argued that human reason could never grasp the infinite or God. Friederich Schleiermacher (1768–1834), considered the father of modern Christian theology, accepted the basic constraints to human reason laid out by Kant, but arrived at a different solution—a Romantic solution. Schleiermacher was a modernist, in arguing that knowledge of God can coexist with our scientific knowledge of the world without conflict because the two belong to different spheres (the inner and outer or private and public). God is experienced in the immediacy of "feeling."

One does not have to deny scientific theories about the world to affirm belief in God. Nor, Schleiermacher argues, does one have to deny the findings of history that were emerging from the application of new critical historical methods to the New Testament. For, contrary to what some Christians think, he argues, the affirmation of faith in the resurrection of Jesus Christ does not depend on historical claims or conclusions. This does not mean that Schleiermacher did not believe that the resurrection really happened. His point is, rather, that when a person does not believe it one day and then confesses such faith the next day, it is not because that person has learned some new historical fact but rather because that person has had a powerful transformative emotional experience of being born again. This emphasis on transformative feeling places Schleiermacher directly in the camp of the tradition of the devotio moderna and evangelical Pietism.

Karl Marx and the Socialist Revolution   In 1851 Karl Marx published his Communist Manifesto and, as we have noted, changed the face of the globe. Marx's vision of history is a mirror image of that of G. W. F. Hegel (1770–1831), by whom he was deeply influenced. Hegel saw history as the dialectical unfolding of Spirit or Mind, leading to an age of perfect freedom; for him, thoughts and ideas shaped the materialistic aspects of life, like economics and politics. For Marx it was just the reverse. Like Hegel, he saw history as passing through three stages on humankind's way to universal freedom. In the Marxist vision, the Hegelian dialectic of thesis, antithesis, and synthesis unfolded as the dialectic of the movement from ancient classless societies through their antithesis, urban class societies, to a new synthesis, at the end of time, a universal classless society. Like a modernist, Marx subscribed to the myth of progress that can be seen as a variation on the biblical millennial myth of history. Yet at the same time, Marx offered a postcolonial vision insofar as the new classless society that was coming would bring an end to the nightmare of suffering and injustice created by modern capitalism and the class conflict expressed in its colonialism. The Marxist vision allowed its adherents a way to both embrace and reject modernity at the same time— bargaining, just as many fundamentalists have, that one can have the scientific-technological benefits of modernity without accepting the modern world view. But unlike fundamentalists, Marx did not want to go back to an earlier world view but forward to a new one.

The Russian Revolution and the Orthodox Churches

The first country to be fully swept up in the Marxist-socialist revolution was Russia, the heart of Orthodox Christianity. Modernization first came to Russia under Peter the Great who, in 1715, moved the capital from Moscow to the new "modern" city he created, St. Petersburg, where it remained until the Russian Revolution. Lagging behind Western Europe by over a century, Russia began its transition out of the medieval world and into the modern. Coming to the throne in 1682, Peter introduced into Russia the intellectual, technical, and industrial ideals of modern Western European civilization. However, neither Czarist Russia nor socialist Russia ever embraced two of the key features of modernity—capitalism and democracy. Instead, political and economic life was ruled from the top down, first by the Czars and then by their revolutionary successors beginning with Lenin, who took command of the socialist revolution in 1917.

After Lenin's death in 1924, Joseph Stalin came to power. He put Russia on the path of industrialization that by the 1940s made it a major economic competitor in the world. This was accomplished at tremendous cost. Between 1934 and 1938 hundreds of thousands of political opponents died in a series of purges, and over a thousand monasteries and convents were closed by 1939 when World War II began. In the end, over 17 million and perhaps as many as 22 million died as a result of Stalin's policies. For the Orthodox church this was an age of persecution and martyrdom. When the persecutions failed to eliminate popular support for the Orthodox religion, Stalin eased off and appointed an Orthodox patriarch and allowed a modest level of religious activity. The churches elsewhere in Eastern Europe fared better. In countries like Romania and Bulgaria, Orthodox clergy were even paid by the state until the end of the cold war. The end of that "war" and the dissolution of the Soviet Union in the last decade of the twentieth century marked the failure of the Marxist model as an alternate religious and political vision, and has allowed the Orthodox churches of Russia and Eastern Europe to once more begin to play a role in public life. The post–cold war world promises to be a post–Marxist-Leninist world as well.

The Existentialist Revolt Against Modernity

Another important contribution to the critique of modernity (alongside that of Marxism) was existentialism. Neither succeeded in completely breaking with modernity. Marxism critiqued individualism and capitalism but remained tied to the modern myth of scientific progress. The existentialists critiqued the myths of science and scientific progress but remained tied to modern individualism. Both were responding to the new revolution in historical and social scientific consciousness that made human beings aware that they lived in a socially constructed world. This awareness led to two radically different types of existentialist response: Søren Kierkegaard's radical Christian existentialism and Nietzsche's atheistic existentialism.

Kierkegaard's Leap of Faith

Writing after Kant, Hegel, and Schleiermacher but before Darwin, Søren Kierkegaard (1813-1855), the son of a pious Lutheran father, offered an alternative solution to those of Hegel and Schleiermacher. Kierkegaard formulated a concept of self that broke with the entire history of philosophy. Since the time of Aristotle (4th century BCE) the human self had been thought of as part of the order of nature. In nature, Aristotle argued, everything has an essence. If you plant an acorn, you know that it will grow into an oak tree. The essence of what it will be is in its beginnings, which determine its purpose and goal. So likewise with human beings. The task of a human life is to become what we were born to be. And, Aristotle added, some were born to be free and some to be slaves. The coming of the social and historical sciences in the nineteenth century undermined that way of understanding human identity. The awareness that different cultures interpreted human nature differently made human beings aware that human identity was not natural but rather self-created. Kierkegaard was the first philosopher to articulate the implications of this for human identity with depth and clarity.

For Kierkegaard, to be human is to be an historical creature, which is to say, to be in a constant state of becoming. Human beings differ from the rest of nature in that *existence precedes essence*. It is this notion that gives rise to the term, "existentialism." Contrary to Aristotle, when a child is born, Kierkegaard might argue, it has no essence, only the possibility of choosing who it will become. We cannot predict who or what a child will become until he or she has breathed the last breath and made the last choice. The life task of a human being is to create a self through its choices. For Kierkegaard, this is both a religious and an ethical task.

Because human beings have no fixed identity, Kierkegaard argues, they experience anxiety and dread as they confront the ambiguity of their existence. The essence of sin is their tendency to flee from their freedom into a false but secure identity. For Kierkegaard, Jesus Christ is the revelation of the paradoxical presence of the infinite in the finite—a paradox that is beyond the limit of thought and so cannot be thought at all but only acknowledged. And only taking the leap of faith to trust this absolute paradox gives the courage necessary to embrace the freedom to create oneself through one's choices. In this we see Kierkegaard's debt to evangelical Christianity with its emphasis on making a mature adult decision for Christ. And yet, like Augustine and Luther before him, Kierkegaard perceived that it is emotion that leads the self to God—not the positive emotions of peace and certainty, like those of John Wesley whose heart was "strangely warmed," but the negative feelings of anxiety, dread, and doubt that force the self continually to abandon its current identity in a restless response to the presence of the infinite within its subjective consciousness. Thus, like Schleiermacher, Kierkegaard offered nineteenth-century European Christians a way of understanding their faith that avoided their having to find some kind of historical proof for the claims of the Bible about what happened in the past. On the contrary, faith was about making a choice in the present—embracing and trusting the absolute paradox, revealed in Jesus Christ, of God's presence as the infinite in the finite.

Nietzsche and the Death of God

Four years after Kierkegaard's death, Charles Darwin published *The Origin of Species*, which gave rise to Social Darwinism. The coming together of the biological, historical, and social sciences in this social Darwinist movement created a far greater shock to human consciousness or self-awareness than anything that had been revealed in the history of science to this point. The Social Darwinism revealed a world of power struggles for domination in which the guiding force was not the hand of God but the forces of competition. Friedrich Nietzsche (1844–1900), the son of a Lutheran minister, was 10 years old when Kierkegaard died. He offered Europeans a way of seeing the world more attuned to the Darwinist world view. Like Kierkegaard, he too wished to affirm the human freedom to continually redefine the self in defiance of all systems. However, for Nietzsche this was not accomplished by making a leap of faith that embraced the absolute paradox of God's presence as the infinite in the finite, but by proclaiming the death of God.

Nietzsche did this in a parable about a madman who entered the public square declaring that God was dead. Modern human beings, the madman suggested, had committed the deed and yet they remained ignorant of its reality because they had not yet experienced its earth-shaking consequences, for like the light of a distant star it takes time for such news to reach its destination.

For Nietzsche, the modern world was incompatible with belief in the biblical God: history had demythologized the sacred stories of biblical history and shown them to be myths, and science had demythologized the biblical views of creation and replaced them with a Darwinistic materialistic determinism. As Nietzsche saw it, European Christians who embraced modernity acted as if Christianity and modernity were compatible, but the day would come when they would realize that in embracing modernity they had killed God. In regarding belief in God and in modernity as incompatible, Nietzsche and modern fundamentalists in the nineteenth century were in agreement. Both wanted to reject modernity, but with an important difference. Fundamentalists wanted to go back to premodern foundations as if modernity had never happened. Nietzsche did not believe that was either possible or desirable. To reject modernity, one must become not premodern but postmodern. Nothing is sacred. One must criticize not only religion but also science, and realize that the human imagination is the creator of all world views.

Like Kierkegaard, Nietzsche believed that human beings must create themselves. But unlike Kierkegaard, he believed they would have to do so without God. For Nietzsche, there is no experience of the absolute paradox of the infinite in the finite, only the historical experience of the struggle for existence dominated by the "will to power." The problem with Christianity, he argues, is that it fosters ideals of compassion and equality. Biblical morality teaches weak values like forgiveness and pity. Such values only lead people to resent persons who are strong and courageous. Therefore biblical values are bad for civilization. They lead to an ideal of "equality" that rewards mediocrity. For not everyone is equal—some have superior values, creative values, and they should dominate and lead society. So Nietzsche welcomed the death of God as the opportunity for humanity to create a new and higher future for itself. The future, he believed, should be in the hands of those superior individuals who were capable of "transvaluing all values."

The End of Modernity: From the Holocaust to Hiroshima

Scarcely more than half a century after Nietzsche's madman had unleashed his prophecy, the Nazis came along to embrace Nietzsche's vision of a will to power. Nietzsche's vision of a world ruled by superior persons was not that of the Nazis. Nietzsche had a somewhat aristocratic view. However, his idea was easily usurped by the Nazis who imagined themselves, the pure Aryan race, as the natural embodiment of those superior human beings who would recreate the world through a will to power. What Nietzsche's vision did have in common with that of the Nazis was a contempt for the ideals of equality and democratic rule that Nietzsche associated with Christendom.

Nietzsche needn't have worried, for during World War II many Christians showed themselves quite willing to abandon their weak values and embrace the ideals of elitism and the will to power. Between 1933 and 1945, Hitler and the Nazi party were in power in Germany and drew Europe and America into World War II (1939–1945). One of the key factors in Hitler's rise to power was his successful appeal to popular anti-Semitism in German and Austrian culture. Hitler was able to achieve power, in large part, because for centuries Christians had viewed Jews as religious and cultural inferiors. The Nazis stripped the Jews of their citizenship, confiscated their property, and sent them off in boxcars to concentration camps. In these death camps, over six million Jews are estimated to have been killed, mostly in the gas chambers.

The Christian churches might have been a powerful force against such barbarity, but they were not. In Germany, by some estimates, only 20 percent of the Protestant churches resisted Hitler and the Nazi message—and even fewer took issue with the treatment of the Jews. Pope Pius XI signed a concordat with Hitler in hopes of protecting the autonomy of the German Catholic churches. Most Christians either actively cooperated or passively acquiesced in the Nazi program of genocide. There were, however, a minority of Christians who held fast to their "weak values" and rescued Jews, but with a few important exceptions they tended to be lone individuals of conscience. Christians in Denmark were an important exception, and most of Denmark's Jews survived because of collective resistance by both church and state. The village of Le Chambon sur Lignon in France is another such exception: this small village of mostly French Protestants saved over five thousand Jewish lives. Wherever the churches led resistance to the Nazis, Jewish lives were saved. Unfortunately that did not happen often. As the church historian Franklin Littell has noted, the irony is that more priests and ministers died in Hitler's armies than died resisting Hitler.

If Nietzsche's prediction of the death of God came too early, as he said, World War I and then World War II may have made his prediction seem more relevant. For what these events represented was the death of what "God" had become in Westerns civilization, namely, the "God of progress." What World War I and World War II did for Western civilization was to finally demythologize the modern myth of history as progress. Stalin's gulags, or labor camps, and the millions upon millions left dead on the battlefields and the shameless reality of the Nazi death camps, gave modern persons good reasons to question whether modernity and "progress" were truly worthy human ideals. With the dropping of the atomic bomb on Hiroshima, Japan, at the end of World War II and the buildup of nuclear weapons in the second half of the twentieth century by the major world powers (Russia, America, and others), with the possibility of nuclear war annihilating the entire planet, belief in the ability to create a better future through science and technology began to disintegrate. The modern world was ready to look for alternatives.

Some forms of Christianity appear to have something to contribute to this quest for alternatives, namely, those forms willing to champion precisely those weak values of dignity and equality that Nietzsche held in such contempt. Among the first signs of this are the changes in Christian teachings about the Jews. Since Vatican II and in response to the Holocaust, both Protestant and Catholic churches have sought to correct past teachings about Jews as a rejected people and have replaced these teachings with an affirmation that the Jewish covenant is an authentic covenant with God—one that exists both prior to and apart from the Christian covenant. After two thousand years of denying the validity of the Jewish covenant, this affirmation of it is unprecedented in the history of Christianity. Moreover, it can be seen as part of an emerging postmodern pattern, linked with the visions of the indigenous mission churches of Africa and Asia and of North American liberation theologies, which have begun to envision a new postcolonial and non-Eurocentric form of Christianity, more open to coexistence with other religions and cultures.

CHRISTIANITY AND POSTMODERN TRENDS IN A POSTCOLONIAL WORLD

From Colonial to Postcolonial Christianity

The Christianity that fostered the rise of modernization was not the Christianity of the Eastern Orthodox churches, which saw Christian civilization as a sacred unity of church and state, but of Western Augustinian Christianity, which saw such a civilization as composed of two cities, one sacred and the other secular. Indeed, the term "secular" comes from the Latin term *saeculum*, which means "worldly," in opposition to the monastic way of life of those who left the world to seek God.

For most of its history Christianity has been predominantly a European religion. Europe gave birth to the largest branch of Christianity, Roman Catholicism, during the Middle Ages, and to modern Christianity with the Protestant Reformation. In 1600 the overwhelming majority of Christians in the world lived in Europe. However, by 1900 only half of all the Christians in the world lived in Europe, and by the end of the twentieth century the majority of the world's Christians resided largely in Latin America, Africa, and Asia (in that order).

Postcolonial Christianity is rapidly becoming predominantly non-European. The reason is that modern Christianity in the nineteenth and twentieth centuries was accompanied by the secularization of Europe, which led to a dramatic decline in the practice of Christianity. Paradoxically, during most of this same period (in the nineteenth and early twentieth century), while Europe was carrying on a program of colonial expansion, Protestant evangelical Christianity was engaged in a massive missionary enterprise whose aim was the Christianization of every part of the world touched by colonization (See Map 1.3 in Chapter 1). Moreover, while reproduction rates among Christians declined in Europe, the reproduction rate among Christians elsewhere increased. The result has been a tremendous geographic shift in Christian populations. From this perspective it seems that even as Christianity was waning in Europe, it was planting the seeds of its possible transformation and renewal in postcolonial forms elsewhere in the world.

The invention of the modern three-masted sailing ship (c. 1500) unleashed a global transformation that began with the colonial expansion of Europe and seems to be culminating in the birth of a global civilization at the beginning of the twenty-first century. The nineteenth century was the great century of Protestant missionary evangelism. Drawing on the same logic that had led St. Augustine to assume that the establishment of the Roman Empire had been the result of God's will so that the Gospel might be spread, the very success of European civilization in the areas of science, technology, and economics gave nineteenth-century European and North American Christians the feeling that the political and economic colonization of the world by Europe was part of God's plan to make possible the spread of the Gospel to the very ends of the earth.

This feeling of the superiority and global destiny of European civilization communicated itself through an attitude of paternalism toward the cultures and peoples that came under colonial rule. At first many in these cultures were impressed with the modern "superiority" of Western science and technology. However, it did not take long for indigenous peoples to feel demeaned and diminished by the Western attitude of superiority. If colonialism brought modernity to the non-European world, the rejection of Western colonialism can be said to mark the beginnings of postcolonial Christianity.

In former colonial areas, whether in Africa, Asia, or the Americas, this inevitably led to a political backlash that included a bid for independence and a rejection of some Western values, such as capitalism and individualism, in favor of a recovery of political and economic independence and a restoration of indigenous values and customs. Paradoxically, at the same time other Western values, such as dignity and equality, lent support to indigenous efforts to undermine colonial domination. We see this paradox for example in Gandhi's campaign to liberate India from English colonial domination.

Latin America

Latin America was colonized by the Spanish and the Portuguese in the sixteenth century, both Roman Catholic countries untouched by the Protestant Reformation and retaining medieval patterns of social order that were hierarchical and antidemocratic. The South American native populations and their civilizations were conquered and overwhelmed. Large numbers died in epidemics, and by the end of the sixteenth century the remainder had become at least nominally Christian, often through mass conversions. Among the native Indian populations and also among the black slave populations, a *syncretism* developed that identified the deities of their own native traditions with the saints and the Virgin Mother of Catholicism. For some this was a genuine melding of religious world views, but for others indigenous Catholicism became a form of resistance to colonial domination, functioning as a mask for their true religious convictions.

Spain and Portugal were the first to establish colonial empires and were also among the first to lose them. By 1830 most of their colonies in Latin America had achieved independence. With independence came a process of secularization. Liberal movements developed that rejected control of society by the church and its representatives, and liberalism came to dominate most of Latin America in the second half of the nineteenth century. This was followed by a backlash against the liberal tradition that has seen the reemergence of a conservative alliance of church and state in twentieth-century Latin America.

This conservative alliance was deeply disturbed when Marxist socialism swept through Latin America in the early twentieth century, giving a voice to the concerns of the poor and those neglected and oppressed by the traditional church-state establishment. By the mid-twentieth century, the forces of secularization and Marxism had taken their toll, and while 90 percent of Latin Americans were baptized, only about 15 percent were estimated to be practicing their faith. This situation set the context of the emergence of postcolonial movements of liberation theology and evangelical-charismatic Christianity.

In the last decades of the twentieth century, Christians (mostly Catholics) exposed to the Marxist analysis of European colonial exploitation developed liberation theology as a revolutionary response to the traditional hierarchical order of society that reinforced privileges for the few and poverty and oppression for the many. First appearing in Latin America, liberation theology rapidly spread to Asia, Africa, and North America. The theologies of liberation have not been confined to developing nations, for even African-Americans, women, and homosexuals in Europe and America began to seek liberation from Western European colonial values that they believed demeaned and subjugated them.

At the same time, in Latin America a backlash among some branches of evangelical and *pentecostalist* Protestant Christianity, which had inspired the missionary zeal of the nineteenth century, led to a rejection of such liberation theologies as the ultimate sellout of Christianity to modern culture. In an effort to return to the premodern spiritual foundations of their faith, these Christians focused less on issues of cultural and economic oppression than on issues of personal conversion (being born again) and/or ecstatic experience (e.g., speaking in tongues) and the transformation of society through the spiritual cultivation of personal virtue within the parameters of whatever civilization they were living in, including capitalism.

For Christians in the liberation movements, the heart of the Christian Gospel is love for the poor and the struggle for social justice. For evangelical Christians it is personal conversion, personal regeneration in the Spirit, and the shaping of a public order that will give priority to these things. Despite their differences, however, both visions of Christianity assume Christianity alone ought to shape the public order of political and economic life. If one wants to find models of Christianity that break with both the premodern and modern visions of a "Christian civilization" one must look primarily to the African and Asian churches, where we see the emergence of a "diaspora" model of Christianity.

Africa

Except for the ancient Coptic church in Egypt and the church of Ethiopia, Christianity in Africa is the result of missionary efforts beginning in the colonial period. At the beginning of the twentieth century there were scarcely any Christians in Africa. At the end of the century it was the fastest growing geographic area for Christianity, and more than a fifth of the world's Christians can be found there today. Almost half of the population of Africa is now Christian, while conversions to Islam are running a close second.

One of the impacts of European missionaries was to undermine the booming slave trade of the nineteenth century. In 1807 Britain, largely due to the efforts of Methodists and other evangelicals, made the slave trade illegal, and in 1833 all slaves were emancipated in British territories. Other European countries began to fall in line. In 1839 Pope Gregory XVI also condemned slavery. Interestingly, many abolitionists argued not only from religious premises but also capitalistic economic premises—arguing for the right of Africans to bring their labor skills to a fair and open market.

As the number of converts to Christianity grew, Africans developed their own indigenous forms of Christianity in revolt against the tight control missionaries sought to maintain over African Christianity. The largest number of such movements occurred in South Africa, where colonial paternalism was stronger than elsewhere. The fewest number of such movements occurred in nineteenth-century Tanganyika, where such paternalism was weakest.

One of the most interesting of the African independent church movements is Isaiah Shembe's Nazareth movement, because it exhibits a genuine longing for a black Christ. Shembe is described as having a miraculous birth and being born of the Spirit—as one who came from heaven so that native Africans might know that God is with them. In general, even among the more traditional denominational native African congregations, Christianity became more and more African and less and less European in the twentieth century, with strong syncretistic elements. This should not surprise anyone, for this parallels what happened when ancient Christianity moved from the Mediterranean world into medieval Europe. The saints of the church coalesced with the gods of the various tribal groups of northern Europe, for example.

There is a liberation theology in Africa but, as the leadership of Anglican bishop Desmond Tutu in South Africa illustrates, it is less on the model of Latin American Marxist theory and more on the model of the nonviolent civil rights movement in the United States led by Martin Luther King, Jr. Indeed, King's movement is an interesting blend of the liberation passion for justice with an evangelical ecstatic piety. This type of evangelical/pentecostalist piety has also left its stamp on African Christianity, commingling with the experiential/ecstatic elements of traditional African tribal religions. African Christianity seems to be finding its own path into the postcolonial world—one that will unite the quest for justice with spiritual ecstasy. In the twenty-first century, African Christianity is likely to be a major contributor to the development of a postcolonial Christianity. However, in Africa, Christianity's success tempts believers to envision a "Christian Africa." It is in Asia that Christianity is most clearly creating models that break free of the Augustinian civilizational model to embrace a diaspora model of creative coexistence with other religions and cultures.

Asia

European expansion into Asia occurred simultaneously with its expansion into Africa. There was a strong British presence in Ceylon (Sri Lanka), India, Burma (Myanmar), Malaysia, Singapore, Hong Kong, and various Pacific islands (also Australia and New Zealand). The French expanded into the Indochina peninsula, including Laos and Cambodia. As in Latin America and Africa, the spread of Christianity that accompanied this colonial expansion was driven by the same Augustinian sense of the providential link between the expansion of European civilization and the spread of the Gospel.

In the West, Christianity had few rivals as a "world religion," and its two main competitors, Judaism and Islam, were variations on the same world view—the myth of history. Asia presented Christianity with interesting new challenges, for unlike the local polytheistic and animistic religions encountered in the Americas and Africa, in Asia Christianity encountered religions that, like itself, had shaped whole civilizations, the great nonbiblical world religions—Hinduism, Buddhism, Daoism, and Confucianism. These traditions were rooted in mythic world views as grand and powerful as its own—the myths of liberation (in India) and the myths of harmony (in China).

The only thing that seems able to stop the expansion of a great world religion is another great world religion. In Asia, Christianity is a distinct minority presence and seems unlikely to ever become the religion of civilizational order. The story of Christianity in Asia is different from its story in Latin America and in Africa in that the Asian story cannot be told as a story of the conquest of the public order in order to create a Christian civilization. In Asia, the Constantinian-Augustinian vision that has been the model for two thousand years of Christianity seems to be unworkable.

Asia's contribution to the development of a postcolonial Christianity may well be the development of a diaspora model of Christianity, one that will transcend traditional Western civilizational and denominational boundaries and be open to creative coexistence with other religions and cultures. A diaspora religion is one in which adherents live not together in one civilization but rather "dispersed" as minority communities among many civilizations. We shall briefly survey four of the most significant instances from South and East Asia—India, China, Japan, and Korea.

India At first Protestant missionaries denounced as heathen idolatry the two major world religions of India: Hinduism and Islam (Buddhism for the most part having died out in India while migrating to other parts of Asia). But when that tactic backfired, missionaries began to portray these religions as divinely inspired preparations for the coming of Christianity. In 1917, the Hindu convert and poet Narayan Vaman Tilak founded a Christian ashram, modeled on the Hindu ashrams, which were communities of spiritual learning consisting of a teacher (guru) and disciples. There were even proposals suggesting that the Hindu Vedas (sacred scriptures) might replace the Old Testament in a Hinduized Christian worship.

Once India had won its independence in 1947, there was increasing pressure on the churches in India to become less European and more Indian. Indeed, Indian Christians were often accused by Hindus of being unpatriotic much the way Christians had accused Jews of being unpatriotic in Europe. In response, Indian Christians began to move beyond European denominational Christianity. In 1947 the Church of South India was formed out of a merger of Anglicans, Methodists, and other Protestant bodies. Much later the Protestant Church of North India was founded and also a Protestant Church of Pakistan (1970). With these changes there was also shift of emphasis from conversion to dialogue, with the goal of showing the compatibility of Hinduism and Christianity. Christians have had to learn how to live as a diaspora religion in a largely Hindu culture, renewing efforts to indigenize Christianity with the appearance of more Christian ashrams (both Protestant and Catholic) and Hinduized forms of worship.

China Nineteenth-century colonialism brought the first large-scale attempts to convert the Chinese. China did not welcome the missionary movements and permitted them only under the military and economic duress that accompanied colonialism. The Chinese were no more able to separate religion from civilization than were Europeans. Chinese civilization was deeply shaped by Neo-Confucianism (a combination of Daoism, Confucianism, and Buddhism). Consequently, Christian converts were often viewed with suspicion as unpatriotic, even as Christian missionaries were distrusted as seditious.

After the Communists came to power in 1949, many missionaries were either imprisoned or expelled. Chinese Christians were persecuted and often forced to undergo "reeducation." All ties between indigenous Protestant Chinese Christians and Western Christian organizations were severed in 1952. The break for Chinese Catholics came in 1958 when bishops began to be elected rather than appointed by the Vatican, despite the latter's protests. With the coming of Mao Zedong's Cultural Revolution in 1966, churches were closed, Bibles burnt, and Chinese priests and ministers sent to work camps for reeducation. All public worship was banned. Nevertheless, Chinese Christians persisted by secretly worshiping in private homes ("house churches"). When Western relations with the Chinese improved in the 1980s, it was discovered that indigenous forms of Christianity had survived and were still being practiced in China.

Japan As in China, the people of Japan considered themselves to be an ancient and sacred civilization, superior to all others. Japan too was deeply shaped by Neo-Confucianism (imported from China), amalgamated with the indigenous traditions of Shintoism. As was true of Europeans and the civilizations of India and China, the Japanese also found it difficult to separate religion and civilization and consequently did not readily welcome other religious traditions. Moreover, the Japanese sought to become the one modern Asian nation to successfully adopt a colonialist strategy, seeking to dominate China and Korea.

Until the nineteenth century Japan was largely closed to the West, including to missionary activity. As early as the 1500s, the Jesuit Francis Xavier (1506–1552) established a Christian community in Japan. The Jesuits were driven from Japan by severe persecution in the next century, but when missionaries returned in the mid-nineteenth century they found a thriving community of "hidden Christians" at Nagasaki. As in China, these believers were considered unpatriotic and subversive by Japanese rulers. Very quickly, Japanese Christians moved to assert their independence from Western forms of Christianity and develop indigenous forms. The Japanese Protestant leader Uchimura Kanzo is famous for having started the "non-church" movement. He saw Western church structures as a cultural appendage not appropriate to Japanese culture and sought to restructure Christianity on the Asian teacher-disciple model. He tried to demonstrate in his life that it was possible to be both a patriotic Japanese citizen and a Christian. Ironically, the atomic bomb dropped on Nagasaki destroyed the oldest center of Christianity in Japan. After the war Japanese Christians turned strongly pacifist and sought to break with the Japanese state by resisting any move toward government involvement with Shintoism.

Korea Korea is the great success story of Christian missionary activity in Asia. A Catholic presence in Korea goes back to the eighteenth century. Protestant missionaries came in the 1870s, but significant growth did not occur until Korea began signing trade agreements with the West in the 1880s. Korean interest in Christianity grew after the Japanese victory in its war with China in 1895, which Koreans rightly felt was threatening to their own autonomy. Christianity became identified not only with modernization and Westernization but also with anti-Japanese sentiments, which only increased once Japan annexed Korea in 1910. The churches were virtually the only independent organized bodies in Korea, and their autonomy was enhanced by their international ties. Christians were persecuted by the Japanese and played a prominent role in anti-Japanese protests.

After World War II, Korea split into North and South and war followed (1950–1953). Christians were driven out of the North by the Communists, although house churches may survive there. Korea has the highest percentage of Christians of any nation in Asia except for the Philippines. Indeed, it is the one Asian country that might be tempted to appropriate the Augustinian vision of a Christian civilization. Nowhere in Asia (except for the Catholic Philippines) has Christianity played as strong a role in public life as it has in South Korea, whose first two presidents were Christians. Since the 1970s a highly political liberation theology similar to that developed in Latin America, known as *minjung* theology, has emerged. And as in Latin America, Africa, India, China, and Japan, Korea too developed its own indigenous forms of Christianity, the most famous of which is the Unification Church of Sun Myung Moon, who is heralded by his followers as a new messiah—in this case an Asian messiah.

Given that the majority of Christians in the world are now non-European, it is likely that much of postcolonial Christianity will draw upon the experience of these "mission churches." The question remains whether the dominant model will be an African model, that is, aspiring to create a Christian civilization, or an Asian model of diaspora churches creatively relating to a world that is religiously diverse.

Postcolonial Christianity—Back in the United States

Although the first explorers and settlers in America were the result of Spanish colonization, and although France later extended its reach to America as well, still the United States of America emerged primarily out of the colonization of America by the British. Indeed, it was a revolt against British colonialism by the citizens of its colonies that led to the Declaration of Independence in 1776 and the Constitution of the United States of America as the foundation for a new nation in 1787.

The citizens of the thirteen colonies that formed the United States of America were largely made up of refugees from the political and religious intolerance toward minorities experienced in the nation-states of Europe after the Reformation. To North America fled not only Puritan Calvinists, but also Anglicans and Methodists (originally an evangelical reform movement within Anglicanism), Moravians, Baptists, Presbyterians, Congregationalists, Unitarians, Universalists, and others. All were seeking religious and political freedom and new economic opportunities. At first the colonies, which were economically, religiously, and politically tied to England and Europe as colonies, offered little improvement, each being founded as a haven for one persecuted group and remaining intolerant of yet other such groups. By the time of the founding of the United States of America it had become clear to the colonists that the uniqueness of America as an alternative to Europe had to lie in its toleration of diversity. Consequently, the very first amendment to the United States Constitution began by declaring: "Congress shall make no law respecting an establishment of religion, or prohibiting the free exercise thereof." This meant that the United States must never declare any religion as the official state religion precisely so that religious freedom might be guaranteed to all. This amendment created a major break with the Constantinian and Augustinian models of Christian civilization and opened the door to diaspora models of Christianity. It was, however, a legal transformation that only very slowly took on cultural embodiment. Only gradually, as non-Christian populations have grown, has American culture begun to reflect this possibility.

From its founding, the United States viewed itself as the great Protestant experiment. Denominationalism emerged as a new pattern, and new denominations emerged and proliferated out of all proportion with Protestant divisions in Europe. Eventually Americans came to think of the church as an invisible reality embracing all Protestants, and denominations as voluntary associations that one joined according to one's preference as to the style or type of Protestant one wanted to be. It was very traumatic, therefore, when in the latter half of the nineteenth century Catholic and Jewish immigrants poured into the United States and tipped the balance away from a Protestant majority. This led to a strong reaction of anti-Catholicism and anti-Judaism, which only disintegrated in the last half of the twentieth century when Protestant, Catholic, and Jew came to be seen by many as the major types of voluntary association within the one body of the civic religion through which good citizens could express their patriotism. As the twentieth century ends, that modern equilibrium is being disrupted by new influxes of immigrants from Asia and from Middle Eastern cultures. These emigrations reflect the emergence of a postcolonial, post-European world, where U.S. citizens are increasingly as likely to be Muslim, Hindu, or Buddhist as they are Protestant, Catholic, or Jew.

This new situation presents yet another level of challenge for a country that has thought of itself as a Christian nation, and for most of its history, even more narrowly, as a Protestant nation.

Consequently, the decision of whether to be a Christian civilization or embrace a diaspora model of Christian life is playing itself out not only in Asian culture but in North American culture as well. For example, in 1976, Jimmy Carter, an evangelical Southern Baptist, became president of the United States and both *Time* and *Newsweek* declared it "The Year of the Evangelicals." But Jimmy Carter was a disappointment to many evangelicals, for he was a liberal democrat who believed in the modernist principle of separation of church and state. The more fundamentalist evangelical groups set about supporting someone more suitable to their vision of a Christian America. In 1980 many believed Ronald Reagan to be that man, because he spoke of America as a new Jerusalem chosen by God for a special destiny, and he questioned the truth of evolution and championed the inclusion of creationism in public school curricula while condemning the secular godlessness and amorality of the public school system. Once in office, Reagan declared 1983 "The Year of the Bible." Fundamentalists in the evangelical camp did their best to revive the ancient Augustinian vision of a Christian civilization.

Two distinct visions of a "Christian civilization" emerged in the United States in the 1980s and beyond. On the one hand, the fundamentalist movement associated with T.V. evangelists like Jerry Falwell and Pat Robertson used their media influence to work within the democratic system to reestablish a "Christian America." On the other hand, during the same period more radical Christian Identity movements, were prepared to resort to violence and replace democracy with theocracy—the direct rule of law by the Bible literally interpreted, as they understood it.

Evangelists like Falwell and Robertson subscribe to a view of Christianity called "dominion theology" that seeks to make America a Christian nation through preaching "Christian values" in order to influence the votes of the electorate. However, a more extreme interpretation of this theology, known as "reconstruction theology," goes beyond Falwell's and Robertson's commitment to working through the electorate, advocating a literal biblical theocracy in America. Reconstruction theology draws on the writings of Nicholas Van Til, whose ultraconservative Calvinism asserts that God's law, as found in the Bible and not in democratic elections, must have literal dominion over all things, even "secular" politics and society.

Reconstruction thinkers are "postmillennialists" who believe Christ will return to rule the earth only after Christians have imposed biblical rule on society for a millennium. While not all reconstruction thinkers endorse violence, many believe that violence may be necessary to establish a truly Christian America. This kind of thinking found a natural affinity with Christian Identity movements, which identify white racial supremacy with the biblical rule of law as the basis for a "Christian nation."

CONTRASTING RELIGIOUS VISIONS

As the following contrasting visions indicate, every religious tradition is capable of generating both visions that encourage peace and understanding and visions that encourage conflict and violence.

MARTIN LUTHER KING JR.

On December 1, 1955, Rosa Parks, a black woman in Montgomery, Alabama, refused to move to the segregated section at the back of a public bus. Her subsequent arrest aroused the churches in the black neighborhoods of Montgomery to organize a boycott of the buses and to demand repeal of the state's bus segregation laws. The Reverend Martin Luther King Jr., pastor of the Dexter Avenue Baptist Church, himself the son of a Baptist minister, was elected to lead the boycott. The boycott came to a successful conclusion when the Supreme Court declared Alabama laws requiring segregated buses unconstitutional. The ruling, on November 13, 1956, took practical effect on December 21, 1956.

This boycott marked the beginning of the struggle to end segregation (c. 1954–1966). Dr. King and the Southern Christian Leadership Conference, which he founded in 1957, were at the forefront of these efforts. Perhaps the major accomplishment of the movement was the passage of the Civil Rights Act in 1964.

Martin Luther King Jr. lived and died by the teachings of the Sermon on the Mount, in which Jesus told his hearers to love their enemies. King argued that the way of violent retribution, "an eye for an eye," leaves everyone blind. Moreover, he was open to the wisdom of other religions, for he believed that God spoke to humanity in every time and in every culture. Indeed, he drew upon the principles of nonviolence and civil disobedience first perfected by great Hindu leader Mohandas K. Gandhi in his struggle against British colonial discrimination.

On April 4, 1968, at the age of thirty-nine, King was assassinated by a sniper in Memphis, Tennessee. His efforts to secure racial justice for black Americans are a valuable legacy for the churches. But King was also an early voice in protest against the neglect of the poor of every race and religion.

MICHAEL BRAY

In May 1989 the Reverend Michael Bray was released from prison after serving time for burning down seven abortion clinics in Delaware, Maryland, and Virginia. Bray is the author of *A Time to Kill*, a book presenting biblical arguments that support the killing by Christians of anyone who performs abortions or assists in providing them.

Michael Bray grew up in a military family and, as a young man, he experienced an evangelical conversion. After studying at a Baptist Bible college and seminary with a strongly fundamentalist orientation, he became assistant pastor of a Lutheran congregation. He soon left to form a splinter group, the Reformation Lutheran Church, arguing that the larger body was not faithful to the literal meaning of the Bible. Bray espoused reconstruction theology, a radical fundamentalist school of thought that rejects the secularization of society and the separation of church and state and seeks to rebuild society around a literal understanding of biblical law. Reconstructionists believe that there is only one truth and one way for all of society. The Christian task, they say, is to establish a Christian civilization in accord with this truth.

Michael Bray rejects the notion that Jesus teaches nonviolence as the appropriate response to injustice. On the contrary, he argues, Jesus demands the justice of "an eye for an eye," like the God of war in the Old Testament (e.g., Leviticus 24:19-20). Bray says that the Sermon on the Mount applies only to Jesus' life as a "suffering servant" up to and including his crucifixion, contending that now Jesus is "a man of war" who reigns from heaven as the divine warrior who will come again to administer justice by the sword.

Michael Bray insists that only those living in conformity with God's law have a right to life and since God's law forbids abortion, those performing abortions have no right to live. He says he does not advocate violence but rather defends the morality of those who feel called by God to engage in the killing of anyone who provides abortion assistance. Bray is considered to have been a decisive influence on a several persons who have stalked abortion providers, including Rev. Paul Hill, who killed Dr. John Britton and his escort, James Barrett, in front of an abortion clinic in Pensacola, Florida, on July 29, 1994.

Christian Identity has its roots in a nineteenth-century British movement, inspired by John Wilson, who argued that the Jews are not the true Israelites. Rather, the British are the real "lost tribe" of Israel. Drawing on the history of Christian anti-Judaism, this movement argued Jesus was not a Jew but an Aryan (an argument some Nazis later also used). This view, transplanted to American soil, saw white Americans as this true Israel and gave birth to such movements as the Ku Klux Klan, the Posse Comitatus and the Aryan Nations, which do not shrink from advocating violence to advance their vision of a Christian America.

Reconstructionist and Christian Identity movements have both played a strong role in inspiring activists such as Michael Bray, Eric Robert Rudolph, and Paul Jennings Hill, who have promoted the murder of doctors who perform abortions, and others like Timothy McVeigh, who bombed the Alfred P. Murrah Federal Building in Oklahoma City in protest against a godless, secular America that rejects these movements' call to be a "Christian nation." Their activities demonstrate the presence of Christian terrorism in the United States. Such groups and individuals see themselves locked in a cosmic battle with the

WOMEN IN THE MODERN CHURCH

Even though the veneration of Mary found in the medieval Catholic tradition was rejected by the Protestant Reformation, Protestants, like Catholics, tended to emphasize the role of women as obedient wife and dutiful mother. Over time, exceptions developed, especially among sectarian Protestant movements with mystical or Gnostic roots. For example, the Shakers and Christian Science church were both founded by women. The pietist/evangelical strands of Christianity, with deep roots in the mystical tradition and its emphasis on religious experience, also provided leadership opportunities to women. This was especially true in the evangelical missionary movements of the nineteenth century, which offered new opportunities for women in leadership roles and contributed to beginnings of the women's emancipation movement. Another major influence was Enlightenment secularization and rationalism. Consequently, in the nineteenth century women began to be ordained in some Protestant denominations, the Congregationalists leading the way in 1853. They were followed by the Universalists, the Unitarians, and other denominations. The mainline churches (Methodist, Presbyterian, Episcopalian, and Lutheran) did not follow suit until the twentieth century. The Roman Catholic and the Orthodox churches still do not ordain women, arguing that the maleness of Jesus and the apostles reveal the divine intent for an all-male priesthood.

The last four decades of the twentieth century also saw the rise of a theologically based feminism. The issue that divides feminists and fundamentalists is whether or not God has created a sacred natural order in which men's and women's roles are eternally defined. Fundamentalists say yes, feminists say no. Feminists argue that fundamentalists confuse the cultural attitudes and common practices of premodern societies with the will of God. Fundamentalists counter by arguing that feminists and other liberation advocates confuse the cultural attitudes and common practices of modern societies with the will of God.

forces of evil that dominate modern secular society. These "forces" manifest themselves in the secular government of the United States that allies itself with multicultural and multiracial organizations that foster globalization through the United Nations. The United Nations, they believe, seeks to destroy a white Christian America by imposing a "godless" "one world government." Their resort to violence is necessary, in their view, if America is ever to abandon is flirtation with modern secularity and globalization and return to its roots as a "Christian civilization."

As elsewhere in the emerging postcolonial world, in the United States the desire to return to the fundamentals of a faith untainted by modernity is counterbalanced by a more postcolonial model of Christianity. This type of Christianity sees the task, not as returning to something lost but as moving forward into a new kind of Christianity. Whereas fundamentalism wants to create a public order focused on creating a "Christian America," American liberation theology seems to be embracing a diaspora model of Christianity that seeks social justice for all in a pluralist society.

Latin American liberation theology was a protest against European political and economic colonialism based on a Marxist social analysis. North American theologians, by analogy, extended the problem of colonial oppression to include other forms of oppression as well. Feminist theologians, for example, argued that they too were the victims of oppression just as real as that suffered by the subjects of colonialism—oppression by male-dominated societies. Indeed, feminists plausibly argued that discrimination against women had been going on longer and was more pervasive in all societies than that which emerged with nineteenth-century European colonialism. Thus feminists, like their black male counterparts, demanded liberation, equality, and justice. By the 1980s the language of liberation theology was also being adopted by some in various groups who felt marginalized, including Native Americans, Asian Americans, homosexuals, and others. While drawing inspiration from the Marxist liberation theology of South America, North American liberation theology was more especially influenced by the civil rights movement and its strategies of social protest and civil disobedience.

What is striking about black and feminist forms of liberation theology is an openness to the wisdom of other religions that is not typical of Latin American liberation theology. Martin Luther King, Jr., who openly drew upon the wisdom of Mahatma Gandhi in developing his philosophy of nonviolence, said that there was truth to be found in all religions, and nominated the Buddhist monk Thich Nhat Hanh for the Nobel Peace Prize. And many feminist theologians draw inspiration from ancient pagan traditions of the goddess. Both have insisted that it is possible to remain Christian and yet appreciate and learn from other religions. These perspectives add new dimensions to a diaspora model of Christianity. From the fundamentalist point of view, however, this openness is a sure sign of the secular decadence of modernism and liberation theology.

CONCLUSION

As we noted in Chapter 1, the decisive event that gave birth to the global debate between fundamentalists and modernists in Christianity was the emergence of the social and historical sciences. The historical and comparative study of different societies and their histories made human beings aware of the diversity of social orders. It became obvious that every social order was not really a part of nature, like trees or mountains, but rather a human creation. The result was the emergence of a growing sense of cultural and ethical relativism by the end of the nineteenth century.

This new awareness produced two extreme reactions—fundamentalism and modernism. The former sees Christianity as an unchanging embodiment of eternal truth, while the latter sees Christianity as an historical community whose growth and transformation is inspired by God's original and continuing revelation. Christian fundamentalists reject the implications of historical consciousness and fear that modern historical and sociological consciousness leads to the anarchy of relativism. Modernists accept historical change as God's will and see Christianity continuing to develop toward a greater understanding of God's will in relation to a changing world.

A significant gulf divides these two ways of affirming Christian faith. For while both share a common scripture with stories of God's action in time, for modernists this means admitting historical change in the development of scriptures and of church doctrine, whereas for fundamentalists it means God's actions can never depart from the models acknowledged by premodern Christianity which embody eternal and unchanging truth. And while both agree that the church should be God's agent for transforming the world, fundamentalists mean that all the world should be converted to Christianity and share a common premodern Christian vision, whereas among postmodern or postcolonial Christians there has emerged a diaspora model that breaks with the Constantinian and Augustinian models of a Christian civilization, welcomes religious diversity, and seeks to live creatively and constructively in a pluralistic world. It is likely that the future of Christianity will be significantly shaped by the contest between these views, each of which has significant but very different social and political consequences.

Standing between these extremes, modern Christians tried to privatize religion and segregate their personal piety from their public life. Religion was a personal and family matter, public life was to be secular and therefore free of religion. Neither fundamentalist nor postmodern Christians are willing to accept that model. Both insist that their faith should affect public life. But the form that public faith takes in each is very different. Fundamentalism champions either a Constantinian or an Augustinian vision of a Christian civilization and a Christian world. Postmodern, postcolonial Christianity affirms a pluralistic world and a diaspora model of Christianity, in which Christians seek to cooperate with others, religious and nonreligious, in creating a pluralistic world with greater compassion and justice for all. We should not expect that Christians will eventually favor one view at the expense of the other. More likely, as in the past, there will be diverse expressions of Christianity in diverse social, historical, and political circumstances.

DISCUSSION QUESTIONS

1. What are the via moderna and devotio moderna and how did they contribute to the development of modernization? Explain by contrasting modernity with the medieval Christian world.

2. It can be argued that Eastern Christianity (Orthodoxy), Western Christianity (Roman Catholicism and Protestantism), and post-colonial Christianity offer three different models for understanding the relationship between church and state and the relation of Christianity to the non-Christian world: a Constaninian model, an Augustinian model, and a diaspora model. Explain these models and identify their strengths and weaknesses.

3. What is secularization and how is it related to the history of Christianity?

4. How did Western colonialism contribute to the emergence of a post-European Christianity ? Define and explain.

5. What were the issues that were resolved by the development of the doctrine of "two natures in one person" (Council of Chalcedon) and of the trinitarian nature of God (Council of Constantinople)? Do these doctrines put Christianity into fundamental disagreement with the prophetic monotheism of Judaism and Islam? Explain.

6. What is "Original Sin" and why does it lead to the need to expect a savior? Is this belief universal among all Christians? Explain.

7. How did the emergence of Protestantism contribute to the development of the secular nation-state?

8. How did Luther's understanding of Christianity differ from that of the medieval church, and what was the political and religious significance of this difference?

9. Who was Jesus of Nazareth and why is he important to the history of Christianity?

10. Explain the issues in dispute between fundamentalists and modernists. How is the argument between them expressed in contemporary Christianity?

11. The idea of "modernity" is deeply rooted in the Christian version of the myth of history as it was interpreted by Joachim of Fiore. Explain how this is so. Give examples.

KEY TERMS

Augustinianism	Constantinianism	evangelical
Catholic	Deism	fundamentalist
Christ	Dominion Theology	Gospel

grace	pentecostal	Son of God
heresy	Protestant	Syncretism
homoousios	Protestant ethic	Trinity
justification by faith	Reconstruction Theology	two natures, one person
Kingdom of God	Sacrament	
Original Sin	Second Coming	

SUGGESTED READING

Henry Bettenson, ed., *Documents of the Christian Church*, 2d ed. (New York: Oxford University Press, 1963).

Walter H. Capps, *The New Religious Right: Piety, Patriotism and Politics* (Columbia: University of South Carolina Press, 1990, 1994).

Justo González, *The Story of Christianity*, Vols. 1&2 (San Francisco: Harper & Row, 1984).

Paul Johnson, *A History of Christianity* (New York: Atheneum 1976, 1979).

Gilles Kepel, *The Revenge of God: The Resurgence of Islam, Christianity and Judaism in the Modern World* (University Park, Penn. :Pennsylvania State University Press, 1994).

Bruce B. Lawrence, *Defenders of God: The Fundamentalist Revolt Against the Modern Age* (Columbia: University of South Carolina Press, 1995).

George M. Marsden, *Understanding Fundamentalism and Evangelicalism* (Grand Rapids, Mich.: William B. Eerdmans, 1991).

John McManners, ed., *The Oxford Illustrated History of Christianity* (New York: Oxford University Press, 1992).

Mark Juergensmeyer, *Terror in the Mind of God* (Berkeley: University of California Press, 2000).

Wade Clark Roof and William McKinney, *American Mainline Religion* (New Brunswick, N.J.: Rutgers University Press, 1987).

Rosemary Ruether, *Liberation Theology* (New York: Paulist Press, 1972).

Paul Tillich, *A History of Christian Thought*, Vols. 1&2 (New York: Harper & Row, 1967, 1968).

CHAPTER THREE

THE MANY FACES OF JUDAISM: SACRED AND SECULAR

Overview

In a neighborhood in Jerusalem, ultra-Orthodox Jews, dressed in black suits and hats, who consider themselves *haredim* ("those of true piety"), close off their streets and neighborhoods to traffic in strict observance of the rules of Sabbath, while the majority of Jerusalem's inhabitants, secular Israelis in modern Western dress, choose to ignore these and most other religious rules while still considering themselves Jewish. Meanwhile, in a New York City neighborhood, a woman rabbi leads her Reform congregation in a Friday night prayer service while three blocks away, a traditional male rabbi leads the worship at an Orthodox synagogue. Secular Israelis reject the attempts of the ultra-Orthodox to impose their strict Sabbath observance on Israeli society and yet, at the same time, the state of *Israel* does not recognize either Reform or Conservative Judaism, the two largest of the three branches (along with the Orthodox) that dominate American Judaism. Paradoxically this is so because of the influence of ultra-Orthodox Jews who dominate religious life there, despite the fact that they are in the minority. And while, since the Holocaust, the majority of Jews worldwide reside either in Israel or in the United States, one can still find communities of Jews throughout Western and Eastern Europe and scattered throughout the Middle East, Africa, Latin America, and Asia, including India and China.

Behind this modern diversity and the conflicts it creates lies premodern *Rabbinic*, or Talmudic Judaism, which provided the normative framework for Jewish life from about the sixth century CE until the emergence of modern forms of Judaism in the nineteenth century. Indeed, ultra-Orthodox Jews see **109** themselves as preserving this premodern Judaism against the onslaught of modern Jewish diversity. The task before us in this chapter is to understand the unity and diversity of Judaism in its response to modernization by tracing its historical origins and transformations.

Judaism is the smallest of the great world religions, comprising less than one-half of 1 percent of the world's population. Yet Jews have had, and continue to have, a major impact on history. Over the millennia Judaism has been many things to many people in different times and places. Moreover, describing the religion of Judaism is made more complex by the fact that some Jews today do not consider themselves religious but do consider themselves Jewish. And yet, such secular or ethnic ways of being Jewish, as we shall see, have had profound effects on the Jewish religion and so must be included in our survey to help us understand the religion of Judaism. We will find great diversity among the Jewish people, and yet we shall look for a common thread that can tie all of this diversity together.

Jews believe that the God of creation and history, who revealed himself at Sinai, is the highest reality, and to act in harmony with the will of this God is the highest goal of life. Indeed, the monotheism of both Christianity and Islam have their roots in this most ancient of the three traditions. They also follow Judaism in seeing the gravest problem in human life as sin—the failure to live in harmony with the will of a God who demands justice and compassion. And as we have already noted in the previous chapter, sin has two dimensions: idolatry and injustice. If the ideal of life is living in harmony with the will of God, and the problem of life is sin as the disruption of that life-giving harmony, then in Judaism the means by which one overcomes the problem and realizes the ideal is *Talmud Torah*—the study and practice of God's teachings or revelation. Judaism, in contrast to Christianity, does not see the sin of the first two human beings, Adam and Eve, as inherited by all their children (i.e., original sin). Rather, each and every human being stands before God in the same relationship that Adam and Eve did. Each is free to choose good or evil just as Adam and Eve were. However, in his infinite mercy, God created the people Israel by giving them the gift of his *dual Torah* (oral and written teachings) to tip the balance between good and evil in favor of good. In giving them the Torah, God established a *covenant* with Israel, making them a holy people, reminding them: "I will be your God and you shall be my people, I will guide and protect you and you will obey my commandments." According to the story of Torah, this God set before Israel the choice between life and death and made it possible for them to choose life by choosing "to walk in the way of God" (the literal meaning of the word for God's law or commands, *halakhah*)—giving them 613 commandments (good deeds or *mitsvot*) by which to embody in their lives the justice and mercy of God as a model for all the world.

It would be misleading, however, to think that this summary sketch of the religious world view of Judaism would be agreed to by all Jews. In the remainder of this chapter we shall try to understand both the unity and the diversity of Judaism as a religious tradition and the profound impact that the emergence of modernity had on its development. We shall try to accomplish this by starting with the twentieth-century encounter of Judaism with modernity that gave rise to ultra-Orthodoxy—an encounter that parallels the fundamentalist response to modernity in Christianity. We will then go back to the historical beginnings of Judaism and trace its history, in order to understand the origins of the diversity of contemporary Judaism and the contemporary struggle to define the future of Judaism. Because our goal is to understand Judaism's encounter with modernity, we shall focus primarily on those aspects that help us understand the diversity of Judaism today, and how that diversity developed.

ENCOUNTER WITH MODERNITY: MODERN JUDAISMS AND THE CHALLENGE OF ULTRA-ORTHODOXY

Premodern Rabbinic Judaism, as we shall see, was a world unto itself, embracing every aspect of life and offering safe haven from a non-Jewish world that largely rejected it and restricted the role of Jews in society to that of aliens. The modern world, by contrast, seems to offer Jews a new option—the possibility of sharing in its citizenship. Thus modern forms of Judaism all draw a line between the secular (i.e., nonreligious) and the religious in such a way as to allow Jews to participate in both worlds.

Two constellations of events have definitively shaped modern Judaism. The first was the Enlightenment, which gave birth to the historical and social sciences and a secular and scientific understanding of society. In response, Judaism splintered into a new diversity that departed in varying degrees from traditional Rabbinic Judaism in seeking to accommodate modern secular life. Reform Judaism sought to embrace modernity, Conservative Judaism less so, and Orthodoxy as little as possible. All of these remained theistic. Other seemingly nonreligious or secular forms also arose, especially ethnic Judaism and *Zionism*. The second constellation of events to shape modern Judaism included the Holocaust and the founding of the state of Israel in the middle of the twentieth century, and the reaffirmation of the latter that occurred in the 1967 Arab-Israel "Six Day War" that Israel miraculously won against overwhelming odds. These events gave rise to still another form of Judaism, the postmodern and postcolonial Judaism of Holocaust and Redemption.

While modern forms of Judaism all draw a line between the secular and the religious in such a way as to allow Jews to participate in both worlds, each tries to preserve an essential core of Judaism while creating space for aspects of life not directly controlled by religion. For Reform Jews the essence is the ethics of Judaism. Consequently all the supernatural beliefs and all traditional ritualistic requirements are seen as negotiable. For Conservative Jews the rituals are not negotiable but supernatural beliefs are. The Orthodox say that neither is negotiable but still allow that some parts of a Jew's life (secular education, job, etc.) can be carried out in the secular world. The new, late-twentieth-century, ultra-Orthodox movements reject even this compromise with the world. They seek to create a segregated Jewish way of life, one totally separate from both the modernizing forms of Judaism and the surrounding gentile world, by creating Jewish ghettos where all of life (the way one dresses, how and where one works, how one spends one's leisure time, etc.) is governed by supernatural beliefs and traditional ritual.

The ultra-Orthodox seek to recapture, as far as possible, the total way of life of premodern Jews. And they hope to see the day (at least in Israel) when all modern forms of Judaism will disappear and their own communities will be the model for the whole of society. The goal of deprivatizing Judaism, so that its religious vision can shape all of public life, sets ultra-Orthodox Judaism apart from modern forms of Judaism and is the one element it has in common with the postmodern/postcolonial Judaism of Holocaust and Redemption. At the same time, unlike the latter, ultra-Orthodoxy rejects a key characteristic of what some call "postmodernity"—pluralism. It does so out of a fear that pluralism leads to religious and ethical relativism. Ultra-Orthodox movements fight a battle similar to that of Christian Fundamentalism. They rebel against the relativity of the modern world by insisting that there is one truth or one way of life to which all Jews must return if they are not to drown in a sea of relativism that will undermine any sense of higher purpose for life. For the ultra-Orthodox there cannot be many ways to keep the covenant—only one way. And that one way is all encompassing. It does not permit a Jew to parcel out his or her life into separate secular and religious portions. Nor does it permit men and women to redefine their gender roles in new and "liberating" ways. Such redefinitions can only lead to moral chaos and the collapse of the family. Although only a minority of the world's Jewish population have opted for ultra-Orthodoxy, their way of being Jewish offers a challenge to Jews the world over to examine the implications of their modern spiritual and political beliefs: Can one be both modern and Jewish, and remain the true Israel called forth by Torah?

The Conflict over Public Order: Religion and Politics in the State of Israel

The conflict created by ultra-Orthodoxy is most obvious in the new state of Israel where public life was shaped during its first two decades by secular Jews with a nonreligious socialist-Zionist world view (about which we will say more later). In the 1990s 80 percent of Israelis remained secular. However, especially since the mid-seventies, the ultra-Orthodox have formed increasingly influential religious parties that seek to undo this secularity and have the public order of Israel be regulated by the *halakhah* (the religious commandments or laws) of the premodern Talmudic tradition.

Ultra-Orthodox Minorities: The Gush Emunim
and the Neturei Karta

Although the ultra-Orthodox remain a minority with considerable diversity and disagreement among themselves, they agree in the strategy of making the public life of the secular state of Israel (founded in 1948) more religiously observant. They insist, for example, that all businesses be closed on the Sabbath, and they forced into law the requirement that all marriages be done by Orthodox rabbis. The ultra-Orthodox echo the radical sentiments of their first-century sectarian counterparts (e.g., the Essenes, the Zealots, etc.), arguing that "we are the true Israel, you (whether secular, Reform, or Conservative Jews) are not." In the eyes of the ultra-Orthodox, all Jews who are not ultra-Orthodox—whether secular, Reform, or Conservative—are not really Jews, and Orthodox Jews are not orthodox enough. They all need to repent and return (*teshuvah*) to the true Judaism. Consequently both the Orthodox and ultra-Orthodox have campaigned to amend the law of return. This law, enacted in 1950, assures all post-Holocaust Jews in the *Diaspora* that Israel is their homeland and grants automatic Israeli citizenship to all Jews, born of a Jewish mother, who apply. The Orthodox and ultra-Orthodox have repeatedly tried to have the law changed so that only Jews who have undergone an Orthodox conversion will be accepted for citizenship.

Religious political movements and religious parties in Israel are too diverse and complex to fully account for here, but we can understand something of the dynamics of their role in Israeli society by looking at some representative groups. Despite their attraction to segregation and aversion to pluralism, the ultra-Orthodox are themselves quite diverse, extending from the religious Zionists like the Gush Emunim (Bloc of the Faithful), at one extreme, to the anti-Zionist haredim like the Neturei Karta (Guardians of the City) at the other. In between stand various compromise movements, like the Agudat Yisrael (Federation of Israel).

The Neturei Karta emulate a way of life (e.g., all-black eighteenth–century style clothing for the men) that comes out of the traditions of the haredim from Eastern Europe. The Gush Emunim, while remaining rigorously ultra-Orthodox in their observance of Jewish law or halakhah, have developed a manner of dress (e.g., jeans, short-sleeve shirts, and a skullcap for the men) that allows them to separate themselves from the haredim and identify with the Sabras (secular Zionists who founded the state of Israel) whom they see as their counterparts.

The Neturei Karta, and most of the ultra-Orthodox movements, have their roots in a strand of vigorously anti-Zionist Eastern European Orthodoxy, which unlike most of Western European Orthodoxy, refused to make any compromise with modernity. These haredim attempt to totally reject modernity. It is because they seek to preserve the way of life of premodern Eastern European Judaism that they refuse to permit even secular education and modern dress. When textbooks on religion want to illustrate Judaism they typically show pictures of this particular Jewish way of life because it is so visually distinctive—with the men wearing long black coats and black hats and curled locks of hair (*pe'ot*) framing their face in a manner they believe is required of them by halakhah.

Unlike their more modern counterparts (Reform, Conservative, and Orthodox), these ultra-Orthodox haredim do not live in mixed communities with *Gentiles*, nor are they willing to mix with other modern Jews. Rather, they live in ghetto-like communities typically led by a rabbi revered for his piety and Talmudic skill—communities where they can live their faith as a total way of life untarnished by what they see as the compromises of "modern" Jews. Scrupulous in their observance of halakhah, they see themselves as the true Israel who lives for God alone, in accordance with *Talmud* and Torah and uncorrupted by the pollution of the modern world. Knowing that only the coming of the messiah in God's own time can bring about a true Jewish polity, they reject the state of Israel as secular and profane. In this they continue the attitude of premodern Rabbinic Judaism, which from the beginning rejected political and Zionist messianic Judaism. This second-century political-messianic Judaism had appealed to the Torah as giving Jews a divine right to the land and authorized holy war against the Romans, until it was crushed by them.

Paradoxically, at the other extreme of ultra-Orthodoxy, this rejection was itself rejected. The Gush Emunim, for example, while not accepting the Jewish state in its secular form, have firmly accepted the emergence of the secular state as in accordance with the divine will as a step on the way to a genuine (*halachic*) Jewish state. Coming into existence early in 1974, the Gush Emunim represent a distinct branch of ultra-Orthodoxy. Unlike the Neturei Karta, they sought not to reject but rather to transform secular Zionism—to put Zionism on the correct path by making public life in Israel conform to halakhah. They demonstrate how difficult it is for ultra-Orthodoxy to keep history out of Judaism. Even ultra-orthodoxy finds itself developing modern forms of Judaism.

The emergence of religious Zionism demonstrates the profound capacity of religious Judaism to absorb even the most secular forms of Judaism. For, as we shall see, modern Zionism, a political movement to develop a Jewish state, was a profoundly secular movement that rejected the traditional belief that only God's messiah could establish such a state. But through the influence of the first chief rabbi of *Ashkenazi* Jews (Jews whose traditions originated in Central and Eastern Europe) in Palestine, Avraham Yitzhak Hacohen Kook (1865–1935), this attitude changed and religious Zionism was born. Kook, who immigrated to Israel in 1904 from Eastern Europe, represents a break with the tradition of the East European ultra-Orthodox haredim in being open to Enlightenment influences, including secular Zionism, in addition to traditional Talmudic studies. Breaking with the anti-Zionism of the haredim, he blended a fundamentalist-style ultra-Orthodox zeal with Zionism to create the very kind of political Judaism that had been rejected by the haredim in their defense of the rabbinic tradition against modernity. While the haredim called for a return to premodern Rabbinic Judaism, Rabbi Kooks' understanding of premodern reached back

THE 1967 "SIX DAY WAR"

It is hard to overstate the impact of this war on Judaism. In June of 1967 the state of Israel found itself threatened by four predominantly Muslim nations: Egypt, Jordan, Syria, and Iraq. Israel found itself overwhelmingly surrounded by 250,000 troops, some 2,000 tanks, and 700 fighter planes and bombers. A U.N. Emergency Force had withdrawn in May, and Israeli diplomatic initiatives seeking intervention from European countries and America met with feeble responses. Israel perceived itself to be alone, without allies and doomed to certain destruction. Israeli armed forces, under the leadership of General Yitzhak Rabin, staged a surprise air attack on the morning of June 5. In a brilliant series of military moves, Israel routed the combined Arab forces in a war that was over in six days.

At the end of the war, Israel occupied territory formerly under the control of the Egyptians and the Syrians—from the Suez Canal to the Golan Heights. In the process Israel had taken control of the entire West Bank area including the Old City of Jerusalem (on June 7), recovering one of the holiest places for all Jews, the Western Wailing Wall of the Second Temple (destroyed by the Romans in 70 CE), which had been under Jordanian control (see Map 3.1). As the dust and chaos of the Six Day War settled, Jews both in the land of Israel and in diaspora were spontaneously overwhelmed with a religious sense of awe at their seemingly miraculous deliverance from almost certain annihilation by the Egyptians and their allies. Even among the most secular or nonreligious Jews, many could not help but see the hand of God in these events.

In response to this unexpected defeat, an Arab Summit Conference was held in Khartoum in August of 1967. At this conference, a policy of no recognition or negotiations with Israel was established. Under new leadership, the Palestinian Liberation Organization, originally organized in 1964, began a long and systematic policy of guerrilla warfare against Israel. During the 1967 war there was a massive exodus of Arabs from the West Bank to the East Bank, increasing the tensions between Israelis and Palestinians. These tensions continue despite the Oslo peace process between 1993 and 2000 that led to the establishment of an independent Palestinian Authority.

before the rabbis to integrate aspects of that Zionism found among the Zealots who had sought to cast out the Romans and reclaim the land of Israel. Rabbi Kook taught that political Zionism, despite its secularity, was unknowingly carrying out the will of God. This message was further developed and promoted after his death by his son, Rabbi Zvi Yehuda Kook, who identified the new

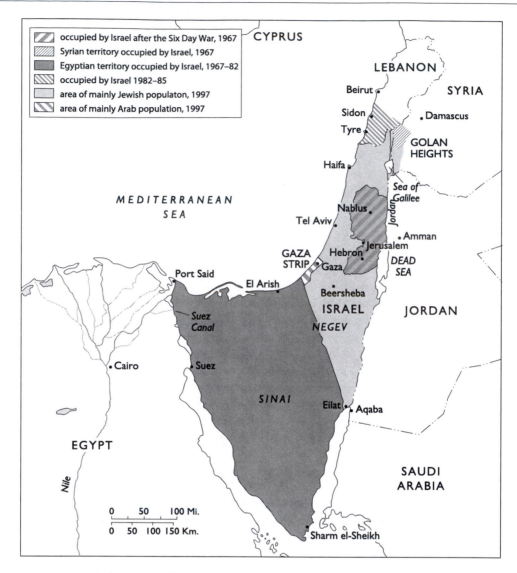

Map 3.1 Arab-Israeli Conflict from 1948.

secular state of Israel as indeed established by the will of God—a fact he regarded as undisputedly established by the Israeli victory in the 1967 war. Indeed, the followers of Rabbi Zvi Yehuda Kook saw 1967 as year one in a new era of Jewish redemption.

Religion and Politics in Israel After the 1973 War

The Gush Emunim, as a form of religious Zionism, was especially influenced by yet another war—the Yom Kippur War of 1973. On October 6, 1973, the

Egyptian army penetrated the Israeli occupation of the Sinai, while the Syrians invaded the Golan Heights. The surprise attack occurred on Yom Kippur, one of the holiest days in the Jewish calendar. Israel, under the leadership of the Socialist-Zionist Labor party, was caught off guard. Israel rallied and successfully rebuffed its attackers, but the event undermined confidence in the leadership of the Labor party. Thus the ground was prepared for both the rise of the conservative Likud party with the election of Menachem Begin as prime minister in 1977, and for a new era of influence from the various ultra-Orthodox religious movements in Israel.

The Gush Emunim were committed to the notion that none of the occupied territories from the 1967 War was to be given back in any peace agreement after the 1973 war. For them, the Jews are the chosen people—chosen by God to inherit the land. They were no more in the mood to share the land with their Palestinian neighbors than many Christian and Muslim Palestinians were to share it with the Jews. Consequently, the Gush Emunim began an intensive program of unauthorized settlements (which they saw as "God's will") in the occupied territory—a program of action that was supported by Menachem Begin when he came to power. In this fashion, religious Zionism began to play an important role in Israeli public policy. However, while the settlements were in their infancy, Begin signed a peace treaty with the president of Egypt, Anwar Sadat, with the encouragement of U.S. President Jimmy Carter at Camp David in 1979. This agreement included the return of occupied territory in the Sinai, which the Gush Emunim saw as a betrayal of God's will. In 1982 their spiritual leader, Rabbi Zvi Yehuda Kook, died, the movement splintered, and some began a program of guerrilla warfare against Palestinian militants. Some even planned to blow up the mosque on the Temple Mount in Jerusalem, but they were discovered before they could carry out their plan. The leaders were arrested in 1984 and the movement lost a large measure of the public support it had enjoyed.

At the end of the twentieth century, Jews in Israel struggle to find a way to live peaceably with their Palestinian neighbors, while Jewish radicals try to undermine such peace with claims of divine privilege and Palestinians talk about holy war. The Gush Emunim illustrate an extreme political interpretation of the Jewish idea of chosenness, one rejected by the apolitical stance of traditional Rabbinic Judaism but one very similar to the traditional Christian and Muslim teachings of supersession. Just as Christians have taught that it is God's will that they replace Jews as the chosen people, and Muslims have taught that they replace both Jews and Christians as God's chosen, so too those ultra-Orthodox who have embraced Zionism tend to see themselves as having a divinely granted right to replace their Christian and Muslim Palestinian neighbors.

The Gush Emunim, and other religious Zionists, embrace just such a belief. However, as we shall see, supersession is not inherent in the biblical understanding of chosenness. For while the biblical stories of chosenness do include promises about the land, the validity of the covenant was interpreted by the great prophets of Israel to be contingent on living a life of justice and compassion. Moreover, while for the most part Christians and Muslims have interpreted chosenness to mean that only "the chosen" enjoy the rewards of the next life, Rabbinic Judaism allowed that righteous Gentiles too have a place in the world to come. And while Christians and Muslims have generally viewed their "chosenness" as divine approval of their right to rule over others politically, Rabbinic Judaism accepted its status as a diaspora religion and held no aspirations to political power. Only with the emergence of modern secular Jewish socialism and Zionism did political aspirations once more enter the picture. The blending of secular Zionism with the zeal found among the haredim has created new minority movements of religious extremists like the Gush Emunim, who seem unwilling to compromise in any way.

In the last decade of the twentieth century Israeli politics is deeply divided between those who believe they have a divine right to supersede all others on the land and those who seek to find a way to share the land in peace. The beliefs of some religious Zionists find a sympathetic response among many secular Israelis, whose memories of the Holocaust as well as of the 1967 and 1973 wars make them feel that if Jews are to survive they must make an absolute and uncompromising claim to the land, and yet many other secular Israelis look for peace and cooperation with their Christian and Muslim Palestinian neighbors.

While religious Jews make up only about 20 percent of the population in Israel, and despite the anti-Zionist stance of most of them, the various political parties that represent them have managed to play a significant role in Israeli public life because typically neither of the major secular parties—Labor and Likud—is able to secure enough votes to form a majority government without entering into a coalition with at least some of these religious parties. This has given such religious parties bargaining power out of all proportion to their numbers.

While some ultra-Orthodox, like the Neturei Karta, reject both the secular state and ultra-Orthodox religious Zionist movements, others, like the Gush Emunim, have sought to force secular Israeli society to conform to their political and religious vision of Jewish life. Still others, both religious Zionists, like the members of the Mizrahi (Spiritual Center) party and the opponents of religious Zionism such as Agudat Israel (Federation of Israel, founded in 1912), have been more moderate, willing to work with the secular state of Israel to find ways of constructive compromise.

Ultra-Orthodoxy as a Type of Fundamentalism

The ascendancy of ultra-Orthodoxy is a part of a larger religious resurgence that has been going on around the globe since the mid-1970s. The late 1960s and early 1970s were a time of radical cultural disruption in Western urban secular societies—a time when the youth of the Western world (who were the children of those who suffered through World War II) were rejecting what they described as the emptiness of modern secularity. In their rejection they turned to various religious movements as a way of recovering a sense of meaning and purpose in life. Indeed, the less modern and secular the movement, the more attractive it appeared.

One form that this religious resurgence took was distinctively fundamentalist. What all religious fundamentalist movements have in common is a desire to return to the foundations of belief and action that existed in the tradition prior to the emergence of modernity. These movements see contemporary culture, in which all truth and all values seem to be viewed as relative, as the logical outcome of modernity. This outcome seems to them to prove the decadence of the modern period—a period in which human beings have lost their way and ended up in a world without standards and norms.

Much of the new strength of ultra-Orthodoxy comes from having made significant inroads among secular Jews and modern religious Jews. Feeling dissatisfied with their lives, many of these Jews have been drawn into the new ultra-Orthodox movements. They have made a leap of faith out of a world that either did not ask them to give their heart to anything (pure secularism) or asked them to give only a part of their heart (modern religious forms of Judaism). They have chosen a form of Judaism that promises to bring order and meaning to the whole of life, not just to a part of it, that requires a full-time commitment, not just a part-time commitment. They have sought to return to the fundamentals of the Judaism of the dual Torah—that is, premodern Rabbinic Judaism.

RABBI MENACHEM SCHNEERSON

One of the most influential of these new ultra-Orthodox religious movements has been the Lubavitch HaBad under the leadership of Rabbi Menachem Schneerson, known as Rabbi Shlita. Schneerson was born in Poland in 1902 and was raised in the Hasidic tradition. He studied engineering in France and immigrated to Brooklyn in 1941. Like many of the leaders of religious movements, Schneerson did not hesitate to use modern technology (especially mass media) to promote a premodern world view. This type of strategy gambles that an ultra-Orthodox movement can use the technology of modernity without allowing it to alter the premodern message it is seeking to promote. In Brooklyn, Rabbi Schneerson used such methods to start what has become a worldwide missionary movement to return Jews to an ultra-Orthodox, totally observant, way of life. This mission has extended into Israel itself, where his movement has been politically influential in the campaign to make the land of Israel religiously observant. This, he preached, is a precondition for the coming of the messiah—a title many of his followers have wished to use of him, especially since his death in 1994.

Therefore, for a significant minority of Jews, the path of rebellion against secular modernity is an attempted return to premodern Judaism as a total way of life. For most of them, there is no compromise. They have rejected a life partitioned between two worlds (secular and religious) and sought, instead, one whole life in total segregation from the modern world and modernist forms of Judaism, in communities of distinctive dress, occupation, and self-governance. In this, they are determined to be more orthodox than the Orthodox, hence—ultra-Orthodox. In this context some rabbis from the United States have begun to establish a new kind of ultra-Orthodox yeshiva or school in Israel.

What these "fundamentalist" movements bring is a challenge to modern forms of Judaism by refusing to reduce being Jewish to historical heritage, morality, and ethnicity. Ultra-Orthodox Jews attempt to recover what they believe has been lost to modern Judaism, namely, the centrality of God, Torah (as divine revelation), and Israel (as an eternal people). Ultra-Orthodoxy rejects all forms of secular Judaism and fears the diversity found in Judaism today. The ultra-Orthodox wish to revert to a time when, in their view, there was one truth and one way. The total immersion in a new way of life engaged in by these Jews represents a definitive break with the "decadence" of Western civilization, as they view it. And while the completeness of their immersion experience parallels that of the premodern tradition of Rabbinic Judaism, its self-consciousness does not. For these "new" Jews are engaged in an experiment and a choice, and in this sense, their religion too belongs to the range of forms of Judaism of the modern/postmodern period. They, like all other religious persons of the modern era, have no choice but to choose. Their choice is either withdrawal from or involvement with the modern world, either back to what they somewhat romantically view as the "one way" of premodern Judaism or forward into pluralism. To understand the implications of this choice we must go back to the beginnings of premodern Judaism in the biblical period and work our way forward.

PREMODERN JUDAISM: THE FORMATIVE ERA—BIBLICAL ORIGINS

The Biblical Roots of Judaism

As we learned in Chapter 1, Judaism, along with Christianity and Islam, is shaped by one of the four major types of myth or symbolic story—the myth of history. Indeed, the myth of history begins with Judaism. Judaism finds its roots in the story of the God who made promises to Abraham and his descendants that were fulfilled centuries later when this God sent Moses to deliver his people from slavery to the Egyptians and lead them into the "land of promise"—the land of Canaan. From these beginnings the story blossomed to tell of the God who acts in time (i.e., in history) and leads his people on a journey through time toward a day of final resurrection in which all injustice, suffering, and death will be overcome.

While all religious traditions pass on their vision of reality through stories, story plays a unique role in Jewish religion. All the great religions of the world have told stories that draw on the metaphors of nature to explain religious experience. For instance, the cycles of nature are used to explain the wheel of death and rebirth in the myths of liberation from India and the rhythms of yin and yang in the myths of harmony from the religions of China. In Judaism, while analogies from nature are not absent, there is a clear shift of emphasis from nature to history. That is, if you want to understand who the God of Israel is, you do not look primarily to nature but to history as the story of the people Israel's journey through time.

Indeed, for Judaism God is the divine storyteller and the unfolding of creation in history is God's story. In the beginning God said, "Let there be light. . .," and the story began. And the story unfolds in history until God brings it—despite many trials and tribulations—to a happy ending when the dead shall be raised to enjoy a new heaven and a new earth at the end of time.

The story of the past, as it was imagined by the people Israel, proceeds from the creation of the first man and woman—Adam and Eve—and the near annihilation of humanity because of their sins as related in the story of Noah and the flood, through the division of humans into many language groups at the tower of Babel, to God's call to Abraham to be a father of many nations and his promise to give the land of Canaan to his descendants (Genesis 15:1–18). It moves on to the descent of the tribes of Israel into Egypt during the time of Joseph and the famine. It relates how the tribes became enslaved in Egypt and how God sent Moses to deliver them from slavery in the Exodus, and how he brought them to Mount Sinai where God gave the Torah to Moses and formed a covenant with the people.

The story of the Exodus is the great founding story from which Judaism draws its identity. It is the story of a people who are freed from slavery against impossible odds and who gather at Mount Sinai in the desert where the God responsible for their liberation addresses them:

> And Moses went up to God, and the Lord called to him from the mountain, saying, "Thus shall you say to the house of Jacob, and tell the people of Israel; You have seen what I did to the Egyptians, and how I carried you on eagles' wings, and brought you to myself. Now therefore, if you will obey my voice indeed, and keep my covenant, then you shall be my own treasure among all peoples; for all the earth is mine; And you shall be to me a kingdom of priests, and a holy nation. These are the words which you shall speak to the people of Israel."
> —(Exodus 19:3–6)

These words are taken from the book of Exodus in the Torah—the bible of Judaism. They are the words said to have been spoken by the God of Abraham to the prophet Moses, as God enters into a binding relationship, called the covenant, with a people he has chosen as his very own and rescued from slavery in the land of Egypt.

This scene at Mount Sinai is a climactic moment in a powerful and dramatic story about a journey that created a people—the people Israel. The God of Abraham sends down ten plagues upon the Egyptians and then parts the waters of the sea to enable the tribes of Israel to escape, closing the waters over the pursuing Egyptian army. It is a story about how a people enslaved by the Egyptians achieved their liberty against insurmountable odds and were led into a new land given to them by their God—in keeping with a promise made to their ancient ancestor Abraham (Genesis 15:18–21). In this way, according to the story, did the God of Israel bring his people out of Egypt to become a holy people, a kingdom of priests. For as the Hebrew word for holy (*qadosh*) suggests, to be holy is to be "set apart." So Israel was *chosen* out of all the nations and *set apart* to be God's people.

The story goes on to tell how the tribes of Israel wandered in the dessert for forty years, and only after the death of Moses did they enter the land of promise under the leadership of Joshua (see Map 3.2). For the next two hundred years they lived on the land as a loose confederation under charismatic leaders called "judges." However, as the threats of military conquest from their neighbors became more frequent, many among the tribes began to demand that Israel have a king like other nations with a standing army to protect Israel. Others, however, argued that there can be only one king over Israel—the God of Abraham, Isaac, and Jacob. God, according to the story, agreed to appoint a king. And so Saul was anointed with oil by a prophet, as a sign that God (not the people) chose the first king over Israel. Indeed, the concept of messiah (*mashiah*) has its beginnings here, for a "messiah" is an "anointed one" chosen to rule over the kingdom of God, the kingdom of Israel.

Saul, however, proved to be a weak king, for he had no independent authority and had to depend on the voluntary cooperation of the tribes, which could be uncertain. It was David, the second king over Israel, that established Israel as a nation. Under David and later his son Solomon, according to the story, Israel became for a brief time the greatest nation in the Middle East. Stories were told of David's rise to power—how even as a young boy he had saved the tribes by slaying the Philistine giant, Goliath. Indeed, Saul, who had taken him in as if he were his own son, soon became jealous of his popularity and turned on him. As a result David had to flee in fear of his life. David then became a kind of "Robin Hood" figure, leading his own private army. This gave him a loyal following and a base of power that Saul never had. When Saul died in battle against the Philistines, David was proclaimed by the people and anointed by the prophets as the next king over Israel.

David used his own army to capture a Canaanite city, Jebus, as his own city, renaming it Jerusalem, which, according to the story, means "God's Peace." Because Jerusalem had not belonged to any of the tribes, it gave David a neutral vantage point from which to rule over all of the tribes. So Jerusalem

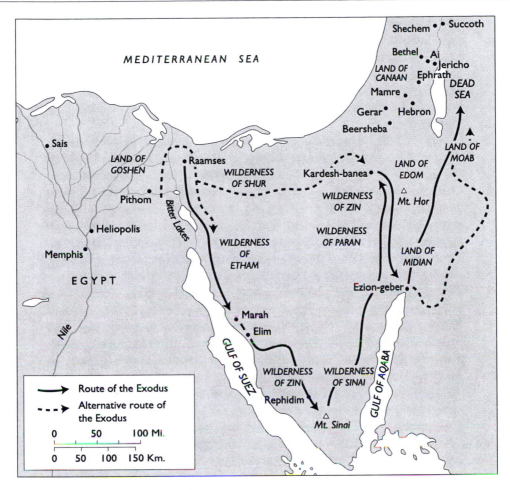

Map 3.2 The Route of the Exodus.

became the capital. Then David gave this capital a religious sanction by bringing the Ark of the Covenant to Jerusalem, making it a holy city. The ark was considered holy because it was believed to contain the tablets God gave to Moses at Mount Sinai. Indeed, it was during David's reign that God is said to have made a new promise—this time to David—that his heirs would rule as messiahs into the far distant future (2 Samuel 7:16). After David's death his son Solomon succeeded him to the throne, and Israel was at the height of its power. It was Solomon who built the first temple so that God could dwell in a splendor greater than that of any of the gods of the other nations.

However, after the time of Solomon there was quarreling about the succession to the throne and Israel was divided into two kingdoms: Israel in the north and Judah in the south. Also prophets like Amos and Hosea (c. 800 BCE) arose in Israel. They reminded the people that ever since they gave up their nomadic life to become an agricultural and urban people, they had been drifting further and further from the tribal values of the covenant made at Sinai. In the cities the people acted as if they were strangers to each other, and the rich mistreated the poor. The prophets warned that God would punish those who offered sacrifices in the temple while continuing to act unjustly. What God wants most of all is the sacrifice of a pure heart committed to deeds of justice and compassion.

It is with the prophets that Jewish monotheism becomes fully formed. For in the tribal days of the time of Moses, Israel's commitment had been "henotheistic"—that is, to one God above all others. Thus the commandment—"I am the Lord your God . . . you shall have no others beside me," did not mean that there were no other gods, but only that Israel was forbidden to follow them. God was their tribal God. But after Israel was established as a great nation in the time of David, the prophets forced Israel to see that they did not own God nor the land of promise—that the covenant conferred not so much privileges as responsibilities. According to the prophets, Israel's God was the God of all the nations and he would use the other nations, if necessary, to punish Israel for any failure to keep the covenant. From the time of the prophets Israel began to think of God not as a tribal deity but in the manner later expressed in the Book of Genesis—as the creator of all things and all peoples. From this time forward, Israel would become progressively convinced that having "no other gods" required more than loyalty. It required affirming that there were no other gods. Out of the prophetic experience came the pure and simple creed of Judaism, the *Shema*: "Hear O Israel, the Lord our God, the Lord is one" (Deuteronomy 6:4). This confession is completed by reminding the people to love this God with all their heart, soul, and strength; to pray the Shema on arising and retiring; and to bind it on their hands, foreheads, and door posts to ensure that the awareness of the one true God might permeate their every thought and action.

The prophets warned the people that if they did not return to the covenant, this God, who is Lord of all creation and history, would punish them. And that is exactly how the misfortunes of Israel and Judah came to be interpreted, For in 721 BCE the Assyrians conquered the kingdom of Israel and carried its inhabitants off into slavery. (Later, the Samaritan tradition would claim that only they had been left behind and had carried on the pure traditions.) In 621, King Josiah is said to have discovered what he believed to be an ancient lost book (the Book of Deuteronomy) in the temple. This book echoed the teachings of the prophets about the need to practice justice in order to please God. On this basis he initiated a reform that included a renewal of the covenant and required that all sacrifices be done only at the temple in Jerusalem. However, according to the biblical story, the reforms were not observed conscientiously and God again allowed the people to be punished. In 586 the Babylonians conquered the Assyrians and their territories, and carried off the inhabitants of the southern kingdom of Judah into exile and slavery.

In exile in Babylonia, the people Israel had to learn how to sing their song in a strange land (Psalm 137:3–4) and without their temple. During and after the exile another generation of prophets arose—Jeremiah, Ezekiel, and Isaiah—who confirmed that God was indeed punishing Israel for its failure to keep the covenant, but then added that the punishment would only be temporary (to teach them a lesson). They would be permitted to return to their land and rebuild their temple. Indeed, the Persians soon conquered the Babylonians and after only fifty years the Israelites were permitted to return to the land (538). This was due to the benevolent policy of the Persian king, Cyrus, who believed in ruling the peoples he conquered by winning their hearts rather than by threats and punishments. Cyrus' permission to return to the land, which included modest funds to rebuild the temple, was seen as so miraculous by the prophet Isaiah that he actually declared that Cyrus was, unknowingly, a messiah, that is, one anointed by God to carry out God's will to return his people to their land (Isaiah 45:1–13). Thus, even in the biblical period, ancient Judaism was capable of finding religious significance in seemingly secular political events.

When the first wave of exiles returned to the land (520–515 BCE), the leadership was weak and the people lacked a clear direction. It was not until Ezra and Nehemiah led a second wave of exiles (458) in a return to the land of Israel that a clear pattern for a postexilic Judaism was laid down. They demanded that the people repent of their past mistakes in consorting with other nations and other gods, rededicate themselves to the covenant, and repurify themselves as a holy people by separating themselves from their neighbors. This meant, for example, that all those who had married foreign wives had to abandon them or be cut off from their own people. Israel must once more be a holy people, set apart from the nations. It is with this priestly reform that Judaism adopted the experience of exile and return as the normative pattern through which to interpret all its future experiences. In this sense, the experience of exile and return gave birth to Judaism.

In the fourth century BCE, Alexander the Great conquered the ancient world, and after his death in 323 his empire was divided among his generals. For over a century the Ptolemies ruled over Israel (301–198). Eventually they were replaced by the Seleucids (198–167), who began a policy of enforced Hellenization, requiring all their conquered peoples to adapt Greek customs and beliefs, including Hellenisitc polytheistic religion. This led to the severe persecution of the Jews, who refused to abandon their worship of the God of Abraham, Isaac, and Jacob for that of the pagan gods. Thus in the middle of the second century, the Maccabean revolt against the cruel Seleucid ruler, Antiochus Epiphanes IV, began, led by Judas Maccabeus and his brothers (167). This revolt was modestly successful in bringing about a status of semi-independence under the rulership of the priestly house of the Hasmoneans, which lasted into the first century CE. However, in a bid to resist new efforts at control by the Seleucids, the Jews in 63 BCE invited in the Romans to protect them. While under the foreign domination of Rome, the second temple was rebuilt in splendor between 20 BCE and 60 CE.

It was in the time of Ezra and Nehemiah that the Great Assembly arose to provide leadership of religious life. And during the next couple of centuries there grew up a considerable diversity of movements within Judaism, leading to the first-century Jewish movements we referred to in Chapter 2—the Sadducees, the Pharisees, the Hellenists, the Samaritans, the Zealots, the Essenes, and the Nazarenes.

More needs to be said about these movements, all of which were engaged in an ongoing debate. Today we would be tempted to say the debate was about the right way to be Jewish, but the idea of Judaism as a religion did not yet exist. They saw the debate rather as about how one must live in order to be the "true Israel" or people of God. To understand this debate it is important to remember that at the beginning of the first century there was no official bible and no agreed upon set of practices and commitments accepted as normative by all Jews. It was only at the end of the first century that the Tanak, or bible of Judaism as we have it today, came into existence, along with Rabbinic Judaism as the normative pattern of Judaism for the next eighteen hundred years.

The *Sadducees* came from the wealthy upperclass, were associated with the temple tradition that was exclusive to Jerusalem, and saw their task as keeping peace with Rome. They accepted only the five books of Moses as sacred scripture and insisted on a literal adherence to the written Torah. The *Pharisees* were teachers associated with the *synagogues* (houses of study and prayer) found in every city and village; they accepted not only the books of Moses but the historical and wisdom writings and those of the prophets. Both the Jewish bible (Tanak) and the Christian Old Testament are largely derived from the Pharisees' selection of scripture. They taught that God revealed himself in the written Torah and through oral traditions that accompanied the giving of the Torah to Moses. Moreover, they insisted that the written word could not be properly interpreted without the oral traditions. In these teachings the Pharisees offered a precursor to the later rabbinic doctrine of God's revelation through two Torahs, oral and written. Politically, the Pharisees were neither cozy with, nor openly hostile to, the Romans. Outside of Palestine, in the Diaspora (Jews dispersed throughout the empire), the leaders in the synagogues were Hellenistic *Jews* who used a Greek translation of scriptures that closely corresponded to the Hebrew scriptures of the Pharisees, with some important exceptions. The *Hellenists* were the great missionaries of Judaism, anxious to promote Judaism as a religion that had a place for Gentiles. They successfully encouraged large numbers of Gentiles to come and worship the one true God of Israel.

Finally, there were the sectarian movements like the *Zealots*, the *Samaritans*, the *Essenes*, and the *Nazarenes* (the followers of Jesus of Nazareth). Some, like the Zealots and Essenes, were openly hostile to the gentile world, and others, like the Nazarenes, were, like the Hellenists, very positive toward Gentiles and sought their conversion. These movements tended to be apocalyptic, believing that God would bring the world to an end soon, and so would send a messiah to judge all human beings and reward the faithful. In the first century there was no single clear definition of "messiah." A wide variety of speculations had grown up, and each sectarian group had its own expectations. Most were expecting a spiritual leader, but some, primarily the Zealots, expected a military leader who would overthrow the Roman oppressors.

What was typical of these sectarian movements was a strong distrust of the Sadducees and the temple tradition in Jerusalem. The Sadducees were viewed as having sold out to the foreign oppressors, the Romans. The Zealots were probably the most hostile of all. They had nothing but contempt for the Sadducees and chose to directly oppose them. If the Sadducees urged "don't rock the boat," the Zealots were committed to rocking the boat as often as possible by staging random guerrilla attacks against the Roman legions. In the second century a Zealot, Simon bar Kokhba, claimed the title of messiah and was executed by the Romans.

Finally, at least some of these sectarian groups practiced baptismal rites, that is, rites of ritual immersion and purification. Such a ritual immersion was already a requirement for any gentile convert to Judaism (along with *circumcision* for males). What was new about their use of this practice was their insistence that not only gentile converts but also Jews must undergo the rite if they had strayed from the true path of Judaism as understood by the particular sectarian movement. This brings us to the historical context in which Rabbinic Judaism first emerged after the fall of the temple in 70 CE, as described in the previous chapter. We will follow up on this emergence in a later section.

Exodus and Exile: The Key Biblical Events

As we saw in our chapter on Christianity, the difference between premodern and modern is the difference between sacred story and secular story or history. Fundamentalists fear the incursion of time and history into their sacred story, whereas modernists welcome it. The biblical writings as we have them are organized to tell a story of God's saving journey with his people through time. This is the story just presented in summary form. It is the story of the myth of history—of the God who acts in time and leads his people through time toward a final fulfillment. This is a grand story that answers questions of origin and destiny for the Jews as a religious people (i.e., where do we come from? where are we going?). When modern historians read this story, they ask different questions. Primarily they want to know if the way things are described are the way things really happened. They try to answer this question by comparing the stories with what else is known about the past through ancient writings, through literary analysis of stylistic changes in the writings, and through archaeological artifacts.

When historians read the biblical stories critically they believe they can identify different layers of historical development in the scriptural writings.

It is on this basis that they identify the four major layers of historical materials: J&E (Jahwist and Elohist, from two different names for "God" in Hebrew) from the period of the monarchy (David and Solomon, c.1000 BCE), D (Deuteronomy, c. 621 BCE) associated with the prophetically rooted reforms of King Josiah, and P (priestly, c. 458 BCE) associated with the priestly reforms of Ezrah and Nehemiah.

The earliest stories (J&E) seem to have been written down in the courts of David and Solomon to tell the story of how God chose Israel, from humble beginnings, to become a great kingdom. Bringing together diverse ancient tribal stories, these royal storytellers constructed a larger and more complex story that begins with the creation of the world and ends with the kingdom of Israel as the greatest nation of the ancient Middle East under David and Solomon. It is an unambiguous story of promise and fulfillment. However, the story had to be revised in light of the Babylonian exile. This Priestly revision tells how Israel is a people shaped by seemingly broken promises that are unexpectedly fulfilled, at least in part, leading to new hope and new life—a story of exile and return. It was this priestly pattern of exile and return that gave Judaism its definitive form—a form that has been able to accommodate yet other stories of Israel as divergent as ultra-Orthodoxy and Kabbalistic Hasidism on the one hand and secular Zionism and the Judaism of Holocaust and Redemption on the other hand.

The core of the story of the people Israel was shaped and reshaped by imagining and reimagining the details and implications of two historical events: the exodus and the Babylonian exile. During the time of David and his son Solomon, the Exodus was viewed as an unambiguous story of promise and fulfillment. Promises made to Abraham are fulfilled in the time of Moses and reaffirmed in David and Solomon's glorious reigns. Indeed, until the time of the Babylonian exile, the story of promise and fulfillment seemed confirmed by experience. Things looked very different by 586 BCE, when the Babylonians were able to carry the people Israel off into exile. That exile was devastating. For now it seemed that the God of Israel had broken his promises and abandoned his people. However, the great prophets of the period suggested an alternative explanation for the misfortune of the people Israel. As we have already noted, the prophets Jeremiah, Ezekiel, and Isaiah reminded the people that the covenant was conditional. Therefore, they argued, if Israel is now in exile it is not because God has not kept his promises but because the people have not kept their promise to obey the commandments of the covenant.

As the biblical stories retell it, the prophets were not only able to explain the tragedy of the people Israel, but were also able to offer hope. For they dared to predict that the exile would be temporary. As a punishment for sin, the exile was meant only to teach the people a lesson, namely, the importance of being faithful to the covenant. Therefore, they would eventually be permitted to return to the land. And we know that, after some fifty years, this did indeed happen. In this situation, leadership in a community subservient to a foreign power and without a royal house fell to the priests of the temple tradition. In their eyes, Israel seemed to be delivered miraculously from an impossible situation.

If the exodus was the founding event of Judaism, it was the exile that was its formative event. As the distinguished scholar of Judaism, Jacob Neusner, has noted, it was the great crisis of exile and the astonishment of return that set the mythic pattern of Judaic thought and experience ever since. The exile and return provided a story pattern through which all past and future events, whether of triumph or of tragedy, could be meaningfully integrated into Jewish identity. "Exile and return" shaped the imagination of all future generations. No longer did Israel think of itself as David did (in 1 Chronicles 22–27), as having an unconditionally guaranteed existence. On the contrary, its existence was dependent on its commitment to the covenant.

Therefore, when the second temple fell at the hands of the Romans in 70 CE, while it was a trauma and a deep blow to the story of the God who leads his people through time, it was not a crisis without precedent and without meaning. For although the power of leadership shifted once more, this time from the priests to the teachers (i.e., rabbis), these rabbis immediately reverted to the priestly pattern of explanation, arguing once more that the cause of the present misfortune was that Israel did not keep the covenant faithfully enough. Consequently, although the fall of the first and second temples were two of the most traumatic events in the long history of Judaism, neither destroyed the faith of Jews. On the contrary, in each case Jews came to the conclusion that the loss of the temple was not a sign of God's failure but a call to the people Israel to be more fully observant of the covenant. Thus today Jews willingly recall these events on the holy day of Tisha B'Av, for remembering brings about not despair and hopelessness but repentance and renewal.

PREMODERN JUDAISM: THE FORMATIVE ERA—FROM TORAH TO TALMUD

The Pharisaic Roots of Rabbinic Judaism

To follow the emergence of Talmudic Judaism we need to pick up at the point we left off, describing the diverse Jewish sects and movements that had emerged by the first century. This diversity was brought to an end by the destruction of the temple in 70 CE. Of the variety of movements that had been vying to provide a model for Jewish life, only a couple survived, and of these it was the Pharisees who provided new leadership. There were at least three reasons for this. First, the political neutrality of the Pharisees in the period before the fall of the temple made them appealing to the Romans. Unlike the Zealots, the Pharisees seemed benign in their views toward the Roman Empire. So the Roman authorities gave them permission to establish an academy at Yavneh on the coast of Israel. There the task of reconstructing Judaism for a new period of exile apart from the land and the temple began.

Second, the Pharisees were well positioned to offer leadership because they were already the leaders of the synagogue tradition and the teachers (rabbis) of the importance of the oral tradition. Third, it was the oral tradition that gave them the flexibility to interpret the requirements of Jewish life for changing circumstances. When the temple priesthood disappeared, everything was already in place for the new leadership. No new institutions needed to be invented. The Pharisees became the natural leaders by default everywhere in ancient Palestine.

The nature of the Pharisaic revolution was to transpose the priestly model focused on the temple in Jerusalem into a new key—one that would allow the people Israel, like their ancestors in Babylon, to sing their song in the strange new lands of the Diaspora after the destruction of the temple. The question facing Jews once again was: How can we survive as Jews apart from the land and the temple? The answer of the Pharisees was that the people Israel (not just the temple) were holy and that every male head of a Jewish household was in fact a priest, even as the table in every Jewish house was an altar. In this new model, the center of Jewish life shifted from written Torah to the oral tradition, from priest to rabbi, from temple to synagogue, and also from temple altar to family table.

The priestly tradition had insisted that Israel was a holy people, set apart for service to the one true God, and had established elaborate rules of ritual separation to keep the people from blending in with the general population around them. The Pharisees, drawing on the prophets, insisted that what God wanted more than cultic worship, with its sacrifices, was deeds of loving kindness (*mitzvot*)—that is, acts of justice and mercy. To this end, then, the Pharisees transferred the rituals of separation from the temple cult to ethics. The prophets had issued sweeping demands, in the name of God, for justice and mercy. The Pharisees took these demands and made them the content for the priestly rituals of holiness, working out their application in all the details of everyday life according to the best insights of the oral tradition. Between the second and fifth centuries, Rabbinic Judaism or the Judaism of the dual Torah, oral and written, emerged as the insights of the oral tradition were written down and incorporated into what became known as the Talmud. And it was this Talmudic tradition, as we shall see, that shaped Jewish life from the sixth century until the advent of Jewish modernizing movements in the nineteenth century.

The heart of the teachings of the Pharisees was that God was a loving personal father who chose Israel to enter into the covenant revealed in the oral and written Torah, so that each and every individual who keeps this covenant can live in hope of resurrection from the dead. Contrary to the stereotype that they were legalists, historians have shown that the Pharisees taught that the Sabbath was made for man and not man for the Sabbath. They taught that the

sacrifices that God wants are not primarily the temple sacrifices but the practice of deeds of loving kindness. They taught that such deeds are not merely a
matter of external observance but must be rooted in a pure heart. The Pharisees
asked Jews to love God above all and their neighbor as themselves. They insisted that what is hateful to oneself must not be done to one's neighbor. They
insisted that humans do not live by bread alone, and therefore one should trust
in God rather than worry about tomorrow. They insisted that those who would
seek the will of God would find it and that those who humbled themselves
would be exalted.

The Rabbis and the Formation of the Talmud

Hillel and Shammai were the two leading rabbis or teachers of oral tradition in
the first century of the common era. Their influence led to the development of
two major schools: the house of Hillel (*Bet Hillel*) and the house of Shammai
(*Bet Shammai*). The disputes between Hillel and Shammai, and their schools,
eventually became the foundation of the Talmud and set the tone of disputa-
tion and dialogue that is characteristic of the Talmud. Both Hillel and
Shammai sought to apply the oral Torah tradition to the details of everyday life.
In general it is said that Shammai interpreted the demands of Torah more
strictly and severely, while Hillel was more lenient and compassionate in his
decisions. He is frequently quoted for saying that the whole of the Torah can
be summed up as: "What is hateful to you, do not unto your neighbor; this is
the entire Torah, all the rest is commentary....Go and study." In general,
although not always, it is the teachings of Hillel that shaped the emerging
Talmudic tradition. And it was the students of Hillel who were the primary
shapers of the Mishnah—the writings that form the core of the Talmud.

It was the disciples of Hillel and Shammai and their descendants who led the
Jews into the new Talmudic era. A disciple of Hillel, Johanan ben Zakkai, initiated the academy at Yavneh after the fall of the temple. There the first task was
to settle one of the key arguments that had been going on in Judaism at the
beginning of the century—namely, which writings of the tradition to consider
holy and therefore as revelations from God. The answer, of course, was settled
by default. Since the Pharisees survived to reestablish Judaism, it was the writings they revered that were selected. This meant that, unlike the Sadducees, they
included not only the Torah, that is, the Pentateuch, or five books attributed to
Moses (Genesis through Deuteronomy) but also the Prophets (Neviim)—which
included not only the great prophets like Jeremiah and Ezekiel but also the
minor prophets and the historical writings like First and Second Kings—and
also the Writings (Ketuvim) or wisdom literature, like Proverbs, Ecclesiastes,
and Job. Thus it was the academy at Yavneh that canonized (i.e., made official)
the books that make up the bible of Judaism, known as the *TaNaK*—an acronym
standing for Torah, Neviim, and Ketuvim.

With the Jewish people's sacred teachings committed to writing in the written Torah, the *Tannaim* ("those who study") began the paradoxical process of

writing down and transforming the oral tradition into the oral Torah. This process occurred in two phases.

First, the Tannaim organized the wisdom of the Jewish oral tradition into six categories or seders, covering the following areas of everyday life: agriculture, sabbaths and festivals, women and property, civil and criminal law, laws of conduct for cultic ritual and temple, rules for maintaining cultic purity. Then the discussions of the rabbis recalling the wisdom of the oral Torah on each of these areas were written down. This collection of materials, known as the *Mishnah*, thus codifies the wisdom of the oral Torah.

The Mishnah was intended to show Jews how they could sanctify life (i.e., make it holy) despite their absence from the temple and the land of Israel. The Mishnah reveals the profound faith of the Tannaim: over half if it is devoted to issues of governance of a land, a temple, and a priesthood that no longer existed. To continue to consider such matters expressed a faith that the exile would someday end, a faith that might be said to bear the seeds of a profound Zionist hope.

In the second phase of Talmudic formation, the successors to the Tannaim, the *Amoraim* ("those who interpret"), set about developing a commentary on the Mishnah that would serve to link the oral to the written Torah. The result of their work was called the *Gemara*, and these writings in combination with the Mishnah form the Talmud (meaning "learning" or "study" as related to Torah).

Two different traditions of Gemara emerged over the next four hundred years, reflecting the work of the Amoraim in both Jerusalem and Babylonia. These schools produced what are called the *Yerushalmi*, or Jerusalem Talmud, and the *Bavli*, or Babylonian Talmud. The latter, three times larger than the former, is considered to be the most complete and authoritative of the two. It contains over 2.5 million words preserved on nearly six thousand folio pages; one English translation comprises thirty-five volumes. Two-thirds of the material is devoted to halakhah (commandments and rules for living) and one-third to *aggadah*, or stories.

Even though the Talmud (Mishnah and Gemara) is said to have been completed by the sixth century, there is a sense in which the Talmud is never complete. For sages in the tradition, the *Geonim* (eminent scholars) followed up the work of the Amoraim by providing the *Responsa*—further commentaries on the Talmud. These writings constitute answers to requests from Jews throughout the Diaspora for insight and guidance in applying the teachings of the Talmud to the problems of everyday life. The tradition of commentary, which continues from generation to generation, is integral to Judaism, leaving the Talmudic traditions, as an expression of oral Torah, open to continuous development.

Because the two-step process that yielded the Talmud is often poorly understood by Gentiles, Christians have been accustomed to think that to compare the scriptures of Judaism and Christianity, all one need do is compare the Old Testament with the New Testament. Such a view, however, is totally misleading.

That is, just as one cannot deduce a Christian world view from reading the Old Testament (or Tanak of Judaism) in isolation, neither can one deduce a Jewish world view from it. For the Talmud is to the written Torah (Tanak) in Judaism what the New Testament is to the Old Testament in Christianity. That is, it is the further divine revelation through which the older revelation is to be understood. So a proper comparison of scriptures would require a comparison of the New Testament with the Talmud.

The faith views embodied in the Talmud and the New Testament are like two different sets of glasses for reading the Hebrew bible (Tanak or Old Testament). If one puts on New Testament glasses, suddenly certain passages of the Hebrew bible seem to become very clear and easy to read, while other parts are fuzzy and unreadable. The parts that appear very bold are, of course, those parts that can be pieced together to tell a story that leads to Jesus of Nazareth as God's messiah. However, if one takes off these glasses and puts on Talmudic glasses, suddenly precisely those passages that were obscure now seem bold and easy to read and those passages that were so bold before are now fuzzy and unreadable. In this case the bold passages are those that help Jews lead a holy life, set apart as a light to the nations.

Thus Christians and Jews who seem to be reading an important body of holy writings in common (the Old Testament or Tanak) might just as well be reading two different books—which, in a sense, they are. Neither tradition reads the Hebrew scriptures as an independent body of literature, but rather each reads them through the eyes of a further revelation (Talmud and New Testament) that tells them how to read the Hebrew scriptures, including what is valid and what can be dismissed. Consequently, Jews and Christians, while using a partially common vocabulary, frequently talk past each other and end up talking about very different things.

To appreciate the uniqueness of the Talmud one really has to look at a page from it and see how it is constructed. For if the Talmud is the writing down of the oral Torah, that surely must seem like a self-contradictory task. And yet the genius of the Talmud is in preserving this oral character despite its written form. For a typical page of Talmud is made up of diverse and distinct parts, all of which coexist on the same page. These parts express the voices of the rabbis throughout the ages all juxtaposed on the same page. The Talmud is not a finished book, but an ongoing dialogue among Jews not only of the same time period but from age to age. So at the core of the page you may find a statement (A) from the Mishnah of the second century outlining the opposing points of view of Hillel and Shammai on some question of appropriate behavior. Then above that, on the same page, is a section of the Gemara (B) from a period two or three hundred years later, relating the Mishnah to relevant passages from the Tanak and to the diverse opinions of the Amoraim who comment on the meaning of the Mishnah in light of the scriptures and of the opinions of the Tannaim. Then you will also typically find a section (C) devoted to the commentary of the greatest of the rabbinic Talmudic scholars, Rashi, from the

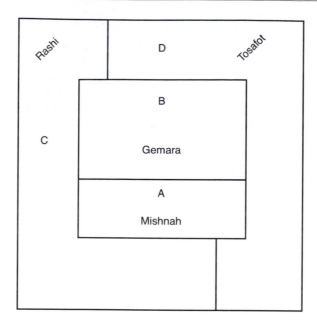

A page of Talmud.

eleventh century. In still yet another section (D), you will find the commentaries of the students of Rashi from a collection known as the Tosafot (12th and 13th centuries). Each of these expresses its own views of the meaning of the passages of the Mishnah in the light of the comments of the others and in light of additional commentaries and writings that supplement the tradition.

Rather than the reader being led to a single conclusion, it is more likely that the total impact will be experienced as an invitation to enter a debate that spans the centuries. Nor is the Talmud really meant to be studied alone. Talmudic study is a communal project that requires at the very least a partner with whom one can interact, dialogue, discuss, and debate the meaning of a given page, drawing on the wisdom of all the dialogue partners through the ages. For this one must also have a rabbinic scholar schooled in the history of that ongoing dialogue to guide one into the heart of the debate.

Although Talmudic decisions are made to guide the life of the Jewish community, it would be a mistake to think that the whole point of Talmud study is to reach a conclusion. For Talmudic study is a form of religious ritual whose purpose is nothing less than to bring the student of Torah to experience God through the thrust and parry of argument about the one thing that matters most in life—God's word, which hallows all life. That is why it is not unheard of for a debating partner to help an opponent who is stumped for a response by suggesting a line of argument that might be able to refute the point he has just made. In this way the Talmud sanctifies doubt and questioning as a medium of religious experience that brings one in touch with God. God is in the questions even more than in the answers. For this reason too, then, the Talmud is never finished so long as there is one more Jew ready to join the debate. It is a tradition of commentary upon commentary that guarantees that the Talmud is always both ancient yet ever fresh and new. For it is always about how one is to make the new day holy.

Accompanying this unique and powerful form of religious experience is a vision of life that sustained Jewish life unchallenged for almost eighteen hundred years—a vision that centers on God, Torah, and Israel. Of the three, Torah is the central category, for it is only through Torah that one can know who God is and who Israel is. Torah, which has the connotation of "revelation," is a word best translated as "teaching." A teacher of Torah is a rabbi. Hence when God gave Moses his oral and written teaching on Mount Sinai, he was Moses' rabbi. And when Moses handed the twofold Torah on to Joshua, he was his rabbi. According to the "Sayings of the Fathers," (known as Pirke Abot), as found in the Talmud, Joshua handed it on to the elders and the elders to the prophets and the prophets to the Great Assembly and so God's revelation is passed on from generation to generation by the rabbis. Indeed, says Abot: "Were it not for the interpretations which Moses received from the mouth of the Almighty, we could not know the true meaning of the written Torah."

The implications of this vision are fairly radical. For it means that since Sinai, the Torah or divine teaching has come down to earth, flowing forth from the mouths of the rabbis themselves. This is illustrated in a story from the Talmud (Baba Metzia, 59b). According to the story Rabbi Eliezer ben Hyrcanos, by working miracles, sought to prove that his interpretations of the halakhah were correct and the interpretations of the other rabbis were incorrect. However, the others refused to accept a miracle as evidence of correct interpretation and instead invited Rabbi Eliezer to wrestle with them over the text. In desperation Rabbi Eliezer called upon God to vindicate his interpretation. As the Talmud tells it:

> Again he [Eliezer] said to them: "If the halakhah agrees with me, let it be proved from Heaven!" Whereupon a Heavenly Voice cried out: "Why do ye dispute with R. Eliezer, seeing that in all matters the halakhah agrees with him!" But R. Joshua arose and exclaimed: "It is not in heaven." "What did he mean by this?"—Said R. Jeremiah: "That the Torah had already been given at Mount Sinai; we pay no attention to a Heavenly Voice, because Thou hast long since written in the Torah at Mount Sinai, 'After the majority must one incline.'" R. Nathan met Elijah and asked him: "What did the Holy One, Blessed be He, do in that hour?"—He laughed [with joy], he replied, saying, "My sons have defeated Me, My sons have defeated Me."

For the rabbis the way of Talmud–Torah was an ongoing discussion and debate about exactly what it was that God expected of them, but it was a debate that included rather than excluded those who disagreed. Indeed, according to Talmudic tradition, when the rabbis disagreed on the observance of halakhah, although the majority opinion was to prevail for the good of order, it did not necessarily mean the minority were wrong. The Torah was large enough to embrace them all.

The moral of the story of Rabbi Eliezer is that even God must participate in the Talmudic debate, and not even God can overrule the majority oral interpretation of the written Torah given on Mount Sinai. The oral Torah is the key to the meaning of the written Torah and the rabbis are the key to the oral Torah. From their mouths and their exemplary way of life flows forth the revelation of God to his people in word and deed.

This view echoes that of the Torah story that explains how Israel got its name. For according to the Book of Genesis:

> And he [Jacob] rose that night, and took his two wives, and his two women servants, and his eleven sons, and passed over the ford Jabbok. And he took them, and sent them over the brook, and sent over that which he had. And Jacob was left alone; and there wrestled a man with him until the breaking of the day. And when he saw that he prevailed not against him, he touched the hollow of his thigh; and the hollow of Jacob's thigh was out of joint, as he wrestled with him. And he said, Let me go, for the day breaks. And he said, I will not let you go, except you bless me. And he said to him, What is your name? And he said, Jacob. And he said, Your name shall be called no more Jacob, but Israel; for as a prince you have power [you have struggled or wrestled] with God and with men, and have prevailed. And Jacob asked him, and said, Tell me, I beg you, your name. And he said, Why is it that you ask after my name? And he blessed him there. And Jacob called the name of the place Peniel; for I have seen God face to face, and my life is preserved. And as he passed over Penuel the sun rose upon him, and he limped upon his thigh.
> —(Genesis 32:22–32)

So the Torah teaches that Israel is the one God has chosen to wrestle with, and that the way of Torah is to wrestle with the God who cannot be named (or for that matter, imaged). And it teaches that the one who wrestles not only with God (and God's Torah) but with other humans (about the meaning of Torah) can prevail. Indeed to wrestle with the Torah is to see God face to face, to be transformed and given a new name: Israel, or "Wrestler with God." Hence in Rabbinic Judaism there is no higher activity than the study of Torah as practiced in the Talmudic tradition. For to engage in Talmud Torah (literally the "study" of Torah) is to wrestle with God and humans—to be wounded and transformed, and to see God face to face.

Indeed, the story of the covenant at Sinai, through which God chose Israel, suggests just such a give-and-take relationship. For, according to the story, the covenant established that day was a *mutual* agreement between two parties, much like a marriage contract that is both a legal agreement and an expression of mutual love and care. In this covenant the people promise to obey the commandments (mitzvot) of God and walk in the way, halakhah, of the Torah, which gives life. And God promises to guide and protect them on their journey through time. Throughout this journey, God and Israel have wrestled with each other—at one moment God reminding Israel that they have strayed from the promise by their sins and at another moment, Israel reminding God that he appears to have strayed from his promises. Within the bounds of the covenant, each can be held accountable by the other.

It is this covenant that makes Israel, Israel—that is, the chosen people. For the rabbis, the identity of the Jews lay not in their national or ethnic history (although within the myth—that is, symbolic story—of Torah they surely embraced that history), nor in their being (by choice) members of a religion called "Judaism" (for there was no word for "Judaism" in their Hebrew vocabulary), but in their being eternally chosen, before all creation, to be God's beloved. The rabbis reminded the people how God had carried them on eagles' wings and brought them to himself to be a holy people (Exodus 19:3–6), set apart to be a witness to the holiness of life. In this lay the ultimate meaning for the rules for *kosher* dining (*kosher*—rules that forbid Jews to eat pork, or mix meat and milk, etc.)—even what one eats and the way one eats should remind the world that life is not meant to be profane and meaningless. Rather, one's life is holy (set apart): it is not one's own but belongs to God. Indeed, every act of one's life, whether in work, in eating, in the bedroom, or in prayer, should be a witness to the One who alone is truly holy and makes all else holy.

"Torah," in the Talmudic tradition, is a multidimensional word. In its narrowest sense, Torah refers to the first five books of the bible, attributed to Moses (from Genesis to Deuteronomy). In a broader sense it refers to the entire bible or Tanak. Broader still is its meaning as the dual Torah, including the entire Talmud. And ultimately Torah is the source and pattern for all creation. For according to the Talmud, when God created heaven and earth he did it by consulting the Torah, which was already with God in the beginning. Hence the Torah provided the pattern for the right order of the universe, a pattern revealed in the halakhah (the way or law or commandments) given through oral and written Torah.

Halakhah told the rabbinic Jew how to sanctify life by walking in the way of life of the Torah. For to choose the Torah and walk in its ways was to choose life over death, walking in accord with the will of God. It is for this reason that the Talmud focuses on the minutest details of everyday life, for it is in the details of everyday life that holiness, justice, and mercy must be embodied if one is to walk in the way of Torah.

Finally, the Torah can be identified with the very being of the rabbinic scholar. The rabbi was viewed as a man so close to God that not only the pattern of his life revealed the meaning of Torah but also his extraordinary powers to work miracles and healings. He was a charismatic figure, capable not only of drawing together a school of disciples (*yeshiva*) for the purpose of studying Torah but also of being the charismatic organizer and leader of the village community in which he lived, providing guidance and wisdom for the most common and unlearned of folks. He was a religious virtuoso to whom everyone looked for guidance. If Torah united heaven and earth in the will and presence of God, it was the rabbi who was that living link—Torah in the flesh.

PREMODERN JUDAISM: THE CLASSICAL ERA

The Premodern Rabbinic World: God, Torah, and Israel

If human beings are not only storytellers but also storydwellers, then the Torah story of the rabbis was a magnificent dwelling indeed. According to the Talmud, the existence of the world is dependent on the study of the Torah—for it is said in the *Pirke Abot* that the "world is suspended in space and has nothing to rest on except the breath of Torah study from the mouths of students—just as a man may keep something up in the air by the blowing of his breath." And if religion (*religio*) is about being "tied and bound" into the cosmic drama of life by one's story symbolically told (myth) and enacted (ritual), then Torah was, and is, just such a story. For the Torah story embraces not only every minute, hour, and day of rabbinic Jewish life, providing a template to make it holy, but also the whole of time from the creation of the world to its final messianic redemption.

The right to live within this story came with birth from a Jewish mother (except for those who were converts). While women thus determined Jewish identity, the primary guardians of rabbinic religious life were men. Males alone had to be confirmed in their religious status through two key rituals: a circumcision shortly after birth and a Bar Mitzvah ceremony in which they demonstrated their knowledge of the faith as they entered adulthood at age 13.

The Jews of the rabbinic age ate, drank, and slept Torah. The men began the day by dressing in garments with fringes (*tzit zit*) to remind them of the commandments of the covenant (Numbers 15:37–34) and wrapping the words of Torah (Exodus 13:1–10, 11–16 and Deuteronomy 6:4–9, 11:13–21) on scrolls in small leather boxes (known as tefillin or phylacteries) on their arms and foreheads as they began morning prayer. Indeed, every act of the day would be couched in prayer. And every Sabbath (the seventh day of the week), all work ceased and eternity pervaded all things as the people recalled both the beginning of creation and its ultimate fulfillment in the messianic era at the end of time. No matter what suffering history brought to Israel, on the Sabbath an eternal people dwelled with their eternal God, providing a foretaste of that messianic day for which all creation was made—when God will be all in all.

The meaning of the Sabbath unfolded in the Torah portion (i.e., assigned reading from scripture) for every week of the year, organized around a great cycle of festivals. From New Year's, which begins with the story of creation on Rosh Hashanah (literally, "Head of the Year") and concludes ten days later with stories of divine judgment on Yom Kippur ("Day of Atonement"), through Passover (liberation/redemption of the exodus) to the Feast of Weeks (the giving of the dual Torah and the covenant) to the Feast of Booths (the wandering in the desert, awaiting the fulfillment of the promises) as well as the commemoration of near disasters averted (Purim) and not averted (Tisha B'Av), the great story unfolded. The story of Torah stretched out over the lives of Jews from the beginning of the day until the end of the day, from the beginning of the year until the end of the year, from the beginning of their lives until the end of their lives, and from the beginning of time until the end of time. In the Torah story, God and Israel dwelled—sometimes in harmony and sometimes wrestling with each other—but always within a drama that gave life meaning in spite of the too often brutal incursions of the profane world that surrounded and rejected the Jews.

The genius of this Talmudic Judaism was that instead of totally rejecting the messianic apocalypticism of the biblical period it transformed it, replacing political Zionism with an apolitical spiritual Zionism. The rabbis argued that Israel had been seduced by the Zealots into trying to force the coming of the messianic era by their own political activity. The truth is, the rabbis argued, that only God can bring the messianic era that will bring the age of exile to an end and restore to Israel the land of promise—and God will only bring that about when all Israel is fully observant of halakhah as required according to the Talmud. This view, as we have already noted, prevailed throughout the Middle Ages and was not seriously challenged until the coming of modern secular Zionism in the twentieth century.

If the Mishnah had come into being through the efforts of the rabbis to provide a way of life for Israel in a new age of exile, the Gemara completed the main contours of the Talmud by shaping a way of life that provided an alternative to the Christianity that had become the official religion of the Roman Empire in the fourth and fifth centuries. Rabbinic Judaism and gentile Christianity grew up side by side in the first six centuries of the common era. Christianity claimed to have the key to the meaning of the scriptures as culminating in the coming of Jesus of Nazareth as the messiah, while at the same time explaining the fall of the temple as God's judgment on the Jews. The Talmud offered Jews a world view that accounted for their situation without having to accept or even acknowledge this story. For in the Talmudic view, the new exile of the Jews was not due to a failure to recognize Jesus as the messiah but to a failure to remain faithful enough to the way of Torah (halakhah). Moreover, since the messiah was supposed to bring a messianic age of peace and justice, in which all suffering and death are overcome, it was obvious to the rabbis, looking through the lenses of their "Talmudic glasses" (so to speak),

RITUALS OF JEWISH IDENTITY AND THE LIFE CYCLE

BRIS OR BRIT MILAH

In accordance with the teachings of the Torah (Genesis 17:10–14), every male child must be circumcised when he is 8 days old, as a sign of the covenant between God and his people. This ceremony is known as the *Bris* or *Brit milah* (derived from the Hebrew for "covenant" and for "circumcision"). During this ritual the child is named and the foreskin of his penis is cut as a sign of the covenant. This ritual ties and binds every male child's life to the eternal covenant between God and his people, renewing that covenant with each generation, child by child. The ceremony generally begins with a prayer calling forth the peace of the covenant. This is followed by a prayer calling upon the prophet Elijah as protector of the sons of the covenant. Then the foreskin is cut. After this another blessing is said over the child, recalling the covenant of Abraham. Finally a cup of wine is raised and a final blessing is said, praising God who has sanctified this child and placed the covenant in his flesh, and asking his protection over the child.

BAR AND BAT MITZVAH

When a male child reaches the age of adulthood, 13, he becomes a Bar Mitzvah (a son of the commandments or covenant) and is expected to demonstrate his ability to carry out his responsibilities in maintaining the religious life of the community. After intense training by his rabbi in the study of Hebrew, and of Torah and Talmud, the young man is called forth at a synagogue service to recite the blessing that precedes the reading of the Torah at every service. Then he reads the Torah portion for the day, and then a portion from the Prophets. He may also be asked to comment on the meaning of the passages. By doing this the boy demonstrates his ability to function as a full member of the religious community. Once he has completed this ceremony he is no longer considered a child but an adult who can form part of the *minyan* (ten adult males) required for any Jewish worship service. In the modern period, Conservative and Reform Jewish communities have extended this ritual, now called the *Bat Mitzvah* (daughter of the commandments or covenant), to female children as well.

MARRIAGE

The Jewish marriage ceremony take place under a *huppah*, a sort of grand prayer shawl stretched over four poles that can be said to symbolize the heavens and God's creation, even as the bride and groom stand in the place of Adam and Eve, the first man and woman created by God. The marriage ceremony sanctifies the uniting of a man and a woman by binding them to each other and to the story of Israel's relation to God, from creation through its exiles and tribulations (customarily the groom steps on and breaks a glass, at the end of the ceremony to symbolize the fall of the second temple) to joyous redemption in the new Zion, through its prayers and blessings. Before entering the canopy the man places the veil over the bride's face. Under the canopy the marriage contract (*ketubah*) is witnessed, the couple are betrothed and married with an exchange of rings, and the words "behold you are sanctified to me by this ring in accord with the tradition of Moses and Israel" are followed by seven blessings said over a cup of wine. The ceremony is generally followed by great festivity and celebration.

DEATH

Jewish death rites are very simple. A person facing death is encouraged to say a prayer of confession, asking for forgiveness of sins and healing if possible, and asking that, if this is the hour of death, the death serve as atonement for all his or her sins. The prayer ends with a request: "grant me a share in the world to come" and "protect my beloved family," and commits the person's soul into the hands of God. After death, the body is buried the same day or the next without embalming. The community places the body in the ground with prayers binding the soul of the deceased to the Eternal One. The immediate family of mourners remains at home for seven days and will continue to recite memorial prayers (*kaddish*) for eleven months, and thereafter on the anniversary of the death.

that Christians were mistaken in thinking Jesus was the messiah. The messiah, they held, was still on his way.

The Medieval Journey of Judaism

Discrimination Against the Jews in the Early Middle Ages

Dwelling in the great cosmic story of Torah, Israel survived its journey through the medieval world of persecutions and expulsions, until it was splintered by the Enlightenment in the nineteenth century and nearly shattered by the Holocaust in the twentieth century. That journey is both a tale of tragic precedents to the coming of the Holocaust and yet a story of amazing spiritual endurance and creativity that enriched and expanded the house of Torah in which Israel dwelled—especially through the emergence of Kabbalistic mysticism and Hasidic piety.

The situation of the Jews deteriorated with the decline of the Roman Empire and the rise of Christianity. While Jews in Israel were under the colonial rule of the Romans in the first four centuries, they were unique in enjoying a

THE DAYS OF AWE AND PASSOVER

ROSH HASHANAH AND YOM KIPPUR

After the Sabbath, which sets the rhythm of Jewish religious life, the Jewish New Year (Rosh Hashanah and Yom Kippur) and Passover are the most prominent of the Jewish holy days or festivals. Unlike Passover, which is focused on the home and family, Rosh Hashanah and Yom Kippur are both days of communal prayer spent in the synagogue. At Rosh Hashanah the story of creation is retold and people are reminded that God is deciding who will be written in the book of life for another year, and who will not—even as he will decide the fate of nations and of the whole world. So the new year raises questions of life and death and of self-examination. This process ends ten days later with a day of total fasting and repentance, Yom Kippur. When Yom Kippur ends at sunset and the fast is broken, the penitent is cleansed and is prepared to face the new year with proper awe and respect for the Lord of the universe who governs the destiny of all.

PASSOVER

Passover or *Pesach* recalls God's deliverance of the tribes of Israel from slavery in Egypt (Exodus 1–15). Passover is celebrated in the home, usually with the extended family and friends. The Passover *aggadah* is an order of service that retells the story of the liberation from Egypt with extensive commentary from the sages of the Talmud. The male head of the household presides at this retelling, which is done around the dining table, but members of the family are invited to participate, individually and collectively, in the recitation. Prominence is given to the youngest child who must ask four key questions—the first of which is: "Why is this night different from all other nights?" In this way the story is passed on from generation to generation. As the story is retold, certain symbolic foods are eaten to remind everyone of the events that led and still lead to liberation from slavery for every Jew.

This festival is also called the feast of unleavened bread (*matzah*), for the story indicated that only bread without yeast was used at the time of the original event, since the tribes left in a hurry and did not have time to make leavened bread. To prepare for Passover all leavened bread must be removed from the premises and all utensils cleaned. Special foods used in the Seder service include wine to celebrate the joy of deliverance; bitter herbs (e.g., horseradish) to recall the bitterness of oppression by the Egyptians; saltwater to recall the tears of the tribes in slavery; celery or parsley as a sign of spring, life, and hope; one roasted or boiled egg and a roasted shank bone to recall both the destruction of the temple and Israel's redemption at the Red Sea by the "outstreched arm" of God; and a mixture of apples, walnuts, and spices, called *Haroset,* to recall the mortar used by Israelite slaves in building the Egyptian cities. After the symbolic foods are consumed during the telling of the story, a full family meal of celebration is eaten, and the meal concludes with further prayers and recitations from the Passover aggadah. During the Passover meal it is said that ordinary time is suspended and every Jew becomes part of the liberating event and so can say, "This day I too have been liberated from slavery."

protected status as a legal religion within the empire, even though they refused to worship the gods of the official state cult. When the emperors and the empire became Christian, the colonial domination of the Jews became more severe. That domination did not really end for Jews until the establishment of the state of Israel in the twentieth century. In 381 the first Christian emperor, Theodosius, declared Christianity the only legal religion of the empire. With that, all pagan religions were outlawed, and Judaism was placed in a restricted legal status. Under the Theodosian law code of the early fifth century, although Judaism was not made illegal, Jews were severely discriminated against, religiously and economically. Then in the sixth century the emperor Justinian produced the Justinian law code, which was even more severe and removed Judaism from the status of a legally protected religion. The Christian view that they superseded or replaced the Jews as God's chosen people led to what in later centuries would be called "the Jewish problem"—namely, why Jews still existed at all. Jews came to be seen as an "obstinate" and "stiff necked" people who refused to see the truth of Christianity and convert (or in later modern secular culture, refused to give up their Jewishness and assimilate).

Due to their impoverished legal status, Jews became extraordinarily vulnerable to discrimination and persecution by the overwhelmingly Christian population that surrounded them. However, by the year 712, an Islamic empire was created that stretched from India into Spain, subsuming the vast majority of Jews under Muslim rule. In general, while Jews did not enjoy full equality under Islamic rule, they usually fared better than under Christian rule. Nevertheless, they experienced sporadic periods of discrimination and persecution from Muslims as well. For example, it was under the Fatimid caliph of Egypt, al-hakim bi-Amr Allah (996–1021) that Jews were first forced to wear special clothing as a "badge of shame" (a practice later adopted by the medieval Catholic church, and later still by the Nazis). Under Islam, Jews moved from agricultural village life into the new urban centers of the Muslim empire where they became craftsmen or else capitalized on their diaspora connections to prosper as traders and merchants. In the Christian West, Jews also embraced trading and selling, but out of necessity rather than choice, since Jews were not allowed by law to have slaves (which were permitted to Christians only), who were at that time essential to success in agriculture.

The Carolingian Era of Tolerance

In Europe, as the Roman Empire collapsed so did the stringency of the laws against Jews. And for a while, under the Frankish Carolingian kings, who (beginning with Charlemagne in 800) founded the Holy Roman Empire, the life of Jews actually improved. Jews enjoyed high positions in the courts and in the professions and experienced new opportunities for wealth. Indeed, the court chaplain under Louis the Pious actually converted to Judaism in 839. This led to an attempted backlash of discrimination, but it was squelched by the emperor. And while Jews were not considered full citizens, they prospered under diplomas of protection from the king's court. They became "the king's Jews." This practice was a benefit as long as Jews were favored by the king. However, in later periods this arrangement often resulted in sudden reversals of fortune whenever a king (or Holy Roman Emperor) found it convenient to rescind his protection.

Centuries of Persecution and Pogrom

In the late Middle Ages Jewish life became truly precarious in Europe. The tide turned against Jews with the papal preaching of the First Crusade in 1096. The announced reason for the Crusades was to free Jerusalem and all of the Holy Land from the Muslims who had taken Jerusalem in 638 as part of the expansion of the Islamic empire. Jerusalem was revered as a holy city by Muslims as well as Jews and Christians. Christians were promised a "plenary indulgence," which guaranteed forgiveness of all sins and entry into heaven for all who participated in the Crusades. However, as the armies raised for this purpose passed through the cities and towns of Europe on their way to the Holy Land to "slay the infidel," they decided to "kill two birds with one stone" and rid the Christian world of its other "enemy" as well—the Jews.

The Christian armies passing through the Rhine valley offered Jews the choice of conversion or death. Many committed suicide, many others were massacred. Few converted. The pattern of persecution and violence against Jews continued in the centuries that followed. In 1215 the Fourth Lateran Council of the Catholic church adopted the Muslim practice of forcing Jews to wear distinctive dress and restricted Jews to living in ghettos. To the pattern of violence was added the periodic practice of expulsion. In 1306, in a single day, all the Jews of France were arrested and ordered to be out of the country within a month—a practice that was repeated in other countries, driving the majority of Europe's Jews into Eastern Europe. In 1348, as the Black Death swept across Europe, Jews were blamed and made the scapegoats, and the Jews of many communities were executed. In Strasbourg, for instance, two hundred Jews were burned alive in the cemetery on the Sabbath. And when the Golden Age of Spain (11th and 12th centuries) came to an end under Christian reconquest, the next two centuries saw intensified persecution, culminating in the

THE POPES AND THE PARADOX OF "THE JEWISH PROBLEM"

The one paradoxical thread in the religious history of Europe was the fate of Jews in Italy. Throughout Christian history, the Jews of Italy, on the whole, fared much better than the Jews of the rest of Europe. Rome was the only major city of Europe from which the Jews were never expelled. Jews experienced no punitive taxes, were free to select their occupations, and could even intermarry with Christians. Nor were Jews objects of persecution in Italy during the Crusades and the Black Death. There were a number of reasons for this. One was that the medieval feudal system ended very early in Italy, and free cities developed. Another was that Jews were not especially prosperous, since usury was practiced by Christian financiers in Italy. Later, the Renaissance brought a new openness toward the Jews as well. But perhaps the most influential factor was the paradoxical relation between the popes and the Jews. Faced with the "Jewish problem"—namely, the question of why God permitted Jews to continue to exist despite the fact that, as Christians saw it, they had replaced the Jews as God's chosen—the popes, from the sixth century on, turned to the negative witness theory, This theory, developed by St. Augustine, suggested that it was God's will that Jews wander the earth without a home, their impoverished existence functioning as a "negative witness" that proved the superiority and truth of Christianity. Consequently, the popes followed a paradoxical policy of preaching that God had rejected the Jews while at the same time acting as their legal protectors and guardians, insisting that they not be physically harmed. This "negative witness" theory became the operative papal strategy for dealing with the "Jewish problem" in medieval Christendom. It required seeing both discrimination against Jews and their protection as in accord with "God's will." During the Renaissance, however, some popes took a more genuine interest in the Jews. Pope Sixtus IV (1471–1484), for example, actually commissioned a Latin translation of the *Kabbalah*. Later Pope Clement VII sought to develop a common translation of the Old Testament by Jewish and Christian scholars, and he suspended the Inquisition's persecution of *Marranos* (Jews who had been forcibly baptized) in Spain.

expulsion of all Jews in 1492. All of this was done under the auspices of the papal Inquisition.

For the Jews, the "Middle Ages" lasted into the nineteenth century when modern Enlightenment thinking began to have an impact. With the Protestant Reformation in Germany, beginning in 1517, Jews experienced a modest reprieve. Indeed, at first its initiator, Martin Luther, wrote favorably of the Jews, convinced that the only reason they had not converted was that the Catholic church had distorted the Gospel by confusing it with Greek metaphysics. But toward the end of his life, Luther, realizing that the Jews were no more receptive to his interpretation of the Gospel than to the Catholic interpretation, turned viciously anti-Judaic, advocating the abuse of Jews and the burning of their synagogues. However, the aftermath of the Protestant Reformation in the sixteenth and seventeenth centuries left Christians too busy fighting each other to make the Jews the central object of their concern. This distraction as well as the further development of ghettos, which put Jews under lock and key at night, served to reduce the violence Jews experienced at the hands of Christians.

However, at the same time, as the Jewish population of Eastern Europe grew by leaps and bounds as a consequence of the expulsions from Western Europe, new waves of violence (pogroms) broke out against Jews in Eastern Europe. Between 1648 and 1658 over seven hundred Jewish communities were destroyed and Jewish deaths numbered in the hundreds of thousands. All of this history helped to create an ethos of Jew-hatred in Europe, which made it plausible to believe that "the Jews are our misfortune" and helped prepare the way for the Holocaust.

From the Golden Age in Spain to the Spanish Inquisition

In the midst of this violent history stands the Golden Age of Spain as an extraordinary interlude, when for a time in the twelfth and early thirteenth centuries, Jews were welcomed as allies against the Muslims in those portions of Spain that had been reconquered by Christians. During this period Jews were encouraged to settle in the reconquered territories and were given unusual freedom both socially and politically, achieving important roles in the royal court and in the professions. Intellectually, it was a period of extraordinary intellectual exchange between the great scholars of Judaism (Maimonides), Islam (Avicenna and Averroes), and Christianity (Aquinas). These scholars sought to express the meaning of their traditions through the newly rediscovered writings of Aristotle, introduced into Europe by the Islamic tradition that had preserved them.

The period came an end in the mid-thirteenth century as Christians reacted to the presence of Jews in high places with alarm, fearing that they were "taking over." This led to a new period of persecution, violence, and forced conversions under the Spanish Inquisition, which began in 1480 and ended in the expulsion of the Jews from Spain in 1492 (see Map 3.3). In this period some thirteen thousand Jews were condemned for practicing Judaism in secret. Many were tortured and burned at the stake.

Two Great Medieval Scholars—Rashi and Maimonides

The period of the late Middle Ages produced two of the greatest scholars in the history of Judaism: Rabbi Solomon ben Isaac (1040–1105), otherwise known as Rashi, and Moses ben Maimon (1135–1204), otherwise known as Maimonides. Rashi's commentaries, as we have noted, are considered so extraordinary that they form an essential component of the Talmud. He is considered the most unsurpassable teacher of Torah in the history of Talmudic Judaism. And Maimonides is famous both for his philosophical work and his commentaries on the Talmud, and especially for his compendium of Talmudic law (halakhah).

Rashi was born in France and educated in the Talmudic academies of Germany. In 1070 he founded his own Talmudic academy at Troyes in France. He wrote commentaries on most of the books of the Tanak and the Talmud in a terse and lucid style that was colorful and descriptive. His commentaries were considered so complete and illuminating that they replaced all commentaries that had preceded them. Rashi's commentaries on the Gemara of the Babylonian Talmud appeared in the first printed edition of the Talmud and has been in all editions since. Not only did his work become an integral part of the Talmud but also the commentaries of his students were included in the Tosafot.

Maimonides was born in Cordova, Spain, but fled with his family at age 13 to avoid an outbreak of Islamic persecution and eventually ended up in Egypt, where he assumed leadership of the Jewish community in Cairo and also became the physician to the viceroy of Egypt. He wrote commentaries on the entire Mishnah and developed a comprehensive compendium of halakhah, the *Mishneh Torah*, in which he indicated his understanding of the normative conclusions on all the issues addressed. The Mishneh Torah became the most influential guide to halakhah in Judaism until the *Shulkan Aruk* replaced it in 1565. Unlike Rashi, Maimonides also drew upon "secular" Aristotelian philosophy to write *The Guide of the Perplexed* as a comprehensive statement of Jewish theology—cast in Aristotelian form and written in Arabic. In the century after his death, a great controversy broke out over his use of philosophy, and his works were forbidden to those under 25 years of age. In later centuries his work became revered by most Jews. His work was also especially revered by the initiators of the Jewish Enlightenment (*Haskalah*) who looked upon him as a model for their own pioneering efforts because of his use of Greek philosophy. Although Judaism is not a religion that emphasizes dogma (right belief) as the test of true faith, Maimonides is credited with giving Judaism a creedal statement known as the Thirteen Articles of Faith.

Kabbalah—Jewish Mysticism

Judaism, like all religions, has a mystical dimension. But in the monotheistic traditions, mysticism has generally been viewed with an element of mistrust because mystical experience is direct and immediate and so tends to undermine traditional lines of authority, whether built on ascribed status (priests) or acquired expertise (rabbis). The mystic finds God without the guidance of a

Map 3.3 Jews in Christian Europe.

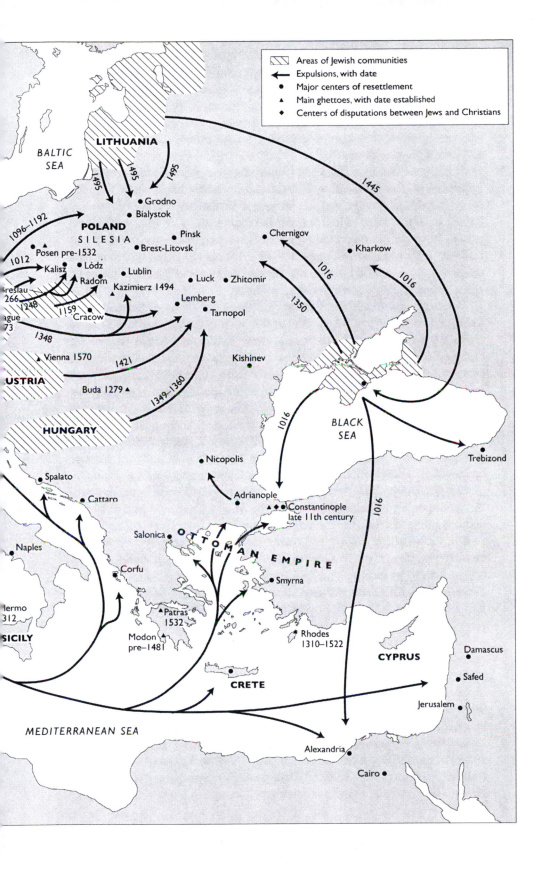

▨	Areas of Jewish communities
⟵	Expulsions, with date
●	Major centers of resettlement
▲	Main ghettoes, with date established
◆	Centers of disputations between Jews and Christians

BALTIC
SEA

LITHUANIA

1495
1495
1495

● Grodno
● Bialystok

POLAND
SILESIA

1096-1192

1012

Kalisz

● Posen pre-1532
● Lódz
Radom
Kazimierz 1494

Breslau
1266
1248

1159 Cracow

ague
73

1348

● Pinsk
● Brest-Litovsk

● Lublin

● Luck   ● Zhitomir

Lemberg
● Tarnopol

● Chernigov

● Kharkow

1445

1016

1016

1350

1016

▲ Vienna 1570

USTRIA

1421

Buda 1279 ▲

1349-1360

● Kishinev

HUNGARY

1016

BLACK
SEA

Trebizond

● Nicopolis

● Spalato

● Cattaro

Naples

● Adrianople

● Corfu

Salonica ●

OTTOMAN EMPIRE

▲◆● Constantinople
late 11th century

● Smyrna

1016

● Corfu

lermo
312

SICILY

▲ Patras
1532

Modon ▲
pre-1481

▲ Rhodes
1310-1522

CYPRUS

Damascus

● Safed

Jerusalem ●

CRETE

● Alexandria

Cairo ●

MEDITERRANEAN SEA

priest or a didactic teacher (rabbi) to lead him or her to God. Moreover, the mystic often speaks of God in ways that are unconventional and sometimes even seem to contradict the nature of prophetic monotheism. For prophetic monotheism emphasizes the difference between God and human beings, whereas mystics tend to speak of achieving a unity with the divine in which all differences seem to disappear.

Although Jewish mysticism goes back to the ancient world and reflects the influences of Neoplatonism and Gnosticism, it was with the explicit emergence of Kabbalah that its presence became a formative influence in Judaism. Kabbalism is that form of Jewish mysticism that emerged in the late medieval period. It sought to explain the mystery of good and evil in the universe precisely at a time (12th–13th centuries) when persecution and pogrom were intensifying. Jews could not help but seek an understanding of God that could sustain them through a new period of suffering.

The most important Kabbalistic work is the *Zohar* (Book of Splendor). For Kabbalists, the God beyond the God of the bible is the *En Sof* ("limitless" or "infinite") who manifests himself in the world through his *Sefiroth* ("fragments of the infinite") or ten qualities such as wisdom, mercy, justice, and so on. The elements of the Sefiroth are fragments that emanate from the spiritual world and are encapsulated in the physical world, finally manifesting in the *Shekinah*. Once God manifested himself in the world through his *Shekinah* ("divine presence") in all things. However, because of the fall of Adam, evil entered the world and the divine presence has been exiled from its unity with the infinite (En Sof). Humans were created for *devekut* ("union") with God, but this was destroyed by Adam's sin and must be reestablished through mystical contemplation (*kavanah*) of the divine through prayer and the devout performance of the requirements of halakhah. The reunion of all with the infinite will bring about nothing less than the messianic kingdom.

The Kabbalistic tradition can be seen as a powerful religious response to the overwhelming tragedy of persecution and expulsion that marked Jewish life in Europe in the late Middle Ages and beyond. It explained the age of darkness in which Jews lived and offered them a hope of transcending that darkness. It was a profound mystical variation on the theme of exile and return. The most important of the Kabbalists was Isaac Luria (1534–1572), whose family was expelled from Spain in 1492 and fled to Palestine. Luria taught that in the beginning God was all in all, but he had "contracted" (*Tzimtzum*) himself, withdrawing his being to make room for creation. In the divine act of creation the *Sephirot* shattered the "vessels," through which the creative divine power emanated, and light became mixed with darkness, the spiritual with the material, good with evil. Human beings must engage in *Tikkun Olam*, or repair of this world, by liberating and returning the divine sparks to the Infinite from which they came. This task can be accomplished through mystical prayer, study of Torah, and the observance of halakhah. Its accomplishment will signal the coming of the messiah. Interestingly, Luria

MAIMONIDES CREED:
THE THIRTEEN PRINCIPLES OF FAITH

1. I believe with perfect faith that the Creator, blessed be Your name, is the Author and Guide of everything that has been created, and that God alone has made, does make, and will make all things.

2. I believe with perfect faith that the Creator, blessed be Your name, is a Unity, and that there is no unity in any manner like unto You, and that You alone are our God, who was, is, and will be.

3. I believe with perfect faith that the Creator, blessed be Your name, is not a body, and that You are free from all the accidents of matter, ant that You have not any form whatsoever.

4. I believe with perfect faith that the Creator, blessed be Your name, is the first and the last.

5. I believe with perfect faith that the Creator, blessed be Your name, and to You alone, it is right to pray, and that it is not right to pray to any being besides You.

6. I believe with perfect faith that all the words of the prophets are true.

7. I believe with perfect faith that the prophecy of Moses our teacher, peace be unto him, was true, and that he was the chief of the prophets, both of those that preceded and of those that followed him.

8. I believe with perfect faith that the whole of Torah, now in our possession, is the same that was given to Moses our teacher, peace be unto him.

9. I believe with perfect faith that this Torah will not be changed, and that there will never be any other law from the Creator, blessed be Your name.

10. I believe with perfect faith that the Creator, blessed be Your name, knows every deed of the human race and all of their thoughts, as it is said, "It is You who fashions the hearts of them all, that give heed to all their deeds."

11. I believe with perfect faith that the Creator, blessed be Your name, rewards those that keep Your *mitzvot*, and punishes those who transgress them.

12. I believe with perfect faith in the coming of the Messiah, and, though Messiah tarry, I will wait daily for his coming.

13. I believe with perfect faith that there will be a resurrection of the dead at the time when it shall please the Creator, blessed be Your name, and exalted be the remembrance of You for ever and ever.

believed in reincarnation as a process whereby, over many lifetimes, this reunion would be accomplished. The mystical impulse of Kabbalism was given further embodiment in the Hasidic movement that appeared in Eastern Europe, partly in response to new episodes of mass violence against Jews, known as "pogroms."

Hasidism

A *hasid* is a pious one, one who lives a life of great devotion. Such piety has always been an important element in the observance of the way of Torah. However, at the beginning of the eighteenth century a movement of enthusiastic piety, *Hasidism*, emerged in Eastern Europe that gave the term a new intensity of meaning.

To understand the role of Hasidism within Judaism, it may be helpful to make a comparison with Hinduism. In the Hindu tradition, it is said that there are four ways to experience the ultimate reality—the four paths of knowledge (*jnana*), duty (*karma*), meditation (*raja*), and devotion (*bhakti*). These four approaches are not unique to Hinduism; indeed they really represent the major possibilities in all religions. Some of these paths, especially the knowledge that comes from studying the scriptures, are so demanding that they become the province of religious specialists who devote their whole lives to studying and interpreting. Such specialization is not really practical for most followers who have to worry about making a living. But the ordinary person also needs a way to deep spiritual experience. In Hinduism that path is *bhakti*—the way of devotion. For devotion is a capacity that even the simplest person can acquire. In Judaism, this need for a way of devotion was fulfilled by the emergence of Hasidism.

In fact, between Talmudic and Hasidic Judaism all four paths are covered. If Talmudic Judaism emphasizes the way of knowledge (Talmudic study) that leads to the way of duty (halakhah), Hasidic Judaism emphasizes the way of devotion fostered by meditative prayer. In the beginning, Hasidic Judaism rejected the elitism of Rabbinic Judaism. For the rabbis and their students were an intellectual elite, trained as Talmudic experts—something the average Jew could not hope to be. Hasidic Judaism offered other ways to reach God beside that of Talmudic study; namely, devotion and prayerful meditation. For unlike the skillful study of Talmud, devotion and prayer were within the reach of every sincere Jew. This path brought into popular practice the deep mystical piety of the Kabbalistic tradition.

This movement of mystical piety was paralleled by a movement of Christian piety that swept through Europe in rebellion against the rationalism of post-Reformation Protestant orthodoxy. However, Hasidism had its own indigenous context as a revolt against the asceticism and rigidity of Talmudic Judaism among some circles in eighteenth-century Poland. It also followed on the heels of a period of pogroms (the Chmielnicki massacres in the seventeenth century and the Haidamak massacres in the eighteenth century) that brought the destruction of hundreds of Jewish communities and cost hundreds of thousands of Jewish lives.

The Hasidic movement first emerged in Poland with the activities of Israel ben Eliezer, who was called the "Besht" by his followers—an acronym for the Ba'al Shem Tov or "Master of the Divine Name." The Besht was an ecstatic healer who worked miracles using magic, amulets, and spells. He taught that joy (*simhah*) is the appropriate response to the world no matter how much suffering Jews experience. The Besht was a charismatic figure whose followers hung on his every word and gesture and who formed a prayer circle characterized by ecstatic singing and dancing and deeply moving spiritual talks by the Besht around the Sabbath dinner table. The Besht taught that essence of the way of Torah is to be found in devotion (*kavanah*), burning enthusiasm (*hitlahavut*), and attachment or clinging to God (*devekut*) rather than in study of the Talmud.

The Besht became a model for the Hasidic notion of the *Tzaddik* or "righteous man." For the Hasidim, the Tzaddik was no ordinary person but one especially chosen by God as a direct link between heaven and earth. He was revered as a savior figure whose holiness was considered so powerful that, like Moses (Exodus 32:11–14), he could intervene on behalf of the faithful and literally change the mind of God. Like the rabbis, the Tzaddik was a religious virtuoso; however he was not a Talmudic virtuoso but a virtuoso of mystical piety and devotion. His virtuosity was said to be spontaneously contagious. Just being near him could enable the Hasidim to catch his piety as the spark to light their own.

Thus the Tzaddik's authority in the Hasidic community was every bit as powerful as that of the rabbinic scholar in traditional Talmudic communities—but it was based on mystical experience rather than on knowledge of Talmud. This was a genuinely new way of Judaism that offered an alternative to the way of Talmud. It is no wonder that the rabbis mistrusted it. And it is not surprising that it garnered an enthusiastic popular following, for it offered a way for even the poor and unlearned to move from the periphery into the heart of Judaism as they understood it.

In spite of its emergence in an era of pogrom and immense suffering in Eastern Europe, for the Hasidim there was no greater sin than melancholy or sadness (*atzut*). For sadness is the root of all sin. It emerges out of a fundamental ignorance of the pervasive and immanent presence of God in all things. Without this awareness humans go astray. According to the Besht, God hides himself in his creation. Therefore, there is no distance between God and humanity for those who have the eyes to see. And once you do see, there can be no excuse for sadness but only simhah or joy—deep, pervasive, passionate joy and celebration. For this reason, asceticism or self-denial is not an appropriate religious response for a Jew so long as each remembers that to enjoy the creation is not a goal in itself but a way of enjoying God.

WOMEN IN PREMODERN JUDAISM

Talmudic Judaism shares with the emerging Judaism of the ancient biblical period a common assumption of premodern urban societies but transposed into a monotheistic frame of reference. There is a sacred natural order of the world revealed by God in which maleness is the normative pattern for full humanity. The second creation story presented in Genesis 2:5 to 3:24 (rather than the first in Genesis 1:1–2:4) was used in the tradition to confirm this, emphasizing how God create Adam first and then Eve from the rib of Adam. Therefore men are given primary responsibility for the order of things and women are created to help men. Indeed, women (like animals and slaves) are the property of men. A father could sell his daughter as payment for a debt (Exodus 21:7), for instance. Basically, a woman belonged to her father until she was given to the man who married her and then she belonged to him. Women had no role in the public worship in the *temple*, but at the same time women were revered as mothers and the mainstay of the family. Nevertheless, during the biblical period there were also exceptional women who were revered for their wisdom and their gifts of prophecy, like Miriam (the sister of Moses), Deborah (one of the judges of Israel), and Huldah (a prophetess during the reign of Josiah).

The biblical attitude toward women was continued in premodern Rabbinic Judaism. For the rabbis too, maleness was the norm for humanness and femaleness was a deviation. The morning prayer for men included: "Blessed art Thou, O Lord our God, who hast not made me a woman." Rabbis looked upon women as inferior to men and as temptresses who must be kept at a distance. Women were viewed as dangerously sensual and were segregated in the *synagogue* during prayer so as not to distract men. Also, women were not obligated to the pattern of daily prayer required of men. Nor could a woman form part of a minyan (the ten men needed for a prayer service in the synagogue). Indeed, women had no ceremonial role at all in public worship. And with the exception of a few dissenting voices, the Talmudic tradition denied women the possibility of the study of Torah. A woman's job was to raise sons to study Torah. In Talmudic law a whole *seder* (order) of the Mishnah is devoted to women and property. Women have status primarily in relation to men, and the primary concern of these laws is to regulate the transfer of a woman from father to husband in marriage and the status of women when marriage ends either through divorce or death.

At the same time, women have always been revered and respected as the center of the home and the givers of life. In the home the women did play an essential ritual role—lighting the Sabbath candles, for instance. The attempt to keep women at a safe distance is a response to the tremendous power of God's holiness that is seen to express itself in the role of women as life-givers. They share in a unique way in God's power to create life. Indeed, for Rabbinic

Judaism, to be born of a Jewish woman is a key test of who is a Jew. (Not the only test, however, since conversion is also a possible way into Judaism.) Women have an awesome role in the natural order of things as created by God. And both rabbinic and later Hasidic traditions also present models of women who were exceptions, noted for their learning and piety. Beruriah, the wife of Rabbi Meir, was noted for her skill as a Talmudic scholar, and Oudil, the daughter of the Baal Shem Tov, for her wisdom and joyous piety. Nevertheless, such women were not the norm. They remained the exception that proved the rule.

What was most extraordinary about Hasidic mysticism was, and is, its communal nature. One cannot achieve this state of joy and selflessness by going off alone to some mountaintop but only by total immersion in the community life of the Hasidim organized around the festive worship made possible by the presence of the Tzaddik. It is this linking of deep mystical spirituality with community life that made Hasidism such a powerful force for renewal.

It was not immediately obvious to the rabbis that Hasidism would benefit Judaism, for Hasidism challenged the authority structure and hierarchy of religious virtues promoted by Talmudic Judaism. At first, Hasidism appeared to the rabbis as just one more attempt to undermine their authority and destroy Talmudic study as the appropriate ritual for the sanctification of Jewish life. Those rabbis who opposed the Hasidim were known as the *Mitnaggedim* ("opponents"). However, despite fears that Hasidism would lead to excesses, Hasidism proved itself capable of bringing genuine renewal and rejuvenation to Judaism. In the nineteenth century, the Hasidic movement moved toward reconciliation with Rabbinic Judaism by incorporating more emphasis on the study of Talmud and was accepted by the rabbis as an authentic expression of the way of Torah.

This integration of the Kabbalistic-Hasidic tradition with the Talmudic tradition, deeply influenced as it was by Neoplatonism and Gnosticism, demonstrates the extraordinary ability of Judaism to absorb and sanctify the "secular" and non-Jewish while reaffirming the practices of the tradition. This is a pattern we see repeated in the twentieth century as many of the movements of modern and post-Holocaust Judaism have moved closer together. Judaism, despite inner tensions and conflicts, shows an amazing ability to absorb conflicting movements, which often form the catalyst for its transformation and renewal. This should not surprise anyone, for this has been true of Judaism from its very beginnings in the biblical period.

Having surveyed premodern Judaism, we are now in a position to look at the emergence of modern forms and understand better how they are both similar to and different from premodern forms of Judaism.

JUDAISM AND MODERNITY

The Emergence of Modern Religious Forms of Judaism

Reform Judaism

From the time Rabbinic Judaism emerged between the second and fifth centuries, until the French Revolution in 1789, Jews in Europe lived as a rejected minority in a religious world—a world dominated by Christians in "the Holy Roman Empire." With Enlightenment secularization, the categories of human self-understanding underwent radical revision. Enlightened Europeans were secular universalists who defined their humanity not in terms of religious myths, which they believed created divisiveness, but in terms of the universality of reason, which they believed all individual human beings have in common. The ideal of this new orientation was to replace the categories of "Jew" and "Christian" with a single category: "human being."

For the first time in almost two thousand years, instead of being treated as a "negative witness" to the truth of another religion (i.e., Christianity), Jews were told that as rational beings they were equal with all other human beings, and they were invited to participate as citizens alongside all other individuals in the modern capitalist nation-states. This message of inclusion was widely accepted by the Jews of Europe. It seemed that a new day was dawning, a day of enlightened tolerance. One of the leading Enlightenment scholars of the eighteenth century, Gotthold Lessing (1729–1781), a Gentile, wrote impassioned works arguing for the humanity of Jews and of Muslims and for their acceptance in society. Lessing befriended Moses Mendelssohn (1729–1786), who became the leading figure in what became known as the Jewish Haskalah or Enlightenment movement out of which Reform Judaism eventually emerged as the first "modern" form of Judaism (See Map 3.4).

Like Hellenistic Judaism in the first century, the Haskalah movement embraced a pattern of partial assimilation into this new gentile world, trying to show that one could be an enlightened citizen of the modern secular world and a Jew at the same time. In doing this, the leaders of the Reform movement had to answer a question that all modern forms of Judaism (including Orthodoxy) have confronted: How can I be both a Jew and a citizen of a secular state? This was a question that was not possible during the age of Christendom, first because the state was not secular but Christian, and second because a Christian state offered the Jews no possibility of citizenship.

In answering this question, Reform Judaism, and all other forms of modern Judaism, have had to make a decision about how to relate to the larger secular

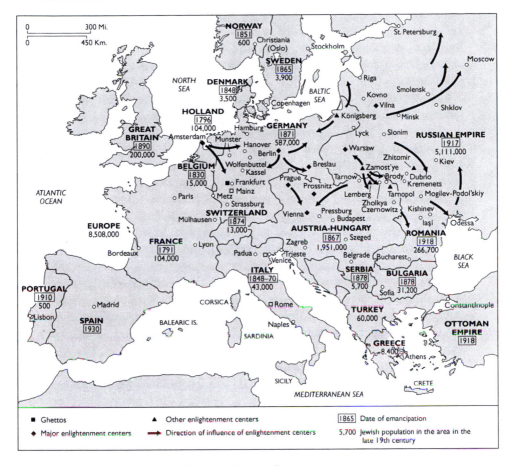

Map 3.4 The emancipation of European Jewry, 1789–1930.

society. They had to decide what belonged to the essence of Judaism and what was an historical accretion that could be safely dispensed with. Embracing the Enlightenment ideal of religion within the "limits of reason," the leaders of Reform Judaism defined the essence of Judaism as a rational-ethical system rooted in the prophetic-ethical ideal of justice—an ethic that was Judaism's gift to humanity. Like their Hellenistic counterparts, they did not think that this ethic was only for the Jews but rather that Judaism was the source and purest form of this universal rational ethic. This was the essence; all other aspects of Judaism were open to compromise.

As Reform Judaism developed it showed a remarkable openness to secular society. For instance, it allowed synagogue prayers and sermons to be said in the vernacular (that is, the local tongue—German, French, English, etc.) instead of Hebrew. As it came to full expression in the late nineteenth century, it was also prepared to abandon the observance of kosher laws restricting what foods Jews might eat and other "historical accretions" as inessential to being a Jew. Indeed, it rejected the Talmud as revelation, seeing it instead as simply a human historical tradition. And it rejected belief in a literal coming of the messiah, replacing it with a belief in a messianic age that could easily be identified with the goal of the modern age of scientific and rational progress. Finally, it renounced any desire to return to the land of Israel, insisting that to be a Jew was not to be a people tied to a specific land but a "religious community."

What especially marks the Reform movement as modern is its openness to secular learning and historical consciousness. In premodern Rabbinic Judaism (with notable exceptions like Maimonides), the only learning worthy of consideration was the study of Torah and Talmud. But among enlightened Jews, secular learning was not only permitted but took precedence. For instance, in deciding what is and what is not essential to Judaism, Reform Judaism argued not from the "revealed will of God," as had premodern Judaism, but from the history of the development of Judaism as a religion. It is "history" and "Judaism," not "God" and "Torah," that are the defining categories. That is, one settles religious disputes primarily by an appeal to the developmental history of Judaism. After all, what history reveals, Reform Jews argued, is that Judaism is a religion not of eternal unchanging truths but of constant change. From this perspective, in the historical progress of Judaism, Reform Judaism is the true Judaism for the modern world and the logical successor to premodern Rabbinic Judaism in the authentic unfolding of the historical tradition.

Reform Judaism explained how one could be a Jew and still be part of a larger secular society. It was Reform Judaism that initiated the journey of Judaism into the modern world. In doing so, it was the pioneer of all modern Judaisms. For some of these, Reform Judaism was a model to be emulated with modifications, especially the more secular forms of Judaism—ethnic Judaism, Jewish Socialism, and Zionism (to be discussed shortly). Indeed, it would be hard to imagine the emergence of the secular state of Israel without the path opened up by Reform Judaism despite an initial lack of interest in Zionism. For others, Reform Judaism seemed to be heading in the wrong direction. Indeed, it was the bold statements of Reform Judaism that caused a second form of modern Judaism to emerge by way of rejection, namely, Orthodox Judaism.

Orthodox Judaism

To call Orthodox Judaism a modern form of Judaism may seem contradictory to many, for orthodoxy claims that it continues the ancient tradition of premodern Rabbinic Judaism. Reform Judaism, of course, also claims to continue the same tradition. The difference was that orthodoxy believed continuity meant resisting all change, whereas Reform Judaism thought it meant being true to the historical law of constant change. The issue between Reform and Orthodox Jews was whether, as Reform Jews held, God was acting through an ever-changing history, progressing toward an age of messianic freedom, or whether God only revealed himself, as the Orthodox held, in the eternal unchanging truths given at Sinai. This reflects the choice modernization puts to all religions—whether to embrace historical change or reject it out of faithfulness to premodern unchanging fundamental truths.

Reform Jews argued for changes that would accommodate the modern world, while the Orthodox wanted to refuse all accommodation, although they seldom fully achieved this. Orthodox Jews wanted to present their choice of orthodoxy as if it were no choice. But clearly, the emergence of Reform Judaism meant that one could no longer just be a Jew, one had to choose to be a Jew of a certain kind. In having to choose, orthodoxy gave evidence that it too was a Judaism of the modern period. Like Reform Judaism, it now was forced to think of itself as one more religious community alongside others. Premodern rabbinic Jews had no such dilemma, for there was no "Judaism" to choose. There was just God, Torah, and Israel—they were the givens of one's birth into the chosen people.

The necessity of having to choose who you are as a self-conscious act is one of the symptoms of being a modern person. As we noted in Chapter 1, the sociologist Peter Berger argues that the emergence of modernity created "the heretical imperative." He notes that the root meaning of the term "heresy," which comes from the Greek, is "to choose," pointing out that modern historical consciousness generates an awareness of the diversity and relativity of all world views, and once one has this awareness one is faced with alternatives and must choose. One has no choice but to choose one's identity. In the case of Orthodox Judaism, this meant being forced to define the relationship to the secular world and to other modern forms of Judaism (neither of which premodern rabbinic Jews had to deal with). Orthodox Jews too were forced to define the essence of Judaism—what must be kept and what can be given up. In reacting to Reform Judaism they were much less generous toward the secular world, holding onto as much of the tradition as they could, changing as little as possible. And yet they did change. Those Orthodox, especially of Eastern Europe who were deeply embedded in village life tried to segregate themselves and resist all change (the haredim we have spoken of at the beginning of this chapter), but those Orthodox who grew up in urban areas, as in Germany and later America, made their peace with the modern world, opting for at least minimal integration. As Jacob Neusner, one of the world's leading scholars of Judaism, explains, unlike the segregationist haredim, whom we have labeled "ultra-Orthodox":

> Orthodox Judaism is that Judaic system that mediates between the received Judaism of the dual Torah and the requirements of living a life integrated in modern circumstances. Orthodoxy maintains the world view of the received dual Torah, constantly citing its sayings and adhering with only trivial variations to the bulk of its norms for everyday life. At the same time Orthodoxy holds that Jews adhering to the dual Torah may wear clothing that non-Jews wear and do not have to

wear distinctively Jewish clothing; may live within a common economy and not practice distinctively Jewish professions...; and may, in diverse ways, take up a life not readily distinguished in important characteristics from the lives lived by people in general. So for Orthodoxy a portion of Israel's life may prove secular, in that the Torah does not dictate and so sanctify all details under all circumstances.... The difference between Orthodoxy and the system of the dual Torah was expressed in social policy: integration, however circumscribed, versus the total separation of the holy people.[1]

Orthodoxy became, in many ways, the mirror image of Reform Judaism, for mirror images reverse the original that they reflect. Thus if Reform Jews prayed in the vernacular, the Orthodox insisted that all prayers be in Hebrew. If Reform Jews insisted on historical change, the Orthodox insisted on eternal unchanging truth. If Reform Jews decided issues of religious practice on the basis of history, the Orthodox decided them on the basis of the eternal word of God given in the Torah and Talmud. If Reform Jews abandoned literal messianic beliefs, the Orthodox reaffirmed them. If Reform Jews dismissed the Talmudic requirements (halakhah) as historical accretions, the Orthodox insisted on continued observance of the requirements of the dual Torah (the written Torah and the oral Torah or Talmud). And if Reform Jews abandoned any ambition to return to the land of Israel, the Orthodox prayed "next year in Jerusalem" while awaiting the deliverance of the messiah to make it possible.

Like their ancient ancestors, the Pharisees, the Orthodox set out to be "separatists" (the literal meaning of "Pharisee"), challenging the integrationism of their Hellenistic-Jewish counterparts, Reform Jews. East European haredim tried to shut out modernity altogether, but this meant doing what no premodern rabbinic Jew ever had to do—become a sectarian. In Western Europe the Orthodox saw the futility of segregating themselves from the world around them and allowed that in "inessentials," like clothing, secular education, and choice of job or career. Jews may be like everyone else. Indeed, Orthodoxy's first great intellectual defender, Samson Raphael Hirsch (1808–1888), sought to show that one can live as a Jew in a secular nation-state and remain fully Orthodox. Therefore, above all, what makes orthodoxy a modern Judaism is that, like Reform Judaism, it divides the world into the religious and the secular, separating religion and politics in such a way as to allow Orthodox Jews to be both Jews and citizens of the secular nation-state.

Conservative Judaism
Once the lines of distinction had been drawn between these two modern ways of being Jewish, it was perhaps inevitable that a third option would emerge, seeking a compromise between them: that option was Conservative Judaism. The

Orthodox saw Jewish life as the life of a supernatural eternal people. Reform Jews saw Jewish life as the life of an historical religious community. Conservative Jews saw Jewish life as the life of an historically ethnic people that included but was not limited to the religious dimension. Conservative Judaism arose among Jews sympathetic to the "modern" intellectual world view of Reform Judaism while being deeply committed to the Orthodox way of life.

The message of the leaders of Conservative Judaism was, "think whatever you like, but do what the law requires." Thus on the question of the relationship to the secular, Conservative Judaism chose to take its stand in practice rather than belief. This compromise gave conservative Jews considerable intellectual freedom of interpretation—one could believe or disbelieve any or all elements of the supernatural world view of premodern Rabbinic Judaism and still be a Jew, as long as one observed Talmudic law in everyday life (although modest compromises in this area were permitted). This position puts the emphasis on orthopraxy (right practice) as opposed to orthodoxy (right belief). Largely an American invention, with intellectual roots in the German Haskalah, Conservative Judaism fits very well with the pragmatic attitude of modern (especially American) culture. Like Reform Jews, Conservative Jews see Judaism as an historically unfolding religion, but unlike the Reform Jews and more like the Orthodox, the Conservatives emphasize (an organic) continuity. Historical change does not produce abrupt reorientations but gradual development—a development of the unfolding essence of Judaism. And that essence is found not so much in belief as in practice. In this way, Conservative Judaism, like Reform and Orthodox Judaism, saw itself as the logical continuation of the tradition. Conservative Judaism, as the third option, has been the most influential and widely embraced form of modern Judaism in America.

Reconstructionism

In addition to these three main strands of modern Judaism, a Jewish movement known as "Reconstructionism" was founded in America in the 1930s by Mordecai Kaplan. Kaplan cast his understanding of Judaism in almost completely secular terms drawn from the modern social and historical sciences, seeing Judaism as the religion of Jewish civilization—understanding religion as the sociologist Emile Durkheim did, not in supernatural terms but as the embodiment of the ideals and group identity of a civilization. But for that very reason the practice of the religious rituals of the tradition were important for preserving the identity and continuing vitality of Jewish civilization. For Kaplan, Judaism must not be about life beyond death but about improving the individual and working for the progress of society. Membership in the Reconstructionist movement remained modest, but many of its themes are found in the three main types of secular Judaism that, as we shall see, found the need for religious ritual less compelling.

The Emergence of Secular Forms of Judaism

Reform, Orthodox, and Conservative Judaism represent the three major ways of Jewish life that resulted from the first wave of Jewish responses to the emergence of a modern world that, instead of treating Jews as a "rejected people" (as premodern Christendom had), offered them the opportunity to be equal members of its new secular order. Each, in its own way, accepted that offer—cautiously for the Orthodox, enthusiastically for Reform and Conservative Jews. On the whole, the dawning of the age of Enlightenment created an optimistic mood among Jews. But that mood did not last, for its promise of inclusion for Jews turned out to be false. The hidden premise of this new offer soon became apparent in the aftermath of the French Revolution, which offered full citizenship to Jews. The offer gave *everything to the Jews as individuals and nothing to the Jews as a people.* To be a citizen in a secular society one had to trade one's religious identity for a secular or nonreligious one.

But even for the considerable number of Jews who paid the high price, the promise of equality proved false. For while the ideals of the Enlightenment were genuine enough, they quickly crashed on the rocks of the intractability of human prejudice. As more and more Jews were "secularized" in Europe (either abandoning or minimizing their Judaism) and entered into European political and economic life, a backlash occurred. Throughout Europe non-Jews began to fear that the Jews were taking over "their" society.

By the end of the nineteenth century a new "scientific" and secular definition had come to replace the old religious definition of the Jews. The Jews became defined as a race—an inferior race whose presence in society was a biologically corrupting influence. Using the new language of race, all the old Christian stereotypes of Jews as a rejected people were resurrected in a new guise. The Jews as a religious people could always be converted—hence, "the Jewish problem" could be solved. But race is not subject to conversion—it is perceived as a biologically unchangeable fact. Moreover, any attempt at assimilation through the mixing of the races was viewed as racial pollution by the advocates of the new "scientific" theory of race. With the emergence of this new racial definition of Judaism, it seemed to the Nazis that the most efficient way to get rid of "the Jewish problem" was to get rid of the Jews. Hence they turned to the "final solution"—the death camps.

The situation of Jews in the United States was different than it was in Europe. America was forged as a nation of many peoples fleeing various forms of religious intolerance in Europe. And while anti-Semitism (and other forms of religious intolerance) were not absent from America's formative history, Jews never experienced the violent pogroms and mass expulsions that they encountered in Europe. American individualism allowed more space for diverse ethnic and religious communal identities.

Jewish immigrants to the United States came in two waves. The first and more modest wave, dating from 1654, was *Sephardic*—primarily *Marrano* Jews (Jews of Spain) seeking religious freedom. The second and much larger wave began in the nineteenth century among the Ashkenazi Jews of Europe and especially Eastern Europe, who were fleeing persecution and pogrom. By the beginning of World War II, approximately a third of the world's Jews lived in the United States. After World War II, twice as many Jews lived in the United States as in all of Europe combined.

While Jews in America were being integrated into society, the Jews of Western Europe were experiencing a new wave of rejection, the backlash of the late nineteenth and early twentieth century. Most of the Jews of Eastern Europe did not experience themselves as having been invited to join a new Enlightenment order of equality and inclusion. On the contrary, the increased persecutions and pogroms they experienced in the nineteenth century seemed more like the continuation of an ancient pattern. The challenge was to devise a strategy toward societies that were replacing religious anti-Judaism with secular anti-Semitism. And it was among the more fully assimilated and secularized Jews that the new responses emerged, responses that would form a bridge from the modern forms of Judaism (Reform, Orthodox, and Conservative) to the postmodern and postcolonial *Judaism of Holocaust and Redemption*. These new secular forms of Judaism were Jewish Socialism, ethnic (Yiddish) Judaism, and Jewish Zionism. Although each of these offered a distinct way of being Jewish, they were capable of combining in interesting and powerful ways that set the stage for the emergence of the Judaism of Holocaust and Redemption.

Jewish Socialism

Some of the strongest currents of Jewish Socialism emerged in Eastern Europe where secularized Jews saw in socialism another way of resolving the tension between being Jewish and being modern. For, as noted in Chapter 1, socialism, especially the later "scientific" socialism of Marx, offered an essentially secularized version of the Jewish and Christian myths of history. It was a view of history as a story of exile and return, in which human beings begin in paradise (primitive communism), only to be expelled from the garden into a world of selfishness and sin (class conflict), but with a promise that at the end of time this world will be transformed into the kingdom of God (a global, classless, communist society)—a kingdom in which all suffering and injustice will be overcome and all will live in perfect harmony. The connections should not be surprising, once we realize that Marx, whose father was a convert to Christianity, was the grandson of a Jewish rabbi.

For the many "secularized" Jews of Europe, the socialist story of history offered them a new, yet very familiar, story through which to understand their place in the drama of history. And it offered them a story that, like the ancient story of exile and return, both deferred yet continued the (Enlightenment) promise of freedom and equality for all (and hence the end of anti-Semitism)—if not now, then in the future messianic age of the classless society. In the meantime, this new secular story gave the new Enlightenment-oriented secular

Jews a secular way of being Jewish. In this, Jewish Socialism adapted the spirit of Reform Judaism, opting for historical development as the key to continuity in Jewish history and for a secular vision of Judaism that favored the prophetic witness of the written Torah (redefined as socialist ethics) over that of the oral Torah traditions of the Talmud. And, like Reform Jews, the Jewish socialists did not need to see their message as exclusive to Judaism. For them it was enough to see Judaism as the unique contributor of the ideal of social justice to an international ethic for the whole human race. However, unlike their Reform counterparts, Jewish socialists no longer felt any need to represent themselves as "religious"—for religion belonged to the prescientific age that was passing away.

Who was attracted to this way of being Jewish? The message of socialism was directed to the "proletariat"—that is, the "workers of the world." So the message naturally took its deepest roots in the poor and impoverished new class of secular Jewish workers created by capitalist societies. In the wake of the Communist Russian Revolution of 1917, it was especially attractive to the Jews of Russia and Eastern Europe and the poor Jewish immigrants from these areas who came to the United States. These were Jews who were not only victims of anti-Semitism but also of economic depression and unemployment. The pivotal date for Jewish Socialism is usually said to be the formation of the "Bund" or Jewish Worker's Union in Poland in 1897.

Yiddish Ethnic Judaism

Many secular Jews, of course, who joined the socialist movement rejected all connections with Judaism in any form. They thought of themselves as purely secular, nonreligious persons. Some even vigorously rejected their own Jewish roots, going so far as to contribute to existing currents of anti-Semitism. Jewish socialists, by contrast, were those who, while not being religious, wished to retain and affirm their ties to the history of the Jewish people. And so they turned to ethnicity as the key to Jewish identity—an ethnicity that was primarily identified with the speaking of the Yiddish language.

Even those secular Jews who no longer knew Hebrew, knew Yiddish, the common language of European Jews that developed from about the eleventh century—an amalgam of primarily Hebrew and German. The focus on Yiddish language, and especially Yiddish literature, which has deeps roots in Talmudic and biblical stories, gave secular Jews a way to identify with Judaism without being "religious" and to still draw on the wisdom of the tradition. Yiddish stood for more than a language. It stood for a way of experiencing and interpreting the world that was still deeply rooted in Judaism. Indeed, ever since the first nation-states emerged in Europe, language had been the key to national identity. Through Yiddish, Jews, otherwise dispersed—without a land of their own—sought to sustain their identity as a people in a secular age. As the language of working-class Jews, Yiddish gave Jews a deep sense of "ethnicity"— of being bound together in a common historical tradition that offered a sense of unique identity. That ethnicity could easily be tapped by Jewish socialists to mobilize Jews, that is, to organize them for the worker's revolution.

The combination of Socialism and Yiddishism gave Jewish Socialism roots in both the Enlightenment and the Romantic reaction to the Enlightenment that characterized the nineteenth century. For if the Enlightenment emphasized the themes of rationality and universality, the Romantic reaction emphasized just the opposite, the nonrational and historically unique aspects of human existence that made each nation or people unique. The socialist dimension of Jewish Socialism retained the Enlightenment ideals of scientific rationality, human universality, and historical progress ending in the classless society. The Yiddish dimension added the contrasting Romantic emphasis on the concrete historical particularity of the Jewish people through the Yiddish tradition—seeing it as the vehicle whereby Jews could participate in the dialectical unfolding of history that would lead to freedom and equality for all in the classless society.

Zionism

From the end of nineteenth century until the end of World War II, Jewish Socialism was the predominant secular response to modernity among Jews, both in Europe and America. But it was not the only response, for there emerged in the nineteenth century another Jewish movement that, in the long run, would be even more influential—Zionism. Zionism was born out of a deep disenchantment with modernity and the promises of the Enlightenment. Unlike Jewish Socialism, Zionism did not hold out much hope for a future in which Jews would be accepted as equals in society. In the Zionist view, the only viable solution for Jews in light of the long history of rejection, first by Christendom and then by modern secular society, was to have a state of their own where they could protect themselves.

The word "Zion" is a biblical term used to refer to the city of David—Jerusalem. While the term "Zionism" was first coined in 1893, it represents a longing to return home from exile to Zion that is virtually as old as Judaism itself. In premodern Rabbinic Judaism, this longing was expressed in a messianic belief that some day God would send a messiah and reestablish a homeland for his people in Israel. For premodern Rabbinic Judaism, as well as for much of modern Orthodoxy and ultra-Orthodoxy, the return of Jews to Israel as their own land can only be the work of God. Any attempt by Jews to create a Jewish state on their own is wholly presumptuous and blasphemous. Thus the emergence of a secular movement at the end of the nineteenth century to organize Jews for the creation of a homeland in Palestine was violently rejected by the Orthodox and ultra-Orthodox. At the same time, Reform Jews, having defined themselves as a religious community rather than a "people," showed little interest in returning to the Middle East. In truth, Zionism came into its own only after the Holocaust, for only then was it clear to Jews everywhere that Jews could never count on being accepted as equals in Europe and

THE DREYFUS AFFAIR

Alfred Dreyfus, a Jew, was a captain in the French army who was accused of having sold secret documents to Germany. In 1894 he was convicted and sent to prison for life on the basis of false documents. The real traitor, a man by the name of Esterhazy, was acquitted in a later trial (1898) of any wrongdoing. Public protests of this travesty of justice were unable to override the tide of popular anti-Semitism that underlay this scandal until a famous novelist, Emile Zola, wrote an editorial protesting the injustice. Zola himself was imprisoned for this. Very shortly after, a French officer admitted forging the documents used to convict Dreyfus and committed suicide. Dreyfus was given a new trial in 1899—a trial that virtually tore the country apart. Dreyfus was again found guilty but with extenuating circumstances and was given a pardon by the president of France. Later, in 1906, when things had calmed down, he was declared completely innocent. Dreyfus, himself, was allowed to finish out his career in the army.

that the only possible protection Jews could count on would be their own homeland—their own state.

A pivotal event in the development of secular political Zionism was the Dreyfus affair in France. Dreyfus' trial had a profound influence on a young Jewish journalist, Theodor Herzl (1860–1904), inspiring him to organize the political Zionist movement that was destined to change the future of Judaism. Herzl, who was born in Budapest and schooled in Vienna, was a correspondent for the *Vienna New Free Press* covering the Dreyfus trial. Herzel was also a playwright whose work explored how Jews ought to respond to the gentile world's perception of "the Jewish problem." At first he flirted with assimilation, but by 1894 he had rejected this option.

After the Dreyfus trial, Herzl became convinced that a radical solution was needed. In 1896 he wrote *The Jewish State*, in which he rejected assimilation as unfeasible and proposed the creation of a Jewish state. While Herzl favored Palestine as the location for a state, he was prepared to seek the establishment of a state in virtually any practical geographic location. From that time forward, Herzl devoted himself to developing a political Zionist movement and negotiating with the various powers of Europe, seeking a homeland for the Jewish people. In 1898 Herzel formed the Jewish Colonial Trust and in 1901 the Jewish National Fund, to raise funds to purchase a homeland.

Herzl convened the First Zionist Congress in Basel, Switzerland, in August of 1897—significantly, the same year as the formation of the Jewish Socialist party or "Bund" in Poland. At this conference the World Zionist Organization was founded. In addition to Palestine, Herzl considered sites for a Jewish homeland in Cyprus and in Uganda. He brought a British offer for a colony in Uganda to the Sixth Zionist Congress, only to have it rebuffed by its members. From that time forward Palestine became the sole option for Zionists. Herzl even wrote a utopian novel, *Altneuland*, imagining a Jewish Palestinian state.

Herzl died in 1904, but not his dream. He left behind a thriving and committed organization of political Zionists embodied in the World Zionist Organization. In 1911 this organization began a modest but persistent program of colonizing Palestine. At the end of World War I as a result of Zionist efforts, the British government issued the Balfour Declaration (1917) granting the right for a Jewish national home in Palestine. France, Italy, and the United States endorsed this proposal. One cannot overestimate the tremendous importance of the organizational infrastructure developed in both Jewish Socialism (embodied in the Bund) and in Zionism (embodied in the World Zionist Organization). The skills developed in these organizations in the Diaspora and transferred to the early settlements in Palestine, with ongoing support from Jews all over the world, made possible the "sudden" emergence of the state of Israel in 1948 with U.N. sponsorship.

Like Reform Judaism, Zionism relied on history and historical change as its link to the premodern traditions of the Jewish people. But unlike Reform Judaism, political Zionism did not think of itself as a religious movement. Therefore, unlike Reform Judaism, Zionism sought continuity in the idea of the Jews as an historical people. Zionists reappropriated the biblical stories of the origins of Israel as part of its story, but was interested in telling these stories not as religious stories of God's actions in history but as "secular" stories of the Jewish people's struggles to achieve and preserve their national identity as a people.

Therefore, Zionists retold the stories of origins from a different perspective than that of the premodern rabbinic tradition of the dual Torah. That tradition had its beginnings in the failure of ancient militant Jewish political messianism (with the defeat of the Zealots) and success of a political policy of neutrality practiced by the Pharisees. The Zionists reacted to what they perceived as the failure (after almost two thousand years) of the rabbinic strategy of accommodation and to the more recent Reform strategy of partial assimilation. They were not content to wait to be emancipated by others (whether God or modern "enlightened" Gentiles). They were looking for Jewish heroes who were prepared to emancipate themselves. Thus they retold the stories of Moses and David as stories of nation-builders and militant revolutionary political leaders. For the Zionists, the interesting stories were the marginal ones of the Maccabean revolts of the second century BCE and those of their successors, the Zealots, who would rather fight for their land, and if necessary kill themselves (as they did at Masada in 73 CE) than surrender. The Zionists were looking for a militant hero who could serve as a prototype for a new kind of Jew, one prepared to fight to

WOMEN IN MODERN JUDAISM

The Enlightenment, as noted in the last chapter, brought with it a gradual change in the status of women in Western culture, and women have progressively claimed their right to autonomy, that is, the right to control their own lives. The role of women has moved toward equality in Judaism to the degree that Judaism has embraced modern secularization. Modern forms of Judaism tend to demythologize traditional Jewish gender roles as inessential historical accretions that may even contradict the fundamental insights of Judaism concerning justice and human dignity. Thus, it is probably fair to say that the greatest equality for women has been among the secular forms of Judaism, especially Jewish Socialism and Zionism and among the most secular forms of religious Judaism—Reform first, then Conservative, and least among the Orthodox.

The Declaration of Independence of the State of Israel, drawing on the state's secular socialist and Zionist roots, declared complete equality of men and women in social and political rights. This was followed by the Equal Rights for Women law in 1951, which guaranteed women equal rights to own property and over their children, and significant protections in divorce. Then in 1964, the Equal Pay for Equal Work law was enacted. The socialist ideal embodied in the kibbutz tradition upon which Israel is largely founded also insisted on equal rights for women. Yet in all these areas (just as in other secular societies), the reality of everyday practice does not measure up to the ideal. For instance, in the kibbutz men still overwhelmingly hold the leadership roles, and job assignments still often suggest the influence of gender stereotypes (e.g., kitchen work is women's work, etc.).

Among the explicitly religious forms of Judaism, the Reform movement has led the way. As early as 1846 a movement to declare women equal appeared in Germany. And about the same time women were admitted to Hebrew Union College in the United States. Nevertheless, the question of women as rabbis did not emerge until the 1920s, and it was not until the 1970s that women began to be ordained (although one private ordination is said to have occurred in 1935 in German Reform Judaism).

Since the late 1960s, Jewish feminist authors have begun to critique the traditional patterns of Judaism, pointing out that the bible offers numerous images of God that emphasize characteristics typically thought of as feminine, especially in reference to the compassion of God. In addition, feminists argue for the primacy of the first creation story (Genesis 1:1–2:4), which affirms that men and women are created equally in the image of God (recall that the second creation story, Genesis 2:5–3:24, has Eve created from Adam's rib).

Conservative and Orthodox Judaism have been slower to respond to issues of gender equality. For in these traditions Talmudic precedent carries more weight than it does among Reform Jews, and progress toward equality has to be done through skillful Talmudic arguments for change. Nevertheless, it is not uncommon in both Reform and Conservative synagogues in America at the end of the twentieth century to see young women celebrating their Bat Mitzvah as a parallel rite to the Bar Mitzvah by which formerly young men alone were permitted to become full members of the Jewish community. Nor is it unusual to see women reading the Torah scrolls at a Sabbath service. And it is even becoming more common to see women cantors chanting such services and women rabbis conducting them. All of this was unthinkable in premodern Judaism. And it remains unthinkable among the ultra-Orthodox.

Against all these developments ultra-Orthodox Judaism takes its stand, insisting that to go forward into gender equality is to violate the will of God while to go back to the premodern foundation of Talmudic Judaism is to reestablish the sacred natural order that God intended for all men and women. For the ultra-Orthodox, the modernists' declaration that there is no sacred natural order to which all men and women must conform is the equivalent of saying there is no God. And such a statement, in their eyes, is the fundamental delusion that underlies all the ills of modern and postmodern society. Thus ultra-Orthodoxy rejects the attempt of the Judaism of Holocaust and Redemption to find a way to permit a pluralism of religious and secular ways of Judaism to coexist. So while both the Judaism of Holocaust and Redemption and ultra-Orthodoxy reject the modern privatization of religion and insist that Judaism should profoundly influence public social and political life, on this issue (and on most others) they have radically different visions of the kind of public order Jews should live in.

the last against all odds. This hero, they imagined, was the kind of Jew who would reestablish a homeland in Israel. And yet, while calling for a new kind of Jew, Zionism was repeating the formative pattern of Judaism, telling a story of exile and return—a people who originated in the land of Israel, were forced into diaspora for almost two thousand years, and now sought to return to their homeland. Moreover, like Jewish Socialism, Zionism offered secular Jews a powerful secular version of the goal of history but unlike Socialism a vision in which the Jewish people were not incidental but essential. This vision recalls the prophecies of Isaiah that God will create not only a new heaven and a new earth but also a new Jerusalem; namely, a reestablished Jewish homeland. All in all, they made a much more comprehensive and creative use of the stories of the biblical past than did the Jewish (Yiddish) socialists.

Like Yiddish Socialism, Zionism created a new way for secular Jews to be Jewish, reappropriating the tradition through story, language (which for Zionists was the recovery and reconstruction of Hebrew as a modern language), and social organization. While Jewish Socialism predominated before World War II, it was clearly eclipsed by Zionism afterward. For after the Holocaust and the destruction of nearly a third of the world's Jews, the truth and the urgency of the Zionist vision seemed self-evident to the overwhelming majority of Jews, both religious and secular. If they were to survive, Jews must have their own homeland.

And yet the Zionist vision did not so much replace the socialist vision as assimilate it into the Zionist story. Israel was founded by immigrants infused with a secular Zionist-socialist vision embodied in the formation of the *kibbutz* tradition (agricultural communes) with its ideals of equality, social justice, hard work, communal self-governance, and self-defense as the basis for building a new nation. This Zionism was a vehicle for the transformation of a people.

Zionism shaped a nation and turned a utopian dream into a reality—the state of Israel. The amalgamation of Jewish Socialism and Zionism represented a powerful, if ambivalent, rejection of the modern era and its ideal of assimilation as defined by the Enlightenment. As such, it forms the natural bridge to the Judaism of Holocaust and Redemption. For without the socialist-Zionist revolution, there would be no state of Israel. And without the state of Israel, there would be only Holocaust and no sense of redemption—no sense of being rescued from the forces of slavery and death as Jews were once rescued from Egypt.

JUDAISM AND POSTMODERN TRENDS IN A POSTCOLONIAL WORLD

The Judaism of Holocaust and Redemption

The Devastation of the Holocaust

Between 1933 and 1945, Hitler and the Nazi party came to power in Germany and drew Europe and America into World War II (1939–1945)—a war of expansion that was meant to give additional *Lebensraum* ("living space") to what the Nazis considered to be the superior Aryan race of Germany. However, the war that mattered most to the Nazis was the war against the Jews. Near the end, when Germany was losing badly and soldiers and supplies were desperately needed at the front, still trains were diverted to haul Jews in boxcars to the death camps. Hitler was more desperate to rid the world of Jews than he was to win the war.

The Holocaust was a singular event in human history that opened the postmodern era of mass death. It was a state-sponsored attempt at genocide, that is, an attempt to eliminate an entire people simply because they exist. Unlike the millions of others who died in World War II, the Jews were not military combatants who died on the battle front. The Jews of Germany were not enemies of Germany, but citizens. There was no military or territorial advantage in systematically killing them. Their only crime was that they were not members of the pure Aryan race. Germans, defeated and humiliated in World War I (1914–1918), and suffering from extreme economic depression as a result of war reparations, sought a reason for their sufferings. "The Jews," they said, "are our misfortune"—they are to blame. The Nazis portrayed them as a racial pollutant or a diseased growth on the healthy body of the German *Volk* ("people") that had to be surgically cut out if the German nation was to be restored to the health and greatness that was its destiny.

Thus, once the Nazi party came to power, the Jews were stripped of their citizenship and all their legal rights, their homes and businesses were appropriated, and they were herded into boxcars that delivered them to an elaborate system of death camps where they were either worked to death as slave labor or murdered in specially designed gas chambers made to order for mass killings. The most famous of the camps, Auschwitz, was established in Poland and is estimated to have killed approximately two million Jews. Ironically, because they no longer had citizenship, Jews had no legal rights and consequently no laws were broken at Auschwitz or at any of the other death camps (see Map 3.5).

One has to ask: Why the Jews? Finding a scapegoat to blame for misfortune is not unusual in history, but what made the Nazis pick the Jews for this role? The answer, unfortunately, takes us back in large part to the story of the beginnings of Christianity (see Chapter 2) as a Jewish sect that came to be dominated by Gentiles who saw themselves as having superseded and replaced the Jews as God's chosen people. The emergence of Christianity as the dominant religion of the Roman Empire in the fourth century led to both legal discrimination and popular discrimination and to violence against the Jews as "the children of the devil"—a people, according to Christians, rejected by God because they had rejected and killed Jesus, the Son of God.

Moreover, as we have seen, Augustine's "negative witness" theory portrayed the Jews as condemned to wander the earth without a home, their misery supposedly offering negative proof of the truth of Christianity. From Augustine forward, through the Middle Ages and into the modern period, Jews were the scapegoats to be blamed for whatever misfortunes occurred in Western civilization. Indeed, Hitler played on popular Christian anti-Jewish sentiments to get himself elected chancellor of Germany. And neither the Catholic nor the Protestant churches of Germany officially protested the Nazi treatment of the Jews—only the treatment of Jewish converts to Christianity. While it took more than Christian anti-Judaism to make the Holocaust possible, it is hard to imagine the Holocaust occurring without it as a significant contributing factor.

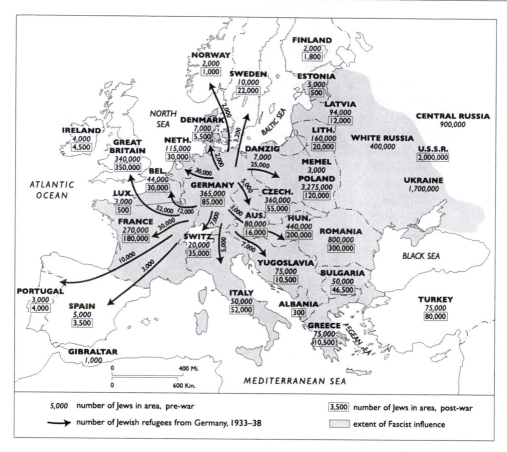

Map 3.5 The Holocaust.

The Holocaust as a Challenge to Jewish Faith

It has been almost two thousand years since a new holy day was added to the Jewish calendar. However, the twentieth century has witnessed two events whose days of commemoration are coming close to just such a status—the Holocaust and the founding of the state of Israel. The Holocaust deeply challenges the faith stories of the exodus and exile traditions. For if these stories promised a God who would always be with the people of the covenant, guiding and protecting them, the Holocaust seemed to prove this promise a lie. God, it seems to many Jews, has failed to keep his promises.

As we have seen, the fall of the first and second temples had challenged Jewish faith in just this way. As the distinguished Jewish philosopher and Holocaust survivor Emil Fackenheim has pointed out, in both cases the Jewish people responded by seeing the tragedy as a punishment for a failure to keep the covenant faithfully enough. In this way they were able to turn a challenge to faith into a reason to renew faith. After the Holocaust, some of the most Orthodox of Jews wanted to treat the Holocaust as a tragedy of the same type as the fall of the first and second temples. In fact, they proposed that the best way to remember the Holocaust was to include it in the period of fasting and mourning of Tisha B'Av. But to many other Jews, both secular and religious, this seemed wholly inappropriate. For in the Holocaust it was not the most liberal and secularized Jews who were its main victims but rather its most orthodox and observant Jews, the Jews of Eastern Europe. To many Jews, the scope of the tragedy was too great and the explanation for its cause as a failure to keep the covenant faithfully enough was too inadequate.

How does one commemorate such an event? What meaning could possibly be found in it? And yet how could one possibly ignore it? Clearly if it were to be commemorated it would require a unique day of its own. It could not be subsumed under Tisha B'Av. But if it were given a day of its own, would not its message be a message of despair so powerful as to wipe out the positive meaning of the exodus event and the Sinai covenant? And how could Jews go on believing the promises of God to guide and protect them on their journey through time after the Holocaust? Indeed, a major debate is being carried out in contemporary Judaism in which a number of important authors offer a variety of suggestions on how Jews should respond to the Holocaust.

One such author, Richard Rubenstein, argues that God died at Auschwitz and Jews will have to go on with their stories and their rituals but without God. Another, Emil Fackenheim, argues that, on the contrary, God is still present in history. How do we know? Because, he argues, it is as if Jews had heard a silent yet commanding voice from Auschwitz, giving them a new commandment, a 614th commandment to be added to the 613 given at Sinai. This commandment demands that Jews remain Jewish lest they give Hitler a posthumous victory by allowing him to kill Judaism after the fact. The evidence for this revelation from Auschwitz, Fackenheim argues, is a spontaneous renewal that is under way in Judaism everywhere. Jews did not give up and slink away. On the contrary, whether religious or secular, Jews have taken great pride in reasserting their Jewishness after the Holocaust.

Elie Wiesel, the Nobel Prize–winning author who is himself a survivor of Auschwitz, sees it somewhat differently. Only the Jew knows, says Wiesel, that one can have the *chutzpah* ("audacity") to argue with God as long as it is in defense of God's creation—as Abraham argued with God over the fate of the innocent at Sodom (Genesis 18:22–33). After Auschwitz, Jews have a right to be angry with God, to call God into question, even put God on trial. After Auschwitz, he argues, Jews have a right to conclude that this time it was not the Jews but God who broke the covenant. And yet, Jews have not despaired. Indeed, according to Wiesel, "Judaism teaches man to overcome despair. What is Jewish history if not an endless quarrel with God?" Wiesel tells the tale of a Hasidic master to make his point.

One day Hasidim came to inform the great Rebbe Nahman of Bratzlav of renewed persecution of Jews in the Ukraine. The Master listened and said nothing. Then they told him of pogroms in certain villages. Again the Master listened and said nothing. Then they told of slaughtered families, of desecrated cemeteries, of children burned alive. The Master listened, listened and shook his head. "I know," he whispered, "I know what you want. I know. You want me to shout with pain, weep in despair, I know, I know. But I will not, you hear me, I will not." Then, after a long silence, he did begin to shout, louder and louder, "*Gewalt, Yiden, ziet zich nit meyaesh!* Jews, for heaven's sake, do not despair.... *Gewalt, Yiden,* Jews, do not despair."[2]

Echoing the Hasidic tradition, in which he grew up in Eastern Europe, Wiesel insists that to be a Jew is to refuse all temptations to despair. Instead, Wiesel argues, Jews, who can no longer be required to keep a covenant broken by God, have chosen to keep the covenant of their own free will.

Another major Holocaust scholar, Irving Greenberg, argues that after Auschwitz Jews are forced to live a "momentary faith"—tossed back and forth between the stories of the Exodus and the stories of the Holocaust. In one moment a Jew might believe in the promises of Sinai, only in the next moment to have them clouded over by memories of the smokestacks of Auschwitz. Moreover, Greenberg agrees with Wiesel that after Auschwitz Jews cannot be required to embrace the covenant and yet they do so freely, but, he adds, in a wide variety of ways, from the extremely orthodox to the extremely secular. And after Auschwitz, he argues, all Jews, from the extremely orthodox to the extremely secular, are obligated to accept each other as Jews. They must accept contemporary Jewish pluralism as an authentic covenantal pluralism. For some Jews to turn their backs on others, as some of the ultra-Orthodox in the state of Israel wish to do, who refuse to acknowledge the Jewishness of nonorthodox Jews, is another way of granting Hitler a posthumous victory. In a post-Holocaust and postcolonial world, Jews find themselves once more facing the question they faced in the first century: Which of all the ways of being Jewish is the right way? Only, after Auschwitz, while Jews are free to observe or not observe the covenant, Greenberg argues, they are not free to reject other Jews who exercise this freedom.

Post-Holocaust Judaism offers an alternative to the "one way" of ultra-Orthodoxy. In a post-Holocaust and postcolonial world, it argues, there is not one single way to truth and to faithfulness but many. This postmodern form of Judaism has transposed the Conservative strategy (i.e., diversity in thought but uniformity in practice) to a new level, where covenantal pluralism (i.e., allowing a great diversity in thought *and* practice, both secular and religious) is affirmed but in which *one practice is not negotiable*; namely, the obligation of

Jews to accept each other in their diversity after the Holocaust. Both ultra-Orthodoxy and the Judaism of Holocaust and Redemption seek a way out of what they see as the spiritual poverty of a modernism that made the Holocaust possible. The choice they offer to all Jews is either withdrawal from or involvement in the modern world, either back to what they view as premodern uniformity or forward to a new age of Jewish pluralism.

Finally, the post-Holocaust Jewish scholar Marc Ellis insists that the suffering of the Jews in the Holocaust must never be an excuse for the oppression of their Palestinian neighbors. They must remember that the covenant relation of the Jews to the land includes a demand for justice and compassion toward the stranger. Not only must Jews accept each other in their diversity, they must accept their Christian and Muslim Palestinian neighbors in Israel in a way that provides justice and peace for all. Such a task is not easy in a world where extremists on all sides seek to undermine genuine efforts at compromise and cooperation, and yet many in the state of Israel continue the struggle to find that middle ground, despite the extremists.

The Holocaust and the State of Israel: Exile and Redemption

This new Judaism of Holocaust and Redemption, which has proven very attractive to American Judaism, Israeli Judaism, and Israeli nationalism, has a postmodern and postcolonial orientation, in that instead of seeking to return to some premodern orthodoxy emphasizing one truth and one way, it attempts to find unity in the diversity of religious and secular Jews. Even its new "holy days" or "holidays" display characteristics of both the holy and the secular. This is evidenced by the fact that the two days that seem to be entering the Jewish calendar are recollections of seemingly secular events—*Yom Hashoah* (Day of Desolation), recalling the Holocaust, and *Yom Ha'Atzmaut* (Independence Day), celebrating the founding of Israel.

One has to realize the devastating impact of the Holocaust on Jewish consciousness. For during the Holocaust the Nazis nearly succeeded in their goal of eliminating Jews from the face of the earth. While nearly a third of all Jews died in the Holocaust, nearly two-thirds of the Jews of Europe died. The Eastern European Jewish communities were hit the hardest. Ninety percent of these Jews, and more than 80 percent of all the rabbis, Talmudic scholars, and Talmudic students then alive, were murdered.

After such a devastating event, Jews might have despaired were it not for an event that gave them hope—the founding of the state of Israel by the United Nations in 1948. The counterbalancing of these two events—the Holocaust and the founding of the state of Israel—fits the great formative story of Jewish existence—exile and return. After two thousand years of exile without a homeland, many Jews experienced the ability to return to Israel as a Jewish state as a miraculous act of divine redemption akin to the return to the land of promise after slavery in Egypt or after exile in Babylonia. That redemption made it possible for Jews to remember the Holocaust without despairing.

In this context we need to review the history of the establishment of the state of Israel, which marks an important turning point in the demise of colonialism (in this case, British colonialism) and the emergence of a post-colonial, post-Holocaust Judaism. In the settlement of World War I, Britain was given control of Palestine, which had been under Muslim control. The Balfour Declaration of 1917 gave the British a mandate to enable the establishment of a homeland for Jews in Palestine alongside the existing Palestinian population. In carrying out this mandate, the British recognized the international Zionist movement as the official Jewish organization to facilitate its implementation. At the conclusion of World War II, Palestine was still under British rule. Britain, as a member of the newly formed United Nations, asked its General Assembly to establish a special committee on Palestine (UNSCOP). The report of this committee led to a resolution to divide Palestine into two states—one Jewish and the other Arab (see Map 3.6). Following the report, the state of Israel was established on May 14, 1948, the date that Great Britain gave up official control of the area. Within a year Israel was admitted to the United Nations, on May 11, 1949.

These events required international political support (including from two key members of the U.N., the United States and the Soviet Union) and represented the triumph of the Zionist movement. The beginning of the new state was itself quite traumatic. The Arab states refused to accept the U.N. partition plan, and on May 15, 1948, the armies of seven Arab states invaded the newly formed nation and the war for independence was under way. Israel, as a new nation, hardly had time to organize, but improvised around established resistance organizations, primarily the Haganah. The war was fought in two phases, with an intervening cease fire, and ended in the defeat of the Arab forces and an armistice with the Egyptians in February of 1949. Later agreements were signed with Jordan, Lebanon, and Syria; however, none was signed with Iraq and Saudi Arabia. Relations with neighboring Arab states remained tense throughout the decades that followed, flaring again into the wars of 1967 and 1973. But the essential fact for Jews has been that Israel exists and has withstood all onslaughts against it. As we have noted, for many Jews the 1967 war was the turning point. From that time forward the meaningful connection between the Holocaust and the founding of the state of Israel could no longer be ignored. The two events became indissolubly linked in Jewish minds, and the days of remembrance of these two events began to assume an ever more prominent place in the Jewish calendar.

Map 3.6 The Creation of the State of Israel.

JERUSALEM: WHERE RELIGION AND POLITICS CONVERGE AND DIVERGE IN AN AGE OF GLOBALIZATION

The present struggle for sovereignty over Jerusalem is symbolic of the convergence of the spiritual and the physical, the religious and the political in the Middle East. This "holy" city is historically as well as scripturally claimed by Jews, Muslims, and Christians. For the Jews, Jerusalem is the "mountain of the Lord." The Mishnah (second-century compendium of Jewish laws) asserts that the Shekinah or divine presence has never left the Western Wall. Jerusalem is a predominant symbol and source of Jewish religious as well as nationalist identity.

In 70 CE the Romans destroyed the Second Temple in Jerusalem and expelled its Jewish population. Jews scattered throughout the world. Although many assimilated into the countries of their diaspora, they retained their faith and Jewish identity. Each year, Jews across the world conclude the Passover ceremonies with the determined wish, "Next Year in Jerusalem." The prophetic idea of an eventual gathering of all Jewish exiles into the land of their origin has influenced the attitudes of Westerners, Jewish as well as Christian, toward Jerusalem. The repeated assertion by Israeli leaders that a united Jerusalem is the eternal capital of Israel is an articulation of this biblical belief translated into a political vision. For 2,000 years, Jews have nursed the idea of returning to reclaim Jerusalem.

For Christians, Jerusalem is the site of their faith's origins and early history, where Jesus preached his message, was crucified, died, and was buried. It was there that in Christian belief Jesus was miraculously resurrected from the grave and ascended into heaven. The religious significance of Jerusalem was translated into the political when Pope Urban II summoned the First Crusade to recover Jerusalem and establish a Christian kingdom there.

Christian political interest in Jerusalem was manifest more recently in the British mandate over Palestine and in continuing U.S. support for Israel. Christian groups and institutions such as the World Council of Churches and the Vatican have also maintained keen interest in the status of Jerusalem. At the same time, Jerusalem and Palestine continue to be the home of Arab Christians, who have lived there for centuries. It is also significant to the many Christians who make pilgrimages to the historical Christian churches and sites in Jerusalem.

Jerusalem is one of the three most sacred places of Islam. It was the first city to which Muslims turned in prayer (subsequently changed to Mecca), and in Muslim belief, it is the place from which the Prophet Muhammad ascended to the heavens (miraj haqq) on a winged horse. According to Muslim eschatology (an aspect of theology that addresses the final events of human history), Jerusalem is the place where the end of time commences. Today, the loss of control of Jerusalem indicates to Muslims their ultimate defeat in what many regard as the unending Crusades launched by Christians against Islam. Failure to regain sovereignty over Jerusalem, they believe, is indicative of the decline of Islamic civilization and the failure of Palestinian aspirations to decolonize their land.

Jerusalem has also become a symbol of Western imperialism for many Muslims who see the continued expansion of Israel as a Western plot to dominate their lands and destroy Islam. They fear that under Israeli rule, Islam's third most important mosque (al-Aqsa/Bait-ul-Maqdis) will eventually be destroyed. Indeed some Jewish religious leaders and groups have expressed plans to rebuild the temple of King Solomon on that very site. The continued settlement of Jews in Arab East Jerusalem and the forced evacuation of Palestinians, both Christian and Muslim, have only reinforced Muslim fears.

Finally, the myth of supersession shared by Christians and Muslims further complicates things. Much as Christians have seen themselves as inheritors of Judaism who supersede or replace Judaism with a new and more complete revelation—Christianity—so Muslims see themselves as the inheritors of Judaism and Christianity. They believe that Islam is a continuation and completion of Abraham's faith and that the Quran is the final revelation sent by the same God who sent his revelations through Moses and Jesus. In that same vein, many believe that they are the true inheritors of the Holy Land, symbolized by the conquest of Jerusalem by Umar ibn al-Khattab, the second of the "Rightly Guided Caliphs," in 637 CE.

The situation became more complicated in contemporary times. In 1948, the status of Jerusalem became a global issue when, in the aftermath of the Holocaust, the United Nations partitioned Palestine to create the state of Israel as a homeland for the Jews.

The struggle for Jerusalem is indeed representative of the intersection of religion and politics in the Middle East, now with global ramifications. It is in Jerusalem that the temporal, spiritual, political, cultural, and territorial converge. Jerusalem is both modern and traditional. It is modern in its status as the aspiration of Jewish and Palestinian nationalism, and it is traditional in its sacred significance to three religions. For many there can be no political solution for Jerusalem without a religious solution. In Israel, where some forms of Zionism fuse religion and nationalism, the modern and the traditional are not distinguishable; neither are the religious and the political.

A particular reading of postcolonial history created the false expectation that the Middle East was well on the way toward secularization. History is not progressing according to the script that modernity had envisaged for the region. Religion has once again become a major theme in the study of world politics, particularly in the context of the Middle East. Rather than receding, religion has returned to the center stage. The region is developing both in political as well as economic terms, but not along the lines that Western social sciences had predicted. The long history of the nexus between power and religion and current conditions in the Middle East suggests that Western-style secularism will continue to be challenged by the contemporary religious resurgence.

In recent years, new Islamic republics have been declared in Iran, Sudan, and Afghanistan. In Morocco, as in Saudi Arabia, the monarchy is strongly legitimized by its close association with Islam. In Jordan, King Hussein never forgot to mention his lineage, which he traced back to the Prophet Muhammad. Muslim rulers remain acutely sensitive to the power of religion, and opposition movements also appeal to Islam for legitimacy and popular support.

Similarly, Israel's very existence and identity remains tied to Judaism. Many believers base their political agenda on issues and sites that their faith holds sacred. Whether to defend the status quo or to condemn it, politicians in the Middle East, Jews as well as Muslims, invoke religious categories. The difference between the role of religion in contemporary politics, in politics in the precolonial past, and in politics in the postcolonial secular era has been one of degree, not of kind.

In the twenty-first century, religion will continue to be a major driving force in global politics. It performs many political functions, just as politics serves many religious functions in the traditional land of God, the Middle East. Religion is a source of identity as well as signification, providing symbols of authentication and meaning for social and political existence. It is the basis for states as well as a source of civil society. It is invoked to give legitimacy to systems and regimes and to provide revolutionary fodder to challenge the legitimacy of states, systems, and regimes. Jerusalem represents the locus where all three Abrahamic faiths have come together in the past and remains the subject of common and at times competing claims. The challenge for the religious politics of the Middle East in coming years, as with the issue of Jerusalem, will be to develop a pluralistic mode of existence based on the recognition of shared principles, values, and interests amid acknowledged religious and political differences.

Adapted from "Religion in the Middle East," (with Muqtedar Khan). In Deborah J. Gerner, (ed.) *Understanding the Contemporary Middle East* (Boulder, CO: Lynne Rienner, 1999).

The existence of the state of Israel represents for many Jews a redemption from two thousand years of powerlessness and exile in which Jews were dependent on the benevolence of others for their existence. The state of Israel represents, for Jews, a new age of politics and power and the ability to protect themselves in a world that has too often been bent upon either subjugating or destroying them. As Jews enter the twenty-first century they continue to struggle to find a way to live constructively with their own diversity in the Diaspora and to maintain the autonomy of the state of Israel, while seeking a just and lasting peace in the Middle East.

CONCLUSION

What we learn from the study of the diverse ways of being Jewish is that religion can either reject the secular or can accommodate it. What form shall the life of the people Israel take in the modern world? That is the issue being debated among Jews as they move into the future. Those like the ultra-Orthodox who reject the secular, see religion as being about a sacred, eternal, and unchangeable way of life that must not be profaned by accommodation with the world. Consequently they are segregationists. The ultra-Orthodox, like fundamentalists everywhere, see modern secular society as profane—a contradiction of the true sacred order of things embodied in its premodern forms. All modern and post-modern/post-Holocaust religious forms of Judaism, by contrast, see the holy and the secular not as opposites so much as complementary, and they tend to see historical change as the medium through which God reveals himself in time.

For modernist and post-Holocaust Jews, knowledge of the historical development of Judaism (in varying degrees) became an inherent component in their self-understanding and has made it possible for each to admit new levels of diversity and change into the tradition. The difference between the modernist forms of Judaism and the post-Holocaust, postcolonial Judaism of Holocaust and Redemption is that the modernist forms (Reformed, Conservative, and Orthodox) tend to see diversity as competition, in which one is right and others are wrong, whereas the Judaism of Holocaust and Redemption sees Jewish diversity as complementary. The ultra-Orthodox, by contrast, see diversity as apostasy and insist that they can only be the true Israel by segregating themselves from the non-Jewish modern world and from all forms of Judaism that compromise with that world.

For most ultra-Orthodox, to admit any change is to admit relativism and with it unbelief. Therefore, Jews must turn back to the fundamental truths and practices of premodern Judaism to truly be Israel. For modernist and post-Holocaust Jews, to admit change is a matter of intellectual integrity. They argue that time cannot be stopped, that some change is inevitable, as is some integration of a Jewish way of life with the surrounding world. They disagree only over how much of each is permissible, with the Orthodox at one end of the scale and secular Judaisms at the other end of the scale. For some (Reform, Conservative, Holocaust, and Redemption), God is found revealing himself in the continued unfolding of history. For others (ethnicists, socialists, and Zionists), the meaning is to be found not in the God of history but in the history itself. Such "secular" Jews are not "religious" in the traditional sense of biblical theism, but they do display one type of religious behavior commonly found in the history of religions—reverence for the ways of the ancestors, ways that are held sacred.

All but the ultra-Orthodox are convinced that the way of Judaism does not require Jews to go back but to go forward. The strength of the modern/postmodern forms of Judaism is in their ability to adapt Jewish life to new environments and situations. The strength of the Orthodox and ultra-Orthodox is in challenging those who would adapt to not sacrifice the heart of Jewish religious existence as a people—God, Torah, and Israel. They would argue that history and Jewish ethnicity are not an adequate substitute.

The adventure continues as Jews everywhere wrestle with each other and the world around them over what it means to be a Jew—especially in the state of Israel where some accommodation both among Jews and with their Christian and Muslim neighbors must be found if there is ever to be peace. And yet the very struggle of Jews everywhere, whether secular or religious, among themselves and with the non-Jewish world around them, is very Jewish. We need only recall the story of how Jacob's name was changed to Israel in the Book of Genesis (32:23–32). For Jacob wrestled with the stranger who would not give Jacob his name but instead blessed Jacob and changed Jacob's name to Israel, meaning "he who has wrestled with God and human beings and prevails." Throughout history, the drama of Judaism has been to wrestle with God and the stranger. Today, whether secular or religious, Jews are still deeply shaped by the stories of Israel, they still wrestle with the stranger, and they still prevail.

DISCUSSION QUESTIONS

1. At what point in history did the fundamental pattern of Jewish experience emerge and what shape did it take? Give two examples from the history of Judaism, one secular and one religious.

2. What are the issues that separate premodern from modern and postmodern or post-Holocaust forms of Judaism, and how do they exemplify the fundamentalist-modernist debate?

3. How does the history of anti-Judaism in Western Christianity and Western civilization relate to the Holocaust, and what was the impact of the Holocaust on the shape of modern and postmodern forms of Jewish life, religious and secular?

4. In what ways have secular forms of Judaism transformed the shape of contemporary religious forms of Judaism? Give examples and explain.

5. What is the Judaism of Holocaust and Redemption and how does it relate to modern and premodern forms of Judaism? Also, why might it be seen as the alternative to ultra-Orthodoxy?

6. What does it mean to say that Judaism is a form of the myth of history? Give examples from both the biblical and postbiblical periods.

7. What is the Talmud and what is its significance for the religion of Judaism?

8. Compare and contrast Enlightenment Judaism (*Haskalah*) and Hasidic Judaism. To what Christian movements are they similar? Explain.

9. It has been said that Judaism is a religion focused more on sanctification than on salvation. Explain what this means and give examples by contrast with Christianity.

10. Whom would you nominate as the three most important postbiblical figures in the history of Judaism, and why?

11. Is Zionism a secular form of Judaism or a religious form, or both? Explain, with historical examples.

KEY TERMS

Aggadah	Halakhah	Sephardi
Ashkenazi	Haredim	Shema
Bar Mitzvah	Hasidism	synagogue
Bat Mitzvah	Israel	Talmud
Circumcision	kosher	Tanak
covenant	Kabbalah	tannaim
Diaspora	Marrano	temple
dual Torah	Mishnah	Tzedakah
Gemara	Mitzvot	Zionism
Gentile	rabbinic	Zohar

SUGGESTED READING

Shlomo Ben-Ami, *Scars of War, Wounds of Peace: The Israeli-Arab Tragedy* (Oxford: Oxford University Press, 2005).

Gilles Kepel, *The Revenge of God: The Resurgence of Islam, Christianity and Judaism in the Modern World* (Pennsylvania State University Press, 1994).

Bruce B. Lawrence, *Defenders of God: The Fundamentalist Revolt Against the Modern Age* (Columbia: University of South Carolina Press, 1995).

Mark Juergensmeyer, *Terror in the Mind of God* (Berkeley: University of California Press, 2000).

Dennis Ross, *The Missing Peace: The Inside Story of the Fight for Middle East Peace* (New York: Farrar, Straus and Giroux, 2004).

Ronald H. Isaacs and Kerry M. Olitzky, eds., *Critical Documents of Jewish History: A Source Book* (London: Jason Aronson, 1995).

Paul Johnson, *A History of the Jews* (New York: Harper & Row, 1987).

Emil Fackenheim, *What is Judaism?* (New York: Summit Books, 1987).

Irving Greenberg, *The Jewish Way* (New York: Summit Books, 1988).

Jacob Neusner, *The Death and Birth of Judaism* (New York: Basic Books, 1987).

———. *Self-fulfilling Prophecy: Exile and Return in the History of Judaism* (Boston: Beacon Press, 1987).

NOTES

1. Jacob Neusner, *The Death and Birth of Judaism* (New York: Basic Books, 1987), p. 116.

2. Elie Wiesel, *A Jew Today* (New York: Random House, 1978), pp.146, 148.

3. Schlomo Ben-Ami, *Scars of War, Wounds of Peace: The Israeli-Arab Tragedy* (Oxford: Oxford University Press, 2005).

4. Ben-Ami, p. 313.

5. Ben-Ami, pp. 270-272.

CHAPTER FOUR

THE GLOBALIZATION OF ISLAM AND MUSLIMS

Overview

"Allahu Akbar.... There is no God but God. Come to prayer...." Five times each day, Muslims throughout the world, in Algiers and Mindanao, in London and Paris, Bosnia and New York, are called to prayer. Shops are closed; office workers adjourn to a prayer room; professionals and laborers simply stop what they are doing and face Mecca to worship God.

On the streets of Cairo, Geneva, Kuala Lumpur, and Jakarta, Muslim women walk, some in stylish Islamic dress, some in dresses and veils that cover their faces and bodies. They join others adorned in Western fashions. While educated Muslim women in some sex-segregated countries are not visible in the work place, in other countries they work as engineers, doctors, scientists, teachers, and lawyers alongside their male colleagues. All of these realities reflect the vitality and diversity of Muslim societies today.

Across the Muslim world in recent years, Muslim activists have marched beneath banners declaring that "Islam is the solution" or "The Quran is our constitution," as they press for the implementation of religion in state and society. Members of Islamic organizations have been elected to parliaments in Turkey, Algeria, Jordan, Egypt, Kuwait, Yemen, Pakistan, Thailand, and Malaysia. They have served in cabinet-level positions and as elected mayors and city councilors in Turkey and Israel and Malaysia. Other Islamic activists are elected officials in professional associations of doctors, lawyers, engineers, journalists, and teachers.

In the slums and many lower-middle-class neighborhoods of Cairo and Algiers, Beirut and Mindanao, the West Bank and Gaza, families that cannot afford state services, or who live under governments that do not provide adequate social services, utilize inexpensive and efficient educational, legal, and medical services provided by Islamic associations.

In September 2001, terrorists attacked New York's World Trade Center and the Pentagon in Washington, D.C. The hijackers who committed these acts reflected a religious radicalism that has threatened many regimes in the Muslim world and Western governments. Post 9/11 in Egypt, Morocco, Iraq, Saudi Arabia, Israel/Palestine, Pakistan, Indonesia, Spain, and England, extremists have been claiming credit for suicide bombings, bombings, kidnappings, and beheadings that kill and maim "the enemies of God" (Muslims and non-Muslims alike) as they attempt to destabilize and overthrow "atheist governments" in what they regard as a global jihad.

The images and realities of Islam and of Muslims are indeed multiple and diverse. This chapter will look at the globalization of Islam and Muslims in terms of faith, politics, and international affairs. It will discuss and analyze the struggles and debates within the Muslim community in defining the meaning of Islam for modern and postmodern life. Thus the history, tradition, and heritage of Islam will be discussed in the context of its significance and impact on Muslim life and society as well as on world events today.

The study of Islam and globalization, yesterday and today, is a fascinating trip across time and space. It requires a bridging of the gap between religion, history, politics, and culture. Let us begin by briefly answering the question: What is Islam and where is the Islamic world?

The word *islam* means submission or surrender. A Muslim is one who submits, who seeks to follow and actualize God's will in history, both as an individual and as a member of a worldwide faith community. Muslims believe that God has given the earth as a trust to humankind and thus see themselves as God's representatives (Q. 2:30, 6:165) with a divinely mandated vocation to establish God's rule on earth. The Muslim community (*ummah*) is a transnational community of believers, God ordained and guided, that is to spread and institutionalize an Islamic Order, to create a socially just society: "You are the best community ever brought forth for mankind, enjoining what is good and forbidding evil" (Q. 3:110).

Islam belongs to the family of great monotheistic faiths, the children of Abraham: Judaism, Christianity, and Islam. Jews and Christians trace their genealogy to Abraham through Sara and her son Isaac; Muslims represent the other branch of the family, which descends from Abraham's son Ismail, and his mother Hagar. While specific and significant differences exist, all three faiths share a belief in the one, transcendent God, creator, sustainer, and ruler of the universe. All believe in angels, Satan, prophets, revelation, moral responsibility and accountability, divine judgment, and eternal reward or punishment. Thus, for Muslims, Islam is the fulfillment and completion of earlier revelations.

Islam is the second largest and one of the fastest growing of the world's religions. Its more than 1.2 billion followers can be found in some fifty-six countries, extending from North Africa to Southeast Asia, and encompass many peoples, races, languages, ethnic groups, tribes, and cultures (see Map 4.1). Because Islam has often been equated simply with the Arabs (only about 20% of the worldwide Muslim community), few realize that the vast majority of Muslims live in non-Arab (Asian and African) societies: Indonesia, Bangladesh, Pakistan, India, and Nigeria. Islam's presence and impact extend beyond what is often referred to as the Islamic world (countries where the majority of the population is Muslim). In recent years, Islam has become a visible presence in the West as the second- or third-largest religion in Europe (in particular, in France, Germany, and England) and in America. Today the capitals or major cities of Islam are not only exotic-sounding places like Cairo, Damascus, Baghdad, Mecca, Islamabad, and Kuala Lumpur, but also London, Paris, Marseilles, Brussels, New York, Detroit, and Los Angeles. However, despite the size, global presence, and significance of the Islamic community, myths, stereotypes, and misinformation about Islam and Muslims continue to abound.

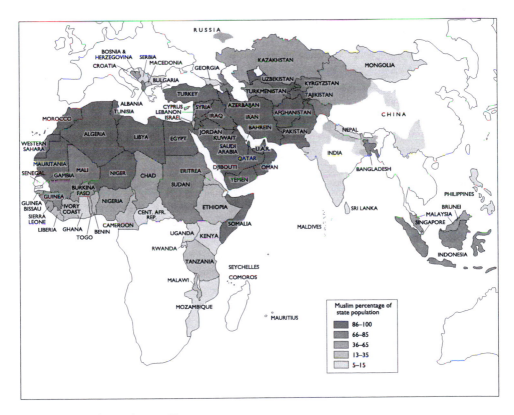

Map 4.1 The Muslim World.

A dynamic religion that interfaces and at times competes with other faiths, Islam has had a significant impact upon world affairs. In contrast to the modern secular belief in the separation of church and state, Islam for many Muslims represents a more comprehensive world view in which religion and society, faith and power, have been and are more closely bound and intertwined. From the creation of the first Muslim community in seventh-century Arabia to contemporary times, Muslims have debated and sought to implement God's will in their personal as well as public lives, in their families as well as states and societies. Thus, throughout much of history, to be a Muslim was not simply to belong to a faith community or place of worship but to live in an Islamic community-state, governed (in theory if not always in practice) by Islamic law. Muslims see their religion as much more than a personal faith. Historically, Islam has significantly formed and informed politics and civilization, giving rise to vast Islamic empires and states as well as Islamic civilization.

From Islam's origins to the present, Muslims have been engaged in a continuous process of understanding and interpreting, defining, redefining, and applying Islam to the realities of life. The process is one of the Word of God (Quran) being mediated (interpreted and applied) through the words of human beings. The development of Islamic law, theology, and mysticism reflects this complex process. Religious doctrines, laws, and practices result not only from clear prescriptions in sacred texts but also from fallible, limited interpreters, whose conclusions reflect their intelligence, political and social contexts, and customs as well as issues of power and privilege. For example, the fact that interpreters and guardians of Islam were males living in patriarchal (male-dominated) societies naturally affected the development of Islamic law and thought, especially its impact on women and the family. Of equal importance, Islamic doctrines and laws developed in response to the political and social questions and issues that arose in the first centuries of Islamic history. Thus, while it is correct to say that there is one Islam, revealed in the Quran and the traditions of the Prophet, as we shall now see, Islamic tradition and heritage reveal the extent to which there have been many interpretations of Islam, some complementing each other, others in conflict.

Muslims today, like other religious believers, struggle with the relationship of their religious tradition to modernity and postmodernity. How does a faith revealing and embodying a God-centered universe relate and speak to a modern, post-Enlightenment human-centered world whose primary criteria are often reason and science? Like Judaism and Christianity, Muslims contend with questions about the relationship of Islamic faith and belief to science and technology on a range of issues from evolution, birth control, artificial insemination, and transplants to ecology, nuclear energy, and chemical warfare. A faith that inspired the creation of vast Islamic empires and sultanate states with a rich Islamic civilization now faces existing and redefining itself and its role in a predominantly modern, secular world. What is the relationship of

Islam to secularization—should Islam today be restricted to personal life or should it be integral to the state, law, and society? At issue are questions regarding the compatibility of Islam and modern forms of political participation such as democracy; secularism, or the separation of religion and politics; human rights; and the status of religious minorities, non-Muslims, and women.

Another set of concerns relate to the relationship of the Islamic world to the non-Islamic world, or, in its sometimes more contentious formulation, the relationship of Islam to the West. If many in the West see Islam and Muslim-Christian relations through the stereotype of jihad and religious extremism, many in the Muslim world see a militant Judeo-Christian West confronting them in a series of successive Crusades. Thus, Western images of a militant Islam are countered by Muslim charges that the real culprit is a militant Judeo-Christian tradition, witnessed in history from the Christian-initiated Crusades and Inquisition to European colonialism and American neocolonialism. Critics of U.S. actions in the Muslim world condemn "anti-Muslim" policies: the creation of Israel, support for authoritarian Arab and Muslim regimes during the cold war and post–cold war, a failure of nerve and will in Bosnia, support for Russia's occupation of Chechnya, and (what they charge is) a bias toward Israel in the Palestinian-Israeli conflict and toward Indian rule over a Muslim majority population in the conflict in Kashmir, and, finally, a propensity to equate Islam with radicalism and extremism. These issues have been reflected by what some on both sides perceive as an "Islamic threat," or an impending clash of civilizations or global confrontation between Islamic countries and the West.

In recent years the question of Islam *and* the West has been joined by that of Islam *in* the West. The presence and growth of significant Muslim populations in America and Europe have required Muslims to address a host of questions and problems, many of which are related to the issue of assimilation. What does it mean to live as a Muslim minority in a non-Muslim majority state in which the *Shariah* (Islamic law) plays no role? Muslims have had to struggle not only to overcome stereotypes arising from the Iranian Revolution of 1978–1979, and subsequent acts of hostage taking and terrorism, but also to gain recognition and respect for their faith and its practice as citizens in the West. American society, however officially secular, recognizes Christian and Jewish Sabbaths (Sunday and Saturday, respectively) and celebrates holy days as holidays (Christmas, Easter, Yom Kippur). An equal recognition of other faiths still does not exist. Muslims have had to seek accommodation for their Friday congregational prayer, celebration of holy days, and respect for women who wear headscarves. They have struggled to open mosques and schools in communities that sometimes have been resistant, and to introduce Muslim chaplains into the armed forces and prisons. They have fought to have their dietary requirements (no alcohol, pork, or foods cooked with certain products) recognized. Like Jews who keep kosher, many Muslims will only eat meat that has been killed in a religiously observant manner. They cannot eat foods prepared in or with non-*halal*, or *haram* ("forbidden") substances (lard, sauces, gravies). This has meant the need to open halal restaurants, meat markets, and stores.

ENCOUNTER WITH MODERNITY: THE CHALLENGE OF WESTERN COLONIALISM

The Islamic world has witnessed a protracted period of upheaval and renewal since the nineteenth century, as Muslims have struggled with the impact of European colonialism; the creation of modern Muslim nation states; the superpower rivalry between America and the Soviet Union; the failures and challenges of their societies; and the religious, intellectual, and moral challenges of rapid change and globalization.

By the nineteenth century, a clear shift of power occurred as the decline of Muslim fortunes reversed the relationship of Islam to the West. The map of the Muslim world in the twentieth century revealed the extent of foreign dominance and Muslim subordination to Europe: the French in North, West, and Equatorial Africa and the Levant (Lebanon and Syria); the British in Palestine, Transjordan, Iraq, the Arabian Gulf, and the Indian subcontinent; and in Southeast Asia, the British in Malaya (Malaysia, Singapore, and Brunei) and the Dutch in Indonesia.

Muslims found themselves on the defensive in the face of a European expansion that constituted a singular challenge to Islam and Muslims, religiously, politically, economically, and culturally. European imperialism threatened both Muslim political and religiocultural identity and history. The impact of Western rule and modernization raised new questions and challenged time-honored beliefs and practices. The political crisis precipitated by European colonialism was accompanied by a spiritual crisis. Colonialism was experienced as a threat to Muslim faith and identity. Implicit in its policies and explicit in the statements of many government officials and missionaries was the belief that Europe's expansion and domination was due to its inherent Christian cultural superiority. Muslim views of the West and their responses to its power and ideas varied from rejection and confrontation to admiration and imitation.

Islamic modernist reform movements responded to the intellectual and political challenge of Western hegemony. Reformers sought to rejuvenate and restore the pride, identity, and strength of a debilitated Islamic community by attempting to bridge the gap between their Islamic heritage and modernity. They emphasized the compatibility of Islam with reason, science, and technology and the need to reinterpret (*ijtihad*) Islam in light of the new questions and issues that were brought by their encounter with modernity. However, Islamic modernism remained primarily attractive only to an intellectual elite and failed to produce a systematic reinterpretation of Islam or develop effective organizations to preserve and propagate its reformist message. This failure led to the emergence of modern Islamic organizations (sometimes referred to as fundamentalist movements): the Muslim Brotherhood in the Middle East and the *Jamaat-i-Islami* (The Islamic Society) in South Asia. Both criticized secular elites for simply emulating the West and Islamic reformers for westernizing Islam. Instead they proclaimed the self-sufficiency of Islam to generate its own, alternative path and responses to the demands of modern life. In particular, they condemned the tendency of most Muslim countries to uncritically adapt Western models of development and thus Westernize Muslim societies. Islam, they asserted, offers an alternative to capitalism and communism/socialism; it is a total, comprehensive way of life. These movements and their many offshoots, from mainstream social and political organizations to radical revolutionary groups, remain major forces in promoting responses to the encounter with modernity and postmodernity.

During the post–World War II era, most of the Muslim world had regained its independence. However, modern nation-states like Syria, Sudan, Jordan, Iraq, Kuwait, Malaysia, and Pakistan were artificially carved out by their former European colonial rulers, who drew their artificial boundaries. Many rulers were appointed by colonial governments or seized power. As a result, much of the Muslim world has witnessed a legacy of autocratic rulers (kings, military, and ex-military) rather than elected governments. Questions regarding the political legitimacy of rulers and issues of national identity/unity have plagued many of these nations to this day and resulted in governments that have relied heavily on military/security forces and outside powers (America, Europe, and the former Soviet Union) for control and stability. Because the West provided the models for development, the presupposition and expectation was that modernization and progress were dependent upon westernization and secularization. Iran's Islamic revolution of 1978–1979 shattered this assumption.

Although Iran drew attention to the reassertion and power of Islam in society, in fact Islam had been reasserting itself in Muslim politics for more than a decade before the Iranian revolution in Egypt, Libya, and Pakistan. The crushing military defeat of combined Arab forces by Israel in the Six Day war in 1967 and the loss of major territories (the Sinai, West Bank, and Gaza, the Golan Heights, and especially Jerusalem, the third holiest city of Islam) was chronicled as "*the* disaster" in Muslim literature and consciousness. This key event triggered a period of doubt and self-examination. The early and rapid expansion of Islam as faith and empire from Africa to Asia and its continued success and power until the rise of European colonialism were attributed to God's guidance and pleasure with the Islamic community. However, modern Muslim history revealed a record of failure. Despite national independence, most Muslim countries remained weak, underdeveloped, and dependent upon the West. To those who asked what had gone wrong, many responded that

Muslim failure resulted from abandoning their God-ordained path and mission. To regain their past power and glory, many Muslims believed that they must now return to the straight path of Islam. The 1973 Arab oil embargo and Iran's Islamic revolution seemed to many to signal the vindication of this position, a return of Muslim economic and political power as a result of the contemporary resurgence of Islam in Muslim politics and society.

During the late 1960s and 1970s, Islam enjoyed a higher profile in personal and public life: greater attention to religious observances (increased attendance at mosques and observance of the fast of Ramadan, more concern with matters of Islamic dress and family values, etc.); the growth of Islamic banks, publishing houses, schools, hospitals; more governments as well as opposition parties appealing to Islam for legitimacy and to mobilize popular support. Despite their differences, an array of Muslim rulers during the 1970s and 1980s found it expedient to turn to Islam in politics: Egypt's Anwar Sadat, Libya's Muammar Qaddafi, Sudan's Jafer Numeiri, Pakistan's Zulfikar Ali Bhutto and General Zia ul-Haq. At the same time Islamic activist organizations mushroomed in number and size throughout the Muslim world. Alongside Islamic organizations like the Muslim Brotherhood in Egypt, Syria, Jordan, and Sudan, there were violent revolutionary organizations with names like the *Jund Allah* (Army of God), *Hezbollah* (the party of God), and Jihad (Holy War).

The 1980s were dominated by fear of Iran's export of its "Islamic Fundamentalist Revolution." Disturbances in Saudi Arabia, Kuwait, and Bahrain and Iran's strong backing of a Shii group, Hizbollah, in Lebanon's civil war, as well as the assassination of Egypt's President Anwar Sadat fed the fears of nervous Muslim rulers and the West. However, no other "Irans" occurred. Yet by the late 1980s and 1990s it was increasingly clear that a quiet (nonviolent) revolution had occurred. Islamic revivalism and activism had in many contexts become institutionalized. From North Africa to Southeast Asia, Islam played an increasingly more visible and important role in the socioeconomic and political life of mainstream society: schools, clinics, hospitals, day care, legal aid, youth centers, disaster relief, banks and other financial institutions, and electoral politics.

In the twenty-first century, Islamic activists and parties are a significant factor in electoral politics in countries as diverse as Egypt, Algeria, Sudan, Lebanon, Jordan, Turkey, Pakistan, Malaysia, Indonesia, and Central Asia. Many authoritarian rulers and secular-oriented elites have experienced the power of religion in Muslim politics through ballots as well as bullets. Islam has become a powerful force in confronting modernity and postmodernity.

Change is a reality in contemporary Islam and in Muslim societies. It may be found at every level and across social classes. The question or issue is not change but the pace and direction of change, not whether there should be any change but, rather, how much change and what kinds of change are necessary and permissible?

In contrast to the past, to speak of Islam in the twenty-first century is to speak not only of Islam *and* the West but also of Islam *in* the West. Islam is the fastest-growing religion in America and in Europe, the second-largest religion in France, Holland, Belgium, and Germany, and the third-largest in Britain and America. Even if Muslim immigration and the rate of conversions were not to increase, birthrates alone assure that Islam will replace Judaism as the second-largest religion in the United States. Integral to the experience of Muslims in America, like other religious or ethnic minorities before them, are questions of faith and identity: Are they Muslims in America or American Muslims? Can Muslims become part and parcel of a pluralistic American society without sacrificing or losing their identity? Can Muslims be Muslims in a non-Muslim state that is not governed by Islamc law? Is the American legal system capable of allowing for particular Muslim religious and cultural differences within the Constitution's broader universal claims?

In the West, it has sometimes been fashionable to speak of a post-Christian society, but for many Muslims, talk of a post-Islamic society is not relevant. The debate is not over whether religion has a place and role in society, but rather what kind of Islam or Islamic presence should exist. Understanding Islam today requires an appreciation of the full spectrum of Muslim responses to the modern world, from those who view Islam as a personal faith to others who wish to see it implemented more formally in state and society.

As Muslims face the challenges of the twenty-first century in their original homelands or in Europe and America, finding answers within historical tradition is a time-honored strategy. Throughout the ages, when Muslims have sought to define or redefine their lives Islamically, the starting point has always been an understanding of the past. As with many of the world's great religious traditions, the time of the founders provides the paradigm or model, the idealized time whose core events reveal the origins, meaning, and mission of the community—its principles and values. Thus, we need to go back in order to go forward, to learn about the history and development of Islam and the Muslim community in order to understand Islam's present as well as its future.

PREMODERN ISLAM: THE FORMATIVE ERA

Islam, like all of the world's religions, places great emphasis on its early formative history, the time of the Prophet Muhammad, the revelation of the Quran, and Muhammad's founding of the first community. Islam's formative period is often seen as the "best of times," a time when the most pristine and authentic Islamic community existed, a society that was to be emulated by future generations. Thus, Muslims today as in the past see their faith and purpose in the world through an idyllic paradigm or model to which all return for inspiration and guidance.

At the core of Muslim belief and faith are the messenger and the message; the two reveal God's will for humankind. As Christians look to Jesus and the New Testament, and Jews look to Moses and the Torah, Muslims regard Muhammad and the Quran as the final, perfect, and complete revelation. In addition, because of the remarkable success of Muhammad and the early Muslim community in spreading the faith of Islam and its rule, an idealized portrait of Islamic history and of Muslim rule became the model for success. They served as a common reference point by which later generations of reformers would measure, judge, and seek to restore their societies. Thus, it is critical to understand how and why Muhammad, the Quran, and the early Islamic community have been the primary sources for Muslim self-understanding, guidance, and reform today.

The foundations of Islam are belief in Allah, in his messenger, and in his message. Since God is transcendent (beyond our ordinary experience), Islam teaches that he cannot be known directly, but only through his messengers and revelations. Thus, Muhammad and the Quran, the final messenger and message, were pivotal to the formation and development of the Islamic tradition, its beliefs, laws, rituals, and social practices. Learning more about the messenger and message will increase our understanding of Islam today and our insights about the sources Muslims use to guide their lives in the twenty-first century.

Few observers in the sixth century would have predicted that Muhammad ibn Abdullah and central Arabia would come to play such pivotal roles in world history and world religions. Most would have seen the future impact of a young orphan raised in a vast desert region marked by tribal warfare and divisions and bounded by two great imperial powers, the Eastern Roman (Byzantine) and Persian (Sasanid) empires, as limited at best. And yet the force of Muhammad's personality and the message he brought from God would quite literally transform Arabia and have a significant impact on much of the world, past and present.

Because Muhammad saw himself as a religious reformer and not the founder of a new religion, it is important to understand the nature of pre-Islamic Arabian society and religion. Arabian society and religion were tribal in structure and organization. Individuals lived in extended families; several related families constituted a clan; a cluster of several clans comprised a tribe. The nature and structure of Arabian society was reflected in its religion. Allah (God), the transcendent creator and sustainer of the universe, was seen as the high god of a pantheon of tribal gods and goddesses who were believed to be more directly active in and relevant to everyday life. Each city or town had its divine patron/protectors and shrine. Tribal gods and goddesses were respected and feared rather than loved, the objects of rituals (sacrifice, prayer, and pilgrimage) and of supplication at local shrines. The tribal polytheism of Arabia was embodied in Mecca's *Kaaba* ("cube," a cube-shaped building) and center of pilgrimage, which housed the idols of 360 tribal gods.

MUHAMMAD: THE FINAL MESSENGER

No prophet has played a greater role in a world religion and in world politics than Muhammad. Both in his lifetime and throughout Muslim history down to the present, Muhammad ibn Abdullah has served as the ideal model for Muslim life, what some Muslims have called the "living Quran," that is, the embodiment in his behavior and words of God's will. He is viewed as the last or final prophet who brought the final revelation of God. He is so revered that the name Muhammad (or names derived from it—Ahmad, Mahmud) is the most common Muslim name. In some Muslim countries, every male child has the Prophet's name as one of his forenames. Thus, the Prophet and his example or *Sunnah* are central to Islam and Muslim belief and practice. Muhammad is not only the ideal political leader, statesman, merchant, judge, soldier, and diplomat but also the ideal husband, father, and friend. Muslims look to his example for guidance in all aspects of life: eating; fasting; praying; the treatment of a spouse, parents, and children; the creation of contracts; the waging of war; and the conduct of diplomacy.

Tribal polytheism was a very "this worldly" religion with little concern about or belief in an afterlife. Individual identity and rights were subordinated to tribal and family authority, affiliation, solidarity, and law. The key virtue, "manliness," included loyalty to family and protection of its members, bravery in battle, hospitality, and honor. There was little sense of meaning or accountability beyond this life, no moral responsibility and accountability beyond tribal and family honor—no belief in an afterlife, divine judgment, or reward or punishment in the next life. Justice was guaranteed and administered not by God but by the threat of group vengeance or retaliation by family or tribe.

Monotheism was not unknown in Arabia. Both Arab Christian and Jewish communities had long resided there. In addition, Jewish, Christian, and Zoroastrian traders regularly came to Mecca, the major commercial center, and Arab traders would have encountered Judaism and Christianity in their business trips throughout the Middle East. In addition, the Quran speaks of Arab monotheists, *hanifs*, descendants of Abraham (Ibrahim). However, monotheism's powerful appeal to the Arabs came only when the Prophet Muhammad received his message from Allah (Al Ilah, "the God"), a message that would change the lives of hundreds of millions of peoples throughout Arabia and beyond.

Muhammad ibn Abdullah (the son of Abdullah) was born in 570 in Arabia in the city of Mecca, a city of trade and pilgrimage. While there is a great deal of information about Muhammad's life after he received his "call" to be God's messenger, the portrait of his early years is drawn from history, legend, and Muslim belief.

Although born into the ruling tribe of Mecca, the Quraysh, Muhammad was among the "poorer cousins." Orphaned at an early age (his father Abd Allah died before his birth and his mother died when he was 6 years old) and raised by an uncle, Abu Talib, he was not among the privileged members of the Quraysh. Muhammad was employed in Mecca's thriving caravan business. At the age of twenty-five, he met and later married Khadijah, a wealthy forty-year-old widow for whom he worked as business manager, and to whom he was married for twenty-eight years, until her death. She was his strongest supporter and adviser, particularly during the early, difficult years after his call to prophethood. Muhammad and Khadijah had three sons (who died in infancy) and four daughters, the most famous of whom was Fatima, who married Ali, the fourth caliph of Islam.

By the age of thirty, Muhammad had become a prominent, respected member of Meccan society, known for his business acumen and trustworthiness (he was nicknamed al-Amin, the trustworthy). Reflective by temperament, Muhammad would often retreat to the quiet and solitude of Mount Hira to contemplate his life and society. It was here during the month of Ramadan in 610, on a night Muslims commemorate as "The Night of Power and Excellence," that Muhammad the caravan leader became Muhammad the messenger of God. Through a heavenly intermediary, later identified by tradition as the angel Gabriel, Muhammad at the age of forty received the first message or revelation: "Recite in the name of your lord who has created, Created man out of a germ cell. Recite, for your Lord is the most generous One, Who has taught by the pen, Taught man what he did not know."

Muhammad became a link in a long series of biblical prophets, messengers from God who served as a conscience to the community and as his messenger. Like Moses, who had received the Torah on Mount Sinai from the god of the Hebrews, Muhammad received the first of God's revelations on Mount Hira: "It is He who sent down to you the Book with the truth, confirming what went before it: and He sent down the Torah and the Injil ["Evangel," "Gospel"] before as a guidance to the people" (Q. 3:3). Also, like Amos and Jeremiah before him, Muhammad served as a "warner" from God who admonished his hearers to repent and obey God, for the final judgment was near:

> Say: "O Men I am only a warner." Those who believe, and do deeds of righteousness—theirs shall be forgiveness and generous provision. And those who strive against our signs to avoid them—they shall be inhabitants of Hell. (Q. 22:49–50)

Muhammad continued to receive revelations for more than two decades (610–632); together they constitute the text of the Quran (literally "the recitation or discourse").

The first ten years of Muhammad's preaching were difficult. At first he revealed his experience to his wife and close friends only. When he finally began to preach God's message, critiquing the status quo, he drew the ire of Mecca's prosperous and powerful political and commercial establishment. In the name of Allah, the one true God, Muhammad increasingly denounced polytheism and thus threatened the livelihood and revenues of those who profited enormously from the annual pilgrimage, which was the equivalent of a giant tribal convention. Equally problematic, Muhammad preached a message strong on issues of social justice, condemning the socioeconomic inequities of his time. The Prophet denounced false contracts, usury, and the exploitation of the poor, orphans, and widows. Muhammad claimed an authority and legitimacy, as God's prophet or spokesperson, that undermined Mecca's rich and powerful masters. He called all true believers to join the community of God, a universal community that transcended tribal bonds and authority, a community led by Muhammad, not by the Quraysh.

As Muhammad continued to preach his message, the situation in Mecca became more difficult. The persecution of the Muslims turned violent:

> Then the Quraysh showed their enmity to all who followed the Apostle; every clan which contained Muslims attacked them [the Muslims], beating them, allowing them no food or drink, exposing them to the burning heat of Mecca, so as to seduce them from their religion. Some gave way under pressure of persecution, and others resisted them, being protected by God.... [1]

After ten years of rejection and persecution in Mecca, Muhammad and his followers migrated to Yathrib, later renamed Medina, "city" of the Prophet, in 622. Invited to serve as arbiter or judge, for Muslim and non-Muslim alike, Muhammad became the religious and political leader of the community. Medina proved a new beginning, as the Muslim community prospered and grew.

The emigration (*hijra*) from Mecca to Medina in 622 was a turning point in Muhammad's life and in Islamic history. Its central significance and that of the community in Islam can be seen in the fact that when Muslims devised their own calendar, they dated theirs not from the birth of the Prophet or from the first revelation but from the creation of the Islamic community at Medina. Thus, 622 CE became 1 AH, "After the Hijra." This act reinforced the meaning of Islam as realization of God's will on earth and the centrality of the Islamic community (*ummah*). Thus, Muslims, then and now, believe Islam is a world religion, a global community of believers with a universal message and mission.

Muhammad did not create a new religion; he was not the founder of a religion but a prophet and reformer. His message proclaimed monotheism, the unity (*tawhid*) or oneness of God. Polytheism or association (*shirk*) of anything with God, putting anything in place of the one, true God, was condemned and suppressed. While Arabian polytheism was ignorant of and violated the doctrine of tawhid, Muslims believe that over time the Jewish and Christian communities distorted the original revelation. Therefore, Muhammad and the Quran were a corrective, a restoration of the true faith (*iman*) and message of God to an ignorant, deviant society. One final time, God had sent Muhammad, the last or "seal" (*khatam*) of the prophets (Q. 33:40), and the Quran, the complete, uncorrupted revelation. All were called by Muhammad to repentance, to turn away from the path of unbelief and false practice and toward the straight path (*sharia*) of God.

Muhammad taught that submission (*islam*) to God was both an individual and community obligation. For in contrast to past primary identification with a tribe, Islam now was to be the primary source of community (*ummah*) identification and solidarity that transcended all other loyalties and bonds. This belief was reinforced by the Quran's emphasis on social justice and the social welfare and protection of the rights of women, orphans, and the poor. Muhammad rejected some rituals and introduced others; he also reformed others, reinterpreting Arab pagan and Jewish rituals. The annual pre-Islamic Arabian pilgrimage to the Kaaba at Mecca was reinterpreted. The Kaaba was cleansed of its 360 polytheistic tribal idols and rededicated to Allah for whom, Muslims believe, it was originally built by Abraham and his son Ismail. Pilgrimage to the Kaaba in Mecca, like prayer five times each day, was reformulated and became one of the Five Pillars, or required practices, in Islam.

During the short decade that Muhammad led the community at Medina, he, in light of continuing revelations, defined its mandate and mission. He forged its identity, consolidated its political base, and established its basic religious law and practice.

The tribes of Arabia were called to submit to Allah and his Prophet. Both force and diplomacy were employed skillfully by Muhammad to defeat the Meccans and subsequently to unite the tribes of Arabia under the banner of Islam. In 624 Muhammad and his followers successfully engaged and defeated the far greater forces of Mecca at the battle of Badr. For Muslims, then and now, this battle has special significance. It was a "miraculous" defeat against overwhelming odds. It pitted the forces of Allah, of monotheism, against those of Meccan polytheism, the army of God against the forces of unbelief. The Quran itself tells of God's sanction and assistance (8:42ff. and 3:123) in victory. Quranic witness of divine guidance and intervention made Badr a sacred symbol that has been remembered, commemorated, and used throughout history. The 1973 war between Egypt and Israel was given the code name "Operation Badr" by President Anwar Sadat in an attempt to use Islamic symbols and slogans to inspire and motivate his forces.

After a series of battles—Badr, Uhud (625) in which the Meccans were triumphant, and the "Battle of the Ditch" (627), in which the Muslims routed the Meccans—a truce was struck at Hudaybiyah. In 630, charging that the Meccans had broken the truce, Muhammad led an army of ten thousand strong; the Meccans surrendered without a fight. Muhammad rejected vengeance or plunder and instead granted amnesty to his former enemies. The majority of the Meccans converted to Islam, accepted Muhammad's leadership, and became part of the Islamic community.

In his early preaching, Muhammad had looked to Jews and Christians as natural allies. As "People of the Book" who had been sent prophets and revelation, they had much in common with Muslims and so he anticipated the approval and acceptance of Islam by the Jews of Medina. Muhammad initially presented himself to the Jews of Arabia as a prophetic reformer reestablishing the religion of Abraham. However, the Jewish tribes of Medina, who had lived there a long time and had political ties with the Quraysh of Mecca, were resistant. While the majority of tribes converted to Islam, Medina's three Jewish tribes, half the population of Medina, did not. At first, Muslims had faced Jerusalem to pray and, like the Jews, fasted on the tenth day (Ashura) of the lunar month. However, when the Jews rejected his claims and proved resistant to conversion, Muhammad received a revelation and changed the direction of prayer from Jerusalem to Mecca. From this point on, Islam was presented as a distinct alternative to Judaism.

Because Muslims encountered and had to live with other believers, Muhammad promulgated the Constitution of Medina that set out the rights and duties of all citizens and the relationship of the Muslim community to other communities. Jews were recognized as a separate community, politically allied to the Muslims, but retaining their internal religious and cultural autonomy. However, political loyalty and allegiance were expected. The Jews' denial of Muhammad's prophethood and message and their ties with the Meccans became a source of conflict. The Quran accuses the Jewish tribes of regularly breaking treaties: "Why is it that whenever they make pacts, a group among them casts it aside unilaterally?" (2:100). After each major battle between the Muslims and Meccans, one of the Jewish tribes was accused of such acts, leading first to exile and finally to warfare. In the end, Muhammad moved to crush the remaining Jews in Medina whom he regarded as a political threat to Muslim consolidation and rule in Arabia.

In 632, Muhammad led the pilgrimage to Mecca. There the sixty-two-year-old leader delivered his farewell sermon, a moment remembered and commemorated each year at the annual pilgrimage to Mecca:

> Know ye that every Muslim is a brother unto every other Muslim, and that ye are now one brotherhood. It is not legitimate for any one of you, therefore, to appropriate unto himself anything that belongs to his brother unless it is willingly given him by that brother.[2]

The Message of the Quran

In contrast to modern biblical criticism in the Judeo-Christian tradition, Muslims believe that the Quran is the eternal, uncreated, literal, and final word

of God revealed to Muhammad as guidance for humankind (2:185). God is the
sole author; no human authorship or editing is admitted. The Prophet Muhammad is merely seen as a conduit, an intermediary, who received God's
message and then communicated it. In size, the text of the Quran is about
four-fifths that of the New Testament. It consists of 114 chapters (*surahs*) of six
thousand verses, arranged in terms of length, not chronology, revealed to Muhammad over a period of twenty-two years.

The God (Allah) of the Quran is the creator, sustainer, ruler, and judge of
humankind. He is merciful and just, the all-knowing and all-powerful, the
Lord and Ruler of the universe. The Quran teaches that God's revelation has
occurred in several forms: in nature, history, and scripture. God's existence can
be known through nature that points to or contains the "signs" of its creator
and sustainer (3:26–27). The history of humankind also contains clear examples and lessons of God's sovereignty and intervention in history (30:2–9).
Finally, God's will for humankind has been revealed through a long line of
prophets and messengers (from Adam and Abraham to Moses, Jesus, and
Muhammad): "Indeed We sent forth among every nation a Messenger saying:
'Serve your God and shun false gods'" (16:36). As a result, throughout history,
people could not only know that God exists but also know his will (what God
desires and commands) for humankind.

Muslims believe that the Quran, like the Torah and Evangel, is taken from
an Arabic tablet, the source or mother of all scriptures, preexisting with God in
heaven. From it, the teachings of the three Abrahamic faiths (Judaism,
Christianity, and Islam) have been taken and revealed at different stages in history: "Every term has a book...and with Him is the essence of the Book"
(13:38–39).

Because Arabic is the language of the Quran, all Muslims, regardless of
their national language, memorize, recite, and pray the Quran in Arabic
whether they fully understand it or not. Much as the Catholic mass until the
middle of the twentieth century was always said in Latin and the faithful
responded to the priest in Latin rather than local languages, across the world
Turkish, French, Pakistani, Malaysian, German, Indian, and American
Muslims stop to pray in Arabic five times each day. Arabic is viewed as the
sacred language of Islam; in a very real sense it is the language of God. In contrast to Christianity, which at an early stage translated its scriptures into Latin
and Greek and which after the Reformation translated the scriptures and worshiped in local languages, Arabic has remained the language of the Quran, the
primary source for religious learning and training, and of formal worship.
Translations, which have only occurred in the past century, are usually accompanied by the Arabic text.

The Quran, like its divine author, is believed to be perfect, eternal, and
unchangeable. Like God it is considered unique and thus inimitable in language, ideas, and style. Muslim tradition is replete with stories of those who,
when challenged to produce a comparable text, failed. The Quran was central

to the development of Arabic linguistics and provided the basis for Arabic grammar, syntax, and vocabulary. For many Muslims the clearest evidence of the Quran's power and uniqueness is its impact upon it hearers; indeed many have been moved to conversion upon hearing the beauty of the Quran recited.

Memorization of the entire text of the Quran is a time-honored act of piety. Recitation or chanting of the Quran is a major art form as well as an act of worship. Muslims gather in stadiums and auditoriums around the world to attend international Quran recitation competitions as many in the West might attend an opera. To win an international competition can be a source of great national pride. Media coverage of the awards would be comparable to coverage for gold medals in the Olympics. The sacredness and the centrality of the Quran are witnessed in a variety of other ways. The Quran is handled in a special way. It should not be treated like any other book, for example, placed in a pile of books, covered with papers, coffee cups, set on the floor, and so on. A devout Muslim will not write in the Quran or mark it up in any other way.

As mentioned earlier, the Quran acknowledges that God's revelation came first to the Jews and then to Christians.

> Say (O Muslims): "We believe in God and in what is revealed to us, and in what was revealed to Abraham and Ishmael and Isaac and Jacob and the Tribes (of Israel), and in what was given to Moses and Jesus, and in what was given to the [other] prophets by their Lord. We make no distinction between any of them and we submit ourselves to Him." (2:136)

Indeed, many Muslims take their names from the biblical prophets Ibrahim (Abraham), Musa (Moses), Sulayman (Solomon), Dawud (David), Yahya (John), and Issa (Jesus). Equally striking to many is the fact that the name of Mary, the mother of Jesus, is cited more often in the Quran than in the entire New Testament.

Throughout history, Jesus and Mary (Maryam), his mother, have been held in high esteem; both are common Muslim names. Jesus enjoys a special place among the prophets in Islam. The Quran affirms the virgin birth of Jesus, the promised Messiah," who declared from his cradle: "I am God's servant; God has given me the Book, and made me a prophet" (19:30).

The Quran's recognition of Christians, like Jews, as People of the Book was counterbalanced by its teaching that over time Christians, like Jews, had distorted their original revelation. Thus, the Quran rejects what it regards to be later Christian doctrines (the Trinity, and the incarnation, redemption, atonement, and resurrection of Jesus) influenced by foreign sources that Muslims believe corrupted the original meaning and message of God's revelation to Jesus and resulted in Christianity's belief in the divinity of Jesus. Although Muslims see Jesus as a great prophet, he is not, according to Islam, the Son of God. The Quran maintains that the doctrine of the Trinity contradicts God's Oneness or monotheism: "The Christians say 'The Messiah is the Son of God.'

...God assail them! How they are perverted!...They are commanded to serve
but One God; There is no God but He" (9:30–31). Islam also denies Jesus' death
on the cross and the collective guilt or sin (original sin) of humankind. Thus,
they believe, there was no need for Jesus' resurrection from the dead nor for his
suffering and death to redeem humankind or atone for original sin. Christians,
like Jews, are invited to become Muslims and accept the final and complete revelation of Allah. Otherwise, they are to be respected and treated justly, as long
as they do not oppose Islam, and will be judged and rewarded by God: "Those
who believe and those who are Jews, Christians and Sabeans, anyone who
believes in God and the Last Day, and does good will receive their reward from
their Lord: no fear will lie upon them nor need they feel saddened" (2:62).

The Quran teaches that the Torah of Moses and the Evangel of Jesus were
corrupted or distorted by human authors and editors in the collection, editing,
and transmission of the Hebrew bible and the New Testament. Thus, the
texts we now have are seen by Muslims as a composite of divine revelation and
human interpolation and fabrication. Therefore, God in his mercy sent his final
revelation through the final prophet, Muhammad. Thus, for Muslims, Islam is
not a new religion but rather the oldest, for it represents the "original" as well
as the final revelation of God to Abraham, Moses, Jesus, and Muhammad.

The Four Rightly Guided Caliphs

The rule of Muhammad and his first four successors or caliphs is seen as a very
special time. These early caliphs (Abu Bakr, Umar, Uthman, and Ali) are
remembered as the "Rightly Guided Caliphs." Muslim tradition has drawn
upon not only the *Sunnah* (example) of the Prophet but also the pious example
of Muhammad's successors. In the eyes of believers, the age of Muhammad
and the early Rightly Guided Caliphs is the normative, exemplary period of
Muslim faith and history for several reasons. First, it is the time when God sent
down his final and complete revelation for humankind through his last
prophet. Second, during this period the Islamic community-state was created,
bonded by a common religious purpose and mission. Third, the sources of
Islamic law, the Quran and Sunnah of the Prophet, originated in this time.
This period of Muhammad and his early Companions (*salaf*, "elders" or
"ancestors") serves as the reference point for divine guidance and historical validation, both used for revival and reform today. Muslims believe that the
revealed message of the Quran and the example of the Prophet and his successors were corroborated in the full light of history by the success and power
that resulted from the "miraculous" victories and the phenomenal geographi-
cal expansion and spread of Islam.

Expansion and Conquest

Through force and diplomacy, Muhammad united the tribes of Arabia under
the banner of Islam. During the next century, the period of the four Rightly
Guided Caliphs, Muslim armies, inspired and motivated by their new faith and

the material as well as spiritual rewards of victory, overran the Byzantine (Eastern Roman) and Sasanid (Persian) empires, which had been greatly weakened by internal strife and constant warfare. Muslim rule was extended throughout much of the Middle East and North Africa, creating an empire greater than that of Rome at its zenith (see Map 4.2).

Victory brought the bounty from richer, more developed societies as well as spiritual reward for obedience to God and his Prophet. Those who died in battle were considered martyrs for the faith and thus were promised the reward of paradise. While there were many motives and forces, economic as well as religious, the spread of Islam, as Fred Donner has said, was "truly an Islamic movement. For it was Islam—the set of religious principles preached by Muhammad, with its social and political ramifications—that ultimately sparked the whole integration process and hence was the ultimate cause of the conquest's success."[3]

Christendom experienced the early conquests and expansion of Islam as a theological, political, and civilizational threat to its religious and political hegemony. Muslim rule, and with it the message of Islam, quickly spread from the Byzantine and Persian empires to Syria, Iraq, and Egypt, and then swept across North Africa and into Europe, where Muslims ruled Spain and the Mediterranean from Sicily to Anatolia.

For non-Muslim populations in Byzantium and Persia, who had been subjugated to foreign rulers, Islamic rule meant an exchange of rulers rather than a loss of independence. Many in Byzantium willingly exchanged Greco-Roman rule for that of new Arab masters, fellow Semites, with whom they had closer linguistic and cultural affinities. Christians and Jews were regarded by Muslims as "People of the Book" (those who had possessed a scripture/revelation from God). As a result of their allegiance to the Islamic state and payment of a poll (head) tax, these "protected" (*dhimmi*) peoples could practice their faith and be governed by their religious leaders and law in matters of faith and private life (family laws).

Islam proved more tolerant than imperial Christianity, providing greater religious freedom for Jews and indigenous Christians; most local Christian churches had been persecuted as schismatics and heretics by a "foreign" Christian orthodoxy. As Francis Peters has observed:

> The conquests destroyed little: what they did suppress were imperial rivalries and sectarian bloodletting among the newly subjected population. The Muslims tolerated Christianity but they disestablished it; henceforth Christian life and liturgy, its endowments, politics, and theology, would be a private not a public affair. By an exquisite irony, Islam reduced the status of Christians to that which the Christians had earlier thrust upon the Jews, with one difference. The reduction in Christian status was merely judicial; it was unaccompanied by either systematic persecution or blood lust, and generally, though not everywhere and at all times, unmarred by vexatious behavior.[4]

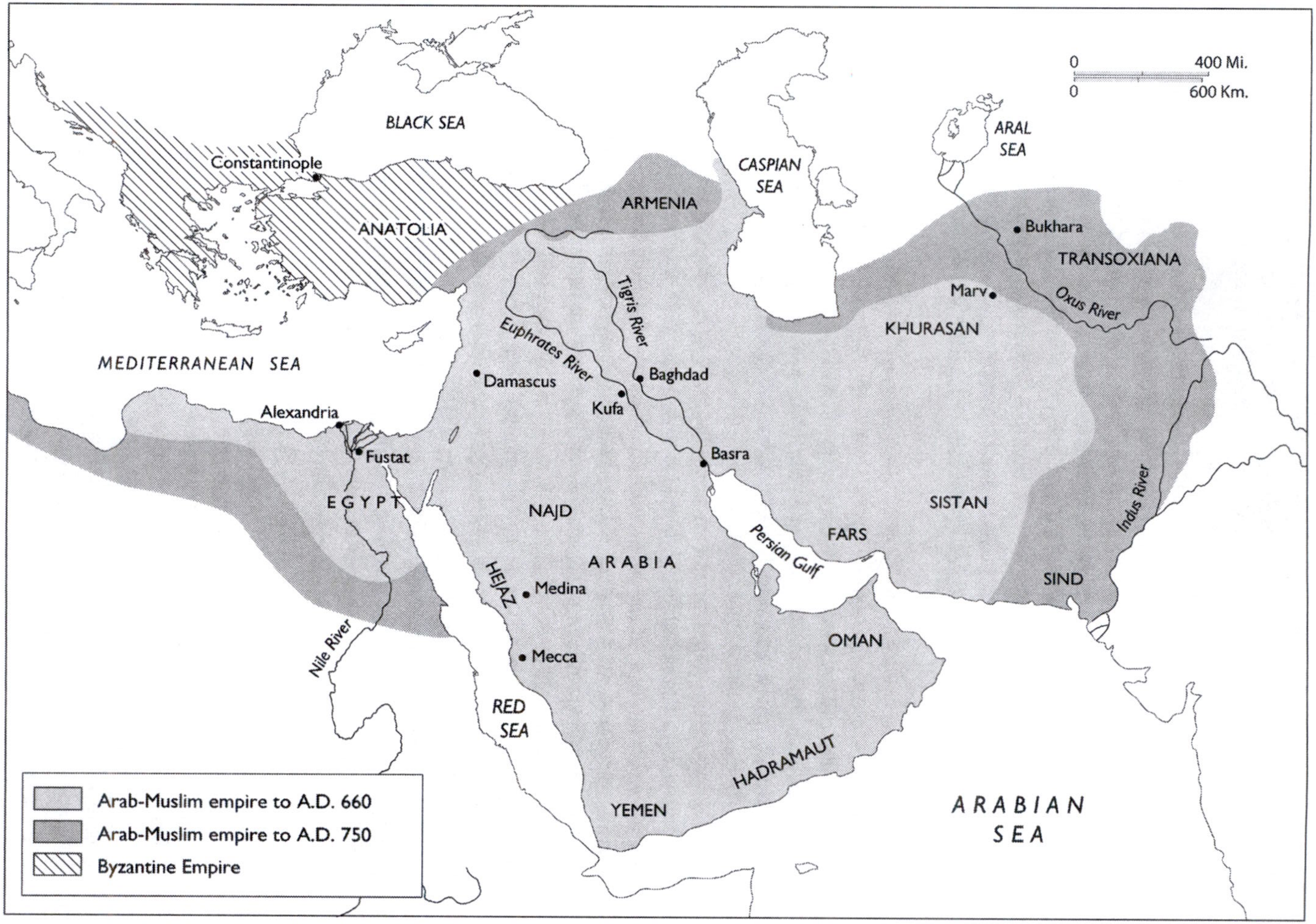

Map 4.2 The Muslim Empire to 750.

Arab-Muslim empire to A.D. 660

Arab-Muslim empire to A.D. 750

Byzantine Empire

The rapid spread and development of imperial Islam produced a rich Islamic civilization that flourished from the ninth to the twelfth centuries. Great urban cultural centers emerged in Cairo, Baghdad, Cordova, Palermo, and Nishapur. With significant assistance from Christian and Jewish subjects, Muslims collected the great books of science, medicine, and philosophy from the West and the East and translated them into Arabic from Greek, Latin, Persian, Coptic, Syriac, and Sanskrit. The age of translation was followed by a period of great creativity as a new generation of educated Muslim thinkers and scientists made their own contributions to learning in philosophy, medicine, chemistry, astronomy, algebra, optics, art, and architecture. These were true "renaissance men," multi-talented men of genius who often developed mastery in the major disciplines of philosophy, medicine, mathematics, and astronomy. Avicenna (Ibn Sina), remembered as "the great commentator" on Aristotle, reflected this pattern:

> I busied myself with the study of Fusus al-Hikam (a treatise by al-Farabi) and other commentaries on physics and mathematics, and the doors of knowledge opened before me. Then I took up medicine.... Medicine is not one of the difficult sciences, and in a short time I undoubtedly excelled at it, so that physicians of merit studied under me.... At the same time I carried on debates with and controversies in jurisprudence. At this point I was sixteen years old. Then, for a year and a half, I devoted myself to study. I resumed the study of logic and all parts of philosophy. During this time I never slept the whole night through and did nothing but study all day long.... Thus I mastered logic, physics, and mathematics.... When I reached the age of eighteen, I had completed the study of all these sciences. At that point my memory was better, whereas today my learning is riper.[5]

The cultural traffic pattern was again reversed when Europeans, emerging from the Dark Ages, turned to Muslim centers of learning to regain their lost heritage and to learn from Muslim advances. The failures and reforms of Muslim societies today, as in the recent past, are often measured against this history, at times romanticized, of an earlier period of brilliant success.

Diversity, Division, and Dissent

The victories and accomplishments during the early history and spread of Islam were also accompanied by deep division and dissent within the Muslim community. During the time of Muhammad the community remained united by Muhammad's prophetic claims, his remarkable leadership skills, and his reception of continued divine revelations. Muhammad's death precipitated crises, dissent, and civil wars as well as continued conquests, expansion, and the development of Islamic law, theology, and mysticism.

Given the pivotal role of Muhammad in the life of the community, his death in 632 was a traumatic event that shook its foundations. What was the

community to do? Who was to lead? Issues of political succession and seces-
sion or civil war were to plague and threaten its survival. Muhammad's senior
Companions moved quickly to reassure the community. Abu Bakr, a close
Companion and trusted adviser of the Prophet, proclaiming his death to the
faithful declared: "Muslims! If any of you has worshiped Muhammad, let
me tell you that Muhammad is dead. But if you worship God, then know that
God is living and will never die." The Companions of the Prophet, the elders
of Medina, selected Abu Bakr as caliph (khalifah, "successor or deputy"). The
caliph was not a prophet but rather Muhammad's successor as political and
military head of the community.

This next stage in the history of the Muslim community, the Caliphate
(632–1258), has traditionally been divided into three periods: The "Rightly
Guided Caliphs" (632–661), followed by the Umayyad (661–750) and Abbasid
(750–1258) dynastic empires. During these centuries a vast empire was created
with successive capitols at Medina, Kufa, Damascus, and Baghdad. Stunning
political and military success was complemented by a cultural florescence,
resulting in powerful Islamic empires and a brilliant Islamic civilization.
However, it was the earliest period, that of the four Rightly Guided Caliphs and
the Companions of the Prophet, which was to become exemplary and normative for later generations of believers.

Abu Bakr (632–634) as the successor of Muhammad was tested almost
immediately when some Arab tribes attempted to bolt from the community.
They declared their political independence, maintaining that conversion to
Islam had nothing to do with their political allegiance, which was based on a
political pact or alliance with Muhammad that ended with his death. Abu Bakr
countered that all Muslims belonged to a single community and that the unity
of the community was based upon the interconnectedness of religion and the
state, faith and politics. In a series of battles, remembered by later historians
as the Wars of Apostasy, Abu Bakr crushed the tribal revolt, consolidated
Muslim rule over the Arabian peninsula, and preserved the religiously based
unity and solidarity of the Islamic-community state.

Abu Bakr's successor, Umar ibn al-Khattab (634–644), initiated a period of
expansion and conquest. One of the great military leaders of his time, he
added "Commander of the Faithful" to that of "Successor (Caliph) of the
Prophet," a title that Muslim rulers would keep. During the reign of his successor, Uthman ibn Affan (644–656) from the Umayyad clan, tribal faction-
alism and rebellion resurfaced. Personally pious but with a weaker presence
and skills than his predecessors, Uthman was a member of a family that had
been among the strongest foes of Muhammad. His election was opposed by
many of the early supporters of Muhammad, who resented the increased
prominence and wealth of his family and accused the caliph of nepotism. In
656 he was assassinated by a group of mutineers from Egypt, an act that was
the first in a series of rebellions that would plague the Islamic community's
development.

A second crisis of leadership occurred when civil war broke out during the reign of the fourth caliph, Ali. Although the majority of the community had supported the selection of Abu Bakr as caliph, a minority dissented, believing that leadership should stay within the family of the Prophet and thus pass to its senior male member. Ali, the cousin and son-in-law of the Prophet, had married Fatima, the only surviving daughter of Muhammad and Khadija, his first wife. Shortly after Ali's accession to power, his authority was challenged by a triumvirate that included Muhammad's widow Aisha, the daughter of Abu Bakr. This was followed by the rebellion of Muawiyah, the governor of Syria. When it looked as if the army of Muawiyah would fall, his soldiers raised Qurans on the tips of their spears, declaring, "Let the Quran decide." Arbitration between all these opposing forces proved inconclusive but did lead to two results that have had a profound impact on the history of Islam. First, a group of Ali's followers, the Kharajites (those who "go out" or secede), broke away. They maintained an uncompromising faith, believing that Ali's failure to subdue his opponents rendered him no better than Muawiyah. Both had sinned against God and were deemed unbelievers whose revolt against God was punishable by death. Second, Muawiyah remained recalcitrant in Syria. He bided his time until Ali was assassinated by a group of Kharajites. He then seized power and established an absolute monarchy, creating the Umayyad dynasty (661–750).

The Umayyad dynasty was responsible for the rapid spread of Islam and the emergence of imperial Islam with its capital in Damascus. However, opposition to what later Muslim historians would characterize as impious Umayyad caliphs also resulted in movements of renewal and reform; some movements like the Kharajites and Shiah were revolutionary, while others led to the development of Islamic law and mysticism (Sufism). All have to varying degrees remained important.

The Kharajites, who had broken with Ali, were the first in a long series of movements to offer a different concept of the nature of the Islamic community and its leadership. Combining rigorous puritanism with an exclusivist egalitarianism, they emerged as revolutionaries who, although ultimately unsuccessful in their own times, continue to inspire contemporary radical groups. The Kharajite world view was simple. Muawiyah had challenged the legitimate authority of the caliph; this grave sin rendered him an apostate or infidel. Thus Ali and all true Muslims had an obligation to wage war (jihad, "struggle") against this "enemy of God" until Muawiyah repented and desisted or was subdued. There could be no compromise.

The Kharajites, like some religious extremists today, interpreted the Quran and the Sunnah literally and sought to follow and impose their beliefs absolutely. They believed the Quranic command to "command the good and prohibit evil" must be applied rigorously and without any compromise. They viewed the world as divided into clear, mutually exclusive categories: acts were either good or bad, permitted or forbidden. The world was divided into realms of belief or unbelief, that is, Muslims (followers of God, or those who agreed with the Kharajites) and infidels (the enemies of God, those who differed with the Kharajites and were therefore excommunicated or cut off from the community).

Like extremist groups today, who have taken such names as Jihad or the Soldiers of God, the Kharajites, claiming to follow the letter of the Quran and the example of the Prophet, adopted their own pattern and interpretation of Muhammad and the early community's hijra and jihad. They withdrew (hijra) from society to live in a bonded community from which they waged war (jihad) against their enemies, seeing themselves as the instruments of God's justice. They were the soldiers of God (or paradise) waging war against the people of evil (hell). Since they were God's righteous army, they believed that violence, guerrilla warfare, and revolution were not only legitimate but also obligatory in their battle against the usurpers of God's rule. Other Muslims, however pious, who committed an action contrary to the letter of the law, as interpreted or understood by the Kharajites, were guilty not of sin but of grave (quite literally mortal) sin. They were apostates and thus guilty of treason against the Islamic community-state. If they did not repent, they were to be fought against and killed. Many of the components of this world view may be found in twentieth-century Muslim extremist writings, including those of the Muslim Brotherhood's Sayyid Qutb and in the ideology of groups in Egypt, Lebanon, and Algeria like Islamic Jihad, the Army of God, the Armed Islamic Group, Muhammad's Youth, and Takfir wal Hijra (Excommunication and Flight).

The Kharajites continued to lead rebellions against Umayyad and Abbasid rulers. A moderate branch, known as Ibadiyya, later established Ibadi *imamates* ("governments") in North (Tripolitania and Tahert) and East (Zanzibar) Africa, Yemen, and Oman, where Islam today remains the official state religion.

A second major revolutionary movement spawned by opposition to Umayyad rule, and with a far more significant impact and legacy today, is the rebellion by followers of the fourth caliph, Ali. Its results would lead to the two great branches of Islam, its Sunni majority and Shiah minority communities.

The followers (*shiah*, "partisans") of Ali had been thwarted first when the Companions of Muhammad bypassed Ali in favor of Abu Bakr in the appointment of the first caliph, and then by Muawiyah's challenge to Ali and later seizure of the caliphate. When Yazid, the son of Muawiyah, came to power, Husayn, the son of Ali, was persuaded by a group of Ali's followers in Kufa (a city in modern Iraq) to lead a rebellion in 680. However, the promised support did not materialize, and Husayn and his army were slaughtered by the Umayyad army at the city of Karbala (a city in modern Iraq). The memory of Karbala and the "martyrdom" of Husayn would shape a Shii world view, a paradigm of suffering, oppression, and protest against injustice. This paradigm was reinforced by their minority status and discrimination against them through the centuries. It inspired and sustained the community throughout history and became a major source of inspiration and mobilization during Iran's Islamic Revolution of 1978–1979.

Sunni Muslims constitute 85 percent and Shiah approximately 15 percent of the global Islamic community. Although united in their common confession of faith in God, the Quran, and the Prophet Muhammad, their histories produced different notions of leadership and history. In Sunni Islam, the caliph ideally (contrary to the reality of the Umayyad and Abbasid caliphates, which were dynastic) is the selected or elected successor of the Prophet, but only as political and military leader of the community, not as prophet. In Shiah Islam, by contrast, the *imam* ("leader") is not selected from among the members of the community but must be a direct descendant of the Prophet's family. He is not only the political but also the religiopolitical leader of the community. Though not a prophet, he is the divinely inspired, sinless, infallible, final authoritative interpreter of God's will as formulated in Islamic law.

Sunni and Shiah also developed differing interpretations concerning the meaning of history. For Sunni, the early success and power of Islamic history were signs of God's guidance, rewards to a faithful community, and historic validation of Muslim belief and claims. In contrast, the Shiah saw these same events as the illegitimate usurpation of power by Sunni rulers. Therefore, for Shiah, history is the theater for the struggle of a righteous but historically oppressed and disinherited minority community, who must restore God's rule on earth under his divinely appointed imam. A righteous remnant was to persist in its struggle against the overwhelming forces of evil (Satan), as Ali struggled against Muawiyah and as Husayn fought against the army of Yazid, to restore God's righteous rule under the imam's leadership. The battle of Karbala became the paradigm for struggle and, with it, sacrifice and martyrdom (that is, the willingness to sacrifice everything, even one's life, in the defense of Islam) if necessary.

Realization of what they believed to be the legitimate claims of the descendants of Ali, and not the Sunni caliphs, to govern the Islamic community was to remain the frustrated Shii hope and expectation for centuries. Despite Shiah opposition and rebellions, the Islamic community remained ruled by the Sunni caliphate. In addition, the Shiah themselves split into three major subdivisions, dependent upon the number of legitimate successors (imams) each acknowleged: the Zaydi, Ismaili (a subsect of whom, the Nizari Ismailis, is led by the Agha Khan), and Twelvers (Ithna Ashari). The Zaydi, who believed that any descendant of Ali could become imam, recognized Zayd ibn Alia, a grandson of Husayn (Ali's son) as the fifth imam. The majority of Shiah, believing that the imamate was restricted to direct descendants of Ali and Fatima, did not recognize him. The Zaydis were the first to gain independence and found a dynasty in Tabaristan on the Caspian Sea in 864. Another Zaydi state existed in Yemen from 893 to 1963.

In the eight century, the majority of Shiah split again over whom the seventh imam, Jafar al-Sadiq (d. 765), had designated as his heir or successor. The Ismaili, sometimes called the Seveners, believed that the line of imams ended in 760 when Ismail, Jafar al-Sadiq's son and the designated seventh imam, died before his father. Others believed that he was in seclusion and would return at some future date as the *Mahdi* ("Awaited One"), while still others recognized Ismail's son as successor. The Ismaili were a political revolutionary movement against Sunni rulers. They established their own Fatimid dynasty (named after Fatima, the daughter of Muhammad), which ruled over areas extending from Egypt and North Africa to the Sind province in India from the tenth to the twelfth centuries. An Ismaili offshoot, the Nizari Ismailis, struck such fear into Sunni Abbasid rulers that they came to be known as the assassins. A descendant fled to India, where a series of imams, known by the honorific title Agha Khan, have ruled over prosperous communities in East Africa, South Asia, Britain, and Canada. The current Agha Khan, who studied at Harvard, functions as a living imam, overseeing the spiritual and cultural life as well as the successful commercial, educational, and social institutions of the community.

The Twelvers, who today are a majority in Iran, Bahrain, and Iraq, recognized twelve legitimate successors of the Prophet from the house of Ali. The twelfth, Muhammad al-Muntazar (Muhammad the Awaited One), disappeared in 874. Shii theology addressed and resolved this dilemma with its doctrine of the absence or occultation (hidden presence) of the imam. The imam was transformed into a messianic figure who had not died but rather disappeared into hiding or seclusion. He will return as the Mahdi at the end of time to vindicate and restore his faithful community and usher in a perfect Islamic society of truth and justice. In the interim, the community is to be guided by its religious/legal experts (*mujtahids*, "those capable of interpreting Islamic law").

Over the years, Twelver Shii Islam in contrast to Sunni Islam developed something of a clerical hierarchy, at whose apex were religious leaders who, because of their reputations for learning and piety, were acknowledged as *ayatollahs* ("signs of God"). In Iran, the Ayatollah Khomeini reinterpreted Shii Islam, maintaining that in the absence of the imam, the religious scholars (*ulama*), as the representatives of the hidden imam and interpreters of Islamic law, should govern. This belief, governance by the jurist (*wilayat al-faqih*), was implemented when the Islamic Republic of Iran was established in 1979. The Ayatollah Khomeini assumed the title of faqih (supreme jurist), and within a short time Iran's parliament and government institutions were dominated by the clergy. The clergy's role in politics remains a contested issue in Iran today.

PREMODERN ISLAM: THE CLASSICAL ERA

Islam today exists both in continuity and in dialectical tension with a rich classical heritage of Islamic law, thought, and institutions. A critical issue faced by Muslims today, like all religious believers, is the connection or continuity of current religious discourse and practice with centuries-old, sacrosanct traditions.

Believers tend to legitimate or justify their belief and practice or their calls for renewal and reform in light of their Islamic tradition and heritage.

Law and Mysticism: The Outer and Inner Paths to God

Dissatisfaction with Umayyad rule also resulted in the development of non-revolutionary reform movements. The rapid expansion of Islam brought the rise of new centers of power and wealth, an influx of "foreign ways," and greater social stratification. The very success of the Umayyads contained the seeds of their vulnerability. With wealth and power came abuse of power and corruption, symbolized by the new lifestyle of its captured capital and the growth of new cities. The contrast between an idealized Medinan community and the realities of Umayyad life gave rise to two Islamic movements or institutions, the ulama (religious scholars) and their Islamic law, and the Sufis of Islamic mysticism.

In contrast to Christianity's focus on doctrine or theology, Islam, like Judaism, places primary emphasis on what believers are to do, on religious observance and obedience to God's law. The message of Islam is rooted in a vision of individual and community moral responsibility and accountability. Muslims are commanded by the Quran to strive or struggle (jihad) in the path (sharia) of God, to realize, spread, and defend God's message and community. They are to function as God's vicegerents or representatives on earth, promoting the good and prohibiting evil (3:104, 3:110). All Muslims are responsible as individuals and as a community for the creation of the good society. The good

ISLAMIC LAW

Shariah literally means the "right" or "straight path" to be followed or pursued. In colloquial Arabic, it means road or street. In Islam, shariah came to mean the divinely mandated path, the straight path of God. Of course, the Quran itself is not a law book; it does not provide a comprehensive set of regulations, but, rather, guiding principles and values. Thus, the desire to discover and set out God's will in a comprehensive systematic fashion led to the development of Islamic law.

Historically, from the seventh to the tenth centuries, Muslim scholars in Mecca, Medina, Damascus, Kufa, and other city centers formulated Islamic law. Early Muslim scholars developed the science of law or jurisprudence (fiqh), the "understanding" needed in order to ascertain, interpret, and apply God's guidance (shariah) as found in the Quran and the Sunnah (example) of the Prophet. Based upon both divinely revealed prescriptions and their own human interpretation (ijtihad), the scholars attempted to delineate a comprehensive blueprint for Muslim life and society.

will enjoy eternal happiness in heaven and the evil will suffer eternal damnation in hell. Despite vast cultural differences, Islamic law has provided an idealized blueprint that has instilled among Muslims throughout the ages a common code of behavior and a sense of religious identity.

Recognition of the need to articulate Islamic law did not simply grow out of an intellectual motivation or inspiration. As in much of Islam's development, it was a response to real religious and political concerns and issues. Those who turned to law did so during the Umayyad dynasty in the eighth and ninth centuries to limit the autonomy and power of rulers by standardizing the law and taking its control out of the hands of the caliph or his appointed judges. Centers of concern could be found in Medina, Damascus, Baghdad, Kufa, and Basra, whose scholars—like Abu Hanifa (d. 767), Malik ibn Anas (d. 796), Muhammad al-Shafii (d. 819), and Ahmad ibn Hanbal (d. 855)—came to be regarded respectively as the founders of the Hanafi, Maliki, Shafii, and Hanbali law schools.

The development of law flourished during the tenth century under the Abbasid dynasty. The Abbasid caliphs, having led a rebellion that overthrew the Umayyads, sought to justify their revolution and legitimate their rule in the name of Islam and so become the patrons of Islam. The study of Islamic sources and the development of Islamic studies in the Quran, prophetic traditions, and law excelled in the hands of a new class of scholars (alim, pl. ulama, "learned ones") during this period. It is important to note that law did not develop primarily from the practice of courts or from government decrees but through the interpretation and formulation of scholars, not judges, who set out a religious ideal or blueprint.

There are four official sources of Islamic law: (1) Quran, God's revelation; (2) the Sunnah, the example or practice of Muhammad, as found in the collections of prophetic traditions, hadith; (3) analogical reasoning (qiyas); and (4) consensus (ijma).

The Quran

Belief that the Quran is the very word of God assured that it would be the primary material source of law. It does not reveal the transcendent God, but God's will for humankind: "Here is a plain statement to men, a guidance and instruction to those who fear God" (3:138) The Quran contains approximately eighty prescriptions that would rank as legal in the strict sense of the term. However, the majority of texts provide general principles and values, moral directives as to what the aims and aspirations of Muslims should be. The bulk of these verses come from the Medinan period, when Muhammad was establishing the first Islamic community-state.

The Sunnah (Example) of the Prophet

Major knowledge about the Prophet comes from the Quran, prophetic traditions, and early biographies. Of these sources, the richest trove of information about Muhammad and his times are the massive collections of prophetic traditions, that is, narrative stories or reports (*hadith*) about what the Prophet said and did, which comprise his model example, or Sunnah. The volumes, of hundreds of thousands of hadith narratives contain stories that seemingly cover every situation. Their centrality yesterday and today cannot be underestimated. As a distinguished contemporary Muslim scholar has noted: "But the Sunnah and Hadith are not simply a heritage from an historical past. They are associated with the person who is 'alive' here and now and who is as revered and loved by all Muslims now as he was fourteen centuries ago."[6]

Analogical Reasoning

Where no clear text of the Quran or Sunnah directly relevant to a legal question or problem existed, jurists used their independent judgment or reasoning in light of principles of justice, community welfare, or local customs. This led to a great deal of diversity. In an attempt to set a limit to this inductive approach, a more deductive method, analogical reasoning (*qiyas*), based upon finding a relevant precedent in sacred texts, was introduced. Thus, when confronted by a question or issue for which no specific, clear text exists in the Quran or Sunnah, jurists were to look for similar or analogous cases in scripture to identify principles that could be applied to a new case. For example, while there is no specific text dealing with the use of mind-altering drugs, jurists nevertheless could condemn them, drawing their conclusion from sacred texts that forbid the consumption of alcohol. The selection of those laws that were to endure and be binding from amidst a vast body of laws developed by the jurists was based on consensus.

Consensus

In theory, the doctrine of consensus (*ijma*) is based upon a tradition of the Prophet that said, "My community will never agree on an error." In reality, it comprises acceptance or consensus by the majority of religious scholars (ulama) who represent religious authority.

The two main divisions of Islamic law concern a Muslim's duties to God (*ibadat*) and duties to others or social transactions (*muamalat*). The former consist of fundamental or obligatory practices, in particular the Five Pillars of Islam, that is, essential observances. The latter include regulations governing public life (from contract and international law to family laws—marriage, divorce, and inheritance).

Islamic law is a source of both unity and guidance and of difference and diversity. The essential agreement of the law schools has often led some to exaggerate the degree of agreement and conformity, which, in turn, tends to reinforce an excessive notion of the rigidity of Islamic law. Differences of opinion did exist, and were acknowledged, debated, rejected, and accepted. While the four schools of law agree in their essentials, they differ in a number of particulars, reflecting the role of individual reasoning and social custom.

Individual jurists differed in their interpretation of texts, their personal opinions, and their notions of equity and public welfare. So too, the diverse social backgrounds and cultural contexts of legal scholars (*faqih*, pl. *fuqaha*) affected their judgments and informed their interpretations. Thus, law schools differed about the grounds on which a woman could sue for divorce or on the amount to be paid for maintenance. The differences and local customs of the more cosmopolitan and class-conscious city of Kufa, a Hanafi center, versus a more conservative Medina, where the Maliki law school developed, can be seen in the varying regulations of these law schools.

Acceptance of contrasting views was reflected in a doctrine that acknowledged the validity of different (*ikhtilaf*) opinions. A similar variance can be found among the official legal opinions or interpretations (*fatwas*) rendered by legal experts/consultants (*muftis*) who advised judges and litigants. We see these differences in recent times when muftis have provided contrasting opinions or fatwas in the Salman Rushdie case and in the Gulf War of 1991. In the Rushdie case, the Ayatollah Khomeini's fatwa found the author of *Satanic Verses* guilty of blasphemy and condemned him to death. With a price on his head, Rushdie went into hiding. Other muftis, while deploring the book, called for a trial by Islamic law. In the Gulf War, muftis' opinions varied in providing supporting positions for either Iraq or a United States–led armada that included Egypt, Kuwait, and Saudi Arabia. Along with differences are key commonalities among Muslims worldwide. The Five Pillars of Islam unite all Muslims in their worship and following of God.

The Five Pillars of Islam

Like all religions or religious traditions, Islam and Muslim practice, influenced by faith, human interpretation, and contexts, have taken many forms throughout the centuries. However, despite diverse historical and cultural contexts and practices, the Five Pillars of Islam have provided a unity and continuity of faith and practice for all Muslims. If God, the Quran, and the Prophet Muhammad unite all Muslims in their common belief (common denominator), the Five Pillars of Islam provide a unity of practice in the midst of the community's rich diversity. The pillars are the common denominator, the five essential obligatory practices that all Muslims are to follow: (1) the profession of faith, (2) worship or prayer, (3) almsgiving, (4) fasting, and (5) the pilgrimage to Mecca.

1. *The Profession of Faith.* A Muslim is one who simply proclaims (*shahadah*, "witness" or "testimony") "There is no God but the God and Muhammad is the messenger of God." This brief yet profound statement marks a person's entry into the Islamic community and is repeated at least five times each day in worship or prayer (*salat*). It affirms Islam's absolute monotheism, an unshakable and uncompromising faith in the oneness or unity (tawhid) of God. The second part of the confession of faith is the affirmation of Muhammad as the

messenger of God, the last and final prophet, who serves as a model for the Muslim community. The action, or doing, orientation of Islam is witnessed by the remaining four pillars or duties.

2. *Salat.* Five times each day (dawn, noon, midafternoon, sunset, and evening) Muslims throughout the world are called to worship (*salat*) God. In many cities of the world, the quiet of the night or daily noise of busy city streets is pierced by the call of the *muezzin* from atop the tower (*minaret*) of the mosque. The voice of a single muezzin is multiplied by those of muezzins from many nearby mosques in the congested urban settings of Jakarta, Karachi, and Cairo.

> God is Most Great (Allahu Akbar)!, God is Most Great!
>> I witness that there is no god but God (Allah)...
>> I witness that Muhammad is the Messenger of God...
>> Come to prayer...come to salvation...
> God is Most Great! God is Most Great! There is no god but God!

Prayer is preceded by a series of ablutions to cleanse the body and symbolize the purity of mind and body required for worshiping God. Facing the holy city of Mecca, Islam's spiritual homeland where the Prophet was born and received God's revelation, Muslims recall the revelation of the Quran and reinforce a sense of belonging to a single, worldwide community of believers. Regardless of race or national language, all pray in Arabic. Muslims may pray in any appropriate place wherever they happen to be: at home, in an airport, on the road. They may do so as individuals or in a group. For Muslims, prayer is an act of adoration of God and remembrance of his word, not one of request or petition.

On Friday, the noon prayer is a congregational prayer that usually takes place in a mosque (*masjid*, "place of prostration"). A special feature of the Friday prayer is a sermon (*khutba*), preached from a pulpit (*minbar*). Since there is no clergy or priesthood in Islam, any Muslim may lead the prayer. In many communities, larger mosques do have an imam who is paid to look after the mosque and who leads the prayer.

3. *Almsgiving.* The third pillar of Islam is the *zakat*, a religious tithe or almsgiving. Almsgiving is linked with prayer in the Quran (9:11). Just as the performance of the salat is both an individual and communal obligation, so too payment of the zakat instills a sense of communal identity and responsibility. As all Muslims share equally in their obligation to worship God, so too they all are duty bound to attend to the social welfare of their community by redressing economic inequalities through payment of an alms tax or poor tithe. The zakat is a tithe on one's accumulated wealth and assets, not just on one's income. Strictly speaking, zakat is not charity, since almsgiving is not regarded as a voluntary offering but as a duty imposed by God, an act of spiritual purification and solidarity. Just as the Quran condemns economic exploitation, so

too it warns against those who accumulate wealth and fail to assist others (3:180). Those who have benefited from God's bounty, who have received their wealth as a trust from God, are required to look after the needs of the less fortunate members of the Muslim community.

In most countries, Muslims determine to whom they will pay the zakat. However, in recent years, some governments such as those of Pakistan, Sudan, and Iran, in the name of creating a more Islamic state, have collected and distributed the zakat. This has proved to be a point of contention, for some charge that the central government misappropriates funds, and others prefer to have the freedom to distribute it themselves to needy relatives, friends, or neighbors.

4. *The Fast of Ramadan.* Once each year, Muslims are required to fast during the month of Ramadan, the ninth month of Islam's lunar calendar. From dawn to dusk, abstention from food, drink, and sex are required of all healthy Muslims. The primary emphasis is not so much on abstinence and self-mortification as such but rather on spiritual self-discipline, reflection, and the performance of good works.

The fast is broken at the end of the day by a light meal (popularly referred to as breakfast). Evening activities contrast with those of the daylight hours as families exchange visits and share a special late evening meal together. There are unique foods and sweets that are served only at this time of the year. The month of Ramadan comes to an end with a great celebration, the Feast of the Breaking of the Fast, Id al-Fitr, one of the great religious holy days and holidays of the Muslim calendar. Family members come from near and far to feast and exchange gifts in a celebration that lasts for three days.

5. *Pilgrimage to Mecca*: the Hajj. Ramadan is followed by the beginning of the pilgrimage season. Every adult Muslim who is physically and financially able is expected to perform the pilgrimage (*hajj*) to Mecca at least once in his or her lifetime. Those who are able to may go more often. Just as Muslims are united five times each day as they face Mecca in worship, so too each year many make the physical journey to this spiritual center of Islam where they again experience the unity, breadth, and diversity of the Islamic community. In recent years, almost two million Muslims from every part of the globe have gathered for the pilgrimage in Saudi Arabia.

The focus of the pilgrimage is the Kaaba, the cube-shaped House of God that Muslim tradition teaches was originally built by the prophet Ibrahim (Abraham) and his son Ismail to honor God. The black stone that the Kaaba contains is believed to have been given to Abraham by the angel Gabriel and thus is a symbol of God's covenant with Ismail and, by extension, with the Muslim community. Like prayer (salat), the pilgrimage requires ritual purification, symbolized by the wearing of white garments, which also symbolizes for everyone, rich and poor alike, the unity and equality of all believers before God. No jewelry, perfume, or sexual activity is permitted. During the following days, ritual actions or ceremonies are held to commemorate or reenact major events in the sacred history of Islam.

JIHAD: THE STRUGGLE FOR GOD

Jihad, "to strive or struggle," is sometimes referred to as the sixth pillar of Islam, although it has no such official status. In its most general meaning, jihad refers to the obligation incumbent upon all Muslims, as individuals and as a community, to exert (jihad) themselves to realize God's will, to lead a virtuous life, to fulfill the universal mission of Islam, and to spread the Islamic community through preaching Islam to convert others or writing religious tracts ("jihad of the tongue" and "jihad of the pen," respectively). Thus, today the term can be used to describe the personal struggle to keep the fast of Ramadan, to lead a good life, to fulfill family responsibilities. Popularly it is used to describe the struggle for educational or social reform—the struggle to establish good schools, to clean up a neighborhood, to fight drugs, or to work for social justice. However, it also includes the struggle for or defense of Islam, that is, holy war. Despite the fact that jihad is not supposed to include aggressive warfare, this association has occurred, as exemplified by early extremists like the Kharajites and contemporary extremists such as Osama Bin Laden and his jihad against America as well as jihad organizations in Lebanon, the Persian Gulf, and Indonesia.

As the pilgrims near Mecca, they shout: "I am here, O Lord, I am here!" When they reach Mecca, they proceed to Mecca's Grand Mosque that houses the Kaaba. There they pray at the spot where Abraham, the patriarch and father of monotheism, stood, and they circumambulate the Kaaba seven times. Finally, they visit the Plain of Arafat, the site of Muhammad's last sermon, where they seek God's forgiveness for themselves and for all Muslims throughout the world.

The pilgrimage ends with the celebration of the Feast of Sacrifice (Id al-Adha). The "Great Feast" commemorates God's testing of Abraham by commanding him to sacrifice his son Ismail (Isaac in Jewish and Christian traditions). Commemorating God's final permission to Abraham to substitute a ram for his son, Muslims sacrifice animals (sheep, goats, cattle) not only in Mecca but across the Muslim world. While some of the meat is consumed, most is distributed to the poor. The Feast of Sacrifice lasts for three days, a time for rejoicing, prayer, and visiting with family and friends.

Women and Muslim Family Law

Few topics have received more attention, are the subject of more stereotyping, and are the source of more contention than that of women and the family. If many Muslims speak of Islam as liberating women, others in the West as well as in Muslim countries decry the oppression of women today. The position of Muslim women must be viewed within the context of both their status in Islamic law and the politics and culture of their societies today. Islamic law itself must be seen as reflecting both the Quranic concern for the rights of women and the family (the greater part of its legislation is devoted to these issues), as well as the male-dominated (patriarchal) society within which Islamic law was developed.

The Quran introduced substantial reforms affecting the status of women both through new regulations and the modification of prevailing customs. In contrast to pre-Islamic Arab practice, the Quran recognized a woman's right to contract marriage, receive and keep her dowry, and own and inherit property. No equivalent right existed in Christianity or in Judaism. Moreover, women in the West did not gain inheritance rights until the nineteenth century. These Quranic reforms and others would become the basis for Muslim family law.

As the Five Pillars are the core of a Muslim's duty to worship God (*ibadat*), so too family law is central to Islam's social laws (*muamalat*). Indeed, Muslim family law has often been described as the heart of the Shariah, reflecting the importance of the family in Islam. Because of the centrality of the community (ummah) in Islam and the role of the family as the basic unit of society, family law has enjoyed pride of place in the development of Islamic law and in its implementation throughout history. While many areas of Islamic law remained unenforced ideals or were circumvented by caliphs and sultans, family law was enforced. Similarly, though the emergence of modern Muslim states has often seen the adoption of Western-oriented civil and commercial laws or legal systems, in most countries Muslim family law has remained in force. While in some countries family law has been reformed rather than replaced, often this reform became the subject of considerable conflict and debate. In the 1980s, the resurgence of Islam often was accompanied by attempts to return to the use of classical family law and to reverse modern reforms. Thus today, as in the past, the subject of women and the family remains an important and extremely sensitive subject in Muslim societies.

The status of women and the family in Muslim family law is the product of many factors: Arab culture, Quranic reforms, foreign ideas and values assimilated from conquered peoples, and the interpretation of male jurists in a patriarchal society. While Islam's sacred texts were the primary sources of law, pre-Islamic Arabia's society, customs, and values informed the world views and social values of those jurists who interpreted and formulated family law as they did all of Islamic law. Regulations developed in the early centuries of Islamic history regarding marriage, divorce, inheritance, and bequests have guided Muslim societies, determining attitudes toward women and the family throughout the history of Islam.

The Quran teaches that men and women are equal before God in terms of their religious and moral obligations and rewards (33:35). However, their function and roles in society and the family vary. Husbands and wives are seen as fulfilling complementary roles, based upon differing characteristics, capacities, and dispositions and their traditional roles in the patriarchal family. Men function in the public sphere, the "outside" world; they are responsible for the financial support and protection of the family. Women's primary role is that of wife and mother; they are responsible for the management of the household, raising and supervising their children's religious/moral training. In light of women's more sheltered and protected status and experience in society and men's greater experience in public life and broader responsibilities, the Quran (and Islamic law) teaches that wives are subordinate to husbands (2:228) and that a woman's testimony in Islamic law is worth half that of a man, that is, the testimony of two women is worth that of one man. Similarly, because men in a patriarchal system were financially responsible for the economic well-being of all women and other dependents in the extended family, the male portion of inheritance was twice that of a female.

Marriage is a primary institution in Islam, regarded as incumbent upon all Muslims. It is a civil contract or covenant, not a sacrament. It safeguards chastity and the growth and stability of the family, legalizing intercourse and the procreation of children. Reflecting the centrality of the family and the identity and role of individuals within the family, marriage is not simply an agreement between two people but between two families. Thus, "arranged marriage," that is, a marriage arranged by the two families or by a guardian, is traditional, although the majority of jurists agreed that a woman could not be forced to marry a man against her will.

While many are ignorant or unaware of Quranic reforms affecting women, most equate Islam with polygamy, or more accurately, polygyny. The common myth is to believe that Islam counsels men to marry four wives. Though the Quran explicitly permits four wives, its purpose was to provide protection to unmarried women as well as to limit and regulate the unfettered rights of men. The Quran limits the total number to four while in the same verse noting that if each could not be supported and treated equally, then only one was permitted (4:3). Islamic modernists in recent years have used this same spirit and another Quranic verse ("You are never able to be fair and just between women if that is your ardent desire," 4:129) to argue that the Quranic ideal is monogamy and that plural marriages should either be restricted or eliminated. In particular they note that the original revelation was given to a community in which losses in battle left many widows who needed protection. More important, many maintain that the demands of modern life make it extraordinarily difficult for any man to provide equally for more than one wife, especially in terms of time and affection.

Islamic law, reflecting the spirit of the Quran (4:35) and a saying of the Prophet ("of all the permitted things divorce is the most abominable"), regards divorce as permissible but reprehensible. One authoritative legal manual calls divorce "a dangerous and disapproved procedure...nor is its propriety at all admitted, but on the ground of urgency of relief from an unsuitable wife."[7]

Islamic law itself, as if to underscore the seriousness of divorce, prescribes that a man must pronounce the words or formula of divorce three separate times to make it irrevocable.

Although Islamic law sought to constrain a husband's liberty to divorce his wife and did enable women to obtain a judicial (court) divorce, the prescriptions of the law itself fell short of the ideal, an Islamic ideal that has often been compromised by historical and social realities. The most common form of divorce is repudiation (*talaq*) by the husband. This could be accomplished by a man's pronunciation of the formula for divorce ("I divorce you") and then a three-month waiting period to enable arbitration/reconciliation and to determine paternity and maintenance obligations. Alternatively, a man could pronounce "I divorce you" three times, once each successive month. However, the law also reluctantly recognized a third undesirable practice, a husband's immediate repudiation of his wife three times at once. This makes the divorce immediately effective and bypasses the Quranically mandated three-month waiting period (65:1). Although regarded as an unapproved innovation or deviation (*talaq al-bida*) and thus sinful, it is nevertheless valid. This disapproved though legal form of divorce is but one example of the extent to which custom was able at times to override or circumvent revelation.

The strong influence of custom can also be seen in the more limited rights of divorce accorded women. In pre-Islamic society, Arab women had no rights. The Quran had declared: "Women have rights similar to those (of men) over them; while men stand above them" (2:228). However, while the ulama extended more limited divorce rights to women, in contrast to men women had to go to court and had to have grounds (physical abuse, abandonment, failure to provide adequate maintenance) for divorce, grounds that, though they varied among the law schools, were limited.

Historically, divorce rather than polygamy has proved to be the more serious social problem. The situation was compounded by the fact that women have often been ignorant of their legal rights or, due to family pressures, unable (as in their other rights) to exercise them in male-dominated societies. Historically, custom often prevailed over Islamic law as well as the letter and spirit of the Quran. As in divorce law and the interpretation of veiling and seclusion, so too a woman's Quranic and legal right to contract her own marriage, receive and control her dower, or inherit often succumbed to the pressures and mores of strong patriarchal societies.

A major example of the interaction of custom and scripture is the veiling or covering (use of *hijab, chador, burqa*) and seclusion (*purdah*) of women. Both are customs assimilated by Islamic practice from the conquered Persian and Byzantine empires, which have been viewed by many, though certainly not all, as appropriate expressions of Quranic principles and values. The Quran does not stipulate the veiling and seclusion of women, although it does say that the wives of the Prophet should speak to men from behind a partition. It also admonishes women (as it does men) to dress and behave modestly (24:30–31).

The extent to which foreign practices were adopted and legitimated by Quranic practice is reflected in this commentary of a renowned Muslim Quranic scholar: "Indeed the whole of the body is to regarded as pudental and no part of her may lawfully be seen by anyone but her husband and close kin, except in case of need, as when she is undergoing medical treatment or giving evidence."[8]

Veiling and seclusion have varied considerably across Muslim societies and in different historical periods. Originally these practices had been meant to protect and honor women in upper-class urban surroundings where they enjoyed mobility and opportunities to socialize. Village and rural women were slower to adopt such measures as they interfered with their ability to work in the fields. Over the centuries as the practice spread, it had serious and deleterious effects upon the status of women religiously and socially. Many women were cut off and isolated from access to the mosque, the social and educational center of the community, an isolation that further lowered their status. Poorer women were often restricted to small houses with limited social contacts. The serious negative impact of this process in modern times was attested to by the noted Egyptian scholar and prominent religious leader Muhammad al-Ghazali (d. 1996) in the 1940s: "Ninety percent of our women do not pray at all; nor do they know of the other duties of Islam other than their names."[9]

A debate rages today in many Muslim societies about defining or redefining the status and character of the "Muslim woman." In the twentieth century, the status and role of Muslim women have changed to varying degrees, depending on the specific Muslim country. With greater opportunities for women's education and employment have also come reforms to address the inequitable legal situation of women. Modernizing governments from the 1920s to the 1960s reformed Muslim family laws in marriage, divorce, and inheritance. Reforms included measures that restrict a male's right to unilaterally divorce his wife as well as to practice polygyny by requiring a husband to obtain permission from the courts. A wife was permitted to specify in her marriage contract that a husband must obtain her permission before taking another wife. Also, a wife's grounds for divorce were increased. These reforms were partial and imposed from above through legislation. They were often resisted or reluctantly accepted by the ulama. However, with the resurgence of Islam, more conservative religious forces (ulama) and many Islamic activists have rejected family law reforms as Western inspired and called for a return to classical Islamic laws.

The Interior Path: Islamic Mysticism

Sufism, Islamic mysticism, began as an early ascetic reform that later grew into a spiritual path to be embraced by hundreds of millions of Muslims. Combining renunciation and detachment from the world with contemplation and loving devotion to God, Muslim mystics were not content to merely know and follow the will of Allah (*Shariah*). They also wanted to experience the presence of God.

The interior path (*tariqah*) of the Sufis complemented and at times conflicted with the more exterior path of Islamic law. Like the mystical paths of all the great religious traditions, the Sufi path offers a way of purification, a discipline of body and mind, whose goal is to allow direct experience of the ultimate reality, God.

Islamic mysticism, like Islamic law, began as a reform movement in the seventh century. With the phenomenal spread and success of Islam in uniting the tribes of Arabia and conquering the Byzantine and Persian Sasanid empires, the Islamic community entered a new phase in its development. The Umayyad caliphs set up court in a new capital, Damascus, amidst an imperial lifestyle and material luxuries resulting from conquest and success. Increasingly, however, some pious Muslims in many locations believed that God and submission to his will were being replaced by dynastic rulers and royal courts whose primary concerns were power and wealth. Reacting with disdain to the materialistic, this-worldly seductions of imperial Islam, these early ascetics combined study of the Quran and traditions of the Prophet and performance of religious duties with an asceticism that rejected the transient vanities of the material world and reemphasized the centrality of God and the Last Judgment. To those who seemed preoccupied with the pursuit of material success, early Sufis emphasized the impermanence of the world and the need to rediscover or become aware of the presence of God: "O you who have attained the faith! Remember Allah with unceasing remembrance and extol His limitless glory from morning to evening" (Q. 33:41–42).

The term "Sufism" comes from the coarse woolen garment (*suf*, "wool") worn by many early ascetics. They did not reject the world so much as dependence on the things of this world, allowing creation to obscure the Creator, forgetting the Absolute Reality as one is swept along and away from God by contingent, transient material realities. Desiring a more faithful return to the purity and simplicity of the Prophet's time, men and women pursued a path of ascetic self-denial and good works marked by: detachment from the material world, which was viewed as an ephemeral, transient distraction from the divine; of repentance for sins; of fear of God and the Last Judgment; and of selfless devotion to the fulfillment of God's will. Hasan al-Basri (643–728), an eminent scholar, embodied the ascetic reaction to the extravagances of imperial Islam:

> The lower (material world) is a house whose inmates labor for loss, and only abstention from it makes one happy in it. He who befriends it in desire and love for it will be rendered wretched by it, and his portion with God will be laid waste.... For this world has neither worth nor weight with God, so slight it is.[10]

The ascetic detachment of the first Sufis was complemented by the practice of Rabia al-Adawiyya, who fused renunciation with an undying devotional love of God. Muslim tradition tells us that although she was a very attractive woman, she refused all offers of marriage, unwilling to permit anyone or anything to distract her from total commitment to God. She became a great Sufi master, who served as an example and guide for her students. Her selfless devotion to God is revealed by the following words attributed to her: "O my Lord, if I worship Thee from fear of hell, burn me in hell, and if I worship Thee in hope of Paradise, exclude me thence, but if I worship Thee for Thine own sake, then withhold not from me Thine Eternal Beauty."[11]

Over the years, a variety of ascetic and ritual practices were developed as part of the mystic way. Fasting, poverty, silence, and celibacy are means of letting go of immersion in and attachment to the world. Sufis employed many techniques to "remember" God, who is always present in the world, such as rhythmic repetition of God's name along with breathing exercises to focus consciousness on God and place the devotee in the presence of God. This same principle may be found in the "Jesus prayer" of Christianity (a variation of which today is the "centering prayer") and in the use of mantras in Hinduism and Buddhism. Music and song as well as dance were also used to express deep feelings of love of God, to feel or experience his nearness, and to show devotion to God and Muhammad. The most well-known use of dance is that of Turkey's "whirling dervishes" who circle their master to imitate the divinely created order of the universe.

Among the popular practices of Sufism is the veneration of Muhammad and Sufi saints as intermediaries between God and humanity. Despite the fact that official Islamic belief emphasized that Muhammad was only a human being and not a miracle worker, his central role as the ideal model of Muslim life had generated stories of his extraordinary powers. In Sufism these stories mushroomed and were extended to Sufi saints, the friends (wali) or protégés of God, who are said to have had the power to bilocate (to be in two places at the same time), cure the sick, multiply food, and read minds. After death the burial sites or

THE SUFI PATH

At the heart of Sufism's world view and spirituality is the belief that one must die (fana, "annihilation of the lower or ego-centered self") to self to become aware of and live in (baqa, "abide") the presence of God. Sufis relied on a teacher or master (shaykh or pir), one whose authority was based not so much on books but on direct personal religious experience, for guidance in the way (tariqah). The master leads his or her disciples through the successive stages of renunciation of the transient phenomenal world, purification, and insight. Along the way, God is believed to reward and encourage the disciple through special blessings and certain religious experiences or psychological states.

mausoleums of Sufi masters became religious sanctuaries—the objects of pilgrimage, miracles, and petitions for success in this life and the next. Sufi theory organized the saints (or friends of God) into a hierarchy at whose apex was Muhammad, the pole of the universe and the perfect man, supervising the world.

Though Sufi spirituality complemented the more ritualistic and legalistic orientation of the ulama and the Shariah, the relationship between the two was often marked by a good deal of tension. The ulama tended to regard Sufi masters and the mystic way, with its spirituality that included but went beyond ulama-defined "orthodoxy," as a challenge to their authority and interpretation of Islam. Sufism offered an alternative religious community with Sufi masters, not the ulama, as religious authorities. Sufis tended to regard the ulama's legalistic definition of Islam as the letter of the law as lesser, incomplete, and subordinate to the Sufi way.

By the eleventh and twelfth centuries, Sufism seemed on a collision course with orthodoxy. These were particularly turbulent times. The Abbasid empire seemed to be unraveling; many feared that Islam was in danger from many sides. The universal caliphate at Baghdad had disintegrated into competing states. Muslim philosophers, indebted to (Greek) Hellenism and Neoplatonism, offered alternative answers to the philosophical and theological issues of the day. The philosophers espoused a rationalism that tested the ulama's belief in the primacy of faith over reason in the debates over the relationship of reason and revelation. Sufism had swept much of the Islamic world, becoming a mass movement with a strong emotional and devotional component and an eclectic tendency to incorporate local non-Islamic superstitious practices. The majority of the ulama, who were threatened by these challenges to their authority and world view, struck back in the name of Islamic orthodoxy. They condemned both Islamic philosophy and Islamic mysticism. At this critical juncture a prominent Islamic scholar emerged to save the day.

Muhammad al-Ghazali (1058–1111) received the best Islamic education available at that time and rose to become an eminent religious scholar. He enjoyed a remarkable career as a leading teacher and scholar, publishing major books that refuted Islamic philosophers like Avicenna in his *The Incoherence of the Philosophers*, maintaining that while reason had an important role to play in logic and mathematics, its application in theology and metaphysics led to confusion and threatened faith. At the height of his fame and career, he experienced a spiritual crisis. The brilliant and accomplished scholar and lecturer saw his world crumbling. He found himself deteriorating physically and psychologically, unable to speak. Despite his brilliance and extraordinary accomplishments, he felt lost, his life seemed meaningless and worthless:

> I saw I was deeply involved in affairs, and the best of my activities, my teaching, was concerned with branches of knowledge which were unimportant and worthless. I also examined my motive in teaching and saw that it was not sincere desire to serve God but that I wanted an influential

position and widespread recognition. I was in no doubt that I stood on an eroding sandbank, and in imminent danger of hell-fire if I did not busy myself with mending my ways....Worldly desires were trying to keep me chained where I was, while the herald of faith was summoning, "To the road! To the road! Little of life is left, and before you is a long journey. Your intellectual and practical involvements are hypocrisy and delusion. If you do not prepare for the future life now, when will you prepare; if you do not sever your attachments now, when will you sever them?"[12]

In desperation, al-Ghazali resigned his position, left his home and family, and went to Syria to study and practice Sufism:

I turned to the way of the mystics....[I] obtained a thorough intellectual understanding of their principles. Then I realized that what is most distinctive of them can be obtained only by personal experience [dhawq, taste], ecstasy and a change of character....I saw clearly that the mystics were men of personal experience not of words, and that I had gone as far as possible by way of study and intellectual application, so that only personal experience and walking in the mystic way were left.[13]

Al-Ghazali spent many years traveling to major Sufi centers in Arabia and Palestine, practicing and studying Sufism. During this time, he wrote what many regard as his greatest book, *The Revivification of the Religious Sciences*, in which he reconciled law, theology, and mysticism. It was a brilliant tour de force that reassured the ulama about the orthodoxy of Sufism and countered the rationalism of the philosophers. In this great synthesis, law and theology were presented in terms that the ulama could accept but they were grounded in religious experience and interior devotion (Sufism). Rationalism was tempered by the Sufi emphasis on religious experience and love of God.

Al-Ghazali came at a critical period in the history of Islam. The religious-intellectual and spiritual currents of Islam were in contention, if not on the brink of mortal conflict. Al-Ghazali reconciled the ulama and the Sufis, producing a religious synthesis and integration that earned him acclaim as one of the great scholars of Islam as well as the title "Renewer (*mujaddid*) of Islam." This title originates from the Islamic belief that in every century an individual will come to restore and revitalize the Islamic community. While the tension between many of the ulama and Sufism continued, and, as we have seen, led to attempts to reform or suppress Sufism in later centuries, al-Ghazali secured an important place for Sufism within Islam. Indeed, Sufism in the twelfth century and later swept across much of the Islamic world. Sufi orders became the great missionaries of Islam, and Sufism became integral to everyday popular religious practice and spirituality.

However, the strength of Sufism as a popular religious force also proved to be its weakness. Its flexibility, tolerance, and eclecticism, which enabled it to incorporate local indigenous religious practices and values as Islam spread to new regions, also led at times to the indiscriminate incorporation of many bizarre and superstitious practices ranging from magic and fetishism to drunkenness and sensuality. Sufism's healthy concern about the dangers in the ulama's religious legalism and ritual formalism gave way to those who rejected the official practices of Islam and engaged in a highly individualistic and idio-syncratic brand of Sufism. Emphasis on the limits of reason and importance of religious practice and experience gave way to an anti-intellectualism that rejected all Islamic learning and authority and led to the growth of supersti-tion, passivism, and fatalism. Some shaykhs became charlatans, who exploited the poor, ignorant, and well-meaning; dispensers of amulets; and wealthy land-holders. The ascetic mendicant mystic ideal (*faqir*) became the faker. Both pre-modern reformers and modernists (secular and Islamic) have blamed Sufism for the ills of the Muslim world. The Wahhabi and Mahdi revivalist movements in the eighteenth century criticized Sufi eclecticism with its resultant absorp-tion of superstitious non-Islamic practices, and in the twentieth century mod-ernists added to this critique Sufism's anti-intellectualism, passivity, and fatal-ism. Yet Sufism has remained a vital spiritual presence and force throughout much of the Islamic world.

Revelation and Reason: Islamic Theology and Philosophy

In contrast to the centrality of theology and philosophy in Christianity, both of these, though important, have never been as central to Islam as is Islamic law. Theology (*kalam*, "speech" or "discourse") in Islam grew out of the specific sociopolitical context of Islam rather than from any theoretical or dogmatic necessity: contexts arising from the Kharajite split with Ali, or early Muslim-Christian polemics, or the penetration of Greek thought during the early Abbasid period. Though it began relatively early, the science of theology did not really develop as a discipline until the Abbasid period (750–1258), when it grew under royal patronage. The first major theological issue faced by the community was raised by the Kharajites: the question of grave sin and its effect on membership in the Islamic community as well as on the legitimacy of a ruler. For the Kharajites' world view, there were only two categories: believer and unbeliever, Muslim or non-Muslim. The majority of the community rejected this position and followed that of the Murjites (to be discussed shortly), who refused to judge and expel individuals from the community, maintaining that only God on Judgment Day could judge sinners and determine whether they were excluded from membership in the community and from paradise. Except for obvious acts of apostasy, the majority concluded, an individual's faith, not specific acts, deter-mined membership in the Islamic community. Sinners remained Muslims, and non-Muslims were part of the universal mission of Islam to call (*dawa*, "the call," propagation of the faith) humanity to worship and service of God.

The Murjia position had political implications; it provided justification for legitimacy and rule. The caliphs had asserted that whatever their sins and injustices, they remained Muslims; they ruled by divine decree and their rule was predetermined by God. This of course raised the question of determinism versus free will: Does an omnipotent and omniscient God predetermine all acts and events and thus constitute the source of evil and injustice, or are human beings free to act and therefore responsible for sins? Determinists argued that free will limited an omnipotent God's power; advocates of free will countered that to deny free will ran counter to the sense of human accountability implicit in the Last Judgment. The Quran could be cited to support both positions. Human freedom is affirmed in passages such as "Truth comes from your Lord. Let anyone who will, believe, and let anyone who wishes disbelieve" (18:29). Many other verses support a determinist position: "God lets anyone He wishes go astray while He guides whomever He wishes" (35:8). The issue of free will versus predestination was a major theological issue, with the majority accepting a divinely determined universe. However, as in other monotheistic faiths, it has remained a thorny theological issue to the present time.

Islam and the State

From Muhammad's establishment of the first Muslim community at Medina in 622 CE and down through the centuries, the faith of Islam became a central force in the development of state and society. Muhammad served as the Prophet-leader of the first Muslim community-state in Medina. The soldiers, traders, and Sufis (mystics) of Islam spread God's word and rule, creating a vast land or region of Islam (*dar al-Islam*). The caliphate with its centralized Islamic empires, the Umayyad (661–750) and Abbasid (750–1258) dynasties, was followed by an extensive series of Muslim sultanates headed by rulers or sultans extending from Timbuktu in Africa to Mindanao in Southeast Asia. During this period great medieval Muslim empires emerged: the Ottoman in the Middle East, Safavid (1501–1722) in Iran, and Mughal (1483–1857) in South Asia.

However different these empires and sultanate states, Islam constituted the basic religious/ideological framework or ideal for their political and social life. Islam provided legitimation, a religiopolitical ideology, and law, informing the state's political, legal, educational, and social institutions. The ruler—caliph or sultan—as head of state was seen as the political successor of Muhammad. Though not a prophet, he was the protector of the faith who was to implement Islamic law, the official legal system, and to spread Islamic rule. Indeed, early in Islamic history religious scholars faced the question of whether the character of the ruler was decisive in determining whether the state was truly Islamic. For example, if a ruler was known to be immoral, did this mean that the state was no longer Islamic and that its citizens were required to rise up and overthrow him? The ulama or religious scholars opted for stability and determined that what made a state and society Islamic was whether it was governed by Islamic law.

The ulama were the guardians of religion, its interpreters, and as such often served as advisers to caliphs and sultans. They were not an ordained clergy, nor were they associated with organized "churches." Rather, they were a major intellectual and social force or class in society: "The ulama regarded themselves as the collective voice of the conscience of society."[14] They played a primary role in the state's religious, legal, educational, and social service institutions. The ulama were theologians and legal scholars and advisers, responsible for the administration and application of the law and the Shariah courts. They ran the schools and universities that provided education for those who aspired to public as well as religious office. They administered funds from royal grants and religious endowments that were applied to a broad range of services, from the construction and maintenance of mosques, schools, student hostels, and hospitals to roads and bridges. In time, they came to constitute a religious establishment alongside and often dependent upon the political establishment. Indeed, in many empires the ruler appointed a senior religious leader, Shaykh al-Islam, as head of religious affairs, a post that still exists in many Muslim countries today.

In an Islamic state, citizenship, or, perhaps more accurately, degree of citizenship, and taxation were also based on religious affiliation. Muslims were full citizens, enjoying all the rights and duties of this position. As discussed earlier, Jews and Christians as People of the Book (those who had previously received a revelation from God) were also citizens, but had the status of protected people (dhimmi). Islam also informed the international relations of the state. The spread of Islam as a faith and a religiopolitical system was legitimated both by the Quran and the teaching/example of Muhammad. Muslims sought to create a "Pax Islamica," much like the "Pax Romana" and what Americans later spoke of as a "Pax Americana." Conquest and diplomacy, force, persuasion, preaching, and alliances were its means. As we have seen, the obligation to strive (jihad) to follow and realize God's will meant the struggle against evil and injustice and included jihad as holy war to defend and spread Islam. As such, jihad became part and parcel of Islam's doctrine of war and peace. As Islam spread, non-Muslims were offered three options: (1) to convert to Islam, (2) to become "protected people" and pay a poll tax, (3) to become subject to "the sword," that is, jihad as holy war.

For the believer, the role of Islam in state and society reinforced a sense that there was a continuum of Muslim rule, power, and success from the time of the Prophet Muhammad to the dawn of European colonialism. Despite the contradictions of life, civil wars, impious rulers, and dynastic usurpers, the presence and continuity of an Islamic ideology and system, however different the reality might at times be from the ideal, validated and reinforced a sense of a divinely mandated and guided community with a purpose and mission. Despite its difficulties and divisions, for many Muslims the history of Islam is that of a vibrant, dynamic, and expansive faith. Islam and Muslim rule were extended over major areas of Africa; the Middle East; South, Southeast, and Central Asia; Spain; and southern Italy. As a result, Sunni Muslim history contains the belief that following the Islamic community's divine mandate to spread God's guidance and governance will lead to prosperity and power in this life as well as the promise of eternal life in heaven. The benchmark of a faithful community is its strength and vitality; the sign of failure, powerlessness or decline.

Islam and Christendom (the West): The Crusades

Despite common religious roots and instances of cooperation, the history of Islam and Western Christendom has often been marked more by confrontation than by peaceful coexistence and dialogue. For the Christian West, Islam is seen as the religion of the sword; for many Muslims, the spirit of the Christian West is epitomized by the Crusades and centuries later by a second crusade, European colonialism.

Unlike Judaism or any other world religion, Islam constituted an effective theological and political challenge to Christendom and its hegemonic ambitions. Muslim armies overran the Byzantine (Eastern Roman) Empire, Spain, and the Mediterranean from Sicily to Anatolia. At the same time, Islam challenged Christian religious claims and authority. Islam took over Christianity's supersessionist claims (to have a new covenant and revelation superseding that of the Jews). Muslims claimed that there had been a third major stage in God's revelation, a third covenant. They called Christians and Jews to recognize that they had corrupted their original revelation from God and that the one, true God in his mercy had sent his revelation one final and complete time to Muhammad. Like Christianity, Islam now claimed to have a divinely mandated universal mission to call all to worship God and to join the Islamic community and live under Islamic rule. From the seventh to the eleventh centuries, Islam spread rapidly, extending Muslim rule over Christian territories and winning Christian hearts, in time creating large numbers of converts. Many who remained Christian were Arabized, adopting Arabic language and customs. Both the mutual religious claims and political rivalry of Christianity and Islam set them on a collision course.

By the eleventh century, Christendom's response to Islam was twofold: the struggle to reconquer (the Reconquista) Andalusia Spain (1000–1492), where the coexistence of Muslims, Christians, and Jews had produced a cultural florescence, and the undertaking of the Crusades (1095–1453).

Jerusalem had been taken by Arab armies in 638. Thereafter, for five centuries, Muslims lived in peaceful coexistence with Christians and with Jews, who were previously banned by Christian rulers but were permitted by Muslims to return, live, and worship in the city of Solomon and David. However, in the eleventh century political events and an imperial-papal power play that pitted Christendom against Islam began a continuing legacy of misunderstanding and distrust.

In 1071, the Byzantine emperor Alexius I, whose army had been decisively defeated by a Seljuq (Abbasid) army, feared that all Asia Minor would be overrun. He called upon other Christian rulers and the pope to come to the aid of

Constantinople by undertaking a "pilgrimage" or crusade to free Jerusalem and its environs from Muslim rule. For Pope Urban II, the "defense" of Jerusalem provided an opportunity to gain recognition of the papacy's authority and role in legitimating the actions of temporal rulers. In addition, Christian rulers, knights, and merchants were driven by the promise of economic and commercial (booty, trade, and banking) rewards coming from the creation of a Latin kingdom in the Middle East. A divided Christendom united, its warriors spurred by material as well as spiritual rewards (the promise of heaven for its martyrs), in a holy war against the "infidel" to ostensibly liberate the holy city. The appeal to religion captured the popular mind and gained its support. This was ironic because as one scholar has observed, "God may have indeed wished it, but there is certainly no evidence that the Christians of Jerusalem did, or that anything extraordinary was occurring to pilgrims there to prompt such a response at that time in history."[15]

Few events have had a more shattering and long-lasting effect on Muslim-Christian relations than the Crusades. Three myths pervade Western perceptions of the Crusades: first, that Muslims were the provocateurs; second, that Christendom triumphed; and third, that the Crusades were simply fought by Christianity for the liberation of Jerusalem. For many in the West, the specific facts regarding the Crusades are but a dim memory.[16] Indeed, many neither know who started the Crusades, why they were fought, nor how the battle was won. In fact, the Crusades were launched by Pope Urban and Christian rulers, for causes as much political and economic as religious, and on balance Muslims prevailed.

For Muslims, the collective memory of the Crusades lives on as the clearest example of militant Christianity, an early harbinger of the aggression and imperialism of the Christian West, a vivid reminder of Christianity's early hostility toward Islam. If many regard Islam as a religion of the sword, Muslims down through the ages speak of the West's Crusader mentality and ambitions. While historians in the West speak of Richard the "Lion Hearted," Muslims remember Richard as the conqueror who, having promised to spare women and children, took Jerusalem (1099) and slaughtered all its Muslim inhabitants indiscriminately in establishing the Latin kingdom. They contrast his behavior with that of Salah al-Din (Saladin), the great Muslim general who in reconquering the holy city (1187) spared noncombatants.

By the fifteenth century the Crusades had spent their force. Although ostensibly launched to unite Christendom and turn back Muslim armies, the opposite had occurred:

> An ironical but undeniable result of the Crusades was the deterioration of the position of Christian minorities in the Holy Land. Formerly these minorities had been accorded rights and privileges under Muslim rule, but, after the establishment of the Latin Kingdom, they found themselves treated as "loathsome schismatics." In an effort to obtain relief from

persecution by their fellow Christians, many abandoned their Nestorian or Monophysite beliefs, and adopted either Roman Catholic, or—the supreme irony—Islam.[17]

Amid a bitterly divided Christendom, the Byzantine capital, Constantinople, fell in 1453 before Muslim armies and, renamed Istanbul, became the seat of the Ottoman Empire.

For Muslim-Christian relations, it is less a case of what actually happened in the Crusades than how they have been remembered. The legacy of the Crusades depends upon where one stands in history. Both Christian and Muslim communities had competing visions and interests. Each community looks back with memories of its commitment to faith and heroic stories of valor and chivalry against "the infidel." For many in the West, the assumption of a Christian victory is predicated on a romanticized history with its celebration of the valor of Crusaders. This is combined with a tendency to interpret history through the experience of Western ascendancy and superiority of the past two centuries, European colonialism, and America and the West's preeminence in recent decades. Each community (Islam and Christianity) sees the other as militant, holy warriors, who were somewhat barbaric and fanatic in their religious zeal, determined to conquer, convert, or eradicate the other—thus an enemy of God, an obstacle and threat to the realization of God's will. As we shall see, the history of their contention continued through the next wave of European colonialism and finally in the superpower rivalry of the twentieth century.

How do we get from Muslim memories of a centuries-long history of vitality, creativity, power, and success vis-à-vis the West to the situation today, in which much of the Muslim world is part of the developing rather than the developed world? How do we get from not only the confrontations of the past but also the coexistence and tolerance of Andalusia to contemporary concerns about a clash of civilizations between Islam and the West? Why is Islam simply equated by many with violence, religious extremism, and terrorism: from hostage taking and hijackings to holy wars, assassinations, and bombings?

Understanding Islam today requires an appreciation of key historical events from the eighteenth to the twentieth centuries as well as of the causes and nature of premodern and modern reform movements. Both sacred texts and long-held religious beliefs combined with the specific sociopolitical contexts of Muslim societies have been critical factors in producing a diversity of Muslim experiences and interpretations of Islam.

Premodern Revivalist Movements

Islam today is an immediate and direct heir to both premodern and modern Muslim responses to the decline and disintegration of Muslim societies and the challenge of European colonialism and modernity. Muslims, like all religious believers, seek to understand and apply their religious beliefs and values to their lives. To the extent that they perceive a serious or dangerous gap between their faith and how they live their lives, many have turned to their religious tradition for new answers.

From the eighteenth to the twentieth centuries, the Islamic world witnessed a protracted period of upheaval and renewal. Muslims in many countries struggled with internal failure and decline in their societies as well as with the external threat from European colonialism. Such crises sparked responses from religious social/political revivalist movements that quite literally spanned the breadth of the Islamic world: from the Mahdi in the Sudan, the Sanusi in Libya, the Fulani in Nigeria, the Wahhabi in Saudi Arabia, to the Padri in Indonesia. Though their political and socioeconomic conditions varied, all shared a common concern about the religious, political, and social disintegration of Islam and a conviction that the cure was a purification or renewal of their way of life and societies.

Islamic revivalist movements draw on a long and rich history and tradition of revival (tajdid) and reform (islah). Throughout Islamic history, the failures of and threats to Muslim societies have given rise to individual reformers and to reformist movements led by scholars and mystics alike. Islamic revival and reform involve a call for a return to the fundamentals (the Quran and Sunnah) and the right to interpret (ijtihad—use independent judgment) these primary sources of Islam. Islah is a Quranic term (7:170; 11:117; 28:19) that describes the vocation and activities of prophets. As in Judaism and Christianity, prophets are messengers or "warners," reformers who call upon wayward or sinful communities to return to God's path. Thus, Muslim reformers called for the realignment of individual and community life with the norms of the Shariah. This Quranic mandate, coupled with God's command (3:104, 110) to enjoin good and prohibit evil, provides the time-honored rationale for Islamic reformism.

The tradition of renewal is based on a saying of the Prophet that "God will send to this umma at the head of each century those who will renew its faith for it."[18] The renewer (mujaddid) is believed to be sent at the beginning of each century to purify and restore true Islamic practice and thus regenerate a community that over time tends to stray from the straight path of Islam. This belief took on popular religious forms; the most important was that of the *Mahdi* (divinely guided one). In contrast to those who simply claimed to be qualified to interpret or reinterpret Islam, a mahdi, though not a prophet, asserted that he was a divinely appointed and inspired representative of God. While Islamic renewers or revivalists claimed simply to return to the original teachings of the Quran and the Prophet Muhammad, in fact they produced new religious interpretations and cultural syntheses needed to guide their age.

Mysticism (Sufism) was a central force in Muslim societies and a concern for some revivalist movements, as it was blamed for the backwardness and failures (the political, moral, and social decline) of many societies. Sufism's flexibility and openness to local, indigenous beliefs and practices proved a great strength in adapting Islam to local cultures and therefore making it that much more effective in attracting large numbers of converts. However, every weakness is an overused strength. Critics, such as Muhammad ibn Abd al-Wahhab in Arabia, charged that the very flexibility of Sufism opened the door to its association with all manner of local "pagan" idolatrous superstitions. He and others charged that Sufism's overemphasis on the next life, its otherworldly orientation, resulted in adherents passively withdrawing from engagement in the affairs of this world.

While Muhammad ibn Abd al-Wahhab sought to suppress Sufism in Arabia entirely, most revivalists wished to reform it. For example, the vast majority of African jihad movements, as they were called, were led by reformist, militant, politically oriented Sufi orders. Reformers sought to reform rather than suppress, to realign Sufism with the guidelines of the Shariah. They redefined

THE WORLD VIEW OF REVIVALISM

Reformers believed that they were reenacting the paradigmatic drama of early Islam, establishing (or, more accurately, reestablishing), as Muhammad had done, God's rule on earth. Thus, they claimed to be restoring or re-creating the ideal, early community-state of the Prophet. Revivalist movements, combining prayer and political action, established Islamic states based upon the Shariah. They waged a jihad to defend, purify, and restore the integrity (orthodoxy) and earthly strength of their community.

The major stages in this process were the creation of a sociomoral reform movement, a religious community-state of "true believers" who waged a jihad against those Muslims who disagreed or resisted; a return to pristine Islam, to the teachings of the Quran and the Sunnah of the Prophet Muhammad and the early Muslim community, through a process of rigorous, fundamental reform; and the right to interpret the Quran and Sunnah. The integral components of the revivalist world view were (1) the belief that the righteous community established by the Prophet at Medina constitutes the timeless and eternal model for the Muslim community; (2) the need for removal of foreign, that is, un-Islamic historical accretions or unwarranted innovations that had infiltrated and corrupted the community; and (3) a critique of established Islamic institutions, in particular, the religious establishment's (the ulama's) interpretations of Islam. In contrast to the Islamic modernism of the nineteenth and twentieth centuries, the purpose of these revivalists was not to reinterpret Islam in order to accommodate new perspectives and yield new solutions. Rather, they wished to reclaim and reappropriate the essentially complete vision of Islam, preserve the Quran and Sunnah, and reestablish an authentic Islamic community modeled on that of the Prophet and his early Companions.

Sufism to emphasize a spirituality that included and stressed a this-world, activist Islam. The sociopolitical dimension of Islam was reintroduced.

The Wahhabi movement in Arabia and the Mahdiyya in Africa are perhaps the best known of premodern Islamic movements. Each has been a formative influence on modern Muslim states (the Wahhabi in Saudi Arabia and Mahdi in Sudan) and, although similar in some respects, represent contrasting styles of leadership and reform. A religious leader, Muhammad ibn Abd al-Wahhab (1703–1792) and a local tribal chief, Muhammad ibn Saud (d. 1765) joined forces to produce a united, militant religiopolitical movement that would subdue large areas of Arabia and leave a religious and political legacy that continues today. Although popularly called the Wahhabi movement, after Abd al-Wahhab, its own self-designation was the "Unitarians" (*muwahiddun*), those who practice and uphold monotheism, worship of the one true God. Abd al-Wahhab, a jurist and theologian, was dismayed by the condition of his society, which he saw as having degenerated to a condition little better than that of pre-Islamic Arabia, the *jahiliyya* or period of ignorance of Islam. He was appalled by popular religious practices such as the veneration of Sufi saints and their tombs, which he believed compromised the unity or oneness of God (absolute monotheism) and that of the Islamic community in Arabia, which had fallen back into tribalism and tribal warfare. He condemned these and other practices as pagan superstitions and idolatry (*shirk*), to substitute anything for God, the worst sin in Islam. They were unwarranted innovations, which he denounced as deviations (*bida*), similar to the charge of heresy in Christianity, from true Islam. Abd al-Wahhab called for a rigorous purification of Islam from all such foreign un-Islamic practices.

The Wahhabi movement waged a rigorous holy war to subdue and once again unite the tribes of Arabia; the warrior-missionaries were called the Brotherhood, *Ikhwan*. Muslims who disagreed with them were not tolerated but rather were declared enemies of God who must be fought. In contrast to the Mahdist and other revivalist movements, the Wahhabi chose to completely suppress rather than merely reform Sufism. Their zeal resulted in a puritan iconoclasm that led them to destroy not only Sufi shrines but also other sacred tombs and shrines, including the tombs of the Prophet and his Companions as well as that of Husayn, a major Shii holy shrine and place of pilgrimage. This act has affected Wahhabi-Shii relations to this day, as witnessed in recent times in adversarial Saudi-Iranian relations as well as clashes and conflict between the Sunni majority and Shii minority within Saudi Arabia in the late 1970s and the 1980s.

In contrast to the Wahhabi movement, the Mahdi of the Sudan, like other African revivalists, was a charismatic Sufi leader who initiated a militant reformist religiopolitical movement. Muhammad Ahmad (1848–1885), the founder of the Mahdiyya order, proclaimed himself Mahdi ("divinely guided one") in 1881. Thus, he went beyond most other revivalist reformers who claimed the right to interpret Islam and instead claimed to be a divinely appointed and inspired representative of God. The Mahdi established an Islamic community, uniting his followers, who like the Prophet's Companions were called Ansar, "helpers," and justified waging holy war against other Muslims (Sudan's Ottoman Muslim rulers) by declaring them infidels who "disobeyed the command of His messenger and His Prophet ... ruled in a manner not in accord with what God had sent...altered the sharia of our master, Muhammad the messenger of God, and blasphemed against the faith of God."[19]

Sufism was reformed, and alcohol, prostitution, gambling, and music were outlawed as foreign (Ottoman Egyptian), un-Islamic practices that had corrupted society. From 1885 to 1889, after Mahdist forces overcame Egyptian forces, an Islamic state was established in Khartoum. The mahdi had supreme power as God's representative and the Sharia was its law.

ISLAM AND MODERNITY

By the nineteenth century, the internal decline of Muslim societies led to their ultimate vulnerability to external powers. Like many parts of the world, they fell victim to European imperialism. The dominant reality in shaping the modern Muslim world politically, economically, and religioculturally was the impact of European imperialism. When Europe overpowered North Africa, the Middle East, South Asia, and Southeast Asia in the nineteenth century, reducing most Muslim societies to colonies, many Muslims experienced these defeats as a religious as well as a political and cultural crisis. Colonialism brought European armies and Christian missionaries, who attributed their conquests not only to their military and economic power, but also to the truth and superiority of Western Christian civilization. Europe legitimated its colonization of large areas of the underdeveloped Muslim world religioculturally. The French spoke of a "mission to civilize" and the British of "the white man's burden." Missionaries accompanied the armies of bureaucrats, soldiers, traders, and teachers to spread the message of Western (Christian) political and cultural superiority and dominance.

Muslim responses to "Christian" Europe's political/religious penetration and dominance varied significantly, ranging from resistance or warfare in "defense of Islam" to accommodation, if not outright assimilation of Western values. Some advocated following the example of the Prophet Muhammad, who in the face of rejection and persecution in Mecca chose to initially emigrate from Mecca to Medina and later to fight. However, the military defense of Islam and Muslim territory generally proved fruitless in the face of the large modernized weapons of superior European forces, and emigration to a "safe, independent" Muslim territory was logistically and physically impossible for most.

The response of many Muslim rulers from Egypt to Iran was an attempt to emulate or adopt that which had made the West triumphant—its knowledge, science, and technology as well as its culture. From Muhammad Ali,

MUSLIM RESPONSES TO EUROPEAN COLONIALISM

In grappling with European dominance, several groups offered alternative ideological models for the revitalization of Islam and the defense of Muslim interests, rooted in contending interpretations of Islam and its relationship to state and society. The four general tendencies or perspectives were (1) the conservative traditionalism of the ulama, who sought to broadly reapply traditional Islamic teachings and law; (2) a Western-inspired secular modernism that embraced the new European-oriented order with its separation of religion and the state (the progressive restriction of religion to private rather than public life); (3) Islamic modernism, which sought to respond to the threat of Western hegemony by resurrecting a debilitated Islamic community through a modern reinterpretation or reformulation of Islam; and finally (4) a modern Islamic revivalist movement (sometimes referred to as "Islamic fundamentalism") that harnessed religion and social and political activism. These models or approaches continue to exist today, although their relative power and influence have changed.

the nineteenth-century ruler of Egypt, to the shahs of Iran in the twentieth century, the goal was development of modernized societies with modern militaries. Even those Muslim rulers who sought to overthrow Western hegemony seemed convinced of its superiority and were drawn by its accomplishments and power. Students were sent to the West to study, to learn the sources of its success. New "modern" schools and institutions, based on European models and curricula, were created in many parts of the Muslim world to provide a "modern" education for a new generation. Alongside traditional Islamic schools and great mosque-universities like Egypt's al-Azhar University, new universities such as Cairo University, Baghdad University, Damascus University, and the University of Malaya, which offered a modern, Western-based curriculum, were established. Major universities were also established by foreign (Christian) missionaries and countries: the Syrian Protestant College (subsequently renamed the American University of Beirut), the French Jesuits' St. Joseph's University in Beirut, the American University in Cairo, and Roberts College (renamed Bogazici University) in Istanbul. As a result, a modern, Westernized elite establishment quickly emerged.

Most modern elites, though politically desirous of throwing off the political dominance of European colonialism, were intellectually and culturally influenced by, if not dependent on, the West for their education and dress as well as for many of their beliefs and values. They regarded the traditional Muslim religious establishment, the ulama or scholars who interpreted Islam, as relics of the past, incapable of inspiring and responding to the demands of the day. Most advocated a Western, secular model of development: not only appropriating Western political, economic, and social institutions but also introducing a process of secularization, separation of church and state, a restriction of religion to private, rather than public, life.

Secular Modernism

Taha Husayn (1889–1973) and Ali Abd al-Raziq in Egypt (1886–1966) represent this liberal secular tendency among emerging modern elites. Taha Husayn epitomized the transition from a traditional religious to a modern secular orientation. Although blind from an early age, he was educated at Cairo's two premier institutions of higher learning, al-Azhar University, the oldest center of Islamic learning, and the Egyptian (Cairo) University, the newly established modern (secular) national university. This was followed by four years (1915–1919) of study in France, where he earned a doctorate from the Sorbonne. Husayn became an internationally known writer and educator, and served as Egypt's minister of education (1950–1952).

Few books represent more the cultural crossroads that Muslims faced in the early twentieth century and the Western orientation of many emerging Muslim elites than Taha Husayn's *The Future of Culture in Egypt*. It embodies the rationale of those who concluded that future strength was best achieved not by a return to an Islamic past or in the path of Islamic modernism but rather by an aggressive pursuit of Western-oriented liberal, secular reform. An unabashed admirer of the West, Taha Husayn attempted to legitimate secularism by claiming that it had long been part of Egypt's Islamic traditions: "From earliest times Muslims have been well aware of the now universally acknowledged principle that a political system and a religion are different things, that a constitution and a state rest, above everything else, on practical foundations."[20]

Ali Abd al-Raziq took the Western, liberal secular tendency to its logical conclusion. Educated as a religious scholar at Cairo's al-Azhar University, he became a judge in the Shariah court. Abd al-Raziq wrote *Islam and the Principles of Government* in response to the "caliphate crisis."

Although the caliphate had ceased to exist with the fall of the Abbasid dynasty (Baghdad) in 1258, it remained a powerful religious symbol of legitimacy. In later centuries, Ottoman sultans appropriated the title "caliph" to religiously legitimate their rule over an area that stretched from Egypt to Iraq. However, Christian Europe's occupation of Constantinople after World War I, in punishment for Turkey's failure to support the Allies in their war with Germany, threatened the future of the Ottoman Empire and its caliph.

Many Muslims from the Middle East to South Asia called for the defense of Islam and the restoration of the caliphate. In contrast to these sentiments, Ali Abd al-Raziq boldly repudiated the belief that Islam and politics were historically intertwined. His denial of a traditional religiopolitical doctrine that Islam required the fusion of religion and political power became a lightning rod for orthodoxy. Critics of Ali Abd al-Raziq's liberal secular position charged that he simply copied the West, denied Islam's comprehensive religious world view, undermined traditional Islamic beliefs and institutions, and contributed to the disunity and weakness of the Islamic community. He was condemned by a council of al-Azhar religious scholars and lost his position in an affair that epitomized the issue of the relationship of Islam and secularism, an issue that has continued to the present.

Islamic Modernism

Both Taha Husayn and Ali Abd al-Raziq had been early students and disciples of Muhammad Abduh, a major figure in the Islamic modernist movement. In the late nineteenth and early twentieth centuries, Islamic reformers sought to bridge the gap between conservative religious leaders and modernizing secular elites, to demonstrate that Islam was not necessarily incompatible with modernization. Islamic modernists advocated the reinterpretation of religious doctrine and practice in light of the needs of modernizing societies through programs of religious, educational, and social reform. Reformers advocated a bold reinterpretation (ijtihad) of Islam to respond to the realities of modern life. They rejected both the tendency of the ulama to cling blindly to past traditions and religious interpretations as well as the indiscriminate Westernization advocated by many secular modernists. Thus, for example, through a process of reinterpreting verses in the Quran, they introduced reforms that enhanced the status of women, introducing measures to restrict polygamy, limit a husband's right to divorce, broaden the grounds for women to sue for divorce, and improve maintenance payments and child custody regulations.

Islamic modernism asserted the compatibility of faith and reason, of Islam and modernity. It provided an Islamic rationale for the reinterpretation of Islamic doctrine and law, for the adoption or adaptation of modern ideas, science, technology, and institutions. Proclaiming that Islam was a religion of reason, science, and progress, reformers called upon Muslims to reclaim those beliefs, attitudes, and values that had made the Islamic community so successful in the past, that had contributed to the creation of Islamic empires and a world-class civilization.

Maintaining that the decline of the Muslim community was not due to Islam but to Muslims' departure from the dynamic faith of Muhammad, Islamic reformers advocated a process of purification and reconstruction, of renewal and reform, to overcome what they viewed as the prevailing static medieval religious world view. Centers of Islamic modernist thought sprang up across the Muslim world from Cairo to Jakarta. Among the more important reformers and movements were those of Muhammad Abduh (1849–1905) in the Middle East and of Sayyid Ahmad Khan (1817–1898) and Muhammad Iqbal (1876–1938) in South Asia. All were pioneers whose legacy informed much of Muslim reformist thought and action in the early twentieth century from North Africa to Southeast Asia.

The debate within the Islamic community concerning appropriate responses to modernity was similar to that of other faiths. Community leaders, traditionalists and reformers alike, offered contending religious interpretations about how to deal with the challenge of European colonialism, the relationship of religion and science, the question of Islamic legal reform, and women's education and rights. Conservative religious leaders maintained that Islamic religious doctrines and practices were totally adequate and relevant. They saw little need for substantive reform and accused reformers (secular and Islamic alike) of seeking to "Westernize" Islam. Islamic modernists countered that Islam was a dynamic faith, capable of responding to the demands of the modern world, but that to do so required that some "medieval doctrines" be replaced by a fresh reinterpretation of Islam and of Islamic law.

The challenge of Islamic modernism to the conservative religious establishment focuses on both their doctrines and their leadership. Modernists rejected blind acceptance (*taqlid*, "imitation") of the authority of the past, distinguishing between the divine, the immutability of that which came from God, and the human, that which was the product of religious scholars' interpretation. Moreover, most of the modernists were not traditionally trained religious scholars, many of whose predecessors had determined by the thirteenth century that, Islamic law having been fully delineated, all that was left for future generations was to follow rather than continue to interpret and to apply the law to changing circumstances. These reformers were modern educated "laymen" who not only criticized the conservatism of the ulama, whom they portrayed as out of touch with modern realities, but also claimed for themselves the right to interpret and reinterpret Islam. They reasserted that Islam knows no clergy and thus rejected both the authoritative role of the ulama as the sole "keepers of Islam" as well as the binding nature of the ulama's legal doctrines/interpretations.

The rationale of Islamic modernism was simple. Reformers insisted that the corpus of Islamic law consisted, on the one hand, of divinely revealed and thus immutable laws and, on the other, of laws that were human interpretations that met the needs of past historical and social contexts and were therefore subject to change. Although such laws were adequate guidelines in the past, reformers maintained that a fresh interpretation of Islam was now required to meet the new circumstances and conditions of the modern world. Thus, they distinguished between the unchanging laws of God (observances governing prayer, fasting, pilgrimage) and social legislation or regulations that were capable of reformulation and change.

Islamic modernists implemented their new ideas and agendas through political action and educational, legal, and social reforms. In Egypt, Muhammad Abduh, a religious scholar, reinterpreted scripture and tradition to provide an Islamic rationale for modern Muslim reform. When Abduh became mufti of

Egypt (head of its religious court system) in 1899, he introduced changes in Egypt's Shariah courts. As a judge he interpreted and applied Islam to modern conditions, using a methodology that combined a return to the fundamental sources of Islam with an acceptance of modern rational thought.

Critical of many religious leaders' inability to address modern problems, Abduh modernized the curriculum at al-Azhar University, the venerable Islamic university whose graduates were religious leaders throughout the Muslim world, to change their training and intellectual outlook. Abduh called for educational and social reforms to improve and protect the status of women, supporting their access to education and arguing that the Quranic marriage ideal was monogamy, not polygamy.

In the Indian subcontinent (what is today India, Pakistan, and Bangladesh), Sayyid Ahmad Khan and later Muhammad Iqbal were among the more prominent voices for Islamic reform. Ahmad Khan rejected the classical formulations of Islam fashioned by the ulama and claimed to be returning to the original Islam of the Quran and Muhammad. Arguing that Islam and nature or science were compatible, he advocated a new theological formulation or reformulation of Islam: "Today we need, as in former days, a modern theology [*ilm al-kalam*] by which we either render futile the tenets of modern sciences or [show them to be] doubtful, or bring them into harmony with the doctrines of Islam."[21] To implement his ideas and produce a new generation of Muslim leaders, in 1874 he established the Muhammadan Anglo-Oriental College at Aligarh, India, renamed Aligarh University in 1920. It was modeled on Cambridge University, with a course of studies that combined the best of a European curriculum with a modernist interpretation of Islam.

Muhammad Iqbal embodied the conflicting agendas of modernists. Educated at Government College in Lahore, Pakistan, he studied in England and Germany, where he earned a law degree and a doctorate in philosophy. Iqbal's modern synthesis and reinterpretation of Islam combined the best of the East and the West, his Islamic heritage with Western philosophy (Hegel, Bergson, Fichte, and Nietzsche). He was both an admirer and a critic of the West. Acknowledgment of the West's dynamic spirit, intellectual tradition, and technology was balanced by his sharp critique of European colonialism—the materialism and exploitation of capitalism, the atheism of Marxism, and the moral bankruptcy of secularism. Iqbal's reformist impulse and vision, embodied in his extensive writings and poetry, were succinctly summarized in *The Reconstruction of Religious Thought in Islam*. Like other Islamic modernists, Iqbal rejected much of medieval Islam as static and stagnant, part of the problem rather than the solution for a debilitated community. He saw Islam as emerging from five hundred years of "dogmatic slumber" and compared the need for Islamic reform to the Reformation: "We are today passing through a period similar to that of the Protestant Reformation in Europe and the lesson which the rise and outcome of Luther's movement teaches should not be lost on us."[22]

Iqbal emphasized the need to reclaim the vitality and dynamism of early Islamic thought and practice, calling for a bold reinterpretation of Islam. He attempted to develop alternative Islamic models for modern Muslim societies. He looked to the past to "rediscover" principles and values that could be reinterpreted to reconstruct an alternative Islamic model for modern Muslim society. Thus, he identified precedents in Islamic belief that through reinterpretation could yield Islamic equivalents of Western democracy and parliamentary government. Because of the centrality of such beliefs as the equality and brotherhood of believers, Iqbal concluded, democracy was the most important political ideal in Islam. He maintained that although the seizure of power by Muawiya after the period of the Rightly Guided Caliphs and the creation of dynastic governments had prevented realization of this Islamic democratic ideal, it remained the duty of the Muslim community to realize it. He did not believe that he was simply appropriating Western values. This is strikingly evident in his conclusion that England had borrowed and embodied this "Muslim" quality (Islam's democratic ideal): "Democracy has been the great mission of England in modern times... it is one aspect of our political ideal that is being worked out in it. It... makes it the greatest Muhammadan Empire in the world."[23]

It was this same belief in the unity and brotherhood of all believers that formed Iqbal's objection to modern territorial nationalism, which threatened the pan-Islamic unity of the Islamic community. However, like many other Islamic modernists, his religious idealism was tempered by a political realism that led him to accept the need for Muslims to gain national independence. However, once that was achieved, he believed that as a family of nations who, however different, shared a common spiritual heritage and values, and a common law, the Shariah, Muslim nations should form their own League of Nations. He applied this same logic in India. During the independence movement, convinced that Hindu-Muslim communal harmony was not possible in a Hindu-dominated state, he called for the creation of a separate region or state for Muslims that allowed them to preserve their distinctive Islamic identity, solidarity, and way of life: "The nature of the Prophet's religious experience, as disclosed in the Quran, is wholly different [from that of Christianity].... The religious ideal of Islam is organically related to the social order which it has created."[24] In contrast to the secularist Muhammad Ali Jinnah, the founder of Pakistan, Iqbal believed that the basis of the state and its source of unity should be the Shariah. However, he did not advocate a simple restoration of classical Islamic law. For Iqbal, just as God has a dynamic, creative life that is both permanent and changing, Islam's way of life as interpreted and delineated in Islamic law is dynamic and open to change: "The early doctors of law taking their cue from this groundwork evolved a number of legal systems. But with all their comprehensiveness, these systems are after all individual interpretations and as such can claim no finality."[25]

Islamic modernism inspired movements for religious reform and national independence but remained primarily attractive only to an intellectual elite. Its major contribution, however, was to provide much of the vocabulary for Islamic reformism and to legitimate a modernist agenda. It provided a general rationale and methodology for reform as well as a vocabulary and agenda. In particular, it stressed the compatibility of religion and reason, the need for ijtihad, and thus for religious, political, and social reforms. Islamic modernism provided the precedent for Islamizing "modern" ideas and institutions (from the nation-state and parliamentary government to women's education) as well as the notion that the category of those qualified to interpret Islam should be extended beyond the monopoly exercised historically by the ulama. However, it failed to produce a systematic reinterpretation of Islam or to develop effective organizations to preserve, propagate, and implement its message. These failures contributed to the emergence of Islamic organizations like the Muslim Brotherhood in Egypt and the Islamic Society in South Asia.

Neorevivalist (Neofundamentalist) Movements

The continued presence and power of Europe in the Muslim world and the seeming failure of reformers to effectively block the spread of Western political and cultural penetration spawned two major Islamic revivalist movements in the Middle East and South Asia in the 1930s, the Muslim Brotherhood (Ikhwan al-Muslimi) and the Islamic Society (Jamaat-i-Islami). Both were to become the models for a host of contemporary Islamic movements and organizations that we read about in the press across the Muslim world today. While all sought and continue to seek to recapture the strength and vitality of an Islamic past, their methods and agendas differed.

Islamic activist organizations have been the driving force behind the dynamic spread of the contemporary Islamic resurgence. Their trailblazers, Hasan al-Banna (1906–1949) and Sayyid Qutb (1906–1966) of the Brotherhood and Mawlana Abul Ala Mawdudi (1903–1979) of the Jamaat, have had an incalculable impact on the development of Islamic movements throughout the Muslim world. Both movements constructed an ideological world view based on an interpretation of Islam that informed social and political activism. They are the architects of contemporary Islamic revivalism, men whose ideas and methods have been studied and emulated by scholars and activists from the Sudan to Indonesia.

Both Hassan al-Banna and Mawlana Abul Ala Mawdudi drew on and were influenced by Islam's theological and historical resources for renewal and reform and by the more proximate example of premodern Islamic revivalism in the eighteenth century. The legacies of Islamic activist movements like the Wahhabi, Sanusi, and Mahdi and of Islamic modernism form the context for the formation of the Muslim Brotherhood and the Jamaat-i-Islami. Both organizations emerged at a time when the Muslim world remained weak and in decline, much of it occupied and ruled by foreign powers. Egypt was occupied by Britain from 1882 to 1952, and the Indian subcontinent was ruled by Britain from 1857 to 1947, when modern India and Pakistan achieved independence.

The linkage of the Brotherhood and the Jamaat with their eighteenth-century predecessors is reflected in the penchant of those who called the Wahhabi and Mahdi movements fundamentalist to dub the Muslim Brotherhood and the Jamaat neofundamentalist, due to their insistence on returning to the sources of Islam. Although referred to as fundamentalist, the Brotherhood and the Jamaat were quite modern-oriented (though not necessarily Western) in their ideological agenda, organization, and activities. Rather than fleeing the modern world, they sought to engage and control it.

Hassan al-Banna, a schoolteacher, established the Muslim Brotherhood in Egypt in 1928 and Mawlana Abul Ala Mawdudi, a journalist, organized the Jamaat-i-Islami in India in 1941. These contemporaries both combined traditional Islamic educational backgrounds with a knowledge of modern Western thought. They believed that their societies were dominated by and dependent on the West, politically and culturally. Both al-Banna and Mawdudi posited an "Islamic alternative" to conservative religious leaders and modern, Western, secular-oriented elites. The ulama were generally regarded as passé, a religious class whose fossilized Islam and co-optation by governments was a major cause for the backwardness of the Islamic community. Modernists were seen as having traded away the very soul of Muslim society out of their blind admiration for the West:

> All these people in their misinformed and misguided zeal to serve what they hold to be the cause of Islam, are always at great pains to prove that Islam contains within itself the elements of all types of contemporary social and political thought and action.... [T]his attitude emerges from an inferiority complex, from the belief that we as Muslims can earn no honour or respect unless we are able to show our religion resembles modern creeds and is in agreement with most of the contemporary ideologies.[26]

The Brotherhood and the Jamaat proclaimed Islam a self-sufficient, all-encompassing way of life, an ideological alternative to Western capitalism and Marxism. They did not simply retreat to the past. Joining thought to action, they provided Islamic responses, ideological and organizational, to their twentieth-century Muslim societies to address such issues as how best to respond to European colonialism and to revitalize the Muslim community and its fortunes. Religious vision or ideology informed, motivated, and inspired their political as well as social activism. In contrast to Islamic modernists who justified adopting Western ideas and institutions because they were compatible with Islam, al-Banna and Mawdudi sought to produce a new interpretation or synthesis. It began with Islamic sources and then found either Islamic equivalents or Islamic sources for new interpretations regarding government accountability, legal change, popular participation in the political process, and educational reform.

For al-Banna and Mawdudi, the religiocultural penetration of the West (education, law, customs, values) was far more pernicious and dangerous in the long run than political intervention, since it threatened the very identity and survival of the Muslim community.

Though opposed to Westernization, the Brotherhood and Jamaat were not antimodernization. They engaged in modern organization and institution building, provided modern educational and social welfare services, and used modern technology and mass communications to spread their message and to mobilize popular support. Their message itself, though rooted in Islamic revelation and sources, was clearly written for a twentieth-century audience. It addressed the problems of modernity, analyzing the relationship of Islam to nationalism, democracy, capitalism, Marxism, modern banking, education and law, women and work, Zionism, and international relations.

Organizationally, the Brotherhood and the Jamaat believed that, like Muhammad and the early Muslim community in Mecca, they were a vanguard, righteous communities within the broader community. Like Muhammad and like later eighteenth-century reform movements, these twentieth-century organizations created an Islamic brotherhood or society that was to be the dynamic nucleus for a true Islamic reformation or revolution in society. Both organizations recruited followers from mosques, schools, and universities: students, workers, merchants, and young professionals who were primarily urban based and from the lower-middle and middle classes. The goal was to produce a new generation of modern-educated but Islamically oriented leaders prepared to take their place in every sector of society. However, while al-Banna worked to develop a broad-based populist (mass) movement, Mawdudi's Jamaat was more of an elite religious organization (with multiple levels of membership), whose primary goal was to train leaders who would come to power. While both viewed an Islamic revolution as necessary to introduce an Islamic state and society, the revolution was to be first and foremost a social rather than a violent political revolution. The establishment of an Islamic state first required the Islamization of society through a gradual process of social change. Muslims had to be "reborn," to reclaim and reappropriate their Islamic identity and practice. The Brotherhood and the Jamaat disseminated their interpretation of Islam through schools, publications, preaching, social services, and student organizations, combining religious commitment, modern learning/technology, and social/political activism. Both the Brotherhood and the Jamaat maintained that Muslims should not look to Western capitalism or communism (white and red imperialism), but solely to Islam, the divinely revealed foundation for state and society. The Brotherhood charged that faith in the West was misplaced. Western democracy had not only failed to check but also contributed to authoritarianism (the manipulation of the masses by modern elites), economic exploitation, corruption, and social injustice. Western secularism and materialism undermined religion and morality, society and the family. These early Islamic activists believed that the inherent

IDEOLOGICAL ORIGINS OF CONTEMPORARY REVIVALISM

Despite differences, both Hassan al-Banna and Mawlana Abul Ala Mawdudi shared the following ideological world view based upon an historical tradition that has inspired and guided many contemporary reform movements:

1. Islam is a comprehensive way of life, a total, all-embracing ideology for personal and public life, for state and society.
2. The Quran, God's revelation, and the example (Sunnah) of the Prophet Muhammad are its foundations.
3. Islamic law (the Shariah, the "path" of God), based upon the Quran and Sunnah, is the sacred blueprint for Muslim life.
4. Faithfulness to the Muslim's vocation to reestablish God's sovereignty or rule through implementation of God's law results in success, power, and wealth of the Islamic community (ummah) in this life as well as eternal reward in the next.
5. The failure and subservience of Muslim societies results from the fact that they have strayed from God's divinely revealed path, following the secular, materialistic ideologies and values of the West or of the East—capitalism or Marxism.
6. Restoration of Muslim pride, identity, power, and rule (the past glory of Islamic empires and civilization) requires a return to Islam, the reimplementation of God's law and guidance for state and society.
7. Science and technology must be harnessed and used within an Islamically oriented and guided context to avoid the Westernization and secularization of Muslim society.

fallacy of Western secularism, separation of religion and the state, would be responsible for its moral decline and ultimate downfall. Finally, the Brotherhood maintained that despite Arab subservience to the West, the West had betrayed the Arabs in its support for Israeli occupation of Palestine: "The Palestine question became the starting-point for attacks on the United States ...[and resulted in] the full identification of Zionism with crusading Western imperialism."[27] In contrast to Islamic modernists, the goal of the Brotherhood and the Jamaat was not to render Islam compatible with Western culture but to create a more indigenously rooted Islamic state and society, through a process of renewal or Islamization. In the final analysis, the renaissance or reformation of Islam would not come from modernity's emphasis on empirical reason and secularism but, as in the past, from revelation.

Radical Islam

The world views and interpretations of Hassan al-Banna and Mawlana Maw-dudi were shaped by their social context as much as by their faith. As a result of the Muslim Brotherhood's confrontation with the Egyptian state in the late 1950s and 1960s, the ideology of Islamic revivalism became more militant and radicalized. Its chief architect, Sayyid Qutb (1906–1966), transformed the ideological beliefs of Hassan al-Banna and Mawlana Mawdudi into a rejectionist revolutionary call to arms.

Like Hassan al-Banna, Sayyid Qutb studied at a modern college established to train teachers. A devout Muslim, he had memorized the Quran as a child. Like many young intellectuals of the time, he studied Western literature and grew up an admirer of the West. Qutb was a prolific writer and an active participant in the literary and social debates of his times. In 1948 he published *Social Justice in Islam,* in which he maintained that in contrast to Christianity and communism, Islam possessed its own distinctive social teachings or social path. Islamic socialism, rooted in Islam's comprehensive vision, avoided the pitfalls of separation of religion and society on the one hand and atheism on the other:

> Christianity looks at man only from the standpoint of his spiritual desires and seeks to crush down the human instincts in order to encourage those desires. On the other hand, Communism looks at man only from the standpoint of his material needs; it looks not only at human nature, but also at the world and at life from a purely material point of view. But Islam looks at man as forming a unity whose spiritual desires cannot be separated from his bodily appetites, and whose moral needs cannot be divorced from his material needs. It looks at the world and at life with this all-embracing view that permits of no separation or division. In this fact lies the main divergence between Communism, Christianity, and Islam.[28]

In 1949, a turning point in his life, Qutb traveled to the United States to study educational organization. Although he had come to the United States out of admiration, Qutb experienced a strong dose of culture shock that drove him to become more religiously observant and also a severe critic of the West. His experiences convinced him of Western civilization's sexual permissiveness, moral decadence, and anti-Arab bias, which he perceived in U.S. government and media support for Israel. Shortly after his return to Egypt in 1951, Sayyid Qutb joined the Muslim Brotherhood.

During the 1950s, Qutb emerged as a major voice of the Muslim Brotherhood, its most influential ideologue, especially among its younger, more militant members. Government harassment of the Brotherhood and Qutb's imprisonment and torture in 1954, for alleged involvement in an attempt to assassinate President Nasser, increased his radicalization and increasingly confrontational worldview. During ten years of imprisonment, he wrote prolif-ically. In his most influential Islamic ideological tract, *Signposts* or *Milestones*, he took the ideas of Hassan al-Banna and especially Mawlana Mawdudi to their literalist, radical revolutionary conclusions.

For Qutb, the Muslim world consisted primarily of repressive, anti-Islamic governments and societies. Society was divided into two camps, the party of God and the party of Satan, those committed to the rule of God and those opposed to it. There was no middle ground between the forces of good and of evil. Qutb advocated a vanguard, a group (*jamaa*) of true Muslims within the broader corrupted and faithless society. The Islamic movement (*haraka*) was a righteous minority adrift in a sea of ignorance and unbelief (*jahiliyyah*). Muslim governments and societies were dismissed as un-Islamic, *jahili*—in effect, atheist or pagan states and societies. Thus, the classical use of jahiliyyah to designate pre-Islamic Arabia's ignorance of Islam was transformed or rein-terpreted to mean anti-Islamic. For Qutb, the cause was the displacement of Islam's God-centered universe by a (modern, Western) human-centered world.

Qutb maintained that the creation of an Islamic system of government was a divine commandment, and therefore not just an alternative but an impera-tive. Given the political realities of authoritarian, un-Islamic regimes, Qutb concluded that jihad, rather than futile attempts to bring about change from within existing repressive Muslim political systems, was the only way to imple-ment a new Islamic order. Islam, he declared, stood on the brink of disaster, threatened by repressive anti-Islamic governments and the neocolonialism of the West and the East. Qutb went beyond his predecessors when he declared Muslim elites and governments atheists, enemies of God, against whom all true believers should wage holy war. Qutb's formulation became the starting point for many later radical groups. The debate over the two options, evolution—a process that emphasizes change from below—or revolution—violent over-throw of established (un-Islamic) systems of government—have remained the contested options for contemporary Islamic movements and societies.

In 1965, Qutb and several other Muslim Brotherhood leaders were accused of an attempt on President Gamal Abd al-Nasser's life and were executed. Thousands of Brothers were arrested and tortured, while others went under-ground or fled the country. Many concluded that the Brotherhood had been crushed, a prediction that was to prove false a decade later.

It is difficult to overestimate the impact of Hassan al-Banna, Mawlana Abul Ala Mawdudi, and Sayyid Qutb. Their ideological world views and organizations became formative influences and models for contemporary Islamic move-ments. Combining religiopolitical activism with social protest or reform, contemporary Islamic movements represent a spectrum of positions from mod-eration and gradualism to radicalism and revolutionary violence, from selective criticism of the West to rejection and attack upon all that it stands for. Indeed, they signaled the multiple issues facing modern Muslims in their struggle to determine the relationship of Islam to modern state and society. Among these issues were overcoming Western political and cultural hegemony, dealing with the seeming challenge of modernity to Islamic belief, redefining Islam and its relevance to modern life and society, and addressing the clash of cultures not only between the West and the Muslim world but within Muslim societies over issues of religious and national identity and development.

ISLAM AND POSTMODERN TRENDS IN A POSTCOLONIAL WORLD

The Impact of the Islamic Resurgence

In the last decades of the twentieth century, the Muslim world experienced the impact of another revival or resurgence of Islam in personal and public life. This Islamic reawakening was and remains visible in mosques and Muslim politics as well as in international affairs. Many Muslims have become more religiously observant, finding in Islam a sense of identity, meaning, and guidance. Mosque attendance has risen, as has the number of those who observe the annual month-long fast of Ramadan, adopt forms of Islamic dress, and reappropriate a strong sense of Islamic values—from a renewed emphasis on family values to social justice.

New Islamic governments or republics have been established in Iran, Sudan, and Afghanistan. Rulers, political parties, and opposition movements have appealed to Islam. Islamic activists head governments: serve in cabinets and in the elected parliaments of Turkey, Jordan, Kuwait, Egypt, Sudan, Pakistan, Malaysia, and Yemen; and serve as senior officials of professional associations of doctors, lawyers, engineers, and professors. At the same time, radical Islamic organizations in Egypt, Algeria, Lebanon, the West Bank, and Gaza have engaged in violence and terrorism to topple governments or to achieve related goals. Extremists have left a legacy of kidnapping, hijacking, bombing, and murder from the Middle East to Southeast Asia, from Paris to New York. Understanding this complex and multifaceted phenomenon is often difficult and requires an awareness of its roots and sources. What were the causes and conditions that led to the contemporary resurgence of Islam?

Islam in Modern State and Society

A map of the modern Muslim world reveals both old and new realities and begins to visually explain the upheaval in Muslim societies. During the twentieth century, Islamic empires and sultanates were obliterated and replaced by modern nation-states. Many countries in the Middle East were quite literally newly created, "mapped out" by European colonial powers (Britain and France) after World War I. For example, as a punishment for its alliance with Germany, the Turkish Ottoman Empire, which encompassed an area extending from

Egypt to Iraq, was divided into separate nation-states. Turkey, Syria, Algeria, Sudan, Libya, Iraq, Jordan, India, Lebanon, Pakistan, Bangladesh, and Malaysia were among the many modern states carved out of what had been Muslim empires or sultanates.

Between World War I and World War II, most of the newly created states won their independence from European colonial rulers (France, England, the Netherlands, Italy). Both the national boundaries of many modern states and their rulers, many placed on their thrones in Jordan, Syria, and Iraq by Britain or France, were artificial creations. Moreover, European education, culture, and values permeated the urban areas and strongly influenced the elites in most states and societies. As a result, issues of government legitimacy as well as of national and religiocultural identity remained unresolved. Rulers, more often than not, rooted their legitimacy in an authoritarian state whose stability was due more to foreign (Western or Soviet) support coupled with strong military-security apparatus rather than to an indigenous culture, political participation, and electoral politics.

Once these modern nation-states were created in the Muslim world, it was expected that they would generally follow a "modern," that is, Western, secular path of development. Outwardly, this seemed to be the general case. While Saudi Arabia proclaimed itself an Islamic state, based upon the Quran and Shariah law, most new nations adopted or adapted Western political, legal, social, economic, and educational institutions and values. In contrast to Saudi Arabia, Turkey positioned itself at the polar opposite end of the religion versus secularism spectrum. Under the leadership of Mustafa Kemal Ataturk, it suppressed Islamic institutions, banned Islamic dress and Islamic law, and transplanted Western secular laws and institutions to create its own version of a secular state. However, the majority of countries, such as Egypt, Syria, Iraq, Pakistan, Malaysia, and Indonesia, created what may be called "Muslim states." These were countries whose majority populations were Muslim but which, despite some religious prescriptions, adopted Western-inspired institutions: parliaments, political party systems, legal codes, educational systems and curricula, banks, and insurance companies. Western dress, movies, and culture became prominent and pervasive among the wealthy and powerful in urban centers.

Throughout much of the twentieth century, progress and prosperity in Muslim societies were regarded by most governments and elites (those with key positions in government and society) as well as by the outside world as dependent upon the degree to which Muslims and their societies were "modern." This understanding of modernity generally presupposed a Western, secular orientation. The degree of progress and success for individuals, cities, and governments was measured by conformity to Western standards and values. This included wearing modern "Western dress," speaking a Western language, earning a degree from a Western-oriented school at home or preferably abroad, working or living in office buildings and homes reflecting Western architecture and furniture, and preferring Western music and movies. Based on these criteria, Turkey, Tunisia, Egypt, Lebanon, and Iran were often seen as among the more modern, advanced and "enlightened," that is, Westernized and secular, countries. Saudi Arabia, the states of the Persian Gulf, Afghanistan, Bangladesh, and Pakistan were generally regarded as more traditional, religious, and thus "backward."

The Failure of Modernity and the Islamic Revival

The 1960s and 1970s shattered the hopes and dreams of many, who believed that national independence and Western-oriented development would usher in strong states and prosperous societies, and proved a powerful catalyst for a religious resurgence and revival. The crises of many Muslim societies underscored the fact that despite the hopes and promises of national independence, many governments and societies had not become strong and prosperous. The hopes and promises of national independence seemed shattered by the realities of Muslim societies (poverty, illiteracy, failed economies, high unemployment, and maldistribution of wealth), raising profound questions of national identity and political legitimacy as well as of religious faith and meaning.

The negative fallout from the effects of modernization is of equal importance in understanding the Islamic resurgence. The fallout included massive migration from villages and rural areas and rapid urbanization of overcrowded cities with insufficient social support systems; the breakdown of traditional family, religious, and social values; the adoption of a "Western lifestyle," enthusiastically pursued as a symbol of modernity, a modernity increasingly perceived by many as a source of moral decline and spiritual malaise, corruption, and the maldistribution of wealth.

The signs of such profound changes would not become fully evident and appreciated in the West until a decade later with the Iranian Revolution of 1978–1979. However, a series of events during the previous decade—the 1967 Arab-Israeli war, the Malay-Chinese riots in Kuala Lumpur in 1969, the Pakistan-Bangladesh civil war of 1971, and Lebanon's civil war of the mid-1970s, as well as the subsequent Arab/Muslim successes in the 1973 Arab-Israeli war and the Arab oil embargo—revealed the pitfalls and failures of many states and societies. Such catalytic events triggered a soul-searching reassessment among many Muslims focused on the reliance on Western models of development in nation building as well as personal life. Disillusionment and dissatisfaction were accompanied by an Islamic revival, marked by a quest for self-identity and greater authenticity as many reaffirmed the importance of Islam and Islamic values in their personal and social lives. Along with a reemphasis on religious identity and practice (prayer, fasting, dress, and values) came an equally visible appeal to Islam in politics and society made by governments as well as Islamic political and social movements. While rulers like Libya's Muammar Qaddafi, Egypt's Anwar Sadat, Sudan's Jafar al-Numeiri, Pakistan's Zulfikar Ali Bhutto, and especially his successor, General Zia ul-Haq used Islam to enhance their legitimacy and to mobilize popular support, opposition movements and political parties in Pakistan, Iran, Sudan, and Egypt did the same to oppose rulers and regimes. Islamic ideology, discourse and politics reemerged as a major force in the development of the Muslim world, a force that both Muslim and Western governments have had to accommodate or contend with for several decades.

The return of Islam as an international economic and political force was seen by many as signaling a return of God's guidance and favor. However, for many Sunni Muslim governments and elites, especially those in Gulf states like Iraq, Saudi Arabia, Bahrain, and Kuwait, which have significant Shii populations, the fall of the shah in Iran and a clergy-led revolution were as repugnant as these events were in the West.

Perhaps the most significant symbolic event, which sparked Muslim disillusionment and dissatisfaction, was the 1967 Arab-Israeli war, which came to be called the Six-Day war. Israel defeated the combined forces of Egypt, Syria, and Jordan in a "preemptive" strike, which the Israeli government justified as necessary to counter a planned Arab attack. The Arabs experienced a massive loss of territory: Sinai, Gaza, the West Bank, and in particular Jerusalem, the third holiest city (after Mecca and Medina) of Islam.

Though for different reasons, Muslims, like Jews and Christians, for centuries have looked to Jerusalem, a city central to Muslim faith and identity, a place of religious shrines and pilgrimage. This sacredness of Jerusalem comes from both its association with biblical prophets (from David and Solomon and Jesus) and a miraculous event in Islamic belief, the Prophet Muhammad's "Night Journey" (al-israh) and ascension (al-miraj).

Muslim tradition teaches that one night in the year 620, when Muhammad prayed in the Kaaba, he was carried by the angel Gabriel on a winged horse, Buraq, from Mecca to the Temple Mount in Jerusalem. There Muhammad met with many of his prophetic predecessors (Adam, Abraham, Moses, John the Baptist, and Jesus), proceeding up a ladder that extended from the Temple Mount to the Throne (presence) of God. There the five daily prayers of Islam were instituted.

When Muslim armies took Jerusalem without resistance in 635, they restored and rebuilt the Temple Mount area (al-haram al-sharif, "noble sanctuary"). First they built a large mosque (al-Aqsa) and then a magnificent shrine, the Dome of the Rock, on the site believed to be "the terminus of the Night Journey and the biblical site of Abraham's sacrifice and Solomon's Temple."[29] Historically, Jerusalem has been a point of contention, first during the Crusades, which were ostensibly called to "liberate" Jerusalem from Muslim control, and then in the twentieth century, with the ongoing Palestinian-Israeli conflict.

Muslim loss of Jerusalem in the 1967 war was a traumatic experience, remembered to the present day, not only for Arabs (Arab Muslims and Arab Christians alike), but also for Muslims worldwide who all revere Jerusalem

RESPONSES TO THE FAILURE OF MODERNITY

As a result of these catalysts for change, several phenomena may be identified as common to the Muslim experience: (1) an identity crisis precipitated by a sense of utter impotence and loss of self-esteem; (2) disillusionment with the West (with its models of development and with the West as an ally) and with the failure of many governments to respond adequately to the political and socioeconomic needs of their societies; (3) a quest for greater authenticity, that is, to be less dependent on the West and to reappropriate a greater sense of indigenous identity, history, and values; (4) a newfound sense of pride and power resulting from the Arab-Israeli war and oil embargo of 1973 as well as the impact of Iran's "Islamic revolution" of 1978–1979.

(*al-quds*, the "holy city") as a site of central religious significance. The loss of Jerusalem made Palestine and the Arab-Israeli conflict not just an Arab but a transnational Islamic issue. Many asked what had gone wrong, and why this had happened. Why had Israel been able to defeat the combined Arab forces? Were the weakness and failure of Muslim societies due to their faith? Was Islam incompatible with modernity and thus the cause of Arab backwardness and impotence? Had God abandoned the Muslims? These were questions that had been raised before.

As we have seen, from the seventeenth to the nineteenth centuries, Muslim societies faced first internal and then external threats, the internal breakdown of societies closely followed by the onslaught (external threat) of European colonialism. However, the failures they now faced occurred during a period of independence and Muslim self-rule. The failures of the "modern experiment" led many to turn to a more authentic, indigenous alternative to nationalism and socialism. Despite significant differences, Islam became a rallying cry and symbol for political organization and mass mobilization worldwide.

The Religious World View of Contemporary Islamic Activism

In the face of disillusionment and crises of identity, many turned to Islam for answers. While all advocated an Islamic alternative to Western capitalism and Soviet Marxism, and a tremendous diversity existed from country to country, nevertheless Islamic activists did share the following beliefs:

1. Islam, a comprehensive way of life, is and must be integral to politics and society.

2. The failures of Muslim societies were caused by departing from the path of Islam and depending on Western secularism, which separated religion and politics.
3. Muslims must return to the Quran and the example of the Prophet Muhammad, specifically by reintroducing Islamic rather than Western laws.
4. Modern development must be guided by Islamic values rather than the Westernization and secularization of society.

As Islamic symbols, slogans, ideology, leaders, and organizations became prominent fixtures in Muslim politics, religion was increasingly used both by governments and by opposition movements. Libya's Muammar Qaddafi, Pakistan's General Zia ul-Haq, Egypt's Anwar Sadat, and Sudan's Jafar al-Numeiri appealed to Islam to enhance their legitimacy and authority and to mobilize popular support. At the same time, Islamic movements and organizations sprang up across the Muslim world. Opposition movements appealed to Islam: the Ayatollah Khomeini led Iran's "Islamic revolution" of 1979–1980; militants seized the Grand Mosque in Mecca in 1979 and called for the overthrow of the Saudi government; religious extremists assassinated Anwar Sadat in 1981. Afghan freedom fighters (*mujahideen*, "holy warriors") in the late 1970s and early 1980s led a resistance movement against the Soviet Union's invasion and occupation. Other Islamic movements and organizations throughout the 1980s created or extended their influence over religious, educational, social, cultural, and professional schools as well as financial institutions.

The leadership of most Islamic organizations (particularly Sunni groups) was and remains lay rather than clerical. Islamists have earned degrees in modern science, medicine, law, engineering, computer science, and education. Most Islamic organizations attract individuals from a spectrum of society. Members range from professionals and technocrats to the uneducated and poor. While the majority of Islamic organizations work within the system, a minority of radical extremists insist that Muslim rulers are anti-Islamic and that violence and revolution are the only way to liberate society and impose an Islamic way of life.

From the Periphery to Mainstream Politics and Society

The 1980s were dominated by fear of "radical Islamic fundamentalism," embodied in Iran's export of its "Islamic revolution" and the activities of clandestine extremist groups. Disturbances by Shii in Saudi Arabia, Kuwait, and Bahrain, and Iran's strong backing of a Shii group, Hizbollah, which emerged in response to the Israeli invasion and occupation of Lebanon; a series of hijackings, kidnappings, and bombings of Western embassies; and the assassination of Egyptian president Anwar Sadat fed the fears of nervous Muslim rulers and the West. However, no other "Irans" occurred.

By the late 1980s and early 1990s, it was increasingly clear that a "quiet (nonviolent) revolution" had occurred in many Muslim societies. Islamic revivalism and activism had in many contexts become institutionalized in mainstream society. From Egypt to Malaysia, Islam played a more visible and important role in socioeconomic and political life. Islamically inspired social and political activism produced schools; clinics; hospitals; day care, legal aid, youth centers, and other social service agencies; private (as opposed to government-controlled) mosques; and financial institutions such as Islamic banks and insurance companies. Islamic candidates participated in local and national electoral politics and assumed positions of leadership in professional associations and trade unions. A new, alternative elite emerged in every sector of society, modern educated but Islamically (rather than secularly) oriented: doctors, engineers, lawyers, business people, university professors, military officers, and laborers. Perhaps nowhere was the impact of the Islamic revival experienced more visibly than in political elections.

The majority of governments in the Muslim world are authoritarian, a legacy of premodern Muslim history as well as European colonial rule and postindependence governments that have not fostered the growth of participatory or democratic governments, institutions, and values. Despite this fact, during the late 1980s, in response to "food riots," protests, and mass demonstrations over the economic failures of governments, elections were held in a number of countries, including Jordan, Tunisia, Algeria, and of Egypt. Islamic organizations such as the Muslim Brotherhood of Jordan and of Egypt, Tunisia's Nahda (Renaissance) Party, and Algeria's Islamic Salvation Front (FIS) participated. They emerged as the major political opposition. In Algeria, the Islamic Salvation Front swept municipal and later parliamentary elections and thus was poised to come to power through the electoral process. Power was being taken through ballots, not bullets or revolution. In response, the Algerian military intervened, installing a new government, canceling the election results, and imprisoning and outlawing the FIS. This set in motion a spiral of violence and counterviolence that polarized Algerian society and produced a civil war costing more than 100,000 lives. By the mid-1990s, Islamic activists could be found in the cabinets and parliaments of many countries and in the leadership of professional organizations (doctors, lawyers, engineers). In Turkey, the most secular of Muslim states, the Islamist Welfare party swept mayoral elections and in 1995 elected its first Islamist prime minister and also the leader of the Welfare party (Dr. Ecmettin Erbakan). The Turkish military, claiming to save Turkish secularism, brought about the resignation of Erbakan, and influenced the outlawing of the party and the imprisonment of some of its leaders.

At the same time, radical extremist groups like Egypt's Gamaa Islamiyya (Islamic Group) attacked Christian churches, businesses, tourists, and security forces. Other extremists were convicted in America and Europe for terrorist acts such as the attacks against America's World Trade Center and the Pentagon in 2001, American barracks in Saudi Arabia in 1995, and American embassies in Africa in 1998, leading some governments and analysts to identify "Islamic fundamentalism" as a major threat to global stability.

The events of September 11, 2001, proved a watershed, signaling the extent to which Muslim extremists had become a global threat, in particular, the magnitude of the threat of Osama bin Laden and al-Qaeda.[30] The wealthy son of a multimillionaire, Osama bin Laden had become a major godfather of global terrorism, suspected in the bombing of the World Trade Center in 1993, the slaughter of eighteen American soldiers in Somalia, and the bombings in Riyadh in 1995 and in Dhahran in 1996.[31]

In February 1998, Bin Laden and other militant leaders had announced the creation of a transnational coalition of extremist groups, The Islamic Front for Jihad against Jews and Crusaders. Al-Qaeda was linked to a series of acts of terrorism: the truck bombing of American embassies in Kenya and Tanzania in August 1998 that killed 263 people and injured more than five thousand, followed in October 2000 by a suicide bombing attack against the USS Cole, which killed seventeen American sailors.

Bin Laden's message appealed to the feelings of many in the Arab and Muslim world. A sharp critic of American foreign policy toward the Muslim world, he denounced its support for Israel, sanctions against Iraq that resulted in the deaths of hundreds of thousands of civilians, and the substantial American (military and economic) presence and involvement in Saudi Arabia, which he dismissed as the "new crusades." To these were added other populist causes like Bosnia, Kosovo, Chechnya, and Kashmir.

Al-Qaeda represented a new global terrorism, associated with the Afghan Arabs, those who had come from the Arab and Muslim world to fight alongside the mujahideen (holy warriors) against the Soviet occupation of Afghanistan in the 1980s. It was also reflected in the growth of extremism and acts of terrorism in Central, South, and Southeast Asia (where also it often has been associated with the influence of Saudi Arabia and Wahhabi Islam). Bin Laden and other terrorists transformed Islam's norms about the defense of Islam and Muslims when under siege into a call to arms, in order to legitimate the use of violence, warfare, and terrorism. Their theology of hate espouses a bipolar view of a cosmic struggle between the armies of God and of Satan, the forces of good and evil, right and wrong, belief and unbelief. Those who are not with them, whether Muslim or non-Muslim, are judged to be against them. These extremists legitimate their acts of violence and terror by "hijacking" the Islamic concept and practice of jihad.

Globalization of "Jihad"

In the late twentieth and twenty-first centuries, the word *jihad* gained remarkable currency, becoming more global and diverse in its usage. On the one hand, jihad's primary Quranic religious and spiritual meanings, the "struggle" or effort to follow God's path, to lead a moral life, to promote social justice, became more widespread. On the other hand, jihad as armed struggle has been widely used by resistance, liberation, and terrorist movements alike to legitimate their cause and recruit followers. The Afghan mujahideen waged a jihad in Afghanistan against foreign powers and among themselves; Muslims in Kashmir, Chechnya, the southern Philippines, Bosnia, and Kosovo have fashioned their struggles as jihads; Hizbollah, Hamas, and Islamic Jihad Palestine have characterized war with Israel as a jihad; and Osama bin Laden, al-Qaeda, and other terrorists have waged a global jihad against Muslim governments and the West.

The importance of jihad is rooted in the Quran's command to struggle (the literal meaning of the word *jihad*) in the path of God and in the example of the Prophet Muhammad and his early Companions. In its most general meaning, jihad refers to the obligation incumbent on all Muslims, individuals and the community, to follow and realize God's will: to lead a virtuous life and to extend the Islamic community through preaching, education, example and writing. Jihad also includes the right, indeed the obligation, to defend Islam and the community from aggression. Throughout history, the call to jihad has rallied Muslims to the defense of Islam.

Jihad as struggle pertains to the difficulty and complexity of living a good life, struggling against the evil in oneself in order to be virtuous and moral, making a serious effort to do good works and help to reform society. Depending on the circumstances in which one lives, it also can mean fighting injustice and oppression, spreading and defending Islam, and creating a just society through preaching, teaching, and, if necessary, armed struggle or holy war.

The two broad meanings of jihad, nonviolent and violent, are contrasted in a well-known Prophetic tradition. Muslim tradition reports that, when Muhammad returned from battle, he told his followers, "We return from the lesser jihad to the greater jihad." The greater jihad is the more difficult and more important struggle against one's ego, selfishness, greed, and evil.

Jihad is a concept with multiple meanings, used and abused throughout Islamic history. Although it has always been an important part of the Islamic tradition, in recent years extremists have maintained that it is a universal religious obligation for all true Muslims to join the jihad to promote a global Islamic revolution.

Bin Laden and other terrorists go beyond classical Islam's criteria for a just jihad and recognize no limits but their own, employing any weapons or means. They reject Islamic law's regulations regarding the goals and means of a valid jihad: that the use of violence must be proportional; that innocent civilians, noncombatants, should not be targeted; and that jihad must be declared by the ruler or head of state. Today, extremists from Madrid to Mindanao legitimate their unholy wars in the name of Islam.

While Bin Laden and al-Qaeda have enjoyed support from a significant minority of Muslims and religious leaders, other Islamic scholars and religious leaders across the Muslim world, such as the Islamic Research Council at al-

Azhar University, regarded by many as the highest moral authority in Islam, have issued authoritative declarations against Bin Laden's initiatives: "Islam provides clear rules and ethical norms that forbid the killing of non-combatants, as well as women, children, and the elderly, and also forbids the pursuit of the enemy in defeat, the execution of those who surrender, the infliction of harm on prisoners of war, and the destruction of property that is not being used in the hostilities."[32]

The Struggle for Islam

The events of 9/11 highlighted the struggle for the heart and soul of Islam that has been going on in recent decades, a war not only within Muslim societies but also transnationally. Subsequent terrorist attacks from Madrid to Bali led many to ask "Why?" and "What is the relationship of Islam to global terrorism? "President George Walker Bush, like the leaders of many religious faiths, carefully distinguished between the religion of Islam and Muslim extremism, but many others did not. Some prominent leaders of the Christian Right—Franklin Graham, Pat Robertson, and Jerry Falwell—disparaged the religion of Islam and the Prophet Muhammad, seeing the roots of extremism and terrorism in the Quran or in the teachings of Muhammad and Islam. However, many others spoke of the need to look for the root causes of terrorism, namely, the political (the authoritarianism and repression of many Muslim governments), economic and social (poverty, illiteracy, maldistribution of wealth, amd rampant corruption), conditions in many Muslim societies. This plus anti-Western, especially anti-American, anger at American and European foreign policies in the Muslim world (uncritical support for regimes, Palestinian-Israeli policies, a double standard when promoting democratization) proved conducive to the growth of radicalism and the appeal of Bin Laden and other terrorist leaders and their theologies of hate.

The fact that Osama bin Laden and many of the 9/11 hijackers were from Saudi Arabia, along with Saudi support for some Islamic groups and madrasas (seminaries) in countries like Afghanistana and Pakistan have raised questions about the role and influence of Wahhabism in global terrorism. Wahhabi Islam, the official form of Islam in Saudi Arabia, is among the most ultraconservative interpretations of Islam. As we have seen, the Wahhabi movement takes its name from Muhammad Ibn Abd al-Wahhab and his revivalist movement. Over time, Wahhabi Islam has been uncompromising in the hands of many of its interpreters, resulting in an ultraconservative, "fundamentalist," brand of Islam: literalist, rigid, puritanical, exclusivist, and intolerant, whose adherents believe that they are right and therefore all others (other Muslims as well as people of other faiths) are wrong. Presenting their version of Islam as the pristine, pure, unadulterated message of the Prophet, Wahhabis have sought to propagate and sometimes impose their strict beliefs and interpretations, which are not commonly shared by many other Muslims, throughout the world.

Since the last half of the twentieth century, militant, violent interpretations of Islam have emerged, from both domestic and foreign sources. In 1979, militants seized the Grand Mosque in Mecca and called for the overthrow of the monarchy. After a bloody battle, they were crushed, their leaders killed or executed. At the same time, Islamic activists mainstream and extremist, from Egypt and other countries, often fleeing their home governments, had found refuge in Saudi Arabia. They found jobs teaching in universities and religious schools, working in government ministries and organizations. As a result, alongside the Wahhabi Islam of the establishment, a militant brand of Islam, from both internal and external sources, infiltrated many of Saudi Arabia's mosques, schools, and society. Their theology and worldview was a theology of militant jihad, domestic and global.

Internationally, Saudis, both government-sponsored organizations and wealthy individuals, exported Wahhabi Islam, in its mainstream and extremist forms, to other countries and communities in the Muslim world and the West. They offered development aid; built mosques, libraries, and other institutions; funded and distributed religious tracts; and commissioned imams and religious scholars. Wahhabi theology, funding, and influence were exported to Afghanistan, Pakistan, the Central Asian Republics, China, Africa, Southeast Asia, the United States, and Europe. At the same time, some wealthy businessmen and organizations in Saudi Arabia and the Gulf provided financial support to extremist groups who follow a militant, violent brand of Islam (also commonly referred to as Wahhabi or Salafi) with its holy war ("jihadi") culture. The challenge is to distinguish between those who preach and propagate an ultraconservative, exclusivist, Wahhabi theology, on the one hand, and terrorist organizations, on the other. Similar divisions between mainstream and violent extremists exist in other fundamentalist forms of religion, including Judaism, Christianity, and Hinduism.

Questions for Postmodern Times: Issues of Authority and Interpretation

Muslims in the twenty-first century, as throughout Islamic history, are called by their faith to worship and to implement God's will for humankind in their lives. This they share in common with all religious peoples. The sources and sacred texts of Islam, the Quran and the Sunnah of the Prophet, remain the same, but the political, social, and economic contexts have changed. While all observant Muslims continue to affirm belief in God, Muhammad, and the Quran, interpretations of Islam today vary significantly. Some believe that Islam, like most faiths in the modern age, should be restricted primarily to private life; others have struggled to implement Islam in public life as well. Recognizing that categories are not clear-cut and may overlap at times, four general Muslim orientations or attitudes toward change may be identified: secularist, conservative or traditionalist, Islamist or fundamentalist, and Islamic reformist or modernist.

Like their counterparts in the West, secularists believe religion is a personal matter and should be excluded from politics and public life. Calling for the separation of religion and the state, they believe that Islam belongs in the mosque, not in politics, and that the mosque should solely be a place of prayer, not of political activism. Sometimes dismissed by their opponents as nonbelievers, most secularists counter that they are religious but believe that religion should be restricted to private life (to matters of prayer, fasting, pilgrimage, etc.).

Conservatives emphasize following past tradition (taqlid) and are wary of any change or innovation that they regard as deviation (bida), the Christian equivalent of heresy. Conservatives are represented by the majority (though certainly not all) of the ulama and their followers who continue to assert the primacy of centuries-old classical formulations of Islamic law and emphasize the importance of continuity of interpretation with the great jurists of the past. Some conservatives prefer to call themselves tradionalists to explicitly identify the primacy of Islamic tradition in their reinterpretation of Islam.

Islamists or fundamentalists emphasize a return to Islam and the Sharia. However, while they respect the classical formulations of law, in contrast to conservatives they are not wedded to them, emphasizing instead a return to "fundamentals." In the name of a return to the fundamental sources of Islam (Quran and Sunnah), they are prepared to interpret (ijtihad) and reformulate Islamic belief and institutions, Islamists and islamic movements range from those who espouse a literalist interpretation of Islam, Wahhabi or Salafi Muslims, to Islamic movements that create an Islamic ideology for state and society. A dangerous and deadly minority, like al-Qaeda and many Jihadist organizations, are religious extremists who selectively reinterpret tradition to justify violence and terror. The majority live and work in mainstream society and are members of the mainstream in Islamic political and social movements. They participate in electoral politics, serve in government, and run educational and social service organizations.

Islamists emphasize the self-suffciency of Islam and the dangers of excessive dependency on the West. The tend to be lay rather than clerical. Like many Islamic revivalist organizations in the twentieth century, such as the Muslim Brotherhood, their wholistic or comprehensive understanding of Islam fosters social and political activism often challenging the political and religious establishment.

Islamic reformers or modernists overlap with Islamists in reinterpreting Islamic sources (ijtihad). However, modernists are more open to substantive change and to borrowing from other cultures. Wbhile they root their reforms in normative Islamic sources (Quran and Sunnah), they are not wedded to classical Islamic law. Their approach to change is more substantive or fundamental, distinguishing more sharply between substance and form, between the principles and values of Islam's immutable revelation and the historically and socially conditioned practices and institutions that can and should be changed to meet contemporary conditions.

The heart of a modernist approach gets at the core issue in contemporary Islamic reformism, the relationship of the divine to the human in Islamic law. In the terminology of classical jurisprudence, they focus on the need to distinguish between the Shariah, God's divinely revealed law, and *fiqh* ("understanding"), human interpretation and application that are historically conditioned. Modernists go further than Islamists in their acceptance of the degree and extent to which enshrined classical formulations of Islamic law may be changed. They place more emphasis on the finite nature of early doctrines or formulations. Just as jurists applied the principles and values of Islam to their societies in the past, they argue that again today, in the words of Muhammad Iqbal, a new interpretation or reconstruction of Islam is needed. Many reformers, after an early traditional or Islamic education, have obtained degrees from major national and international universities in the Muslim world and the West, combining an appreciation of Islam with modern disciplines and knowledge.

The issue of Islamic reform is especially evident in the current debate among many Muslims over such key issues as the relationship of Islam to the state, political participation or democratization, reform of Islamic law, promotion of religious and political pluralism, and the rights of women.

Muslim experiments have run the spectrum: from conservative monarchies like that of Saudi Arabia to the more radical approaches of Libya, Sudan, and Iran; from an Islamic social and political activism that works within society as part of a gradual process of change (creating schools and hospitals, providing social services, participating in elections in Egypt, Turkey, Jordan) to violent revolutionaries (the Gamaa Islamiya in Egypt, and jihad organizations in other Muslim countries) who have sought to topple governments and impose authoritarian versions of Islamic rule.

The contemporary Muslim experience reveals a grappling with multiple challenges and issues, many of which continue to face other faiths as well. However, because of the close association of religion, state, and society in Islam and in Islamic history, the relationship of Islam to the state and in particular the place and role of the Shariah in modern Muslim countries have become a hotly contested issue. The primary question is not change, for most accept its necessity. Rather, it is how much change and what kind of changes; and even more important, how

"WHOSE ISLAM?" AND "WHAT ISLAM?"

Two all-encompassing questions facing Muslim communities today as they seek to define the relationship and relevance of Islam to their lives are "Whose Islam?" and "What Islam?" In other words, who should (has the authority to) interpret Islam, and what are the relevant and acceptable interpretations of Islam for today's world?

much change is possible or permissible in Islam? This issue is central to virtually all the questions and issues that Muslims face regarding the relationship of their faith to contemporary life: gender relations; the status and role of women; family values; medical ethics (contraception, abortion, in vitro fertilization); Islamically appropriate dress, music, and other forms of entertainment; interest in banking and investments; and relations with non-Muslims.

As in the past, both the ulama, the religious scholars of Islam, and Muslim rulers continue to assert their right to protect, defend, and interpret Islam. The ulama remain persistent in regarding themselves as the guardians of Islam, the conscience of the community, Islam's only qualified interpreters. They continue to write religious commentaries, run schools and universities, and promote their ideas not only through publications but increasingly through the use of modern media and technology.

Many rulers, through co-optation and coercion, combine their obligation to protect/promote Islam with the state's power to influence, control, and promote an acceptable "brand" of Islam. Governments control and distribute funds used to build mosques, pay the salaries of religious officials and functionaries, approve the topic or outline for Friday mosque sermons, and appoint religious leaders and judges. Saudi Arabia, Kuwait, Libya, and Iran, among others, through the creation and funding of international Islamic organizations, promote not only Islam (building mosques, schools, hospitals, sending imams to serve as mosque leaders/preachers, distributing Qurans and Islamic publications) but also their "brands" or interpretations of Islam internationally among Muslim communities in the Muslim world and in the West. The result has been the promotion and propagation of a broad range of interpretations from the conservative to the revolutionary.

Today, many argue that the laity and parliaments not rulers or the clergy, should be major actors in the process of change. As we have seen, the ulama have often come under criticism from diverse sectors of Muslim society, viewed as out of touch with the demands and realities of the modern world and as a religious establishment too easily co-opted by governments or too compliant. At the same time, as in Christianity and Judaism, an educated laity has increasingly asserted its role in the community. While the ulama base their authority on their training in traditional Islamic disciplines (Quran, hadith, and Shariah studies), the laity counter that they possess the expertise (legal, economic, medical) necessary to address contemporary issues and should be counted among qualified "experts" along with the ulama. Just as the vast majority of Islamic political and social organizations (such as the Muslim Brotherhood, the Jamaat-i-Islami, Algeria's Islamic Salvation Front, Turkey's Welfare party, and Tunisia's Renaissance party) are lay rather than clerically led, so too, in the latter half of the twentieth and early twenty-first centuries, the authors of contemporary Islamic literature increasingly represent lay as well as clerical experts offering their interpretations of Islam on political, social, and economic issues.

The primary issue underlying all discussions is the relationship of tradition and change or, in more classical Islamic terms, that of simple acceptance and following (*taqlid*) of past practice versus reinterpretation (ijtihad) and reform of the tradition. Broadly speaking, the question is "Should the process of renewal and reform be one of restoration or reinterpretation—the reimplementation of classical Islamic law or a bold reformulation and reconstruction of Islam?" Some who call for a return to Islam mean simply reclaiming and reapplying the traditional legal blueprint for Muslim society in all its details. Others argue that times have changed and that it is necessary to replace or supplement laws formulated centuries ago with fresh interpretations that respond more adequately to conditions today. They wish to return to the sources of Islam, to the principles and values of the Quran and Sunnah of the Prophet, upon which new laws and institutions can be constructed. This discussion, debate, and, at times, battle can be seen across the Muslim world from Egypt and Morocco to Malaysia and Indonesia.

The status of non-Muslims and of women are two examples of viewpoints in the current debate. Many who call for greater implementation of Islam in state and society, as in Islamization programs in Pakistan, Iran, Afghanistan, and Sudan in the 1980s and 1990s, simply wish to reinstate the traditional doctrine of non-Muslims as "protected" (dhimmi) people. While this notion was well ahead of its time in the past, in today's world it consigns non-Muslims to second-class status and has exacerbated tensions between Muslims and non-Muslims. Thus, for example, most non-Muslim citizens wish to enjoy full and equal rights of citizenship, from the right to vote to the right to hold senior government positions.

Similarly, the resurgence of Islam has often compounded rather than alleviated the situation of Muslim women. On the one hand, many have "returned" or reappropriated their Islamic identity and integrated it more effectively in their personal, professional, and family lives. Women have developed their own prayer and Quran study groups, adopted modern forms of modest "Islamic" dress, and established or participated in Islamic social and political activities. However, in many other cases women have become a "quick fix" for those who wish to Islamize society. It has proven difficult to define and implement Islamic political or economic systems. However, given the centrality of women and the family in the formation and development of a strong Islamic community, many have found it easier simply to make the status and role of women the primary symbol of Islamization. This has often meant countering modern reforms or paradigms, dismissing them as simply Westernization, with a restoration of a more traditional paradigm that in the name of the restoration of family values subordinates women in society with requirements that range from veiling and seclusion (sex separation) to restrictions on women's educational and employment opportunities.

Islam in the West

The globalization of Islam has meant the extraordinary expansion of Islam beyond the borders of what is generally regarded as the Muslim world, the

ISLAM AND DEMOCRACY

A primary example of Islamic reformism and its method today is the debate over the relationship of Islam to democracy. Some Muslims reject any discussion of the question, maintaining that Islam has its own system of government. Others believe that Islam and democracy are incompatible, claiming that democracy is based upon un-Islamic Western principles and values. Still others reinterpret traditional Islamic concepts like consultation (shura) and consensus (ijma) of the community to support the adoption of modern forms of political participation or democratization such as parliamentary elections. Thus, just as it was appropriate in the past for Muhammad's senior Companions to constitute a consultative assembly (majlis al-shura) and to select or elect his successor through a process of consultation, Muslims now reinterpret and extend this notion to the creation of modern forms of political participation and government, parliamentary governments, and the direct or indirect election of heads of state. This process is sometimes called "Islamization." Similarly, in legal reform some Muslims believe that Islam is totally self-sufficient; they demand the imposition of Islamic law and reject any outside influences. Others argue that Islamic law can be reinterpreted today to incorporate new interpretations or formulations of law, as well as laws from elsewhere that do not contradict the Quran and Sunnah.

fifty-six Muslim majority countries. As noted earlier, Islam is now the second- and third-largest religion in Europe and America, respectively; Muslims have become part and parcel of the American and European landscapes.[33] Today, the capitals and major cities of the world of Islam include not only Cairo, Damascus, Islamabad, and Kuala Lumpur but also Paris, Marseilles, London, Manchester, New York, Chicago, Detroit, and Los Angeles.

Muslims have for some time been an invisible presence in the West. Most came as immigrants. Many wanted to fit into their new societies, be accepted, gain employment, raise families, and live quietly in their adopted countries. Others wished to live apart, to avoid any prospect of assimilation and loss of identity in a Western, non-Muslim society. Political events in the Middle East reinforced a desire for a low profile in a newly adopted country and in some cases put Muslims on the defensive. The 1973 Arab oil embargo with its negative impact on Western economies, as well the Iranian Revolution of 1978–1979, transformed old stereotypes and hostilities into new ones. Images and stereotypes of camels and harems from the past were replaced by modern impressions of violence and terrorism associated with the threat of militant

"Islamic fundamentalism." The result has often been Muslim bashing and what some have called "Islamophobia."

Today, Muslims in Europe and America are no longer primarily immigrant but, rather, second- and third-generation communities, participating in professional and civic life. Nevertheless, many continue to face issues of faith and identity as a religious minority.

The Muslims of Western Europe

More than eighteen million Muslims may be found in Europe, nine million in western and southeastern Europe, respectively. Because many, though certainly not all, wish to retain their religion, culture, and values, the presence and citizenship of Muslims in Western Europe, as in America, have made assimilation, acculturation, integration, and multiculturalism major religious, social, and political issues.

In contrast to America, in Western Europe the Muslim presence is due in large part to labor and family immigration and a vestigial colonial connection. After independence, many professionals and skilled laborers from former European colonies in Africa, South Asia, and the Arab world immigrated to Europe seeking a better life. In the 1960s and 1970s, unskilled laborers flooded into a Europe whose growing economies were in need of cheap labor. At the same time, from the 1970s onward, increasing numbers of Muslim students came to Europe, as they did to America, to study. While many returned home, others for political or economic reasons chose to stay.

France, with five million Muslims (almost 10% of the population), has the largest Muslim population in Western Europe, many of whom come from North Africa. They may be found in most major cities and towns. The Muslims of France now exceed Protestants and Jews in number and are second only to France's Catholic community. There are grand mosques in major cities like Paris and Lyons and more than a thousand mosques and prayer rooms throughout the country. Britain's one to two million Muslims come primarily from the Indian subcontinent, although others are from Africa, Malaysia, and the Arab world. More than six hundred mosques serve as prayer, education, and community centers in Britain.

Despite differences, Muslims in Europe and America have shared common concerns though different experiences, depending on the policies of specific European countries, regarding the practice of their faith, the retention of Islamic identity in the process of forging new national identites (especially for their children), and the preservation of family life and values. Issues of religious observance include the ability to take time out from work to pray daily, to attend mosque on Friday, to celebrate the great feasts of Islam (Id al-Adha and Id al-Fitr), to have halal foods available in schools and the military, and, for those women who wish, to freely wear a headscarf (hijab).

The issue of identity has been particularly acute in France where, after a long battle, the government took a firm stand in favor of total assimilation rather than the more multicultural approaches of Britain and America. The issue was symbolized in 2004 in a celebrated case in which the wearing of a headscarf by Muslim female students was outlawed. Both the government's ministry of education and teachers' unions united in claiming that wearing the hijab violated France's secular constitution and traditions. A similar position had not been taken regarding the wearing of Christian crucifixes or the Jewish yarmulke. After several years of bitter debate, the French Constitutional Council ruled in October 2006 that despite the education ministry's ban, students could not be expelled for wearing headscarves if no proselytizing occurred.

Islam in America

Islam is the fastest growing religion in the United States; more than one million Americans (Caucasian and African American) have converted to Islam. While estimates of the number of American Muslims vary significantly (4–12 million), it is safe to say that there are four to six million Muslims in America. The American Muslim community is larger than that of the Episcopalians and will soon be larger than the American Jewish community. Many believe that in the first half of the twenty-first century, Islam will become the second-largest religion (after Christianity) in America.

Muslims were present in America prior to the nineteenth century. Perhaps twenty percent of the African slaves brought to America from the sixteenth to the nineteenth centuries were Muslim. However, most were forced to convert to Christianity. It was not until the late nineteenth century that significant numbers of Muslims became a visible presence in America. Waves of immigrant laborers initially came from the Arab world. In recent decades many more have come from the Middle East and South Asia. In contrast to Europe, where large numbers of Muslims came as immigrant laborers needed by the booming economies of the 1960s and 1970s, many who have come to America in recent decades have been well-educated professionals, intellectuals, and students. Many have come for political and economic reasons, leaving behind the constraints of life under authoritarian regimes and failed economies.

Unity of faith is tested by the American Muslim community's rich, and at times divisive (racial, ethnic, and cultural), diversity. About two-thirds (60%) of America's Muslims are immigrants or descendants of immigrants from the Middle East, Africa, and South and Southeast Asia. The other third is composed primarily of African American converts to Islam plus a smaller percentage of white American converts. The majority of American Muslims are Sunni, but there is a strong minority of Shii. These racial, ethnic, and sectarian differences are often reflected in the composition and politics of some mosques. While many mosques incorporate the diversity of Muslims in America, the membership of others is drawn along ethnic or racial lines.

African American Islam

African American Islam emerged in the early twentieth century when a number of black Americans converted to Islam and established movements or communities. Islam's egalitarian ideal, in which all Muslims belong to a brotherhood of believers transcending race and ethnic ties, proved attractive. While Islam was seen as part of an original (African) identity, Christianity was associated with the legitimation of slavery and thus a legacy of white supremacy and oppression of black Americans that extended to the twentieth century and the civil rights movement. In the early twentieth century, quasi-Islamic groups emerged, combining a selective use of Islamic symbols with black nationalism. Timothy Drew (1886–1929), one of the first black American converts to Islam, changed his name to Noble Drew Ali and founded the Moorish-American Science Temple in Newark, New Jersey. However, the most prominent and lasting movement, the Nation of Islam, was associated with Elijah Muhammad (formerly Elijah Poole, 1897–1975) in the 1930s.

Elijah Muhammad had been the follower of Wallace D. Fard Muhammad, who claimed to be the "Great Mahdi" or savior. He preached a message of black liberation in the ghettos of Detroit in the early 1930s. After Fard mysteriously disappeared in 1934, Elijah Muhammad became the leader of the Nation of Islam. Adopting the title of the Honorable Elijah Muhammad, he claimed to be the messenger of God. Under his leadership the Nation of Islam, popularly known as the Black Muslims, was redefined and transformed into an effective national movement. Elijah Muhammad preached black liberation and nationalism, black pride and identity, strength and self-sufficiency, black racial supremacy, and strong family values. The spirit and ethic of the Nation of Islam was embodied in the phrase "Do for self," a doctrine of economic independence that emphasized self-improvement and responsibility through hard work, discipline, thrift, and abstention from gambling, alcohol, drugs, and eating pork.

Under Elijah Muhammad's leadership, hundreds of temples as well as small businesses (grocery stores, restaurants, bakeries) were established nationally. His message of black pride, self-respect, and militancy proved particularly attractive to black youth, many of whom were recruited from ghetto streets and prisons.

The Nation of Islam differed significantly from mainstream Islam in a number of basic beliefs. It claimed that Allah (God) is human, a black man named Wallace D. Fard, and that Elijah Muhammad (not the Prophet Muhammad) was the last messenger of God. The Nation taught black supremacy and black separatism, whereas Islam teaches the brotherhood of all believers in a community that transcends racial, tribal, and ethnic boundaries. The Nation did not follow major Muslim rituals such as the Five Pillars of Islam.

Three individuals epitomize the development and transformation of Elijah Muhammad's Black Muslim movement: Malcolm X, Wallace D. Muhammad (Warith Deen Muhammad), and Louis Farrakhan.

Malcolm X (1925–1965), born Malcolm Little, the product of the very social conditions (white racism, poverty, broken families, drugs, and crime) he would later seek to change, exemplified the personal and religious transformation for which the Nation of Islam was noted. His experience of racism and prejudice led to his alienation and rejection of American society. His life of drugs and crime in the ghettos of Roxbury, Massachusetts, and later Harlem, New York City, led to his imprisonment. It was during his incarceration (1946–1952) that he became self-educated, reading widely in history, politics, and religion. Malcolm became convinced that Christianity was the "white man's religion" and that the Bible "[in the] white man's hands and his interpretation of it, have been the greatest single ideological weapon for enslaving millions of non-white human beings."[34] In 1948 he formally turned to Elijah Muhammad and accepted the teachings of the Nation of Islam. Malcolm Little became Malcolm X. A gifted speaker, dynamic and articulate, and a charismatic personality, Malcolm X rose quickly through the ranks of the Nation of Islam to national prominence in the 1950s and early 1960s, a time when America was in the midst of the civil rights movement. He organized many of the Nation's temples, started its newspaper *Muhammad Speaks,* and recruited new members (such as the boxer Cassius Clay, renamed Muhammad Ali). However, Malcolm's increased involvement in domestic and international politics, as well as his contacts with Sunni Muslims in America and in the Muslim world, led to a gradual shift in his religious/ideological world view. This development put him increasingly at odds with some of Elijah Muhammad's teachings. While Elijah Muhammad advocated a separation and self-sufficiency that excluded involvement in "white man's politics," Malcolm came to believe that "the Nation of Islam could be even a greater force in the American Black man's overall struggle if we engaged in more action."[35] He spoke out forcefully on a variety of issues: the civil rights movement, the Vietnam War, solidarity with liberation struggles in colonial Africa. Such statements made him an easy target for those within the Nation who were jealous of his prominence, and as a result he found himself increasingly marginalized.

In March 1964 Malcolm X left the Nation of Islam to start his own organization, and a month later went on pilgrimage to Mecca. Here Malcolm underwent a second conversion—to mainstream Sunni Islam. The pilgrimage brought Malcolm and the religious/separatist teachings of the Nation face to face with those of the global Islamic community, vividly exposing their conflicts and contradictions. He did not know how to perform Islam's daily prayers (salat), nor had he observed the other prescribed practices of the Five Pillars of Islam. Malcolm was profoundly affected by the pilgrimage's emphasis on the equality of all believers: "We were truly all the same (brothers)—because their belief in one God removed the 'white' from their minds, the 'white' from their behavior, and the 'white' from their attitude."[36] He returned a Muslim rather than a Black Muslim, changing his name to El Hajj Malik El-Shabazz. As Betty Shabazz, his wife, commented: "He went to Mecca a Black Muslim and there he became only a Muslim. He felt all men were human beings; we must judge a man on his deeds."[37] On February 21, 1965, Malcolm Shabazz was assassinated as he spoke to an audience in New York.

The 1960s were a transitional period for the Nation of Islam. Not only Malcolm X but also Wallace D. Muhammad (the son of Elijah Muhammad), each in his own way, questioned the teachings and strategy of Elijah Muhammad. At one point, Wallace was excommunicated by his father. However, upon the death of Elijah Muhammad in February 1975, Wallace D. Muhammad succeeded his father as supreme minister. Despite their disagreements, Elijah Muhammad had designated Wallace as his successor. With the support of his family and the Nation's leadership, Wallace set about reforming the doctrines of the Nation and its organizational structure. He simultaneously integrated the Nation within the American Muslim community, the broader American society, and the global Islamic community.

The Nation and its teachings were brought into conformity with orthodox Sunni Islam. The name of Nation was initially changed to the World Community of al-Islam in the West (WCIW); *Muhammad Speaks* became the *Bilalian News*, named after the first black convert to Islam. Wallace Muhammad made the pilgrimage to Mecca and encouraged his followers to study Arabic in order to better understand Islam. The community now observed Islam's Five Pillars. Black separatist doctrines were dropped as the community proceeded to participate within the political process and system. The equality of men and women believers was reaffirmed; women were given more responsible positions in the ministry of the community. In 1980, as if to signal his and the community's new religious identity and mission, Wallace changed his name to Warith Deen Muhammad, renamed the WCIW the American Muslim Mission, and the *Bilalian News* became the *American Muslim Journal* (later renamed *Muslim Journal*).

The integration of the American Muslim Mission within the country at large did not lessen its concern with issues of racism and injustice. However, its critique of racism has been articulated within its primary function as a religious community, framed within its twin foci, black identity and following the straight path of Islam:

> You can't live in America without hearing the message. The message of white supremacy is everywhere. You are conscious that Jesus is in a white body even if you don't go to church.... Every American knows that apostles and saints and angels are made European by Church society.... We are not to see God in a racial image. As long as white (Caucasian) people think that their physical image is in the world as the image of God, and as long as non-white people see and know that the Caucasian image is in the world as the purported image of God, there will be no real coming together and no peaceful meeting of the minds of Caucasians and non-Caucasians.[38]

The transformation of the Nation of Islam under Warith Deen Muhammad did not occur without dissent. Louis Farrakhan (1933–), a bitter foe of both Malcolm X and Wallace, broke with Wallace in March 1978. Maintaining that he and his followers had remained faithful to the message and mission of Elijah Muhammad, Farrakhan retained the name and organizational structure of the Nation of Islam as well as its black nationalist and separatist doctrines. However, from 1986 onward, while retaining much of the political and economic teachings and program of Elijah Muhammad, he moved the Nation closer to more orthodox Islamic practices.

While the militancy and at times anti-Semitic statements of Farrakhan brought condemnation and criticism, the effectiveness of the Nation in fighting crime and drugs in ghettos and in rehabilitating prisoners earned the Nation praise. Farrakhan's leadership of the Million Man March on Washington in 1995 received widespread media coverage and support among Christian as well as Muslim leaders and organizations. Though the Nation of Islam membership is far less numerous than that of Warith Deen Muhammad's American Muslim Mission, Farrakhan's persona and actions have given him a disproportionate amount of visibility and recognition.

Issues of Adaptation and Change

Islam and Muslim identity in North America reflect the diverse backgrounds of the community: from immigrants who came to America in pursuit of political, religious, or economic freedom to native-born African Americans seeking equality and justice. They are challenged by an America that, despite separation of church and state, retains a Judeo-Christian ethos. Jewish and Christian holidays are officially recognized holidays, and Christian values are regarded as integral to American identity and values, from its currency and morality to its culture. The tendency of some in America, as in Europe, to contrast American (a Judeo-Christian) "national culture" with Islamic values further complicates the process of Muslim assimilation. Finally, the American media's portrayal of Islam or Muslims as militant, the identification of Islam as a global threat, and talk of a clash of civilizations in the post–cold war period has often led to the equation of Islam with extremism and terrorism. Despite their numbers and religious heritage as one of the three branches of the Children of Abraham, Islam and Muslims have yet to be fully recognized as neighbors and equal partners in American society. Islam in America provides many examples of significant change and reform. Both mosques and mosque leaders (*imams*) have been transformed by the American experience. In contrast to many parts of the Muslim world, mosques in America serve not only as places of worship but also as community centers. Because Friday is a workday and a school day in America, many Muslims are not able to attend the Friday congregational (*juma*) prayer. Therefore, for many, Sunday at mosques and Islamic centers has become a day of congregational prayer, religious education ("Sunday school"), and socializing. Imams in America are not only responsible for the upkeep of mosques and leading of prayers, but often take on the activities of their fellow clergy of other faiths, ranging from counseling to hospital visits.

Since Islamic law (Shariah) provides the ideal blueprint for Muslim life, a primary question facing Muslims in America is "Can Muslims live in a non-Muslim territory?" For many raised in Muslim majority countries, this is a particularly vexing question. Muslim jurists in the past, writing during the days of expansionist Islamic empires, encouraged Muslims to migrate from non-Muslim areas lest they contribute to the strength and prosperity of non-Muslim states. However, while the ideal was to live in a Muslim territory, Islamic jurisprudence did allow Muslims to live outside the Islamic territory (*dar al-Islam*) provided they were free to practice their religion. In the twenty-first century, Muslim minority communities have become a global and permanent phenomenon. If some religious leaders continue to counsel emigration from non-Muslim territories back to Muslim lands, many others have redefined the conditions under which Muslims can live permanently as loyal citizens in their new homelands while preserving their faith and identity.

In North America, as in France, wearing of the hijab symbolizes legal/religious issues of religious and cultural pluralism. In contrast to France, where the hijab issue primarily concerned Muslim students, in America it has been an issue for Muslim teachers and other professionals. Although Muslims are equal members of the societies in which they live, societies that protect freedom of religion, it is an ironic fact that the rights of Muslim minorities are often compromised or denied. Thus, for example, despite the guarantees of freedom of religion, American courts have at times refused to regard the wearing of the hijab as symbolic of personal religious conviction, but instead regarded it as an attempt to proselytize in the public sphere.

Today, American Muslims increasingly seek to empower themselves, responding rather than simply reacting to life in America. Like American Jews and other minorities before them, Muslims are developing institutions that are indigenously rooted and responsive to their realities. Attempts to adapt and apply Islam in America can be seen in mosque architecture that reflects the landscapes of American contexts, the appointment of local (rather than foreign) imams, the creation of mechanisms to obtain legal opinions (fatwas) from local rather than overseas muftis, and the creation of Muslim advocacy and public affairs organizations that promote and lobby for Muslim rights and community interests. Muslim educational associations monitor textbooks and the teaching of Islam to assure accuracy and objectivity. Public affairs organizations monitor publications and respond to misinformation in the media and to objectionable policies and actions by legislators and corporations. Islamic information services develop and distribute films, videos, and publications on Islam and Muslims in America to further better understanding. In some communities, Islamic schools (primary and secondary) have been created; teaching materials and syllabi on Islam and Muslim life have been and are being created for the instruction of children and adults at mosques and in schools.

Emigration and globalization have transformed the religious and cultural landscape of our world. There are more muslims living in diaspora communities than at any time in history. Muslim minority communities have faced many hurdles in making the transition.

Osama bin Laden and the Threat of Global Terrorism.

Muslim issues, like those of other religious minorities, are those of identity: assimilation or integration, the preservation and practice of religious faith in a society based upon Judeo-Christian or secular values, empowerment in politics and culture. The situation is complicated by the problematic historical relationship between Islam and Christianity, in particular between the West and Muslim societies from the period of European colonialism to what many Muslims perceive to be American neocolonialism.[39] At the same time, many Americans' and Europeans' experiences of contemporary Islam have been through the prism of revolution and violence: hijackings and hostage taking, attacks against embassies, the World Trade Center bombing, Osama bin Laden and the threat of global terrorism.

The psychological fallout from post-9/11 and the subsequent attacks from Madrid and London to Bali has had a negative impact on the image of Islam and Muslims. Too often the line between the religion of Islam and the mainstream majority has been blurred by the terror committed by a minority of religious extremists and terrorists in the name of Islam. Muslims have been faced with a growing Islamophobia, and increase in hate crimes, racial profiling, and the erosion of civil liberties.

Muslims and non-Muslim citizens and communities alike face the challenges of living in a multicultural, multireligious pluralistic society. Can the majority of Muslims both retain their faith and identity and do so in a manner that enables them to also accept and function within the secular, pluralistic traditions of Europe and America? The pluralism of countries in the West is likewise being tested. Is Western pluralism a limited form of pluralism? Is it inclusive or exclusive, primarily secular or Judeo-Christian? Can Muslims (as well as Hindus, Sikhs, Buddhists, and others) come to be fully accepted as no longer sojourners, not simply worshippers of foreign religions, but truly and fully as fellow citizens and neighbors?

An International Superhighway

The globalization of Islam has not only produced global terrorist networks but also new networks of religious thought and authority. The flow of knowledge and authority has been expanded and transformed from a one-way road (Muslim world to West) to a multilane superhighway with two-way traffic (between Muslim countries and the West and vice versa). It is a movement encompassing diverse people, ideologies, institutions, and mass communications. Two-way communication and exchange occur through scholars' and activists' travel and speaking engagements, publications, video- and audiotapes, and, increasingly, cyberspace. The process is multi-leveled, involving individuals (scholars, preachers, activists), movements, and countries. Muhammad Arkoun, Algerian-born Sorbonne Professor; Rashid Ghannoushi, leader of Tunisia's Ennahda (Renaissance Party), who is in exile in London; Khurshid Ahmad, Founder of the Islamic Foundation in Leicester and member of Pakistan's Senate; Yusuf Islam, the singer/songwriter formerly called Cat Stevens, and prominent Muslim spokesmen, such as Tareq Ramadan, a Swiss academic, Oxford Fellow and Egyptian-born grandson of Hassan al-Banna, founder of the Muslim Brotherhood; Seyyed Hossein Nasr at George Washington University in Washington, DC; Abdulaziz Sachedina of the University of Virginia; Mahmud Ayub of Temple University; and Sulayman Nyang of Howard University, all based in Europe and America, speak to Muslims overseas through their writings, their influence on their former graduate students, and/or audiotapes and videotapes. At the same time, diverse voices in the Muslim world, such as Egypt's al-Azhar Grand Shaikh Muhammad Sayyid Tantawi; Shaykh Ali Juma, Mufti of Egypt; and Amr Khaled, popular preacher and NGO leader; Qatar's Yusuf Qardawi; Lebanon's Faysal Mawlawi and Muhammad Fadlallah; Turkey's Fetullah Gulen; or the Amir of Pakistan's Jamaat-i-Islami have a similar presence and impact in Europe and America. Muslim European and American diaspora communities can have almost instant access to the fatawa (legal opinions) of muftis (legal experts) throughout the Muslim world and can obtain answers to their own specific questions on Internet sites that feature segments like "Ask the Mufti."

ISLAM: POSTMODERN CHALLENGES

Islam and Muslims today, as in the past, are again at an important crossroads. The history of Islam has been intertwined with the realities of Muslim politics, as Muslims struggle to define themselves and the place of Islam in their lives and societies. The wars of national independence have been fought. The struggle today from Egypt, Sudan, and Algeria to Malaysia and Indonesia, from London, Paris, and Marseilles to Boston, New York, Detroit, and Los Angeles, is one of religiocultural identity. What does it mean to be a Muslim in contemporary society? What is the relevance of Islam to everyday Muslim life?

In the early centuries of expansion, conquest, and settlement, Islam was interpreted and applied to provide a framework of faith, meaning, and guidance. Throughout the ages, believers, wherever they might be spread across the world and however different their cultural contexts, have found in Islam a core of belief and practice that provided a sense of unity and identity, of faith and purpose.

As Muhammad brought his reformist message to Arabia, at critical points in history when the Islamic community was threatened or in danger, great religious leaders and revivalist movements responded to the religious/intellectual and political challenges of the community with a variety of reformers and revivalist/reformist movements. The cry "Islam in Danger!" has served as a battle cry to encourage Muslims to rise to the religious and political defense of Islam. Just as it was used by early caliphs, throughout history by Islamic revivalists and reformers, and in the twentieth century in anticolonial/independence struggles, so too in recent years it has been a source of inspiration and popular mobilization in Palestine, Afghanistan, Bosnia, Kashmir, and Chechnya.

Today Islam continues to reflect that same unity and diversity. Although believers continue to affirm their belief in God, the Quran, and the Prophet Muhammad, they differ in their understanding and interpretation of what that should mean. The political resurgence of Islam has been accompanied by a ferment in which contending voices and paradigms have emerged. If modernization brought widespread political and economic reforms in the twentieth century, the pace of religious reform lagged behind. Change has been more visible at the top, for a small group of elites rather than for the masses of Muslims. The political and economic failures of Muslim societies in the 1970s and 1980s have contributed to an Islamic revival that has challenged political and religious establishments alike and called for an Islamic solution, the implementation of an Islamic alternative in personal and community life, in faith and politics. This call has divided as much as united Muslims, precipitating discussion, debate, and confrontation within Muslim societies and, at times, between the Muslim world and the West. Key to this process has been the question of the meaning and relevance of Islam in today's world. Contending voices (clerical and lay, government and opposition, secular and Islamically oriented elites) and their interpretations of Islam press their claims and compete for authority and legitimacy.

Like their Jewish and Christian cousins (like all the Children of Abraham), Muslims today, in facing the challenges of secularism and materialism, of faith and social justice, continue to bear witness to the fact that monotheism does not mean monolithic. While the revolution occurring in contemporary Islam is often seen through the prism or lens of explosive headline events, of radicalism and extremism, the real revolution is the quiet revolution in Islamic discourse and activism. As in the past, the unity of Islam (as in all faiths) embraces a diversity of interpretations and expressions and is a source of dynamism and growth as well as contention and conflict, both among believers and at times with other faith communities. The challenge for all believers remains the rigorous pursuit of "the straight path, the way of God, to whom belongs all that is in the heavens and all that is on the earth" (Q.42:52–53) in a world of diversity and difference.

While the Quran and Sunnah of the Prophet Muhammad remain normative for all Muslims, questions of interpretation, authenticity, and application have become contentious items. If some Muslims see little need to substantially redefine past approaches and practices, others strike out into new territory. Muslim scholars distinguish the eternal, immutable principles and laws in the Quran from those prescriptions that are contingent responses to specific contexts. Others distinguish between the Meccan and Medinan *surahs* (chapters). The former are regarded as the earlier and more religiously binding; the latter are seen as primarily political, concerned with Muhammad's creation of the Medinan state and therefore not universally binding. Still other Muslim scholars have distinguished between the eternal principles and values of the Quran, which are to be applied and reapplied to changing sociopolitical contexts, and past legislation that was primarily intended for specific historical periods.

Although the example (*Sunnah*) of the Prophet Muhammad has always been normative in Islam, from earliest times Muslim scholars saw the need to critically examine and authenticate the enormous number of prophetic traditions (hadith) in order to distinguish between authoritative texts and pious fabrications. In the late twentieth century, some scholar questioned the historicity and authenticity of the hadith, maintaining that the bulk of the Prophetic traditions were written much later. Most Muslim scholars and some Western/non-Muslim scholars have taken exception to this sweeping position. If many of the ulama continue to accept the authoritative collections of the past unquestioningly, other Muslim scholars have in fact become more critical in their approach and use of tradition literature.

New approaches to the study and interpretation of Islam's sacred sources have been accompanied by similar debates over the nature of Islamic law, the Shariah. As noted earlier, many of the ulama continue to equate Shariah, God's law, with its exposition in legal manuals developed by the early law schools. Other Muslims, from Islamic modernists like Muhammad Abduh, Ahmad Khan, and Muhammad Iqbal to Islamic revivalists and neomodernists today, have distinguished between those laws based on clear texts of the Quran and hadith and other laws that are the product of human interpretation and application, the product of reason and social custom. Some express this distinction as between the eternal law (Shariah) of God and its human interpretation and application (fiqh) by early jurists. The distinction is often articulated in terms of the classical division of law into a Muslim's duties or obligations to God (ibadat) and his or her duties to others (muamalat). The former (for example, performance of the Five Pillars of Islam) are seen as unchanging; the latter are contingent upon historical and social circumstances.

Contemporary Muslim discussion and debate over the role of Islam in state and society reflect a broad array of questions: Is there one classical model or many possible models for the relationship of religion to political, social, and economic development? If a new Islamic synthesis is to be achieved that provides continuity with past tradition, how will this be accomplished—imposed from above by rulers and/or the ulama or legislated from below through a representative electoral process?

Legal reform remains a contested issue in many Muslim communities. Many emerging Muslim states followed a pattern of implementing Western-inspired legal codes. The process of legal change did not reflect widespread social change so much as the desires of a small, secular-oriented sector of the population. Governments imposed reforms from above through legislation. The process, contradictions, and tensions inherent in modernization programs in most Muslim societies were starkly reflected in family law (marriage, divorce, and inheritance) reforms. Family law, which is regarded as the heart of the Shariah and the basis for a strong Islamically oriented family structure and society, was the last area of law to be touched by reformers. Even then, unlike most areas of law that implemented Western-inspired legal systems and codes, Muslim family law was not displaced or replaced but instead was subjected to selective reform. Officials often employed an Islamic modernist rationale, in an ad hoc and haphazard manner, to provide an Islamic facade and legitimacy to new laws.

In more recent decades, the debate over whether the Shariah should be part of or the basis of a country's legal system has become a sensitive and at times contentious issue. If this is so, to what degree? Does Islamization of law mean the wholesale reintroduction of classical law as formulated in the early Islamic centuries or the development of new laws derived from the Quran and Sunnah of the Prophet, or can it include the acceptance of any laws, whatever their source, that are not contrary to Islam? Who is to oversee this process: rulers, the ulama, or parliaments?

As Iran, Sudan, Afghanistan, Pakistan, and Saudi Arabia demonstrate, the implementation of Shariah has not followed a fixed pattern or set interpretation, even among those countries dubbed conservative or fundamentalist. Women in Saudi Arabia and in Afghanistan under Taliban rule were not able to vote or hold public office. In Pakistan and Iran, despite other strictures and problems, women vote, hold political office in parliaments and cabinets, teach in universities, and hold responsible professional positions. However, Islamization of law has underscored several areas that have proved particularly problematic: the *hudud* (Quranically defined crimes and prescribed punishments for alcohol consumption, theft, fornication, adultery, and false witness), the status of non-Muslims (*dhimmi*) and minorities, and the status of women. All involve the question of change in Islamic law.

While many conservatives and revivalists or fundamentalists call for the reimplementation of the hudud punishments (punishments of amputation for theft or stoning for adultery), other Muslims argue that these are no longer appropriate. Among those who advocate imposition of the hudud, some call for its immediate introduction and others argue that it should be contingent on the creation of a just society in which people will not be driven to steal in order to survive. Some critics charge that while appropriate relative to the time they were introduced, hudud punishments are unnecessarily harsh in a modern context. If many Muslim rulers and governments try to avoid addressing the issue of the hudud directly, Malaysia's former prime minister, Dr. Mahathir Mohamad, directly criticized the conservatism of his country's ulama, their legal opinions (fatwas), and religious courts. He refused to allow the Malaysian state of Kelantan, the only state controlled by PAS (an Islamic opposition political party) to implement the hudud.

The reintroduction of Islamic law has often had a particularly pronounced negative impact on the status and role of women and minorities, raising serious questions about whether it does not constitute a setback in the gains made in many societies. During the postindependence period, significant changes occurred in many countries, broadening the educational and employment opportunities and enhancing the legal rights of Muslim women. Women became more visible in the professions (teachers, lawyers, engineers, and physicians) and in government. Admittedly, these changes affected a small proportion of the population and varied from one country or region to another, influenced by religious and local traditions, economic and educational development, and government leadership. The contrasts could be seen from Egypt to Saudi Arabia, Iran to Malaysia.

As we have seen, one result of contemporary Islamic revivalism has been a reexamination of the role of women in Islam and, at times, a bitter debate over their function in society. More conservative religious voices among the ulama and many Islamists have advocated a return to veiling and sexual segregation

WOMEN AND EMPOWERMENT

Muslim women in the twentieth century had two clear choices or models before them: the modern Westernized lifestyle common among an elite minority of women and the more restrictive traditional "Islamic" lifestyle of the majority of women, who lived much the same as previous generations. The social impact of the Islamic revival produced a third alternative that is both modern and firmly rooted in Islamic faith, identity, and values. Muslim women, modernists, and Islamists have argued on Islamic grounds for an expanded role for women in Muslim societies. Distinguishing between Islam and patriarchy, between revelation and its interpretation by males (the ulama) in patriarchal settings, Muslim women have reasserted their right to be primary participants in redefining their identity and role in society. In many instances, this change has been symbolized by a return to the wearing of Islamic dress or the donning of a headscarf or hijab. Initially prominent primarily among urban middle-class women, this new mode of dress has become more common among a broader sector of society. For many it is an attempt to combine religious belief and Islamic values of modesty with contemporary freedoms in education and employment, to combine a much-desired process of social change with indigenous Islamic values and ideals. The goal is a more authentic rather than simply Westernized modernization.

as well as restrictions on women's education and employment. Muslim women are regarded as culture bearers, teachers of family faith and values, whose primary role as wives and mothers limits or excludes participation in public life. The imposition of reputed Islamic laws by some governments and the policies of some Islamist movements reinforced fears of a retreat to the past. Among the prime examples have been the Taliban enforcement of veiling, closure of women's schools, and restriction of women in the work place in Afghanistan; Pakistan's General Zia ul-Haq's reintroduction of hudud punishments and a law that counted the testimony of women as worth half that of men; restrictions on women in the Islamic republics of Iran and Sudan; and the brutality of Algeria's Armed Islamic Group toward "unveiled" or more Westernized professional women. In fact, the picture is far more complex and diverse, revealing both old and new patterns.

Islamic dress has the practical advantage of enabling some women to assert their modesty and dignity while functioning in public life in societies where Western dress often symbolizes a more permissive lifestyle. It creates a protected, private space of respectability in crowded urban environments. For some it is a sign of a real feminism that rejects what is regarded as the tendency of women in the West, and in many Muslim societies, to go from being defined as restricted sexual objects in a male-dominated tradition to so-called free yet exploited sexual objects. Western feminism is often seen as pseudoliberation in reality, a new form of bondage to dress, youthfulness, and physical beauty, a freedom in which women's bodies are used to sell every form of merchandise from clothing to automobiles to cell phones. Covering the body, it is argued, defines a woman and gender relations in society in terms of personality and talents rather than physical appearance.

New experiments by educated Muslim women to orient their lives more Islamically have also resulted in more women "returning to the mosque." In the past, the restriction of women to the home and their limited education had resulted in their not participating in public prayer in mosques. While some, separated from the men, attended the Friday congregational prayer, it was more common for women to pray at home and to leave religious learning to men. Today, in many Muslim countries and communities, particularly those that have been regarded as among the more modernized, such as Egypt, Jordan, Malaysia, and America, women are forming their own prayer and Quran study groups, which are led by women. They cite as justification for their present public activities the example of Muslim women in early Islam who fought and prayed alongside their men and of women who were held in high repute for their knowledge and sanctity. Women from the United States to Malaysia, as individuals and organizations, are writing and speaking out for themselves on women's issues. They draw on the writings and thought not only of male scholars, but also, and most importantly, a growing number of women scholars who utilize an Islamic discourse to address issues ranging from dress to education, employment, and political participation.

Contemporary Muslim societies reflect both the old and the new realities. Traditional patterns remain strong and are indeed reasserted and defended by those who call for a more widespread return to traditional forms of Islamic dress and sexual segregation or seclusion (purdah) in public life. However, at the same time, Muslim women have also become catalysts for change. They have empowered themselves by entering the professions, running for elective office, and serving in parliament (in countries as diverse as Egypt and Iran), becoming students and scholars of Islam, conducting their own women's study groups, and establishing women's professional organizations, journals, and magazines. Women's organizations from Egypt and Iran to Pakistan and Indonesia, such as Women Living Under Muslim Laws, based in Pakistan but international in membership, and Malaysia's Sisters in Islam, are active internationally in protecting and promoting the rights of Muslim women.

The Place and Status of Non-Muslims

The simultaneous call for greater political participation and for more Islamically oriented societies has not only had a negative impact on non-Muslim communities in some Muslim countries but also sparked a lively discussion and debate among Muslim intellectuals and religious leaders over the status of non-Muslims in an Islamic state. The traditional doctrine of non-Muslims as protected people, elaborated in the early history of Islam, enabled many to practice their faith and hold positions in society; it was advanced relative to its times and to the far more exclusivist approach of Western Christendom at that time, which was intolerant of other faiths. However, by modern standards of pluralism and equality of citizenship, it amounts to second-class status. More conservative Muslim voices continue to celebrate and defend this doctrine, while other Muslims from Egypt to Indonesia have advocated a redefinition of the status of non-Muslims in terms of their right to full and equal citizenship, which would enable an egalitarian and pluralist society of Muslims and non-Muslims. This is reflected in debates in Egypt over whether the Copts can serve in the army or should have to pay a special tax, and similar discussions over issues of religious and political pluralism in countries such as Lebanon, Pakistan, Malaysia, and Indonesia.

Ironically, questions of citizenship and the exercise of political rights have become increasingly significant for Muslim minorities in the latter half of the twentieth century. At no time have Muslim minority communities been so numerous and widespread. Both the swelling numbers of Muslim refugees and the migration of many Muslims to Europe and America, where Islam is now, respectively, the second- and third-largest religion, make the issue of minority rights and duties within the majority community an ever-greater concern for Islamic jurisprudence. Can Muslim minority communities accept full citizenship and participate fully politically and socially within non-Muslim majority communities that are not governed by Islamic law? What is the relationship of Islamic law to civil law? What is the relationship of culture to religion?

Are Muslims who live in America American Muslims, Muslim Americans, or simply Muslims in America?

CONCLUSION

Islam has always been a world and therefore global religion. However, in the twenty-first century the globalization of Islam has extended to Europe and North America and elsewhere. Today there are more Muslims living in permanent minority communities than at any time in history. Thus, Islam in the contemporary world, as throughout much of history, continues to be a religion of dynamic change. Muslim societies have experienced the impact of rapid change, and with it the challenges in religious, political, social, and economic development. Muslims continue to grapple with the relationship of the present and future to the past. However, in contrast to Judaism and Christianity, Muslims, due to centuries of European colonial dominance and rule, have had only a few decades to accomplish what in the West was the product of centuries of religious and political revolution and reform, a process that included the Enlightenment, Reformation, Counter-Reformation, and the French and American Revolutions. Like believers in other faiths, the critical question today facing Islam and Muslim communities globally is the relationship of faith and tradition to change in a rapidly changing and pluralistic world. Across the Muslim world today, many have taken up the challenge articulated by Fazlur Rahman, a distinguished Muslim scholar, who noted that Islamic reform required "first-class minds who can interpret the old in terms of the new as regards substance and turn the new into the service of the old as regards ideals."[40]

DISCUSSION QUESTIONS

1. Identify and describe the Five Pillars of Islam.

2. Describe the diverse meaning of *jihad*. How has it been used by different Islamic movements to justify their activities?

3. What are the differences between Sunnis, Shiah, and Sufis?

4. What is the difference between the Shariah and *fiqh*? What impact have they had on modern revivalism and reformism?

5. What are the origins of the Crusades? Explain their long-term effects on Muslim-Christian/Western relations.

6. Discuss the impact of European colonialism on the Muslim world. What are some of the ways in which Muslims responded to it?

7. What are *taqlid* and *ijtihad*? Why are these concepts at the heart of the question of the relationship between Islam and modernity?

8. Describe the different themes and techniques used for the revival and reform of Islam in the eighteenth century.

9. Discuss the basic tenets and significance of the Muslim Brotherhood and the Jamaat-i Islami.

10. What are the causes and conditions which led to the contemporary resurgence of Islam?

11. How is Islam used both to support and to oppose the state? Give examples.

12. Discuss the origin and development of the Nation of Islam. Do African American Muslims differ from mainstream Muslims?

13. How has Islam affected or changed the status of women? How are women influenced by and influencing Islamic movements today?

14. What are some of the issues facing Muslims living in non-Muslim majority countries today, particularly in Europe and America?

KEY TERMS

Allah	jihad	Shiah
ayatollah	mahdi	Sufism
caliph	mosque	sunnah
dhimmi	mufti	Sunni
fatwa	People of the Book	tawhid
hadith	Quran	ulama
hajj	ramadan	ummah
hijab	salat	zakat
hijrah	shahadah	
ijtihad	shariah	

SUGGESTED READING

Leila Ahmad, *Women and Gender in Islam* (New Haven, Conn.: Yale University Press, 1993).

Karen Armstrong, *Muhammad: A Biography of the Prophet* (San Francisco: Harper, 1993).

Muhammad Asad, *The Message of the Quran* (Gibraltar: Dar al-Andalus, 1980).

John J. Donohue and John L. Esposito, eds., *Islam in Transition: Muslim Perspectives* (New York: Oxford University Press, 2005).

Khaled Abou El Fadl, *The Great Theft: Wrestling Islam from the Extremists* (San Francisco: Harper, 2005).

John L. Esposito, *Islam: The Straight Path*, 3rd rev ed. (New York: Oxford University Press, 2005).

———, *The Islamic Threat: Myth or Reality?* 3rd ed. (New York: Oxford University Press, 1999).

———, ed., *The Oxford Encyclopedia of the Modern Islamic World*, vols. 1–4 (New York: Oxford University Press, 1995).

———, *Unholy War: Terror in the Name of Islam* (New York: Oxford University Press, 2002).

———, ed., *The Oxford History of Islam* (New York: Oxford University Press, 2000).

The Quran: A Modern English Version (Majid Fakhry, trans.). (Berkshire: Garnet Publishing, 1996).

Martin Lings, *What is Sufism?* (London: I.B. Taurus, 1999).

Seyyed Hossein Nasr, *The Heart of Islam: Enduring Values for Humanity* (San Francisco: Harper, 2002).

Vali Nasr, *The Shia Revival: How Conflict Within Islam Will Shape the Future* (New York: W.W. Norton., 2006).

———, *Ideals and Realities of Islam*, 2nd ed. (Chicago: Kazi Publications, 2001).

Fazlur Rahman, *Major Themes of the Quran*, 2nd ed. (London: Bibliotheca Islamica, 1989).

Tariq Ramadan, *Western Muslims and the Future of Islam* (New York: Oxford University Press, 2004).

Olivier Roy, *Globalized Islam: The Search for a New Ummah* (New York: Columbia University Press, 2006).

John O. Voll, *Islam: Continuity and Change in the Modern World*, 2nd ed. (Syracuse: Syracuse University Press, 1994).

NOTES

1. Ibn Ishaq, as quoted in F. E. Peters, *Muhammad and the Origins of Islam* (Albany, N.Y.: SUNY Press, 1994), p. 172.

2. Ibn Hisham, as quoted in Philip K. Hitti, *History of the Arabs*, 9th ed. (New York: St. Martin's Press, 1966), p. 120. For the text within the context of a major biography of the Prophet Muhammad, see Ibn Ishaq, *The Life of Muhammad*, A. Guillaume, trans. (London: Oxford University Press, 1955), p. 651.

3. Fred R. Donner, *The Early Islamic Conquests* (Princeton, N.J.: Princeton University Press, 1981), p. 269.

4. Francis E. Peters, "The Early Muslim Empires: Umayyads, Abbasids, Fatimids," in *Islam: The Religious and Political Life of a World Community*, Marjorie Kelly, ed. (New York: Praeger, 1984), p. 79.

5. Bernard Lewis, ed., trans., *Islam: From the Prophet Muhammad to the Capture of Constantinople* (New York: Harper & Row, 1974), pp. 179–181.

6. Seyyed Hossein Nasr, *Muhammad: Man of God* (Chicago: Kazi Publications, 1995), p. 90.

7. *The Hedaya*, Charles Hamilton, trans. 2d ed. (Lahore, Pakistan: Primier Books, 1957), p. 73.

8. As quoted in Rueben Levy, *The Social Structure of Islam* (Cambridge: Cambridge University Press, 1955), p. 126.

9. Muhammad al-Ghazali, *Our Beginning in Wisdom*, Ismail R. al-Faruqi, trans. (Washington, D.C.: American Council of Learned Societies, 1953), p. 111.

10. John Alden Williams, ed., *Islam* (New York: George Braziller, 1962), pp. 138–139.

11. Margaret Smith, *Rabia the Mystic and Her Fellow-Servants in Islam* (Cambridge: Cambridge University Press, 1926), p. 30.

12. W. Montgomery Watt, *Muslim Intellectual: A Study of Al-Ghazali* (Edinburgh: Edinburgh University Press, 1963), p. 136. See also W. Montgomery Watt, *The Faith and Practice of Al-Ghazali* (London: George Allen & Unwin, 1953).

13. Watt, *Muslim Intellectual*, p. 135.

14. Roy Mottahedeh, *Loyalty and Leadership in an Early Islamic Society* (Princeton, N.J.: Princeton University Press, 1980), p. 138.

15. Francis E. Peters, "Early Muslim Empires," p. 85.

16. For a history of the Crusades, see S. Runciman, *A History of the Crusades*, 3 vols. (Cambridge: Cambridge University Press, 1951–1954), and J. Prawers, *Crusader Institutions* (Oxford: Oxford University Press, 1980).

17. Roger Savory, "Christendom vs. Islam: Interaction and Coexistence," in *Introduction to Islamic Civilization*, Roger Savory, ed. (Cambridge: Cambridge University Press, 1976), p. 133.

18. John O. Voll, "Renewal and Reform in Islamic History: Tajdid and Islah," in *Voices of Resurgent Islam*, John L. Esposito, ed. (New York: Oxford University Press, 1983) p. 33.

19. John O. Voll, "The Sudanese Mahdi: Frontier Fundamentalist," *International Journal of Middle East Studies* 10, 1979, 159.

20. Ibid., p. 74.

21. Sayyid Ahmad Khan, "Islam: The Religion of Reason and Nature," in *Islam in Transition: Muslim Perspectives*, John J. Donohue and John L. Esposito, eds. (New York: Oxford University Press, 1982), p. 42.

22. Muhammad Iqbal, *The Reconstruction of Religious Thought in Islam* (Lahore, Pakistan: Muhammad Ashraf, 1968), p. 163.

23. Muhammad Iqbal, "Islam as a Political and Moral Ideal," in *Thoughts and Reflections of Iqbal*, S. A. Vahid, ed. (Lahore, Pakistan: Muhammad Ashraf, 1964), p. 52.

24. Muhammad Iqbal, as quoted in "A Separate Muslim State in the Subcontinent," in *Islam in Transition*: Donohue and Esposito, eds., pp. 91–92.

25. Iqbal, *Reconstruction of Religious Thought*, p. 168.

26. Abul Ala Mawdudi, "Political Theory of Islam," in *Islam in Transition*, Donohue and Esposito, eds., p. 252.

27. Mitchell, *Society of Muslim Brothers*, pp. 228–229.

28. M Sayyid Qutb, "Social Justice in Islam," in *Islam in Transition*, Donohue and Esposito, eds., pp. 125–126.

29. Francis E. Peters, "Jerusalem," Oxford Encyclopedia of the Modern Islamic World, vol. 2, p. 368.

30. For perceptive discussions of Osama bin Laden, see A. Rashid *Taliban* and J. K. Cooley, *Unholy Wars: Afghanistan, America and International Terrorism* (London: Pluto Press, 2000).

31. Transcript of Osama bin Laden Interview, CNN/Time, *Impact: Holy Terror?* August 25, 1998.

32. *Al-Hayat*, November 5, 2001.

33. This section is adapted from John L. Esposito, *Islam: The Straight Path*, 3d ed. (New York: Oxford University Press, 1998) and *Muslims on the Americanization Path* (New York: Oxford University Press, 1999).

34. Malcolm X with Alex Haley, *The Autobiography of Malcolm X* (New York: Ballantine Books, 1973), pp. 241–242.

35. As quoted in Clifton E. Marsh, in *From Black Muslims to Muslims: The Transition from Separatism to Islam, 1930–1980* (Metuchen, N.J.: Scarecrow Press, 1984), p. 76.

36. Malcolm X, *Autobiography of Malcolm X*, pp. 316–317.

37. As quoted in Marsh, *From Black Muslims*, p. 82.

38. Ibid., p. 74.

39. Yvonne Y. Haddad, in "Dynamics of Islamic Identity in North America," *Muslims on the Americanization Path*, Yvonne Y. Haddad and John L. Esposito, eds., (New York: Oxford University Press) ch. 1.

40. Fazlur Rahman, *Islam and Modernity* (Chicago: University of Chicago Press, 1982), p. 139.

CHAPTER FIVE

HINDUISM: MYRIAD PATHS TO SALVATION

Overview

"*Namaskar.*" Millions of Hindus every day extend this ancient Sanskrit greeting to holy seekers and other respected individuals, as well as to gods whom they honor. In a suburb of Calcutta, devotees lead a goat toward the small temple where a priest sprinkles pure water on its head; after seeing it "consent" to its fate by shivering, the priest skillfully wields a sharp knife to slit the animal's throat, severs the head, and pours the spurting blood on the icon of goddess Kali, saying, "*Om namaskar Kali-Ma*" ("*Om* homage to Mother Kali"). In a desert oasis town in western India, a *sadhu* who has renounced all family ties in quest of salvation walks slowly down a narrow byway, wearing a humble robe and carrying an alms bowl; noticing a white cotton cloth covering his nose and mouth, indicating the sadhu's vow to complete nonviolence (the mask preventing his accidentally inhaling any unfortunate insects), a housewife offers some fruit to him, bows, and says, "*Namaskar baba-ji*" ("Homage to respected father"). Despite the apparent contradiction, no one would dispute that both animal sacrificers to Kali and absolutely nonviolent ascetics are following ancient and legitimate Hindu traditions. Nor can we ignore the fact that other venerable Hindu traditions empower holy men to take up weapons to defend their faith, or that in countless temples across the Hindu world today priests accept only the purest, vegetarian offerings designed to nourish and please the deities.

As can be surmised from this admittedly bewildering set of examples, Hinduism is unlike the traditions surveyed already. It lacks both a single canonical text accepted by all followers and an elite who exert control over the development of its fundamental beliefs and practices.

Ancient Hindu traditions continue to thrive today amidst all the changes brought by colonial rule, independence, and the advent of science. There are newly built monasteries for study (*mathas*) in the traditional way, at the feet of recognized masters, or *gurus*. And there are also yoga centers in the major urban centers, catering to India's new middle class, that resemble those found in London or Chicago. New Hindu sects have arisen, usually around charismatic teachers, that combine classic doctrines with ideas from other Asian traditions or the West, using video and Internet media to extend their outreach. Yet in India today there are also communities of very conservative priests in which the earliest hymns and rituals (some dating back 3,000 years) are still memorized, recited, and passed down orally and in secrecy to their sons. In the great centers such as Varanasi and Hardwar, pilgrims come by the hundred thousand each year to make offerings and see the deities enshrined in their magnificent temples, while musicians and dancers in their traditional training studios nearby continue to perfect their dramatic renditions of religious themes. In many villages across the Indian subcontinent, where 70 percent of the population still lives, ritual practices within families and in local temples remain vigorous. What we label "Hinduism" ranges from monotheism to polytheism, from monism to materialism and atheism; from nonviolent ethics to moral systems that see as imperative elaborate blood sacrifices to sustain the world; from critical, scholastic philosophical discussion to the cultivation of sublime, mystical, wordless inner experiences. In this chapter, we will survey this broad spiritual tradition, a tradition that spans almost every conceivable religious orientation—in belief and practice—that has ever been recorded in human history.

Religious Unity Underlying Diversity?

"Hinduism" is the term used to indicate the amalgam of spiritual traditions originating in South Asia that comprise the third largest world religion today. The term owes its origins to *Sindhus*, the Persian word for the great Indus River. Conquering Muslims used "Hindu" to designate people who lived east of the Indus, and later the British applied the term to the non-Muslim natives, whom they characterized as "the idolaters."

The power of this singular name Hinduism eventually induced South Asian intellectuals and politicians to accept it to stand for a separate religious identity of Hindu amidst the apparent singularities of the Muslim and Christian. What is meant, or what should be meant, by "true Hinduism" has remained contested throughout history, especially in the modern and postcolonial eras.

Religion in South Asia has been the most pluralistic and least centrally organized in the world, a characteristic dating back at least a millennium when the Arab geographer Alberuni identified forty-two discrete "religions" in South Asia. While conservative religious ideology still is used to justify caste and social inequality, there are other ancient traditions that argue forcefully—in ways similar to those in the Western prophetic faiths—for the reform of society and for "God-given" egalitarianism. Hinduism thus incorporates differences at least as fundamental as those between Judaism, Islam, and Christianity. Therefore, it is only by distinguishing the various "Hindu" traditions from the more general and monolithic term "Hinduism" that comparability with other world religions can be intelligible.

One Sanskrit expression for dominant high-caste religion is *Sanatana Dharma*. Its meaning, "eternal teaching," is very broad, drawing on the term "Dharma" that signifies "truth," "practice," "duty," "way of life." As used in India today, Sanatana Dharma usually describes the attitude of "orthodox" believers who accept the superiority of the *brahmin* caste and the earliest scriptures called the Vedas; adherents of the "heterodox" South Asian traditions, who do not accept these beliefs, are excluded. However, many modern Hindus regard Buddhists, Jains, and the Sikhs (c.1500 CE to the present)—as co-religionists. As we will see, there are many "Hindu" traditions in India that do not fit the Sanatana Dharma mold.

The Geography and Demography of Modern Hinduism

Though the great majority of Hindus live on the South Asian subcontinent, an important postcolonial development has been the global diaspora of South Asians. Their transplantation to other parts of the world has made Hinduism a global faith today. By the turn of the millennium, the number of Hindus is estimated to surpass 800 million; after Islam, it is the second fastest growing world religion.

Among the contemporary nation-states, India remains the heartland of Hinduism (see Map 5.1). The modern nation has been a secular democracy since its inception in 1947. It has over eighteen major culture regions, whose ethnic groups speak over one thousand distinct languages and divide into four major groups. These regions each have their distinctive religious traditions as well. The most profound differences are seen between the traditions of North and South India.

Among the other South Asian states, Nepal was the world's last Hindu nation (until 2006), with a majority of its twenty-two million people identifying themselves as "Hindu." Two Muslim nations, Pakistan and Bangladesh, contain large Hindu minorities (3% and 16%, respectively), most of whom remained despite the chaos and bloodshed occasioned by partition of British India in 1947. Fifteen percent of Buddhist Sri Lanka's population of twenty million is Hindu. Small communities of Hindus are also found in Burma, Malaysia, Indonesia, Fiji, and the Caribbean.

In North America there are over one million Hindus, mostly immigrants. In the United States, as across Europe, Hindu temples serve as centers of religious teaching and ritual practice. The yoga traditions that involve training the body for flexibility and mental peace have been the most influential vehicle for spreading Hinduism among non-Indian peoples. The most well-known Hindu traditions that have attracted Euro-American converts are the so-called Hare Krishna movement (ISKON) and Transcendental Meditation (T.M.).

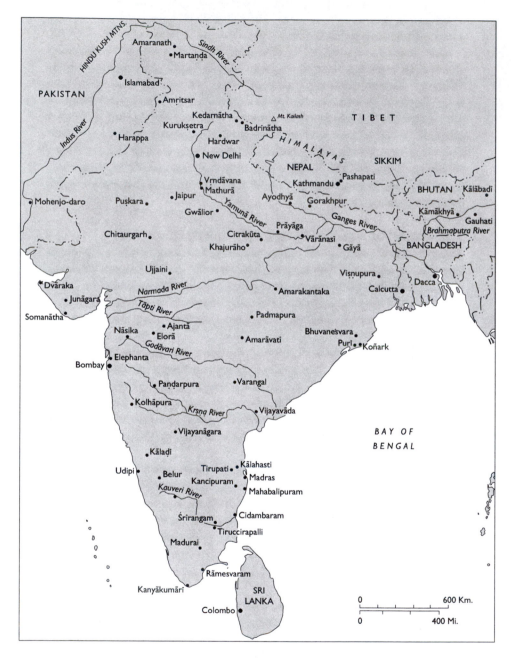

Map 5.1 India with Major Ancient and Holy Places.

ENCOUNTER WITH MODERNITY: HINDU CHALLENGES TO INDIA AS A SECULAR STATE

Religion in South Asia has undergone a continuous, additive process throughout its pluralistic history, one that has tended to preserve the past even amidst striking innovations. Traditions have thrived and multiplied without any single priestly group, theologian, or institution ever imposing a universal or reductive definition of the core beliefs. Hindus have since antiquity respected the remote past as a more refined era of spiritual awareness. There have been no heresy trials or inquisitions in South Asia's long history; in fact, debating spiritual truths, often with great subtlety, was a regular feature of premodern court life and in society at large. Hindu kings did impose laws that required respect for the "orthodox elite," that is, for brahmin priests and ascetics, just as they protected and supported the temples in return for religious sanction of their rule.

The additive pattern continues to the present, with the result that Hinduism's multiplicities are continuously extended: very ancient traditions are preserved alongside those originating in the medieval era, and these threads exist in interaction with the traditions introduced by nineteenth- and twentieth-century reformers.

But although in many respects South Asia preserves elements of premodern religious culture with a vigor matched in few other places across the globe, there is no "unchanging East" in South Asia—or anywhere else! Religions have changed as the circumstances of individuals and societies have changed: the scientific ideas associated with the Enlightenment have affected nearly everyone through education, technology, and medicine; the views and practices of Christian missionaries as well as the political practices introduced through the modern state impacted most regions as well. Most important, the pattern of reform and synthesis that has kept Hinduism so flexible and fluid has continued, as leading exponents have entered the global religious arena and adopted mass media to serve the faith. (In 2007, there were over 19,500 Web sites dedicated to the various forms of Hinduism!) Both classical and reformed Hinduism as well as political movements emphasizing religious identity have proven extremely successful at attracting the loyalty of believers of every sort, from highly educated intellectuals to illiterate villagers. Despite the many inducements that Christian culture offered in the days of British rule, few Hindus abandoned their indigenous faith.

Leaders such as Gandhi and Nehru who led South Asia to independence (1947) subscribed to the prevailing norm in Western political thought, insisting that for India to be modern it should be a secular democracy, formally favoring no religion. In the beginning of the twenty-first century, however, this stance has been questioned by an increasing number of Hindu citizens.

In reacting to threats perceived as coming from modern secularism and non-Hindus, Hindu revivalist groups have created new organization styles based on Western prototypes. Among the many responses to British colonial rule and the changes it brought to South Asia, one of the most enduring has come from institutions calling for thoroughgoing reform of "Hindu-ness" (*Hindutva*) in national life and the reconstitution of India as a Hindu state (*Hindu rashtra*). With roots among nineteenth-century reformers, this ideology began to be forcefully articulated in 1923 across the nation by the Rashtriya Svayamsevak Sangh ("National Union of [Hindu] Volunteers," the RSS), a group that proposed a nativist definition of "Hinduism" as devotion to "Mother India." Members have worked in the political arena to promote candidates wishing to repeal the secular rule of law India instituted in 1947, when the country gained independence from Great Britain. By 1989, RSS membership had grown to two million.

It was only with the most recent incarnation of an RSS-allied political party, the Bharatiya Janata party (BJP), that Hindu nationalists finally found success in electoral politics across the nation. In the elections of 1995, the BJP won more seats than any other party in the national Parliament, defeating the Congress party that had dominated Indian politics since independence. In the 1998 elections, the BJP finally ascended to national rule; it fell from power in 2004.

The BJP is controlled by high-caste politicians and appeals primarily to middle-class urbanites. It has risen in prominence as its leaders have sought to symbolize the unity of a militant and revived Hindu India through a series of motorized "chariot festivals" across the nation, culminating in reworked traditional rituals in which all the waters from all the country's sacred rivers were brought together and merged. The BJP and its allies have also stoked resentment over government-sponsored affirmative action initiatives aimed to break high-caste control over the nation's civil service and educational institutions.

Most stridently, the BJP has also fomented disrespect for South Asian Muslims by accusing the secular government of favoring them in its civil laws and of protecting medieval-era mosques that were purportedly built on North Indian sites sacred to Hindus. The BJP seeks to have the Hindu majority strike back at Muslims today for actions of centuries past. The first and most violent focus was on Ayodhya, where in 1528 the Mughal ruler Babar built a mosque on a site that modern BJP partisans claim was the birthplace of Rama, the human incarnation of the god Vishnu. Responding to the call made by many Hindu groups, one that was dramatized in a widely distributed video production suggesting that the activists had been miraculously given Rama's blessing for this "service," thousands of volunteers converged on the site in December 1992. They attacked and subdued government troops protecting the site, then broke up the building with hammers, steel rods, and crowbars. In the aftermath, rioting broke out between Muslims and Hindus in other Indian towns and in Pakistan.

The RSS- and BJP-led movements advocate paths to religious modernization found elsewhere in the world: they adopt the latest technological media, yet reject the Enlightenment-inspired critiques of religious belief and insist that the secular political systems established in the colonial and postcolonial eras give way to a religious state. They have used the ancient idea of Mother India to express symbolically their sense of colonial and postcolonial secular rule "raping" the Mother Goddess. As Guru Golwalkara, the former RSS chief (1940–1973), stated,

> When we say this is a Hindu nation, there are some who immediately come up with the question, "What about the Muslims and Christians?" But the crucial question is whether or not they remember that they are children of this soil. . . . No! Together with the change in their faith, gone is the spirit of love and devotion for the nation. They look to some distant holy land as their holy place. It is not merely a change of faith, but a change even in national identity.[1]

Yet beyond declaring loyalty to the land and the Hindu state, fundamentalist-nationalist literature remains elusive and necessarily vague on what exactly "Hindu-ness" means, and for good reason: Hindus have remained divided on this question since antiquity and certainly throughout the era of colonial rule and up to the present.

Yet the appeal of the Hindu-India movement has grown stronger, providing a political expression for the guru-oriented sects with their emphasis on personal devotional enthusiasm (discussed later in this chapter), and for the neo-yoga centers with their rigorous challenge of mastering inner discipline (also discussed later), both of which offer their own versions of "essential Hinduism." Hindu nationalist groups appeal to the simplest level of religious identity. As Daniel Gold has concluded, "If personal religion entails among other things the identification of the individual with some larger whole, then the Hindu Nation may appear as a whole more immediately visible and attainable than the ritual cosmos of traditional Hinduism."[2] To better understand the significance of the Hindu nationalist challenge to the modern secular state of India we must go back to the beginning and trace the historical development of Hinduism.

PREMODERN HINDUISM: THE FORMATIVE ERA

The Aryans and Religion in the Vedic Era

The recounting of South Asian history until recently included legends of an invasion of the subcontinent by an aggressive light-skinned people who called themselves "Aryans" and spoke an Indo-European language. Mounted on their horse-drawn chariots, these warriors were imagined destroying cities of the Indus valley nearly as ancient as those of Egypt and Mesopotamia, and subduing the darker skinned speakers of Dravidian languages inhabiting the northern subcontinent. This rendition of history was used to explain the modern distribution of "north" and "south" India as separate linguistic and racial zones. The Aryans, supposedly culturally superior, then allegedly forced the invaded people to migrate southward over the Vindhya Mountains to settle in the lower peninsula.

Built on very forced readings of thin textual evidence, this view of history contained a racial assumption welcomed by early European scholars and by high-caste Hindus in the modern and postcolonial era. Just as Sanskrit, the language of the Vedic hymns, was discovered to be related to most languages of Europe, so it was also concluded that the ancestors of the modern Hindu elite are distantly kin to the now superior British. Western archaeologists and the British colonial government supported such research and found this imagined history attractive. The British, in particular, welcomed support, however tenuous, for their view of modern Hindus as inept and modern Hinduism as corrupt.

Although migration in prehistory is accepted by objective historians as explaining the linguistic geography of Eurasia, such scholars now find no justification for understanding "Aryan" as a racial term, and they reject utterly any suggestion that the ancient Aryans, or their descendants, were or are culturally superior to darker skinned South Asian people. The Indus valley cities are now thought to have declined not through conquest but due to regional climatic changes. There are also signs that the Indus valley culture in fact shared many continuities with subsequent "Aryan" culture. Indeed, "Aryan" in social terms really had no meaning beyond designating participants in early Vedic sacrifices and festivals. By 700 BCE, "Aryan culture" had been adopted by most politically dominant groups across the Indo-Gangetic plains, but most of the religious beliefs and ritual practices of Hindus today are those recorded from texts that were composed *after* the original four Vedas, to which we now turn.

Vedic Religion

Knowledge of early Indic religion comes from the four Vedas, a collection of over one thousand hymns of praise and supplication addressed to the gods, the oldest of which is the Rig Veda. Composed in archaic language and set in complicated poetical form, these hymns show no systematic development, ordering, or single mythological framework. It is likely that the Vedic hymns were collected and appreciated by only the most elite social groups of that time.

Early Vedic religion was centered on the fire sacrifices (*yajna* or *homa*). The sacrifice depended upon the knowledge of a special, hereditary group of priests called brahmins, who chanted the Vedic hymns and orchestrated highly intricate and time-consuming rituals intended to gratify the numerous Aryan deities. Accompanied by carefully cadenced chants, the brahmins offered grain, animal flesh, and clarified butter into a blazing fire, thereby transforming them into fragrant smoke that could nourish and please the gods. The entire universe was thought to be maintained by this sacrifice: if kept happy, well fed, and strengthened through these offerings, the deities would sustain creation and ensure the prosperity of the Aryan sacrificers.

The language of the Vedic hymns, called Sanskrit, was thought to be divine in origin. Command of Sanskrit was essential, and the hymns were memorized by brahmin priests and taught to men in succeeding generations. The Vedas existed for over two millennia in oral form only; the earliest extant written manuscripts, which date back only to the eleventh century of the common era, include annotations showing proper accent and ritual context.

The major deities of the Vedic world, all male, were those connected to sacrifice, martial conquest, mystical experience, and maintenance of moral order. Agni, the fire god whose flaming tongue licks the offerings, was essential for the successful ritual. The Aryan warrior deity par excellence was Indra, and he has the greatest number of hymns dedicated to him. It was Indra who subdued alien deities, and it was Indra who was called upon to lead the Aryan men into battle. Soma was conceived to be a divine presence dwelling within a psychoactive substance of the same name, possibly a mushroom, and it was drunk by humans and deities before battle and at the end of other ritual celebrations. Perhaps it was Soma who inspired the early Hindu seers to probe deeper into the nature of reality. But *rita*, the moral order of the Vedic universe, was thought to be enforced by another strong deity, Varuna, who could mete out punishment or reward. The hymns indicate that humans felt they could approach Varuna with personal petitions for forgiveness.

Death and afterlife in the early Vedic era were envisioned as two alternative destinies. There was the possibility of becoming an ancestor (*pitri*) and reaching a heavenly afterlife (*pitriloka*) if one lived morally, but only if one's family in the after-death year performed special rituals (*shraddha*). These were designed to embody the initially disembodied spirit in its arduous journey to become, as several hymns poetically describe it, one of the twinkling evening stars. Alternatively, those whose deeds were immoral or whose families failed to do the proper shraddha rituals lost their individual identity and merely dissolved back into the earth.

Vedic religion was marked by faith in the power of the gods, ritual acts to influence them, and the spiritual resonance of Sanskrit words. The Aryans believed with absolute certainty in the primacy of their deities. In later eras, however, all of the central deities of the earliest pantheon fade into minor roles: Indra is the king of the minor heavenly hosts, Agni is confined to be a guardian of ritual, Soma is seen as the deity residing in the moon, and Varuna becomes the lord of the ocean. Similarly, the concept of *rita* is replaced by others that dominate subsequent Hinduism: reincarnation, the law of *karma*, and the concept of *dharma* (duty).

Karma, Yoga, and the Quest for Liberation

Scattered references in the final stratum of Vedic hymns indicate that a very different spiritual orientation had entered the Aryan world. The practice of asceticism—involving retreat into the forest, silent introspection, and the cultivation of trance states—was likely the first indigenous spiritual tradition absorbed into the dominant religion. Such practices found a receptive community in certain circles among the Aryans, and their synthesis of this spirituality emerges clearly in the Upanishads, the remarkable tracts that began to be appended to the Vedic hymns after 1000 BCE. The dialogues recorded and the very name given to these texts—*upanishad* means "sitting near devotedly"—indicate a context of disciples learning at the feet of masters who have gone beyond the Vedic sacrificial framework to adopt ascetic practices aimed at realizing the more fundamental realities underlying all existence. These gurus articulated both new teachings and practices.

The fundamental paradigm introduced is that of *samsara*, "the world," in which all phenomena are inspired by the existence of an unchanging soul (*atman*) that wanders from birth to death again and again, until it finds release (*moksha*) from the cycle.

An individual's destiny in samsara is determined by the actions (deeds and thoughts) an individual performs. This natural law affected by and inscribed within the atman is called *karma*, a complex term whose meaning is often oversimplified by Westerners. It is important to note here that all of the world religions that emerge in India accept this samsara paradigm: the "orthodox" traditions that accept the authority of the Veda as well as the "heterodox" Indic religions that do not, primarily Buddhism and Jainism. Although the latter two do hold different doctrines about the precise nature of the soul and the mechanisms of karma, all advocate specific yoga practices designed to realize the highest truth.

The teachers in the Upanishads argue that the ultimate reality of the world is the universal spirit called *Brahman*.[3] Through a process that is inexplicable, this unitary ultimate reality became subdivided into myriad individual atmans. They are the truly real entities in the world, however subtle and difficult to perceive they may be. All beings, then, are spiritual beings, sharing with one another and the forces that move the universe a common metaphysical essence. This truth is stated concisely in the Chandogya Upanishad when the teacher simply states, "That [i.e., Brahman] thou art." As we will see, it is not enough simply to know intellectually that Brahman equals atman, one must realize this truth in one's own life, and this is accomplished through yoga.

Yoga

Yoga refers to the disciplined practices by which human beings can unify and focus their bodily powers for the purpose of realizing their true spiritual essence, the atman within. First surfacing in the late Upanishads, these practices were codified in a text, the *Yoga Sutras*, attributed to a sage named Patanjali. The yoga tradition is for the highly advanced spiritual elite, for those attempting to escape samsara by their ending or "burning up" all past karma. (As we'll see, in contrast, most "good Hindus" are householders who define their spiritual orientation as managing karma toward the good, with self or atman realization relegated to a future rebirth.)

The *Yoga Sutras* assume that only individuals of high moral character, who have renounced most material possessions, live in simplicity (including

First appearing in the Upanishads, where it is described as the "seed sound" of all other sounds, OM (also written in full phonetic rendition as AUM) is one of the most prominent symbols of Hinduism. Repeated as part of almost every *mantra* for offerings and meditation, as well as written calligraphically on icons and other symbols, OM has become an ever-present and multivalent symbol, often reflecting sectarian differences. Upandishadic interpretations were carried on and developed in both yoga and Vedanta, where OM is seen as a symbol of cosmic origination and dissolution, and past-present-future-dissolution (A+U+M+ silence) in its one resonating sound. OM's components also include all four states of consciousness in yoga theory, with A as waking, U as dreaming, M as dreamless sleep, and the syllable as a whole "the fourth," i.e., OM is the sound-form of *atman-Brahman*. Repeating OM is thus the key to meditation that leads to *moksha*.

The theological schools (discussed in the text) suggested yet further meanings: the three letters AUM representing Brahma, Vishnu, and Shiva; Vaishnavites identify OM with Vishnu; Shaivites see Shiva as Lord of the Dance creating from OM all the sounds for musical notes from his drum. OM adorns all the major deities in their popular art forms.

vegetarianism), and study the teachings regarding the "inner reality," have any chance of success in meditation. Advanced practice then turns to: first postures (*asana*) designed to make the body flexible and free its energies, and breath control (*pranayama*) to harness and direct the body's primal energy; then, after focus on a single object for long periods (*dharana*), a series of increasingly refined states of consciousness as the mind is withdrawn from external sensation. These experiences culminate in a trance state (*samadhi*). It is in samadhi that one develops a direct and unbroken awareness of the luminous origin of consciousness itself: the life-giving, pure, and blissful atman.

The *Yoga Sutras* assume that the progressive sensing of the commanding reality of the spirit within reverses the power of ignorance and egotistic desire to distort human consciousness. The ultimate goal in yoga meditation is to dwell for extended periods in trance, reaching the highest state, *kaivalya*, an awareness that is perfectly at one with and centered in the atman. The *yogin* who reaches this state is said to experience *moksha*, or release, putting an end to all past karma. This adept, freed from desire and ignorance, is thought omniscient and capable of many *siddhis*, which are supernormal feats such as telepathy, clairvoyance, extraordinary travel. This "enlightenment" experience and the capacity to know others' tendencies and thoughts makes the yogic sage an ideal spiritual guide for seekers.

The great majority of householders from the formative period onward have oriented their religious lives around the reality of karma. Although subject to various interpretations, Hindu karma doctrine asserts that all actions committed by an individual set into motion a cause that will lead to a moral effect in the present and/or future lifetimes. This belief holds that a natural mechanism functions to make the cosmos orderly and just. One Sanskrit name for India—*karmabhumi*, "realm of karma"—reflects its centrality in Hindu life. This has meant that inclinations to do good and avoid evil were backed up by the belief in karmic retribution for one's actions. Since old karma is coming to fruition constantly and new karma is being made continuously, it is—in most explications—incorrect to see karma doctrine as fatalism. Further, not all events in life are due to karmic causes; Indic religious philosophies and medical theory have all recognized natural causalities as part of the human condition.

What is implicit in karma theory for typical human beings is that one's karma in daily life is in fact unknown. In practice, this uncertainty principle (similar to the belief of some Protestant Christians that no one can be certain about his or her salvation) has sustained a strong tendency for Hindus to resort to astrology for guidance at times of important decisions such as when to first plant the fields, the choice of marriage partner, or when to set off on a journey. As Indian society developed, other ideas were tied to karma, weaving tighter the socioreligious fabric of classical Hinduism.

Sacred Sound and Brahmins

One of the great continuities in Hinduism is the focus on sound for religious purposes. From antiquity, priests chanted Vedic hymns in very precise cadences. The early brahmin sages believed that their language had divine origins and that uttering Sanskrit rightly had efficacy to please, even move, the deities to action. In the Upanishads, teachers suggest that chanting repeatedly certain Sanskrit words (that they called *mantras*) can activate a spiritual force within human consciousness. By the time the Yoga texts were written down (300 CE), the practices engaging the kinesthetic and visual senses were combined with mantra recitations. Faith in mantras and the practice of their repetition (called *japa*) continues to be at the center of Hinduism for many today, whether the chanting is done for worshiping the gods or as an essential component in Hindu meditation. We will see that this belief is the reason that song and music became so much a part of Hindu ritual practice.

PREMODERN HINDUISM: THE CLASSICAL ERA

There were very few periods in South Asian history when expansive empires unified the subcontinent. The first great empire was that of the Mauryas (300–180 BCE), whose emperors helped to spread Buddhism and its ideal of compassion as a principle of just rule. As Buddhism expanded and thrived, it competed with early brahmanical tradition.

Classical Hinduism, the product of the response by the orthodox brahmin priests and spiritual teachers to Buddhism, absorbed and synthesized aspects of this heterodox missionary faith while also embracing pre-Aryan deities and other indigenous Indic traditions. In the same way that modern Hinduism defined itself in relation to the West, classical Hindu traditions took form through relations between yogins, brahmins, and the exponents of heterodox faiths. One result was that nonviolence and vegetarianism became ideals of high-caste religiosity, Hindu monasteries for training and meditation were begun, and the theistic dimension of Hinduism (not part of early Buddhism) found vast elaboration and increasingly popular acceptance. This tradition was so compelling that by 1200 CE, by which time Hinduism had slowly absorbed the Buddha within its panoply of gods, Buddhism had virtually disappeared from South Asia (except for the Himalayan [Nepal] and Sri Lankan peripheries). The brahmins composed Sanskrit literature that codified and disseminated expressions of this new synthesis in the realms of philosophy, theology, and law. These texts and leaders gave the subcontinent a source of unity. It did this through one fundamental paradigm: defining an individual's place in society in terms of karma doctrine.

The Reality of Karma and Caste

As we have seen, the idea of karma provided a way of explaining the destiny of beings according to their moral pasts. Evil deeds lead to evil destiny and vice versa; people get what they deserve, although not necessarily in this life. As this idea of karmic retribution had become widely accepted by the classical era, brahmin social thinkers built upon it to formulate the basis of the ideal Hindu society in a series of texts called the *Dharmashastra* (*Treatises on Dharma*). These texts, the most famous of which is known by the English title *The Laws of Manu*, make a series of arguments about karma while charting a host of practices and social policies designed to keep the world in order.

The *Dharmashastras* assume that one's birth location is the most telling indication of one's karma. They also argue that high-status birth gives one a higher spiritual nature, reflecting one's good karma past. Rebirth, then, is assumed to fall into regular patterns, and this cyclicity justifies seeing society, like the animal kingdom, as broken down into groups with very separate natures and capacities. These groups have come to be called "castes" in English, although the Sanskrit term is *jati* ("breed" or "birth").

Hindu social codes, which became the law of the land in India in the early classical period, prescribed that those born into a caste should marry within their group. Such individuals were believed to have closely matching karma, so that if they segregated themselves to bear and raise children, reincarnation patterns should be consistent and clear. Those born into a caste were also expected to perform the traditional tasks of that group. The four main groups were called *varnas* (classes): *brahmins*, who were to master the Vedic and ritual practice; *kshatriyas*, who were to rule justly and protect the Aryan society, especially the brahmins; *vaishyas*, who were to specialize in artisanship and trade, multiplying the wealth of the society; and *shudras*, the workers needed to perform laborious and menial tasks for those in the upper jatis.

The *Dharmashastras* also identify the top three classes as *dvija*, "twice born," meaning "born again" through a Vedic initiation. Despised groups such as *chandalas* were assigned to perform polluting tasks such as street sweeping and carrying dead bodies. Under each varna, hundreds of caste subgroups were arrayed, and to this day these vary regionally in names and traditional social functions.

Each caste was thought to have a singular proper duty to perform in life; the term for this, *dharma*, is central throughout the subsequent history of Hinduism. The *Dharmashastra* texts argue that one must live in accordance with one's place in the world, which has been assigned retributively. Only by doing so does one make the good karma needed to move "upward" in samsara. As one famous passage in *The Laws of Manu* (10:97) warns, "Better to do one's own *dharma* badly than another caste's *dharma* well."

Hindu religious law, therefore, does not see all human beings as having the same value, nor as being subject to the same code of law. While religious views underlie this system of social inequality, Hindu social theorists argued that in the fullness of time—beyond a single-lifetime framework—samsara and its law of karmic retribution allows for certain, inescapable cosmic justice, matching karmic past to social function. In the end, every soul will move upward through samsara to be reborn as a brahmin and reach salvation. Individual freedom is sacrificed for harmony and for society's ultimate and eventual collective liberation.

Thus, in theory, the religious underpinning of the caste system has served to legitimate the social hierarchy beyond that in Vedic times. It preserves the purity and privileges of the highest castes and argues that society depends upon brahmins with their ritual mastery to worship the gods properly and so to ensure the divine grace necessary to sustain a fruitful, nonthreatening environment.

Consistent with this belief system, Hindus, like Jews, Christians, and Muslims, came to regard themselves as "chosen people." The next logical step was to use religious doctrine and caste ideology to justify their efforts to convert and subjugate other groups in their midst. As we will see in what follows, this ideological complex sanctioning high-caste privilege had early critics among Buddhists and Jains, and later Hindus as well. Some modern reformers from the "Scheduled Castes" (a colonial euphemism used to refer to the lowest social groups retained in India's constitution) point out that these Hindu doctrines were and are an apology for the high-caste minority to rule over the low-caste majority. As Bhimrao Ambedkar, one of the modern legal reformers stated,

To the untouchables, Hinduism is a veritable chamber of horrors. The sanctity and infallibility of the *Vedas*, *Smritis* and *Shastras*, the iron law of caste, the heartless law of *karma* and the senseless law of status by birth are to the Untouchables veritable instruments of torture which Hinduism has forged against the Untouchables.[4]

The classical brahmin writers also prescribed other spiritual disciplines to realize the ideal Hindu life; the need for an individual to fulfill his or her dharma fully explains the extraordinarily precise attention shown to the ideal human lifetime, to which we now turn.

The Four Stages of Life (*Ashramas*)

The twice-born man becomes a full person only after he has passed through the stages known as student, householder, forest dweller, and homeless wanderer (sadhu). A student studies in the house of his teacher, learning to the extent appropriate to his caste and individual aptitude a curriculum that formerly included memorizing the Veda as well as archery, medicine, astrology, and music. Upon completing the student phase, a man returns to be married as a householder whose duty it is to perform the traditional rites and raise children in the proper manner to continue his father's lineage. The *Dharmashastras* require women to subordinate themselves to men, although husbands are required to respect their wives and maintain happiness within the household. Marriage is treated as a sacrament and divorce is not allowed.

Once the couple "sees their son's sons," finds the household well handled by them, and notices their hair turning white, they are instructed to become forest dwellers. In this stage, they focus on spiritual matters by retreating to the forest, living only on wild foods and with bare necessities, renouncing sensuality and sex, with rituals and meditation the chief concern. The fourth portion of life, the homeless wanderer, builds on the third, on the supposition that knowledge and discipline have led the forest dweller to the gateway of moksha realization. Persons now wander alone; no rituals need be done and they renounce all but what can be carried, as the remaining days become a pilgrimage to holy sites and dedicated to yoga practice.

From the classical era onward, the widespread dissemination of teachings about caste and stages in life, called *varnashrama Dharma*, has given "Hindu doctrine" its area of strongest consensus. Thus, if asked to name their religion, both modern villagers and learned theologians today define what we call "Hinduism" as "Varnashrama Dharma."

The Four Aims of Life

Since individuals differ in their karma-determined capabilities according to their caste and stage of life, the classical Hindu theorists in the *Dharmashastras* also identified four legitimate aims or ends that could be the focus of human striving. The first aim, *artha*, can be translated as material gain or worldly success. A vast folk literature of animal stories and human parables exists in South Asia that imparts instructions toward this goal in life, an indication that belief in karma has never stifled pious Hindus' interest in "getting ahead."

The second, *kama* ("sensory pleasure"), was seen as an acceptable goal for embodied beings, especially householders seeking to fulfill the duty of propagating the family line. Although the *Kama Sutra*, the text that treats the cultivating of pleasure explicitly, is known in the West as a sex manual, many chapters are devoted to achieving "the good life" in other spheres as well. The third aim, *dharma*, we have already discussed; the other ends of life are justly pursued only if they remain consistent with one's caste and gender-appropriate duties. The last of the four goals, *moksha*, is adopted by few, but the texts counsel that true ascetics should command everyone's respect and support through almsgiving. Hindus still venerate the sadhu saints, who follow this path of spiritual wandering. For the majority of Hindus, the ideals of the law books and the theologies of classical Hinduism are conveyed in the plots and characters of the great epics.

Epics and the Development of Classical Hinduism

By the classical era, the two great Hindu epics had been composed from oral sources that doubtless originated in heroic accounts of early battles fought by warriors in the Aryan clans. The longer of the two, the *Mahabharata*, records an escalating and ultimately devastating feud between rival clans as they vied for control of the northern plains, each one aided by supernatural allies. This rivalry ended in a war of immense carnage that in theological interpretation marks the onset of the current age, the *Kali Yuga*. The *Mahabharata* and its most famous portion called the *Bhagavad Gita* allowed for diverse and nuanced evaluations of dharma, especially that pertaining to warriors, kin, and women and the role of divinity in human affairs. The epic reveals the many difficulties, paradoxes, and ambiguities that face those who wish to apply the lofty religious ideals of the *Dharmashastra* to real-life circumstances.

The same quality of "speaking with many voices" is true of the second great epic, the *Ramayana*. Here, the underlying historical circumstance is the rivalry between Aryan clans—symbolized by the hero Rama—and the non-Aryans of the south who are portrayed as powerful demons subject to unbridled lust and who rudely disrupt the Vedic sacrifices. Rama does succeed in defeating the demon Ravana and establishing a unified Hindu kingdom. The tale has proven very malleable in giving groups across South (and Southeast) Asia a narrative to express their own views on ethnic relations, the good king, gender relations, the relationship between northerners versus southerners. In fact, there is no one *Ramayana* today, as through its tellings and retellings hundreds of groups have claimed it as sacred and central to their own Hindu ideal.

When the modern television production of the *Ramayana* (discussed later), based upon that recomposed in Hindi by the North Indian poet Tulsidas (1532–1623), debuted in 1987, for the first time all Hindus across the modern state of India saw the same version of this drama. Modern interpreters link this

media event (and its continuation through videotape showings) to the successful resurgence of Hindu fundamentalist parties since then, as they have championed the restoration of Rama's putative birthplace in the city of Ayodhya and
called for changing India's identity from secular state to a Hindu kingdom
(*Ram-Raj*) following the "dharma of Rama." Whatever the merits of fundamentalist politics or history, such groups do hearken back to the epics originating in classical South Asia, in particular the belief that a just Hindu king is
essential for sustaining the sacred order of a brahmanical society and its prosperity. We now examine other beliefs about securing divine blessings and salvation characteristic of devotional Hinduism.

Mainstream Hinduism and the Rise of Devotion to the Great Deities

The deities who dominated Hindu life by the classical age differed in name and
conception from those of the earliest Vedic hymns. An entirely new collection
of Sanskrit texts called *puranas* was composed to extol the glories of the emerging deities, specify their forms of worship, and celebrate the early saints who
worshiped them. The purana stories recount examples of human incarnation, instances of divine omniscience, and episodes of grace. Heroes in these stories
become models of exemplary devotional faith, or *bhakti*. Just as Hanuman the
monkey king serves Rama, or Radha the consort loves Krishna without limit, so
should one's own bhakti practice receive the full commitment of heart and mind.

All the puranas—which many Hindus revere as "The Fifth Veda"—share an
important assumption about humanity living in the Kali Yuga, the post-Vedic
age: this era, said to have begun in 3102 BCE, is defined as a period of degeneration in which human spiritual potential is declining. In view of this, the
puranas declare that the deities have extended their grace to humanity in ever-
increasing measure in return for the people's unselfish devotion. While the
ascetic practices of yoga do not end (and not all Hindus accepted Kali Yuga
theory), this ideal of bhakti became the predominant one for Hinduism
throughout the centuries until the present day.

Hinduism's shift toward bhakti follows its characteristic "add-on pattern" in
merging a new theology with the fundamental paradigm of the formative era:
the samsara-karma-moksha system. The devotional tradition accepts the early
cosmic model but builds upon it by asserting that the great deities like Shiva,
Vishnu, and Durga have the power to reward devotion by altering the karma of
the *bhakta* (devotee). Thus, the deities, although omnipotent and omniscient,
are seen as augmenting the earlier tradition, not challenging it. By absorbing
human karma, they can bring their grace to persons seeking liberation from
worldly suffering and ultimately from samsara. This view is most dramatically
expressed in the *Bhagavad Gita*, where Krishna argues that desireless action is
possible only through ego-neglecting bhakti faith and that the true suspension
of all action (that produces additional karma) is impossible. The *Gita* (18:56)
states that salvation is made possible only through dedicating all karma to

THE HINDU DEBATE ON GRACE
BY FAITH OR WORKS

In the theoretical ideas that describe the means of deities granting grace to devotees, two models emerge among Vishnu devotees: that of the Cat and that of the Monkey. Some theologians argue that no force, including human action, can interfere with the divine's omnipotence, so that salvation comes from the side of the deity entirely, just as a mother cat carries her kittens away from danger into safety. Other Hindu theologians insist that human beings have an essential part to play in effecting their own *moksha*: the baby monkey fleeing danger clinging to the mother's stomach as she moves toward certain safety will fall unless it fulfills its duty of holding on.

Krishna: "Those who dedicate all of their actions to ME, intent on ME, with un-wavering discipline, meditating on ME, who revere ME—for those I am the savior from samsara."

Among theologians, the terms and mechanisms for such salvific acts of grace vary; in many of the puranas, rebirth in one's chosen deity's heaven—not exit from samsara—is stated to be the highest goal. Nonetheless, belief in the great deities and the common forms of worship directed to them gave Hinduism coherence amidst its polytheistic diversity. From the classical period onward, too, we see the shift to bhakti faith embodied in the widespread building of the great temples characteristic of the postclassical age, as devotees focused on expressing their faith through rituals and on icons of the deities.

By the classical era purana texts asserted the existence of 330 million deities. How could the theologians account for such mind-numbing diversity? Drawing upon the received teaching that each individual bears his or her own karma, the bhakti gurus argued that polytheism simply is the grace of the divine trying to meet the diverse needs and temperaments of pluralistic humanity in the Kali Yuga. The crucial goal facing each Hindu is to find and focus upon the one deity whose form is most appropriate to his or her level of spiritual maturity.

The common principle of simplification in Hinduism's postclassical poly-theistic theologies was that each devotee should choose a deity (*ista deva*) to be at the center of his or her religious life, a focus for personal communion through an emotional relationship. Although most teachers (and families) be-lieved that "good Hindus" should respect all the great deities as well as the lesser spirits thought to dwell in each locality, it was nonetheless essential for each person to establish a single divinity to meditate upon and venerate as a channel for grace.

The concept of "chosen deity" entailed commitment to knowing extensively and loving selflessly that particular god. This meant making offerings (*puja*, to be discussed later), meditating, and studying the purana stories to be able to discern as completely as possible the divine personality. One formula for the stages of bhakti progress described the stages of devotion moving from listening, singing, and worshiping to self-surrender.

Each of the great deities of Hinduism has come to be known through the purana texts, and theologians have drawn slightly different theories for each to explain how and why they manifest themselves to save humanity both from mundane dangers and to bestow ultimate salvation.

Shiva

Does a figure seen on one of the Indus valley seals (datable to 1800 BCE)—a male sitting in a cross-legged position, surrounded by four animals, with an erect phallus—show a proto-form of the great deity Shiva? Later traditions that developed in the formative era suggest a link with this figure such as his name, Pashupati ("Lord of Creatures"), and the widespread use of a phallic icon, the *linga*, to represent Shiva.

While the question of the origins of the Hindu deities is intriguing, the "Shaivite," or one whose chosen deity is Shiva, focuses on two beliefs: that Shiva's essence is found in all creative energies that saturate this world, and that one can find one's own divine nature by dedicating bhakti practice to this lord. Shiva's identity in the puranas merges opposing sides of Hindu practice: he is the ideal ascetic revered by yogins, the god who in the Himalayas underwent long penances while dwelling with cobras, clad in deer skin, and covered in ash. He is also conceived of as a divine householder after he was roused by the god of desire (Kama), and then consorts with the goddess of the snow mountains (Parvati) and fathers divine sons Ganesh and Kumara (who become important deities as well). For believers who understand the linga symbolism on a deeper level, the icon marks the world's cosmic pillar as well as the great god's universal presence emerging from unusual rocks, ice formations, and mountain peaks.

In Hindu legend, Shiva saves the world repeatedly and requites devotion with his grace. However, Shiva is unique among the great Hindu gods in having a wrathful side that can punish humans as well. In the periodic cosmic upheavals that return the universe to a resting state "without form and void," the puranas say Shiva carries through this final destruction. The sectarian Shaivite theologians see the linking of world creation, fertility, and destruction as signifying Shiva's omnipresence, making him the supreme "Great God."

Vishnu and His Avataras

Although they may respect Shiva, Vishnu devotees ("Vaishnavite") believe that their chosen deity is the one who truly underlies all reality. Vishnu is the one who alone sleeps atop the cosmic ocean in the universe's era of dissolution, and he alone is the one who begets the god Brahma who then begins another cycle of creation.

THE DANCE OF SHIVA

One of the most lyrical and evocative symbols of Hinduism, especially in the sweeping design of South Indian artisans, is that of Nataraja, Shiva as Lord of the Dance. The upper right hand holds the twin-sided drum, from which sacred sound emerges, counting time and originating sound's creative resonance. The opposite hand shows on it a flame so that in Shiva's holding a fire, he points to his being a refuge in the fires of *samsara*. Fire also alludes to this deity's role as destroyer at the end of a great world era. Both hands move together in Shiva's great dance, ceaselessly integrating cosmic creation and destruction, including all the gods. Another hand shows the "fear-not gesture," and the last points to his upraised foot, the place where Hindu devotees take their refuge in ritual. Shiva dances while treading on a demon who symbolizes heedlessness. Thus, to enter into the Dance of Shiva means to brave the circle of rebirth, transcend the limitations of time and apparent opposites, and join with the divine powers of the great deity whose grace and eternal energy can remove spiritual obstacles. Because the cosmos has become a manifestation of Shiva's power, a dance done simply for the purpose of his own entertainment, wherever individuals can cultivate artistic pleasure, they can find union with Shiva.

The great paradigm of Vishnu theology is that of incarnation. The puranas dedicated to him recount many episodes in the earth's history when demons or evil threatened creation. It is at these times when Vishnu assumed the form of just that being needed to smash the threat. Many of these incarnations or *avataras* (lit. "descents") likely were local heroes or tribal deities who were consolidated under one name, most often "Vishnu."

Vishnu remains alive and connected to the human community of devotees through temple icons and rituals and through the singing of songs recounting his greatness. The texts also sense his being poised for future salvific work, and one avatara, Kalki, is expected to come riding on a white horse to guide humanity as the Kali Yuga turns darker.

Avatara theology provides one avenue through which Hinduism absorbed Buddhists back into its fold across South Asia. Specifically, the puranas describe Shakyamuni (Gautama Buddha) as another descent by Vishnu, a divine teacher who saved the world either (1) by teaching the people about asceticism and nonviolence or (2) fooling those with evil karma to follow false teachings, hastening their decline to lower births.

Vishnu avatara theory thus provides the most systematic example of Hinduism's ecumenical theological pattern that spawns a profusion of sects, moving readily from the acceptance of multiple particular deities to arrange them in hierarchical pantheons whose exact superior Lord varies (for some) according to the sect involved. But most Hindus, intellectuals and commoners alike, will assent to the same theological understanding that avers that "ultimately all the gods are one." There is also a long history of Hindus (and Buddhists) refraining from staking out one final dogmatic position, since many traditions hold that Ultimate Reality is beyond all human naming or philosophical comprehension. Accepting this limitation has given Hinduism its flexible strength and its adherents an openness to ongoing revelation.

Rama

We have already encountered Rama, hero of the *Ramayana*, who slays the demon Ravana and reveals the ideal of proper filial obedience to parents, loyalty to brothers, and the exemplary conduct of Hindu kings. His alliance with the monkey leader Hanuman also signals the ideal of harmonizing the divine with the natural world. A second form of Rama is one dedicated to destroying any evil kings who would molest brahmins or their rituals.

Krishna

The most complex and multifaceted of the avataras, Krishna is revered as the infant whose every prank and gesture reveal his underlying divinity; the child who as "the butter thief" also steals the hearts of the world's mothers and fathers; the brave youth who rescues villagers from the poison of evil serpent deities (*nagas*) and from the cruel rains sent by the Vedic god Indra; the divine paramour and consort of the female cowherds (*gopis*). Finally, Krishna is the mature guru who offers counsel about the necessity of serving the world according to one's dharma, clarifying choices among the many spiritual practices, and revealing that he is in fact the reality from which all the gods originate. This last orientation is expressed in the *Bhagavad Gita*, a "song" incorporated into the *Mahabharata* that is recognized as one of the spiritual masterpieces of Hinduism.

Devis

The consolidating pattern in Hindu theology is readily apparent in the development of the myths of the goddess. Early Indian art depicts the fertile, creative power of the universe in scenes where a young woman touches a tree, her innate energy (*shakti*) causing it to burst into bloom. Hindu goddesses are born of the earth and can bestow its wealth. Rivers are all goddesses. From ancient times onward each locality had its own local *devi* who protected it. Those who worship the goddess are thereby called "Shaktas" and theirs is the third major group among Hindu deity worshipers alongside Vaishnavites and Shaivites.

The earth goddess may be addressed as Ambika ("Mother"), Sita ("[born of the] tilled furrow), or Sati ("The Virtuous"). All of these forms draw upon the creative, mothering female force. Another widespread and primordial sense of female divinity is that associated with destruction; this has been primarily in the form of the smallpox goddess (called in the north Shitala or Ajima). Yet another related female form is that of the martial goddess associated with the killing of demons, whose name is Durga or Kali. Those needing to confront death to arrive at mature spirituality can make Kali their "chosen deity": to visualize the dance of Kali means seeing that life inevitably becomes encircled by death and so the gift of human life should not be frittered away.

By the late classical era, devotees and theologians had developed a "Mahadevi ("Great Goddess") theology" that projected an essential female divinity who manifests in all these different forms, calling her as well Bhagavati ("Blessed Goddess"), seeing her as the one dwelling in the powers of rivers (such as the Ganga, Yamuna, Saraswati), on the mountains (Parvati), existing in the lovely dawn (Ushas) and night sky (Ratri) and present in smallpox (Shitala Mata). So alive is this devi theology today that with the disappearance of this disease, Shitala has become the deity to appeal to against the rising scourge of HIV/AIDS. Devi theology even saw the power of the male deities coming from their consorts' shakti, without which, as one saying goes, "Shiva is merely a corpse."

Hindu theology also views the pantheon as balancing the distinct powers that are uniquely those of male and female. The cosmos, like the human species, is seen as created and sustained by the same combination of gender energies: the male shakta and the female shakti. Each is incomplete and even dangerous without the balancing influence of the consort. Thus, Shiva has his consort Uma or Parvati, Vishnu has Lakshmi (important as the wealth goddess), Brahma has Saraswati (goddess of learning), Krishna–Radha, Rama–Sita, and so on. Tantric Hinduism (discussed later in the chapter) carries on the implications of this theology into individual yoga practice.

Situating and Sighting the Sacred: Hindu Icons

Matching the rich theology of sound in mantra practice, Hinduism from the classical period onward has emphasized that sight, too, can be an experiential avenue for spiritual awakening. Many traditional practices draw upon this belief by calling on *darshan*, the power of focused religious viewing. One is said to "take darshan" of one's guru as often as possible in person; when separated from him, one should carry a picture and include it in personal rituals, viewing the image of the guru as often as possible. This Hindu theory about sight and the spiritual powers of seeing point to a universal pattern: consider how many terms of spiritual importance draw upon vision, light, and the open eyes: "enlightenment," "insight," "awakening." The saints who are released from samsara are "people of vision" and they "give darshan" of themselves to disciples so that, with the disciples' own eyes and minds, they, too, might see reality clearly.

Diagrams are also used as aids in Hindu meditation: there are geometric designs called *yantras*, the visual equivalent of the mantra for each deity in the pantheon. Yantras are symbols of integration, as are *mandalas*, the more complicated spaces arrayed around a divinity. Both are used for visualization, the advanced meditation practices in which one places the symbol in one's mind's eye. Hindu theories of karmic effect hold that one can be transformed by seeing something sacred and opening oneself to it with faith and concentration. The *Shri yantra* (A), for example, symbolizes the tantric union of opposites, the downward triangle signifying *prakriti* ("matter"), water, and womb and the upward triangle symbolizing *purusha* ("spirit"), fire, and the male organ. The most common Hindu spiritual sights are temple icons. The minimal ritual done at any Hindu temple is *darshan*, making eye contact with the image. Early Muslim and later Christian encounters with Hinduism were marked by great misunderstanding on this issue. Indeed, the adherents of Abrahamic faiths, both influenced and limited by their own histories and theologies, charged Hindus with "gross idolatry." South Asia's polytheism does present a bewildering array of deities, each of which can be depicted in a variety of forms. Belief about icons varies, but many Hindus would find it laughable to have anyone think that they identify an icon of wood, metal, or stone as "Shiva" or "Kali."

The consecration of a Hindu icon involves a long series of ablutions, to make it an abode for a portion of the divine essence, and many thousands of chants, to activate the divine life force (*prana*) believed to reside within the image. Hindus take seriously the immanence of their deities and believe that divine omnipotence gives a deity the potential to dwell anywhere. Thus, for example, an icon can make the god Vishnu's presence available to devotees at a particular place. One ritual invokes the deity at an icon's birth as follows: "Oh Vishnu, approach this image and wake it up with thy embodiment of knowledge and divine energies, which are to be concentrated in this one image."[5] The last act of image consecration, the opening of the eyes, is done with great care. (The artisan usually uses a mirror to avoid direct darshan at this moment, when the power of the deity first blazes forth.)

The Circles of Time in Hindu Thought

Having surveyed the major Indic deities and the ways of devotionalism, we must now consider the Hindu understanding of cosmic time, since the gods, like humans, must conform to its irresistible force.

Cosmic Eras

The Hindu view of time articulated in the ancient texts represents a web binding beings together to the eternal dance of life, death, rebirth. The Vedic texts contain a multitude of creation accounts, and later texts enfold them in a more circular vision of successive eras of cosmic dissolution followed by equally long eras when the created world undergoes a regular series of transformations. Once creation has begun, the earth evolves through four eras called *yugas*.

The first and longest era, the *Krita Yuga*, is a golden age bereft of suffering and wants: meditation and virtue come naturally to all beings. In the second

TABLE 5.1   The Hindu *Yugas*

Age	Dominant Activity	Duration
Krita ↓	Meditation	1,728,000 years
Treta ↓	Dharma practice	1,296,000 years
Dvapara ↓	Dharma practice	864,000 years
Kali	Bhakti/Giving	432,000 years

and third *yugas*, people are strongly inclined to proper duty (*dharma*), yet the inclination to virtue slowly slips downward and eventually there is the need for castes to be formed to keep order and the *Vedas* to be composed to aid those striving for truth and goodness. But in the *Kali Yuga*, which in the current cycle began in 3102 BCE, human life moves from bad to much worse: brahmins become unworthy, the Vedas are forgotten, castes mix unlawfully, and life spans decrease due to famine, war, and hunger. Certain bhakti groups, however, proclaim a dissenting, triumphal alternative to this pessimistic scenario, and the grip of evil on this era has been (or will be) ended through the devotional practices of true believers.

The Kali Yuga ends with the destruction of the earth after a series of natural disasters culminating in a great flood, when Vishnu will again sleep on the resulting waters. Some texts recount that after one thousand of these eras, a greater destruction will take place, one in which all matter will be consumed in a great fire that will reduce all reality to pure spirit.

The Lunar and Solar Cycles

The cycle of the moon's waxing and waning, which governs the Hindu reckoning of time's passage, was explained poetically in the Vedas as follows: beings, including the gods, are strengthened by beams given freely by the moon, and when they are depleted, the sun renews them through an equal fortnight of infusing it with its golden elixir. Then sun as well directly nourishes plants, humans, and gods with its radiance. Hindus believe that the full moon is the best time for meditation and rituals, for then there is bounteous energy throughout the "triple world" of the heavens, earth, and the netherworlds. Most rituals are held during the waxing or brightening fortnight due to such considerations.

Ancient Hindus were aware of the regular movement of sun and moon through the sectors of the sky called *nakshatras* ("constellations") and the regular movement of planets (*graha*) across them. Hindu astronomers were adept at predicting eclipses, and elaborate theories of auspicious periods suitable for specific actions by individuals were developed. For this reason, one's birth date and birth time have been carefully recorded by parents since antiquity so the chart could be used for precise astrological calculation throughout life.

PREMODERN HINDUISM: THE POSTCLASSICAL ERA

The Formation of Hindu Schools of Thought

During the late classical era, the brahmin elite concerned with philosophical views (called *darshana*) consolidated their positions in systematic expositions, which became authoritative for the tradition from this time onward. Every school's texts sought to explain the nature of matter and causality, the boundaries of individuality, the basis for establishing human knowledge, and the means to salvation.

The orthodox schools formed in response to the Buddhist and Jain heterodoxies, as well as to refute the pesky agnostics of the materialist school, the Lokayata. Some of the classical schools were confined to small circles of high-caste scholastics. The remaining classical schools, discussed here, came to dominate the subsequent tradition.

Sankhya

One of the first systematic schools to appear, and one whose ideas were especially important in subsequent Hindu thought, was the Sankhya ("Analysis"). The Sankhya posits a dualistic universe of matter (*prakriti*) bonded in various combinations with spirit (*purusha*). Both matter and spirit are eternal, with an infinite number of purushas eternally distinct from one another. Sankhya is atheistic, seeing the purpose of human life as isolating purusha from prakriti by escaping the bondage of deluded identification. Although its goal is to go beyond the material world, the Sankhya nonetheless developed a powerful analysis of material formations, specifying twenty-five gunas ("qualities") by which matter can be clearly understood. Sankhya's threefold differentiation of spirit-matter combinations has informed Hindu culture to the present, and is applied to the analysis of human personality, gender, species, the seasons, aesthetics, and even foods.

One typical use of Sankhya theory is to assess the spiritual status of human beings. All beings are combinations of three material qualities or "strands" that bind spirit to the material world: *sattva* (associated with purity, goodness, subtlety), *rajas* (passion, raw energy), and *tamas* (darkness, inertia, grossness). It is desirable to live to be *sattvic* in one's dwelling, diet, and activities. In the Sankhya view, too, even the gods are qualitatively similar to humans, different only by having more sattva. This school thereby sees the incarnation of divinities in human form as part of the universe's natural processes.

Advaita Vedanta

The Advaita Vedanta school is monistic, that is, it regards the singular reality of the universe as impersonal spirit, a view we have encountered in the Upanishads' formula Brahman = atman. Indeed, the systematic monism of Vedantic thought became the prevailing scholastic philosophy of South Asia after 800 CE, through both the intellectual and institutional innovations of its postclassical exponents. (It is the school most often emphasized by modern Hindu reformers as well.) Advaita Vedanta's enduring central place among Hindu philosophies was due to the brilliance of the great religious virtuoso Shankara (c. 780–820). His succinct commentaries and original works received additional exposure through public debates with proponents of other schools (including Buddhists).

Shankara argued that the apparent diversity of a self-separate phenomenal world is pure illusion (*maya*). Only study and yoga practice could reverse the "superimposition" of dualistic perception and analysis on pure spirit and allow a seeker to gain true knowledge. This path came to be known as *jnana yoga*, "union through discriminating knowledge."

Shankara admitted that one could in elementary and intermediate stages of spiritual development relate to Brahman as a personal divinity with characteristics ("*sa-guna*") such as power and grace (saguna Brahman). But ultimately, moksha can be achieved only by going beyond this anthropocentric projection to experience Brahman without characteristics, merging one's own soul with nirguna Brahman, that reality "without characteristics."

Shankara also organized the first great network of Hindu monasteries (*mathas*) that supported male ascetics who had to abide by a rule of conduct that specified vegetarianism, dress in an ochre robe, use of a walking staff, and horizontal forehead markings. At monasteries established originally at Dvaraka in the west, Puri in the east, Badrinath in the north, and Shringeri in the south, this order grew, expanded, and survives to this day.

Later teachers, such as the great Vaishnava teacher Chaitanya (1485–1533) and his predecessors Ramananda (active 1300), Madhva, and Nimbarka (both active 1162), provided—at least on the elite level—the formative layers of organized institutional Hinduism.

The Theology of Qualified Monism: Vishishta Vedanta

While Shankara's monistic thought and practice appealed to intellectuals and ascetics, it was quite distant from the religious experience of most devotees who revered the gods. It remained for later theologians, particularly Ramanuja (c. 1020–1137), to link scholastic theology with popular theistic practice. Ramanuja argued that human beings could not claim to perceive the divine beyond attributes and that the religious path to moksha should be content with saguna Brahman. Like Shankara, Ramanuja wrote his own commentary on the Upanishads, but he reached a very different conclusion about the ultimate

spiritual truth. He emphasized Vishnu as the form of Brahman most effectively worshiped.

Ramanuja asserted that each individual is ultimately a fragment of Vishnu,
wholly dependent upon him, and that this perfect continuous intuition could
be realized only through concentrated and intense devotion (bhakti yoga). This
theology also holds that souls do not ultimately merge with Brahman, maintaining a "separate nondifference" even in moksha.

Tantric Hinduism

Postclassical-era Hinduism produced two major innovations: sectarian monasticism and *tantra*. Like the bhakti exponents already mentioned, the tantric
tradition built upon earlier ideas and practices but advocated new forms of
spiritual experience. The name "tantra" relates to weaving, signifying "warp
and woof," in this case likely indicating the interweaving of teaching/texts that
together create a distinctive and esoteric pattern. The emergence of tantra can
be seen in both Hinduism and Buddhism, indicating how thoroughly these
later traditions affected each other.

Tantric teachers accepted Kali Yuga theory and their texts (*tantras*) typically
begin by underscoring how the tantric path to salvation in this lifetime is
suited for the Kali Yuga age, when individuals and the world itself are in spiritual decline. The assumption is that what was normative for the Vedic sages is
too subtle for today. What would have been prohibited to the seeker then is
needed today to break through spiritually. Still, tantric teachings are not given
openly or universally, but are bestowed by teachers only to those deemed capable of practicing methods that contradict the dharma-based morality of the
upper castes. The method of transmitting the teachings from guru to student,
of course, goes back to the ancient period. However, the vows not to reveal the
teachings to noninitiates imposed by the teacher are more highly restrictive
than in earlier practice.

There are many tantric schools, each deriving from an enlightened saint
called a *siddha,* who discovered in an intensive personal quest a method of meditation and understanding that culminates in moksha. This personal lineage
was passed down in small circles following specific forms of praxis and explanation deriving from the original master. All the tantric paths are rooted in the
ancient yoga traditions we have discussed. Tantric yoga, too, regards the body as
a microcosm of the universe; all bodily energies are regarded as capable of producing a transformative religious experience if harnessed and focused. What is
distinctive in tantric yoga is that the energies of male and female become essential and focal in the path to realization. Thus, tantra incorporated the devotional worship of female deities in union with their consorts. Many tantric
teachings prescribe the practice of ritualized sexual union during which both
partners visualize themselves as divinities in order to cultivate in each other an
enlightened awakening through the transformative energy that arises through

their union. The goal is realization of the one spirit that is beyond gender and is both universal and blissful.

Most tantric traditions invite practitioners to experience this ultimate reality, one that can be found only by suspending the norms imposed by the Hindu social law and caste-determined individual conduct. Tantric yoga entails mastering complex rituals and practices that invert status and gender hierarchy norms, breaking down a person's construction of his or her identity on such conventional lines. Thus, one can select a tantric partner from a lower caste, and practitioners perform rituals that involve ingesting foods such as meat, fish, and alcohol that are otherwise unacceptable for high-caste groups. Places of tantric practice include cremation grounds, the most polluted ritual sites; ritual implements include human bones and skulls. The sexual elements and the use of gruesome items shocked orthodoxy, but they were employed for the highly traditional goal of realizing moksha.

Ritualized union in Hindu tantra seeks to arouse an otherwise dissipated primal power conceived of as a serpent coiled at the base of the spine; this force, called the *kundalini*, is made to rise up the spine through a series of centers (*cakras*) visualized as wheels or lotuses. These centers are found proximate to the genitals, navel, heart, throat, eyes, forehead, and the top of the skull. If the energy can be raised to this topmost center, the "1000-petaled lotus," one's spirit is perfected and a host of supernormal powers unfold.

Tantric practice is considered difficult but unerringly successful if one adheres to the path of one's master with full energy and commitment. But it was also considered dangerous, and the tantric texts warn that one who enters into the practice for mundane results or for profane pleasure will spend many world eras reborn in purgatory. The unorthodox practices and extraordinary experiences were also thought dangerous for those unready for them; this made the *siddha* teachers wary of initiating unproven individuals and led them to prescribe similar dire penalties for anyone breaking the vow of silence imposed on initiates for revealing anything about tantric practice to outsiders.

While early on tantra grew to become a "counterculture" juxtaposed against– orthodox/orthoprax Hinduism, its influence slowly grew even among the high castes. Later, in fact, tantric ideas shaped Hindu life-cycle rites and temple ritualism, as priests over the centuries who delved into tantric practice revised rituals to be multidimensional, adding meaning for the general public as well as for those attuned to more esoteric tantric symbolism. Tantra also inspired the flowering of later South Asian music and dance.

The Early Islamic Era: Delhi Sultanate

Soon after the conversion of Central Asian and Turkic peoples to Islam in the first centuries after the death of Prophet Muhammad (632 CE), South Asia began to absorb Islamic influences. Muslim traders entered through caravan and port towns, built mosques, and eventually brought religious scholars and clerical authorities to guide their slowly growing communities. Missionaries preaching the tolerant and mystical tradition of Sufi Islam won an especially strong reception in some quarters. The conquest of northern India by Ghuride armies from Central Asia (1192) ended Hindu *kshatriya* resistance and resulted in Muslim armies torching the remaining Buddhist monasteries of the Gangetic plain, sending the monks who survived into the Himalayas. The over five hundred years of Muslim rule that followed was an era of strong, increasingly centralized rule. In many areas, Muslims displaced kshatriyas as heads of regional states; in many other places, Hindu rulers continued as their vassals. The Delhi Sultanate was the Muslim administrative unit, including the northern sections of modern Pakistan and India, from the Indus to the upper Ganges. In general, authorities of the sultanate did not molest indigenous traditions in their own regions or in kshatriya-ruled states, and Hindu traditions continued strongly. Indeed, the saints who rose to prominence in this era have dominated the popular Hindu imagination ever since, and we turn to them now.

Hindu Saints During the Centuries of Muslim Rule

The popularity achieved by the saints of this era do reflect their times: with Islam's political power ascendant in the north, the traditions of high-caste Hindu orthodoxy (and Hindu law) were inevitably weakened. Dissidents within many orthodox schools, as well as women and teachers from low castes, arose and were heard as never before. Their medium was not Sanskrit but the spoken vernacular languages; their teachings were conveyed in hymns and songs that could be widely disseminated orally and outside of high caste control. Bhakti also originated early in the south, where Muslim influences were least and latest in coming.

The theological positions articulated by these great bhakti figures do divide on the fault line of one of Hinduism's oldest debates: whether impersonal monism or dualistic theism is the highest spiritual truth. Notable exponents of the former, *nirguna*, were called *sants*. Among them are Ravidas, Kabir, Ramananda, and Nanak, the founder of Sikhism. Still-renowned exemplars of *saguna*, the most accessible of devotional Hinduism, called *bhaktas*, include Chaitanya, Mirabai, and Basavanna, and their "chosen deities" Ram, Krishna, or Shiva. Unlike the earlier bhakti exponents, these saguna saints did not see Ram or Krishna as mere avataras of Vishnu, but as themselves the Lords of the Universe. We will close this section on Hindu saints with the remarkable sect founded by the already-mentioned Ramananda, one that spans both poles in the nirguna-saguna spectrum.

Ravidas   Ravidas (active c. 1450) was born into an untouchable tanner family. He composed hundreds of songs pointing out how the ultimate reality transcends all conceptual boundaries. He taught that singing was a way of abandoning all ego, creating an opening to divine truth. Ravidas explicitly addresses his social marginality, using it to challenge brahminical privilege and practices: true bhakti community dedicated to a formless ultimate must itself transcend all caste discrimination. In some of his songs, Ravidas claims that the untouchables suffering discrimination can have the unparalleled spiritual advantage of making the ego empty. As one song proclaims:

> A family that has a follower of the Lord
> > Is neither high caste nor low caste, lordly or poor.
> The world will know by its fragrance.
> > Priests or merchants, laborers or warriors,
> > half-breeds, outcastes, and those who tend cremation fires—
> > their hearts are all the same.
> He who becomes pure through love of the Lord
> > exalts himself and his family as well.[6]

The All India Adi Dharma Mission, established in 1957, and now with satellites in Europe and North America, reveres Ravidas as its founding saint.

Kabir   Kabir (1440–1518), one of the most critical and original religious figures of his era, was born a Muslim weaver in Benares. Exhorting all who would listen about the necessity for a personal experience of the formless reality underlying all existence (which he labeled "Ram"), Kabir exhorted Muslims and Hindus alike to avoid the trap of lazy conformity to time-honored customs and he encouraged them to seek directly the salvific potential of intense personal experience with the divine. According to legends about him, Kabir's fearless iconoclasm and social criticism directed at both brahmins and Islamic judges earned him much hostility and persecution. To the brahmin priests he said:

> Vedas, Puranas—why read them ?
> > It's like loading an ass with sandalwood!
> Unless you catch on and learn how Ram's name goes,
> > how will you reach the end of the road?[7]

To the Muslim jurist, he issued the same unyielding challenge:

> Hey *Qazi*,
> > What's that book you're preaching from?
> And reading, reading—how many days?
> > Still you haven't mastered one word...
> Fool,
> Throw away that book, and sing of Ram.
> What you're doing has nothing to do with him.[8]

Kabir has been revered by reformist Muslims and Hindus; in the modern and postmodern era, Kabir has been held up as an "apostle of Hindu-Muslim unity."

Nanak   A contemporary of Kabir was Nanak (1469–1539), founder of a religious sect that was significantly influenced by Islam. Nanak and his *Sikhs* ("disciples") began the most significant new religious traditions to emerge

within South Asia since the start of the Islamic era in South Asia. We will discuss Nanak and the Sikhs shortly in connection with the Mughal era, when the
movement experienced spectacular development.

Mirabai Through the songs and legendary life of Mirabai, a woman born
around 1540 in Rajasthan, Hindus see revealed the full letting go of ordinary
life characteristic of popular bhakti. Love for Krishna drew Mirabai to renounce
husband and the householder's life, to migrate to Krishna's city Brindavan
near Mathura, and to dwell near his home in mystical communion as a *gopi*
("cowherdess"), lover of the youthful deity. Like the gopis in the puranas, Mira
in her unorthodox asceticism moved from feeling loving intimacy with
Krishna to dejection at the separations, only to be intoxicated by the thought of
expectant reunion. Despite the emotional turmoil this intense bhakti practice
imposed upon her, Mirabai in powerful verses testified that her form of yoga
with Krishna is far superior to that of male ascetics:

> Let us go to a realm beyond going,
> Where death is afraid to go,
> Where the high-flying birds alight and play,
> Afloat in the full lake of love.
> There they gather—the good, the true—
> To strengthen an inner regimen,
> To focus on the dark form of the Lord.9

In this saint, Hindus encounter a woman who defied their society's norms of
female dharma and renunciation yet achieved moksha: legend recounts her
merging at death with her beloved icon of Krishna.

Chaitanya Chaitanya, the most influential bhakta of Krishna in Bengal
(1486–1533), was an extraordinary revitalizer and systematic theologian who
renounced the world at age 24, went on a long pilgrimage across the subcontinent, and founded a devotional community in the town of Puri.

Over his lifetime, Chaitanya was a passionate advocate of the bhakti path and
an innovative practitioner. He debated Vedantin saints and scholars, arguing
for the superiority of the devotional path. Most innovative was Chaitanya's
method of singing songs (*kirtan*) and chanting the names of Krishna—both
long-established forms of devotional expression—done in more dramatic style in
public processions. Chaitanya's goal in this was to push the devotee to empty ego
and mind so that nothing else but Radha and Krishna were in the consciousness. His disciples devised new pilgrimage traditions and extended dramas associated with the youthful god, all to further the disciple's quest to find beauty
and singular at-one-ness with Krishna. To this day, these forms of worship endure and have been emulated across India in communities devoted to Krishna.

A new twist in avatara theology is associated with Chaitanya as well: it
begins with Krishna in heaven wishing to experience Radha's ecstatic love
for him by incarnating himself as Chaitanya, who himself is capable of fully

experiencing Radha's love. For his school, then, Chaitanya himself is the incarnation of both Radha and Krishna. The International Society of Krishna Consciousness (ISKON), popularly known as Hare Krishna, traces its spiritual lineage back to Chaitanya.

Basavanna Basavanna (1106–1168) founded the bhakti movement called Virasaivism that began in Mysore state (South India). Virashaivas, centered in the founder's passionate devotion to Shiva and to the personal unmediated experience of Shiva as Lord, have been critical of many orthodox practices, even to the point of denying the doctrines of karma and samsara. Basavanna's only measure of spiritual life is pure devotion that leads to knowing the Lord Shiva; there is only one useful or meaningful offering, and one of Basavanna's poems expresses it as follows:

The rich
will make temples for Shiva.
What shall I, a poor man, do?

My legs are pillars,
the body the shrine,
the head a cupola
of gold.
Listen, O lord of the meeting rivers [Shiva],
    things standing shall fall, but the moving
        ever shall stay.[10]

Basavanna was surely among the most antiestablishmentarian among the bhakti teachers, as he denounced the caste system and high caste practices in his poems. Following the teacher's injunction to ignore caste in making marriage alliances and any conformity to brahmanical ritual rules, this sect has survived periodic episodes of repression for its antiorthopraxy. The Virashaivas endure as a separate caste group in modern Karnataka where they constitute 20 percent of the population, with members mostly among the poorer classes who keep the sect vital.

Ramananda Ramananda, the fourteenth-century teacher and founder of a sect that still bears his name, inspired a devotional tradition that quite strikingly merges in its two divisions the sant and bhakta sides of postclassical Hinduism. Like Kabir and Ravidas, whom the group's later sectarian historians identified as his disciples, Ramananda taught meditation through mantras focused on Rama's name. Ramananda, like the sants of the nirguna community, was also a fearsome critic of caste prejudice; he is still remembered for his saying that sums up the protest bhakti tradition of postclassical Hinduism: "Do not ask anyone's caste or sect, whoever worships Vishnu belongs to Vishnu." Humanistically inclined Hindus today see in him a man ahead of his time, a "democrat" among medieval ascetics.

This group rivaled mystical Islam in its early missionizing among the lowest castes living across the north. Perhaps it was the logic of missionary appeal that led to the Ramananda sect developing an allied twofold division: its ascetics were devoted to the nirguna ultimate and the householders focused on classic saguna bhakti practices. What unites them is that they see themselves as being vessels of an identical "Ram mantra" going back to the guru himself.

Religion in the Mughal Era (1526–1707)

The great Mughal Empire that controlled northern and central India from 1526 until 1707 represented the second era of Muslim rule across much of South Asia. In its first century, Mughal rule was prosperous and peaceful, ushering in an efflorescence of Indo-Islamic culture in architecture and the fine arts. The Taj Mahal is the most famous among hundreds of magnificent buildings erected in this period. There was a significant rise in converts to Islam across the north, especially in the western region and in Bengal.

Guru Nanak and the Rise of Sikhism

A contemporary of some of the bhakti saints we have mentioned, Guru Nanak achieved unparalleled success as founder of the last great religious tradition to originate in India, Sikhism. The number of disciples committed to this faith now number over twenty million, eclipsing the number of Buddhists in South Asia and the number of Jews globally.

Guru Nanak (1469–1539) was born before the beginning of Mughal rule. He was a civil servant with a wife and two children until at age 30 he underwent a three-day religious experience that changed his life. His first pronouncement as a spiritual man was definitive and indicated the path he was about to embark upon as founder of a new faith: "There is neither Hindu nor Muslim, so whose path shall I follow? I shall follow God's path. God is neither Hindu nor Muslim and the path that I follow is God's."[11]

For the next twenty years, Nanak wandered far and wide as an ascetic. His teachings, many conveyed in song form, record encounters with animals, rulers, commoners, and holy men among both Hindu sadhus and Muslim Sufis. Legendary accounts of Nanak's life describe his visiting Tibet and setting forth to Mecca, where his spiritual understanding and supernormal powers surpass those of all others. Sikh tradition avers that Nanak's mission was to reveal the full spiritual truth and the proper path to realize it, correcting the mistaken practices and partial truths of both Hinduism and Islam.

When he returned home from his wandering at age 50, Nanak set out to do just this. Back in the Punjab, he taught all who were interested and soon attracted many disciples—*Sikhs*—who were drawn by the charismatic guru as well as by the community whose rules and rituals he established. Clearly many disparate Hindu groups—disciples following the tradition of sants such as Kabir, Ravidas, and others—were drawn to this community that offered an indigenous alternative to Islam. After designating a successor, Nanak died in 1539.

The Ten Gurus and the Development of the Sikh Community Nine other gurus followed, who managed the burgeoning communities being established across the region. They gathered the songs and sermons composed by Nanak, adding hymns attributed to other like-minded saints, forming a text called the Adi Granth or Guru Granth Sahib. This work, 1,430 pages in its final form, remains the unique focus of Sikh worship to this day. The gurus also refined the community liturgies that unified the group, keeping the group a compelling alternative to and socially separate from similar Hindu groups. The town of Amritsar was built and became a second center of the faith, with the Golden Temple set in a lake the crown jewel of Sikh architecture. The last guru, Gobind Singh (1666–1708), declared that in the future, the guru of the Sikhs in spiritual matters would be the text itself, while in political leadership it would be the *Khalsa,* an elite group that had adopted a strict and determined lifestyle as guardians of the faith.

In the early years of Mughal rule, the Sikhs gained popularity and were welcomed at court. The ecumenical emperor Akbar (1561–1605) found in the faith a tolerant monotheistic theology and regarded the followers as a disciplined moral community. Akbar's successors, however, felt distrustful about the Sikhs' growth and political influences. The fifth guru, Arjan (1581–1606), was killed on the order of one emperor, and in 1669 when another Mughal ruler ordered all Hindu temples and schools demolished, Sikhs resisted, and many were martyred. It was in response to this growing persecution that the Khalsa was formed, dedicated to struggling for the defense of the faith (*dharma yudha,* much like the doctrine of *jihad* in Islam). The Khalsa marked themselves by their appearance: uncut hair (covered with a turban), short trousers, steel wristlet, comb, and sword. Sikhs also adopted the names *Singh* ("lion") for men and *Kaur* ("lioness") for women, essentially eliminating caste distinctions within the community.

Sikh Theology and Spiritual Practices

Nanak's spiritual path contained elements of both Hindu and Muslim traditions. As in Islam, Nanak taught that there is only one "God" who never walked the earth as a man (i.e., had not had an incarnation); but Nanak also set his teaching firmly in the Hindu nirguna sant tradition, mystically affirming that this God (that he called *Om-kar* or *Sat Guru* ["true teacher"]) is entirely beyond form and human categories.

Anticipating reformers of colonial and postcolonial Hinduism, Sikhs deny that asceticism is necessary or of value, holding that householders are perfectly capable of realizing the highest goal of salvation. Similarly, they say that ritual acts and pilgrimages have no spiritual effect. In addition, they reject the authority of the Vedas and the innate sanctity of the brahmin caste, positions that have caused high-caste Hindus to regard them as heterodox.

Residing in the human heart and communicating with those who live rightly and develop their spiritual faculties, Sat Guru freely bestows grace that ends individual karma and rebirth. In Sikh spiritual understanding, the human struggle involves rejecting ego-centered life and embracing the inner life of opening to the divine Sat Guru within. Revelation occurs through the effect of divine sound on one's consciousness. Therefore, Sikh religiosity is centered on listening to and congregationally singing the hymns composed by Nanak and other saints whose very words both reflect and impart this grace.

Consciously rejecting the norms of caste Hindu society while living among a Hindu majority, Sikhs have had to make accommodations yet establish separate boundaries through their rituals. Festivals mark the birth or death of the Ten Gurus, but Sikhs join Hindus in observing the major Hindu festivals. Instead of Vedic or brahmanical texts, passages from the Adi Granth are used in community life-cycle rites for naming, marriage, and death. Sikhs find their salvation in combining public and private worship with social action, earning an honest living, giving alms, and doing community service. Sikh temples, called *gurudwaras*, are focal points where these activities are centered.

Furthermore, every male and female must be initiated into the faith, repeating a recitation that summarizes the Sikh sense of the divine:

> There is one God, his name is truth eternal
> He is the creator of all things, the all-pervading spirit
> Fearless and without hatred, timeless and formless.
> Beyond birth and death, he is self-enlightened.
> He is known by the Guru's grace.[12]

HINDUISM AND MODERNITY

Hinduism under British Colonialism

The first Europeans known to have settled in South Asia in Mughal times were missionaries, initially the Dominicans in the Portuguese colony of Goa by 1510 and later the Jesuits after 1540 led by Francis Xavier. Early merchants also arrived by sea to trade for spices, silks, indigo, and cotton goods. Although they had competitors among early Dutch, Portuguese, and French traders, the British under the East India Company eventually were the most successful at establishing themselves permanently. As the Mughal Empire over its last fifty years slowly disintegrated and the region's "Hindu states" asserted their independence, civil disorder increased, causing trade and tax revenues to decline. Growing instability led the British to transform their trade missions into garrisoned fortresses, so that by 1730 military detachments were integral to the British mercantile presence. From these centers, the British leaders were eventually drawn into conflicts; when they defeated local rulers in battle, they made alliances and extended their command and control inward. South Asia soon became a patchwork of British territory and "Princely States" that submitted to the British but were still ruled in their internal affairs by Hindu royalty or Muslim sultans.

Modern scholarship on India and Hinduism originated in this context of Europeans seeking to learn about native peoples in order to tighten imperial control. British officials believed that it was their duty as white Europeans to spread enlightened civilization to the "primitive peoples" of South Asia. This message was, in turn, repeated back in Europe to justify the expanding colonial enterprise as "the white man's burden."

British schools were also established to train young Indians to serve in the lower echelons of the colonial bureaucracy. In large part, it was this new class that made first in-depth contact with modern ideas from Europe, especially in political thought, the natural sciences, and Christianity. This process unfolded in the colonial urban centers, the first of which was Calcutta. English quickly became the lingua franca of the subcontinent; knowing English and the now-global culture of Englishmen became the necessary path for any ambitious Indian subject in the British domain.

By 1813 missionaries had arrived from every major Christian denomination, challenging Hinduism on every front, from theology and ritual practices to morality and caste norms. Many ministers suggested that the British triumph in India represented God's judging Hinduism to be an idolatrous and demoniac heresy. In a not unrelated development, many Hindus came to regard the missionaries as in league with the colonialists.

In 1857, widespread civil disturbances swept across British-held territories. Styled "The Mutiny" by the British and regarded by many Indians as "The First War of Independence," Indian troops and peasants gave vent to resentments over colonial law and administrative insensitivities, executing some British officers and murdering their families. Colonial troops and their loyal mercenaries put down the rebellion, and after brutal reprisals against Indian citizens, the British Parliament in 1858 dissolved the company that had held the royal charter for trade with Asia and declared the Queen's rule over India directly. India became "The Jewel in the Crown" of the British Empire until 1947.

Challenges and Responses to Colonialism

The early modern era thus presented individual Hindus and Hindu institutions with a series of challenges that they shared with other colonized peoples across the globe. Powerful outsiders were arriving in significant numbers, proclaiming new truths and boldly denouncing the eternal Hindu verities. This ideological challenge occurred on several fronts simultaneously: the materialist scientific world view of the European Enlightenment, humanistic critiques of religion, proponents of racial theories of European superiority, and the outspoken Christian missionaries with triumphalist Gospel teachings.

The denominations of Christianity in India were largely Protestant. As a result, the ideas of nineteenth-century Protestantism exerted special impact on Hindus who sought to reform their own traditions. Protestant emphases that were significant among Hindu reformers included the search for core scriptures and doctrines using historical and scientific methods; criticism of ritual that was not consistent with these doctrines; distrust of priests as purveyors of "blind superstition"; promotion of spiritual individualism whereby each person is responsible for his or her own spiritual destiny; reliance on new lay-run institutions to organize new religious movements; the linking of social uplift initiatives with religious reform; the prestige of monotheism. (With the exception of monotheism, the same ideas had an impact in the colonial Buddhist territories of Asia, as we shall see in Chapter 6.) In India, too, "Protestant Hinduism" mobilized the colonized *to protest* against British imperialism.

Although most South Asians did not convert to Islam or Christianity, the states in which Hindus lived were ruled by non-Hindus (Muslims and the European successors). This state of affairs contravened the norms of proper social organization outlined in the ancient texts, for conquest by outsiders naturally suggested that the power and grace of the Hindu deities had been eclipsed by those of the non-Hindu conquerors. Further, the economic dislocations due to imperialism in many instances undermined the traditional channels of support for Hindu temples and hermitages.

The colonial government's political practice was to use religious identity as the basis for official dealings with "native constituencies." Thus, "Muslim," "Hindu," "Sikh," became units of perception and action. This created a problematic postcolonial legacy, although it gave the British a convenient manner in which they could "divide and conquer" groups that arose to oppose their policies, or (eventually) their very presence as overlords of South Asia. As a result, too, Hindus, Muslims, and Sikhs competed against one another for favorable treatment at the hands of the colonial government. Since 1947, tensions between these religion-delimited groups have resurfaced, sometimes tragically.

The nineteenth century saw a variety of Hindu responses, making it an era of tremendous cultural vitality and synthesis. The early influential leaders were mainly brahmins, the traditional priestly caste that had long emphasized literacy and education, and whose "rank and file" caste members supported change-resistant and old-fashioned orthodoxy. Yet among this elite group, especially those in areas of most intense contact (Bombay and Calcutta), the initial reaction to the British shifted from indifference to more engaged positions: either hostility or curiosity. Some Indians quickly developed a genuine interest in European civilization, and increasing numbers traveled there for education. We turn now to examine prominent examples among these Hindu responses.

Rammohan Roy and the Brahmo Samaj
The widespread issue that Hindus were forced to confront, one shared by Muslims and Buddhists elsewhere, centered on asking the question: How could it be that the world-preserving great deities have allowed non-Hindus to so utterly eclipse Hindus and defame Hindu society? Some Hindus gave an answer similar to that heard from time to time in Judaism and in other faiths

struggling under colonialism: "Revelation has not failed, but the community has lost true belief and practice. It needs, therefore, to be reformed." The first to articulate this position for Hinduism was Rammohan Roy (1772–1833), who is regarded as the "father of modern India." Roy was a remarkable brahmin educated in Sanskrit, Persian, and both classical Hinduism and Islam. He also learned English, read avidly, and worked within the British administration. Convinced that "true Hinduism" was found in the Upanishads, being both monotheistic and rationalist at root, Roy called for the reform of certain Hindu beliefs and practices prevalent across India, including superstition, caste discrimination, and the practice of widow immolation (sati). He argued for education in English so Indians could study modern math, science, and medicine. Roy was equally outspoken in defending Hinduism against missionary attacks, drawing on his study of the Bible and rational analysis to critique Christian dogmas. In public debates, Roy heaped scorn on the Christian doctrine that another person could win redemption for one's own sins and he argued (in the Muslim fashion) that the trinity is really a form of "polytheism."

In 1828, Roy founded an organization to further his reformist views. Initially called the Brahmo Sabha, in 1841 its name was changed to the Brahmo Samaj, whose official English title—"Fellowship of Believers in the One True God"—indicates its goal of uniting Hindus of all castes to proclaim a reformist, monotheistic ideology. The Brahmo Samaj also formulated simple and refined group rituals consistent with Roy's revivalist and rationalistic teachings. In roughly sixty years, the Brahmo Samaj organization spread across India. It has influenced subsequent generations of Hindu reformers and revivalists.

Dayananda and the Arya Samaj

Similar in many respects to the Brahmo Samaj but centered in Bombay and Lahore, the Arya Samaj was founded in 1875 by the brahmin teacher Swami Dayananda, honored also as Saraswati (1824-1883). Dayananda held that only the four Vedas were valid sources for true Hinduism and that they were in fact "infallible," containing all knowledge, even the root ideas of modern science. India in fact needed nothing from the West. For him, as for Roy, the essential Hindu theological idea, one he insisted is found in these earliest texts, was monotheism. Accordingly, he rejected post-Vedic scripture and saw later polytheism as the reason for Hinduism's decline. Dayananda tirelessly denounced practices such as child marriage, untouchability, and the subjugation of women. He composed his own simplified list of ethical norms and a description of properly reformed Vedic rituals.

Aryas sought to reform Hinduism's caste discrimination, but their dramatic purificatory rites made little impact nationwide. The Samaj also was open to women as full members, a radical innovation for the times. Although one might see in the Arya Samaj's reform program acceptance of the missionary criticisms of Indian society, Dayananda was also one of the most outspoken and effective critics of both Islamic and Christian missionary preaching. The

Arya Samaj promulgated the view that both Islam and Christianity were impure and alien religions out to undermine Hinduism. While such a teaching ran against the premodern pattern of toleration characteristic of Hindu traditions, the Arya Samaj's reformism provided a strong and decisive answer to the demoralization inherent in British colonialism.

Swami Dayananda's successors made the Arya Samaj especially influential once it developed village institutions and schools. The many Dayananda Anglo Vedic colleges and high schools continue the Arya Samaj revivalist tradition to the present day. Many of the current Bharatiya Janata Party members and leaders have been influenced by the Arya Samaj. Its work was taken abroad after 1900 by émigrés from South Asia who settled across the empire in Africa, the Caribbean, and the Pacific.

Sikh Reform and Resurgence

Through their resistance to the Mughals, the Sikhs eventually carved out their own kingdom in western India that lasted from 1799 until 1849, when it was absorbed into British India. After this, Sikh men were recruited into the colonial army from 1870 to 1947, becoming renowned for their disciplined character and martial abilities. Sikhs also entered into many of the new colonial educational institutions, finding success as civil servants, educators, and businessmen. Soon, Sikhs were serving across the British Empire, and upon retirement many settled outside India, from Singapore and Hong Kong to England. These migrants brought their faith with them, making Sikhism a global faith in the modern era.

Sikhs also responded to the religious challenges posed by South Asia's colonial situation and the aggressive Christian missionaries who appeared in the Punjab. A Sikh reformist organization, the Singh Sabha ("Lion Society"), was formed in 1879 to implement socioeducational uplift programs and defend the faith. The Singh Sabha sought to vitalize Sikhism through educational and literary activities as well as political agitation, founding a college in Amritsar and sponsoring magazines and newspapers that encouraged ethnic and religious pride among the Sikh communities that were spreading across India and abroad.

Ramakrishna and His Mission

A brahmin like Roy and Dayananda, but with a much more humble educational background, Ramakrishna (1834–1886) was a charismatic guru who attracted reform-minded Hindus. In Ramakrishna's revivalism, however, the teacher emphasized mystical experience and ecumenical theology. His spiritual experiences included long periods of trance in which he reported being possessed in turn by Kali, Sita, Rama, Krishna, Muhammad, and Jesus. Ramakrishna's teaching emphasized that the entire universe is permeated by the paramount divine spirit, a reality that is called different names by the world's different people, but whose essence is one. In articulating this view, Ramakrishna was

THE SAME WATER, DIFFERENT NAMES: A PARABLE BY RAMAKRISHNA

God is one only, and not two. Different people call on Him by different names: some as Allah, some as God, others as Krishna, Shiva, and Brahman. It is like the water in a lake. Some drink it at one place and call it *"jal,"* others at another place and call it *"pani,"* and still others at a third place and call it "water." The Hindus call it "jal," the Christians "water," and the Muslims "pani." But it is one and the same thing. Opinions are but paths. Each religion is only a path leading to God, as rivers come from different directions and ultimately become one in the ocean.[13]

updating on a global scale the teaching of the classical Hindu school we have already discussed, that of Vedantic Hinduism. The power of the mission that formed around Ramakrishna's teaching was based on his charismatic and personal witness to this essential truth.

It was Swami Vivekananda (1863–1902), Ramakrishna's foremost disciple, who became a guru in his own right and presented this theology in a forceful and systematic manner. He also defended Hinduism against its critics by contrasting its tolerance with the narrowness of dogmatic Christianity, pointing out that the church's complicity with racist and imperialist British attitudes was hypocritical. Vivekananda was the first great missionary representative of Hinduism on the global stage. His popularity grew through lectures on Hinduism across America and Europe. Most Westerners' first acquaintance with Hinduism is largely a product of the teachings of Vivekananda and his later followers.

Vivekananda organized the Ramakrishna Mission, whose institutions spread across India. The Mission advocated reformist traditions and embraced a global ecumenical awareness. Its highly organized order of monks cultivated inner spiritual development through yoga, taught "the Gospel of Ramakrishna," and established educational institutions, hospitals, and hospices open to all. Some monks trained as doctors. As of 2007, there were 16 Mission hospitals, 120 dispensaries, and 6,500 educational centers in India. Vivekananda and his successors also built distinctive ecumenical temples, composed rituals and vernacular texts, and created pilgrimage traditions drawing upon the experience and charisma of Ramakrishna.

The Ramakrishna Mission became the first great global Hindu organization with a vision of ecumenical Hinduism as the savior of the world, not merely of India. The Mission's disciples in the West now support its global reach. It has published many books and built retreat centers, libraries, and sanctuaries in major cities that by 2007 were found in fourteen countries.

The Work of Gandhi: Hindu Elements in Indian Nationalism

By the turn of the twentieth century, Britain's command over the subcontinent had grown with increasing trade and the presence of Christian missions had increased, as had the extensions of the colonial government's bureaucracy. Indian leaders and organizations seeking to strengthen and reform Hinduism were also multiplying through this period, however, and religious reformism and political activism frequently converged.

Religious identity and pride were often drawn upon in the growing independence movement. Nationalists committed to forcing the British to "quit India" advocated a broad spectrum of remedies, from revolutionaries who assassinated British officials, to moderates who sought to negotiate gradual assumption of political self-rule, to loyalists among those merchants and indigenous royalty who were prospering under the Colonial system.

An important player in the independence movement was the Indian National Congress, founded in 1880 in Bombay. Although dominated by brahmins and a few Muslims who were urban, English-educated lawyers, Congress sought to speak for all Indians. While it proclaimed loyalty to the Raj, as the British colonial government was called, Congress increasingly agitated non-violently for greater economic development and the incremental growth of self-rule. Thus, it gained acceptance as the party to articulate an Indian voice vis-à-vis the colonial government.

The spiritual background motivating many of the Congress leaders was that of the reformists who sought to regenerate Indian culture (both Hindu and Islamic). Indeed, many were convinced that India had a spiritual message for the future of humanity. Such a sentiment was heightened, of course, by the great world wars, whose devastation suggested that neither science, European political systems, nor Christianity was to be triumphant in global history.

It was Mohandas K. Gandhi (1869–1948) who became the most significant leader to guide South Asia to independence. Gandhi himself embodies the changes and syntheses affecting South Asia as the era of globalism under colonialism was brought to an end. As a paradigmatic reformist Hindu who merged European and Indian cultures, Gandhi became one of the greatest world figures of the twentieth century.

On the national stage, Gandhi linked the Congress elite with the masses. Although some disagreed with his stands, he was a nationally venerated guru, an activist who creatively reinterpreted Hinduism in an ethical, this-worldly manner. Gandhi at times went on hunger strikes to move British officials (or, at times, other Indian leaders) to reconsider their positions. His London-derived knowledge of British law and culture was also integral to his unparalleled success. (The honorific "Mahatma" applied to his name, meaning "great-souled [one]" expresses the profound spiritual respect he garnered.)

Carrying on the work of earlier reformers, Gandhi decried high-caste discrimination toward others and he especially highlighted untouchability as a blight on Hinduism. He also extended the Hindu and Jain notion of *ahimsa*

GANDHI

M. K. Gandhi was born in a merchant family in the western region of Gujarat. As a young man he was interested in secular subjects, and he eventually traveled to London to study law. While there he encountered for the first time the classical Hindu texts, all in English translations. They were introduced to him not from an Indian *guru* but through meetings at the Theosophical Society, a group of European mystics interested in the secret doctrines they felt were at the root of all world religions. While in England, Gandhi also read the Bible avidly, as well as books by Western intellectuals like Tolstoy, Thoreau, Ruskin.

After becoming a lawyer, Gandhi settled in South Africa, then a British colony with a large Indian minority. He was soon drawn into political activism in opposition to the racist and discriminatory imperial practices directed toward South Asians as "coloreds." From experiences with protests and community organization, Gandhi developed his central principle, one that guided his future life. He called it *Satyagraha* ("Grasping the Truth"). This concept has roots in both Hindu doctrine of nonviolence (*ahimsa*), and in Christianity's injunctions to "love one's enemy" and "turn the other cheek." Gandhi required those opposing the government to confine their protests to nonviolent acts, accept suffering for the cause, love the opponent, and be disciplined in personal life. Gandhi's work in South Africa among Indian immigrants transformed him and drew attention to his teachings back in India, where Congress leaders urged him to return. He did so in 1915.

Although Gandhi always retained respect for British law and the moral ideals articulated in Western religions, back in India he abandoned the dress of the Western barrister for the humble *dhoti* (loincloth) of the Indian peasant. Gandhi's greatness as a political leader was likewise built upon his connection with the Indian masses, a relationship that developed through his wide-ranging tours of the countryside, his involvement with a series of peasant protests, his self-imposed poverty, and an effective organization (including a daily newspaper) that he developed with those who lived in his *ashram* (the traditional Hindu religious commune).

(nonviolence) to require an entire way of life guided by this ideal. Through following ahimsa in all spheres, Gandhi argued that the modern Hindu could find the truth in humble daily work. It was a principle that could transform the individual and society, imbuing each with a spiritual center. For this reason, Gandhi promoted small-scale cottage industries such as spinning, urging individuals to use a spinning wheel to make their own cotton thread. By adopting this practice, he brilliantly found a symbol and practice that could simultaneously protest imperial monopolies the British had enforced (on salt, loomed cloth, etc.), prod elite political leaders to keep touch with the lower classes, and give individuals a disciplined personal activity.

Gandhi's life work was crowned in 1947, when India finally gained its independence. However, celebration of this long-anticipated moment was shattered by the violence that accompanied it. The British allowed no time for the orderly implementation of their partition: dividing India, a new secular nation, from the new Muslim state of Pakistan. A civil war broke out in which an estimated four million people perished. Nearing the age of eighty, Gandhi traveled to many of these areas in an attempt to quell the chaos, but largely in vain. He was murdered in 1948 by a member of a fundamentalist group that had opposed partition as well as Gandhi's "concessions" to Muslims and the lowest castes.

India in many respects abandoned Gandhi's vision of spiritually centered development. Only in civil law did India continue to embrace Gandhi's vision, albeit haltingly, in its rhetorical commitment to eradicate caste discrimination and by holding fast to India's fundamental identity as a secular—not Hindu—nation. Even this last legacy of Gandhism has been under attack by the high-caste-dominated Hindu parties that have enjoyed increasing success during the last decade of the twentieth century, as witnessed by the rise of the BJP.

HINDUISM AND POSTMODERN TRENDS IN A POSTCOLONIAL WORLD

The Persistence of Traditional Religious Understandings

Despite the modernization of India that daily reaches ever further into the rural regions, there has been remarkable persistence of traditional beliefs and practices in postcolonial India. While we cannot point to any one school or theology as representative of "Hinduism" in all its many expressions, it is possible to trace broadly shared understandings and central ideas among the traditions that have remained influential to the present.

The Presence of the Divine

Whatever specific doctrines or practices an individual Hindu follows, it is the widely held conviction that underlying the material world there is "something more" than that seen in waking or our ordinary consciousness that gives the tradition a measure of unity. For humans, therefore, life entails more than satisfying the needs dictated by survival. There is the presence of a divine cosmic spirit from which all the created world proceeded. A divine reality enfolds human reality, interpenetrating the material world and human experience, primarily the soul (*atman*) that animates an embryo in the womb and whose presence energizes human life.

HINDUS DISCERNING THE DIVINE

Within the human being and in many natural places, Hindus see immaterial spirit as alive and accessible to humans who seek it. This is not to say that the often confusing gap between commonsense understanding and deeper perception does not go unnoticed, as indicated in the following parable told by a modern guru:

> A sage had a number of disciples. He taught them his deepest belief: "Brahman is everywhere and dwells in everything. So you should treat all things as Brahman and bow before them." One day a disciple was out on errands, a mad elephant was rushing through the marketplace, and the elephant driver was shouting, "Get out of the way!... This is a mad elephant!" The disciple remembered his guru's teachings and refused to run. "Brahman is in this elephant and in me. How can Brahman hurt Brahman?" he thought, and just stood there full of love and devotion.... The disciple did not move an inch. The mad elephant picked him up with his trunk, swung him around, and threw him in the gutter. The poor fellow lay there, bruised, bleeding, but more than all, disillusioned that Brahman should do this to him. When his guru and the other disciples came to help him and take him home, he said, "You said Brahman is in everything! Look what the elephant did to me!" The guru replied, "It is true that Brahman is in everything. The elephant is certainly Brahman. But so was the elephant driver, telling you to get out of the way. Why didn't you listen to him?"[14]

Hindus also perceive the divine in the bearing of holy ascetics, whose mere presence inspires beatitude, and in the periodic miracles of temple images "sweating," miraculous icons emerging from the earth, or—as we note later—through icons "drinking" milk.

In traveling across the villages of South Asia, one senses that the culture is unique in terms of the veneration of the sacred expressed in the daily rhythms of life. Rituals honor the rising and setting sun, temples have been erected at any unusual or aged natural feature (stones, trees), and reverence is shown to rivers, mountains, and animals (elephants, snakes, monkeys, and of course cows). There are shrines for the protectors of houses, families, artisans, and castes; there are guardian deities of the settlement and of the agricultural fields. Goddesses control the outbreaks of disease; possession by ghosts and demons explains certain illnesses. Even the distant deities who appear in the night sky as planets are thought so immanent as to influence human destiny.

There is, thus, little acceptance of the notion made popular in post-Enlightenment Western theology that suggests that God set up creation as a mechanism and then retreated to let it tick away, like a detached watchmaker. Across Hindu South Asia, the immanence of spirit is respected and the gods live next door. It is the human task to find harmony with them and eventually to seek salvation from rebirth by finding the spirit in whatever guise one is most suited to discover. Thus, even in modern cities and among individuals who are highly educated, the wish to connect with and worship the divine remains strong today.

There is likewise a widespread view that through the key moments in one's life—especially birth, coming of age, marriage, death—one should strengthen one's own and one's family's collective spirit by seeking divine blessings. As a result, Hindu life-cycle rites are extensive undertakings. Full marriage ceremonies, for example, last two weeks. In fact, to whatever extent Hinduism has unity, it is not belief but the ritual practices that sustain it.

Syncretism, Coexistence, Sectarianism

Another distinctive and enduring characteristic of Hinduism today is the broad range of ideas about the sacred and the widespread tendency for individuals to accept alternative, opposing views. The coexistence of so many competing theologies and religious practices, and even the toleration of nonbelievers, have been based upon two notions. First is the belief that every human understanding of the highest truth, whatever that is held to be, whether monotheistic or monistic, is never complete or perfect. Second is the expectation that as individuals learn and practice more deeply, they will see reality more clearly. As a result, those thought to hold false views are simply located in a hierarchy, not rejected. A wrongheaded person may be ignorant, immature, or incomplete, but not evil. Beginning with Islam, and extended into the modern era with other "Western" religions, Hinduism's acceptance of pluralism has certainly endured. Most South Asians have placed Christianity into a now-global hierarchy, albeit below various Hindu traditions. As we will see, the exponents of Hindu nationalism have rejected any accommodationist stance, even questioning the loyalty of Muslims and Christians.

Muslim-Hindu relations continue to be contentious in modern India. Communal enmity on religious lines was rare after the establishment of Islam in South Asia (1000 CE) because group identity developed predominantly according to caste, region, and political loyalties. It was an acceptance of coexistence, as historian Ainslie Embree has pointed out, that characterized this relationship:

> Two great cultures and religious systems, the Hindu and the Islamic, while borrowing much from each other along the margins of their existence, retained their separate, core identities for 1,000 years. Coexistence, not assimilation, was the characteristic behavior of both

communities, and it was made possible by the nature of Hindu society as well as the political policies of the Muslim rulers.[15]

Religious enmity is not eternal, inevitable standpoint in South Asia or elsewhere; in the past as today, it is the product of a specific historical context, that is, it is shaped by human actions and political policies.

The inclusivist religious attitude still shared by many Hindus has encouraged ever new spiritual searches and the appearance of new religious sects that combine beliefs and practices from various traditions, including astrology, Buddhism, and "secular" traditions such as psychology.

This general characteristic of Hindu groups accepting others, Hindu and non-Hindu, as having value should not cloud the recognition that many Hindus are indeed sectarian in their religious orientation. While the view "all the gods are one" is widely expressed, sometimes seriously and at other times as a polite cliché, it is not a view shared by everyone. Adherence to the ecumenical strategy of inclusivity, of accepting the legitimacy of competing religious standpoints, does not oblige one to abandon one's own sect's truth claims. As the Christian missionaries in India who first encountered this viewpoint recognized when it was applied to them, inclusivity is ultimately a means of subordinating other truth claims, be they Vaishnava theism, Vedanta monism, or Christian trinitarianism. Using this method, Hindu world views have held their primacy from the modern era through the postcolonial era; it has mainly been in reforming and modernizing their social institutions that Hindus have adopted non-Hindu ideas.

Contemporary Hindu Practices

The Guru-Disciple Relationship

Dating from the time of the Upanishads, one central Hindu tradition has been the relationship connecting gurus and disciples (chelas). Just as Hindus perceive the divine in their natural and settled environments, it is equally important to note that they find spirit alive in the unbroken fact of its realization by those who reach moksha, achieve spiritual powers, and share their experiences for the benefit of humanity. Charismatic saintly gurus still hold central place in both traditional and reformist Hinduism today.

We have noted the lasting forms of organized Hinduism that emerged in the postclassical era. Then as now, numerous spiritual teachers have emerged independently in the traditional manner of undergoing long periods training with independent gurus, then attracting their own disciples. Guru residences called ashrams sustain the community that performs rituals, meditates, and learns together under the guru's direction. Many Hindu guru-centered institutions tend to be short-lived, and the "school" that emerges lasts only as long as the charismatic teacher lives or only through his first generation of designated successors. Others continue, and in these cases we see the central Hindu notion of *parampara*, meaning "lineage, tradition, pedigree," that is, the genealogy of teachers back to the enlightened sages.

The circle of intimate disciples must master the guru's instructions on the key spiritual practices (meditation, worship, etc.), most often memorizing them through intensive repetition. They may also collect their guru's teachings, sometimes only in memory, sometimes through writing, or today, even on video! Eventually, the tested and trusted disciples are also designated gurus by the teacher, usually once he or she reaches an advanced age, and so the parampara continues.

Many Hindus believe that karma directs one to find a proper teacher and that one should be open to the need to find a new teacher if one's spiritual growth stagnates. Some gurus also guard their circle of disciples by subjecting eager students who present themselves to certain tests to ensure that they are sincere and trustworthy.

MEETING THE GURU

In the postcolonial era, Americans and Europeans who have sought Hindu teachers have left rich accounts of their first encounters. Richard Albert, the former Harvard researcher who became a popular Western interpreter of Hinduism as Ram Dass, describes his initial meeting with his guru Maharaj-ji in this manner:

> Some time later we were back with the Maharaj-ji and he said to me, "Come here. Sit." So I sat down and he looked at me and said, "You were out under the stars last night."
> "Um-hum."
> "You were thinking about your mother."
> "Yes." ('Wow,' I thought, 'that's pretty good. I never mentioned that to anybody.')
> "She died last year."
> "Um-hum."...
> "Spleen. She died of spleen."
> Well, what happened to me at that moment, I can't really put into words. He looked at me in a certain way at that moment, and two things happened—it seemed simultaneous. The first thing that happened was that my mind raced faster and faster to try and get leverage—to get a hold on what he had just done.... And at the same moment, I felt this extremely violent pain in my chest and a tremendous wrenching feeling and I started to cry. I cried and cried and cried. And I wasn't happy and I wasn't sad.... The only thing I could say was it felt like I was home."[16]

The true guru is one's soul-mate, and the disciple can expect the guru's full grace and loving guidance only through the complete abandonment of ego. The new identity that accepting a guru entails is symbolized in the widespread practice of each disciple receiving a new name. The common affix of *-dasa* ("slave, servant") in such names signifies the expectation of submission and letting go of ego that marks this fundamental relationship.

Given the many material and psychological rewards bestowed upon gurus, it is small wonder that there has been no shortage of clever charlatans who have cultivated followings and fortunes. This possibility, too, has been long recognized by the Hindu community. Yet even up to the present, most will show respect for all who conform to the role, acknowledging that, as one proverb goes, "Only the Lord Shiva can discern who is the genuine ascetic."

Living with Karma: Rituals, Astrology, and Rebirth

The classical doctrines associated with karma, reincarnation, and salvation are the center of Hindu (and Buddhist) belief, regardless of the school one follows or one's focus on a particular chosen deity. Karma is thus the most important spiritual force in the universe, determining one's place in the cosmos (animal, human caste, etc.). What one does in a particular incarnation, however, then shapes future destiny so that, properly speaking, Hindu belief does not posit a closed fatalistic world view. Nonkarmic causalities (natural forces, biological reactions, chance) also shape human life, so that Hindus can say (like many Americans), "it was meant to be," as well as, "things just happen." Only enlightened saints are thought capable of knowing their karmic past and future; everyone else remains uncertain. For this reason, a steady menu of meritorious ritual is a sensible approach to living with karma, as is consultation with astrologers (again, a practice some Americans incline to).

Karma doctrine assumes a natural causal mechanism conditioning individual destiny, but destiny can be shaped by group actions, too. Husbands and wives worship together and act together in many ways. Marriage ritual ties couples for life and can include a vow to be reborn together in future incarnations (a popular motif in South Asian folklore). Entire families are thought to be shaped by the actions of elders for the better (e.g., through their sponsoring special rituals) or for the worse (e.g., through their neglecting proper ritual norms).

Hindus today, in the extent to which they vary considerably, may explain their individual and collective destiny in terms of karma causality. It is true that stretches in life may seem to be inscrutable except through a past-karma explanation; some individuals do indeed see everything in life fated from the past. But the great majority of Hindus believe that their destiny today and in future lifetimes is also determined in significant part by their moral actions and ritual acts. The puranas and guru parables often state that being human and being Hindu are rare incarnations in samsara and should not be wasted. There are rebirths as beings inhabiting this world, there are purgatories (*naraka*) that receive evil human beings, and there are heavenly realms (*svarga*) created by each great deity reserved for good and devout devotees. Being born in heaven, not in the disembodied realm of moksha, is understood by most Hindus today as the highest destiny.

There is much more unity today among Hindus in their ritualism than in their beliefs. The ritual practice called *puja* is nearly universal and thus is an essential aspect of Hinduism. We have discussed the ideas associated with icons that "channel" the divine presence and the broad consensus among believers that the spiritual reality/realities exist and that they are in daily and intimate connection to our human world. Simply stated, being human in the Hindu way means acknowledging this. Respectful gestures and puja are the means by which Hindus relate to the divine wherever and in whatever form they find it.

Gestures of Respect for the Divine

Namaskara/Namaste   Hindus greet each other by raising the joined palms to the shoulder level and repeating this term, sometimes bowing. Some gurus teach that saluting other humans in this way is a theological statement: "I center my physical self in the atman located in my heart, and salute your same holy center."

Pranam   The core gesture of *namaskara* can be multiplied into any number of prostrations (*pranam*), principally either with the knees touching the ground or the body moving to face down while fully prone. This gesture, too, is one humans may do to other humans by, for example, grasping the feet of the one honored such as a guru, a priest, an elder in the family, a mother-in-law (for a daughter-in-law), a husband (for a wife), parents (for children).

Pradakshina   Another Hindu perception of the body is that between sides of the body: the right side is the pure side and one eats with the right hand; the left hand is used to wash after calls of nature and is regarded as impure. As an extension of this, whenever circumambulating an icon or temple, one should do *pradakshina* in a clockwise manner, keeping one's right side closest to the sacred object.

Puja

Puja ("homage") is also built on the assumption that humanity and the divine must maintain an intimate connection, one marked by respectful hierarchy. For humans, the great deities (such as Shiva, Durga, and Vishnu) are superiors. Devotees address them as "Lords" and "Masters" while referring to themselves as their "servants," "disciples," or "slaves." Puja involves all the expressions by which an inferior can welcome, show respect for, and entertain a distinguished guest. Ideally, all ritual acts express a faithful bhakta's submissive, adoring, and self-negating service to the divine.

Materially, one doing puja seeks to please the deity as if the divine personage were human, that is, possessed five senses. All that Hindus offer as puja can be seen accordingly: incense pleases the sense of smell; flowers please the senses of sight and smell; foods gratify the taste; mantras and music please the hearing; cloth and pastes please the deity's tactile sense.

The inseparability of worldly and mundane blessings is seen in the full process involved in making a puja offering and then receiving back the remains, *prasad*. These substances, having been proximate to the image, carry a subtle infusion of divine blessing, turning all prasad into "medicine." In addition to food, flowers can be worn in the hair, incense smoke wafted around the body, and holy water (*jal*) sipped. Colored powders that come back from the icon are mixed with water and used to mark the forehead with a *tika*, the mark made in the center of the forehead above the eyes.

In puja offered to specific deities, devotees usually connect the particular offerings made with the divine personality and mythology. Some deities have favorite colors, such as Lakshmi (goddess of wealth) preferring gold; others have favorite foods, such as the pot-bellied Ganesh who craves the round gooey sweets called *laddu* or the youthful Krishna who adores butter.

While the norms of different dharma and of following one's own chosen deity have led Hindus to accept differences in religious orientation even among close family members, this "spiritual individualism" is balanced in most instances by the widespread and daily custom of families worshiping all the major gods in their midst (home and neighborhood), then sharing from the same plate the prasad returned from the common family puja.

A good Hindu today, like a good Muslim, need never worship in public and may make all puja offerings to icons in the home shrine. In temples with priestly attendants, devotees usually place on the puja tray coins or uncooked rice to be taken by the priests, a meritorious service donation called *dakshina*. It is through the medium of puja therefore that Hindu householders contribute to the subsistence of their priests and temples.

It is literally true that all the fine arts of South Asia developed as offerings made to the gods: instrumental and vocal music, dance, sculpture, and painting all have their connection to temple rituals. Hindu temples, which are simply homes for ritually empowered icons, can be humble thatched buildings sheltering crude stones with no attending priesthood or magnificent palaces built to house jeweled images attended by hosts of priests and other temple servants, with the sanctuary proper surrounded by monasteries, music pavilions, pilgrim hostels, sacred ponds. The great temples are the preeminent centers of Hindu culture; to visit them is to see all these cultural forms directed toward serving the gods with beauty, grace, and dedication.

Vratas

For devout (and usually more affluent) Hindus, there are more intensive ritual programs that require the services of a brahmin priest. The *vrata* combines these forms but adds group participation in fasting and maintaining celibacy throughout the ritual, while individuals are led by the priest to make detailed

offerings, repeat mantras associated with the deity, and listen to a series of sacred stories. Most vratas today last one or two days.

Vratas are the most common communal ritual Hindus perform; some may
be done less for their spiritual uplift and more for specific boons associated
with the rite, such as for financial benefit (Lakshmi), for success in school
(Saraswati), for couples wishing to have a son (Shiva). The *Satyanarayan vrata*
dedicated to Vishnu is the most widely done in North India today. It has
Vishnu make these promises:

> This *vrata* can pacify sorrows and sufferings: it can increase the amount
> of wealth and land, it can also give good fortune, children, and victory in
> all spheres of life. And any day when man is filled with devotion and
> feels like doing the *puja* of Vishnu, he can worship him in the evening
> of that same day. He should do the *puja* along with priests, relatives, and
> his friends.... After offering it he should listen to the *katha* (story) along
> with friends and relatives. Then he should give *prasad* and then *dakshina*
> to the priest.... Obviously, people can get their desires fulfilled by per-
> forming the *vrata* in the way described. Especially in the *Kali Yuga*, this
> is the best and easiest way on earth for people to get rid of their sorrows
> and for the fulfillment of their desires.[17]

Hindu Samskaras: Life-Cycle Rites

Being Hindu means following the proper path in life determined by the dharma
codes set forth by the ancient sages, so that the individual's life—like society's
groups—should be properly organized. The *Dharmashastra* lists over forty life-
cycle rituals, *samskaras*; they are most observed and elaborated today by families
at the top of the caste hierarchy. We summarize the most popular contemporary
practices briefly here, using North India terms and culture as representative.

Birth Rituals Pregnant women are given empowered charms to protect the
fetus and are kept isolated from sources of pollution, demons, and nonfamily.
Despite the spilling of the mother's blood and bodily fluids, birth is a time of
"happy pollution," and for the period of the mother's recovery (up to 10 days),
the family abstains from puja and does not interdine with outsiders. A special
"release from birth pollution" ritual (*chati*) must be done in which the house is
cleaned and purified, mother and family bathe, the father shaves, and the family holds a feast.

Childhood Rituals The ritual called *namkaran* serves to gives an infant its
formal name. Naming children after the deities is a common practice and this
can be done according to a parent's chosen deity, for the day on which the child
is born, or simply for auspiciousness. The horoscope with the carefully noted
birth time must be finished and kept for lifelong consultation. Infants at this
time are often given amulets empowered by mantra recitations by the family
priest or guru. Before the first birthday, the final childhood rite of first rice
feeding introduces the baby to solid food.

Coming of Age   Boys and girls are led on different ritual paths emphasizing male dominance and female fertility. The rites marking adulthood for both establish expectations and responsibilities of full Hindu personhood; most significant is the assumption of accountability for actions, as these now "count" in karmic retribution. Since the *Dharmashastra* forbids teaching Vedic verses to women, adult females are not assigned brahmanical rites but participate in their husband's rituals. Womens' ritual customs nonetheless developed.

Girls are initiated as women once they have their first menstruation, usually by going through a week of strict isolation, being prohibited from seeing the sun or males. During this time, elder females in the family instruct the girls on aspects of adult religious practice, the duties of Hindu women, stories of the deities.

Boys of the top three castes have a sacred thread investiture (*upanayana*) after which they receive the first teachings from the family guru, including those rituals associated with the wearing of a multistranded thread (*janai*) over the left shoulder and right hip, a burden taken on from this day until death. (In modern times, this "wearing the thread" is held to most consistently among brahmin families only.) Boys are also given their first mantra to memorize, the Rig Vedic Gayatri that one should repeat daily at the rising and setting of the sun:

> We meditate on that excellent light of the divine sun
>> May he illumine our minds. (Rig Veda 3.62.10)

In adult initiation, boys become "twice-born" through this second birth into the knowledge of the Veda and Vedic ritual.

Householder   Marriage is a bond usually arranged by the couple's families, although many young people today can veto the choice proposed for them. The relatives setting up the match must be satisfied that the individuals' horoscopes match harmoniously, which ensures that their characters and karma are compatible. This is a judgment usually requested of an astrologer.

Upon marriage, a Hindu woman leaves her home, often with a dowry, to live with her mother-in-law, shifting forever her ritual center to the husband's family line. (This pattern is breaking down today in the urban middle classes where employment patterns require transfers; among the rural population that is drawn to migrate to cities in search of jobs and education, nuclear families are common.)

Death   The best possible death, religiously speaking, occurs on the banks of the Ganges, soon after the dying one has earned a large store of good karma through a last donation ritual. Death produces a crisis in the family and a state of corporate pollution that for immediate kin endures for an entire year. When someone dies, the family out of love wishes to perform all the rites carefully and ensure that the soul goes to its best possible rebirth. However, the death of a loved one also produces fear that the soul might reincarnate as a dangerous ghost. Thus, families are motivated by love and fear to attend to these rituals with the greatest dedication.

The corpse should be cremated as soon as possible after death, and before sundown. Carrying the body to the cremation site, the *ghat*, is men's work, with the eldest son lighting the pyre for the father and the youngest doing so for the mother. When the skull bursts, Hindus believe that the soul has been released to go to its next birth. The women who stay at home during the cremation must remove their ornaments and sweep the house, beginning to repurify the house polluted by death. The men who cremate must collect the burned remains so that the family can immerse them in the Ganges in the course of the after-death rituals.

After-Death Rites   Before the family may reestablish purity in their homes and resume social life, they must perform the first rites of feeding the departed soul who is thought to wander as a ghost (*preta*) from twelve days up to one year. Here, Hindu tradition is preserved in the performance preservation of the ancient Vedic *shraddha* rites: the mourners offer *pinda* puja, ritual rice ball offerings, to feed the soul and build up its intermediate-state body to be a preta and continue on its afterlife journey. The rites should be done at the riverside (every river is understood to be connected with the divine Ganges, a means of conveying the offering to the "other world" in whatever realm the soul is wandering). Shraddha rites for parents and especially fathers are done yearly on the death anniversary, or on the one day each year in the spring called *Akshaya Tritaya* ("Inexhaustible Third") that is felt particularly propitious to combine all mourning rituals dedicated to the ancestors.

Utsavas: *Hindu Festivals*

Many Hindus today carry a small pocket almanac that organizes the Western, lunar, and solar succession of days. Why are these so popular? Since the year is punctuated by a succession of great and small festivals, or *utsavas*, some lasting only a day, others stretching over ten days, Hindus must harmonize personal, family, and business affairs with the religious celebrations.

Part of the reason for this extravagant festival agenda is that across South Asia, it is customary for each important deity to have a procession (*jatra*) that is the occasion for extraordinary acts of devotion. At these times, the god or goddess is felt to be more accessible to devotees and more inclined to extend grace to those who demonstrate their faith. The Hindu utsavas traditionally offer a dramatic break from the mundane routines of life, making times for puja, feasting, and rest. They offer the chance to live in a profoundly different and sacred time, when the great salvific deeds known from legend and myth are retold by *pandits* or enacted through live cultural performances. In many of the utsavas, special foods, drinks, and decorations are made that appear at no other time. Some festivals are reserved for fasting, ascetic acts, or other penances.

The greatest festivals celebrated in the notable religious cities of India are immense spectacles that involve thousands in arranging for the myriad cultural performances and sideshows. These gatherings can create a marvelous sense of community among *bhaktas* (devotees), drawing pilgrims from afar to witness and seek blessings. The time chosen to visit the great pilgrimage sites often coincides with the major festival celebrations.

Diwali   In India, the new year begins at the vernal equinox, a date also marking for Hindus the moment when creation in each world era begins anew. But across the north, the year begins with *Diwali*, the festival around the autumnal equinox that focuses on Lakshmi, goddess of wealth. On the main day families wear new clothes, sweep their houses clean, arrange a special altar with puja laid out for the goddess, and set up lamps (now, most are "Christmas lights") to guide her. On a subsequent day, brothers and sisters honor their kin ties and individuals may do other special pujas to strengthen their health for the year ahead. Middle-class families now send "Diwali cards," akin to Christmas cards.

Sri Panchami   The festival of *Sri Panchami* is dedicated to Saraswati, the goddess of learning and the fine arts. Students, scholars, and artists all will flock to her temples. Some temples set up a whitewashed wall on which young children are to write their first letters, for traditional Hindu parents wait until this day to begin to teach their offspring to read and write.

Shiva Ratri   Shiva Ratri ("Shiva's Night") is the end of winter festival, one of two festivals each year dedicated to Shiva. This festival emphasizes fasting and grand offerings to Shiva's phallic icon, the linga. Shiva Ratri also in some localities connects with the god's identity that imagines him controlling the myriad ghosts and goblins that occupy the lower portions of the Hindu pantheon. It is also the time for ascetics to make offerings at his great temples, which accordingly fill with thousands of sadhus and yogins who meditate, instruct devotees, receive donations, and demonstrate their powers.

Holi   Holi inaugurates Hinduism's "Feast of Love." It is the year's primary festival honoring Krishna in his guise as the playful trickster god. In harmony with the theology called *lila* ("divine play"), devotees establish a set period for honoring the youthful Krishna. For the primary three or so days, all of society is at play and normal caste and gender rules are suspended. In imitation of Krishna and to find harmony with his spirit that transcends the mundane, all society should join in the lila, inverting established hierarchies and expectations. Women may sing lewdly in public or douse male passersby with buckets of water, and public officials such as policemen suffer usually playful subordinations; in villages, an untouchable may be declared "headman" for the duration of the festival. Through the modern period, reports on Holi mention that some followed Krishna's example to slip away for extramarital liaisons. There is also the custom of ingesting an intoxicating hashish concoction called *bhang* to help devotees enter more deeply in the shifting sense of reality. On the last day, bonfires are lit to consume evil, commemorating Krishna's defeating a female demon who sought his demise.

Naga Panchami   Naga Panchami, "the Fifth Day [Worship] of the Serpent Deities," or *nagas*, is a time to clean wells and set up shrines for offerings to snake deities (who have hoods like cobras) associated with the fertility of the earth and the bringing of the rains. At this time, when the young rice plants are nearing their time of transplantation, farmers await the first monsoon showers to begin setting out their essential crop. Nagas are thought to reside in underground palaces and claim ownership of the ground as well. The pujas offered to them can be described as "rental payments" for human presence and with requests for their welcoming their allies, the rain clouds. Devotees also give peace offerings so that the nagas of their locality will not move during the upcoming year and cause earthquakes or wander up to earth where, if angered, they can cause illness.

Guru Purnima   The festival day for honoring one's spiritual guide is *Guru Purnima*, "Teacher's Full Moon." This is a day for disciples to make the year's largest material donation to the guru and ideally the disciple should make *darshana*, that is, see the guru. This is also the day each year when high-caste Hindu men change their sacred threads (*janai*), and the brahmin also dispense to householders special protective threads that are tied around the wrists. Disciples of great teachers who have "left the body" (i.e., died) will often arrange for pujas before a garlanded commemorative photo.

Gai Jatra   A festival specifically dedicated to honoring "mother cow" is *Gai Jatra*. Real cows, one of the unique and provocative symbols of Hinduism, are to be feasted on this day and garlanded like icons. In some places, children can be dressed up as cows, taken in procession, and honored. As the gift of a cow is one of the most ancient and meritorious gifts one can make to a brahmin, some Hindus choose this day to do so. Families who are in the first year of mourning are those most often seen doing this puja and making the cow donation (*godana*). Why? Because they dedicate the merit earned to the deceased in case the soul has not yet been reborn and so needs an infusion of good karma.

Tij   *Tij* is the festival for women, who can act in imitation of Parvati, the incarnation of Devi, who fasted, meditated, and underwent purification in the hopes of winning the husband she deserved. In her case, this was Shiva; for unmarried women, the hope is for a good human husband; for those already married, it is for the long life of one's spouse. For Tij, some women join to spend the night at a temple, one ideally situated beside a river or having a large bathing tank, where they sing devotional songs and dance to secure divine blessings. As they pass the night they also fast, listen to stories associated with Parvati and other exemplary women, then immerse themselves in the sacred waters to repurify themselves before sealing their vows.

Dashara   *Dashara* usually falls just before the first rice harvest. It has become the occasion for marking two separate divine events. For Rama bhaktas, this festival is *Rama Navami* ("Rama's Ninth"), the time for celebrating both Rama's birth and his victory over the demon Ravana, rescuing his consort Sita, and instituting an era of proper Hindu rule. *Durga Puja* similarly enfolds the community in the goddess' "Nine Nights" of struggle against Mahisha, the demon who could not be killed by a man and so threatened the gods and all creation. The "Victory Tenth Day" commemorates Durga's finally slaying of

SACRED COWS AND HINDUISM

One of the striking first impressions of South Asia is the free-ranging movement of cows in villages and on city streets. Up through the 1960s, when India suffered its last major famine, it was widely stated in the West that "if only Hindus would eat beef, all their food needs could be met." What is certainly true is that cows are integral to Hinduism in many respects: one *purana* text suggests that all the divinities exist in the cow, and another sees the cow as an incarnation of Devi, the goddess. Killing a cow is thereby unthinkable. The cow's centrality is further seen in ritual practice: to mark and purify any space and make it suitable for *puja*, cow dung is a necessary ground coating; in addition, the five products of the cow (milk, curds, butter, urine, dung) are one of the most potent sources for the inner purification for humans when they are ingested. Anthropologists have also sought to link the logic of "mother cow" veneration with its crucial contributions to South Asia's subsistence agriculture. Dried cow dung is an essential cooking fuel; composted cow dung is irreplaceable in the reinvigoration of the soil for intensive rice and wheat crops; cows are also capable of eating nearly everything and recycling chaff, odd roadside vegetation, even garbage; finally, the gelded oxen born of cows are also the most reliable beasts of burden for plowing deep enough to turn over the soil. Thus, for a subsistence farming family to harvest its (typically) sole cow at times of food shortage risks its long-term survival. Here, argues the cultural ecologist Marvin Harris, lies the reason for the cow's sacrality: it is holy because it promotes survival. And besides, the initial supposition is in fact false: tanner castes (ranked as untouchables because they collect dead cows) do eat beef. Modern fundamentalist groups have chosen the cow to symbolize "Mother India" and agitate for a ban on cow slaughter to define their religio-nationalist goals.

Mahisha as he took the form of a buffalo demon. To imitate the goddess in her moment of triumph and to bathe her images in the blood offerings that she most loves, devotees still perform animal sacrifices at her temples, beheading primarily goats, fowl, and water buffaloes. Durga Puja ends the festival year at the time of the rice harvest: tradition evolved so that divine and human feasting on animal meat coincides with the time that farmers need to cull their herds, especially of old and young males, who can wreak havoc in the luxuriant rice paddies if they escape human confinement.

Pilgrimage (Yatra)

From earliest times, Hindus believed the land bounded by the Himalaya mountains and the oceans to be graced by the highest revelation. The subcontinent's mountains and rivers thus were imagined to be abodes of the deities and the places where sages have realized the highest truths. From then until now, devotees have gone on pilgrimage to see these sacred persons and places (for *darshan*, viewing the divine) and to dwell in their precincts that are blessed with spiritual powers. On their journeys, today Hindus do the rituals described for temples, make elaborate offerings and countless expressions of respect, and bring home treasured prasad. Modern transport has facilitated the expansion of pilgrimage for many Hindus today.

Himalayas   The most dramatic and famous among the myriad Hindu sacred sites are located in the Himalayas, the world's highest mountain chain, where the very names of the snow-clad peaks (from which the name "Himalaya" is derived) reflect the perception of divine residence. According to one passage in the *Skanda Purana*, seeing any of the Himalayan peaks is transformative of one's karma: "As the dew is dried up by the morning sun, so are the sins of mankind by the sight of Himalayas."

Ganges   Other focal areas for pilgrimage are rivers. The Ganges and its tributaries that reach up to the Himalayan glaciers all are associated with divinity: the Ganges itself, conceived as a goddess, was sent by the gods to succor humanity in the midst of a horrific drought. The Ganges is thus a divine entity; as such, many bathing rites are done along its banks, where devotees hope to draw upon her capacity to "wash away" bad karma. Ganges waters are seen as the best source for purifying a ritual space, so that pilgrims collect it and store it for future ritual use.

All rivers in South Asia are identified with the Ganges, with a common myth known across the region stating that each river shares a subterranean connection with it. The points on the river best suited for human pilgrimage and ritualism are tributary confluences called *tirthas*. The literal translation of tirtha, "ford, river crossing," also refers more metaphorically to their being places making easier the task of crossing the great river of samsara to reach heaven or moksha. Many of the great religious cities of South Asia are located along rivers, based upon the multiplicity of religious beliefs and practices possible there.

The Kumbha Mela   The largest single religious gathering on earth is not Muslims assembling in Mecca for the Hajj but Hindus congregating for the twelve-year Kumbha Mela at Prayag ("Place of Sacrifice"), the tirtha near modern Allahabad where the Ganges, Yamuna, and invisible Saraswati rivers meet. At the 2001 event, thirty million gathered to bathe at the exact auspicious moment connected with a story in the puranas in which the gods once battled the demons over possession of a pitcher (*kumbha*) containing an immortality-giving elixir. After a long struggle, the gods finally won and became immortal; during the course of the battle, however, four drops of the elixir fell to earth at four places between which the yearly site of the Kumbha Mela shifts in succession. Hundreds of thousands of sadhus emerge from their retreats to immerse themselves in the hyper-divinized river waters, where they are joined by pilgrims seeking the infusion of grace.

KASHI

Kashi, also known as Varanasi or Benares, is arguably the most important center of Hinduism today, whose prominence was recognized as early as the Buddha's lifetime (c. 500 BCE). Located on the western bank of the Ganges and with its riverside *ghats* dominating the urban settlement, Kashi has five *tirthas* where other tributaries join the great river and where pilgrims congregate. Prominent *bhakti* poets and visionaries such as Ravidas, Chaitanya, and Kabir (as we have seen) were associated with the city, and the finest Hindu artisans, musicians, and dancers have lived and performed there. Kashi's narrow lanes lead to over 1,500 temples and countless small shrines dedicated to all the deities of the pantheon. Most are proximate to the river, and there are numerous pilgrim hostels (*dharmashalas*) that serve the thousands of pilgrims who arrive from all over India. Some of the elderly come to the great city to make their "final pilgrimage," death; others come to perform special mourning rites and deposit the cremation ashes of a loved one into the broad Ganges. Brahmin priests and professional guides (*pandas*) thrive there, as they earn their living by serving the pilgrims. Hindu belief is that every religious act done in Kashi is multiplied karmically, meaning that the merit of giving, bathing, fasting even once there, is worth several lifetimes of the same acts done elsewhere. Shiva, called Vishvanath ("Lord of All"), is regarded as the city's chief deity; his *linga* surmounted by a gold-roof temple is the one shrine that all pilgrims will visit and pour Ganges water over.

Pilgrimage in Hinduism is not a requirement of the faith as in Islam, but the benefits are elaborately outlined in the later Hindu texts: healing, good karma, personal transformation. Pilgrims can go alone on foot or in highly organized groups using airplanes and buses. The goal may be to perform a ritual, such as a mortuary rite for a kin member, or the more typical goal of general benefit through darshan and puja. One popular idea about pilgrimage holds that as a pilgrim a householder becomes a "temporary sadhu" who does only life's essential tasks while focusing on spiritual matters, depending on the divine for sustenance.

Pilgrims are expected to bring back prasad for family and friends, for example, Ganges water, flowers from the distant icon, sacred ash (*vibhuti*), or a protective thread. Each major site usually has a resident priesthood and a local text that describes all the shrines and the legends associated with them, including tales of past devotees who won boons through their devotional attentions. By entering into the sacred pilgrimage center to encounter the central and subsidiary deities, the devotee seeks grace through bhakti. Today as yesterday, the Hindu pilgrim joins a temporary community seeking grace and personal transformation from connection with a deity, a sadhu saint, or a teacher.

The Religious Institutions of Contemporary Hinduism

Although there is no single formal institution that unifies all Hindus, there are standard relationships that support the regular practice of ritual and the transmission of religious ideas. Most families have a relationship with a brahmin family priest (*purohita*) whom they call upon when there is the need for a life-cycle rite or when someone wishes to perform a special puja. Some family priests only do rituals; others also give extensive religious instructions. This relationship, one that may go back many generations, is one that the family renews yearly with a special offering to the brahmin *purohita* on the Guru Festival; a stipend (*dakshina*) is also given for each ritual performed.

The predominant religious institution of Hinduism, however, is the temple, and it is thought highly meritorious to build one that houses a living icon. Hindus from all classes, alone or collectively, have done so, with those built by the great kings constructed as the most complete expressions of Hindu religious culture. Yet the major temples are more than shrines: they include lands given to the deity and endowment funds that are continually augmented by the cash offered with puja.

Temple lands are usually rented out to tenant farmers, with part of the harvest going to the temple; other properties adjacent to the temple are often rented to merchants or artisans. Both rentals provide income for the upkeep of the temple buildings and payment for the priests. In the premodern period, slaves and indentured servants were given to great temple deities as well and were bound to farm the lands or keep up the grounds. Smaller temples were often granted the taxes collected from an entire village; larger institutions such as the great temple at Kanchipuram in Tamilnadu, received the taxes from over one thousand villages. Through these relationships, Hindu temples have been integral to the local economies of South Asia, sometimes as the major landowners. Modern land reform has cut back on many of these holdings, forcing temples to find other means of support.

Another widespread institution, the *matha*, or "monastery," is important to the more organized sects and sadhu orders as a venue for schooling and training for ritual service under an abbot (*mahant*). Some modern groups such as the Ramakrishna Mission have built their panregional reform movement through a network of *mathas*.

The *ashram* is a residential retreat center whose lifestyle includes the spiritual activities, especially meditation, study, and devotional practice, that fall under the guidance of a guru. As the institutions dedicated to support teachers and their disciples, ashrams maintain the relationship that is one of the central lifelines of Hindu culture.

Changing Continuities: Examples of Postcolonial Hinduism

Across the Hindu world each day, brahmins memorize, recite, and pass on to their sons the Vedic rituals and hymns, devotional songs composed a half a millennium ago. Ancient rituals are vigorously practiced in millions of households. Increasing numbers of pilgrims flock to the great temples, some consulting their Web sites for guidance.

Although they constitute only 3.5 percent of the population, brahmins remain very influential in postcolonial Hinduism and contemporary India. Across the subcontinent and in global diaspora, they perform many tasks and are "called upon to recite mantras, perform or advise on life-cycle rites, inaugurate a new house, provide horoscopes, sanction marital arrangements, advice on illness, counteract the evil eye, arbitrate disputes, perform accounting, or administer the age-old ritual attention to the images of the household shrine."[18] Brahmin influence in the modern countries India and Nepal has been extraordinary. Most strikingly, while under the British, brahmins had 3 percent of government jobs, today they hold roughly 70 percent of government jobs, and by one estimate about 50 percent of all the elite jobs in the country.[19] For this reason, political and religious reformers, especially those from lower castes, frequently point to the need to end the undue influence of brahmins on national life.

Gurus, the second great figures in Hinduism, continue to attract millions of followers. Ascetic communities in ashrams train in yoga and foster silent meditative retreats. Religious innovations within the Hindu fold have multiplied further through the colonial period and after independence New gurus continue to emerge and gather followers, a source of vitality and innovation that gives Hinduism today the impression of being "a sea of ever-shifting eddies and vortices that catch up individual believers in various aspects of their devotional lives."[20] A 1986 gathering of nearly one thousand abbots of Hindu monasteries, one of the first ever held, assembled teachers representing 165 different organized spiritual traditions.

Yet modern medicine, mass media, and expanding transportation technology have changed how millions of Hindus understand and encounter venerable Hindu doctrines and myths, and how they perform the rituals. Within major Indian cities today, an increasing middle class of diverse origins is emerging, whose lifestyle and experience have been highly influenced by Euro-American media culture, education, and connections. Institutions and "Yoga Centers" among this elite are developing newly synthesized approaches to Hindu spiritual practices, in forms similar to those found in European and American cities. The global spread of Hinduism now impacts the faith back in South Asia. Audiotapes and videos with sermons by gurus reach the middle class, affording traditional doctrinal teachings far wider exposure than was ever possible by word of mouth.

Thus, Hinduism has assumed more forms today than ever in its history, and the linkage of religion to politics is growing. Since there is no one version or center of Hinduism that can stand alone for the entire era, we will draw upon a series of representative case studies to suggest the broad sweep of Hinduism in the postcolonial era. First cited will be the modernizers; second, those who have *not* been influenced by science; finally there are those who are articulating Hindu nationalism, a change that would end the postindependence character of India as a secular state.

Some teachers and movements begun in the modern era (such as the Ramakrishna Mission) make strong assertions about the compatibility between scientific thought and venerable Hindu doctrines. The "big bang" hypothesis of creation, relativity theory, and the cosmological theories of multiple universes are referred to by these modernizers as congruent with or anticipated in the ancient scriptures. Hindu exponents have also proposed scientific explanations for rebirth and karma doctrines. Even the Veda has been interpreted to credit the seers with awareness of contemporary technological possibilities (e.g., airplanes, genetics, brain waves). Hindu confidence that the venerable teachings will stand up to whatever science discovers is striking among modernists. Just as many scientists around the world (including many in India) refrain from suggesting that their discoveries are ever likely to disprove the existence of God or the reality of spirit, many educated Hindus have found no reason to abandon the essentials of their faith. Those with technological savvy have been energetic to express their articles of faith on the World Wide Web, and by 2007 almost ten thousand Web sites were dedicated to the many sides of Hinduism. A sample of recent events and developments gives an indication of how Hinduism has endured so strongly among such modernists.

Ganesh's Milk Miracle

A deity who attracts the devotion of nearly all Hindus is elephant-headed Ganesh, divine son of Shiva and Parvati. Ganesh is beloved for his earthy character, his pot-bellied appetite, and his reputation as a remover of life's obstacles. Ganesh temples are found in nearly every locale where Hindus live. On September 21, 1995, at temples across North India, priests and devotees reported that icons of Ganesh had begun to "drink" the cows' milk that was being offered to them as part of the daily puja. Word of this "miracle" soon spread across the subcontinent through telephone and press accounts, so that thousands of Hindus from all walks of life rushed off to visit their local temples to offer milk and to participate in the phenomenon. Telephone and the Internet just as quickly spread the news across the globe so that Hindus in London, Jersey City, Los Angeles, and Toronto confirmed it.

For believers, this event was merely the latest in a long-running series of demonstrations that the divine is alive, connected to humanity and capable of conferring grace upon those who serve the gods. From uneducated peasants to brahmin priests, people were citing the event as ample proof of the existence of a Supreme Being who accepts the offerings of his disciples. Whatever else this incident reveals about the role of media and the Hindu diaspora, it also demonstrates that modern believers hold the conviction that the divine is immanent, a traditional view that has shifted little amidst all the changes wrought from the modern era.

The reaction was interesting, too: the "miracle" gave rise to widespread public debate and rallies organized by Hindu societies (such as New Delhi's "Guru Busters") whose purpose is to expose charlatans and promote rational faith. Predecessors for these modern agnostics and atheists can be traced as far back as the time of the Buddha (5th century BCE). Although the popular Western imagination about India and Hinduism has been informed by romantic accounts highlighting mysticism and exotic theistic spirituality, it is important to note that there is an equally long-established South Asian tradition of hard-nosed skepticism.

Comic Books and Televised Epics

The modern printing press gave early Hindu reformers a means by which they could reach a mass audience across the subcontinent more quickly than ever before. Ritual manuals, vernacular translations of texts, tracts on saints, interreligious debates, or even reformers' reductive definitions of "true Hinduism" (such as that proposed by the Arya Samaj or modern fundamentalists) reach the literate masses through such publications. South Asia's religious environment during the modern era has also been unified by the lithography of religious poster art that has spread common inexpensive images of the deities.

An important mass media format appearing well after the end of colonialism is the religious comic book. Adopting reformist doctrines and linking far-flung Hindu communities is the Amar Citra Katha series of over two hundred titles, in which newly standardized versions of the great stories of Hindu scripture are offered in colorful illustrated formats, the text written in English and in various vernaculars. Under the editorship of Anant Pai, more than 280 million copies of Amar Citra Katha texts have been sold. These have emphasized for middle-class readers that "true Hinduism" is rational, opposed to violence and superstition, upheld by heroic devotees, and based upon the respectful accommodation of other spiritualities (Hindu and non-Hindu) in the interest of national integration.

Television broadcasts of religious epics have also been pivotal cultural events. In 1987, India's national broadcasting system Doordarshan began showing in weekly installments its Hindi version of the *Ramayana*, one of the two great religious epics that date back to the early classical era. Although most Indians do not own televisions, groups crowded in to tea houses or banded together to rent TVs and view the series. Many treated the experience of viewing the transmitted image as like a visit to a temple. Bathing beforehand, they arrived carrying incense and garlanded the television sets. Some watched with their hands joined together, using the namaste gesture directed to the divinities on screen, and some muttered prayers as they viewed the sacred scenes unfolding weekly for over a year.

An estimated audience of eighty million watched the weekly one-hour Sunday morning program, and the pace of life on India's streets visibly slowed.

The media's *Ramayana* gave the nation its first "national version" of the epic, one that celebrates the glories of the legendary Hindu king Rama and how he struggled to establish a just and prosperous Hindu nation. Doordarshan had to extend the series due to popular demand. It subsequently produced and broadcast since then an even longer series on Hinduism's other great epic, the *Mahabharata,* as well as dramatizations of other devotional stories centered on the great deities such as Krishna and Shiva.

The accessibility of TV productions of religious epics, lavishly produced, complete with special effects, has in places undercut the relation between priest, teacher, and laity. Many argue that the cause of Hindu nationalism has been strengthened by the common experience of viewing these sacred scenes.

The Dilemmas of Reform: A Young Bride Commits Sati in 1987

Following Hindu traditions, Roop Kanwar, an 18-year-old bride, went to live with her husband's family in Deorala, in the western Indian state of Rajastan. But seven months later, on September 4, 1987, her husband Mal Singh died suddenly. Following ancient custom, his kin prepared to cremate him on a pyre outside the town boundaries immediately before sunset. What happened next shocked India: Roop Kanwar was burnt alive atop her husband's funeral pyre, becoming a *sati* ("Virtuous [one]"), one of forty-two known cases since 1947. Five hundred people reportedly witnessed the act. What remains unclear were the widow's motivations and how freely she went to this death.

Rajastan state officials were called to act on the basis of India's National Penal Code that holds widow immolation under any circumstances to be illegal. Reformers argued that those connected with Roop Kanwar's death should be prosecuted as murderers. Eventually, under pressure from national politicians and womens' groups, members of Mal Singh's immediate family were arrested and an investigation ensued. Several months later they were released on bail, but no charges were ever filed. Few witnesses could be found who were willing to testify.

Sati is one of the few Hindu practices that the British had sought to reform through explicit legal prohibition. The immolation of widows was held up for ridicule by many Hindu modernizers as evidence of how Indian society needed to break with blindly followed traditions and to reform its ways. Yet in 1987, over fifty thousand devotees gathered for a commemorative ceremony for Roop Kanwar held thirteen days after her death. The site where the pyre burned has been transformed into a shrine, outside of which artisans sell ritual photos of the site and other mementos. Since 1987, the Singh family has received many thousands of rupees from donations. Throughout the town, the young widow is now celebrated by drummers and chanting youth as a brave *Sati-ma,* a divine figure who was blessed by and merged with the mother goddess, Devi. This act put Roop Kanwar, her husband's family, and Deorala in the tradition of devout adherents; as a Sati-ma, she became identified with part of the Hindu pantheon, a righteous suicide like the divine goddesses Sita and Savitri.

All India became caught up in the debate about whether this was truly a voluntary act, as the Singh family maintains, or whether murder was concealed under the veil of religion. Should the role of the secular state be to regulate this religious practice? As reformers urged, should the state enforce its legal code that defines sati as barbaric and prohibits this custom? Or as Hindu traditionalists insisted—and many in this camp were local citizens and state politicians—should the state respect freedom of religion and allow Hindus to follow whatever path they choose to seek salvation?

The Spiritual Marketplace for Neotraditionalism: Popular Guru-based Movements

Most conspicuous over the last decades has been the rise of cults and sects catering to the urban middle class. What is it like to live in the urban middle class today in South Asia? It involves confronting conflicting claims on one's identity and loyalty, as loyalty to one's "primordial" allegiances (caste, kin, region) clash with the cosmopolitan and socially fluid urban culture that aspires to "being modern" and part of the global culture of CNN, the Internet, and designer clothing. Traditional ties need to be honored at some level, but they no longer can fully contain the individual's deepest feelings of belonging.

Focused on holy men and drawing inspiration from the reformists and revivalists of the nineteenth century, most of the new sects that have attracted the support of this new elite have proclaimed their own view of "essential Hinduism" as belief oriented and not ritualistic. Just as modern technology has undercut to some extent the roles of priest and guru, the new sects have diminished the relevance of caste and regional social identity as relevant to spiritual seeking. Several utilize mass media to promote the teacher's message and link distant communities. A number of the new sects have quickly built an international membership. In some cases they have benefited from praise and support for Hindu gurus active abroad, which has whetted an appetite for their teachings back home in South Asia. Most also emphasize women's participation. Many foster spiritual individuality and encourage the lay members to lessen their dependence on a priestly or monastic elite. Many of these neotraditional groups use modern media to propagate their basic beliefs and practices. All engage their society and include community development, medical service, and educational initiatives, combining various traditional Hindu doctrines and practices with certain tactics adopted from Protestant missionaries.

We highlight next a famous guru and a prominent group that are especially active at the turn of the millennium. Each blends the rich possibilities of Hindu devotional culture with the organizational forms and technologies drawn from religious communities across the globe.

Sathya Sai Baba No modern Hindu saint has drawn devotees from as far and wide across India's urban middle classes as Sathya Sai Baba, a teacher known as much for the miraculous feats credited to him as for his instruction. A vigorous opponent of Western cultural influences on Hindu civilization and individual Hindus, Sai Baba advocates an active life informed by scriptural study and charitable giving; he teaches a form of classical silent meditation involving fixing one's gaze on a flame.

Sai Baba's trusts have established a vast network of service organizations: there are junior and senior Service Corps that feed the poor, act when disaster strikes, visit the sick, and so on. There are at present four Sai Baba colleges (three for women, one for men) that include educational outreach programs aimed to help small children.

Sai Baba's fame and stature is based on accounts of his supernormal feats of multiple presence, miracle cures, and materializing of items out of the air, including sacred ash, food, books, and even Swiss watches. Devotees see these powers of the traditional yogin saint as evidence that Sai Baba is an avatara of a divinity. Indeed, he has said that he is Shiva and his consort Shakti in a single body. The cult center uses Shiva iconography and identifies the ash he "manifests" as marking grace from Shiva. For devotees, the guru imparts a "Sai Outlook" of positive confidence toward the world and life's possibilities. (Accordingly, disciples are encouraged to place Sai Baba's picture on the home shrine for regular darshan.) Through Sai Baba, disciples can see one of the perennial themes nurtured in the myriad South Asian traditions: that the divine is alive and appears in human form, and that this world is still enchanted with grace.

Brahma Kumaris In India today, the most ardent sectarian proselytizers (especially across the northern states) are from the group called Brahma Kumaris. Their Raja Yoga centers, also called "Spiritual Museums," are the organizing points around which each local chapter draws interested individuals and publicity, primarily among urban dwellers. The museums' displays of doctrine-oriented pictures provide a common text, with a member providing commentary; those who show interest are invited to attend meditation sessions and classes. In 1997, these institutions were being maintained by eight thousand fully "surrendered" full-time priests.

This is another group that stems from a charismatic teacher. The visions and spiritual experiences of the founding guru Lekhraj (1876–1969), a jeweler from Hyderabad, inspired an early following. In 1936 he established the Brahma Kumari sect and turned his entire wealth over to the first community.

Lekhraj attributed his vibrant visions portending the end of the world cycle to the grace of Shiva (the deity who commands the group's ritual attention). He also insisted that individuals need to engage in radical purifications to survive and inherit paradise. Such cleansing could come only through celibacy, vegetarianism, abstinence from tobacco and alcohol, and specific yoga practices. These traditional disciplines became the core practices of the Brahma Kumaris. The vow of celibacy, long an ideal for Hindu ascetics, is extended to all householders. As a result, housewives and their husbands who become disciples have to transform their marital relations to expressions of pure, noncarnal spiritual love. This teaching created serious domestic strife in the early community, forcing Lekhraj and his initially small circle of devotees to move to Karachi and later, after partition (1947), to Mount Abu in western India. Once there, the movement was transformed from a reclusive sect to an aggressively outgoing one. Soon missionaries had established centers across the major North Indian cities. Suspicion endures to the present over the group's claims of celibacy, and some have accused the Brahma Kumaris of providing refuge for women who abandon their husband's households.

Although its bhakti doctrines and cosmology could be characterized as drawn from premodern Hinduism, Brahma Kumari social practices are reformist. Although founded by a man and admitting men as members, the sect from the outset has focused on women. Brahma Kumari doctrines and practices challenge Hindu society's patriarchal doctrines and ethical norms; it invites women to awaken to their divinity through a feminist reading of the powers of traditional Hindu goddesses. In recent years, the Brahma Kumaris have won recognition from India's leading politicians for supporting the establishment of a "value-based society," as members work with U.N. agencies on educational projects across South Asia. In the last decade, the Brahma Kumaris have claimed status as an independent religion, rejecting the label of "Hindu." In 1997, the group counted membership at 500,000, with four thousand centers that are found mostly in India; there were also Brahma Kumari centers in sixty other countries.

Pandurang Shastri Athavale and the Swadhyaya *("Truth Seekers")*   Son of a brahmin scholar and educated both in the traditional style as well as in modern subjects, Pandurang Athavale (born in 1920) grew up in a family that was active in movements sponsored by the great Hindu reformer Mahatma Gandhi. In 1956, he began organizing Gandhi-inspired social uplift programs for the poorest low-caste groups, drawing as well upon a modernist reading of Hinduism's great spiritual classic, the *Bhagavad Gita.*

Living modestly as a householder, meditating and worshipping the Hindu gods daily, yet accepting no donations for himself, Athavale prefers to be called *Dadaji* ("Elder Brother"), resisting the usual trappings of the title "guru." His social programs have reached an estimated twenty million people living in 100,000 villages. The scope of this movement is due to the practice of *bhak-tipheri* ("devotional visits") in which he or his followers spread the message of human service to new communities. His message is simple:

> It is my experience that awareness of the nearness of God and reverence for that power creates reverence for self, reverence for the other, reverence for nature and reverence for the entire creation. And devotion as an expression of gratitude for God can turn into a social force to bring about transformative changes at all levels in the society.[21]

Acting on this conviction, Swadhyaya members facilitate settlements to build new temples that are ecumencial, open to all, and community centers for cooperative activities. There is little concern for regulating the cult beyond the conviction that some form of devotion is essential; choice of the divinity is likewise left to the individual. The Swadhyaya also does not collect donations, but only requests that individuals respond from their hearts and serve their communities as they wish. Athavale has thus inspired fisher folk and farmers to work a few days each year to produce foods for the needy. Swadhyaya volunteers have set up dairies and orchards for this purpose as well. The group's Women's Centers and Children's Ceters promote education, economic advancement, and spiritual development. There are also educational centers offering two-year courses on the Veda and comparative religion.

The group has been especially savvy in its use of media, ancient and modern. Specially composed songs reveal both the practical and spiritual aspects of the work at hand. The organization has produced very professional viedotapes showing teachers lecturing and experts coordinating training for uplift programs. Video and audio media link the dispersed followers with Athavale, and they provide a common and consistent series of messages that span the subcontinent... and beyond. Indeed, Swadhyaya has become a worldwide movement, with 350 centers in America. The magnitude of the work and the authentic spirituality of the movement was the reason Athavale was awarded the 1997 Templeton Prize, the "Nobel Prize" for excellence in religious pursuits.

Religious Nationalism: Secular India and Its Discontents

We recounted earlier how India's anticolonial nationalist leaders, many of whom were educated in England, remained unalterably committed to creating modern India as a secular democracy. Surely knowing the history of religious strife in Europe that led to the formation of most modern Western nations, they foresaw endless problems among the complex and competing religious communities in India if any form of favoritism were shown. Although most of the early political leaders were high-caste Hindus, they feared what civil and partisan strife the Hindu majority might bring to the subcontinent. In the end, they succeeded, with British help, in marginalizing groups such as the RSS that wanted to establish India as a Hindu nation.

Yet in a curious and paradoxical development, and despite the state's administration being heavily skewed toward their interests, high-caste politicians have been successful at convincing growing numbers of citizens that Hindus have been discriminated against by the laws and policies of secular India. As noted at the beginning of this chapter, the BJP throughout the 1990s promised to establish a strong Hindu nation and won state and national elections.

The first year-long national BJP government (1998–1999) led India to explode its first atomic bomb and encouraged rhetoric by Hindu leaders criticizing the patriotism of Indian Christians. There have been incidents across the nation in which Hindu terrorists have burned down churches and murdered Christians.

The BJP and its high-caste supporters also campaign to reverse the secular state's successful efforts to promote low castes and introduce democratic elections into India's villages. Recently, in regions where dominant and rich land-holding, high-caste elites control most local politics, lower castes have mobilized, using their great demographic plurality, to elect their own members, including many women, to become village council leaders. As we have seen, this is an inversion of ancient Hindu caste law norms and karma theory. During the first months of BJP rule, high-caste–led massacres in lower caste settlements were reported across North India; in most cases investigated, these were found to represent efforts to intimidate groups that had voted against high caste candidates or had sought state intervention to enforce lower caste rights. Will such incidents of communal violence, like earlier attacks directed against Muslims and mosques, convince the Indian electorate that the imposition of a Hindu state portends a descent into chaos and national disintegration?

The VHP: Hindu Leaders in Search of a Religious Nation

Linked to the RSS and the Bharatiya Janata party, the Vishva Hindu Parishad ("The Council of All Hindus") was founded in 1964 as an organization of religious leaders who, while still retaining their own disciples and spiritual agendas, wished to promote the interests of Hindus and a general kind of spiritual Hinduism. In agreement with earlier reformers and actually internalizing some of the criticisms made by European colonialists, the VHP accepts the decline of Hinduism as fact, seeks the roots of the faith in the earliest texts, considers the *Bhagavad Gita* to be Hinduism's preeminent scripture, and seeks to promote among the popular gurus.

Although we have spoken of the lack of a central institution as a characteristic of Hinduism, one measure of the VHP's rise is its increasing success at securing unity among hitherto fiercely independent spiritual leaders. Projects undertaken in common include religiopolitical festivals, missionary projects in tribal areas (including campaigns to "reconvert" some back from Christianity or Islam), and uplift initiatives among the "untouchable" castes. Critics have noted that such VHP efforts serve to add to the number the group can count as members of the "Hindu majority" in the state of India. But VHP supporters point out that uplift projects among the "untouchables" act on Gandhi's exhortation of Hindus to work to end the "evils of caste society."

VHP outreach also extends to Hindus worldwide. It now has centers in twenty-five countries and has sponsored periodic "World Hindu Conventions" since 1966. Its "success-oriented" interpretation of Hindu belief and practice helps to explain why the rising middle class (at home and abroad) is the core group of its supporters.

The VHP argues that the era before Muslim rule (1200 CE) was a golden age for Hinduism, a time when there was social egalitarianism, prosperity, just rulers, and a wealth of enlightened seers. But with the Muslim conquest and such actions as the razing of temples to build mosques, Hindu culture

A CALL FOR UNITY AMONG
HINDU GURUS

The greatest curse of Hinduism throughout the ages has been it disunity—and more than that—its betraying each other. The British did not conquer India, it was given to them by warring Hindu princes, jealous of each other. I know there is something mysterious and unfathomable in the manifestation of the Divine upon earth, and that each guru has a defined task to fulfill and that the combined task of all the gurus may solve the great puzzle that is this ignorant and sufftering earth. Thus, it may not be necessary for each guru to communicate with each other. But nevertheless, it is of the greatest urgency today that Hindu leaders unite to save Hinduism, rather than "each one for his own" that we see today.

The Catholics have their Pope and his word is binding on all Catholics. Muslims have Prophet Mohammed's words and that binds all of Islam together. Indian Communists have the words of Marx and Lenin, even if it has become irrelevant in Russia, Germany, and also in China. But the poor Hindus have nobody to refer to, so as to defend themselves.

Yet, if you take the combined people power of Satya Sai Baba, Amritaanandamayi, Sri Sri Ravi Shankar, Swami Ramdev, Guruma of Ganeshpuri, the Shankaracharya of Kanchipuram, and so many others I cannot mention here, it runs in hundreds of millions. I propose that a Supreme Spiritual Council, composed of at least seven of the most popular Hindu leaders of India, be constituted...It should be a non-political body, and each group would keep its independence but nevertheless it could meet two three times a year and issue edicts, which would be binding on the 850 million Hindus in India and one billion over the world.[22]

declined; subsequent British domination of India made matters worse, causing further stagnation and division among all groups. The VHP views the secular state of India created at independence as a further means of dividing Hindus and thwarting the establishment of a great civilization centered on "Vedic spirituality." It further argues that if this secularism can be overthrown, and with it a mindset of inferiority induced during the colonial period, a golden age can be restored. Such VHP views represent a continuation of reform thought originating with nineteenth-century activists such as the Arya Samaj and Vivekananda.

VHP leaders have also embraced traditional rituals shared widely by Hindus, very creatively redesigning them to express their causes: Hindu unity, martial strength, the sacrality of the "motherland." Beginning in 1983, a series of nation-spanning pilgrimage processions (*yatra*) were orchestrated. Involving millions of participants, different groups converged on RSS headquarters in Nagpur, in central India, for its carefully choreographed final rites. Processions beginning from distant cardinal points were led by new trucks decorated to resemble the chariot used by Arjuna, warrior hero of the *Bhagavad Gita*. Each also carried an image of "Mother India" and sacred water vessels containing Ganges water.

Cow veneration and protection are another VHP theme, with leaders drawing on classical religious views on the bovine sacrality. The treatment of cows is an emotional issue used to demonstrate how the secular state continues to disrespect cows (allowing slaughter), just as the British did, while also serving as an issue to instigate anti-Muslim feelings (since they work as butchers and eat beef).

In similar fashion, the VHP has voiced support for dismantling any mosques that were (in their historical determination) built over Hindu temples in centuries past. The destruction of the mosque in Ayodhya in 1992 attracted attention to the group and support from ultranationalists, as did the VHP's marketing scheme to raise funds by selling bricks for the construction of the new Hindu temple planned for the site. The VHP leaders have expressed their plans to destroy other Muslim shrines as well in Benares and Mathura.

Through its campaigns, the VHP has sought to establish popular identification with its views of history, unity, sacred geography, and destiny. The success of the BJP in the national elections demonstrates that support for secular India is being eroded by the rising tide of Hindu nationalism.

Sikh Separatism and Globalization

Because the British invested heavily in irrigation and infrastructure in the Punjab, by the postcolonial era the Sikh home territory had become one of the most productive agricultural regions of India. Already dominant in the region, Sikhs became one of the wealthiest ethnic groups in postcolonial India.

Following up on agitations aimed to win British support for allowing Sikhs (not brahmins) to administer their own temples (dating back to 1925), the community had established a reformist modern ecclesiastical organization, the Shiromani Gurudwara Pradandhak Committee. This body acted in consort with the Akal Takht, the group whose leaders manage the Sikh Golden Temple in Amritsar, the crown jewel of their culture.

Despite Sikh prosperity, radical leaders in the 1980s revived a preindependence demand for a Sikh homeland in Punjab, following the logic that had led to the creation of Pakistan as the homeland for South Asian Muslims. Guerrillas tried to transform this region into a de facto separate state they called Khalistan, extorting contributions they identified as "taxes" from Sikh farmers and merchants while randomly murdering Hindus living there. The movement had support in the Akal Takht and was funded as well by contributions from Sikhs abroad. In 1984, after armed secessionist leaders occupied the Golden Temple in Amritsar, the Indian government sent troops to invade this shrine, killing many and declaring martial law in Punjab. This sacrilege led two Sikh bodyguards to assassinate Prime Minister Indira Gandhi later that same year, causing many episodes of anti-Sikh rioting and antistate terrorist attacks in Delhi and other large cities. Over three thousand Hindus died in 1987 and 1988. By the turn of the millennium, the separatist agitation had largely dissipated as moderate Sikhs came back into power in national politics and international support for an independent state declined.

Through the last decades of the century, the Sikh global migration continued, and now almost 10 percent of Sikhs live outside of India. With over twenty million followers worldwide, including a growing number of Western converts, Sikhism is slowly being recognized for its distinctive spiritual development and as the youngest of the three great heterodox faiths that originated in India.

CONCLUSION

Recalling the initial caution about taking any religious tradition as standing for all of "Hinduism," we can only generalize about the broad patterns of change affecting the religion in South Asia. There is no doubt that India is changing in the manner that other parts of postcolonial Asia are. Newly built roads, transport, education, mass media, and industrialization are developing the economic system of the country, drawing migrants from rural settlements to burgeoning urban areas and transforming the life experiences of individuals. In these settings, the Hindu traditions of the premodern world decline as new institutions and teachers arise to meet the needs of those living under these new circumstances.

But even with so much change, the belief in the spiritual presence of the gods, in yoga, in the guru-centered spiritual life, remain strikingly strong. It is easy to be misled by surface changes to overestimate religious change: do cement buildings replacing cut stone temples or electric lights replacing the butter lamps set out in the Diwali festival represent Westernization and the decline of traditional values? . . . or simply the transposition of new technologies in the service of the centuries-old wish to please the divine with artful decoration?

In the cities, among the rapidly expanding middle class as well as among slum dwellers, there are numerous new incarnations of "organized Hinduisms." Hitherto independent groups such as sadhus from different regions have formed new organizations to work for common interests. Likewise, laity and priests associated with major temples have pressed for the establishing of management committees to orchestrate rituals and festivals as well as for supervising temple accounts.

Thus, what in rural India was a largely preordained relationship with a family priest and local guru, in urban settings has become a matter of individual choice. Hindus in ever-increasing numbers, then, are faced with the "heretical imperative" (as discussed in Chapter 1) of making their own choices about their own religious paths. There are now media-savvy gurus who appear on television, use video recordings and Web sites to link far-flung communities, and draw upon a global network of disciples to build their movements. One of the most popular English-language magazines dedicated to promoting reformist Hinduism in India and abroad (*Hinduism Today*) is now published in Hawaii.

A Growing Global Tradition

Hinduism has entered into Western awareness strongly. As we will also see in the case of Buddhism, this interest is selective, centered on yoga and meditation, with much less focus on ritual. Many Westerners have been trained as yoga teachers by Indian masters, and nearly every major American city and college town has centers where one can go to practice. For many, of course, this interest is confined to the athletic or health benefits, with the religious beliefs underlying the practices often downplayed or tailored to fit into the person's existing belief system. To see the panoply of traditions and applications of yoga in the West, one need only pick up a copy of *Yoga Journal*, a magazine that in 2007 counted over 350,000 subscribers and reported that ten million Americans now practice yoga.

The ubiquitous Indian diaspora is increasingly important in this Hindu globalization process. First and second generations of Hindus settled in the United States are the nation's richest ethnic group in terms of per capita income, and their affluence has enabled them to support the internationalization of the faith. For example, the Hindus of the greater Boston area have organized and collected several million dollars to build a large South Indian-style temple in Ashland, Massachusetts. They hired artisans from Chennai and had the chief icons made to order; they also created an endowment that pays for the lodging and full-time employment of two brahmin priests, who are recruited for long-term assignments to serve patrons of the temple. Similar institutions exist in Austin, Texas, Los Angeles, and elsewhere. Temples also are the natural centers for cultural awareness and revitalization movements among immigrant Hindus. For example, the Arya Samaj of North America regularly sponsors conferences in Hindu temples which seeks to "empower the next generation with Vedic values" by having youth "practice those values in daily life, maintain a linguistic link to Sanskrit,...inculcate a spirit of humility, give back to the community," and live by the founding motto, *Krivanto vishvam arya* ("Make this world noble").[23]

Converts and immigrant groups also have supported the global tours of notable Indian gurus. In the West there are over a dozen Indian teachers, in fact, who have shifted their own lives to ashrams dedicated primarily to Westerners who have converted to Hinduism. Perhaps the most successful of these gurus is the *sadhu* Maharishi Mahesh Yogi, who in the 1960s came to

GLOBAL HINDUISM: TM

For the past fifty years, Maharishi Mahesh Yogi has brought mystical Hindu teachings to the West. Having introduced mantra-centered meditation to over six million seekers across the world, each of whom paid for the initiation (in 2006: $2,500), Maharishi's TM has established yoga centers around the world and founded a Vedic University in Fairfield, Iowa. TM now seeks to implement the guru's vision of rebuilding the world's spirituality and healing humanity according to his interpretation of Vedic principles combined with the principles of quantum physics. With assets of $300 million in the United States, the group focuses on (1) training advanced yogis in forty countries whose levitations can "produce quantum shifts to heal humanity's overstressed minds," coordinating sessions across the globe in which mediators numbering the square root of the world's population (eight thousand, according to Maharishi's theory) will positively alter the planet's atomosphere and so the planet's humane consciousness; and (2) building three thousand "marble peace palaces" in major cities to offset the disharmonious locations. Having turned eighty-nine in 2006 and living in an ashram in the Netherlands, Maharishi expressed his aim: "My coherence-creating groups are going to put out all this mischief-mongering in the world. The world is going to come out to be a neat and clean world. All these countries will fade away."[24]

prominence by giving spiritual instruction to the Beatles. His movement, Transcendental Meditation (T.M.), has taken Hindu tradition across the globe and inspired utopian initiatives.

Funds from Indian devotees in the West and Westerners who take teachings from touring gurus have also helped support the institutions run by these teachers back in India. Overseas Indians have been strong supporters of religious nationalism among the Sikhs and as advocated by the VHP. Hindu nationalists have spread their activism in the America as well, establishing summer camps for youth, raising funds for causes back in India, and even seeking to have public school textbooks in California rewritten to conform to their ideological interpretations.

Older Hindu institutions and new movements have adopted the Internet technology. For example, a famous Ganesh temple in Bombay has set up a World Wide Web site in which viewers can have live darshan of the main icons, hear hymns being sung, and with a few additional mouse clicks, make credit card contributions to sponsor pujas. A Vishnu shrine in the northern state of Jammu offers similar scenes and services, adding maps, regularly updated

weather reports, and hostel bookings to aid the estimated four million pilgrims who visit the temple annually.

As Indian workers and entrepreneurs have become important in the global economy, especially in the computer and software industry, observers have discerned the rise of "karma capitalism." Here we can recognize Hindu teachings exerting a new and powerful influence in the global marketplace. Indian philosophies have been integrated in elite business schools in a variety of ways: "self-mastery" courses that now help to train managers "to boost their leadership skills and find inner peace in lives dominated by work;" Hindu "business gurus" like C. K. Prahalad now teach that executives should conceive of companies in more holistic ways, to redefine success as larger than monetary profit, including the well-being of employees, customers, and the environment. Classical Hindu teachings have now become a creative influence on the culture of modern business, with many now explicitly managing their enterprises to generate "good karma."[25]

The Fate of the Ganges: A Test Case Regarding the Power of Hindu Reform

In addition to relying on belief to measure the future of Hinduism, one might propose examining what Hindu reformers collectively are *doing*. One case study would be the Ganges River, which flows from the slopes of the Himalayas into the highlands through sites associated with all the great gods. The Ganges has a central place in the Hindu religious imagination, with every confluence with a tributary considered a sacred site. Texts describe the Ganges as a gift from the gods to humanity and symbolize it by a goddess; in practice, its holy waters remove bad karma and receive the ashes of one's dead kin. In addition, this great river flows through the most densely populated states of India, from which countless farmers draw water directly to irrigate their fields and grow the food that feeds over five hundred million people.

Yet, as elsewhere in the world where industrial development has proceeded, people have used the river as a sewer and dumping place for factory wastes. The Ganges has been increasingly polluted over the last several decades, with dangerous water toxicity and pollutant levels recorded in many sections. In 1985, with great fanfare, a coalition of religious and political leaders announced a campaign to restore the purity of the Ganges, with a multimillion dollar budget and international support. Here is the powerful convergence of spiritual need and ecological necessity, with the moral goal of protecting the health of millions.

Yet over twenty years later, most of the planned water filtration plants have not been completed, funds have been misspent, and raw sewerage and untreated wastes still flow directly into the river from most cities. If anything, the Ganges has gotten worse as new industries have added their discharges to the flow. So pernicious has this problem become that at the end of the great Kumbha Mela in 2007, thousands of Hindu holy men staged two days of protest, threatening to lead others to boycott the festival unless the government immediately began corrective actions to clean up the river.

The Connection of Religion with Social Reform

The impact of Christianity on Hinduism, as we noted earlier, was not primarily doctrinal but more in the arena of modeling the role of modern religious institutions and the scope of religious service in society. Just as the missionary Christians had shown that churches could be linked with schools and hospitals, most Hindu reformers (e.g., the Ramakrishna Mission and Sai Baba) who have begun spiritual movements almost without exception include social welfare initiatives to address the nation's undeniable needs. Initially, perhaps, this was done in competition with the Western missionaries; but the idea also found support from Hindu theologies promoting the spiritual power of selfless compassionate service and exhorting individuals to engage in humanitarian works.

As a result, most Hindu *mathas* (monasteries) have started educational institutions and many, like the Ramakrishna Mission, continue to expand their network of clinics and hospitals staffed by their own trained monks. Hindu gurus cite a variety of reasons for the motivation that mathas now display for social work. A swami influential in the early VHP remarked long ago that the Indian people required inspiration from leaders who do not merely retreat to caves and meditate. Likewise, the leader of one of India's largest monasteries described his work in education as necessary to make democracy a success. Another prominent swami, while acknowledging a desire to serve the people and foster humanitarianism, admits that his monastic order engages in social work primarily to dispel the impression that only other religions do it.

As middle-class South Asians have raised their educational level, experienced rising prosperity, and encountered religions and societies elsewhere, they have been inevitably forced to consider "Hinduism" in global comparison. This process was very poignant in the summer of 1997, when the Indian elite was drawn into thinking about where their nation had traveled in the fifty years since independence and how they now measured up against both their earlier expectations and in comparison with the other great nation founded at roughly the same time, China. The widespread opinion expressed in the popular press was that while democracy was treasured and never to be surrendered, there was also the hard truth to be faced that Hindu culture and religion have failed to transform Indian society in many of the positive ways evident in contemporary China. How could caste discrimination endure? How could India's extreme poverty be tolerated among the masses while the rich get richer? How could the nation's leaders, drawn largely from the high castes, accept these failures? While no uniform answer emerged, and while not only religion was blamed, the frequent and often intense debates that swirled through that year signaled support for the view that Hinduism is part of the problem and needs reform. One representative example of this self-scrutiny, by the Nepali social critic Dipak Gyawali, incorporates many of the issues discussed above, perhaps foreshadowing the direction of future change:

> In the social field, several things need to be done. The first is that modern Hindus need to rediscover the origins and rationale of Hinduism and its rituals because they are as ignorant as anyone. This is probably easier to do for a modernist Hindu because Hindu literature is now more readily available in English than in native languages or in incomprehensible Sanskrit. The second is that modern Hindus need to reject the archaic, the irrational, and the inefficient to make living a Hindu life less full of contradictions. The third is that they need to redefine the religion's core in a manner that is not exclusive but allows non-Hindu neighbors to participate as well. Finally, and most important, there is a need to reassert moral outrage rather than escape into flaccid tolerance whenever justice is being denied.[26]

Among the many voices of Hinduism today, those advocating against secularism and for reform have garnered unprecedented political power. Their daunting task in India is to demonstrate how Hindu values, beliefs, and conscience can serve the needs of all its now one billion citizens.

DISCUSSION QUESTIONS

1. What reasons might be ascertained for the transformation of the polytheism of the early Vedic peoples into the monism and theism of later Hinduism?

2. Why would the lowest castes regard the doctrines of karma, caste, and duty as a system designed to subjugate them?

3. What reasons would a woman have for abiding by her dharma?

4. To what extent can karma theory be considered a doctrine of fatalism? Do humans still have freedom of action?

5. If you were an Islamic judge in medieval India, how would you advise the local sultan who asks if his subjects who follow

Krishna (as depicted in the *Bhagavad Gita*) are in fact monotheists?

6. What are the strengths and weaknesses of the Hindu tradition due to the fact that no religious group ever acquired the power to define what was true doctrine and what was heresy?

7. How does ritualism relate to the ideals of bhakti Hinduism?

8. Why was the influence of colonialism on the religions of India powerfully conveyed as "Protestant Hinduism"?

9. What reasons are Hindu nationalists giving to support their view of secularism as being the perpetuation of colonialism

and a betrayal of the great modern Hindu reformers?

10. Explain why Mahatma Gandhi's biography contains a paradigmatic study of the factors shaping modern Hindu reform.

11. Critique the following statement, coming from an ecumenical Hindu organization: "We can follow Jesus without

contradiction, for he is none other than another *avatara* of Lord Vishnu."

12. What does it say about the power of ideas regarding the sacred versus the power of profane modern economic interests that Hindu leaders and politicians have been unable to reverse the trend of their most sacred Ganges becoming a nearly dead and toxic river?

KEY TERMS

ahimsa	*Kali Yuga*	*saguna Brahman*
atman	*karma*	*samsara*
avatara	*moksha*	*satyagraha*
Bhagavad Gita	nirguna Brahman	*shankara*
bhakti	puja	*tantra*
BJP	*puranas*	*Upanishad*
Brahman	Ramakrishna	*Vedas*
brahmin	Mission	*yatra*
dharma	Ramanuja	*yoga*
guru	RSS	*Yoga Sutras*

SUGGESTED READING

Lawrence Babb, *Redemptive Encounters: Three Modern Styles in the Hindu Tradition.* (Berkeley: University of California Press, 1986).

————. *The Divine Hierarchy* (New York: Columbia University Press, 1975).

Ram Dass, *Be Here Now* (Kingsport, Tenn.: Hannman Foundation, 1978).

William Theodore de Bary, ed., *Sources of Indian Tradition*, 2nd ed., 2 vols. (New York: Columbia University Press, 1988).

Cornelia Dimmitt and J. A. B. van Buitenen, *Classical Hindu Anthology: A Reader in the Sanskrit Puranas* (Philadelphia: Temple University Press, 1978).

John Hawley and Mark Juergensmeyer, *Songs of the Saints of India* (New York: Oxford University Press, 1988).

Thomas Hopkins, *The Hindu Religious Tradition* (Belmont, Calif.: Wadsworth, 1982).

Christophe Jaffrelot, *The Hindu Nationalist Movement in India* (New York: Columbia University Press, 1996).

Kenneth W. Jones, *Socio-Religious Reform Movements in British India* (Cambridge: Cambridge University Press, 1994).

Gerald James Larson, *India's Agony over Religion* (Albany: State University of New York Press, 1995).

Heinrich Zimmer, *Myths and Symbols of Indian Art and Civilization* (Princeton, N.J.: Princeton University Press, 1970).

NOTES

1. *India Today*, 1/15/96, p. 22.

2. Daniel Gold, "Organized Hinduisms: From Vedic Truth to Hindu Nation," in *Fundamentalisms Observed*, M. E. Marty and R. Scott Appleby, eds. (Chicago: University of Chicago Press, 1991), p. 581.

3. For the sake of simplicity, in this text we use *brahmin* to indicate the priestly caste and *Brahman* to indicate the "world spirit," although in fact they are similar Sanskrit words: *brahman* and *brahmana*, respectively.

4. Bhimrao Ambedkar, *What Congress and Ghandhi Have Done to the Untouchables* (Bombay: Thacker and Company, 1934), pp. 307-308.

5. Diana Eck, *Darshan* (New York: Columbia University Press, 1998), pp. 52–53.

6. John Hawley and Mark Juergensmeyer, *Songs of the Saints of India* (New York: Oxford University Press, 1988), p. 25.

7. Ibid., p. 51.

8. Ibid., p. 52.

9. Ibid., p. 140.

10. A. K. Ramanujan, *Speaking of Shiva* (Baltimore: Penguin, 1973), p. 88.

11. W. Owen Cole, "Sikhism," in *A Handbook of Living Religions*, John R. Hinnells, ed. (New York: Penguin, 1984), p. 240.

12. W. Owen Cole, "Sikhism," in *A Handbook of Living Religions*, John R. Hinnells, ed. (New York: Penguin, 1984), p. 253.

13. Ramakrishna Mission Pamphlet (Calcutta, 1976).

14. A. K. Ramanujan, *Folktales from India* (New Delhi: Penguin Books India, 1993), p. 175.

15. "Hinduism," in *Understanding Contemporary India*, Sumit Ganguly and Neil De Votta, eds. (Boulder, Colorado: Lynne Reiner, 2003), p. 204.

16. Richard Albert, *Be Here Now*, (Kingsport, Tenn.: Hanuman Foundation, 1978), p. 55.

17. Susan S. Wadley, "*Vratas*: Transformers of Destiny," in *Karma: An Anthropological Inquiry*, Charles F. Keyes and E. Valentine Daniel, eds. (Berkeley: University of California Press, 1983), p. 153.

18. David Knipe, "Hindu Priesthood," in *Encyclopedia of Religion*, M. Eliade, ed. (NY: Macmillan, 1987), p. 541.

19. Khushwant Singh, *Sunday Magazine*, December 23–29, 1990, p. 19.

20. John Stratton Hawley, and Mark Juergensmeyer, *Songs of the Saints of India.* (New York: Oxford University Press, 1988), pp. 44–45.

21. *Hinduism Today,* June 1997, p. 35.

22. Francois Gautier (Hindu convert), in *India Abroad,* January 9, 2006, 26.

23. *India Abroad,* August 4, 2006.

24. Lily Koppel, "Outer Peace," in *New York Times Magazine,* October 8, 2006, p. 24.

25. "Business Filfer," Section E, page 2 in *Boston Globe,* October 30, 2006.

26. Dipak Gyawali, "Challenged by the Future, Shackled by the Past," *Himal South Asia,* May 1997, p. 19.

CHAPTER SIX

BUDDHISM: WAYS
TO NIRVANA

Overview

For over two thousand years, this simple recitation of "going for refuge" has been used to mark conversion to Buddhism, to affirm one's devotion, and to start Buddhist rituals:

- *Buddham Saranam Gacchami*   I go for refuge in the Buddha
- *Dharmam Saranam Gacchami*   I go for refuge in the teachings
- *Sangham Saranam Gacchami*   I go for refuge in the community

Today these three repetitions are heard across Asia and increasingly beyond, in Japan and Nepal, from Mongolia to Thailand, by immigrants and converts from Moscow to San Francisco. But for the student first encountering Buddhism, how different those who "go for refuge" appear! High in the Himalayas, a Tibetan monk wearing a humble red woolen robe seals himself into a cave retreat for three years, three months of meditative solitude; in the heart of urban Seoul, Korea, the layman heading the largest Buddhist reform organization, wearing a stylish three-piece suit, stages a press conference in its ultramodern headquarters, declaring the opening of a twenty-four-hour Buddhism cable TV channel. In tropical Singapore, as householders gather to view the 2,500-year-old bone relics of the Buddha, monks in yellow robes chant and extol the blessings of worshiping his mortal remains. For Mrs. Wong of Taiwan, being a Buddhist means chanting set phrases in hopes of rebirth in the heaven of a Buddha; for Mr. Khatt of Cambodia, being a Buddhist means bestowing charity and doing good in order to achieve a better life in his next 367 rebirth; for Mr. Vajracarya of Nepal, being a Buddhist means performing intricate rituals to honor the gods and Buddhas who out of their boundless compassion can bless his community; for forest monks in Thailand and American disciples of a Japanese Zen master practicing in his monastery in the Catskills, being a Buddhist means only meditating in order to reach enlightenment. It is true that each of these Buddhists reveres an image of the Buddha who is seated in meditation, serene and exemplary; but one cannot help but wonder what the historical Buddha might say if he heard how differently each of these disciples now construes his teachings!

Buddhists today are becoming ever more aware of this diversity of Buddhist paths. Although modern activists and intellectuals may contest exactly "what the Buddha taught," and many are eager to reexamine the texts for reinterpretation, Buddhism's basic teachings about life, mortality, and spiritual development have remained compelling amidst the often traumatic changes wrought in recent centuries. In every land, both venerable institutions and reformist groups are seeking to adapt the faith to the changing world and to revive the essential practices that lead to Buddhism's perennial threefold goals: establishing moral community, securing worldly blessings, and realizing *nirvana*. This chapter will examine how Buddhism in its creative global diversity has sought to direct devotees to secure these goals.

The oldest of the world's missionary religions and perhaps the most accommodating in adapting to widely varying communities in its wide-ranging global diaspora, Buddhism is in modest revival in most areas of the world today after having suffered debilitating setbacks throughout the modern era. Understanding Buddhism thus entails knowing about most of the peoples and cultures of Eurasia: from the homeland on the Ganges in South Asia into the high Himalayas, across the tropical states of Southeast Asia and over the Central Asian deserts, and throughout the imperial domains of China, Korea, and Japan.

Besides this geographic complexity, Buddhism, unlike the other world religions, has but a few universally accepted doctrinal formulae. Beyond the "Three Refuges" cited at the beginning of this chapter, Buddhists have adopted varying subsets of the Buddha's teachings and many rituals, always keeping the monastic community (the *sangha*) as its central institution. How could a world religion achieve such pluralism in the course of demarcating its essential doctrines? First, Buddhists (like Hindus) assume that humanity contains many sorts of persons and needs many different avenues to reach the state of salvation called *nirvana*. Its teachers therefore formulated myriad practices to reach nirvana, and intellectual writers offered multiple interpretations of the truth the Buddha revealed.

The second reason for Buddhism's pluralism lies in an instruction from the Buddha himself: that after his death, no one person or institution be allowed to fix a single canon or set a single norm of orthodoxy in doctrinal interpretations (the opposite extreme of premodern Christianity). As a result, by six hundred years after the death of Shakyamuni Buddha (whose dates are either 563–483 BCE or 440–360 BCE), adherents aligned themselves under two main divisions, those of the "elder traditionalists," called Sthaviravadins (the sole surviving school of which is called Theravada) and those of the "Great Vehicle," who called themselves the Mahayana (among which many schools survive today such as Pure Land and Zen, each with many subgroups). Thus, in many respects it is quite artificial to posit a single "Buddhism" based upon a common code, text, or catechism of belief. Buddhism in popular practice among the laity, however, does show many continuities, as we will see.

The Global Diaspora of Buddhism Today

Rough estimates place the number of Buddhists at 350 million, making it the fourth largest among world religions. Over 98 percent live in Asia. Globally, there are as many Buddhists as there are Protestant Christians. Among Buddhists, these sources estimate that 62 percent are adherents of the Mahayana and 38 percent are Theravada followers. With most modern Mahayanists located in the countries north of the tropics, the label "Northern Buddhism" is also used for this grouping, as opposed to the "Southern Buddhism" of the Theravadins. In a half dozen Asian states (Sri Lanka, Myanmar, Thailand, Laos, Cambodia, Japan), Buddhists comprise the overwhelming majority of the population. They are significant minorities in Nepal, China, South Korea, and Singapore, while their presence in Malaysia (10%), Indonesia (3%), and India is less marked. (It should be noted that specific percentages, figures taken from Western almanac sources, are at best rough estimates, with wide margins for error.)

A recent survey of Buddhist clergy worldwide also estimated that there are about 700,000 "renunciants," as monks and nuns are called in Buddhism. Officially ordained men outnumber women in this vocation by six to one. Almost one-half of the world's modern ordained sangha are in Thailand.

ENCOUNTER WITH MODERNITY: SOCIALLY ENGAGED BUDDHISM

The Karma of Buddhist Renewal: "Engaged Buddhism"?

After the end of World War II, the rebuilding and renewal of Buddhism began across Asia, as most Asian nations faced the need to recover from colonialism and reinvent their societies politically and culturally in light of the new reality of the cold war that set America and Western Europe against the Soviet Union and China. For most Asians, the encounter with Western culture continued, especially in the Christian, scientific, and political domains. Every Buddhist community across the globe had to reorient and renew its beliefs and practices, with the communist bloc taking a new direction. In post–World War II China, Mongolia, Vietnam, and North Korea, rulers regarded Buddhist doctrine as superstition and Buddhist institutions as parasitic on society and so engaged in

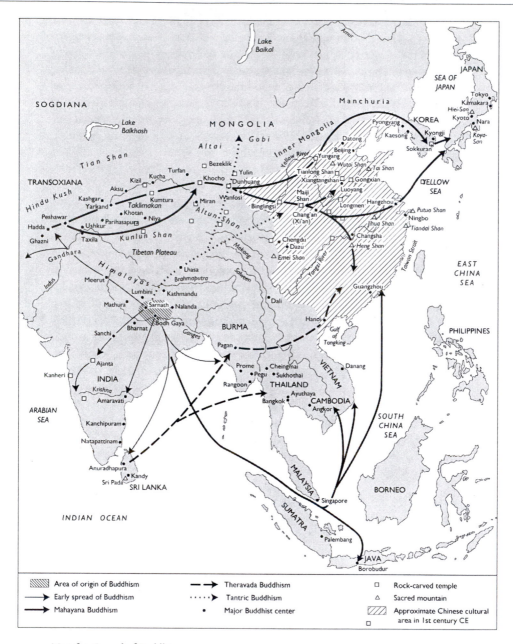

Map 6.1 Spread of Buddhism.

"revolutionary campaigns" aimed at disbanding the sangha, destroying its buildings and images, and discrediting all forms of Buddhist belief and practice. "Buddhist-Marxist dialogue" did arise in some of these countries, but mostly among philosophers and for the communist states' external relations with other Asian nations. In the noncommunist nations, Buddhist nationalism continued to be a force in the postcolonial era. The last major development in Buddhism since World War II has been the global establishment of the faith on a scale unprecedented in world history.

As Asia's rapid industrialization and urbanization have created new forms of social dislocation and wealth, there have been dramatic increases in landless wage-dependent workers, an unprecedented number of ecological crises, an expansion of higher education, and the rise of educated classes alongside new commercial elites. As a result, Buddhism today has been transplanted and drawn into entirely new social contexts, political struggles, and global dialogues.

For example, one image of modern Buddhism is that of a Vietnamese monk sitting cross-legged, engulfed in flames. This and other suicides in 1963 protested the South Vietnamese government's failure to respect Buddhism and to urge policies of national reconciliation. Among the many Buddhist monks who challenged the corrupt South Vietnamese state was Thich Nhat Hanh, who argued that when faced with immense suffering, Buddhists must take action and engage their society. While Buddhism's ascetic traditions advocate renunciation of the household life and retreat to nirvana-seeking meditation, Hanh drew upon other sides of the tradition to urge both monks and nuns to defer solitary individualistic practice in order to stage nonviolent confrontations with the governments and other agencies responsible for profound suffering.

Inspired by the monks of Vietnam and underlining the fact that compassion (*karuna*) and loving kindness (*maitri*) are as ancient and as fundamental to Buddhism as the ascetic and solitary practices of the spiritual elite, contemporary Buddhist activists in Asia, and now in the West, are responding to the crises posed by environmental despoliation, political corruption, and global hunger. "Engaged Buddhists" have accordingly refused to turn away from suffering and now seek "mundane awakening" by eliciting the compassion of individuals, villages, countries, and eventually all people.

Buddhists engaging with society in political arenas now span the world, offering examples of revival from India to Japan: there is the Trailokya Bauddha Mahasangha Sahayaka Gana of India that has since 1956 worked to convert low-ranked castes in India and help raise them out of poverty (with the motto: "Educate! Agitate! Organize!"); the Sarvodaya Shramadana movement in Sri Lanka seeking to promote rural development through harnessing the service commitments of lay volunteers; monk reformers such as Buddhadasa of Thailand and the Tibetan Dalai Lama who have connected with those of other faiths to mobilize mutual seeking of the common good; and various postwar Japanese Buddhist groups such as the Soka Gakkai that work to transform society through political activism informed by Buddhist ideals. By 1989, Sulak Sivaraksa, a Thai lay activist, formed the International Network of Engaged Buddhists to foster connections and develop this latest interpretation of traditional Buddhism.

SOCIALLY ENGAGED BUDDHISM: SOME EXAMPLES

"In Buddhist terminology, the world is full of dukkha ["suffering"], i.e., the dangers of impending world destruction through nuclear weapons, atomic fallout, air, land and sea pollution, population explosion, exploitation of fellow human beings, denial of basic human rights, and devastating famine....World dukkha is too immense for any country, people, or religion to solve. We can only save ourselves when all humanity recognizes that every problem on earth is our own personal problem and our own personal responsibility....The language of Buddhism must offer answers which fit our situation. Only then will Buddhism survive, today and tomorrow, as it has in the past, influencing humankind positively and generating love, peace, and nonviolence.
—Sulak Sivaraksa[1]

"The word 'Buddha' comes from the root 'budh,' which means 'awake.' A Buddha is one who is awake. Are we really awake in our daily lives? That is a question....Society makes it difficult to be awake. We know that 40,000 children in the Third World die every day of hunger, but we keep forgetting. The kind of society we live in makes us forgetful. That is why we need exercises in mindfulness....Our earth is like a small boat. Compared with the rest of the cosmos, it is a very small boat, and it is in danger of sinking. We need a person to inspire us with calm confidence, to tell us what to do. What is that person? The Mahayana texts tell us that you are that person."
—Thich Nhat Hanh[2]

Buddhist social activism has made the tradition more attractive to many in the West. In Asia, engaged Buddhists have no shortage of traumatic provocations given the region's rapid industrialization, the explosion of urban slum settlements, the alarming degradation of forests and watersheds, the predations of corrupt politicians, and the bloodshed from ethnic conflicts and civil wars. These profound changes and crises have disrupted the regions' rural societies, including many of the communities that harbor established Buddhist institutions.

The engaged Buddhists, predominantly in the urban centers, now offer new understandings of Buddhism and Buddhist action, often confronting politicians and corporations. Can this movement revitalize the tradition back down to the rural hinterlands and mitigate suffering without reducing or compromising the faith? To understand their importance today and to discover the "engagement" this movement advocates, we must start with the founder and trace the historical development of his teachings.

PREMODERN BUDDHISM: THE FORMATIVE ERA

The Buddha

The most famous man ever to become an ascetic was born the son of warrior-caste parents who ruled a small state in the Himalayan foothills. According to the legendary accounts, this boy's birth was accompanied by auspicious celestial signs and a wiseman's prediction that he would be successful as either a universal monarch or a great ascetic. (The personal name given as a result, Siddhartha, means "the one who attains the goal.") The young prince, whose mother died a week after giving birth, grew up in a palace where his father did everything in his power to ensure the first destiny. The son was trained in the martial arts, isolated from life's unpleasantries, and pampered with all the pleasures of rule, including marriage, a harem of concubines, and every form of artistic distraction.

We saw in Chapter 5 that North India at the time of the Buddha's birth (560 BCE) was a place of spiritual questioning and ascetic searching unmatched in the history of religions. In the dominant Aryan society that was evolving from small pastoral settlements to city-states and a more diverse economy, the old religion controlled by members of the brahmin caste was becoming for some much less plausible in its providing the ultimate explanations for humanity's deepest connection to the universe. In remote retreats and in areas proximate to the emerging urban centers, there were many seekers called *shramanas* who pursued ascetic practices (*yoga*) to realize the true essence of life, reality, consciousness. The society in which Siddhartha was born was ordered by caste and brahmin ritualism, but there were also ardent, nonconformist shramana seekers in this region who questioned everything brahminic tradition asserted about spirit, morality, and social hierarchy. Some lived naked, in silent retreat, or even sealed in clay pots; most explored various trance states and adopted renunciatory lifestyles. Still other ascetics advocated materialism, nihilism, agnosticism, or fatalism.

Like certain devotees of the Upanishadic seers, most shramanas believed in a new spiritual paradigm that life consists of a countless series of rebirths (*samsara*); that these are determined by an individual's *karma*, a natural and moral causal force that accrues according to one's deeds; and that rebirth continues until through moral perfection and *yoga* practices one "burns off" one's karma to reach a state of liberation, which in Buddhism is variously styled *moksha*, *nirvana*, and *mukti*. Shramanas differed widely on the exact means of reaching this state and debated the details of personhood and universe. They were contrasted with the priestly brahmins in terms of the mortal enemies "cobra and mongoose."

Siddhartha's life changed when he followed his inclination to go with his faithful chariot driver to see the world beyond the palace walls. All the textual legends describe the profound impact of seeing a sick man, an old man, a dead man, and a shramana. These "four passing sights" overturned his rosy assumptions about life and also offered an idea about the personal path he could take to escape the spiritual emptiness he felt in his sheltered existence. Within days, Siddhartha ran away, abandoning his palace and family, including a newborn son. He began at that moment his search for a teacher among the forest-dwelling ascetics. The legends state that he was 29 years old.

He found a shramana *guru*, Arada Kalama, whose meditation technique allowed one to achieve a "state of nothingness." Siddhartha soon mastered it, but he also recognized this state as a limited accomplishment. His quest led to a second teacher, Udraka Ramaputra, who taught a method of attaining trances that brought an experience of "neither perception nor nonperception." But again Siddhartha found that his fast-won mastery of this yoga had left him short of the highest goal.

He set forth alone again, and soon joined five other ascetics who vowed to explore together a rigorous ascetic practice involving fanatical fasting (down to a few rice grains daily), breath control, and spending of long periods seated in unmoving meditation. He adopted this lifestyle for several years, but eventually rejected this method also as too extreme, much to the dismay of his fellow seekers who then cursed and abandoned him. Through this experiment, Siddhartha did come to understand that the spiritual life is best undertaken as a middle path between the extremes of sense indulgence (the life in the palace) and the asceticism (of the forest) so zealous that it weakens the body. (One name for Buddhism, "the Middle Way," stems from this experience.)

Although he lacked bodily strength and felt dismayed, Siddhartha did not quit. He was buoyed by a gift of rice and barley gruel from a village woman, and he came to sit beneath a great ficus tree by a river outside the town of Gaya. He vowed to find either success or death. The legendary accounts relate that his revitalized meditations were disturbed by Mara, a supernatural being regarded by Buddhists as the personification of death, delusion, and temptation; his minions appeared as armies to elicit fear and as alluring females to elicit lust. Siddhartha's gesture of touching the right hand to earth, asking it to bear witness to his merit and eventual success, brought forth earthquakes and a cooling stream that washed away Mara and his hordes. (The earth-touching gesture is one of the most common depictions of the Buddha in art.)

Later that night, after resuming his meditations, Siddhartha reached more subtle and blissful perceptions and then the attainment of superfaculties such as memory of his former lives, psychic vision that allowed him to survey the destinies of all beings according to their karma, as well as the powers of levitation, telepathy, and superhearing. Finally he completely extinguished all desire and ignorance by fully realizing his capacity for insight (*prajna*). This "awakening" or "waking up" to the nature of reality under the bo (or *bodhi*, "enlightenment") tree, poetically recounted as being completed just as the dawn broke, provides the root meaning of the term "Buddha" that from this moment onward we can properly apply to Siddhartha.

The references to him have assumed many other forms: Mahashramana, "the Great Ascetic", Tathagata, "the one who has come [or gone] thus"; and Jina, the "conqueror" (i.e., of karma, ignorance, death, etc.). He is also "Gautama Buddha," called using his family surname, and Shakyamuni: "the sage," or *muni*, from Gautama's clan, the Shakyas.

For seven weeks the Buddha remained in the vicinity of the bodhi tree, enjoying the bliss of nirvana. The texts recount a story that his very first disciples were householders, merchants who made offerings and received his benediction for their continued worldly success. He also received the veneration of *nagas*, the snake deities thought to own the earth, control the rains, and normally reside underground; their submission came to symbolize Buddhism's claim of "spiritual conquest" over all deities in every locality where the faith missionized. Mara returned to tempt the Buddha not to teach and so remain isolated, enjoying his solitary nirvana, citing humanity's hopeless stupidity to support his exhortation. But the high gods also intervened to request that the Buddha live on to share his doctrine because, they assured him, there were people everywhere capable of understanding his *Dharma* (the ultimate truth). This request stoked the Buddha's compassion and he vowed to engage the world through teaching.

He walked first to Sarnath, a deer park outside the city of Varanasi, where he found his former ascetic colleagues. After he overcame their initial disdain for his quitting their practice, he taught them the "Four Noble Truths" that end in the "Eightfold Path." This formulation by which the Buddha first "turned the wheel of the Dharma" enlightened each of them. The circumstances of this first sermon led to the creation of several universal symbols of Buddhism: deer flanking an eight-spoked wheel—🕉—representing the eightfold path, which will be discussed shortly. These ascetics were the first members of the sangha, and they were instructed to share the Dharma with others and to travel to different places in the four directions to do so.

For the next forty or so years, the Buddha empowered his enlightened disciples, called *arhats*, to act on his behalf, to admit seekers into the sangha, guide those who wished to meditate, and teach the Dharma to whomever would hear it. They converted other ascetics, sometimes whole assemblies of them, as well as solitary shramanas, householders, and rulers. All textual traditions state that the Buddha's faculty of psychic knowledge allowed him to preach according to the exact capacity of his audience.

Slowly the movement grew as the Buddhist shramanas found interested audiences among the forest-dwelling ascetics and urban householders.

Shakyamuni traveled almost continuously, except for the period of the summer rains when he, like his monks, retreated to one place both out of compassion for the creatures who suffer with the monsoon and to engage in a period of more intensive meditation.

As the Buddhist movement grew, new situations arose that required adaptation, so that in addition to his skill at teaching, the Buddha also managed the successful creation of an entirely new institution in ancient India. The sangha was established on the basis of an extensive set of rules that adapted this institution to the many environments it reached.

After much urging (at least in some legends), Shakyamuni also gave permission for the creation of a *bhikkhuni* sangha of female renunciants, bequeathing a mixed message by emphasizing that women are capable of realizing enlightenment but also specifying rules forcing the bhikkhunis to subordinate themselves to the monks in social etiquette. In subsequently allowing the sangha to receive lands, buildings, and other communal resources that were donated initially to make the rain retreat well observed, the Buddha established the means by which the sangha shifted its focus over time from wandering to settled cooperative communal existence, a development that also gave the householder disciples a fixed focus for their patronage.

Late in life the Buddha began to suffer from various ailments, and he died in Kushinagar, a rural site, at the age of 80. His body was cremated and the remains, divided into eight portions, were enshrined in relic mound shrines (*stupas*) that became the focus of Buddhist ritual and the visible symbol of the Buddha's presence across the world.

Shakyamuni's life story became for Buddhists a paradigmatic example of an individual's quest for enlightenment, and his exemplary role for subsequent generations was elaborated in hundreds of didactic stories that describe incidents from his previous births as human, animal, or spirit. These narratives, called *jatakas*, along with stories of his final ascent to Buddhahood inspired vernacular arts and literatures across Asia that conveyed the essential doctrines in explicit, personified form. The Buddha, thus, embodies the Dharma, the ultimate truth.

Buddhism as the Path to Nirvana

The spiritual tradition we refer to as "Buddhism" arose from the Buddha's wish to help others realize the transformative experience of nirvana. The Buddha emphasized the practical goal-directed orientation of his way and urged his disciples not to engage in idle speculation or mere intellectualism. He taught his disciples to be teachers and to recognize that there are very different kinds of persons who bear different forms of karma. According to whether they are "ordinary persons," "learners," or "adepts," each is to be instructed differently. Regardless of the individual's level, the tradition underscores that the rare opportunity of human birth should not be wasted and that life therefore should be lived with purpose.

The word *nirvana* (Pali: *nibbana*) is based upon the Sanskrit verb meaning "to cool by blowing" and refers to one who has "cooled" the feverish *kleshas* ("hindrances," "poisons")—greed, hatred, delusion—that create karma and bind the individual into *samsara*, the world of rebirth and suffering. The simile often employed in Buddhist texts for nirvana realization is the extinction of a fire, for as this phenomenon was understood in antiquity, extinguished flames were released to return to a diffuse, unagitated, and eternal state. The state of nirvana thus carries similar associations: freedom and existence in an eternal state beyond all material description. Both men and women can realize nirvana through the cultivation of *prajna* ("insight") through moral living and proper meditation.

The Four Noble Truths

The earliest and most enduring formulation of the Buddha's doctrine, the Four Noble Truths, provides a definition and analysis of the human condition as well as a diagnosis: the path toward *nirvana*. The biographies recount that through the realization of these truths in his own experience, Gautama reached final enlightenment. The Four Truths were also the subject of the Buddha's first sermon. The medical methodology of diagnosis and treatment used in their presentation contributed to yet another epithet of the Buddha: "The Great Physician."

The first Noble Truth, "All life entails suffering," calls the Buddhist not to deny the inevitable experience of mortal existence: physical and mental disease, loss of loved ones, the bodily degeneration of old age, and the inescapability of death. The intention of this first truth is not to induce pessimism but to hold up clear, realistic observation. Even pleasure and good times, however enjoyable, have a fundamental inadequacy since they are only temporary. The appropriate response to this truth is to make the most of the spiritual opportunities of human birth and to show compassion *(karuna)* and loving kindness *(maitri)* to alleviate the suffering affecting all other beings.

The second Noble Truth states, "The cause of suffering is desire." The term for "desire" *(trishna)* literally means "thirst" and this covers all that human beings "thirst after" far beyond mere liquids: food and drink beyond biological need, possessions, power, sex. (At the advanced stages of Buddhist practice, desire for doctrinal learning and even the wish for one's own enlightenment must also be rejected to reach the final goal.) The emphasis on desire in the second truth makes plain the need for renunciation, detachment, and asceticism in Buddhist tradition.

The third Noble Truth, "Removing desire removes suffering," provides a terse reference to the central Buddhist focus on spiritual causation: the same pattern of cyclical cause and effect by which desire leads to further suffering can also be reversed and eventually extinguished in nirvana. The twelvefold formula of dependent origination (*pratityasamutpada*, discussed later) is a more extended treatment of this important (and universally accepted) Buddhist doctrine of causality. The emphasis on renunciation also signals the importance of the sangha as a refuge for individuals who wish to live the most complete approximation of the nonattachment ideal.

The fourth Truth, "The way for removing desire is to follow the Eightfold Path," specifies the treatment needed to be "cured" of the human condition's continuous cycle of rebirth, suffering, and redeath. This entails eight specific elements in the progressive path to nirvana: moral practice, meditation, and the cultivation of the prajna that leads to salvation. As the Buddhist progresses toward enlightenment, his or her understanding of the Four Noble Truths deepens through meditation and critical reflection.

The Eightfold Path

Among the many doctrinal lists compiled to describe Buddhist practices, The Eightfold Path has been the most widely disseminated summary compilation. It outlines the necessary means for achieving the realization of nirvana. The usual order is: (1) *Right Views*, especially of the Noble Truths; (2) *Right Thought*, thought that is shaped by detachment from hatred and cruelty; (3) *Right Speech*, speech that refrains from falsehood, gossip, frivolity; (4) *Right Action*, defined negatively, as action free of killing, stealing, harming; (5) *Right Livelihood*, refraining from earning a living through astrology, casting magic spells, or careers that involve inflicting harm or killing; (6) *Right Effort*, effort to clear and calm the mind; (7) *Right Mindfulness*, the distinctive form of Buddhist meditation that observes clearly the mind and body and cultivates detachment; and (8) *Right Concentration*, another form of advanced meditation that attains the mastery of trance states.

An important arrangement of the Eightfold Path was made according to another schema, the three central categories of Buddhist practice:

Morality (Shila)
entails Speech, Action, Livelihood

Meditation (Dhyana)
entails Effort, Mindfulness, Concentration

Insight or Wisdom (Prajna)
entails Views and Thought

The Theravadin commentator Buddhaghosa (5th century CE) organized his entire summary of the faith based upon this division; he refers to the two legs of Buddhism as Morality and Meditation, upon which the body of Insight stands. The Eightfold Path emphasizes that moral progress is the essential foundation to successful meditation and that the measure of successful meditation is the awakening and deepening of prajna. Its different elements underscore Buddhism's practical emphasis on effectiveness, whether in the foundational goal of improving moral standards, good conduct, and the material welfare of society, or the more advanced ideal of deconditioning desire-driven behavior, restructuring cognition, and liberating consciousness for enlightenment realization.

The First Community and Its Development

Life in the Buddhist sangha was a true refuge for those "sons and daughters of the Buddha" (as monks and nuns were called) who wished to leave behind their homes and seek enlightenment. The ideal was simple: material needs were managed by the institution and by householders such that meditation and study could be practiced without encumbrances.

Texts of the early monastic schools, called *Vinayas*, that record the monastic rules show that criminals, runaway slaves, debtors, or army deserters were not eligible to join a sangha, for the Buddha was sensitive to the state laws under which he lived. He also specified principles to govern the community (by seniority, as reckoned from the time since ordination) and insisted that a group ritual be observed each fortnight involving the collective recitation of the sangha rules (called the *pratimoksha*) to certify that each individual was in conformity with them. The Buddha's genius as community founder can be seen as well in his cultivating a householder community that provided for the needs of the sangha. It was good Buddhist householders who joined the sangha and whose merit-earning patronage established the faith's monasteries and shrines across India and, over time, throughout Asia.

After the Buddha's death and following his instruction that authority over his community was not to reside in a single person or institution, the monks and nuns settled in separate monastic colonies and these became the centers that perpetuated the faith. These renunciants repeated and memorized the sets of sermons they had heard and worked out a distinctive form of communal life. Within the first three centuries there were several "conferences," which came to focus on the exact rules of monastic orthopraxy. Although the early sanghas also found considerable common ground in collecting the earliest doctrinal pronouncements gathered in the *Tripitakas* ["three baskets"—i.e., divided among Discipline, Teachings, and Advanced Doctrine], no conference achieved consensus on matters of discipline. Dissenters went off to practice as they felt proper in their own monasteries, but the monastic codes in the *Vinayas* are remarkably similar and the disagreements that led to schisms seem have involved relatively minor points. The Tripitakas are often referred to today as the first Buddhist scriptures. After the first two conferences recorded in the first century, it is not even certain that all monks and nuns in northern India ever gathered together again! This early fact of sangha autonomy and divergent understandings of the Dharma became precedents that shaped the continuation of regional pluralism found across the Buddhist world right up to the present. As Chinese pilgrim Fa-Hsien noted in 400 CE, after traveling extensively in India, "Practices of the monks are so various and have increased so that they cannot be recorded."[3]

How Buddhism Became a "World Religion"

In the first two centuries after Shakyamuni's death, Buddhist monks and converts spread slowly across the Gangetic plain as simply another one of the many shramana groups that emphasized asceticism and rejected the brahmin caste's privileged status, its ritual system, and especially its claim to hold a monopoly on advanced spiritual practice. It was the conversion of Ashoka, the Mauryan emperor (273–232 BCE), that shaped and propelled Buddhism's emergence as a broad-based religion that reached beyond the ascetics, one that could unify the social classes of a civilization and link the householder majority population with its monastic elite.

Just as the Mauryan Empire extended across most of the subcontinent, Ashoka through his imperial edicts, patronage of notable monks, and prestige helped spread Buddhism from Afghanistan to the Bay of Bengal, from the Himalayan foothills to the island of Sri Lanka. As a result, the first definite traces of Buddhist monuments (monasteries, and stupa shrines) can be dated to this era as can the first extensive and systematic oral collections of the teachings. Within a century after the end of the Mauryan period, Buddhist institutions dotted the major trade routes going north and south, east and west from the Buddhist holy land, with sites associated with the Buddha the places where major shrines, monasteries, and pilgrimage traditions developed.

The expansion northwest into the upper Indus River, in the region called Gandhara and into the Kashmir valley, and then beyond them up the trade routes crossing the mountains north into Central Asia made these areas a Buddhist stronghold for the next millennium. It was here that the Indic world had already met the Hellenic: hundreds of settlements across the upper Indus were populated by descendants of Alexander the Great (355–323 BCE). Alexander's campaign of world conquest faltered on the Indus, easing the expansion of the Mauryan Empire. Moreover, many of the descendants from Alexander's army settled, established small states, and became prominent regional traders. Many converted to Buddhism.

To understand Buddhism's successful rise to popularity among kings and commoners, however, we must comprehend how the sangha (monastic community) provided the strongest common thread in the history and practice of Buddhism across Asia.

Sangha and Monastery: The Institutional Vehicles of Buddhism's Expansion

The community of monks, nuns, and devout lay followers established monasteries and shrines that rooted the faith in every locality. When Buddhist monasticism spread across Asia, it introduced independent, corporate institutions that transformed local societies and regional polities. In ancient India, the early sangha disregarded caste as a social category for its members. In Buddhism's subsequent missionary migrations, acceptance into the sangha offered ordinary citizens an opportunity for spiritual seeking and educational advancement that was otherwise unavailable.

Buddhism could not have existed in society at large without the support of the householders: by making donations to the sangha to earn merit to improve their karma and to garner worldly blessings for themselves, their families, and their communities, they ensured the viability of the monastic institution. It was this central exchange, maintained between sangha and society, that kept Buddhism vibrant.

Varieties of Buddhist Monasticism

The typical Buddhist community had its center in a monastery (*vihara*), where monks (or nuns) would take their communal vows and recite fortnightly the pratimoksha, as well as meditate and study. These institutions also supported monks who practiced medicine, performed rituals essential to the Buddhist lifestyle of the locality, or managed the institution. Over time, a distinction developed within Buddhist monasticism: there were forest monasteries, where meditation and optional ascetic practices (*dhutanga*) could be undertaken (often under the leadership of a charismatic monk teacher), and monasteries in settlements (village and urban), which offered the opportunity to blend compassionate service to the community (ritual, medical, educational) with individual cultivation and study. A Buddhist monk or nun typically moved between village and urban monasteries, with many going out for periods "in the forest."

In many areas, the focus and inspiration for followers was a monk whose spiritual charisma and exemplary teaching ability drew ascetic disciples and meritorious donations from the laity. The common biography of such monks mirrors that of Shakyamuni (the Buddha): disillusion, renunciation, retreat to the wilderness mark the path to the Dharma, nirvana realization, then returning to teach.

Practical Mechanisms of Expansion

Successful monasteries expanded. The pattern was to send out monks to establish satellite institutions of that lineage. This template of Buddhist expansion created "galactic systems" that extended Buddhism into unconverted frontier zones. This network of "mother-daughter" monasteries shaped all sorts of alliances, religious and otherwise, providing the pattern of new Buddhist institution building found from Ladakh to Bali, and more recently from Bangkok to Los Angeles, Dharamsala to New York. The logic of this institutional system also resulted in the tendency for aristocratic/dominant caste families to control local *viharas* or monastic lineages, a pattern of ethnic group dominance that was visible until recently in Buddhist Tibet and continues in the Kathmandu valley, in Japan, and Sri Lanka. In other contexts, Buddhist viharas also broke down ethnic and class boundaries, blurring divisions between peoples, creating transregional communities.

Rulers across Asia were drawn to support Buddhism because of its emphasis on individuality morality, its rituals designed to secure prosperity for the state as well as themselves, and the powerful legitimization that respected monastics could bestow on them. History has also shown that states favoring Buddhism often placed controls on the sangha's development. For example, to orchestrate the early expansion of Buddhism in China and Japan, emperors ordered each provincial governor to build a monastery, a command that was reissued eventually down to the subunits in each province, as Buddhist institutions came to mirror the state's own administrative networks. Buddhist exponents, in turn, held up Ashoka as a model for the ideal Buddhist ruler. A just, generous king (governor, local official, etc.) could be called a *bodhisattva* ("future Buddha"), a *dharmaraja* ("just king"), or a *cakravartin* ("wheel-turning just ruler and zealous devotee"). Thus, leading monks in the sangha could offer those wielding political power the highest terms of legitimation in the eyes of the faithful. In this manner, Buddhist doctrines, officials, and patrons entered into the secular and political lives of the societies Buddhism entered. This ancient and fundamental dynamic of institutional expansion, moral leadership, and ethnic integration has continued in modern Asia (especially in Burma/Myanmar and Thailand), as nations still struggle to integrate tribal peoples and ethnic minorities into their state's society.

In places where Buddhism thrived, some monasteries in cities and villages evolved to be complex institutions that were much more than refuges for ascetics. The monastery was often the only local school, and members of the sangha served their societies by spreading literacy. Many urban monasteries also became lending institutions, appointing treasurers to see that monies donated at shrines that exceeded the sangha's requirements were reinvested (usually in trade loans) back into the secular community. Interest earned through this practice was reinvested as well. On the trade routes especially, this practice, combined with renting monastery-owned buildings to merchants for warehousing or retailing enterprises, garnered considerable income for the monastery treasuries. Such developments, which are attested from 200 CE onward in India and China, explain the economic foundations for Buddhism traveling across the Asian landscape on the basis of trade, supported by traders, and in cities along the commercial routes.

Another component in the spread of vibrant Buddhist institutions across Asia was the accumulation of lands donated by individuals and the state as perpetual endowments. Since monks were forbidden to till the soil, the sangha (as typically organized by lay managers) would rent out the cultivated lands it was acquiring. Whether its laborers grew rice and wheat or cultivated orchards, the monastery derived the food or cash needed for the sangha's upkeep. Until the twentieth century, many of the large Buddhist institutions were given indentured workers or slaves (usually entire families). Finally, shrines located within or adjacent to the monasteries would also earn income for the sangha in the form of offerings left behind and from levies imposed upon artisans who sold icons and votive amulets around the monastic precincts. All of these elements made the management of major monasteries a demanding and influential job.

These practices of "monastic landlordism," banking, and shrine management were also very central to Buddhism's successful missions across Asia, creating the means to endow the faith with reliable income and a strong material culture. Buddhists attracted a following in societies across Asia with spiritual teachings but also with well-built, often remarkable buildings, shrines, and image halls that complemented them. Tied to the productive base of society, Buddhist monasteries were ornamented with masterful art works, their libraries grew with manuscript production, and their leaders could develop an effective presentation of the Dharma. Many viharas also organized endowed charities that fed the poor and dispensed free medical care.

Allied with monasteries was a common institution that unified monks and householders for religious pursuits: the lay committees (Skt.: *gosthis*). These would stage periodic festivals (image processions, chariot festivals), arrange for regular public recitations of popular narratives, and organize other rituals designed to cultivate both devotion to the Buddha-Dharma-sangha and ritual blessings for the local community.

Monastery autonomy and the lack of an overarching body that supervised the monks' and nuns' obedience to the monastic norms made the integrity of Buddhist institutions dependent upon political leaders, who had to "purify the sangha" periodically, that is, remove those not properly ordained or acting contrary to the *Vinaya* norms. Rulers undertook this task especially after periods of great piety, when more and more lands in their realm were dedicated to the sangha, in effect removing them from the tax rolls. For Buddhism's strength through concentrating wealth and human resources was also its historical weakness: viharas were vulnerable to the vagaries of state patronage and royal protection, as well as to the devastating effects of internal corruption and civil disorder.

New officials often supported alternative monastic schools or non-Buddhist religions. Thus, the reaction to abuses and nature of "reforms" carried out within the sangha by rulers—yesterday and today—must be understood in this wider context of wealthy monasteries weakening the economic power of the state and their involvement in the politics of religious legitimation.

PREMODERN BUDDHISM: THE CLASSICAL ERA

The Pan-Asia Expansion of Buddhism

In the first sermon after his enlightenment, Shakyamuni Buddha told his audience of five monks to spread the teaching (Dharma) in the four directions and to use the local dialects. Thus, from its inception Buddhism has been a missionary religion teaching a message directed to and thought suitable for all peoples. As the first missionary religion in the world, Buddhism initially spread to places similar to where it began, among the urban peoples and merchants. Within the first millennium of the common era, Buddhism was found throughout South Asia and far beyond it into Central Asia on the overland routes. Monks also traveled on the maritime trade routes to Sri Lanka and across Southeast Asia. Monasteries welcomed all who would observe the rules of residence. The small circles of philosopher monks had divided into more than twenty schools of doctrinal interpretation. What gave the religion unity was a common reverence for the Three Refuges. Thus, Buddhism has never been a unified faith either doctrinally or institutionally.

By the year 100 CE, Buddhism had entered China through Central Asia on the silk routes; as it grew more popular and spread across East Asia over the next six centuries, monks and pilgrims traveled on the land and oceanic routes between the two great ancient civilizations of Asia. The conversion of this region to Buddhism constitutes one of the greatest instances of cross-cultural transmission and conversion in world history, parallel in scope only with the transformations wrought by the world's other great missionary faiths, Christianity and Islam. Buddhism added wholly new conceptions of space, time, psychology, and human destiny that challenged indigenous notions; it also introduced a new social institution that fostered its missionary success: the land-grant monastery whose members could be drawn from diverse social classes.

The Core Doctrines

While textbooks always emphasize the division between Traditionalists (Theravada) and Great Vehicle (Mahayana) adherents that grew among intellectuals in Buddhism's first millennium, for the lay majority who focused on morality, merit, and blessings, doctrinal disputes were mostly irrelevant. For householders as for the sangha, conformity to the *Vinaya* code was the major concern because having upright monks and nuns guaranteed that householders could rely on their rituals and would earn merit by making donations to them.

We have seen that an individual's beliefs and meditation practices were largely personal matters and that from the earliest days, monks (or nuns) following very different interpretations of the Dharma coexisted under the same monastery roof. We now consider doctrines and ethical norms that all Buddhists shared, then move to discuss those teachings that were different.

Prajna *and* Nirvana

Necessary for the attainment of nirvâna and often translated as "wisdom," *prajna* (Pali: *panna*) is better rendered as "insight," since it refers to the active capacity for spiritual discernment, that is, "seeing into" the nature of reality as it truly is: marked by suffering, impermanence, and self-lessness: the Three Marks or Characteristics of existence. All Buddhist schools have held that the full development of prajna is essential to salvation, as discussed later. The Theravada schools today emphasize *vipassana* meditation as the most important practice to see "life as it is." The Mahayana schools also define the path of the bodhisattva in reference to prajna, as it is the culminating *paramita* ("perfection") "realized" only through meditation.

Buddhist salvation is often referred to as "enlightenment" because this fullness of prajna eliminates ignorance and clears the mind to see reality clearly. The state a Buddha or an arhat, a fully enlightened follower, achieves at death is referred to as *parinirvana* ("final nirvana"), although the texts say that strictly speaking this after-death state is beyond conception. Nirvana has been described in both negative and positive terms: a realm where there is neither sun nor moon, coming nor going; but also a state that is tranquil, pure, and deathless. Most of the early scholastic treatises recognized nirvana as the only permanent reality in the cosmos. It is not, as erroneously depicted by early Western interpreters, to be seen as "annihilation," which is an extreme position rejected by the Buddha.

Non-Self Doctrine

The concept of *anatman*, "no-*atman*" or "non-self," is used to reject any notion of an essential, unchanging interior entity at the center of a person. The "*atman*" the Buddha rejected is the physically real and indestructible soul posited in the Upanishads and subsequent Hinduism, as described in Chapter 5. Buddhists argued that the law of impermanence, one of the three marks of existence, most certainly applies to human beings. As a result they analyzed the human "being" as the continuously changing, interdependent relationship between the five aggregates (*skandhas*).

Seeking to see all reality as process, the Buddhists begin with the person as really a collection of the five skandhas: the physical body (*rupa*) that is made of combinations of the four elements (earth, water, fire, air); feelings (*vedana*) that arise from sensory contact; perceptions (*samjna*) that attach the categories good, evil, neutral, to these sensory inputs; habitual mental dispositions (*samskaras*) that connect karma-producing will to mental action; and the consciousness (*vijnana*) that arises when mind and body come in contact with the external world.

The spiritual purpose of breaking down any apparently unchanging locus of individuality is to demonstrate that there is "no thing" to be attached to or to direct one's desire toward. The anatman doctrine, however, presented exponents of Buddhism with the perpetual problem of explaining moral causality: how can the doctrine of karma with its emphasis on moral retribution operate without the mechanism of the soul (as in Hinduism or Christianity)? Early texts show that this question was clearly posed to Shakyamuni Buddha: if there is no soul, how can the karmic "fruits" of any good or evil act pass into the future of this life or into a later incarnation? The standard explanation given is that karma endures in habitual mental energies (samskaras) that are impressed in the fifth skandha, consciousness (vijnana). Although always evolving and so impermanent, vijnana endures in this life and passes over to be reincarnated in the next.

While the no-self or no-soul doctrine was at the center of Buddhist thought for the philosophical elite, householders across Asia nonetheless typically conceived of themselves in terms of a body and a soul. In fact, the term for "soul" is common in most vernacular languages, as in the Burmese *leikpya* ("butterfly soul"), the Thai *khwan* ("spirit"), or the Chinese *hun/p'o* ("soul"). This contradiction may indicate how peripheral philosophers were to the mainstream of popular Buddhist understanding!

Impermanence and Interdependence

A doctrinal formula as universally accepted among Buddhists as that of anatman describes how antecedent psychic and bodily states condition a being's future evolution. Known as dependent, or conditioned, co-arising (*pratityasamutpada*), this causal definition views reality as an ongoing, impermanent, and
interdependent flux in the form of a circle. Whatever point of entry you take to
diagnose the cause-and-effect conditioning acting on human experience, the
next clockwise element is that experience conditioned and the next element
in the counterclockwise position is that condition affecting the present. Without spiritual exertion, we spin around, life after life, under these conditioning

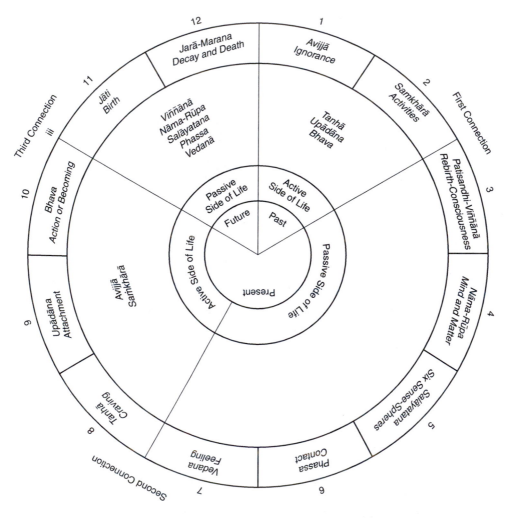

Diagram showing the formula of dependent origination, with several interpretative schemes.

patterns. Used in this way, the twelvefold formula reiterates the basic doctrines already cited: craving (*trishna*) as well as ignorance (*avidya*) are the core causes of suffering (Noble Truths 2 and 3); and no soul exists to center the human being, only changing units (skandhas). Conditioned co-arising also dismisses the role of God or gods in shaping human life, rejects merely materialist theories of reality, and undermines the assumption that life "just happens" in random fashion.

Buddhist Moral Precepts

The early doctrinal formulae specify that moral practice is the first and necessary foundation for moving further on the path toward nirvana. Buddhist ethics entails an "ideology of merit" in which making good karma and avoiding bad is the only sensible approach to life. Popular Buddhist stories focus on imagining the reality of rebirth and seeing that since all contemporary beings have been one's parents and children throughout a vast number of rebirths, acting morally toward them should be natural and logical.

Buddhist morality emphasizes the wisdom of cultivating detachment, discernment, and compassion (karuna). In Buddhist ethics, unlike most Hindu schools, only intentional acts are held to produce karmic results. The varying lists of precepts across the Buddhist world reflect the different doctrinal and praxis emphases.

The five precepts likely are the earliest the Buddhists developed in ancient India and are found in most scriptures. In South and Southeast Asia, they are chanted regularly in modern Theravada rituals by both monks and laity. In these communities, the precepts are regarded as general ideals applicable to everyone. Mahayana schools tended to regard the precepts more as vows, to be chanted only if one intends to follow them completely. (One can omit reciting a precept if one cannot expect to observe it.) The five precepts are listed here, with the corresponding positive traits that counteract the chance of transgression:

1. Not to destroy life intentionally || ← kindness and compassion
2. Not to steal || ← generosity and renunciation
3. Not to have sexual misconduct || ← seeking "joyous satisfaction with one's spouse"
4. Not to lie || ← loving the truth, seeking it, pursuing discernment and insight
5. No intoxication || ← mindfulness, contentment, awareness via meditation

The eight precepts are usually taken and rigorously observed by householders on holy days. They entail a stricter interpretation of the original five along with three additional renunciations:

6. Not to eat (solid) food after noon
7. Not to participate in shows, dancing, singing, or to wear garlands, perfumes, jewelry
8. Not to sleep on high or wide beds.

To observe the eight precepts regularly is one mark of being an *upasaka/upasika* ("devout lay man/woman").

The ten precepts are observed by novice monks and are undertaken as a long-term commitment. They comprise the eight, but split one of these into two parts and add a final prohibition against handling money. This final rule ensured that begging should be the norm for monks and nuns and this exchange between laity and sangha binds the Buddhist community. In this formulation, the moral duty of Buddhist householders to give generously found special emphasis: only by their giving can renunciants keep the precepts.

In East Asia, where Buddhists had to adapt to the Confucian and ancestral traditions, householders were exhorted to fulfill their filial and familial duties. Such expectations of moral treatment toward parents, children, and teachers were also present in South Asia. But Buddhist texts composed in China were much more emphatic in stating that the essence of personal and social morality is the mutuality between parent and child, especially the child's "repayment of filial debt" to the parents. East Asian Buddhists expanded the manner of this "repayment" to include service to the Buddha/Dharma/Sangha in their name.

Karma *and Causality*

One can make the case from textual sources that karma doctrine is not fatalistic since one is continually making new *punya* ("merit") or *pap* ("demerit") to change the ongoing calculus of karmic destiny. Buddhist philosophy indeed stresses the potential for certain strong karma effects to set off mechanistic causal connections between past and future; but a person's karma, like all phenomena, nevertheless changes every instant.

Further, the Buddhist understanding of causality is that not all contingencies in life are karma dependent. In fact, according to the Theravadins, events are more likely than not to have been due to causes other than karma. Since only Buddhas can ascertain whether karma or other contingencies are at work in ongoing life, individuals are faced with uncertainty in evaluating events in life. What is clear is that Buddhists can make a "general reading" of karma from birth station and biography. But for the future, the logic of the karma doctrine has motivated Buddhists everywhere to seek guidance through astrology and to keep making punya. Indeed, texts for householders emphasize that accumulation of wealth is the fruition of good past karma, that giving away wealth to earn merit is the best expenditure, and that this giving is of benefit to all, in a sense the social application of interdependence doctrine. These principles have been incorporated into "Four Conditions" and "Four Good Deeds," doctrinal statements that have been as influential for the laity as the Four Noble Truths were for the philosophers:

Four Conditions (to seek):	*Four Good Deeds (to use wealth for):*
Wealth gotten by lawful means	Make family, friends happy

Good renown in society	Ensure security against worldly dangers
Long life	Make offerings to family, friends, gods,
Birth in heaven	and ghosts
	Support worthy religious people

The provisions and actions articulated as core doctrines were "normative Buddhism" for the householder, fostering family ties, cultivating the ethos of "energetic striving" after economic success, encouraging the worship of hungry ghosts and local gods, applauding the rightful seeking after worldly happiness and security, seeking the cultivation of faith, and promoting heaven-seeking.

The question still remains as to how individual Buddhists and Buddhist communities have focused on the fatalistic or free-will elements affecting individual life. This issue has great significance for assessing Buddhist history, making historical comparisons with other religions, and understanding the modernization of Asian societies.

The Classical Ideal: Buddhist Civilization

Buddhist civilization was sustained by ritual exchanges between householders and renunciants, the monks and nuns whose advanced ascetic practices entailed abandonment of worldly comforts. Many formulations of proper Buddhist practice were made in the course of early Buddhist history to guide the faithful among the spiritual alternatives specified by the Buddha. The traditional and progressive triad of moral practice (*shila*), meditation (*dhyana*), and insight cultivation was an early organizing schema.

Buddhist monasticism arose to provide refuge and support for renunciants seeking enlightenment, but the tradition survived by building multifaceted relationships with lay followers who provided for the monks' and nuns' subsistence. Solidifying the loyalty of a cross section of society's economic classes, Buddhists eventually articulated the foundations for a society with spiritual and moral dimensions. Buddhism adapted to myriad local traditions, yet still—when vital—its community focused on the Three Refuges: Buddha, Dharma ("teachings"), Sangha ("monastic community"). All who take these refuges are members of "the assembly" of ordained monks and nuns, and householders.

The general ideals of Buddhist civilization were articulated very early. Monks and nuns served the world through their example of renunciation and meditation, by performing rituals, and by providing medical service. As preservers, transmitters, and exemplars of the Dharma, the sangha's duty was to attract the lay community's merit-making donations by being spiritually worthy; complementing this, sangha members were to follow the *Vinaya* rules and seek out *prasaditas* ("dedicated sympathizers") and *danapatis* ("generous donors"). Based upon these guidelines, Buddhist cultures came to exhibit an array of common traits: stupas as centers of community ritual; viharas as refuges for meditation, study, and material resources; sangha members who assume leadership of the community's spiritual instruction and ritual life.

Thus, Buddhism developed a broad vision of the spiritual community and of proper practice: one text speaks of the devout layman's duty to help others grow in faith, morality, knowledge, and charity; another enjoins householders to maintain the traditions of family and lineage, to live a life worthy of their heritage, and to make offerings to the spirits of the dead. Finally, the Buddha cited certain short texts (called *mantra* and *paritta*, later *dharani*) that, when chanted, would help householders achieve blessings and protections needed for a good worldly life. All Buddhists are instructed to listen to the Dharma and make exertions to resist its decline. Given the variety of possible practices, the only sound definition of a "good Buddhist" is simple: one who takes the three refuges and practices accordingly.

The Mahayana: Philosophies and East Asian Monastic Schools

Despite their prolific writings, Mahayana philosophers and followers were in fact a minority in ancient South Asia, as monks of this persuasion lived in monasteries alongside Sthaviravadins. Mahayana became the dominant strain of Buddhism only outside the heartland, being a small but vibrant subculture only in India (until its extinction), in Burma, in the Khmer and Funan regions of medieval Southeast Asia, and in Sri Lanka. "Reforms" across this region by kings had nearly eliminated the broad pluralism of Buddhism in the tropical regions by 1300; at the same time the once dominant presence of Mahayana schools in insular Southeast Asia (notably Java) was ended with the fall of the Srivijaya empire. But for roughly a millennium, Mahayanist practice was a significant force in the Buddhism of Southeast Asia.

The contrast between Traditionalists (Theravadins) and Mahayanists seems to reflect a universal human tendency to divide religious communities between those inclined to a literal approach (holding to the letter within a conservative tradition) and those inclined to a more open-ended, experimental, and expansive approach to the spiritual that finds "keeping the spirit" essential. The Mahayana in this light might be compared to the Sufis in Islam opposed to the strict scholars of the law (*ulama*); the Christian analogy would be the Gnostics and mystics in opposition to the official church.

On the philosophical level, there were fiercely contested disagreements that we know of chiefly from the Mahayana side. For the most part, the traditionalists ignored their opponents' polemics: the term found in the Theravada commentaries for the Mahayanists, "Illusionists" (*Vaitulika*), is representative of the traditionalists' evaluation of the arguments raised. The label the Mahayanists applied to their opponents, the "Lesser Vehicle" (Hinayana), suggested diminished religious effectiveness, commitment, and vision.

We shall discuss the Madhyamaka and Consciousness Only schools of Mahayana thought, as well as some minority sects that happen to be well known today and an esoteric tradition called the "Thunderbolt vehicle."

The Madhyamaka

Among the earliest texts expressing Mahayana ideas are those called the *Perfection of Wisdom* (*Prajnaparamita*). These texts of varying length have the Buddha or notable monks poke fun at the arhats and poke holes in their scholasticism. Applying the adjective "empty" (*shunya*) to all perceived experiences, the *Prajnaparamita* texts seek to deconstruct mistaken scholastic analysis and search for the ultimate truth behind the words of the older scriptures. In the Mahayana view, erroneous ideas propounded by the traditionalists discredited the arhats' enlightenment as false or incomplete.

Since Mahayana thought emphasizes interdependence, its exponents saw the Theravadins' focus on the individual pursuit of nirvana as "selfish" and reflecting ignorance of the Buddha's highest teaching. The Mahayana exponents held that the laity as well as monks could attain enlightenment, and thus they elevated the bodhisattva ideal above the arhat, recognizing the inseparability of personal and universal enlightenment.

Opposition to the Traditionalists coalesced in the writings of the monk Nagarjuna (born c. 120 CE), one of India's greatest philosophers and founder of a school called the Madhyamaka. Nagarjuna developed a deconstructive method that reduces all assertions to arbitrary propositions and applied the system to a wide-ranging subject matter. In one of the most courageous explorations in the history of religions, he argued that all language is conventional and all oppositions set up by it are mere constructions, including all Buddhist constructs, even "nirvana" and "samsara." It is through understanding how humans construct reality arbitrarily from no-thing-ness (*shunyata*) that one is released from all illusions and desires, and from the cycle of rebirths. Nagarjuna also interpreted the dependent origination formula to show how the Buddha had argued that all reality lacks essential self-existence (*svabhava*) and is inherently empty (*shunya*), that is, that every entity entirely depends upon others for its meaning, as no thing can be shown to have its own independent reality.

Nagarjuna stated that the purpose of his deconstructive philosophical effort was religious: to clear away all false assumptions and even the subtle attachment to language and scholastic categories, opening the way to find true refuge and final enlightenment only in meditation practices that transcend words.

"Consciousness Only" School

The other major school of Mahayana thought continued from Nagarjuna's standpoint. The "Consciousness Only" (*Cittamatra*) school largely agreed with the Madhyamaka critique of experience but asserted that the real arena of spiritual transformation can therefore be further specified: within human consciousness. This school's great thinkers were the brothers Asanga and Vasubandhu (active c. 320 CE), who developed intricate theories of consciousness and causality, especially in terms of how karma works within the stream of consciousness, "seeded" by past actions that block pure, passionless seeing.

Further, as mind or consciousness is all that truly exists, the spiritual life must be devoted to purifying it. Again, the practical effect of such theories was to promote the traditional Buddhist practice of meditation, as indicated by this faction's other name, Yogacara ("Yoga Practice" [School]).

Buddha-Nature School

Yet another Mahayana school grew from Madhyamaka roots: the Buddha-Nature (*tathagatagarbha*) school. These proponents held that if it is true that nirvana and samsara cannot be separated in any meaningful way, then nirvana interpenetrates all reality. And if this is so, then one might say that all beings have a portion of it and so possess the latent potential for nirvana realization. One text that developed this idea at great length was the Avatamsaka, a work on which an early Chinese school, the Hua-yen, centered its teachings. Among the many similes developed to convey the interdependence of all reality with the Buddha nature, that of Indra's Jeweled Net had great appeal. As each jewel in the net reflects every other one, including their reflections of each jewel, ad infinitum, even the tiniest thing contains the mystery of the universe. Although the Hua-yen school eventually declined in China, its ideas and metaphors influenced Ch'an/Zen Buddhism. The Buddha-nature doctrine appeared to some as a backdoor admission of soul theory into Mahayana thought; but it, too, reinforced the need for traditional meditation practices.

The Lotus Sutra and Its Schools

One of the most popular Buddhist scriptures in East Asia was the *Lotus Sutra*. Originally written in Sanskrit by 100 CE, this work was later translated into every East Asian language spoken by Buddhists. The Chinese T'ien T'ai school, like its Japanese descendant (the Tendai) several centuries later, based its interpretation of Buddhism on the *Lotus* and popularized it greatly in the early centuries through art and preaching. The *Lotus* develops another important and popular realm of Mahayana doctrine: the theory of cosmic Buddhahood. Through parable, accounts of astounding magical display, and hammering polemics, the text recounts how amazed and confused the arhats became when Shakyamuni Buddha revealed that the human Buddha to whom they were so attached is in fact the embodiment of a more universal Buddha reality that can materialize in many forms simultaneously throughout the cosmos. The *Lotus* describes how the Buddha's preaching skillfully adapted the Dharma to suit the level of the audiences. Even his dying was a show, performed to encourage the active practice of devotees so that they would take seriously the shortness of mortal life. The *Lotus* asserts that the nirvana of arhats is merely a preliminary stage in enlightenment seeking, with all beings destined for Buddhahood through eons of rebirth in samsara.

The religious ideal in the *Lotus Sutra* and in other Mahayana texts shifts from the arhat to the bodhisattva, or "future Buddha." Disciples following the Great Vehicle are encouraged not to be satisfied with the arhats' limited nirvana, when

Buddhahood is the proper, final religious goal. Why? Mahayana teachers point out that given the reality of interdependence, no one can be an enlightened "being" somehow independent of others. Bodhisattvas should therefore not imagine ending their careers until all beings are enlightened, a mind-boggling and very long-term commitment. The aspiring bodhisattva should advance by developing clear and calm insight (*prajna*) merged with skillful practices (*upaya*). The Mahayana framework for achieving such insight has set a profoundly challenging spiritual ideal, one of the most altruistic articulated in the history of religions.

The *Lotus Sutra* is only one among a large class of texts that focus on bodhisattvas who have garnered the merit necessary to earn rebirth as divinities. These "celestial bodhisattvas" continue to serve humanity by offering compassionate intervention to secure worldly blessings and even the means to salvation. In the popular imagination, they became the Buddhist parallels to Hindu or Chinese deities by the end of the faith's first millennium. The most popular and universal of these was Avalokiteshvara, who came to be known as Guanyin in China, Kannon in Japan, Chenrizi in Tibet, Karunamaya in Nepal. Wherever Mahayana Buddhism spread, texts recounting the local deeds of this and other celestial bodhisattvas were commonly disseminated through storytellers, art, and popular texts. Temples with their icons, monastic priesthoods, and ritual traditions all evolved to maintain these Mahayana cults. Advanced meditators used their forms in visualizations and repeated mantras to identify with them. For the great majority of householders, being a Mahayana devotee meant performing rituals and asking for blessings from these compassionate divinities.

Pure Land Schools

Perhaps as an extension of the Buddha's injunction that the sangha should "show the householders the way to heaven," Pure Land Buddhism arose as yet another "cabin" within the Great Vehicle. This school's texts describe how certain bodhisattvas vowed to create celestial paradises upon reaching Buddhahood. These "Pure Lands" supplied all requisites for the enlightenment of individuals reborn there. The popularity of this Buddhist orientation that deferred enlightenment seeking from the human state until rebirth in a heaven had been earned, probably had its origins in Shakyamuni's predictions of Buddhism's decline after a thousand years. This expectation legitimated a new spirituality to match the changed times, and Pure Land Buddhism gained wide popularity.

The most important and highly developed of these traditions was that associated with the paradise *Sukhavati* skillfully created by the Buddha called Amitabha in Sanskrit, Amitofo in Chinese, Amida in Japanese. An ordered system of Pure Land doctrine and practice, developed in China, featured chanting Amitabha's name (*Namo A-mi-t'o Fo*) as a meditative act and communal ritual. Exponents assured Pure Land followers that by drawing upon this Buddha's distinctive cosmic power through chanting and other devotional practices, even those with bad karma could be reborn in Sukhavati. It was the monk Shan-tao (613–681) who effectively brought the Pure Land teaching to its widest audience, preaching to both court officials and the masses.

In Japan, Pure Land Buddhism continued to evolve as devotees were taught that their own "self power" was insufficient to reach nirvana and only the "other power" of celestial Buddhas and bodhisattvas could be relied upon. Rituals at death were dedicated to having an individual's lifetime accumulation of merit (punya) be directed to attaining rebirth in the Pure Land. Eventually, these schools were widespread, and hopes for Pure Land rebirth became extremely popular. These schools were also the first to deemphasize the requirement of monastic celibacy by its ordained sangha.

The Meditation School

In response to the Pure Land emphasis on "other power," a more "traditionalist Mahayana" school called Ch'an formed by about 600 CE in China. Its teachers insisted that individual effort to reach nirvana was the Buddha's true teaching. Ch'an stressed meditation, this-life realization, and "self power." Its authority is asserted through an unbroken line of patriarchs from Shakyamuni onward. Each enlightened master in turn, wordlessly by "mind to mind," transmitted enlightenment to well-prepared disciples.

Less concerned with a single text and formed in close association with Daoist concepts and aesthetics, Ch'an lineages respected the Mahayana scriptures but used as pivotal texts the stories recounting the teachings of their own patriarchs and masters, including their unlocking the doors of nirvana realization. This school also developed the use of particular problems called koans ("cases") that masters forced their disciples to ponder and answer. Resolution of the koans—with words, roars, bodily gestures, or composed silence—could lead to small awakenings of prajna or even complete nirvana realization. Ch'an masters also insisted on the necessity of mindfulness meditation.

The paradigmatic figure of this school is Bodhidharma, the patriarch who reputedly brought the mind-to-mind transmission tradition from India to China. He is depicted as a fierce meditating monk dispensing terse spiritual admonitions. Later known as Zen in Japan, this school also developed in monasteries upholding strict monastic rules. Its lineages eventually split on the lines of those believing in gradual versus those believing in sudden enlightenment.

The Thunderbolt Vehicle

One additional branch of elite doctrine and practice that had emerged among Mahayana Buddhists was the Vajrayana, a tradition that some scholars would highlight (as did later Tibetan scholastics) as a third division of the faith. Also called "tantra," it developed after the faith's first millennium in South Asia and was initially centered among the wandering mendicants whose spiritual seeking on the fringes of society began in the Buddha's era. Perhaps in reaction to the spiritual orientation that had evolved in the devotional traditions that had come to the fore—the assumption that final enlightenment would not be achieved until after many future lifetimes—the tantric traditions emphasized realizing salvation speedily and in this lifetime.

Tantric Buddhism is also called "Thunderbolt" or "Diamond Vehicle" (*Vajrayana*) or "Mantra Vehicle" (*Mantrayana*), terms indicating the esoteric spiritual traditions that developed principally within later Mahayana Buddhism. Using pan-Indian yoga techniques and unorthoprax means under the guidance of an accomplished teacher (*siddha*), tantric Buddhism drew upon the philosophical understandings from Mahayana philosophy that equated samsara with nirvana. It agreed that all beings partake of the Buddha nature (*tathagatagarbha* doctrine) and found the essence of the Buddha's teaching (the experience of unshakable diamondlike (hence, *vajra*) insight (prajna) to be the pursuit of this ultimate goal by whatever means brought immediate success.

There were in fact many recognized paths to enlightenment within tantric Buddhism: dozens of traditions cohered around separate texts (*tantras*) that specified interrelated forms of initiation, ritual, and medical practice, mantra recitation, and visualization meditation.

The central experience of tantric Buddhism is *sadhana*, communion with a celestial Buddha or bodhisattva through the experience of identification with his (or her) body, speech, and mind. Based on the assumption that the siddha who discovered each path had experienced the deity as the embodiment of enlightenment, an initiate is taught to place the deity (with entourage) in his or her mind's eye, repeat mantras that resonate with that form, and build an existential connection with it, even performing *mudras* (hand gestures) and other rituals that help to solidify the identification. When complete, one's identification ultimately implies the attainment of enlightenment coequal with that of the divine form.

Some tantric traditions consciously break the norms of orthodox caste society. Men and women assume identities as divine, enlightened consorts and their sexual union is developed as a unifying experience of the dual energies of *prajna* (the feminine, as insight) and *upaya* (the masculine, as means of practice). Sexual consort yoga was doubtless once an element in some tantric traditions. (In Nepal and Tibet, consorts are often spouses.) But as these traditions were systematized in textual form by Buddhist monks after 900 CE in North India, the requirement of literal sexual yoga practice was often reinterpreted to allow its replacement by symbolic visualization.

PREMODERN BUDDHISM: BUDDHIST EXPANSION

As Buddhism expanded across Asia up to the early modern era, in each cultural region monks, nuns, and disciples sought to adapt the faith to local material and cultural conditions. It is important to note that the philosophical teachings of the doctrinal schools were not the concern of most Buddhists, for the typical householder was free to choose a teacher, a set of personal devotional practices, and one or more objects of meritorious donations. Across Asia, all the sanghas developed Buddhist rituals to help individuals through their lives, from birth to death. In applying the faith's resources to fulfilling the religious needs of the householders, monks and nuns from all Buddhist doctrinal schools served their parishioners in a similar manner. In this section we survey the wide-ranging pilgrimage of the faith by geographic region, then note the distinctive beliefs and practices that gave the faith its local appeal.

South Asia

With the decline of the great Gupta dynasty in North India by 650 CE, small regional polities controlled the Hindu-Buddhist societies of South Asia. Buddhism survived mainly in the northeast under imperial patronage, yet its presence contracted mostly to large university monasteries. The largest, Nalanda and Vikramashila, fostered a vigorous articulation of Mahayana Buddhist philosophy, meditation, and popular piety. Ties to Tibet, Nepal, and centers in the Srivijaya kingdom of Sumatra-Java extended the influence of the Great Vehicle.

The Sthaviravada school remained the strongest in central and southern India, with Sri Lanka eventually most influenced by its Theravada branch. This school's textual traditions had been well established by the beginning of Buddhism's second millennium as the Pali Canon, whose three divisions total roughly twice the size of the Christian Bible. Monk scholars in Pali there had compiled the materials and closed the Canon by 800; the subsequent work of Theravadin scholasticism was concerned primarily with compiling commentaries. It was the commentaries and treatises of Buddhaghosa, the great monk who settled in Sri Lanka in the fifth century, that established the conservative ethos of this school, an approach that remains authoritative to the present day in all Theravada countries.

By 600, the Mahayana *Sutras* were more diverse, with a growing number of commentaries and treatises swelling the monastic libraries. The Great Vehicle has no single canon, but the texts that were written remain extant today in Sanskrit, Tibetan, Chinese, Mongolian, and Japanese versions. (At most, 15% of these texts have been translated into English.)

After Buddhism's successful transplantation in China, Sri Lanka, and Southeast Asia, monks and householders from there traveled to study in South Asia, bring back texts, and complete pilgrimage visits where they could venerate the "sacred traces" (cremation relics, begging bowls, etc.) of the Buddha and arhats that were housed in the stupas. The enlightenment tree in Gaya and the temple erected nearby were at the center of such visits. Distant rulers from Sri Lanka and Burma are recorded as sending funds and artisans to renovate this site until 1296. Such support was needed, because many Buddhist monasteries across North India had been abandoned for centuries and many shrines had been left to decay. The decline of the faith in South Asia was caused in part by the successful development of popular devotional Hinduism and by Hindu monasticism that was originated by the Vedantin saint-scholar Shankara.

Another factor in Buddhism's decline was the arrival of Islam in South Asia in the first century after its birth (by 750 CE), when converts introduced another missionary faith that slowly spread throughout South Asia from the west. Early conquests and conversions to Islam in Central Asia and the northwest undermined Buddhism. As we have seen, Buddhist monasticism was strongly tied to trade and mercantile patronage, and as the trade moving along silk routes was overtaken by Muslim merchants, the monasteries lost a major source of support. In addition, 1152 marks an era of raids across North India that culminated in the first period of Muslim rule from Delhi. Across the Gangetic plain, almost all remaining Buddhist institutions were plundered, and the destruction dispersed Indian monks into the Himalayas, to coastal urban centers, and across the seas. In the southern peninsula of the Indian subcontinent, Buddhism declined slowly, its monasteries existing as late as the seventeenth century.

Buddhism's center moved to the east after its sacred centers on the Gangetic plain were ravaged, a misfortune that resulted in the loss of many early versions of the first Buddhist textual collections. (Only one full *Tripitaka* survives intact, that of the Theravadins in Pali.) Across the Buddhist world after 1200, many of the regional schools had to look at their surviving texts and scholastic traditions to set their standards of doctrinal authority. Once Bodh Gaya was no longer accessible, pious donors built "replica Bodh Gaya temples" now found across Asia for regional pilgrims. In Southeast Asia, it was Sri Lanka that was regarded as the center of scholarship and disciplined practice. In East Asia, China remained the prime second center of the faith, although after 1250 Tibetan Buddhists at times exerted strong influences within China, south into the Himalayas, and north into Mongolia.

The island of Sri Lanka embraced Buddhism, and its early kings after 100 BCE supported the sangha and built monuments to express their devotion. Although both Mahayanists and Sthaviravadins practiced there throughout the first millennium, the Theravada school eventually prevailed. As indicated earlier, "reforms" instituted by kings in the 1300s ensured the dominance of Theravada traditions in Southeast Asia that continues to the present day.

China

In East Asia, Buddhist schools formed around charismatic teachers whose interpretations favored one or another of the many texts as the Buddha's highest teaching. Mahayana Buddhism flourished, translated in terms compatible with Daoist mysticism, the indigenous pantheons, and aspects of Confucian morality and state governance.

SELECTIONS FROM A MERIT ACCOUNT SHEET[4]

100 Merits: Save one life; save a woman's chastity; prevent a child from drowning; continue family lineage

50 Merits: Prevent an abortion; provide for a homeless person; prevent someone from committing a serious crime; give a speech that benefits many

30 Merits: Convert another to Buddhism; facilitate a marriage; take in an orphan; help another do something virtuous

10 Merits: Recommend a virtuous person; cure a major illness; speak virtuously; save the life of a good animal; publish the Buddha's teachings; treat servants properly

5 Merits: Prevent a lawsuit; cure a minor illness; stop someone from slandering; make an offering to a saintly person; save any animal; pray for others

3 Merits: Endure ill-treatment without complaint; bury an animal; urge those making a living by killing to stop

1 Merit: Give an article to help others; chant a Buddhist scripture; provide for one monk; return a lost article; help repair a public road or bridge

100 Demerits: Cause a death; rape; end a family lineage

50 Demerits: Induce an abortion; break up a marriage; teach someone to do great evil; make a speech that harms many

30 Demerits: Create slander that dishonors another; disobey an elder; cause family to separate; during famine, fail to share food grains

10 Demerits: Mistreat an orphan or widow; prepare a poison; kill an animal that serves humans; speak harshly to parent or teacher

5 Demerits: Slander spiritual teachings; turn away a sick person; speak harshly; kill any animal; write or speak lewdly; not clear an injustice when possible

3 Demerits: Get angry over words spoken; cheat an ignorant person; destroy another's success; be greedy

1 Demerit: Urge another to fight; help another do evil; waste food; kill insects; turn away a begging monk; take a bribe; keep a lost article

Under the weak states of the pre-T'ang era (up until 645 CE), Buddhism found widespread support. With the consolidation of the T'ang state in Chang-an (modern Xian) and its revival of the traditional Confucian literati class, the destiny of Buddhism rose and fell with the vicissitudes of imperial support. Despite the generosity of imperial patrons and wealthy donors who profited from silk route trade, the Confucian officials who manned the permanent state bureaucracy never ceased their harsh critiques of Buddhism. They were especially zealous in highlighting the problems involved in tolerating Buddhist institutions whose wealth was tax exempt and whose members were free from the tax or *corvee* requirements due from other citizens.

Anti-Buddhist sentiment culminated in the great persecution of 841–845. Nearly every Buddhist monastery was dismantled, metal images were melted down for the state treasury, members of the sangha were ordered to return to lay life. Buddhism eventually rebuilt and rebounded, but the faith never permeated Chinese society so thoroughly again, nor did all the early Chinese doctrinal schools truly recover. From the Sung era onward, it was the Ch'an and Pure Land Schools that survived, as both depended less on scholasticism, official recognition, or aristocratic patronage. Leading monks repositioned the faith in Chinese society by emphasizing their disinterest in political concerns, the faith's compatibility with Daoism and Confucianism, and their insistence on a disciplined lifestyle by the clergy.

During the short-lived Mongol conquest of China marking the Yuan Dynasty (1271–1368), Tibetan Buddhism became the state religion and its distinctive Mahayana-Vajrayana traditions were granted strong support across the empire, primarily in imperial strongholds. The Mongols' conversion to Buddhism, soon after their campaigns of violent conquest and rule across Eurasia (1217–1293), marks another point in which Buddhism changed world history, in this case by undercutting Mongol martial values and expansionism.

With the return of native Chinese rule under the Ming (1392–1644), Mahayana traditions were embraced by a large sector of the population: worship of the celestial bodhisattva Guanyin (Skt.: Avalokiteshvara); veneration of the sixteen *lohan* (Skt.: arhats) designated as protectors of Buddhism until the coming of the next Buddha; pilgrimage to Mount Wu-t'ai as the home of another celestial bodhisattva, Manjushri; and the practice of releasing animals (typically fish or birds) to earn merit. From the early Ming, too, the practice of householders keeping detailed merit account books gained in popularity. In China as elsewhere, merit making and ritual observances dominated the religious scene in most Buddhist communities. Indeed, there was little meditation among either monks or laity.

Southeast Asia

Southeast Asia in the post-1200 era was ruled by regional states that sought their legitimacy in supporting the Theravada Buddhist monastic system they introduced from Sri Lanka. Buddha relics were imported as well, and stupas in the Sri Lankan style were also built across the region. The "reforms" already mentioned effectively reduced the presence of the Mahayana to a few isolated communities and all of these eventually disappeared. The Khmer state (including the region of modern Cambodia) for several periods was ruled by kings who favored Mahayana Buddhism, and they constructed magnificent temples and monasteries.

The Srivijaya Empire in Sumatra and Java likewise supported the efflorescence of both Hinduism and Mahayana Buddhism. These rulers created the
colossal stupa at Borobodur, the crowning monument of this era. But after the
empire's decline, the smaller states ruled by regional kings favored local religions or (later) the mystical schools of Islam mediated through India.

It should not be imagined that these Buddhist states, each formed by different ethnic groups (Mon, Burmese, Thai, Khmer), always lived in peace with
their Buddhist neighbors! On the contrary, wars were waged across Southeast
Asia. Armies plundered religious monuments for the usual treasure as well as
for Buddha images and relics, causing each new dynasty to build entirely new
capitals.

In these distinctive Southeast Asian polities, the faith thrived under rulers
who claimed legitimacy under the cosmic law of karma, whereby they were
reaping past merit to rule. Their states supported the sangha and sponsored
rituals designed to have the powers of the Buddhist universe continually re-
generated. In turn, they expected their subjects to emulate their example by
following the Dharma, supporting a just Buddhist order in the territory, and
accepting their place in the karma-determined social hierarchy. The sangha
was compelled to support these regional rulers and live by the highest standards, ensuring that the society would earn the greatest merit from donations.
The many hundreds of grand stupas, image halls, and monasteries built in
these prosperous states show the success of premodern Theravada Buddhism.
In them, Buddhist moral law unified the scattered ethnic groups, since state
sponsorship of religious building projects around the capitals served, in effect, as a continuous large-scale public works program. The great monuments
legitimated the state, created spectacular sanctuaries, employed artisans and
the masses, and lent prestige to the sangha. Across Theravadin Southeast
Asia, this form of "cosmological Buddhism" survived even after the great kingdoms gave way to smaller regional states. It was this "state Buddhism" that
was challenged in the modern era, as new ideas and political systems
emerged.

Japan

Mahayana Buddhism triumphed across East Asia. In Japan by 1230, monks
again had traveled to China to undertake the last transplantations of Chinese
schools: two forms of the Ch'an became the Soto Zen School (instituted by the
monk Dogen [1200–1253]) and the Rinzai Zen school (under the monk Eisai
[1141–1215]). Both vied for popularity among the aristocrats and warriors who
controlled Japanese society in the post-Kamakura era (after 1350).

The Pure Land school found widespread popular acceptance through the
public preaching campaigns undertaken by charismatic monks. Since their
simplification of Buddhist practice entailed only the *nembutsu*, the chant of an
honorific repetition of Amitabha Buddha's name imported from China, householders could hope for nirvana in Pure Land rebirth. A thirteenth-century

monk named Shinran continued the basic practices and textual interpretations imported from Chinese Pure Land teachers and added a Japanese component, *mappo,* the so-called decadent age doctrine. Shinran argued that human beings were completely dependent upon the Buddha's grace to reach nirvana and had simply to acknowledge their grateful acceptance of it to enter the Pure Land. Shinran's school, the Jodo Shinshu, became a vital separate lineage, and its sangha was the first in Japan to drop the requirement of celibacy.

A third track in this era of new Japanese schools is represented by Nichiren (1222–1282), a prophetic and charismatic monk who emphasized that the *Lotus Sutra* is the only true Buddhist text. Like Shinran, Nichiren also subscribed to the "decline of Buddhism doctrine," and argued that the instability of the turbulent times confirmed it. He also accepted the ultimate reality of an omniscient cosmic Buddha immanent in the world and in persons. Practice in the Nichiren school was simplified to three practices: *daimoku,* a short honorific repetition of the *Lotus Sutra*'s title (*Nam-Myoho Reng-e Kyo*); *gohonzon,* the meditation on a mandala of the cosmic Buddha designed by Nichiren; and *kaidan,* pilgrimage to the school's national shrine. His followers taught that Nichiren himself was a bodhisattva. Their interpretation of Buddhism emphasized Japan's special significance in leading Buddhism through the declining next stage of history, a visionary view that has inspired several splinter movements in the modern and postwar eras. The Nichiren school also introduced two new elements into the Japanese context: a pattern of intolerance expressed through outspoken denunciations of other schools, and a style of aggressive proselytizing called *shakubuku* ("break and smash"), which was felt to be necessary to awaken individuals in the degenerate contemporary era.

The Himalayan Region

In Tibet, Mongolia, and Nepal, Mahayana schools again found supremacy. Across the highland frontiers, Vajrayana traditions came to be regarded as the Buddha's highest teaching, and the monks who domesticated Buddhism there taught that Buddhist belief and practice has both outer and inner levels of understanding, the highest of which was accessible only through tantric initiation and practice. In these regions, Vajrayana tradition developed in rich elaboration, where exhaustive meditation regimens were practiced by dedicated elites. Scholars translated a vast corpus of Sanskrit texts, commented upon them, and composed their own interpretive tracts. Ritual masters also applied the texts and teachings to many aspects of life, including rituals designed to promote the best possible rebirth. Even flags, watermills, and hand-turned wheels were adapted to broadcast the Buddha's words, continuously earning merit for individuals and communities.

In Tibet, too, the celestial bodhisattva doctrine was domesticated as nowhere else: extraordinary monks and nuns came to be identified as their incarnations (Tib.: *tulku)* of these divinities. Indeed, after 1250 as these "incarnate lineages" became institutions endowed with lands and households, some tulkus assumed power as both religious and political leaders of their regions.

Leaders of the major Tibetan monasteries ascended to rule over central Tibet, a situation unprecedented in any other Buddhist society. With the triumph of the Gelugpa school under the Dalai Lamas, Tibetan polity assumed its modern form that was dominated by large monasteries (joined by roughly 15% of the male population).

BUDDHISM AND MODERNITY

Early Modern Buddhist Polities: Monks, Nuns, Householders, Kings

One decisive factor in Buddhist history has been its relations with political power, an issue that has been a recurring source of controversy from the colonial period until the present. Buddhists have always looked to the legend of Ashoka (273–232 BCE) to define their exemplary relationship with rulers as protectors and patrons. Only with such support can the sangha's integrity be assured, the Buddha's monuments maintained, and the teachings passed down. In premodern Sri Lanka, the king was considered the *sangharaja* ("ruler of the sangha"); in every Theravada country today, leadership and jurisdiction over the sangha is found in the form of a single individual or council appointed by the state.

A dramatic modern instance of this exemplary royal support was Burma's King Mindon who convened the Fifth Buddhist Council (in Theravada reckoning) in 1871. The whole Pali Canon was recited and corrected at this conference, and every passage was inscribed on marble slabs set out in Mandalay. Postcolonial Buddhist governments across the world sponsored similar activities in 1956 on the occasion of the 2,500-year anniversary of Shakyamuni's parinirvana.

For most of its history, however, the Buddhist sangha has existed in polities ruled by kings or emperors. As a result, the tradition developed an exchange synergy: the sangha adopted rules in harmony with those of states and would applaud the monarch's moral leadership if exemplary. In premodern times, monastic Buddhism usually served to promote social stability, accommodating itself to local traditions. The monks also performed long-life rituals for rulers, a custom of mantra chanting and merit-making ritualism that continues in modern Japan, Thailand, and Nepal.

Buddhist Monasticism

A monastery (*vihara*) can be of humble construction or built to imperial, aristocratic standards. Each, however, must have a place for the monks to sleep and a building marked with special boundary stones (*sima*) in which they gather for ordination, fortnightly recitations, and other legal proceedings. Most monasteries also have one or more stupas, a "*bodhi* tree," a meditation hall, an image hall, and memorial stupas for enshrining the ashes of deceased notable monks.

MONASTIC RAIN RETREAT: *VARSAVASA*

In conformity with the lunar-month system, the most prominent yearly Indic Buddhist observance is the monsoon rain retreat called *varsavasa* ("residence due to the [monsoon] rains"). The rain retreat practice curtails the monks' and nuns' mobility outside the monastery and encourages meditation and study for its three-month duration. It is likewise a time for intensive lay devotional exertions, as it is until today in Burma, Sri Lanka, and Thailand. In the Theravada world still, ceremonies mark the beginning, formal ending (*pavarana*), and new robe donations (*kathina*) to monks who complete their rain retreat.

The special ceremonies defined in antiquity for monastic initiations for novices (*pabbajja*) and full monks (*upasampada*) have continued. Adolescent, premarital short-term monastic ordinations evolved in Theravadin Burma and Thailand, and in Mahayana communities of Nepal. It is striking to note here, as in the East Asian adaptations of Buddhism generally, that most Mahayana schools did not follow Indic monastic precedents.

The subsistence of the monks and nuns has remained dependent upon the donations of food and shelter by the lay community. Originally, all sangha members gathered their food in morning begging rounds, and the day's solid food had to be eaten by noon. By the modern period, however, the community developed more routinized methods: in some places the laity worked out systems of their coming to the monastery by rotation with food donations; in other places, monks cooked their own foods. (Today, the begging round is still practiced regularly only by certain Theravadin and Zen monks.) Mahayana monasteries of East Asia interpreted the moral rules to require vegetarianism of the monks and nuns, but in recent centuries the restriction against alcohol was taken to mean "no intoxication," not complete abstinence.

A formal division that endured within the sangha was that between village monks and forest monks. Forest and village were the two poles of the monastic orientation. As a rule, male and female renunciants in the former domain were dedicated to service and study, while forest dwellers meditated. (Buddhists in Sri Lanka many centuries ago debated whether the monk's most important pursuit should be meditation or learning; citing the danger of the faith's decline at the time, it was decided that the learning was more important.)

Meditation Practices

As we have noted, meditation remained essential for all aspirants, lay and ordained, seeking to move on the final path to nirvana. This practice by monks and nuns, even if only by a few, certifies Buddhism's continuing spiritual vitality, inspiring layfolk to respect and take refuge in the sangha. Until late into the modern era, however, it was almost entirely the elite among monks and nuns who practiced meditation.

Buddhism inherited and extended the spiritual experiments of ancient India. The practice of trance (*samadhi*) is accepted, even encouraged, but the state(s) achieved is seen as a diversion from nirvana realization, hence is not given highest priority. The key salvific practice is mindfulness meditation (*vipashyana*): a careful attending to the three characteristics of existential reality—suffering (*dukkha*), impermanence (*anitya*), non-self (*anatman*). Attention to, and comprehension of, these conditions in direct personal experience has a critical twofold effect: it develops nonattachment that stills desire and it cultivates spiritual insight (*prajna*) that dispels ignorance (*avidya*). The development of prajna and the removal of ignorance eliminate bad karma and create good karma. Perfection eventually leads to the fullness of *prajna* in a breakthrough, transformative experience (Jap.: *satori*) of an enlightened mind (*bodhi*).

Mahayana meditations elaborated upon these precedents. Ch'an (Jap.: Zen) mindfulness meditation (Jap.: *zazen*), like Theravada vipashyana practice, focuses first upon the breath. Given the Mahayana teaching that all beings possess the Buddha-nature (*tathagatagarba*), meditation practice can comprise any activity practiced with mindfulness, from chopping wood to tea ceremony, from martial arts to the art of flower arranging.

In Pure Land meditation, the fervent wish for nirvana attainment in an otherworldly paradise (*Sukhavati*) encourages devotees to visualize that extraordinary paradise as described in the texts. These practices are especially important as death nears, for individuals who can visualize this realm are promised painless passage into heavenly rebirth there through the boundless grace of the Buddha Amitabha.

Schools devoted to esoteric Vajrayana innovations developed yet other forms of meditation under the heading of *sadhana* ("communion [with an enlightened deity]"). The exact procedures and instructions were passed from teacher to student, with an initiation (*abhisheka*) necessary for beginning. Sadhana practices also utilize visualizations of enlightened beings (bodhisattvas) along with mantra recitations linked to them to awaken the mind's powers and foster disciplined spiritual development. By controlling the appearance of mental images, one sees all experience as mind constructed and thus empty (*shunya*) of any ultimate reality.

Again, however, it is necessary to emphasize that most Buddhists concentrated their devotional activities on rituals and on accumulating merit (*punya*), and so we turn to an early doctrinal formulation called the graded teaching that established gift giving as the foundation of Buddhist practice.

Punya and Dana: The Fundamental Buddhist Exchange
The "graded teaching" (*anupurvikatha*) legitimated a Buddhist community's diverse cultural activities by setting up a format for merit-making donations

(*punya/dana*). The anupurvikatha, still used as a guide for modern Buddhist teachers, counsels progress through the following stages of religious striving:

1. *Dana* ("self-less giving" to diminish desire)
2. *Shila* ("morality")
3. *Svarga* ("heaven")
4. *Dharma-deshana* ("instruction on doctrine") on the Four Noble Truths

This hierarchy of progressive practices defines a "syllabus" for advancing in spiritual attainment. Stages 1 and 2 lead to heaven birth (3), the fruit of merit; the doctrines in 4 are those instructions concerning reaching enlightenment, beyond good karma making.

As merit has provided the chief orientation point and goal in the Buddhist layperson's world view and ethos, dana has always been the starting practice for accumulating it. Merit-making for most Buddhists, including most monks and nuns, was the central measure of spiritual advancement. Merit-making remained the universal, integrating transaction in Buddhist settings through the modern era, regardless of the respective intellectual elite's orientation toward competing Theravada, Mahayana, or Vajrayana doctrinal formulations or spiritual disciplines.

The wish for merit leading to rebirth in heaven has remained the most popular and pan-Buddhist aspiration; indeed, monks from the beginning of the faith were instructed to "show the laity the way to heaven" by acting as what modern physics might define as a "field of merit." Punya is needed for a good rebirth, and although Buddhist doctrine holds that heaven is a temporary state, the reward of heavenly rebirth has motivated many to be "good Buddhists."

Merit-making can lead one close to nirvana, but it has practical, worldly consequences, impacting destiny in both this lifetime and across future lifetimes. Therefore, Buddhists seek punya to change their karma "account" that affects this life as well as future rebirth destiny.

To maximize punya and so the course of spiritual advancement, popular texts urge all disciples, monastic and lay, to cultivate such practices as venerating images, fasting, taking the precepts (as described at the beginning of this chapter), organizing compassionate actions and charitable institutions, arranging public recitations of the texts, and encouraging meditation.

The most universal expression of lay Buddhist faith and punya seeking has been through dana. Making donations for spiritual purposes and time for moral observances remained the foundation for householder practice; these still comprise the most visible Buddhist activity today. Passages in the Mahayana texts also articulate the value of dana to the individual as an expression of compassion (*karuna*) and as a renunciatory practice that undercuts desire and attachment.

Merit transfer also became a popular pan-Buddhist practice, albeit one whose mechanisms philosophers have had to explicate. Texts exhort persons doing something meritorious to share the good deed's karma effects with family, community, and all beings simply by announcing the intent; such sharing increases the initial merit earned by helping others. The calculus of merit transfer becomes very complex. In Theravada countries, it is common for humans to make merit, then transfer it to the local gods—who need merit infusions to stay in their heavens—on the expectation that the deities will grant mundane aid to the devotees who were generous with their merit "currency."

Unsurprisingly, by the modern era people had recognized the need to standardize essential donations (dana) and to ensure a consistent flow of punya to the laity.

Buddhist Rituals, Individual and Communitywide

Buddhist monasteries developed ritual procedures (*puja*) and a yearly festival calendar precisely for the purposes of imposing some uniformity on the widespread sangha network. The monk's vocation came to include priestly duties, performing rituals that linked the Buddha's spoken words with simple gestures. The simplest (and still most popular) universal Buddhist ritual has monks pour water into a vessel as they chant words revealed by the Buddha. Imbued with healing powers, the liquid can now be drunk or sprinkled over the bodies of those needing assistance. All Buddhist schools also render offerings of food, incense, and flowers to Buddha images, bodhi trees, and stupas.

Mahayana rituals are seen as a bodhisattva's service to others, and most emphasize mastery of word chains called mantras known for their spiritual powers. These can be spoken to bless and protect the speaker, the sangha, and entire settlements. Ritual chanting of the canonical works is thought to further the foundations of spiritual practice and provide infusions of good karma for towns, domiciles, and at moments of life-cycle passage. Ritual service thus came to dominate Mahayana Buddhism in its missionary program, especially mantra recitations that expressed the faith's spiritual ideals and activated the unseen powers promised in the Mahayana texts.

Each fortnight on the new and full moon days, Indic sangha members had to recite the *pratimoksha*, a summary of the community's *Vinaya* regulations. This recitation came after any transgressions of the rules were confessed in private to the monk's superior. This day, called *Uposatha*, continued in the modern era to serve as the regular occasion to review, correct, and certify the proper standards of monastery discipline in Theravada societies. Emphasizing the fundamental interdependence between sangha and lay community, householders visit the local vihara on these days to make dana offerings. On these days, too, devout layfolk (*upasakas*) take the opportunity to don white robes and observe eight of the ten monastic rules while residing continuously on the monastery grounds. They join with many more layfolk who may come there to release animals, make offerings to Buddha images, and remain to hear monks preach the Dharma. Thus, the lunar fortnight rhythm dominates the festival year. There is the regular succession of uposathas and the two half-moon days when Buddhists typically undertake meritorious actions, perform rituals, and engage in meditation practices. Thus, each week has a special day for Buddhist observances.

Festival Traditions and Public Religious Observances

Like other great world religions, Buddhist cultures came to order and shape time through regular monthly and yearly festivals. Some festivals orchestrate the reliving of classical Buddhist events "in the beginning": celebrations of the Buddha's birth, enlightenment, and nirvana are universal, although differing as to season. Other more regional sacred events likewise mark the year, as different communities assigned their own definitions for these "auspicious days." These include: Shakyamuni's ascent/descent from heaven to preach to his mother, events marking a key point in a popular bodhisattva's life, or the death anniversary of a local saint.

The Universal Buddhist Shrine

For all Buddhist schools, the stupa (or *caitya*, a term that can also signify any Buddha shrine) became a focal point and the singular landmark denoting the tradition's spiritual presence. Early texts and the archaeological record link stupa worship with Shakyamuni Buddha's life and especially the key venues in his religious career. Buddhism eventually recognized "Eight Great Relic Caityas" for pilgrimage and veneration in South Asia. Stupa worship thus became the chief focus of Buddhist ritual activity, and this has continued through the modern era to the present. The Buddhist relic cult began early, inspiring monks, nuns, and householders to circumambulate the shrines (in clockwise direction) and to have their own cremation ashes deposited in the same great stupa or in smaller votive stupas located nearby.

The elaborations on stupa ritual in Buddhist history are extensive: a place to go to recall the Buddha's great acts; a "power place" tapping the Buddha's (or saint's) relic presence and its healing potency; a site to earn merit through joyful, musical veneration; a monument marking the conversion and control of local gods and spirits. In the Mahayana schools, the stupa came to symbolize other ideas: of Buddhahood's omnipresence; a center of Mahayana text revelation; and an archetypal form showing the unity of the five elements with the Buddha nature.

Later Buddhists identified stupas as the physical representations of the eternal teachings and expanded the possible sacred objects deposited to include Buddha's words in textual form. Despite the many understandings, Buddhists of every level of sophistication believe that ritually correct veneration of stupas will earn them merit; in practice, all converge at them to mark events associated with the Buddhas or saints. Stupas thus remain the natural sites for Buddhist festivals of remembrance and veneration.

Pilgrimage to Worship Sacred Relics
and Revealed Texts (Sutras)

Travel to venerate the stupas marking important events in the Buddha's life also defined early Buddhist pilgrimage. This meritorious veneration of the Buddha's relics was organized into extended processional rituals, and their ordering was informed by the early biographies of Shakyamuni. Buddhists in South and Southeast Asia also revere sites such as Adam's Peak in Sri Lanka, where legendary visits of Shakyamuni occurred through supernormal travel. Yet other sites were identified as those where Shakyamuni in an earlier rebirth lived, as described in the narratives recounting his previous lives (*jatakas*).

Sites identified with celestial bodhisattvas became pilgrimage destinations for Mahayana devotees. Accordingly, each missionized region of Asia developed its own Buddhist overlay of pilgrimage involving mountains, and sites for saint veneration; in fact, monasteries and stupas were often built to "colonize" the sacred venue for the faith.

The most extraordinary Indic form of Buddha image veneration noted in numerous locations was the chariot festival (*ratha jatra*). The Chinese pilgrims noted that in ancient India and Central Asia there were images of Buddhas and bodhisattvas placed on twenty-four-wheeled, five-story chariots made of wood and bamboo and then pulled through the city. Beginning on the eighth lunar day and continuing for eight nights, the local merchants made vast donations to monks and others from specially erected dwellings along the path. Nepal's surviving ratha jatras dedicated to the bodhisattva Avalokiteshvara continue the tradition.

Death Ritualism

In all Buddhist countries today, and despite many regional differences, death rituals are the exclusive purview of the sangha and a key time when monks expound core teachings and receive dana. Buddhist mourners carefully dispose of the corpse, relying on ritual to ensure that the dead person does not become a hungry ghost (*preta*) or, worse, a demon (*yaksha*). They also seek to avert bad destiny for the deceased by making punya, then transferring it to the dead person. In adopting such practices, Buddhists straddle both alternatives to the ancient Indic question of whether destiny is based strictly upon an individual's own karma from past and present lifetimes, or whether the proper performance of rituals during and immediately after death can override unfavorable karma, hence manipulating rebirth destiny. Since Buddhism is conceptually centered on the doctrine that the cosmos is governed by karmic law, ritual traditions naturally surround death as it is the critical time when such causal mechanisms operate. Both Theravada monks and—more expansively— Mahayana ritualists apply ritual expertise to this time. The tradition's dependence on after-death ritual service for sangha donations is evident in all modern Asian traditions; even when people are otherwise hardly observant in modern urban areas of Japan, death rituals performed by the Buddhist clergy endure.

Buddhism Under Colonialism

The modern era was one of widespread decline for Buddhism across Asia, as medieval states either lost their autonomy or were destabilized by colonialism, first by European powers (the British in Burma, India, Sri Lanka, Tibet, and China; the French in Indo-China; the Portuguese and Dutch in Sri Lanka; the Dutch in Indonesia) and later (in the early twentieth century) by the Japanese. In East Asia, the imperial Chinese state was weakened by the colonial powers (primarily Britain) whose aggressive trade practices backed by military intervention had disrupted the Chinese economy; the civil disorders that followed also undermined Buddhist institutions. (These events are discussed in Chapter 7.)

The impact of European colonialism on Buddhism can be summarized under two broad domains, institutional and doctrinal. Although Dutch, British, and French colonial governments had somewhat different ideologies guiding their rule in Asia, all administrations eventually adopted the position that they would not fulfill the traditional native monarch's role of patron and protector of local religions, including Buddhism. As a result, the means of accommodation that had evolved over the centuries to perpetuate Buddhism were ended, sometimes precipitously, in every colonized polity. When the Portuguese and Dutch took power in Sri Lanka (1505–1658), for example, they seized the ports and lowlands, destroyed monasteries, persecuted Buddhists, forcibly converted many to Catholicism, and caused the Sinhalese king to flee to the central highlands. Once all the island became its colony (1815), the British moved to end state donations to the sangha and discontinued patronage dedicated to the upkeep of Buddhist buildings; colonial administrations also typically ceased enforcement of indigenous land tenure relations and taxation, withdrew from supervision of standards of monastic ordination, and halted ceremonies according respect to venerable monastic leaders, sacred symbols, and temples. The roots of modern crisis and Buddhism's decline across the region are easily traced to this abrupt deprivation of resources and withdrawal of political support.

Early Challenges from Colonialism

In the realm of ideas, the colonial powers introduced two alien and often contradictory systems of thought: on the one hand, the materialist scientific notions derived from the Enlightenment, and on the other, theories of racial, cultural, and religious superiority that were used in attempts to explain and legitimate the triumphant expansion of Euro-Christian peoples. European medicine, often effective where folk remedies and rituals had unpredictable results, presented another challenge to every local culture's world view.

The ideas of the Enlightenment—science, technology, democracy—were imported into Asia through schools built by the colonial governments. One motivation for establishing the schools was to provide sources of native people who spoke the language of the colonizer. The reach of the colonial government

DISINTEGRATION OF IMPERIAL CHINA AND THE WEAKENING OF BUDDHISM

Among the masses, in fact, Buddhist sects were at times the vehicles for rebellion against the imperial state. The White Lotus Society, a secretive underground order, staged periodic insurrections, the last of which (1796–1804) took ten years to suppress. The army of the Christian-inspired Tai Ping Rebellion (1850–1864) looted and burned most of the great Buddhist monasteries of central China; in response, monks and laity afterward abetted the recovery by forming text-printing societies, Buddhist schools, and study associations. Buddhist monks from the reformist Chinese *sangha* such as T'ai-hsi (1890–1947) did succeed at setting up schools that taught ancient canonical languages and secular subjects, and established relations with other Asian Buddhist reformers.

was broader, however, for in fact they were the official and secular extensions of the European home states. In addition, the colonial administrators were for the most part supportive of the expansion of the Christian missionary presence. (For example, in many places colonial law recognized as legitimate only marriages conducted by Christian ministers.) It was with such backing that the first modern global missions were created: across Asia, lay and ordained Christians built churches and established educational institutions, hospitals, and charities; some proselytized aggressively through public preaching and pamphlets attacking Buddhist beliefs and practices.

After the fall of the Ching dynasty in 1912, socioeconomic conditions remained unstable under the Republic of China, only to worsen further with the rise of the communist movement and the Japanese invasion, first in Manchuria (1931), then southward into the Chinese heartland. Throughout the twentieth century, the traditional Buddhist schools and Buddhist thought were subject to criticism not just by the communists, but also by leaders of a modernizing faction called the May 4th Movement. Though critiqued fiercely by the elites, the Chinese sangha still endured: in 1930, there were 730,000 monks and nuns who maintained 267,000 registered temples. The sustained Communist Party policy of thoroughgoing destruction, denigration, and disestablishment that followed 1949, however, had no precedent in modern Chinese Buddhist history.

Although at first disturbed and demoralized, Buddhists recovered from and responded to colonial-era challenges in various ways. Few converted to Christianity, despite such obvious advantages and inducements as access to charitable services and an inside track to promotions into government service. Despite being hampered by the disruption of their institutions, Buddhist intellectuals and preachers emerged to engage in the dialogue with science and Christianity. In Sri Lanka, for example, early Protestant missionaries, having assessed Buddhist monks as uniformly indolent and ignorant, felt themselves on the verge of mass conversion. Yet a series of public debates ended badly for missionaries, a reversal that restored public faith in the ongoing relevance of Buddhist doctrine.

It was indeed in Sri Lanka where the dialectic between the West and Buddhism was most intense and where decisive new directions for Buddhist modernization were identified. Reformers involved the lay society more fully in Buddhist institutions and spiritual practices (primarily meditation), motivating some among the laity to take the place of former royal patrons. The lay reformers, in turn, insisted that monks respect the integrity of sangha rules and discipline, and they supported the revival of monastic meditation practice, usually in newly created reformist monastic schools. Finally, Buddhist intellectuals carried out historical investigations, offering modern demythologized reinterpretations of the Buddha and Buddhist doctrine analogous to the scholarly search for "the historical Jesus" that was emerging within Protestant Christianity at the same time. To publicize these reforms, Buddhists adopted one aspect of Christian missionary methodology: they began by investing in printing technology and initiating publication series that defined reformed doctrine and practice. They also rediscovered the practice of public sermonizing.

Reformers in Thailand as in Sri Lanka also articulated new interpretations of "true Buddhism." They taught that Buddhism in its pure form was not concerned with communal rituals or harnessing the cosmic powers of Buddhism to support the secular kingdom. Rejecting the adaptive local traditions that had developed in the globalization of Buddhism, reformers insisted that the only genuine center of the faith was the individual's quest for mind cultivation and salvation. Doctrines describing the interdependent and impermanent nature of existence were emphasized, while the teachings about hungry ghosts and a four-continent mythological cosmology were rejected. Most reform leaders were critical of—even hostile to—"superstitions," rituals, and other local accommodations. Meditation was now the heart of "true Buddhism" and it was not restricted to monks and nuns: all Buddhists could and should feel capable of seeking nirvana.

The Buddhist Revival Gains Strength

By the turn of this century, reformers created new institutions to advance the revivalist goals directly. Also supporting the revival process in Asia was the first generation of Europeans sympathetic to Buddhism, who saw in the faith a nontheistic spirituality that was a compelling alternative to dogmatic monotheism. Many interpreted Buddhism as encouraging spiritual experimentation through meditation rather than requiring blind faith. Its philosophy was seen as ancient wisdom marvelously preserved and still accessible. The exigencies of imperialism had resulted in easier travel for Westerners and this development enabled sympathetic Europeans and North Americans to assist native Buddhist modernists as they argued back against Christian ministers. Westerners both educated native intellectuals on Christianity and shared with them Enlightenment critiques of Christian dogma. Individuals from the Theosophical Society, a group formed to pursue the secret, mystical teachings thought to underlie all the world religions, created new institutions including English-medium Buddhist schools and lay organizations such as Buddhist teaching programs modeled after Christian Sunday schools. Buddhist nationalists also became involved in politics, seeking more favorable relations—and eventually independence—from the European colonial governments. This experience in Sri Lanka was eagerly shared across Asia with modernists from Japan to Burma.

Early Western scholarship also added to the awareness of modern Asian Buddhists. It was due to British archaeology that sites associated with Ashoka and many long-forgotten early monuments were discovered. European scholars used modern critical methods to translate and interpret the earliest canonical texts and then disseminated them globally. In fact, it was common for the newly educated indigenous intelligentsia in Buddhist countries to read their first canonical passages from a Buddhist text in English translation. (As in medieval Europe, only the elite among monk-scholars could read the original sacred texts.)

As Buddhist literature in English became available and was assimilated, voices from outside the sangha joined the contested discussion of "what the Buddha really taught." Thus, throughout the Buddhist world, the leaders of the old Buddhist establishments were often challenged to conform to the standards of discipline set forth in the monastic texts, with instances of corruption, family control of monasteries, or moral lapses exposed. In most Buddhist countries, colonial and postcolonial governments sought more completely to regulate the sangha both to "keep pure" local Buddhist institutions and, at the same time, to eliminate any centers of possible political dissent.

Buddhism Tailored for Western Consumption: Meditation and Atheism

These efforts by the colonial powers to control Buddhism and Buddhists had a paradoxical effect. The global diaspora of Buddhism flowed "backward" on the networks of empire and through Western converts who became aware of Asian religions due to expanding communications and travel. For some Euro-Americans, the Enlightenment-based critiques of the Western monotheistic religions were persuasive and led to their search for religions that did not depend upon belief in the Abrahamic God. By 1920, Buddhist centers in the West had been established by Euro-American converts and immigrants. As depicted in early popular and sympathetic accounts, the Buddha was a rationalist who rejected ritual and a heroic social reformer; his movement was not religious but based on philosophy only; Buddhism was seen as atheistic and compatible with science; and Buddhist meditation was an authentic, ancient spiritual practice. The latter aspect also attracted Westerners interested in the new field of psychology. Finally, those interested in comparative religion found in Buddhist doctrine important critiques of religion based upon Judeo-Christian paradigms.

Euro-American contact with Mahayana Buddhism came strongest and earliest with Japanese Zen. Westerners were drawn to the spirit of iconoclasm and to meditation, and to Zen's connection with the fine arts conveyed by early exponents such as D. T. Suzuki (1870–1966). In the years immediately following the Second World War, Zen Buddhism particularly attracted segments of the bohemian and intellectual Western society, leading to a revival in interest that has grown throughout our day. It was less than a century before World War II, however, that Japan embarked on an imperialistic course that not only obscured the peaceful face of Zen Buddhism but also saw it contribute to Japan's causing death, dislocation, and destruction throughout Asia.

The Effects on Buddhism and on Asia of Japanese Imperialism

As already indicated, the role of Japan in twentieth-century Asia was pivotal. Once it opened itself to the modern world with the restoration of the emperor to power in 1868, Japan's leaders sought to create a modern industrial state based on nationalism that promoted Shinto as the shared national faith, with the emperor revered as a living god at the apex. This movement also involved the conscious diminishment of Buddhism. Despite its 1,400 years in Japan, Buddhism was criticized as "a foreign religion" inferior to Shinto; many Buddhist monasteries and temples had their lands confiscated and state patronage withdrawn as Buddhist doctrines and practices were critiqued as "unnatural." Amidst these rapid changes, some Buddhist organizations did institute reforms that involved undertaking social work, educational initiatives, and the renewal of global missions. Some schools such as Zen issued strong public pronouncements in favor of nationalism and militarism, with prominent monasteries even raising money for armaments. Many new Buddhist movements also began, but outside the older schools.

Led by the former samurai and others who studied in Western countries, Japan's rapid and successful modernization effort also fomented nationalism and imperialism. In the attempt to magnify the empire, the Japanese annexed neighboring Korea (1910) and northern China (1934), and eventually invaded more distant Asian countries (Indochina, 1940; Burma, 1942). Soon after the Pacific phase of World War II began with the attack on the U.S. base at Pearl Harbor in 1941, the Japanese occupation extended from Manchuria, Korea, and China south to Micronesia and as far west as the borders of India through Southeast Asia.

BUDDHISM AND POSTMODERN TRENDS IN A POSTCOLONIAL WORLD

By the mid-twentieth century, Asians had begun to recover from World War II. In addition, many people had reclaimed their independence, though often in new countries drawn along haphazard lines sensible only to imperial convenience. Indeed, many Asian states still struggle with an illogical arrangement of boundaries and ethnic divisions, and with the ideal of secular states that the early nationalist leaders had adopted from the West.

Buddhist leaders and movements today span the same approaches seen across the globe in other faiths. Some reject modernity, seeking to return to practices thought "corrupted" in the colonial era by modernizers. Others strive to move Buddhism to an entirely new plateau to adapt to the global realities of the postcolonial era. Still others blend traditionalism and reform, "rescuing" what in their view is the essence of Buddhism from the past while employing modern technologies to propagate the Dharma. New institutions have been created to champion strict adherence to monastic norms, scholastic learning, and meditation. Most commonly, it is organizations led by lay persons that have been the most active and effective in adapting Buddhist teachings and practices to the world today.

South Asia

South Asia is the "holy land" where the Buddha was born, was enlightened, and died and where Buddhism has endured over 2,500 years. Among the contemporary countries of the region—India, Pakistan, Bangladesh, Sri Lanka, Bhutan, and Nepal—only in the Himalayan regions of the north and in the island of Sri Lanka to the south has Buddhism remained strong.

The Remnants of Buddhism in India: Reconstruction in the Land of Origin

Today, Buddhism is found in modern India in only very small communities. Most important for the faith's revival in the land of its origins are those sacred sites that have been rediscovered through the archeological discoveries initiated by the British colonial government (c. 1800–1947). Among the hundreds of sites that were abandoned or that sank into oblivion after the Muslim conquest of South Asia (since 1200 CE), the site where the Buddha was enlightened under the bodhi tree became the most significant and controversial. Identified by British officials in the mid-1800s and "restored" through colonial excavations and constructions (in the modern city of Gaya, Bihar), the temple built at the site, called the Mahabodhi ("Great Enlightenment") temple, has again become a focal point for Buddhists. Reformers in the colonial era focused on reestablishing the sanctity of this temple as their first step in reviving the faith; in recent decades, over twenty Buddhist sanghas from around the world have erected branch monasteries there as well as libraries, study centers, and pilgrim hostels. Reformist Buddhists are also attempting to reestablish the site's importance as it was in antiquity: Buddhism's holiest center and pilgrimage destination, a shrine that unifies all Buddhists. Even after decades of work by reformers, this remains a distant goal.

Despite decades of negotiations, even control over the Bodh Gaya temple has eluded the Buddhist organizations, as Hindu priests and politicians have failed to turn over ownership of the shrine. By 1992, frustrations at unfulfilled promises peaked, so that monks residing there were moved to take extreme measures. Two threatened to immolate themselves, and several others began fasts unto death. What provoked this confrontation was the priests' treatment of five Buddha images in the temple as the five Pandhavas, heroic deities cele-brated in the Hindu epic, the Mahabharata, as well as their enthronement of a phallic icon of Shiva, a *lingam*, on an altar. On the full-moon day celebrating the Buddha's birth, enlightenment, and death in 1992, Buddhist demonstrators entered the temple and ripped off the cloth draped over the idols. Though this demonstration ended without further violence or suicides, the shrine through 2007 has been the focus of regular demonstrations and still remains contested and under Hindu control. In 2002, UNESCO declared the temple a World Heritage Site.

The All-India Action Committee that has led this movement in Bodh Gaya has drawn many of its members from the activist Buddhist communities in contemporary India: "untouchable" Mahar caste communities from Maha-rashtra; intellectual Buddhists attracted to reformist institutions from among the urban areas; and from among the hundred thousand Tibetan refugees who have settled in India since fleeing Chinese rule after 1959.

"Protestant Buddhism": An Enduring Colonial-Era Reformation of the Faith

Anthropologist Gananath Obeyesekere has described the modern re-formation of Buddhist tradition begun in colonial Sri Lanka as "Protestant Buddhism" and uses the term to convey two distinct but connected historic trends: (1) the *protest* of modernizers against Christianity, the arrogance of missionaries, and British colonial discrimination against Buddhism; and (2) the adoption of as-pects of missionary Protestant Christianity into the Buddhist framework to re-vitalize its institutions, practices, and doctrines.

The early influential mediator of such "Protestantism" in Sri Lanka was Henry Steele Olcott (1832–1907), who came to the country and helped activist Buddhist leaders organize their efforts, and reputedly became the first American convert to take the "Three Refuges." Olcott emphasized the impor-tance of the laity in revitalization and the founding of Buddhist publications and schools. He also composed a *Buddhist Catechism* (1881) and invented a five-color Buddhist flag, both of which are widely used across the world today. Modern Protestant inclinations were evident in the reformist insistence that spiritual and scientific truth must be compatible, that true practice was more worthy than rote observance of ritual, and that—in agreement with the Protestant missionaries—the practice of Buddhism in Sri Lanka had been corrupted by idolatry, Hindu polytheism, and an undisciplined and corrupt monastic "priesthood." "True Buddhism" could be reestablished by adhering to the pure philosophy and meditation practices taught by the human Buddha. Popular texts and village traditions were strongly critiqued and two new sangha schools were started with ordination lineages from Burma, both requiring strict adherence to Vinaya rules.

A Sri Lankan protégé, who adopted the name Anagarika Dharmapala (1864–1933), continued Olcott's initiatives and went beyond them, preaching and publishing tracts to spread his vision of revitalized Buddhism. At the age of 29, Dharmapala addressed an ecumenical "Parliament of World Religions" held in Chicago in 1893, impressing hearers from all over the world with his definition of modernist Buddhism as compatible with science, free from dogma and superstition, tolerant of other faiths, and committed to social reform.

Dharmapala also found an enthusiastic reception among the Sri Lankan laity, especially those among the newly educated professional elite and the merchant middle class, who owed their rising positions in the world to the changes wrought by the colonial modernization of the country. Dharmapala energized the Buddhist reformers in Sri Lanka; his speeches and writings also contributed to the linkage between the faith and the nationalist struggles.

Dharmapala celebrated Sri Lanka as a uniquely pure Buddhist country, elevated the Sinhalese ethnic group as a "chosen Buddhist people," and harshly demonized those opposing the country's Buddhist restoration. Scholars today see these influences as having set in motion the cultural forces that have made postindependence Sri Lanka a zone of extremes where ideologies justifying bloody conflict and uncompromising reform have taken deep root.

Dharmapala's founding of the Mahabodhi Society in Calcutta extended "Protestant Buddhist" reform into other countries in Asia. In recent times, "Protestant Buddhism" has fostered an individualist ethos among those whose ties to village and traditional sangha have ended through urban migration. Those influenced by its reformist ideas see it as their own responsibility to practice meditation and study the Dharma (usually in English translations) in the quest for nirvana. Joining the sangha or seeking spiritual guidance from an ordained monk is also not necessarily the norm for those whose view of Buddhism has been affected by "Protestantism." Curiously, as this approach with its rationalism and individualism has penetrated the growing middle class in the expanding towns and cities, new types of bhakti religious practices have arisen outside the monastic precincts, especially among the lower classes.

Buddhism in the Himalayas: Shangri-La?
Many Westerners first became aware of Buddhism through fictional works such as *Lost Horizon*, the film version of which showed the faith in an idyllic,

tropical valley amidst the scenic, snow-blown Himalayan peaks. It is true that, in fact, Tibetan Buddhist communities have survived in the remote and picturesque settlements nestled among the world's highest mountains, but this region has hardly been a utopian zone for Buddhism in the post–World War II era.

Three nations have remained refuges of the faith. *Nepal*, the world's only Hindu kingdom but one of the world's poorest nations, has several million Buddhists among the highland-dwelling Tibeto-Burman peoples, in its settlements of Tibetan refugees, and among the Newars of the Kathmandu valley, the modern capital; this valley is also Asia's largest center for international institutions connected with the major schools of Tibetan Buddhism. Mountainous areas of northern India (in Ladakh, Himachal Pradesh, and Arunachal Pradesh) have also been places where Tibetan Buddhism has survived. India has likewise accepted Tibetan refugees, for since 1959 the Dalai Lama's government in exile has been located in picturesque Dharamsala. Finally, there is Bhutan in the eastern Himalayas, a nation formed in 1907 as the royal kingdom ruled by the Wangchuck family. It is the world's only nation that has Tibetan Buddhism, and particularly that of the Druk-pa school, as its state religion.

But it is the Tibetan plateau on "the roof of the world" that was most transformed. In 1949, most of the territories ruled by the Gelugpa school, whose leader bears the title of Dalai Lama, were declared part of the People's Republic of China, which sent its army to enforce its claims; the peripheries once oriented to Lhasa were soon annexed into adjacent states, while central and western Tibet have been ruled by China as "The Tibetan Autonomous Region." Until the end of China's Cultural Revolution (1976), all religious practices in the region were repressed and most Buddhist temples, monasteries, and shrines were destroyed.

After 1980, official toleration of limited worship and monastic ordination returned, as did state-sponsored rebuilding of select monasteries. But increasing Tibetan protests since 1987 have been met with further restrictions and arrests, while increasing Chinese migration into the region has reduced Tibetans to being a minority in their homeland. Today around the Jokhang, the ancient temple complex at the center of old Lhasa, garish Chinese-sanctioned massage parlors and strip joints have sprung up along the pilgrims' circumambulation route in the old bazaar. (Such subtle undercutting of sacred precincts can be seen as well in many places in China.)

Elsewhere along the southern Himalayan region, the isolation of the Tibetan frontier states (Ladakh, Sikkim, Bhutan) enabled them to retain their independence until the end of the Second World War, as the traditional Tibetan Buddhist schools dating to the Middle Ages endure. However, religious conservatism also kept the monks and leaders of these states isolated and ignorant about the modern world, and this gave little cause for reform or adaptation to the postwar international political order. Unsurprisingly, then, these Tibetan Buddhist areas have lost political autonomy. Central, northern, and eastern

Tibet was absorbed by China, while Ladakh and Sikkim were absorbed into modern India; Bhutan alone remained independent from India, but only in its internal affairs. In exile and in the isolated enclaves, Tibetan Buddhist institutions have sustained the faith, but these Buddhists struggle as refugees in poverty and with minority status within the larger states.

Yet amidst the destruction of tradition and the tragedies of exile, there has been a paradoxical development that has been possible only in the present context: the end of independent Tibet, the persecution of the faith, and the exile of many Tibetans has also led to the extensive migration of Tibetan Buddhist teachers into almost every country of the world. Now publishing houses, learned lamas, Internet Web sites, and charismatic meditation teachers cross the globe to spread Buddhist teachings. The Fourteenth Dalai Lama, Nobel Peace Prize winner in 1989, is now well known as a world leader and is certainly the most recognized Buddhist in the world.

Southeast Asia

The first regions missionized in antiquity by Buddhist monks have remained the stronghold of Theravada Buddhism. In Sri Lanka and Burma, a new era began with the withdrawal of the British (1947). Buddhism became a pillar of the new nations' identity, and the Buddha was elevated to the status of cultural hero and ancestor.

While supportive of the respective struggles for independence, Buddhism in these states had also been enriched and enlarged by revival movements throughout the colonial period. Most of these involved the laity in the administration of its institutions and saw the establishment of new monastic schools emphasizing revival through strict discipline, meditation, and social service. Buddhist leaders in the first decades after World War II were also at the forefront of addressing the relationship between socialism and communism, the political ideologies that had risen to popularity as alternatives to capitalism in guiding the newly independent states. Some monks were highly suspicious of communism and allied themselves with aggressive anticommunist campaigns; some political activists and high civil servants, however, were quite creative in using Buddhist rhetoric to justify participation in communist regimes. Typical of this is a 1951 speech by a minister in newly independent Burma:

> I declare that I have implicit faith in Marxism, but at the same time I assert that I am a true Buddhist. Both of these philosophies are correlated.... In the beginning, I was a Buddhist only by tradition. The more I study Marxism, however, the more I feel convinced in Buddhism. Thus I have become a true disciple of Lord Buddha by conviction and my faith in Buddhism has grown all the more. I now believe that for any man who has deeply studied Buddhism and correctly perceived its tenets there should be no obstacles to become a Marxist. Vexed by anxieties and fears in respect to food, clothing, and homes, human minds cannot dwell

on old age, disease and death. But with the satisfaction of men's material needs, humans can boldly face these three phenomena. Marxism cannot provide an answer to spiritual liberation. Neither can science. Only Buddhist philosophy can. It must, however, be conceded that material satisfaction in life can only be attained through Marxism.[5]

A Tooth Relic Visits Myanmar

The Buddha's cremation relics have always been the most sacred and precious objects for devotees from the faith's very beginnings. Not only are they the sole remnants of the enlightened one, a "sacred trace" of his earthly existence; they are also objects thought to be infused with immense power, the mere proximity of which confers spiritual and worldly blessings.

In 1994, a tooth relic loaned by the Chinese government was brought to Myanmar (formerly Burma). Consider the irony of this exchange, not uncommon in today's global political environment: the Communist party of China finds it politically expedient to utilize a Buddhist relic for advancing its goals in international relations. For their part, the junta ruling Myanmar is supplying many of the images being used across China to rebuild the temples destroyed by Red Guards several decades ago. Placed in a jewel-embellished palanquin and conveyed from the Boeing 757 to a silk-draped float pulled by an elephant, the relic was taken to its shrine in the Maha Pasana cave in Rangoon where over the next six weeks a half million devotees came to pray and make offerings. SLORC, the country's ruling junta, used the state-controlled media to emphasize its role as exemplary Buddhists sponsoring this visit; in 1995, it underwrote the construction of a new temple in the capital where the relic has been displayed in later visits. Displaying and respecting Buddha relics has been a sign of just rulers in Buddhist states since antiquity, and the SLORC generals no doubt intend their sponsorship of tooth relic veneration to win popular approval and counter dislike of its authoritarian rule, including keeping under house arrest Nobel Peace Prize winner Aung San Suu Kyi. Still, Myanmar remains a troubled Buddhist country. After regaining independence from the British empire in 1948 and undergoing a short period of experimentation with "Buddhist socialism," the country deals harshly with monks and monasteries suspected of fostering dissent.

Three Faces of Thai Buddhism

A constitutional monarchy since 1932 and a country never ruled by a European nation, Thailand (formerly Siam) is another predominantly Theravada country. Thai reformist monks and laity have assumed active roles in working for the modernization of the country through government development programs in infrastructure building, agricultural innovation, education, and health care. Several notable independent monks have opposed the state's toleration of corruption, pollution, and environmental destruction. However, Thai Buddhist monastic institutions have benefited from royal patronage and the rising wealth that has come with the economic boom over the last two decades. Certain charismatic monks and a host of new lay-oriented independent Buddhist institutions are active in offering leadership to revitalize the faith. The burgeoning urban areas, where neither old community ties nor traditional monasteries effectively meet the needs of the migrants, have been fertile ground for such reformists. Three examples suggest the gamut of reformists active in contemporary Thai Buddhism: the Dhammakaya, Santi Asoke, and the work of Phra Boonsong.

The Dhammakaya   The Dhammakaya is the fastest growing Buddhist reform group in Thailand, attracting the well-educated and newly affluent classes, including the royal family. Founded by the charismatic monk Phra Monghon Thepmuni in 1978 and run from a single national center in Wat (monastery) Dhammakaya located 30 miles north of Bangkok, the nation's capital, Dhammakaya spreads its teachings and meditation practices through the sophisticated use of publications and mass media. The movement has established a presence in every major city and town across the country, where its very highly educated monks administer a program of rigorous training for the laity. Another binding force of Dhammakaya is Phra Thepmuni's meditation practice, one that has more in common with Mahayana traditions of the Himalayas than with the long-established Theravada methods. (In this, individuals visualize a glowing crystal at the "center of the body" behind the navel, the practice of which induces trance and spiritual visions and promises a rapid ascension to nirvana once it gives one a direct experience of "the eternal essence of the eternal Buddha.") For its followers, the Dhammakaya has reduced the ritual complexity of the traditional monastery to a few simple practices. It has also emphasized that money-making is compatible with Buddhism and has translated utopianism and interdependence teachings through the slogan "World Peace Through Inner Peace." As of 2007, the group numbered its supporters at over one million, with branches in twenty foreign countries.

Santi Asoke   Santi Asoke differs in many respects from Dhammakaya: it has won a much smaller following (perhaps 100,000 estimated in 2007) and has garnered much less wealth, but its activists since its founding in 1976 have played the role of prophetic critics of the complacent established monastic schools and the compromises it feels Buddhists are making in modern Thailand. Santi Asoke ("People of Ashoka") are named after the first lay ruler in Buddhist history, the Indian emperor who (in Buddhist accounts) spread the faith across India and ruled according to the Buddha's ethical norms. Accordingly, this group seeks to reform Thai Buddhism through a return to austere ethical norms such as abstaining from meat, alcohol, and tobacco as well as avoiding gambling and hedonistic entertainment. Santi Asoke grew out of the forest monk reformers who in the 1920s and 1930s sought to revitalize the sangha by a return to having the monks adopt a rigorous meditation and ascetic lifestyle. Santi Asoke's monks wear white robes instead of the traditional yellow because their founder, a charismatic but confrontational

Phra Bodhiraksa, was defrocked by the government's monk-monitoring body in the 1980s. The "Protestant" influence is evident here in his criticizing traditional rituals as "superstition and magic" and his outspoken rejection of worshiping Buddha images.

Phra Boonsong Not all reformers in Thailand have been new institution builders. Take for example Phra Boonsong (1941–) who has been the head monk of Phranon Wat in central Thailand since 1972. When he arrived in the area, the river was sick, river runoff from the Chin River which flows by the monastery was polluting paddy fields, and agriculture and fishing yields were declining, a fact sending men and women to the cities to seek employment. Phra Boonsong has worked in the last two decades to improve the region's ecological balance. Appealing to the traditional Thai prohibition against killing inside a monastery, he began by declaring that the river adjacent to it is a "pardon zone" for all water creatures. Soon, by selling fish food to parishioners (who in turn gave it to the fish, earning merit), fish stock were added and the fish multiplied in that nearby stretch of the river, slowly adding to the breeding population available for harvest by fishermen living along the river for miles. This success enabled Phra Boonsong to convince the National Assembly to enact laws allowing monasteries nationwide to establish similar breeding zones, and over one hundred have done so. More recently the monk has begun establishing fruit trees on long-deforested hills, and in doing so reducing the use of expensive, watershed-polluting chemicals. This sangha's expertise in species use, grafting, fertilizers, and marketing is now being shared across the region, allowing other monks to spearhead similar efforts and promote environmental awareness across the rural hinterlands. A similar Buddhist response to the scourge of HIV/AIDS is evident in the growing movement of monasteries having monks devote themselves to the prevention of the disease as well as the care of infected individuals, with monasteries serving as hospices for the dying.

Buddhist Revival in Postwar Indo-China

By 1985, all the countries of Indo-China had begun to liberalize their economies and relax restrictions on religious observances. As communist governments retreat from dogmatism to pragmatism and accept the enduring popular attachment to Buddhism and indigenous religions, civil authorities in Vietnam, Laos, and Cambodia are accepting the place of Buddhism in national culture and politics.

A French colony until 1953, Cambodia has suffered through the Vietnam wars against the French and the United States, and in the aftermath, the genocidal conflicts under the rule of the Khmer Rouge led by Pol Pot (1975–1979). Under the latter's Communist regime, Buddhist monks and institutions were targeted for murder and destruction. While several Cambodian Buddhist centers were relocated among refugees over the border in Thailand, only after the withdrawal of the Vietnamese in 1989 did the restoration of Buddhism begin.

Several prominent figures seeking national reconciliation have been Theravada monks.

Landlocked Laos, although still ruled by a communist government, has also undergone economic reforms; rising wealth in the cities and the liberalization of government regulations have supported the revival of monastic Buddhism there.

Once Vietnam was reunited in 1975, the country's communist government increasingly tolerated the restoration of Buddhist monasteries and temples. The government has imprisoned monks it regards as involved in politics, but the officially sanctioned (and so-named) Vietnam Buddhist Church has won only minimum popular acceptance. Vietnam's population of seventy-five million more resembles China in its religious orientation, with Buddhism the most widespread tradition existing alongside Chinese Taoism and Confucianism, indigenous cults, and both Roman Catholic and Protestant Christianity. Vietnamese Buddhism today is predominantly Mahayana in the north, with Theravada monasteries found in the south.

The modern state of Indonesia in its western islands of Sumatra and Java, was once at the center of an empire that supported both Hinduism and Buddhism. Although it contains the largest Muslim population in the world, the government is committed to respecting all faiths. Today, Buddhists are a small minority (2% of 205 million) but the faith has undergone a vigorous revival since 1950. Small communities dedicated to predominantly Mahayana Buddhism likewise exist among minority ethnic Chinese communities in Malaysia and in Singapore, the city-state that separated from Malaysia in 1965.

East Asia

Since its introduction almost two thousand years ago, Buddhism took root in every province in China and has survived, but its history has seen periods of strong support followed by eras of fierce persecution. The Communist government of the People's Republic of China since the end of the Cultural Revolution (1966–1976) has slowly allowed a limited number of Buddhist institutions to be reopened. It also has approved monks and nuns resuming many traditional practices, and now permits lay devotees to perform various rituals and pilgrimages. This turnaround is remarkable after the years of stern repression by the Communist party, which had sanctioned the destruction of thousands of Buddhist temples and monasteries.

The Return of Guanyin and Daoist Deities to China

Mahayana Buddhists have for fifteen centuries shared a common faith in the celestial deity Avalokiteshvara (Ch.: Guanyin; Jap.: Kannon), whose cult was found from Central Asia to Japan in shrines located in almost every settlement and home. Over the centuries, this divinity's depiction changed from male to female; with Buddhism's missionary transplantation across East Asia, she became the refuge for all who desired rebirth in the Western Buddhist paradise, met dangerous life circumstances, and especially for women who wanted the birth of a son and safe childbirth. As Daoism organized and was systematized in response to Buddhism in China by the Tang era (617–907), so popular was Guanyin (and so eclectic Daoism) that it was not considered unorthodox to find icons of Guanyin in Daoist temples or in clan temples otherwise dedicated to the veneration of ancestors.

The iconoclasm of Mao Zedong's Cultural Revolution nearly eliminated Guanyin from such public places all across China, and in private shrines as well: Red Guards who found icons in their house-to-house searches claimed them as sure indicators of "reactionary elements" who could be deemed "enemies of the people," publicly humiliated and even killed. Since the mid-1980s, however, Guanyin has returned to favor and even state-run factories have produced a large variety of images for sale, many at newly opened temple votive supply stores. The government's acceptance of (and earning of income from!) the revival of Buddhist devotionalism—in contrast to its combating the more diffuse popular religion and guru-led cults—can be noticed in the opening of pilgrimage sites for Guanyin as well. Indeed, it is evident that even party members, especially among its younger and professional generations, show a tendency to believe in the efficacy of worshiping this Buddhist divinity.

The Return of the Buddha to Mongolia

The modern country of Mongolia (properly styled "Outer Mongolia" to distinguish it from China's northern province, "Inner Mongolia") came into being with the fall of the Chinese Empire in 1911, when the Mongolian Communist party established a separate government with strong Russian backing. Buddhism was severely repressed for the following decades, as all of its 100,000 monks had to disrobe, more than three hundred monasteries were confiscated, and its many shrines were destroyed. Thousands of monks were executed and the material structures of Buddhist culture were nearly destroyed, but the faith stayed alive in the popular imagination.

After the fall of the Soviet Union (1989), Mongolians voted to end the party's monopoly of power in the state in 1990. The concomitant return of religious freedoms has led to the ongoing and vigorous restoration of Buddhism in its traditional Tibetan Buddhist form. Monasteries are now being rebuilt, each settlement has seen the construction of at least one Buddhist temple, and many young men have taken monastic vows. The Dalai Lama and other leading Tibetan monks regularly visit to aid in the Mongol quest to retrain a monastic elite and reestablish ritual practice. Most of Mongolia's 2.5 million citizens, the great majority of whom still live as nomadic pastoralists, are Buddhists.

Buddhist Revival in South Korea

The formerly unified Korean culture area, artificially split into North Korea and South Korea after World War II, has been strongly influenced by Chinese cultural borrowings, including Buddhism, throughout its history. In the early years after independence from China (1911), the traditional Buddhist monastic system was wracked by a struggle over whether monks could marry or should remain celibate, with the courts finally deciding that the group favoring celibacy had the right to inhabit the monastic estates.

As South Korea experienced rising economic prosperity from the 1970s onward, this group has attracted patrons and activists who have sought to build the spiritual programs of the monasteries, present Buddhist teachings in modern media, and oppose the slide of Buddhism in the face of Christian proselytizing and government policies that subjected it to discrimination.

Despite many setbacks over the last century, the surviving Korean Buddhist institutions with landed income have created an important niche in Korean society by establishing schools and lay meditation centers. As in other Buddhist countries undergoing successful economic modernization, Korean Buddhism is experiencing a renewal, with modern institutions upgrading monastic education, creating modern mass media publications, and developing an urban, middle-class Buddhist identity based upon householder rituals, meditation, and youth organizations. The latest Korean innovation is the "All-Buddhist Network Television," whose programs offer a mix of sermons, chants, rituals, and chefs teaching vegetarian cooking.

Finding Kannon Amidst Japan's "Rush Hour of the Gods"

Japan, like the United States, has recently sustained a broadening of religious interests, with Buddhism contributing to this through its classical monastic institutions and by its doctrines providing starting points for many of Japan's "new religions." In the century before the Second World War, the Meiji state's ultranationalist governments (1868–1945) deliberately weakened Buddhism through ideological campaigns and institutionally; many abbots among the co-opted "establishment schools" in fact actively fanned the flames of war. World War II left many monasteries in ruins and prominent clergy in disgrace. But after the war, the sanghas of the oldest schools still retained their nationwide presence under a system of head and branch monasteries developed in the late Tokagawa era (1600–1857), and some worked to restore their spiritual integrity. Today, almost every Japanese family is still registered as parishioner of a monastery branch of one or the other Buddhist schools for, at the very least, the performance of family death rituals.

But for many Japanese, Buddhism has remained part of their lives, and belief in the deities endures. A visit any morning to the Sensoji Buddhist temple in Tokyo would give an example of commonplace observance today. Here the scene would be dominated by (usually older) women who, upon arrival, approach the long temple corridor bearing incense and offerings, recite mantras and prayer requests, ascend the stairs to the main shrine to throw coins and continue their recitations. Many pause to do a divination by shaking a cylinder and having one stick inside protrude out through a small hole; the number on this stick will reveal an answer to the devotee's question once a matching printed sheet is obtained from a nearby attendant and consulted.

Other devotees purchase an *ema* board distinctive of this temple, write a formal request addressed to the bodhisattva on its back, then tie it to a long cord on stands that bear thousands of similar *ema*. At subsidiary shrines, the temple visit continues, with offerings made to the local deities, the *kami* protectors of the shrine or healers of specific illnesses. For example, at the cast-iron image established in a side courtyard of the great monk Kobo Daishi (or Kukai [774–835], the founder of the tantric Shingon Buddhist school), women congregate, lining up for their turn to touch various parts of the statue and then their own bodies, as the local belief is that this promotes healing, especially of arthritis.

Another indicator of the symbolic presence in modern Japan of the Mahayana bodhisattva Avalokiteshvara, here called Kannon, is the great number of individuals undertaking pilgrimage circuits across the heartland of historical Japan to honor this deity. The Saikoku route has pilgrims visit some thirty-three sites, including some of the greatest and most magnificent temples in Japan, a sacred journey organized as far back as the thirteenth century. This route through the Kyoto-Nara-Osaka area, popularized by the Tokagawa shoguns (1600–1868) in their attempts to foster national awareness, has risen from postwar obscurity to reach thirty thousand participants in the late 1960s and over ninety thousand by last count in the late 1990s. This "pilgrimage boom" (*junrei bumu*), as the popular religious revival has been labeled by Japanese scholars and journalists, was aided by the rapid expansion of facilities to support the pilgrims in their travels. Moreover, this example of the Saikoku Kannon pilgrimage has inspired the formation of thirty-three-stage Kannon pilgrimage routes in at least seventy-two other regions of Japan. The number of those undertaking journeys to these temples has also increased in recent decades. There is some debate about how much this rapidly increasing interest in pilgrimage relates to religious dedication to Kannon and how much it relates to a much less pious "cultural tourism" whose main ingredient is "nostalgia."

Three examples of recent revival show the continuing relevance of Kannon in Japanese life. The first is lighthearted: the Zenshoji temple northwest of Tokyo has brought the bodhisattva into the Japanese craze for golf by erecting a 6-foot Kannon who holds various golf clubs in her hands. Hundreds of golfers come daily to pray for the mercy of lower scores. More serious is the recent creation of a thirty-three-stage pilgrimage route with a focus on worship of a completely new form of this bodhisattva: *Boke Fuji Kannon* ("Senility Kannon").

A final example of a new form of Kannon devotionalism in Japan is that concerned with the cult organized to worship the spirits of aborted fetuses (*mizuko*). Buddhist temples throughout Japan have seen a revival in rituals on their memorial grounds as women have set up icons to which they offer food and other ritual gifts to those spirits they denied birth to in human form. Kannon as well as another popular bodhisattva named Jizo are the main focuses of worship at the temples; Japanese women typically request that the

BOKE FUJI ("SENILITY") KANNON: A NEW INCARNATION OF A BUDDHIST DEITY

In the later 1980s, new icons were first noted that depicted the goddess Kannon holding a flower in one hand and opening the other in a gesture of mercy to two elderly people, one male and one female, who clutch at her robes in supplication. Consistent with her renown developed over one and a half millennia for compassionately "mothering" her devotees and bestowing this-worldly boons to those who call upon her, this new form has arisen as senility or Alzheimer's disease has caused many in Japan (as elsewhere) great emotional distress. Both for the elderly and their families who share a Confucian responsibility for parental care at this stage of life, old-age suffering has surfaced as a weighty problem, leading Buddhist temples to respond with both social and spiritual programs in developing amulets, shrines, and pilgrimage routes for devotees to visit in search of preventive blessings. The priests involved also state that as physicians have counseled that the best way to keep senility at bay is for the aged to keep active, encouraging the pilgrimages is one way to direct the elderly to find enjoyable, stimulating, and hopeful activity, one in which they can both articulate their worries and acquire peace of mind.

compassionate deities guard and bless these spirits until they fulfill their destiny and continue on to another human rebirth, as in classical Buddhist teachings. Japan's national government, which bans oral contraceptives, has estimated that one-half of pregnancies in the country end in abortion.

The mizuko cult has spread widely over recent decades, promulgated by many temples that benefit from the income derived from the ritual services provided. This ubiquitous cult points again to the strength of Japanese belief in the central Buddhist doctrines of karma, rebirth, and the intermediate state between births; it also indicates the laity's focus on living life with regard to making merit, minimizing demerit, and acting decisively to aid and respect the dead.

Buddhism in Diaspora and in Asia Today

Buddhism in the West

The economic boom of the 1990s that swept Asia and the increasing migration of Asians across the globe are other recent developments affecting Buddhism in the world today. To a large extent, newly affluent Buddhists in

"CHANGE YOUR MIND DAY" IN CENTRAL PARK, NEW YORK

Each year in late May, the Buddhist magazine *Tricycle* sponsors a gathering on the Central Park lawn that draws a variety of teachers active in America. The other attendees—"longtime practitioners, meditators-for-a-day, Dharma bums, and dog-walkers"—are led through a series of guided spiritual exercises through the half-day program. In 2007, following 108 gong strikes, American abbots from Zen monasteries and Westerners initiated as teachers in Tibetan lineages gave sermons, Japanese monks led chants, and an American meditation master directed the group in Theravadin-style vipassana meditation. A friend of the late Allen Ginsberg read poems by this famous convert to Buddhism. A perennial favorite followed: a spirited debate in Tibetan scholastic style punctuated by hand-slapping exclamations between a Tibetan lama and an American convert who argued about the nature of nirvana. A T'ai Chi teacher directed a group exercise using martial arts and Japanese dance movements. After a musical interlude, a Tibetan monk gave teachings on loving-kindness, a Sri Lankan abbot discoursed on discipline in Buddhist practice, and a Chinese monk talked about the centrality of compassion. Another round of gongs ended the extraordinary inter-Buddhist ecumenical event attended by 1200 people.

these societies have done what Buddhist householders have always done with a portion of their surplus wealth: make merit through pious donations. This infusion of new wealth has been used to rebuild venerable monasteries and temples, support new reform sects, and modernize Buddhist institutions through the creation of schools, periodicals, and mass media. The most affluent and internationally minded, particularly those in East Asia, have shifted the traditional missionary ideal from national to global outreach, building on the migration of the home ethnic group (e.g., Taiwanese, Thai, or Japanese), but often seeking a wider audience beyond. One exception to the trend of new Asian affluence pushing the international expansion of Buddhism is the Tibetan diaspora that has depended largely upon donations by affluent Euro-American supporters, including a galaxy of Hollywood actors and rock stars.

The global migration of Buddhist monastic institutions and ideas has reached the point that a school is found on every continent, and non-Asians have been initiated into the sanghas of every major school. In addition, an awareness of basic Buddhist doctrines (karma, nirvana, Buddhahood) among the educated classes of the world has spilled over into the global mass media.

In the Zen and Tibetan schools in North America especially, converts now speak of the emergence of new "Western schools of Tibetan (or Zen) Buddhism," with an explosion in publications, educational programs, and meditation sessions marking the unmistakable deeper adaptation of the faith within Western societies. Such Western Buddhist schools are selective in their adoption of Asian Buddhist traditions: they have eschewed celibate monasticism, featured meditation, and downplayed ritualism, much like the "Protestant Buddhists of Asia." As of 2007 there were over five thousand Web sites devoted to Buddhism alone. Even the Pure Land Schools in East Asia that do not feature meditation, even for the sangha, find themselves offering such programs for laity in the West.

The modern diaspora of Buddhism in some respects can be seen as the global continuation of the faith's ancient missionary spirit. In North America, Buddhist missionaries have been led by teachers of Japanese and Korean Zen, all lineages of Tibetan Buddhism, Theravadins emphasizing vipassana meditation with ties to the countries of Southeast Asia, Japan's Soka Gakkai sect, and the various Pure Land schools (in rough order of importance).

The perceived iconoclasm of Zen found an audience among Americans in the 1950s who were drawn to the "Beat Generation" culture of jazz, poetry, and experimental literature; the lure of Zen meditation practices drew Western practitioners from the 1960s onward; Zen's connection with Japanese fine arts and martial arts also helped to draw such Zen-oriented teachers and their institutions across the globe to reach a wider athletic and artistic audience.

The Japanese Soka Gakkai, a modern religiocultural offshoot of the Nichiren school of Japan, has attracted an international following drawn by its calls to reinterpret Buddhism and take political action to foster the world's developing a more enlightened civilization. Pure Land Buddhism has been transplanted among East Asians who have migrated to the West Coast of North America and into urban areas worldwide. Indeed, as migrants from every Buddhist country in the world have settled in sufficient numbers, they have contributed to the globalization of their home faith by establishing temples and monasteries. The largest block of Buddhist immigrants in America has arrived from Southeast Asia.

Outside of Asia, Buddhists remain a small minority in the census figures and usually are found in urban areas. Among the immigrants and Western converts, as in Asia, "being a Buddhist" does not necessarily imply an exclusive identity. Thus, the census figures, which show, for example, roughly one million Buddhists in North America, are unlikely to describe accurately the penetration of Buddhist concepts and practices.

With intellectuals worldwide, however, awareness of Buddhist thought and practice is widespread. Buddhism's penetration of popular advertising since 1999 found the Dalai Lama's image being used to sell Apple computers, a Nike sneaker called "Nirvana," and a designer sandal called "Buddha." "Zen" is now appended to hundreds of objects, certain to elicit consumer curiosity.

Buddhism in Asia

In the postcolonial period, then, Buddhists have had to determine how to situate the tradition in the new secular polities: reconstructing the sangha-state relations after the colonial neglect of their institutions, responding to scientific thought and modern medicine, reckoning with religious pluralism introduced by Christianity and other faiths, and revising law codes in relation to national minorities. The results have been mixed. In Bhutan and Sri Lanka, the dominant ethnic groups have promoted Buddhist nationalism at the expense of non-Buddhist minorities, while in Burma and Thailand, the military has manipulated Buddhist monks and symbols to impose authoritarian regimes. Yet Buddhists in each country have also led democratic movements resisting extreme policies and violence.

Reformist monastic schools and lay movements begun in the modern era have continued to the present, with recent initiatives arising to address problems confronting the widely differing national contexts: forest monks in Thailand respond to environmental crises, lay organizations in Japan campaign in elections to insert Buddhist values into the political culture, Mongolian leaders rebuild monuments and restore the clergy's scholastic and ritual expertise, Burmese monks stage sit-ins to protest the restriction of democratic rights.

As ethnic identity has held the loyalty of local communities, often against the demands of modern secular states, "being Buddhist" has drawn individuals to value, rediscover, and embrace Buddhism across Asia. In many cases, the postcolonial web of global interaction has shaped the process: the "Buddhism" reformers discover has been filtered through and drawn from Euro-American scholarship. An interesting example of this phenomenon has occurred in Maharashtra, the modern state in central India. Since 1956, Mahar "untouchable" caste groups relegated to the bottom of the caste system have held mass ceremonies to convert to Buddhism, declaring their rejection of Hinduism and its system of social inequality.

The Mahars' knowledge of Buddhism was informed in part by colonial scholarship; the presence in Maharashtra of ancient Buddhist sites revealed by British archaeology has obvious importance as well. The founder of this movement, Dr. Bhimrao Ambedkar (1891–1956), learned about Buddhism from his studies in the West, particularly at Columbia University where Euro-American scholarship on Buddhism then held up the image of the Buddha as a social reformer. Statues of Ambedkar abound in Maharashtra villages today, monuments to the reinvention of tradition in the service of a late-twentieth-century social reform movement.

CONCLUSION

As a refuge of intellectual freedom and spiritual imagination, Buddhism historically nurtured and enriched the civilizations of Asia through teachers who articulated myriad traditions that formulated and analyzed the Buddha's Dharma. Surveying the belief patterns of the world's Buddhist communities, one is still challenged by both the sheer diversity of doctrinal expression and the complexity of Buddhism's systematic thought. Such an outpouring of conceptualization from a tradition that held the ultimate to be beyond conception! Buddhism's subsequent domestication across Asia and beyond has entailed the literal translation of texts, ideas, and rituals into non-Indic languages and cultures. In becoming a world religion, Buddhism in practice has promoted compassionate, medically advanced, disciplined, mercantile, and literate societies. Like other world religions today, Buddhism has shown that its definition of the human condition and its solutions addressing suffering and mortality have enduring value, even in the midst of changes that have shaken the modern and postcolonial world.

State Buddhism: Compassion or Ethnic Passion?

Few areas of Asian Buddhism have been removed from the crises and changes of the modern era: scientific thought and technology derived from the European Enlightenment that challenged traditional doctrines, cosmologies, and medical theories; the impact of European colonialism that forced (to varying degrees) economic transformations that undermined traditional rulers and patronage; the ideologies of Christian missionary triumphalism and cultural racism that conflicted with indigenous notions of Buddhism's own superiority.

With colonialism now gone, fundamental shifts in the political, socioeconomic, and intellectual spheres have inevitably changed individuals and caused Buddhist adherents to confront a transformed world and to adapt Buddhist beliefs and practices to it. A transregional question for countries with Buddhist majorities centers on how to shape society—in economic and political spheres—to best realize the Buddha's ideal of a compassionate civilization. Exponents still debate if Buddhism should endorse military authoritarianism (on the model of the benevolent dictator Ashoka) or representative democracy (on the model of the sangha's democratic norms). Is it most compassionate to establish a "pure Buddhist state" that privileges Buddhism and Buddhists, or opt instead for a secular state that guarantees evenhanded tolerance of a multireligious and multiethnic society? Can Buddhist ideals be most effectively implemented in a socialist or free-market system?

Colonialism also caused modern states to draw fixed boundary lines and enact national laws where before there were ethnic regions, regional law, and small-scale spheres of influence. In areas like Myanmar and Sri Lanka, where adherence to Buddhism was a powerful force of anticolonial struggle, reform movements within the sangha had varied effects: introducing state supervision in some cases or weakening the older institutional lineages in others. In some quarters (such as modern China and Myanmar), Buddhist monks have been called upon to withdraw, study, and meditate; elsewhere, monks have been encouraged to serve as leaders in political reform movements and in the implementation of development projects.

In revolutionary China and Outer Mongolia, Buddhism was identified by revolutionary regimes with the old feudal order and was fiercely disestablished; across China's Tibetan and Inner Mongolian regions, the policy of the People's Republic of China, especially during the Cultural Revolution (1976–1986), was to destroy Buddhist monasticism, punish believers, and repress any public expressions of devotion. Just reestablishing stupas, ordination lineages, and traditional sangha life has been a challenge over the last decades in these nations.

In Sri Lanka, once the nationalistic Buddhist movements had ushered in independence they turned their efforts inward; by seeking to legislate a "purer Buddhist state" and a restoration of past glories, they created the environment where activist political monks flamed unprecedented ethnic conflict with non-Buddhist minorities long resident in their societies. Paradoxically, Buddhist universalism and the ideology of compassion have not prevented modern attempts at "ethnic cleansing" there as well as in Burma and Bhutan. Some social historians see the further weakening of Buddhist ethics in the future; as populations rise and resources grow scarcer, they argue, Buddhism can be used, as have other world religions, to unify majorities that repress minorities.

The Sangha: Adaptive Reformism?

Given the repeated emphasis placed on the role of the sangha in maintaining the traditional goals of Buddhism in every society, it should not be surprising that we underline the role that ordained exemplars, scholars, teachers, and meditators will play in determining Buddhism's future into the third millennium of the common era.

Arguing that the sangha cannot keep Buddhism alive unless the monks keep pace with the educational level of the nation's population, countries like Thailand have invested to make higher education available to individuals in the sangha. This opportunity attracts many young men from poor rural backgrounds to take ordination; becoming a monk, paradoxically, gives many individuals the chance to live in better material circumstances and gain skills that can be taken back into lay life. But at the same time, these same modern states have bureaucratized the nation's sangha, scrutinized the preaching and personal lives of monks and sought to control the political activities of the monasteries. In recent times as in antiquity, the freedom accorded one "in the robes," the refuge afforded by the monastery, and the high regard extended to charismatic monks have caused political leaders to weaken Buddhist institutions even while honoring them. In countries like Myanmar and China, the monks cannot escape the fear of repression or hope to exert traditional political influence. It is hard to imagine Buddhist monks regaining this power in most of modern Asia.

Since World War II, many developments have undermined the classical patterns and exchanges within Buddhist societies. Monastic schools were once an important part of the sanghas' service to local communities and a source of their recruitment, but today popular education has been removed from the monastery almost everywhere. If connection with and awareness of modern changes is essential to an institution meeting the needs of the lay majority, is the traditional Buddhist sangha across Asia capable of keeping Buddhist ideas and identity vibrant in the whirl of changes sweeping modern Asian societies?

Many progressive Buddhists think not. Pointing to the hierarchical nature of the modern sangha, they see little opportunity for young monks to fashion innovative applications of the Dharma in thought or action; noting how powerful elder monks typically lack vision, purpose, or inspiration beyond the guardianship of ceremonies and tradition, many Asian laypersons look to lay institutions for more promising avenues to keep Buddhism vital.

Recent demographic trends do not portend vitality in the sangha recruitment: the number of men taking ordination across Asia has fallen far short of what population increases would predict. As a result, many rural monasteries are understaffed, a trend reflecting the breakdown of rural communities that has contributed to the urbanization of Asia. The Asian schools that have countenanced sanghas of the "married ordained" (Nepal, Korea, Japan), though they have solved the problem of recruitment by making monasteries family property, show even less inclination to revitalize or innovate. Again, it is easy to see why Buddhist reformers have almost always gone outside the boundary of the modern sangha to move ahead with their programs, at times even having to face opposition from the establishment monastic community.

A Role for Buddhist Women?

Related to the issue of the sangha's adaptability and leadership is the question of the status of Buddhist women renunciants. In 1987, an international conference held in Bodh Gaya was attended by 150 devout women who formed a worldwide women's organization called *Shakyaditya* ("Shakya Daughters") dedicated to the restoration of the full ordination of *bhikkhunis* (nuns) among the Theravadins, a lineage most Buddhist monks of this school today view as having died out almost a millennium ago. Throughout the Buddhist world today, there are several hundred thousand highly committed women who have adopted an unofficial and unheralded ascetic lifestyle involving meditation, service, or study. It is also true that in every country there is also a male-dominated sangha that controls the Buddhist institutions and whose great majority has shown strong resistance to changes in the gender status quo. At a conference held in 1996 in Sri Lanka, the male establishment again rejected the idea of reinaugurating the nuns' ordination lineage.

Yet some women who have gone ahead and adopted the lifestyle of the nun do not even wish to take the full bhikkhuni ordination. Why? According to the *Vinaya* rules, fully ordained women admitted into the sangha must accept the formal supervision of the senior monks. Presently, in their unofficial status, these "nuns" enjoy near-complete autonomy to manage their living arrangements and spiritual training. They argue that since their real loyalty is to the Dharma and their true concern is nirvana-seeking discipline, it is pointless to seek to be attached to such formal recognition. Yet remaining "unofficial" places severe limitations on the women's ability to build their institutions, since they are not recognized for state patronage and householder donations to them do not yield the same prestige or merit return that donations to the monks do. As a result, in most instances, most of the unofficial "nuns" remain impoverished, without special honor in their societies at large, and marginal to the dominant Buddhist community. Yet can Buddhist traditions facing so many future challenges afford to relegate to the margins of their societies the energy, compassion, and merit of such women?

Buddhism's Elective Affinity for Modernization?

At the beginning of this century, Western scholars such as Karl Marx and Max Weber questioned whether Buddhism could prove compatible with economic modernization. Since the end of the Second World War, such skepticism has been laid to rest by the success of the Buddhist nations of Southeast and East Asia. We can now see that Weber erred in exaggerating the "other-worldliness" of mainstream Buddhism, unaware of the unambiguous and early doctrinal emphasis on "good Buddhists" attaining worldly success, an ethos that traveled well across the trade routes of Asia and, it seems, into the twenty-first century. Modern reformers have had many texts to draw upon to promote the compatibility between economic development and Buddhism. As an influential reformist monk of Thailand asserted, "Education breeds knowledge, knowledge breeds work, work breeds wealth, and wealth promotes happiness."[6]

The economic renewal under way in Asia since World War II has clearly benefited Buddhism as newly wealthy patrons have sponsored various renewal initiatives. These works in almost every case do not involve the sangha's leadership. For example, there are under way now Thai and Korean projects that have transcribed their canons into electronic media form (CD-ROMs), a new mode of spreading the Dharma locally and globally to all with computer technology. Translation of the sacred texts into English is another form of innovation. The Buddhist Publication Society founded in Sri Lanka in 1956 has offered hundreds of translations and interpretive tracts on the Pali texts; its work overlaps with that of the Pali Text Society founded in nineteenth-century England, the latter a group that continues to extend its translations into the commentarial and extracanonical southern Buddhist tradition. A more recent project has been undertaken by the Japanese industrialist Yenan Numata's foundation, the Bukkyo Denko Kyokai: it is underwriting the scholarly translation into English of the entire Taisho edition of the Chinese canon. Begun in 1991, the plan is to translate all 3,360 scriptures, a work estimated to span the next one hundred years! Each of the four Tibetan monastic schools now has a modern publishing house in the West that yearly prints dozens of texts promulgating explanations of Buddhist doctrine by its own teaching lamas.

Globalization of Buddhism: Monks, Migrants, and Global Culture

Another postcolonial avenue of revival proceeds through the global migration of Asian Buddhists. As these groups grow and prosper in their new societies, they naturally channel a portion of their savings back to the home region. But these immigrants have also paid to sponsor monks and build storefront monasteries in the West, in the process internationalizing their home country's institutions through a slow grass-roots process of development. As Buddhist clergy and expatriates move between their new and old countries, innovations and resources are being shifted as well. This immigrant-induced exchange also includes the cross-fertilization of ideas moving between Buddhist schools from distant areas of Asia and their Western exponents. It may well be that the future success—or perhaps even survival—of the modern national lineages and schools of Buddhism back in Asia will depend upon their internationalizing their memberships, funding, and interpretive awareness. To date, only the Tibetan Buddhists in exile have been truly successful at linking the material support and ritual practice by Western converts to their traditional schools; otherwise North American immigrants and converts remain in separate worlds.

An especially promising domain is Buddhism's presence in the emerging global culture. In the area of human rights, Asian Buddhist exponents have made impressive contributions. Buddhist doctrine offers many traditional ideals that have been rearticulated powerfully by reformists and activists who styled themselves, in a term utilized by the Vietnamese Zen monk Thich Nhat Hanh, as "engaged Buddhists." These ideas include compassion, nonviolence, selflessness, interdependence, detachment. There is no shortage of examples today that show how the existential "poisons" that Buddhists have always located at the center of their wheel of life—human greed, lust, and delusion (as we have seen)—continue to produce suffering to individuals, communities, and the earth itself.

An example of this determined insistence on applying Buddhist norms to modern crises is seen in the writings of the Thai activist Sulak Sivaraksa, founder (in 1989) of the International Network of Engaged Buddhists:

> When Prince Siddhartha saw an old man, sick man, a dead man, and a wandering monk, he was moved to seek salvation, and eventually he became the Buddha, the Awakened One. The suffering of the present day, such as that brought about at Bhopal and Chernobyl, should move many of us to think together and act together to overcome such death and destruction, to bring about the awakening of humankind.[7]

Uniting Asian Buddhists with Western converts, bringing together the energies of householders, monks, and nuns, as well as finding issues that connect

Buddhist activists with similarly committed reformers from other faiths, Engaged Buddhism holds the promise of advancing the cause of the faith in the emerging global culture. It remains to be seen if Buddhist revivalists can offer a compelling interpretation of the Dharma as Buddhists find themselves drawn into the global markets of multinational capitalism and its doctrines of individualism, ruthless competition, and the virtue of consumerism.

DISCUSSION QUESTIONS

1. Buddhists past and present have looked to the incidents in Gautama Buddha's life for inspiration. Pick three major episodes in the Buddha's life and discuss what they impart to a typical Buddhist householder.

2. Many modern Buddhists regard the Buddha as a reformer. What teachings can be used to support this interpretation? What historical arguments can be made against this position?

3. Which of the Buddha's teachings are shared with post-Vedic Hinduism?

4. Explain how Buddhist doctrine can argue for reincarnation but against the existence of an "immortal soul."

5. Why is compassion a human ideal that is a logical extension of core Buddhist doctrines?

6. What is the relationship between the Three Marks of Existence, *prajna*, and *nirvana*?

7. In what senses can the Buddha be called "The Great Physician"?

8. Describe at least three reasons for which Buddhism can be rightly known as "The Middle Way."

9. How might the Vajrayana school be viewed merely as an application of basic Mahayana Buddhist doctrines?

10. Why is the *Lotus Sutra* so important in China and Japan?

11. How does Mahayana Buddhism resemble and differ from devotional Hinduism?

12. How is the Mahar revival of Buddhism in India indicative of the Protestant and postcolonial movements within the Buddhist world?

13. Name five aspects of Protestant Christianity that were adopted by Buddhist reformers, shaping the nineteenth- and twentieth-century revitalization movements called "Protestant Buddhism."

14. In your opinion, how would a modern Buddhist revivalist present the Dharma and argue that it remains a religion relevant to life in the twenty-first century.

KEY TERMS

anatman	Four Noble Truths	*sangha*
arhat	*karuna*	*shramana*
bhikkhu/bhikkhuni	*koan*	*skandha*
Bodh Gaya	*Lotus Sutra*	*stupa*
bodhisattva	Madhyamaka	Theravada
Buddha	Mahayana	Three Marks of Existence
caitya	*maitri*	Three Refuges
dana	*mantra*	Thunder Vehicle
dependent co-arising/	Mizuko cult	Triratna
origination	*nirvana*	*trishna*
Dharma	Pali Canon	Vajrayana
Eightfold Path	*prajna*	*vihara*
"Engaged Buddhism,"	"Protestant Buddhism"	*vipassana* meditation
Enlightenment	*punya*	Zen
Four Good Deeds	Pure Land	

SUGGESTED READING

Heinz Bechert and Richard Gombrich, eds., *The World of Buddhism* (New York: Thames-Hudson, 1987).

Richard Gombrich, *Theravada Buddhism: A Social History from Ancient Benares to Modern Colombo* (New York: Routledge, 1988).

———— and Gananath Obeyesekere, *Buddhism Transformed: Religious Change in Sri Lanka* (Princeton, N.J.: Princeton University Press, 1988).

Peter Harvey, *An Introduction to Buddhism: Teachings, History, Practices* (Cambridge: Cambridge University Press, 1990).

Donald Lopez, ed., *Buddhism in Practice* (Princeton, N.J.: Princeton University Press, 1996).

Walpola Rahula, *What the Buddha Taught* (New York: Publisher Resource, 1978).

Frank E. Reynolds and Jason A. Carbine, eds., *The Life of Buddhism* (Berkeley: University of California Press, 2000).

Caroline A. F. Rhys-Davids, tr., *Stories of the Buddha* (New York: Dover, 1988).

Richard Robinson and Willard Johnson, *The Buddhist Religion: A Historical Introduction*, 4th ed. (Belmont: Wadsworth, 1997).

David Snellgrove, *Indo-Tibetan Buddhism* (Boulder, Colo.: Shambhala, 1987).

John S. Strong, ed., *The Experience of Buddhism* (Belmont, Calif.: Wadsworth, 1995).

Donald Swearer, *The Buddhist World of Southeast Asia* (Albany: State University of New York Press, 1996).

Kevin Trainor, ed., *An Illustrated Guide to Buddhism* (London: Duncan-Baird Publications, 2001).

Mohan Wijayaratna, *Buddhist Monastic Life* (Cambridge: Cambridge University Press, 1987).

Paul Williams, *Mahayana Buddhism: The Doctrinal Foundations* (New York: Routledge, 1989).

NOTES

1. "Buddhism in a World of Change," in *The Path of Compassion: Writings on Socially Engaged Buddhism,* Fred Eppsteiner, ed. (Berkeley: Parallax Press, 1988), pp. 16–17.

2. "Call Me by My True Name," in Ibid., pp. 34–37.

3. Samuel Beal, Si-Yu-Ki, *Buddhist Records of the Western World.* New Delhi: Munshiram Manoharlal, 1983, p. xxix.

4. Guide formulated by Liao-Fan Yuan (1550–1624), a Zen master of Jiang-su Province. Translated in *The Key to Creating One's Destiny* (Singapore: Lapis Lazuli Press, 1988), pp. 43–46. Passages edited and in places paraphrased.

5. U Ba Swe [Defense Minister of Burma], in *The Burmese Revolution* (Rangoon: Pyida Press, 1957), pp. 14–15.

6. Phra Kummsaen, as quoted in Kenneth Landon, *Thailand in Transition* (Chicago: University of Chicago Press, 1939), pp. 67–68.

7. Sulak Sivaraksa, *Seeds of Peace* (Berkeley: Parallax Press, 1988), p. 9.

CHAPTER SEVEN

EAST ASIAN RELIGIONS: TRADITIONS OF HUMAN CULTIVATION AND NATURAL HARMONY

Overview

On public holidays and lunar days traditionally deemed efficacious for approaching the gods, temples in China, Japan, and Korea are packed with morning visitors, the air thick with incense smoke. In Beijing, newly married couples flock to the White Clouds Daoist temple to light candles, requesting divine aid to ensure the birth of a son; in Seoul, honor students approach the family shrine to report their successful admission to Stanford University at their ancestors' altar; in rural Japan, farmers gather at the village Shinto shrine for the annual harvest festival, clapping their hands to punctuate their prayers of thanks, then offering *sake* and preparing the sacred *sumo* wrestling grounds with salt. Buddhist monasteries have also attracted new patronage as economic prosperity has enriched the region: old women hoping for medicinal cures sip blessed water, executive trainees sent by corporations for "toughening up" sit in meditation, and children desperate for assistance on an upcoming exam light incense sticks, all enlivening these precincts.

It is more difficult to find public shrines for the sage Confucius, but there is no doubt that Confucian tradition has survived the wars, political tumult, and scathing denunciations of the twentieth century. Blamed in the colonial era for retarding the region's development, now Confucianism's emphasis on education, strong families, individual discipline, and harmonious group relations is seen as holding the center of East Asia's stable societies and orchestrating this region's predicted ascendancy in the world economy.

This religious pluralism sets East Asia apart. Throughout the region's history, the great majority of East Asians regarded Confucianism, Daoism, deity cults, 439 and Buddhism as complementary, dealing with different aspects of life, enriching their spirituality with useful and interrelated beliefs and practices, offering individuals the chance for melding the traditions harmoniously to solve life's problems and questions. It was rare for individuals—elite or common folk—to feel that "being religious" meant choosing one tradition to the exclusion of the others.

In East Asia, more so than in South Asia, there has been a popular and strikingly common "diffuse religious tradition" that most individuals still share. It had its roots in the ancestor veneration and spirit worship of earliest antiquity, and over time this was melded with general and basic elements of Daoism, Buddhism, and Confucianism. In contrast to the common Western belief that "being religious" means signing on to an exclusive creed or seizing upon one "either/or" alternative, except for small groups of sectarians, this was not the nature of "being religious" in East Asia. Given that roughly 40 percent of humanity is East Asian, no full reckoning of human religious life, both in universal consideration or in contemporary analysis, can be made without taking into account China, Korea, and Japan.

Modern East Asian Countries and Their Demography

What is today referred to as China is the People's Republic of China (PRC), the country with the world's largest population of over 1.3 billion citizens. China from antiquity has sought to pacify and incorporate the oasis regions of Central Asia and the peoples of the Mongolian grasslands. Different dynasties up to the present have struggled to unify the dozens of minority peoples of the periphery regions with those of the core region who have called themselves Han and whose descendants speak the (originally) northern Chinese dialect called Mandarin. Although spoken Chinese contains over twenty major dialects, the literate culture of China has used the same written language for more than two thousand years. This has made the classical literary tradition (including all religious texts) accessible to the learned throughout the East Asian region. Mandarin language and Han culture effectively wielded by state officials did prove capable, at times, of unifying vast domains. The power of the civilization dominated by Confucianism and Daoism was such that even when foreign conquerors established themselves as China's rulers, they themselves submitted to the power of this culture and adopted its traditions.

The formerly unified Korean culture area, artificially split into the separate countries of North Korea and South Korea since the end of the Second World War (1945), was most strongly influenced by Chinese cultural borrowings, including Buddhism. In the early modern period until the end of the Yi dynasty (1392–1910), Confucianism was the state religion, and the ancestral cult became central in Korean society. At the same time, the Buddhist *sangha* (monastic community) was forced to withdraw to the mountains away from major cities. Although this isolation kept alive in such peripheral areas strong monastic and spiritual practices among the elite, the overall influence of Buddhism on Korean society waned. Shamanic traditions, which are today strongest in Korea compared with other parts of East Asia, are found throughout the peninsula and are resorted to by most individuals regardless of other religious affiliations. In the modern isolationist and communist state of North Korea, little traditional religious activity is sanctioned or reported among its 24 million people.

The island nation of Japan was Sinicized in countless waves throughout its recorded history, but beginning later and penetrating less intensively overall than in Korea. Now a constitutional monarchy headed in practical governance by a prime minister, Japan has for centuries been ruled by an emperor and a single imperial line (albeit sometimes only as a figurehead) that is distinctively Japanese in its mythological origins. Since the end of World War II, Japan's 120 million people have produced the world's fourth largest national economy through its "economic miracle." As elsewhere, this rapid transition has worked in contradictory directions, enriching devotees of every persuasion who have rebuilt institutions and created new ones, while changing the society profoundly and so leaving individuals seeing the world in ways unimagined back in the premodern era. "New Religions" continue to spring up, offering new spiritual orientations.

The Chinese Core and the Periphery of East Asia
China has been the formative center or "culture hearth zone" of the East Asian region from earliest antiquity. The emergence of a central state there predates the unification of the states along its periphery (Korea and Japan) by at least twelve and fifteen centuries, respectively. Most modern country boundaries that demarcate the region date back to the premodern era, with the exception of the divide between the two Koreas, the region of Tibet, and the republic of Taiwan.

In the broadest terms, all regions beyond China's early core region can be seen as the frontier peripheries of Chinese civilization, where states and individuals selectively and creatively adapted the essential Chinese cultural forms. These forms encompass the full range of what "culture" entails, from written Chinese characters used to record the spoken languages, to the fundamental material technologies needed for subsistence (intensive rice production, iron making, porcelain pottery), to of course the beliefs and practices of its great religious traditions. As we have seen, even Buddhism, which the Chinese themselves adopted despite its "barbarian" origins, was transmitted to the East Asian periphery in the same pattern through China.

Yet despite the overwhelming magnitude of Chinese culture and the nearly irresistible power of the Chinese states that dominated the region due to its geographic size and population, it is still true that Koreans, Japanese, and Vietnamese established and preserved their own separate identities. While importing and synthesizing much from China, each nonetheless developed its own distinct spoken language, mythology, and spiritual connections to their native lands. In all these periphery states, too, the national cultures inspired their peoples to identify with being separate culturally and politically from China, however much their cultural elites admired Chinese culture. (In some cases, especially given the destruction and changes that have swept modern China, the best places to find Chinese cultural forms of earlier eras are now in Korea or Japan.) Further, as is all too plain in the modern era, the extensive and long-standing cultural ties connecting East Asian peoples did not prevent colonization, genocide, or other expressions of enmity between the modern states.

ENCOUNTER WITH MODERNITY: POSTCOLONIAL CONFUCIAN ECONOMICS

The Postcolonial Challenge of Confucianism

By 1980 it was clear that modernity theorists who had predicted the decline of religion with the advent of science were incorrect in every instance, as we have seen. Nowhere have the flaws of this analysis been more striking than in East Asia, where indigenous intellectuals and reformers since the mid-nineteenth century blamed Confucianism for the region's decadence and its failure to defend itself against the imperialist West. The region's political despotism, social disintegration, economic retardation, scientific stagnation, poverty, and disease were all ascribed to its blind adherence to Confucian ideals and practices.

The quicker Confucianism could be abandoned in favor of Western cultural borrowings, reformers argued, the sooner would East Asia be on the road to recovery. For this reason, many welcomed the fall of the Chinese (1912) and Korean (1910) imperial states, and with them their domination by Confucian officials and intellectuals. Yet as events transpired, not only has religion survived, it has revived and expanded with the rising development and wealth of hitherto colonized world areas, often in surprisingly strong forms.

For example, early modernity theorists once attributed Japan's postwar prosperity to its successful and rapid Westernization. Although the war fomented by European-styled fascism destroyed many of their material accomplishments through Japan's first era of modernization (1868–1945), the Japanese after World War II were still able to rebound and build what is today one of the world's strongest economies.

Scholars now see the success of Japan as the result of much more than its early and rapid Westernization: the Meiji era facilitated the region's first union of Western technology and reformed Confucian social policy (as we'll discuss in this chapter), one that was accomplished, too, in postwar South Korea, Taiwan, and Singapore and is now under way in post-Mao mainland China.

Thus, the socioeconomic analysis has been completely reversed. That is, we now find many scholars *explaining* the East Asians' success as due to the region's possessing a family-centered "bourgeois Confucianism" (as distinguished from the "high Confucianism" of the former Mandarin ruling elite).

The East Asian revival has been allied in each instance with a strong post–World War II state that defines its duty in terms of providing leadership for the national economic causes. This recent reinvention of Confucianism has produced societies marked by low crime, social harmony, and efficient economic behavior, which in turn has led to unprecedented success, an accomplishment rightly called an "economic miracle" given the disastrous state of the region right after World War II.

Now what reformers had identified as Confucianism's intractable flaws have been reanalyzed in positive terms: family-based businesses are efficient in maximizing scarce capital; tightly woven kin/family relations are excellent building blocks for supply and product distribution; an education system that fostered group cooperation, memorization, and imitation has proven adept at producing individuals able to master existing technologies and make them remarkably better. With strong states focusing initiatives guided by experts dedicated to achieving collective economic success, by 1990 it was clear that East Asian peoples with this reformed Confucian orientation had risen to top global positions in all the major manufacturing sectors of the postmodern world. After East Asians had acquired Western know-how, they effectively mobilized indigenous social resources and created political systems that ensured the social cohesiveness needed to promote national prosperity.

Not only does this success challenge the West's historical monopoly of wealth and economic power; it raises doubt about another tenet of modernity theory: is Westernization an inevitable consequence of modernization? Stated differently: must all nations Westernize to modernize? Or is the Confucian route through strong authoritarian states an alternative for Asia, heralding a "Third Confucian Epoch?" To better understand the significance of this encounter with modernity we must go back to the premodern era and trace the historical development of East Asian religion.

EAST ASIAN RELIGIONS IN THE PREMODERN ERA

East Asia is extraordinary among the world's regions because many beliefs and practices documented from earliest antiquity (1500 BCE) survive there in the present. To convey just how strong this conservatism has been, consider the example of deities worshipped by China's imperial court: a list of the gods sacrificed to by the last Ching emperor in 1907 *exactly* matches the deities mentioned in a Shang-era record (c. 1100 BCE), with the sole exception of Confucius (who lived almost six hundred years after the Shang court!). Therefore, it is important to survey the emergence and early development of Chinese religions to discern religion's pivotal importance in Chinese civilization and to see how its religious beliefs and practices spread to other East Asian societies.

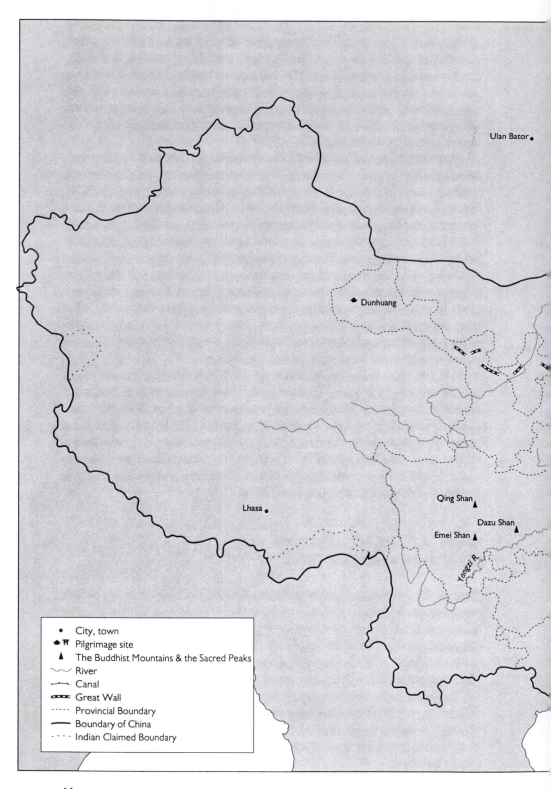

Map 7.1

Yellow R.

Yungang
Miaofeng Shan
Beijing
Heng Shan
Tianjin
Wutai Shan
Dalian

Jinan
Tai Shan
Lao Shan
Taian
Qufu

Longmen
Luoyang
Kaifeng
Hua Shan
Song Shan
Chang-an (Xi-an)
Xionger Shan
Nanwictai Shan

Wudang Shan

Nanjing
Suzhou
Shanghai

Jinhua Shan
Upper Tianzhu Monastery
Poyue Shan
Hangzhou
Putuo Shan
Huang Shan
Ninpo
AyuWang Monastery
Lu Shan
Tiantai Shan

Shao Shan
Longhu Shan
Heng Shan
Wuyi Shan

Jinggang Shan

Nanhua Monastery
Caoxi Shan
Lofu Shan
Guangzhou

Hong Kong

Grand Canal

SEA OF
JAPAN

Kumgangsan

Pyongyang
Seoul

Kwangji
Tóngdo-Sa

Nagasaki

Tokyo
Kamakura
Fuji
Okyoto
Nara
Izumo
Tenri
Ise
Hiroshima

Amaterasu Jinja

TAIWAN

PACIFIC
OCEAN

0   500   1000 km

DEFINING TERMS

Given our treatment of East Asian religions together, a brief explanation of the central terms, figures, and features is needed. Each topic highlighted here will be developed later in the chapter.

We use *Confucianism* a Western term originating in eighteenth-century Europe, instead of the corresponding Chinese term *rujia*, meaning "literati tradition." The literati (for intellectuals) tradition is rooted in the system of moral observance and ritual performance established in the sixth century BCE by Master K'ung (or in English rendering, "Confucius"), whose teachings were commented upon by subsequent sages. The Confucian tradition, which was made China's state ideology over two millennia ago, became noted for its wisdom books, political institutions, social teachings, and attention to self-cultivation. In this cumulative form, and as adapted by medieval scholars influenced by Buddhism known by Westerners as Neo-Confucianists, the rujia became the most common shared spiritual tradition of China, Korea, and Japan. A mastery of the tradition's classical texts and central doctrines was at the center of the educational system and government bureaucracy until well into the modern era (1905 in China, 1868 in Japan, 1910 in Korea). Reflecting this diversity, we use "Confucianism" without imputing to the tradition a singular creed, ritual, or institution.

Daoism refers to both a philosophical and a religious tradition and so always needs further specification. Philosophical Daoism is centered on cultivating an immediate sense of personal connection with the primal force or reality of the universe, one that is labeled "the *Dao*." In religious Daoism, these sages themselves are revered as humans who had realized supernatural physical powers or spiritual immortality and had become divine. Through meditation or alchemy, this strand of Daoism advocated the sage's path to immortality, and eventually (on the example of Buddhism, imported centuries later) developed monastic traditions to sustain its seekers. Many aspects of "applied" Daoism were developed to manage worldly life in East Asia: acupuncture to adjust the flow of the life force flowing in the human body; *feng shui* to help humans live their lives in harmony with the natural energy flowing in the natural and built environment; *I-Ching* and other forms of prognostication to know the proper moment to perform important tasks (marriage, travel, etc.); *wu-shu* or the martial arts to focus human powers to overcome enemies.

Deity cults in traditional east Asia were universal. Springs, rivers, remarkable geographic features—particularly mountain peaks—are thought to have extraordinary divine inhabitants whose spiritual force, or *ling*, is imminent in their dwelling localities. The same ling is evident and personified in wind, rain, the stars, and legendary figures whose souls endured and who became deities. Each sector of the earth, in fact, is thought to have a resident deity who serves as the counterpart of the government official in charge of the village, town, province, and the state itself, with the pantheon's hierarchy mirroring the human civil service. Across East Asia, the common popular perception is that the deities exist, and they can be contacted at temples, asked questions, and will provide answers through ancient divination rituals. In the popular conception, deities, like local officials, can be bought to provide favors, the big gods may be induced to discipline lesser gods (or demons) who cause troubles, and humans out of mutual respect are obliged to show thanksgiving to them regularly for life, health, prosperity.

Diffuse religion is the useful term that indicates what for most East Asians consists of a spiritual life that was centered within the family unit and immediate locality. It has its roots in the ancestor veneration and spirit worship of earliest antiquity and then draws upon general and basic elements of Confucianism, Daoism, and Buddhism. The unity of a region's diffuse religion derives from the explicit use of state bureaucracy to promulgate full expressions of the selected traditions; at times, scholars are assigned to codify the myriad texts and practices to give them coherence. Traditional printed almanacs have been important texts that record such teachings and orchestrate yearly practices for families. The major elements of the diffuse religion include belief in deities and in rituals relating to them as well as a sense that the universe has fundamental forces and powers, requiring humans of necessity to seek harmony with them to achieve health and long life. The world is believed to have certain natural hierarchies that must be acknowledged and respected as prescribed by ancient traditions, a linkage that extends to one's departed kin, and the ways of the past should be revered and studied to discern the proper path to the future. The strength of the diffuse religion can be traced to the great respect Chinese since Confucius have accorded to past traditions, and so there has been a very long period in which the core elements were absorbed across the region.

The sectarian religions in East Asia were institutional Buddhism and Daoism and the sects that arose periodically, often with the goal of overthrowing the state. Such separate religions were meaningful primarily for the very small elites who might have joined an order, adopted a singular discipline within one tradition, or sought individualistic sectarian goals. But even among these sects, many over time ceased advocating the singularity of their approach alone, as we will see.

Thus it is hard to find any firm boundaries separating the spiritual traditions of East Asia. The *Dao* is a concept shared by all schools, for example; indeed, the Buddhists used the term to define the Buddha's teaching (*Dharma*) in early translations. The goal of harmony is common in each spiritual path. It is the commonality of this "diffuse borrowing," the nexus of the diffuse religion in home and among kin rather than large institutions, and the attempt by elites and commoners alike to harmonize these rich traditions that enable us to treat East Asia's religions under a single heading. In each nation, this inclusive harmonizing trait has been expressed with only slight variation: in Japan, "Shintoist in youth, Confucian as an adult, Buddhist in old age"; in Korea, "Confucian by obligation, shamanist at heart"; in China, "Confucian in the office, Daoist outside."

Earliest History: Shang (1575–1050 BCE)

In the fertile valleys of the Yellow River, urban societies formed by 2000 BCE, and their settlements reveal a distinctive complex of advanced metal technologies, writing systems, and religious practices. Among the northern peoples who lived within walled cities and called their dominant families "the Shang," early Chinese character writing was discovered that describes a connection between all three of these aspects of civilization: the practice of oracle bone divination. On dried large bones of animals, questions were posed in inscribed form. A ritualist then applied a hot metal bar to them, and the answers were discerned by the cracking patterns produced. Among the over 150,000 Shang oracle bones found and deciphered to date, "this-worldly" concerns predominate, namely questions regarding whether to undertake military action, hunts, journeys, or ceremonies, as well as regarding omens, weather, illness, or the sex of unborn children.

Among the Shang, too, were master metal casters who made a host of elaborately decorated bronze vessels that were used for ceremonies to worship the deities, including the ancestors. Elaborate offerings of drink and food, including animals dispatched on altars, were arrayed at burial sites. Inscriptions on the vessels indicate that the Shang legitimated their rule by claiming the unrivaled supernatural power of the Shang ancestors to act on their and the society's behalf. This Shang notion of reciprocity between dead and living—food and honor bestowed by the living in return for blessings showered on them by the dead—remains to the present a central aspect of East Asian religions.

The cult of the dead assumed vast proportions in the case of the ruling elite, for whom large tombs were dug and around whom were buried all the essentials for life in the "next world." In Shang times, there was the practice of interring sacrificed human servants alongside the nobles; in the case of the later emperors, similar grand tombs were built but with terra-cotta replicas of servants and animals replacing actual living beings.

Another important religious belief known from earliest antiquity is that of easy access and intimacy between humans and divinities. Gods must have been seen as immanent in rain, mountains, and rivers in Shang times, as early Chinese attributed significance to patterns and events in nature and made offerings to them. The spirits were thought to affect all areas of life, from military battles and interstate relations to business fortunes, marriage, and illness. The presence of gods and ancestor spirits was most dramatically attested to by spirit mediums called *wu/hsi* (women/men). Through their possession by the deities, the *wu/hsi* made ready contact with the supernatural and through them Chinese sought to solicit divine aid as well as to exorcise the demons blamed for causing personal sicknesses and disasters. Over time, this notion of spirit agency became a central characteristic of the popular religion, although a more complex pantheon and more systematic means of contact developed.

There is an interesting Shang concept of a high deity called *Shang-di*, "The Lord Above," regarded as so powerful that only the Shang rulers could petition him. The name signifies the elevation of one Shang ancestor to divine status, though Shang-di endured subsequently in popular imagination as the superior deity who monitors and provides cosmic sanction for human behavior. (The term has been used by modern Chinese Christians to translate "God.")

Thus, the foundation of later East Asia's diffuse religion stems from beliefs prevalent in early China: an organic view of the interconnected universe, one peopled by spirits including dead ancestors and the belief that unseen forces in the heaven and in the earth could be influenced by the petitions of shamans, oracle readers, and kings.

Formative Era: Chou, Chin, and Han Dynasties
(1027 BCE–220 CE)

The millennium from the Chou dynasty (1027–256 BCE) until the fall of the Han (205 BCE–200 CE) can be defined as "formative" in the sense that most of the ideas and practices inherited from the past were developed in more systematic and definitive forms, including textual compilations; further, it is in this era when the great sages arose whose teachings set the terms of subsequent discourse and action not only for the Chinese elite, but for the entire region.

The practices surrounding ancestor veneration, the worship of deities, and the important role of the spirit medium all spread as the population of China increased and dispersed southward into the Yangtze River basin. Some extensions of early concepts can be noted. There was the development of *yin-yang* theory and the five substances theory (*wu-xing*: water, fire, wood, metal, earth) to order observations of nature and natural signs into systematic form. The cult of *Tu Chu*, the "Earth Ruler" who controlled fertility, became widespread among the largely agricultural population; by Han times, he was addressed in legalistic petitions that reflect the growing rationalization of state law in Chinese society. At court and among commoners, Chinese polytheistic theology has regarded the deities as neither good nor evil but as potentially both: they can be agents of illness and disaster as well as agents bringing blessings.

Most of the notable deities by the late Chou were viewed with both hope and fear, as with the Lord of the Yellow River, whose waters usually bring lush harvests but whose floods can cause widespread death and destruction. The popular view of well-disposed deities pitted against chaos-disposed demons is one that contrasts strongly with views of the elite that emphasized rationalism.

Ancestor veneration developed further in the formative era, with more elaborate concepts and practices surfacing regarding the afterlife and the tomb as the key place of connection between the living and the dead. Texts left in excavated tombs mention belief in a soul that survives into an afterlife, calling it a *chao-hun* ("cloud soul"). Dead notables were often buried with a jade cicada in their mouths, symbolizing a parallel between the insect and the dead: just as the cicada has a long dormancy period underground (12 years) before rising to life again, so too does the soul continue the individual's life after burial. With the notable dead, too, were buried objects needed by a revived soul, including ritual vessels for consumption (such as wine flasks) as well as models of musicians, attendants, animals. Also placed in late Chou tombs were texts with prayers, blessings, and ritual instructions to be utilized by the soul.

By the Han era, texts deposited in the tombs suggest the notion that a supreme overlord, called *Tian di* or *Huang Shen*, keeps records on each individual, as tomb scrolls note individual acts that seem intended to verify celestial records and ensure that the deceased be released from blame for any evil conduct. The belief that proper tombs can facilitate beneficial exchanges between living and dead grew stronger, as rulers had texts compiled to describe the proper rites and these practices were adopted across the society.

It remained for the sages of the later Chou to develop systems of thought in harmony with their by now ancient traditions. In their scope and vision, these great figures created the terms of understanding that captured the imagination of East Asia's civilizations.

Although it was a time of growing material prosperity, the Chou era was one marked by considerable political instability and militarism as regional states often vied for control of territory and revenues. Amidst the chaos of the times, when rulers and officials conducted themselves with little regard for moral order or respect for human life, there arose individuals who tried to formulate the principles necessary for establishing a just society and enhancing the humanity of its leaders. Their ideas would eventually become the central pillars of East Asian life, and the emergence of these visionaries at roughly the same time as the Greek philosophers and Indian sages makes them part of the world's "axial age," as future history turned due to their teachings. Those who advocated individualistic retreat and the state's noninterference as the best way to ensure humanity's flourishing were called "Daoists." Those who called for the cultivation of their own humanity through disciplined learning, ritual practice, humility, and active social service were called "Confucians."

Confucius and the Literati Tradition

Although one of the most influential figures in world history, Master K'ung (551–479 BCE), failed to realize his own goal of securing an influential position as a state adviser. It was as a teacher and through his students' collecting and passing down his oral teachings to their own students that his ideas took hold: the concepts of righteousness and of *ren*, a term that has many shades of meaning, but captures the sense of "being fully human." The chief means to ren was *li*, which consisted of ethical propriety, good manners, and the cultivation of traditional ritual performances on musical instruments, in sacrifices, and in ancestor veneration. The Confucian ideal was to be a *jun-zi*, a cultivated gentleman who learns from his teacher in youth and then continues to study constantly, both to develop his virtue and to serve others.

The most important aspect of the li is the individual's conduct within the family. Here the central principles are filial conduct (*hsiao*) and brotherly love (*t'i*).

The key domain for hsaio is the bond between child and parent, a relationship that implies mutual obligations on both parties within a hierarchical framework (protection and nurturing in return for selfless service and obedience). Classical Confucianism conceived of this bond as the fundamental human connection and identified four other bonds as extensions of it. These are the ties between husband and wife, between elder and younger brother, between friend and friend, and between ruler and minister. The entire set comprised the Five Hierarchical Relationships, which, properly served, were to lead the entire society toward harmony and "human flourishing." If hsaio began with serving one's parents, it was to continue with serving one's ruler, and to be completed with the establishment of one's own character.

In East Asia, family metaphors are likewise applied to community, state, and heaven based upon this idea. Confucius' theory was that if those who ruled and ministered both followed and encouraged the society's adherence to maintaining these ideals, all would benefit and the state's harmony would be ensured. Through the *Analects*, the compilation of the Master's teaching episodes, anecdotes, and aphorisms, Confucius for subsequent generations became a model for emulation: at ease but showing careful respect, firm but kindhearted, an advocate for the practice of moderation and finding the natural balance in all endeavors. In one passage, the *Analects* describes Confucius' own search for the ideal:

> At fifteen I set my heart on learning; at thirty, I firmly took my stand; at forty I came to be free from doubts; at fifty I understood the decree of Heaven; at sixty my ear was attuned; at seventy I follow my heart's desire without overstepping the line."[1]

Although he is described as being agnostic on the reality of the spirits, Confucius was emphatic on the need for individuals to perform funeral and ancestor rituals to develop respect for others deeply in their character as well as to establish harmony in the personalities of their immediate kin.

The success of Confucius' teachings was largely due to their systematic and forceful advocacy by several great disciples, notably Master Meng (or Mencius, 371–289 BCE) and Master Xun Zi (298–238 BCE). The sayings of Mencius, recorded in a book bearing his name, argue that human nature is essentially good, that humans are naturally compassionate, dutiful, courteous, and inclined toward learning. Mencius also developed the Confucian view that the well-being of society depends upon the virtue of the rulers, and that it is the state's responsibility to ensure the flourishing of its citizens.

An especially influential theory of Mencius applied Confucian theory to the destiny of a state: if a dynasty rules by virtue then it receives the "Mandate of Heaven," an authorization that can be revoked if rulers cease to be virtuous. Rebellion, too, also received powerful legitimization based upon the view that, "Heaven sees with the eyes of the people; Heaven hears with the ears of the people."[2] Under Mencius' influence, too, the philosophers replaced the god

Shang-di with the impersonal *Tian* ("Heaven") in their discussions about the ultimate reality of the cosmos.

Xun Zi, the third of the classical Confucian sages, bears a more pessimistic, mechanistic, and hard-edged application of Master K'ung's ideas. In his view, humans are inherently antisocial and the universe turns on impersonal forces. But since people can be trained, once shown the good they will inherently adopt practices that lead in that direction. Hence, he turned Confucians toward the careful study of the past, its ancient sages, language itself, and the texts that record the history of human experience. Xun Zi's approach to the state was similar to that of the others in conception, although he also called for very strict laws. Several of his students became founders of a legalist school that advocated highly authoritarian laws and ruthless forms of government.

By the end of the formative era, the two interrelated elements of the literati tradition were established: "inner sagehood" and "outer nobility." Dynasties recorded their histories, officials and the discontented argued about the Mandate of Heaven, scholars revered the past and sought to both safeguard and study its records, and all looked to the earliest sages to model their own lives. We must also note that the notion of Confucius as merely a human and this-worldly sage was not all pervasive in China. By the late Han, literature had already appeared across the empire describing him as a demigod.

Early Daoist Philosophy

The formative era saw many other teachers who proposed alternative philosophies to meet the needs of organizing society harmoniously. Yet the most important and long-enduring critique of Confucian doctrine came from those who argued that social relations would be harmonious only after humanity had synchronized itself with nature and with the *Dao*, the mystical reality underlying it. This school in English is rendered "Daoist."

Daoist ideas were being expressed in antiquity at roughly the same time as those of Confucius, and the first great expression of Daoism is the terse and poetic *Daodejing* (*Tao Te Ching*). This often-translated work, traditionally attributed to an anonymous "Old Sage," or Lao Zi, aims to express the nature of the Dao, while paradoxically beginning with the proviso that "the true Dao" cannot be spoken or adequately defined. Various cryptic passages suggest that the Dao that pervades all reality can be known only through silence and through experiences that transcend words.

In this philosophical system, Dao is the prime source of creation, from which the yin and yang forces emerge in ever-shifting harmonies. Dao determines all things and flows naturally as the mysterious and spontaneous energy (*te*) of the universe, functioning without the will or purpose of a creator god. To experience the Dao, one must let go and pursue the path of noninterference (*wu-wei*) as in Lao Zi's dictum, "Do nothing and nothing will be left undone." The best teacher is (to use the example of the *Daodejing*) the example of water that flows with the natural forces and circumstances, yet can overcome all obstacles.

The Daoists felt that the Confucians harmed society through the imposing of rules and artificial practices that interfered with humanity's natural inclinations. Its political message was to return to primal simplicity, with the state interfering as little as possible with the lives of the people. The highest calling for humans, argued the Daoists, is not state service but retreat into the mountains where the reality of the Dao can be felt most clearly.

The second Daoist classic, the *Zhuang Zi*, is attributed and named after another sage who lived several centuries later, Zhuang Zi (Chuang Tzu, 365–290 BCE). Through lively parables and mind-boggling paradoxes, his work explores the mysterious reality of the Dao in everyday human experiences. The most famous example perhaps is his meditation on waking from a dream of being a butterfly. He asks: Which is "real" ? Was Zhuang Zi dreaming of being a butterfly or is the human Zhuang Zi instead merely that butterfly's dream? This text also explores death and advocates accepting the changes the mysterious Dao brings, including the naturalness of death's transforming us into other life forms. Such acceptance is the necessary step toward experiencing transcendent freedom.

Daoist mysticism provided a balance against the bounded rules and regulations of strict Confucianism, offering a rich lore of parables as well as spiritual guidance to those who retreated from government service or active social life. Daoist refuge in nature and the natural inspired subsequent artists, including poets and painters.

Foundations of "Religious Daoism" (Dao Jiao)

As indicated earlier, Daoism contains both a philosophical and a religious tradition. The tradition we refer to as religious Daoism has its origins in the formative era and its proponents respected the state and Confucius, typically building their spiritual programs on the foundations of filial piety.

But the many schools had far more specific goals that they approached through a number of different spiritual disciplines. Some sought immortality and emulated sages who reputedly ride the clouds and have established a paradise for immortals on islands in the eastern seas. Those questing immortality followed two different paths. The first required meditation aimed at strengthening and multiplying the life force (*qi*), typically through breathing exercises, fasting, and sexual practices. A second path involved alchemy, the art of combining such substances as mercury, gold, and cinnabar into an elixir, that when finally perfected could render body and soul of those ingesting it invincible to decay or death. Doubtless the Daoist mystics and alchemists, a minority of single-minded teachers who lived in secluded retreats, contributed to the development of Chinese science and medicine, as well as to the martial arts traditions, all of which applied Daoist terms and theories to specific and more worldly endeavors.

On the popular level, religious Daoism developed by systematizing the indigenous pantheon, defining formal ritual roles for priests in temples while focusing on the divinity of Lao Zi and *Huang-Di* ("Yellow Emperor," the first immortal). Later, the Buddha and Guanyin, appropriated from Buddhism, were incorporated into the Daoist pantheon.

Philosophical Daoism: Basic Beliefs

Scholars have demonstrated that philosophical Daoism evolved from the *Daodejing* (or *Tao Te Ching*) and through subsequent thinkers, and indeed, certain basic ideas from this elite tradition remained important as general propositions across the region. First, there is in Daoism the "organic" notion that humanity is interconnected in a web of interacting natural forces, some visible, some unseen, all shifting and reversing direction when they reach their apex. The opposing yet complementary yin-yang forces became the means of comprehending and analyzing the phenomenal universe so conceived, as its forces affected human destiny. Reality is best perceived when this interconnection is comprehended, for in this movement the dynamic power of the mysterious and determining Dao can be discerned, or indeed tracked from moment to moment. The classic text determining "the state of the moment" is the *I-Ching*, and it has helped East Asians make such determinations, using trigrams to depict the various combinations of yin (▪▪) and yang (≡) forces at work in a given setting. It is perhaps Song-era landscape paintings influenced by Daoism that best convey to outsiders this sense of human beings finding their proper place in the vast natural world: amidst the great mountains and flowing waters, humans—inevitably dwarfed by the landscape—can find transcendent harmony.

The second central Daoist notion is that some individuals can attain a state of ultimate transformation, transcending mortality via alchemical, dietary, or meditative practices that impart the power to know and control unseen forces. The human condition is thus one of great positive potential; the human body is a potentially perfectible vessel, even though those who truly attained this state were few. Here, Daoists join with Confucians in seeing the world as redeemable through human agency, with nature seen as humanity's home and teacher. In China, then, what many other religions refer to as 'secular' as seen as sacred.

The third Daoist conviction is that the pursuit of simplicity is essential for spiritual development as well as for the betterment of society; it is only the "natural person" who "goes with the flow" (wu-wei), avoiding unnatural action, who can find the truth and only a society living in a simple manner can find true peace and justice. Daoism thus, with Buddhism, provided a counterculture to the Confucian establishment, one that served those who wished to go into retirement or to critique the legalistic excesses of those in power, and even, at times, bolstering a rebel group's intention to overthrow the regime.

State Religion: The First Confucian Epoch

The first full unification of China—from Central Asia to the eastern coast—was brought about by the first Qin emperor who instituted a central bureaucracy

Yin	Yang
Dark	Bright
Earth	Heaven
Female	Male
Autumn	Spring
Valley	Mountain
West	East
Po Soul (Grave)	*Hun* Soul (Heaven)

The symbolism of the *I-Ching* was the main system for East Asians conceptualizing the incessantly changing universe, much like math equations are used to express the essential truths underlying the discoveries of modern science. The most common *yin-yang* symbol above should be viewed as ever in motion, with the opposite circles in each sector expanding to cause a reversal in the shade.

and state religion. The latter served, in part, to express state unity, while also seeking to harmonize the forces of nature with imperial rule. China's first emperor, though making good on many of his lofty ambitions, obsessively sought personal immortality through Daoist alchemy and ruthlessly suppressed viewpoints he considered deviant. His Mandate of Heaven lasted only fifteen years (221–206 BCE).

The next unification of China culminated in the rule of the Han emperor Wu (140–86 BCE), who established an imperial university and examination system (121 BCE) that was based exclusively upon Confucian teachings and texts. By the later Han (about 175 CE) the official "Five Classics" had been fixed for the first time, and synthesizing treatises drawing upon them guided the spiritual cultivation of Chinese life thereafter. Once fixed in literary form and connected with the authority of Confucius, the Five Classics provided the literati of subsequent centuries with a multidisciplinary and holistic perspective on humanity. The canon comprises the *I-Ching* (*Book of Changes*), *Shu Ching* (*Book of Documents*), Shih Ching (*Book of Poetry*), Li Ching (*Book of Rites*), and an historical work that records events in early Chinese states for the purpose of assessing "blame and praise" and so promoting a tradition of learning from the past to guide future governance. The gist of these works is that at its fullest development, humanity must integrate historical, social, political, and metaphysical awareness.

The state religion developed in the Han placed the emperor as chief priest, advised by Confucian experts on ritual performance and by other specialists who used Daoist techniques to interpret signs in the natural world. On behalf of the kingdom, the emperor alone could sacrifice to the spirits of the departed imperial ancestors; as the "Son of Heaven," he worshiped Heaven and Earth as his symbolic parents and as the primary cosmic spirits. The emperor held the Confucian Mandate of Heaven as long as he acted for the well-being of the empire; earthquakes, eclipses, and unusual weather marked Heaven's potentially withdrawing its mandate.

Being Human: The Individual, the Family, and the Ancestors

The Confucian world view fostered a sense of being human in terms of the self as a center for multiple relationships, with the most fundamental determined by the individual's gender, generational location in the family, and status in the empire. The notion of individualism that dominates the West and has spread through modernization globally is quite the opposite from this East Asian understanding. According to the norms of filial piety, the young owe obedience to parents, women to men, citizens to rulers.

The Confucian vision is that society will be in maximum harmony if individuals mute their individualistic desires to conform to the dictates of the Five Hierarchical Relationships, listed earlier. The ideal was for all the family to benefit in old age from the reciprocities that required their deference earlier in life and to have their political obedience rewarded by Heaven's blessings. What Daoism contributed to support this understanding was that since human beings are a combination of heaven (yang) and earth (yin), which in their exact balance determine gender, personality, and health, they must pursue harmony in their social relations and so respect these primary relations.

All persons are also seen as benefiting after death from the Confucian ordering of life, when the living descendants attend to all the necessary rites to ensure the best possible destiny in the afterlife. Indigenous beliefs going back to the Shang (1500 BCE) era later merged with Buddhist notions to create a composite (and not completely integrated) understanding of the individual's fate after death. What emerged in China (and was accepted in Korea and Japan, too) was a belief in the Buddhist concept of karma (see Chapter 6) and an understanding that after death all souls underwent processing in purgatory. In this netherworld, magistrates carefully calculated karma by means of rigorous bookkeeping methods, then sent the soul on to its proper destiny. In this way Chinese and Buddhist ideas coexisted.

In East Asia both Buddhism and institutional Daoism (the latter only in China) developed their own rituals for manipulating the death passage. In Japan, the great Buddhist monasteries included within their vast estates family grave sites where the remains are kept and where ritual offerings can be made for departed kin.

In conception and in practice, then, ancestors live on in the East Asian family's presence and receive ongoing ritual attention: one portion in the grave, one in an ancestral tablet (located in the home altar or clan temple), and that one is assumed (especially in the first years after death) as potentially in the underworld. The Korean and Chinese practice of burning "spirit money" and other paper replicas of items considered useful there (foods, appliances, etc., in this mourning period) is thought to send relief to loved ones who are undergoing their intermediate state before a next reincarnation.

Although popular texts reveal that many viewed Confucius as a deity by this era, it is also true that the centuries of Han state support had caused Confucian ethics centered on hierarchy and mutual obligation to thoroughly permeate Chinese society through proverbs, storytelling, theater, and songs. The key elements of the "diffuse religion" were widely shared and had come to include the notions of yin-yang theory, geomancy (*feng shui*), the major deities of the pantheon, and the understanding of the multiple souls. The Confucian literati were also aware of the need to craft the state laws in broad strokes, convinced that they could unite the society around a common ritual discipline, with ancestor rites the universal and civilizing norm. Acceptance of multiple meanings in Chinese ritualism was recognized as early as the time of the Confucian master Xun Zi (298–238 BCE), who wrote, "Among gentlemen, [rites for the dead] are taken as the way of man; among the common people, they are taken as matters involving demons."[3]

Development of the Multiple Traditions in Post-Han China, Korea, and Japan (64–784 CE)

In the waning years of the Han empire, military leaders extended the crumbling dynastic reign with brilliant strategies and brave fighting; one general, Guan Yu (Kuan Yu), was so respected for his might and bravery that after his death he became the Chinese god of war in the popular Chinese pantheon. The general's apotheosis is representative of a pattern characteristic across China since antiquity: prominent ancestor spirits transcend their families to receive wider recognition, petitions, and state veneration.

We now move into the fractured Chinese polity of the post-Han centuries (220–617), a time when the Confucian tradition so tied to Han rule fell into disfavor, allowing Buddhism to enter into and secure its permanent place in China. It is in this period, as well, that Japan and Korea enter into the region's religious history.

Expansion of Buddhism

The expansion and domestication of Buddhism from India into East Asia is one of the greatest cultural "conquests" in world history, matched in importance only by the people of Europe and the Americas converting to Christianity. Buddhist monks reached China through the silk route through Central Asia by 120 CE, later through the sea routes. Once established in China's major urban and cultural centers, Buddhism spread to Korea by 372 and then to Japan from Korea by 552, as discussed in Chapter 6.

Buddhism entered Asia through merchants and missionary monks, but became firmly established due to the patronage of emperors and aristocracy. Throughout its history the faith remained dependent upon state support and protection, suffering decline when this was withdrawn. As its influences extended beyond the princes and literati, Buddhism's vision of the multitiered cosmos connected by reincarnation, its addressing of human suffering directly, the promise of the aid rendered by its compassionate celestial deities, and life's destiny turning on the unfolding of karma captured the east Asian imagination. Buddhism was accepted as well for its highly developed artistry and for the pageantry and proficiency of the monks' elaborate ritual performances that included healing rites, rain-making, and guiding the dead in the afterlife. By 400, Chinese monks had composed rituals to provide Buddhist services to venerate and assist the ancestors, a facet of the tradition that was important in South Asia as well; most East Asians came to believe in karma and to worship the great Buddhist deities, and many came to think of the highest spiritual goal as enlightenment.

The power of Buddhism was institutional, concentrating the efforts of its monastic elite, providing artful temples for popular worship, and drawing upon the wealth of donated lands and bonded laborers to expand into every region. For those wishing to become monks or nuns, the monastic life provided a second family of renunciants, opening access to branch monasteries in both urban centers and in splendid rural locations.

The indigenous Chinese literati from the beginning recognized Buddhism's deviance from Confucian values and criticized it on several grounds, including its rejection of family life and service to one's kin, and the worship of deities who originated from outside China, hence from "barbarian" peoples. The Buddhist ideal of monastic retreat for personal enlightenment was construed as antisocial behavior. But in splintered China after the fall of the Han, the literati tradition had no strong state backing. In Korea and Japan, the literati tradition itself was newly introduced, although Buddhist monks and nuns had to overcome suspicions from supporters of the indigenous deity traditions who attributed national misfortunes and natural disasters to their acceptance of Buddhism within the nation.

The Confucian anti-Buddhist arguments would eventually be reused at various times, but for almost all of its first five hundred years in East Asia, Buddhism was widely and deeply incorporated into the region's religious life, finding support in the imperial courts and eventually among all segments of society, from philosophers to farmers. Its success was fueled by its attracting some of the most talented individuals in these societies. The work of translating thousands of texts from Sanskrit to Chinese took centuries and the determined efforts of many hundreds of dedicated intellectuals. Once this task was completed, Chinese, Korean, and Japanese monks would eventually formulate their own interpretations of the many teachings, creating in many respects a distinctive East Asian branch of Buddhism.

Organized Religious Daoism

Another effect of Buddhism's rise to prominence was to motivate the hitherto disorganized adherents of Daoism to systematize their texts and teachings and to create institutions modeled after Buddhist monasteries. The regularized meditative regimes and elaborate rituals eventually developed in the Daoist monasteries gave individuals many avenues for being Daoist in their spiritual development and for propitiating local gods.

By 300, one may speak of several branches of "Neo-Daoism" that extended and further interpreted all levels of early practice. Guo Hong (283–363) was the most prominent figure in developing Daoist thought systematically and he is known both for his attempt to harmonize the tradition with Confucianism and for the further explication of Daoist theories based upon his own spiritual experiments. Beginning with the notion that Heaven's greatest creation is that of life itself, he argued that pursuing longevity and immortality must be the greatest human goal. Guo's innovation was to prescribe a very specific path to that goal based upon moral goodness, social service, diet, and advanced practices. He emphasized alchemy utilizing gold (a substance that doesn't corrode or diminish if buried or melted) and cinnabar (that keeps changing as long as it is heated). This "inner alchemy" culminated in ingesting the perfectly refined substances, reversing Lao Zi's formula of creation: through this pursuit, one turns from the *myriad things* to the *three*—essence (*ching*), life energy (*qi*), spirit (*shen*) (each "fixed" through alchemical practices), to the *two*—yin and yang in perfect harmony (through taming the thought processes via meditation) to the *one*—a state of eternal union with the Dao.

Revived Daoism competed with Buddhism for favor at the imperial courts, and devotees among the emperors spread the reformed tradition across China. This successful effort, building on criticisms of Buddhism's declared antiquity, served to strengthen Daoist traditions, enabling them to survive through monasticism. In 471, Master Lu Xinjing (406–477) completed the first cataloguing and organization of the Daoist scriptures; calling the work *The Three Caverns*, he found 1,226 texts for inclusion. Later commentaries expanded the tradition's literature by thousands of additional works.

"Organized Daoism" never penetrated Korea or Japan through monasticism, but organized Buddhism did. We now turn to this important cultural export from China.

Early Korean Buddhism

Respect for and emulation of Chinese civilization was much stronger in Korea than in Japan, as contact between the states was more regular, with Korea until 1910 a tributary of China. Confucian teachings were slowly introduced and eventually Korea adapted them, along with those of Daoism and Buddhism, to its distinctive environment. The triumph of Confucianism in Korea occurred only with the Choson dynasty (1392–1910); for the first millennium of the Korean state, it was Buddhism that dominated the spiritual formation of the nation. Mahayana Buddhism entered Korea through missions by Chinese monks to the peninsula. A Chinese monk ordained the first Korean monks in 384, and by 554 its monks and artisans had brought Buddhism to Japan along with Korean immigrants.

In Korea, Buddhism's pliability enabled the monks to assimilate the indigenous snake and dragon cults with Mahayana Buddhism as *bodhisattva* (future Buddha) protectors. National ancestors were also accepted by identifying them with Indic gods regarded as "protectors of the tradition." Buddhist exponents produced evidence to argue that Buddhas were found in Korea during previous world eras, with the claim made that Korea was a primordial Buddhist land.

From roughly 700, the Korean version of the classical Buddhist formula of "state-protection Buddhism" was in place. The state protected the tradition in return for monks employing rituals by which Buddhism benefited the state. Lavish patronage enabled Buddhism to flourish; all the Chinese scholastic schools were introduced, and Koreans journeyed to China where some became influential monks. In Korea, the scholarly assimilation of the faith did not lead to competition but to attempts to find common ground. As a result, Korean Buddhism became the most ecumenical in Asia, although the Sön [Chi.: Chan; Jap.: Zen] became by 650 the most popular school.

Religion Under the Early Japanese Imperial State

The formative era in Japan is marked by the introduction of Confucianism from China and, as we have seen, Buddhism from Korea. Although Buddhism has always been the stronger of the two in "the land of the rising sun," Confucianism entered deeply into Japanese life as well.

In Japan, as elsewhere, Buddhism began among the elite, who saw in the faith a means to unite a fragmented land. Indeed, it was under the royal sponsorship of Prince Shotoku (d. 622) that Buddhism became the state religion, and by 741, an edict called for officials to establish a Buddhist monastery and temple in every province, enroll at least twenty monks and ten nuns, and recite texts and perform rituals for the benefit of the emperor and state. Theories were promulgated identifying and honoring the indigenous Japanese deities, the *kami*, as protectors of Buddhism; some were even identified as bodhisattvas.

But Buddhism was not the only foreign belief system to shape the development of Japan: Confucian texts and teachers from China were also influential in the early courts. A seventh-century reform established a Confucian bureaucracy modeled after that of China. Daoist ideas of natural harmony and energy flow, both in the environment and within the person, along with yin-yang analysis, were part of this broad cultural influence. Neither a Daoist priesthood nor a monastic network was ever established, however. Moreover, the Japanese

AMATERASU: KAMI OF THE SUN

In Shinto mythology, a primordial couple creates the physical world and the numerous *kami* deities who inhabit it. Most important among them were the moon goddess (Tsuki-yomi-no-mikoto), a male earth god (Susa-no-ono-mikoto), and his sister the sun goddess, Amaterasu. In the earliest myths, after her brother's impertinence and rudeness, Amaterasu hid in a cave, darkening the world. Only after the other *kami* gathered offerings, put on entertainments, and attracted her with a mirror did she restore light to the world. The reformed earth god and his ally, the *kami* of Izumo, then blessed the people of the islands. A grandson of Amaterasu, having received training from the gods and blessings from the Izumo *kami*, was designated the divine ruler of the nation, and he established the chief shrine for Amaterasu on the seashore at Ise, with a mirror as her symbol. The sun goddess' descendant rules until today as Japan's emperor. Most Shinto shrines include a mirror, where devotees can honor the sun goddess.

never ceased to worship their own distinct divinities, always honoring the notion of Japan itself being established by native deities who remain eternally present. This tradition is called Shinto.

The Shinto Pantheon of Japan

In many respects, the Shinto tradition in Japan shares basic assumptions and practices regarding deities found throughout East Asia. Shamanism, as a tradition of arranging human access to the gods as well as to one's ancestors, also took root in Japan, and pilgrimages to mountains thought to be divine abodes were common expressions of piety. However, as Shinto mythology developed, it was disseminated, systematized, and adapted by the state. These accounts portrayed Japan as a unique spiritual territory filled with distinctive deities called kami. The existence of an extensive set of legends focused on the kami enabled the Shinto priests to retain and relate to a unique pantheon and helps explain why the Japanese did not adopt Chinese deities and folk traditions so readily, despite the importation of many other aspects of the country's religious life from China and Korea.

The Shinto pantheon is headed by *Amaterasu*, the kami of the sun, credited in Japanese myth with having aided in the creation of the country and honored as the progenitor of the royal family. Other kami exist in profusion. Some are associated with the natural forces of wind, thunder, lightning, and rain; some are thought to dwell in natural objects such as mountains, rivers, trees, and rocks; some are ancestral spirits; and some dwell in certain animals such as cows and foxes. Exponents of Shinto emphasize the "this-worldly" and positive perception of life, society, and nature that their indigenous faith has imparted. Shinto shrines often display mirrors as symbols of Amaterasu and for their symbolic meaning: free from dust and capable of reflecting images with natural clarity, these symbolize the Shinto ideals of purity and brilliance. For this reason, too, Shinto shrines are traditionally located in bright, sunny areas.

Classical Imperial China

Tang Dynasty

With the era of the Tang, when China was again unified after centuries of fragmentation that followed the fall of the Han, Buddhism reached its maximum development on the continent. In its early centuries Buddhism in northern China appealed to non-Han conquerors and in the south succeeded through the effective polemics of the popular and charismatic monk and nun exponents. But in the Tang era there developed a more unified, panregional monastic network of seven doctrinal schools, each of which interpreted the confusing welter of texts from India using a different prime text for discerning the Buddha's highest teachings.

Tang China, with its capital in Chang'an (modern Xi'an), was the world's most advanced civilization of its time. Living within the high city walls were merchants from across the Asian world, with communities of Nestorian Christians, Hindus, Manicheans, Zoroastrians, and Muslims found in its neighborhoods and mixing with Buddhists and Daoists who had their own numerous monasteries and temples. The wealth from trade, efficient taxation, and imperial patronage underwrote a golden age that found expression in all the fine arts while spreading Buddhist influences and religious practices across the empire and into both Korea and Japan. Chinese monks, such as the renowned Xuan Zang (d. 664), even traveled to India in search of additional texts and teachers.

However, in 845, imperial edicts by Emperor Wuzong abruptly and destructively halted an era of religious toleration in China. Imperial soldiers quickly destroyed the churches and mosques, and confiscated most of the Buddhist monuments, liquidating the possessions of the faithful. Part of the emperor's motivation involved manpower and finances: with the success of Buddhism more lands were being donated to the monastic community, thereby losing their taxable status, and ever more men and women were joining Buddhist orders, by ordination exempting themselves both from taxation and, in the case of the men, from military service. In the expansion of Buddhism, doubtless there were abuses of these privileges, and earlier governments had in fact tried to regulate ordination and institute laws to ensure that lands donated to the Buddhist sangha were used as intended. (The same tensions and cycles of government intrusion marked Korean and Japanese history as well.) Wuzong's second motivation was religious. He was an ardent Daoist and eager to advance the Daoist tradition's standing.

Within one year, Wuzong forced 250,000 Buddhist monastics to return to lay life and confiscated all but forty-nine monasteries throughout the empire; officials destroyed sacred texts by the tens of thousands and melted down the images for the imperial mint. Although the aggressively anti-Buddhist policy was reversed by the next emperor, the damage was quite severe: Buddhism's predominance across China's landscape was drastically reduced, never again to rise to its pre-845 pinnacle. Only the populist Pure Land and the more independent Chan schools survived.

The later Tang was a time marked by the resurgence of Confucianism. This tradition had continued to guide the familial life of commoners, and Confucius himself was used as a symbol of national unity. The development of Confucianism as a concern of philosophers waned, however. The literati tradition's triumph, through a selective assimilation of Buddhist and Daoist elements, lay ahead.

During the Tang prosperity, the Daoist canon was compiled and printed, as was the collection of Buddhist scriptures, all at state expense. (The latter required eleven years and 130,000 woodblocks!) The theologians on the popular level organized the various Daoist immortals, Buddhas, and bodhisattvas, as well as local deities and spirits, into a bureaucratically linked pantheon, mirroring the state reforms instituted across the empire.

Song Dynasty: The Second Epoch of Confucianism (960–1271)

The "Second Epoch of Confucianism" erected for the literati a profound metaphysical edifice that rivaled Buddhist and Daoist philosophies, while supporting the older social ideology of human relatedness based upon hierarchy, age, and gender. Thus, Confucianism moved to the center of Chinese religious life for all sectors of Song society, a pattern that was later true for Korea and Japan as well. Significantly, the Song dynasty administrators adopted mastery of Confucian learning as the basis for winning a position in its burgeoning civil service. This measure, coupled with relative neglect of Buddhism by the authorities, provided a strong inducement for a return to the Confucian classics as a subject for study and further scholarship, as the best minds of the day once again were drawn into reinterpreting the indigenous tradition. Aiding in the area of scholarship was the expansion of literacy, and the invention of block printing made possible increased dissemination of the canonical works. Private academies that sought to instill virtue and erudition flowered; anthologies of Confucian teachings compiled by leading Song literati were influential not only in China but across the entire East Asian region.

The works compiled and commented upon by the tradition's great "Second Master" Zhu Xi (also written Ju Xi and Chu Hsi) (1130–1200), entitled *Jinsi Lu*, (*Reflections of Things at Hand*), gave students a curricular order in which to study the classics and reproduced long-standing polemics against Buddhism and Daoism. Zhu Xi also added brilliant reinterpretations of Confucian doctrines, thus rendering the thoroughgoing system of thought that has been labeled "Neo-Confucianism" in the West.

Despite its apparent criticism directed against Daoism and Buddhism, Neo-Confucianism in fact was strongly influenced by both. Of equal importance in securing the success of Neo-Confucianism was Zhu Xi's compilation of a ritual manual that imparted Confucian procedures and cogent rationales for all life-cycle rites, giving non-Buddhist and non-Daoist alternatives on which the Chinese people could order their lives. This work, too, was influential across East Asia.

Neo-Confucianism's strength was that it provided a convincing framework for understanding the world, for both the individual and the state. Song thinkers argued that Confucianism was built upon the interconnected unity of humanity with the natural world. They tried to understand phenomena through a series of polarities that systematically associated counterbalanced yin-yang forces in the context of the trinity of Heaven, Earth, and Humanity. The neo-Confucian philosophers emphasized that education was needed to perfect human awareness of li, and that inner meditative cultivation (a borrowing from Buddhism), which Zhu Xi called "investigating the nature of things," was needed to perfect the qi, or vital force essential for taking action in the world. Almost all the neo-Confucians assumed the reality of karma as causal agent for changing life's qualities.

Neo-Confucianism Order, Hierarchy, and Relatedness
The established Confucian notion of the self that became reinforced in family norms and in state law is decidedly not that of the isolated individual but of the person as "a center of relatedness." It can be understood in terms of a series of concentric circles, with the assumption that to reach their highest potential, persons must cultivate harmonious relations with and act within their families, local communities, and states, with Heaven beyond. This scheme clearly implies that engagement in culture and community is necessary for both the person and humanity overall to flourish. As the Confucian classic, the *Great Learning*, states:

> The ancients who wished to bring order to their states would first regulate their families. Those who wished to regulate would first cultivate their personal lives. Those who wished to cultivate their personal lives would first rectify their minds. Those who wished to rectify their minds would first make their intentions sincere. Those who wished to make their intentions sincere would first extend their knowledge. The extension of knowledge consists of the investigation of things.... Only when the personal life is cultivated, the family will be regulated; when the family is regulated, the state will be in order; and when the state is in order, there will be peace throughout the world.[4]

The elaboration of meditative practices and multidisciplinary studies by the Neo-Confucian masters established a rich tradition designed to develop the individual's integral relations with each circle, as illustrated on the next page.

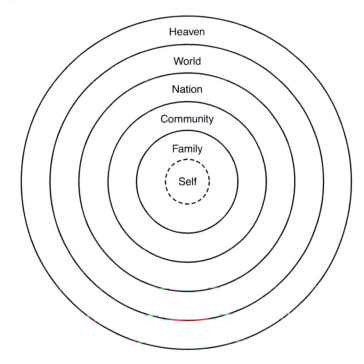

Diagram showing the concentricity of individual relatedness in Confucian moral theroy.

Such later figures as Chang Tsai (1020–1077) went on to merge this conception with Daoist utopianism and anthropocosmic understanding, according to which the ideal of finding "full humanity" is connected to the task of understanding of the universe:

> Heaven is my father and Earth is my mother, and even such a small crea-ture as I finds an intimate place in their midst. Therefore that which fills the universe I regard as my body and that which directs the universe I consider as my nature. All people are my brothers and sisters, and all things are my companions."[5]

The popular convergence of the classical traditions in late traditional China was inspired by these and other figures who sought harmony by learning from all orientations. The "diffuse religion" still extant in contemporary East Asia stems from their brilliant syntheses of ancient sources.

Developments in Korea and Japan

In Korea, Buddhism flourished under imperial support once the country had been united under the Silla rule (668–918). Ties to Chinese Buddhism were strong and almost all of the Chinese scholastic sects had Korean counterparts. Korean monks were notable in China and their commentaries on major texts were studied in both Japan and Tibet. Yet over time, Korean monks were most successful at syncretizing the various schools and teachings, finding harmony rather than division in their development of the tradition.

Religion in the Koryo dynasty (918–1392) continued in the syncretistic mode established under the Sillas. Uniquely Korean was the dominance of the Chogye-chong branch of Sön (Chan/Zen) Buddhism, which was to become the most influential in subsequent Korean Buddhist history. This time was one of ecumenism in which the scholastic schools introduced from China were as-similated and merged into new entities that more closely reflected Korean interests.

The assimilation of Buddhism in Japan had ecumenical aspects as well. It had continued strongly with the movement of the capital to Kyoto by 800 CE, as various elements of imported Chinese culture—Mahayana and tantric Bud-dhism and Daoist theories of yin-yang—were effectively integrated with in-digenous Shinto practices to meet the needs of an expanding state.

The later Kamakura era (1185–1333) ushered in almost seven hundred years of rule by military leaders called shoguns, who usurped the power of the em-peror to rule the nation under a social system closely akin to that of European feudalism. This period was one of widespread contact with China, as trade grew and Buddhist monks were instrumental in bringing new ordination lin-eages from the schools that had survived the persecutions in post-Tang China: Pure Land and Chan/Zen. The notable monks of this era also brought expo-nents of Neo-Confucian learning and their literature to Japan.

The disorder and suffering in the Kamakura also led to dramatic changes in Japanese religions, especially Buddhism. It was widely believed that the world had entered into a period of *mappo*, "decline," in which human capacity for spiritual pursuit had become degraded. This perception was used to justify new interpretations of Buddhism appropriate for the bad new age. Thus, as in Song-dynasty China, the Kamakura in Japan established the framework for sub-sequent nationwide religious practices and beliefs that remained relatively sta-ble until the modern era.

The most popular Buddhist school was Pure Land, and in Chapter 6 we en-countered its polemical advocate Shinran (1174–1262). Shinran and other Pure Land exponents taught that an individual's salvation was completely in the hands of Amida (Skt.: Amitabha), the Buddha of the Pure Land. They empha-sized the practice of uttering the *nembutsu*, that is, repeating Amida's name, and the belief that faith alone was efficacious in the mappo era. Shinran's school ended the requirement of monastic celibacy, and it remains one of the largest religious organizations in Japan today.

Another remarkable Buddhist leader of this era was Nichiren (1222–1282), a monk who opposed the Pure Land schools and in fact all the other Buddhist or-ders. He attributed the decline in Japanese life to the neglect of the *Lotus Sutra*, which he viewed as containing the supreme teaching. The Nichiren-shu advocated chanting the name of this text as the means for personal transformation as well as national renewal, a practice continued to the present day in the Soka Gakkai, a modern Nichiren-derived school that now spans the globe.

The last school established during the Kamakura era was Zen, and it, too, was brought from China by two Japanese monks, Eisai (1141–1215) and Dogen (1200–1260). In adopting sitting meditation, mind-puzzles (*koans*), and unusual teaching methods, Zen represented an innovative lineage of Buddhist practice. It also was very traditionalist, however, rejecting the concept of mappo and resisting the other schools' radical simplification of Buddhism into mere ritual repetition and reliance upon faith. Zen teachers insisted that each individual had to win his or her own salvation on the meditation mat through persistence and self-power alone.

In the Kamakura era, ideas regarding Shinto-Buddhist accommodation were articulated from both sides: Shinto exponents argued that the Buddhas and bodhisattvas were really kami, and the Buddhists built Shinto shrines within their monastic courtyards with the view that the kami were in fact bodhisattvas. This urge to harmonize the various spiritual traditions Japan shared with Korea.

Religions in the Late Classical Era (1400–1800)

The four centuries preceding the modern era find little in the way of religious innovation across East Asia. It was a time when certain ideas among the literati were more fully commented upon, printed, and disseminated, as in the case of Neo-Confucianism in Japan. For Buddhism, this era is characterized by unsteadiness in both state support and in spiritual vibrancy, with Korea the most prominent among those acting to reduce the political power of Buddhism.

Across East Asia, the diffuse religion endured, as ancestor ritualism, local cults to important deities, and the role of the spirit mediums defined the religious field, in cities and villages alike. The *Feng Shen Yan-yi* (The Canonization of the Gods) for Ming-era China (1368–1644) was especially influential and popular in promulgating the idea of the folk pantheon comprising an orderly celestial hierarchy that includes local spirits. Throughout China, a standard organization for the state's official religion was fixed in each province: a Confucian temple with major disciples; a military temple featuring the war god Guan Yu and other notable heroes; and a City God temple to whom all local earth gods "report" and who represents the province in the court of the Heavenly Jade Emperor, who rules all the gods.

China: Late Ming to Early Ching

The Chinese emphasis on harmony was also extended to "the unity of the three faiths" (*san-jiao heyi*, still a widely used phrase) meaning Confucianism, Daoism, and Buddhism. Many philosophers committed to one of these faiths exclusively still argued that their tradition was superior in answering the fundamental spiritual questions. But more popular were teachers such as Jiao Hong (1540–1620) who taught that all three teachings could be regarded as in fact "a single teaching," that each merely uses separate language to articulate its truth, and that all three of them can and should be believed. Other formulae were used to express the era's syncretism and compartmentalization between these faiths:

> Use Buddhism to rule the mind, Daoism to rule the body, Confucianism to rule the world.[6]
> —Emperor Xiaozong (1163–1189)

> Although the Three Teachings are different, in the arguments they put forward, they are One.[7]
> —Liu Mi (active 1324)

> If someone is a Confucian, give him Confucius; if he is a Daoist, give him Lao Zi; if he is a Buddhist, give him Shâkyamuni; if he isn't any of them, give him their unity.[8]
> —Lin Zhaoen (1517–1598)

Among Confucians who conveyed this ecumenical ethos was Wang Yangming (1472–1529), whose view of the "true gentleman" was based on the assumption that everyone can know the good and that "self perfection" means knowing this goodness to the maximum. Wang argued, in language mirroring the "all beings have the Buddha-nature" doctrine of Mahayana Buddhism, that all humans have the potential to achieve self perfection, since all share a primordial awareness:

> Forming one body with Heaven, Earth, and the myriad things is not only true of the great man. Even the heart-mind of the small man is no different....Therefore when he sees a child about to fall into the well, he cannot help feeling alarm and commiseration.[9]

For Wang, since the mind in its essence is beyond good and evil, it is only selfish desires that are the obstacle. His students articulated various forms of meditation such as "quiet sitting" that aimed at extirpating this fundamental human flaw. Wang's views did shock other Confucians, especially in his conviction that external sources—even the words of Confucius or Mencius—are suitable guides only if matched by the truth of one's own time and experience.

This ecumenical attitude was found also within Buddhism, as exponents of the two major schools, Pure Land and Chan, found terms of allegorical accommodation: Chan advocates regarded "the pure land" as a metaphor for the clear mind, and Pure Land followers employed Chan meditation as a means of emptying the ego so as to be able to receive the grace of A-mi-to-fo (Amida Buddha). Both also emphasized practice over doctrinal elaboration. Still, Chan

BUDDHISM AND NEO-CONFUCIANISM IN A POPULAR MING TALE

The *Journey to the West* (or "Monkey Story") written by the Confucian scholar Wu Cheng-en (1500–1582) is a prime example of the Ming-era harmonization of the "three faiths." It recounts the journey of the great Buddhist monk Xuan Zang (d. 664) to search for texts in India. In this dangerous quest, he is assisted by the Monkey King, Sun Wukong, a figure from the Chinese folk pantheon. While ostensibly the account of a great Buddhist monk's journey, the incidents in the long tale (spanning four hefty volumes in English translation) are employed to teach self-discipline—a personal trait valued by both traditions—to the Monkey King and Confucian wisdom to the monk. In many episodes, the success of Xuan Zang's mission depends on the Monkey King's aid and on the monk's timely learning of the ways of the world. Translated into opera and folk ballads, the monkey story became one of China's most popular narratives, its major characters defining important personality stereotypes while conveying the pattern of accommodation under Confucian dominance accomplished by the literati elite of the Ming.

was mainly the school of the literati, artists, and those inclined to asceticism, while Pure Land was the religion of the masses, appealing to the poor, women, those lacking in Confucian education. Thus, Buddhism came to function for many as a nonthreatening counterbalance to Confucian ideology, providing themes and examples through which to spread Confucian ethics. The triumph of Neo-Confucianism in the dominant culture is best seen in the extremely popular narrative, the "Monkey Story."

Buddhism by the late Ming had secured its permanent place in Chinese civilization, as its monastic leaders taught Buddhist doctrine in ways to ensure that there would never be grounds for another imperial persecution. We thus find influential teachers such as Chu-hung (1535–1615) preaching that the essence of Buddhism was social activism as expressed through charity, moral action, and world affirmation. He also emphasized that to be a filial child or a loyal subject was the first step in being a "good Buddhist." This view was carried on by later Chinese revitalizers.

From the late Ming onward, new developments in Buddhism were found mostly outside the monastic sector, as lay associations proliferated that were dedicated to ritual practices such as chanting the Pure Land Buddha's name and promoting vegetarianism by "releasing life," that is, animals that were destined for slaughter. The laity also sought to rationalize Buddhist moral practice by codifying merit and demerit in ledger books.

The Ming dynasty saw the beginning of regular contact with Europe, first with the Portuguese in 1514. With these traders and then with the first wave of missionaries, the Chinese found little to admire and much to resent in the "barbaric manners" of their guests. The failure to institute good relations with the Europeans or to attempt to understand the world beyond China in this early era of small-scale contact set up the problematic and confrontational modern relations of the colonial era.

The Ching dynasty (1644–1912) brought outsiders again in control of China, this time in the form of the Manchurians, who continued most of the forms of state administration. Confucian imperial ritual remained central to the state, and mastery of the classics was the basis for the selection of the literati who ran it.

The strengthening of Confucian ideas and practices throughout all levels of Ching society occurred through the wide-ranging dissemination of *Sheng-zhi tu* ("Pictures of the Sage's Traces"), captioned accounts of Confucius' life. They appeared at this time in a variety of media: on stone tablets installed in temples (Daoist as well as Buddhist), on silk paintings, and in inexpensive and widely disseminated block-printed books. Many versions appeared, offering alternative views of the great teacher. Some were in the ethical-humanistic tradition, others depicted miracles and magic, while still others emphasized the sage's command to make great ritual exertions. Many of these publications were also exported to Japan, where they influenced the efflorescence of Confucian studies and related arts in the Tokugawa era (1600–1867). The Confucian temples of each Chinese locality were also recognized as sites to worship the sage and places where civil service candidates would go to pray for success in the yearly examinations.

Japan in the Shogun Eras (12th to 19th Centuries)

In Japan during medieval and early modern times, there were no Daoist temples competing with institutional Buddhism or Shinto shrines, nor did the deities of "diffuse Chinese popular religion" find their way across the ocean. Instead, Shinto theologians saw the nation's deities in their own connected pantheon, although the relationships between them varied by region and were not thoroughly systematized nationwide until the modern era.

Zen Buddhism, however, also exerted a strong ecumenical influence in the shogunate era. The Zen school's strong relationship with China fostered studies in both the texts of Daoism and the Confucian classics. It also promoted the acceptance of a syncretistic approach to Daoist concepts and Confucian morality. Zen was the vehicle for Japan's cultural elite adopting other art forms derived from China, but Japanese masters soon took them to new vistas of originality in such fields as ink painting, poetry, and tea ceremony. Zen and the other Buddhist schools were closely tied to the ruling elites, who patronized their favorite sects and teachers. This relationship also led Buddhists in Japan throughout this era to vie for support among the factions at the top ranks in society, which they tended to view uncritically. This stance continued right into the modern period, as most monks were more concerned with accommodation with the elite than with reforming Japanese society.

Persecution of Buddhists and Christians

Although Buddhism enjoyed official support during most of the shogunate, Nobunaga (1534–1582) waged an anti-Buddhist campaign, going so far as to burn the great center where Japanese Buddhism was first established on Mount Hiei outside Kyoto. It was dislike of Buddhism that probably led this shogun to be receptive to the first Jesuit missionaries, giving Christianity early support of the sort that it received nowhere else in East Asia. Much to the chagrin of the European missionaries, however, the Japanese had trouble seeing in Christianity anything but an obscure form of Buddhism! Catholic rituals were seen as similar to monastic rites, and the concept of a heavenly Lord whose "son" became incarnate to serve humanity was not unlike Mahayana Buddhism's doctrine of the cosmic Buddha whose "sons," the compassionate bodhisattvas, also served humanity.

In any event, squabbles that developed between Spanish Franciscans, Jesuits, and later Protestants, as well as some missionary attempts to manipulate Japanese politics in the name of their home countries, convinced the first Tokugawa shogun Iyesu to outlaw Christianity in 1606. When in 1616 he acted to expel all missionaries, there were an estimated 300,000 Japanese converts. The next decades saw attempts by the Japanese state to extirpate Christianity. Some officials penned concerted polemics against Christian doctrines that pointed out how the foreign faith clashed with the region's "common sense" spiritual understandings and its norms of secular order. For example, they questioned the logic of a system in which a reputedly omnipotent, benevolent God would allow "original sin" and they objected to biblical passages that seem to undermine loyalty to kin and ruler (e.g., Luke 12:53, 20:37).

Other efforts at removing Christianity were gruesome, as converts who would not recant their faith were tortured. A rebellion in 1637–1638 that resulted in over 37,000 deaths confirmed for its Japanese opponents the disruptive potential of Christianity in Japan. From this time onward, too, every Japanese family by law had to be registered with a Buddhist temple, an effort to regularize ties with Buddhism and emphasize that in Tokugawa times being Buddhist was inherently part of being Japanese. (We will see, however, that in the post-Tokugawa era, nationalists argued the reverse, that is, that Buddhism was a "foreign religion" in Japan!)

The Spread of Confucianism

Although Japan never instituted a Confucian-based civil service system, Confucian thought spread under the Tokugawa shoguns. Confucianism—long present among scholars, in state ritualism, and as part of Buddhist moral teachings from China—finally found its own strong supporters in a succession of prominent philosophers, many of whom were not part of the samurai elite.

For some, Confucian teachings gave those of lower birth an ideal to uphold against the hierarchical system instituted by Japan's hereditary nobility. Unlike in China, Confucianism flourished among both the merchant class and the samurai. Japanese intellectuals throughout the Tokugawa era eventually studied and defended the positions of all the major Neo-Confucians of the Song period and thereafter. There were even some Japanese exponents who came to reject the Neo-Confucian system and urged return to original classics! Efforts were also made to rationalize Shinto beliefs with Confucian doctrines, as in the synthesis of Yamazaki Ansai (1618–1682).

One prominent religious group that arose from the newly affluent merchant class, the *Singaku* ("Heart Learning"), drew upon Buddhist doctrine to emphasize that all occupations offered the individual a means to spiritual development. Its founder, Baigan Ishida (1685–1744), attracted a considerable following in the new towns of Osaka and Edo through teachings that combined elements of Shintoism and Confucianism, extolling traditional morality centered on honesty, frugality, and devotion to one's trade.

Spiritual Training for the Religious Elites
By 1600 CE, all the religious traditions of East Asia had systematically developed institutions and courses of training for those wishing to become adepts in both ritual and meditative proficiency. Although a small percentage of the entire populations actually were initiated into such disciplines, it is useful to understand something of the spiritual training that the region's different religious leaders (priests, monks, and nuns) had to undertake to fulfill their roles.

Confucianism   Only under the guidelines set forth by the Neo-Confucian masters did the literati tradition acquire its own systematic regime. The first stage of training was "disciplining the body" (*shen-chiao*). It involved taking up with zeal the six arts of Confucian education: ritual, music, archery, calligraphy, horsemanship, and mathematics. All were defined very broadly. For example, "ritual" means conducting religious rites as well as mastering the proper ways of eating, walking, asking questions. The *Analects* provides many instances of seemingly trivial events associated with Confucius, but they had their use in just this context of providing the sage's life as a model for disciplined training.

Beyond this foundational training, all of the Neo-Confucian subschools called for the "rectification of the heart-mind" and prescribed new practices: discipline manifested by outward zeal in investigating the external world as well as the personal goal of knowing oneself. The aim is now to become a perfected person, a *sheng-ren*, who achieves fully one's complete human nature. A common practice to realize this is called "quiet sitting," one that its proponents were adamant on distinguishing from forms of Buddhist or Daoist meditation. This Neo-Confucian meditation was not based upon stopping discursive thought but upon calming the mind from the flow of events, perceiving the goodness of the in-dwelling primal human nature, and becoming aware of selfish desires.

Daoism Like the Buddhists (as covered in Chapter 6), Daoists sought a more individualistic "ultimate transformation" through practices that originated in antiquity. For philosophers such as Chuang Tzu, only through the practice of detaching from the mind (*wai-wu*) and ceasing to distinguish separated things could one find union with the Dao. In this text, one also finds cryptic references to a "heart-fast" (*hsin-chai*) that starved the mind of all externalities, allowing one proficient in the practice to forget his senses, ideas, feelings, and wishes and so reach "a zero point" at which only the experience of the primordial and mysterious Dao remains. Having reached this stage, the practice of "free and easy wandering" in nature can be fully undertaken whereby the spiritual adept can "ascend the cloud vapors, ride the flying dragon, travel to the infinite." Facing death involves no travail and only blissful transformation.

The religious Daoists' two paths to immortality we have outlined in an earlier section: the pursuit of the outer elixir (*wai-tan*) via an alchemy of special substances for ingesting that overcomes death; and the practice of inner alchemy (*nei-tan*) that develops a subtle inner spiritual essence (correlating bodily organs and substances with physical elements) through meditation practices. One of these requires secret sexual union with a consort designed to divert the male's semen and the woman's "blood" back into their life force (qi), then inducing it upward to the reservoir within the head, activating yin and strengthening yang. If done as prescribed only on certain days of the year, after purifications, and with a sequence of initiated adepts, masters promise that the qi in the form of a refined fluid shall diffuse cloudlike throughout the body, and practitioners shall become like adolescents and then cease aging altogether.

Shintoism Until the modern era, Shinto priests of major shrines had to be males from aristocratic families, as they inherited their positions and learned the rituals from their fathers. Over the last 150 years, priests have had to pass a prescribed course of training at an institution such as Kokugakuin University founded for this purpose. The role of the *shinshokoku*, as the priests are usually called, involves mastery of the daily gestures of respect offered to the kami, the annual rituals of the shrine, calligraphy, and complex forms of ritual purification. Shinto has never developed any "inner" spiritual practices, but its exponents consider the artful rituals oriented to the deities throughout the seasons as a means to refined sensitivity and moral transformation.

EAST ASIAN RELIGIONS AND MODERNITY

The Disruptions of Imperial Domination

Post-Enlightenment colonialism, also called "imperialism," represents the modern first attempt to establish a global world order. Europeans forced Asian societies to change on their terms, abruptly imposing new ideas, technologies, and institutions that had undergone natural evolution in Europe. European imperialism caused chaos and crises that undermined most institutions in pre-modern East Asia, with "organized religions" especially subject to disruption and decline. Imperialism's impact in Asia can be likened to that of a strong earthquake, one that levels many structures, leaving only the strongest foundations upon which to rebuild.

Colonialism forced other unprecedented breaks with the past. Understanding the world's religions today requires an awareness of this legacy, for East Asian religions and cultures were decisively altered over the period as never before. The effect was overwhelmingly destructive, but the fusion of older traditions with modern changes at times rendered religious innovations that were compelling and original.

By the beginning of the nineteenth century, European civilization had ascended as the supreme force on the global stage. The various forces of the Renaissance had culminated powerfully to transform Europe, driven by innovations in the intellectual, political, economic, and military cultural spheres. The socio-political dynamism and expansion of wealth unseen in the world before accelerated further in the eighteenth century, by which time the major states (England, Netherlands, Portugal, Germany) vied, often militarily, to exert their newfound political-economic power around the globe. Internally, of course, Europe was diverse, transformed by its own class and ethnic conflicts, and facing newly arising problems; new ideologies competed with old to provide solutions to these crises. Some of these, too, were exported to Asia. On every level, social and cultural, as regions came in contact with modern Europe's imperialism, they became subject to the accelerating forces of change.

The emerging nations of Europe were above all self-assured as to their being superior in every aspect of life, be it morality or intellectual understanding. For many this included belief in the white race's superiority, and many, too, saw in the march of colonialism confirmation that Christianity would ultimately triumph on the world stage. Thus, some European leaders felt they were the vehicles of triumphant Christianity; their merchants were soon dedicated to making their fortunes through overseas trade, ready to make alliances with whomever they needed to pursue their often risky ventures, and to do so quite ruthlessly.

Colonialism, like revolution (to paraphrase Mao Zedong), was anything but a dinner party. It forcibly changed the economic systems of East Asia, trafficked in narcotics when the opium trade was profitable, challenged the people's fundamental understandings regarding humanity and cosmos through science and Christian missions, and undermined the long-held view of Asia's ruling classes that their civilizations were the world's greatest.

The crisis of colonial presence and imperial challenge led the national elites away from their own indigenous traditions and on a forced march directed toward understanding the Western world. From about 1850 across the region, the best minds and most talented individuals in East Asia chose to learn about the West first and about their own traditions little, with the result that the Enlightenment mentality, with its revolutionary terms of analysis, began to dominate the cultural heritage of the modern East Asian cultural elite. Among a large portion of the elite, Western-influenced agnosticism replaced identification with the indigenous spiritual traditions.

On the popular level as well, the era of colonialism has been perceived as a time of crisis. The common terms used to express the peoples' sense of inundation and powerlessness across East Asia were "humiliation" (*chi*) in Chinese, "bitterness" (*hahn*) in Korean, and "patient endurance" (*nin*) in Japanese. In sum, they give an overview of the modern era for East Asians as a time of trial, with each set of difficulties representative of the separate nations' slightly different reaction to their respective experiences of modernization.

In many respects, this pattern of Euro-American challenge begun several centuries back continues—as reality and perception—into the present for many East Asians in the conduct of nations, missionaries, and tourists and in today's corporation-dictated global culture based upon consumerism, individualism, and mass–media technology.

It would be wrong, however, to see the history of East Asia as solely dictated by European actors and external forces. There were important internal dynamics at work in Korea, China, and Japan, and the different processes already under way in each shaped their emphatically different destinies under colonialism.

Traumatic Transitions of the Modern Era

The Decline of Confucian Ideology and Exponents

The crisis and rapid changes brought by the onslaught of imperialism ultimately ended the rule and unchallenged influence of the Confucian elite in China, Korea, and Japan. The Confucian world view and social ideology were also subjected to scathing critiques by the native reformers of each nation, who took up the task of saving state sovereignty and attempting to match the wealth, knowledge, and power put on display by the Western imperialists. In addition, many young people abandoned the traditional curriculum to pursue "Western learning," honing their intellectual development by critiquing the disabilities imposed on society under the Confucian tradition. The fall of the Korean and Chinese empires, whose political and economic resources supported Confucianism in many domains, made it certain that this tradition would lose its central place in the region's early modernization.

Confucianism was blamed for every ill visible in the region. The failure to develop modern trade was blamed on the classical ranking of social classes by occupation, which in the Confucian view of the good society placed at the top scholar-officials who administered the bureaucracy and taught in schools;

below them were the farmers, followed by artisans, and finally were the merchants who were held in disrepute as "parasites" (to use Confucius' own term), taking advantage of others and motivated by greed, inclined to dishonesty.

The traditional Confucian educational system was also blamed for stifling the nation's technical development, as it valued generalists over specialists and rewarded rote memorization and imitation, not independent thinking. For the critics, the Confucian view of history as cyclical had made the elite prone to stagnation and uninclined to pursue innovation or progress.

The strongest terms of rejection were directed toward Confucian social norms and at their center, family relations. The classical formula for social harmony that East Asians had incorporated from the ancient period was framed in two triads: the three bonds (ruler>minister; father>son; husband>wife) and the three principles (hierarchy, age, gender). Reformers found these principles an obstacle to modernization in many respects: by placing loyalty to family first, individuals were unable to extend trust to others as needed in the more impersonal workings of a modern economy; filial deference to elders made individuals dependent on the collective family, thwarting the creative thrust toward individuality, and encouraging a "Confucian personality" that either (in the young) followed authority blindly or (in the elders) gave too much power to those who were merely of senior rank. All such relationships were seen as stifling innovation. On the national level, reformers saw the "three bonds" held supreme merely in the service of authoritarian political control. By the time of the "May 4th Movement," many of the brightest intellectuals in China directed their energies to criticizing the shortcomings of the Confucian family, typically accusing it of denying basic rights to the individual, exploiting women, and wasting the energy of the young. Both East Asian reformers and Western social scientists until the 1970s agreed, accusing Confucianism of being the key obstacle to the region's modernization. We have noted above that this critique has been questioned in recent years after the rapid emergence of the successful modern economies in the highly Confucian East Asian countries and in the Chinese subcommunities in Southeast Asia.

A reconsideration of the characteristics fostered by Confucian humanism— for example, the high emphasis on education, careful study of problems before taking action, the expectation of the state acting for the good of the whole, and the intellectual elite taking responsibility for the nation's well-being—reveals that these Confucian elements were also involved in the region's ultimately successful response to the challenges that have flowered in the postcolonial era. But what is certain is that the imperial system that supported the literati tradition was overthrown completely in China and Korea; by contrast, the emperor-led state of Japan endured by melding nationalism with "mutant colonialism." Whatever Confucianism means in the present day, a break with the past had irrevocably occurred. We must first turn to the exception of Japan in its distinctive fusion belief system: melding modernization with Confucianism in the form of nationalist Neo-Shintoism.

State and Civil Religion in Japan: Neo-Shintoism

By 1882, a decade and a half after the demise of the shogunate and the restoration of the Japanese monarchy in the person of the first Meiji emperor, the Shinto tradition was officially divided into shrine Shinto and sect Shinto. Most establishments were integrated into the former under state supervision. The emperor was regarded as a divinity on earth, whose presence was felt a blessing to the nation, a notion that was expressed at the national shrines in the capital and then in rituals regularly conducted in every local shrine as well, as Japanese daily turned to worship the emperor in Tokyo just as Muslims face Mecca. The reformed educational system also centered its curriculum in the sanctity of emperor, which all citizens were expected to honor by working for the good of the nation. As we'll see, this is one of the Confucian elements in Japan's modernization.

The new constitution was finally adopted in 1889. It did limit the freedom of expressing any opinions critical of Shinto doctrines and practices, especially the imperial ties to the indigenous deities; but it guaranteed religious freedom to followers of other religions as long as they did not undermine Shinto and were loyal to the nation. Those affected included the "new religion" sects that multiplied throughout the modern era, as well as Buddhism and the Christian denominations (that had been legalized again in 1873).

The Meiji state cult can be labeled Shintoist (or better, Neo-Shintoism), for it was associated with the religious tradition of ancient origins that reveres the indigenous deities of the Japanese islands. It is also fundamental to see, however, that the "civil religion" constructed around it by the Meiji oligarchy was thoroughly Confucian in character. It emphasized loyalty to the state, the norm of filial piety, self-sacrifice, dedication; it imagined the necessary contributions of individuals to make the modernization of Japan a success; the emperor's and the nation's mission was stated in terms of Confucian vocabulary, especially in its following the Mandate of Heaven. The Meiji reforms were built on Confucian group orientation and communal participation, not on individual self interest. Thus, Japan's stunning success by the early twentieth century among all the East Asian nations has its foundations in its emperor-led religious development. Meiji Japan was the first to successfully harness reformed Confucian values to meet the challenges of modernizing and adopting the technologies pioneered in the West. Across the region, as in Japan, Buddhism was seen as either irrelevant to modernization or an obstacle to it.

Institutional Buddhism

As we have noted in Chapter 6, institutional Buddhism took root in Asia by way of a monastic system in which monasteries became landlords reliant upon lay believers to till the lands while depending as well on charitable donations from the faithful. At times of economic hardship or subsistence crisis, or when the state could not extend customary protections, Buddhism tended to decline. In general, the crises of the modern era across East Asia also deprived

Buddhism of economic support, of donations, and of individuals who in other eras might have joined a monastic order and contributed to its vitality. Now the most gifted were for the most part drawn into the need to learn about the West and lead their nations to modernize their industries, governments, and militaries.

In nineteenth-century China, there were few signs of innovation and few Buddhists who rose to contribute to the national struggles. In Japan's long Tokugawa era (1600–1868), on the other hand, the shoguns had supported Buddhism strongly, including the promotion of Buddhist pilgrimage as a means of having Japanese acquire a sense of national integration. But the Meiji reformers felt it essential to reverse course both to weaken former foes and because they believed that Buddhist influences were inimical to Japan's revitalization.

Zealous attempts in the first Meiji years to prohibit Buddhism outright were abandoned, but the Buddhist tradition sustained considerable damage: from 1871 to 1876, the number of temples throughout Japan was reduced from an estimated 465,000 to 71,000, with the number of monks declining from 75,000 to 19,000. In 1872, the government decreed that Buddhist monks were free to marry and follow nonvegetarian diets, a move that undermined discipline and popular regard for them. The Buddhists successfully rallied support against further acts directed against them, but the Shinto-based nationalism and the state-encouraged challenges to institutional Buddhism forced followers to shift their emphases and rethink their doctrines in light of the changes under way in their society.

The Buddhist establishment in the Meiji period strove mightily to prove its patriotism and relevance, as a host of writers and lay organizations arose to explain why charges of disloyalty and obsolescence were unfounded and to implement social and national programs. By the century's end, organized Japanese Buddhists, too, fanned the rising flame of anti-Western feelings, supported the successive war efforts (in public statements and with funds), and translated into positive doctrinal terms the rationale of imperial expansion.

Compared with elsewhere in Asia, movements led by Japanese householders to reinterpret Buddhism in terms of modern philosophy were sporadic and weak. Instead, religious reformers were more likely to found their own sects, drawing upon doctrines as they liked, without trying to work through the Buddhist establishment.

In Korea, Confucianism was strongly supported in the nineteenth century and Buddhism was increasingly marginalized, as the government tried to limit the economic power of monastic estates by consolidating schools and taking back lands. State decrees actually went so far as to prohibit Buddhist monks from even setting foot in the major cities! Early Western accounts of Korean Buddhism describe monastic buildings falling down and the monks as ignorant and undisciplined.

After Japan annexed Korea in 1910, attempts were even made to merge the Soto Zen school with the Korean Son school, but these did not succeed. Often heavy-handed attempts by the Japanese colonial officials to restore ancient

Buddhist buildings and aid monastic schools served only to disaffect many Koreans from their monks who accepted such gifts from the hated occupiers.

The same remarks about monastic Buddhism in the modern era apply to Daoist monasticism in China as well. The institutions carried on, but they brought little to the discussion about creating the new China in the iconoclastic intellectual climate of the early twentieth century. Daoism, too, was attacked from the standpoints of science and democracy. (One reformer, Liang Qichao, described the religion as "a great humiliation whose activities have not benefited the nation at all."[10]) Institutional Daoism is far from discredited, however, since in the modern era links remain with many village rituals, major temples have been preserved despite all the turmoil of the twentieth century, and the core ideas of Daoism are very much alive.

Christian Missions in China, Japan, Korea

The Jesuits were the first Christians to proselytize in Ming China, although their strategy was not to address the masses, but to convert the elite. Unlike their co–religionists in Japan who were expelled after an era of toleration, they did succeed at winning residence not so much for their religious teachings as for their cogent introduction into China of European sciences, particularly astronomy and military technology. The failure of early Catholic missionaries can be attributed to their inability to explain their theology in terms of traditional Chinese language or logic (for example, they never found an agreed-on Chinese term for translating "God") and to the very bitter controversies that broke out between the different Christian groups, particularly on the issue of whether to tolerate Confucian morality or ancestor veneration. An imperial edict proscribed Christianity in 1724, but the censure was not as extreme or as thoroughly enforced as in Japan.

With the Protestant presence growing in significant numbers after 1800 through Canton, there followed missionary efforts to reach the masses, and a Chinese translation of the complete Bible first appeared in 1815. As elsewhere, the missionaries were hardly successful at proselytizing but made much more impact in transmitting Western secular subjects, particularly modern medicine, in introducing the use of the printing press, and in setting up modern schools. By 1877, there were 347 missionary schools and an estimated 400,000 Chinese converts.

Missionary writings of the late imperial era, especially those of Protestants working in the treaty ports and therefore associating with people on the margins of society, contributed to the rather negative construction of the Chinese among many in the West. These unfavorable characterizations, in turn, reinforced the racist underpinnings of colonialism by suggesting Asia's need for Western civilization.

In addition to the earlier issues of Chinese receptivity, Christianity was associated with the bullying of colonialists and the Taiping Rebellion. Resentments over these situations eventually led to virulent mass-media propaganda such as a depiction of Jesus as a pig (based upon the Chinese phonetic name's homo-nym). Christianity did appeal to those finding in it a religious framework for protest against the weight of traditionalism, and conversion offered a means of success for those needing charity or wishing to do business with Westerners. But despite these potential advantages for proselytizers, and despite massive in-vestments in time and money, Christianity made only modest gains in China.

Outlawed in Japan back in 1606, its missionaries expelled in 1616, and its followers persecuted, Christianity survived underground in Japan among re-markably faithful converts. Once granted religious freedom in 1863, Japanese Christians built churches and asserted their faith in the public domain. Soon, however, the same effort to prove relevance and nationalistic credentials that co-opted the Buddhists also infected the newly recognized Japanese Christians. They joined the nationalistic chorus supporting the war efforts launched by the state, proclaimed its role as strengthening Japan by supporting ethics in na-tional life, resisting radicalism, and (later) combating communism.

Korea remained closed to Christian missionaries until the mid-nineteenth century, when representatives primarily from American Methodist and Pres-byterian denominations settled and attracted converts amidst building schools and hospitals. Korean Christians, like those in Japan, emphasized their inde-pendence from Western churches.

The Appearance of New Religious Movements and Religions

The phenomenon of "new religions" emerging across Asia from the imperial era until the present underscores this period as one of social dislocation, dis-satisfaction, and cross-traditional synthesis. Their propagation also signals the extent to which the "established religions" of the region (Confucianism, Daoism, Buddhism) had lost their allure for some who were increasingly drawn to ideas from the West.

For the majority of peasants and artisans, the crises that resulted from for-eign domination in many places had undermined subsistence economies with disastrous effects on society's misery. Peasants continued to have faith in their local deities, shamans, and ancestors, and indeed turned to them in times of trouble. Yet given the turmoil of the modern era, it is not hard to imagine that countless ritual prayers went unanswered. For all these reasons, the modern era in East Asia is marked by the unprecedented flowering of "new religious movements," some turning into armed uprisings such as the Taiping Rebellion that did not rely on the old practices or old deities. They most often arose from the lower classes through sects created entirely independent from the tra-ditional institutions of Daoism, Buddhism, and (premodern) Shinto.

Taiping Rebellion in China (1850–1864)

Beyond the challenges provoked by the foreigners in their midst, a rebellion led by a Chinese convert to Christianity nearly ended Manchu rule a half cen-tury before the actual fall of the dynasty that succeeded the Ming.

After an illness during which he experienced several weeks of delirium, Hong Xiuquan (1814–1864), with the help of an American Southern Baptist missionary, interpreted his fevered visions as Christian revelations. Despite limited knowledge of the Bible, Hong proceeded to found his own form of Sinicized Christianity, convinced that he had seen God, who had charged him with saving humanity and destroying demons, and had met Jesus, who was revealed to be Hong's "older brother." A charismatic preacher whose apocalyptic predictions captured the imagination of many, Hong organized his followers into a militant sect. To them he offered a prophetic, utopian vision of a future "Heavenly Kingdom of Great Peace" (hence the name *Taiping Tianguo*) based upon egalitarianism, shared property, and gender equality. One of his Old Testament-inspired proclamations was that all idols be destroyed, be they Buddhist, Daoist, or even Confucian ancestor tablets. He also insisted on those joining his group adopting a puritanical moral code that entailed abstention from alcohol, tobacco, and opium.

Hong vilified the ruling Manchu elite as demons that stood in the way of the sect's millenarian transformation. The state, in turn, persecuted the group, stepping up its efforts after 1850, by which time the Taipings had over ten thousand members. Thus provoked, Hong gathered an army whose bloody campaigns likely comprised the most destructive civil war in world history. Most of China was affected, and an estimated twenty million people perished.

China had already been humiliated and weakened by the European powers, which offered many reasons for discontent in addition to those initially proposed by Hong, and the forces of rebellion mushroomed. The Taiping army captured Nanjing in 1853, and occupied it for ten years.

Ultimately, however, the movement fell owing to internal divisions, refusal to cooperate with potential allies, the leadership's ruthless brutality and paranoia in governing the Taiping community, and an initial hostility to the Confucian elements deeply embedded in China's population. Nanjing was retaken in 1864, all Taiping members not killed in battle were executed, and the first Chinese-Christian "new religion" was eradicated.

Another effort to establish a group to foster religious revival and resist outside influences on a region, in this case a group based upon indigenous teachings, met with greater enduring success. We now turn to Korea and the Ch'ondogyo.

"Religion of the Heavenly Way": Ch'ondogyo in Korea

The Ch'ondogyo, which merges elements of Confucianism and Daoism, was founded by Ch'oe Suun (1824–1864) in 1860. Its original name, Tonghak ("Eastern Learning"), signals its origins as an indigenous response to the challenge of newly imported Christianity (called "Western Learning" in Korean). The Ch'ondogyo movement reaffirms the belief that a reformed indigenous religion, not religions from elsewhere, is most suitable for the Korean masses. According to the sect's scriptures, Suun received a direct revelation of a new "Heavenly Way" (*Ch'ondo*) from the Heavenly Lord, who is conceived of as the totality of life or as the universe, immanent in each person and all creation. Suun attracted a large following but was martyred by the government. Under his successors, the Ch'ondogyo continued to grow, becoming one of the major religions of the Korean peninsula. Like Korean Christians, Ch'ondogyo members were especially active in resisting Japanese rule. Although banned in North Korea since 1949, the movement is very popular in the south. There is an institutional center in Seoul and by 2000 its membership, governed by an elected body, numbered over three million.

The collected writings of the first three leaders became the sect's chief scriptures. Ch'ondogyo's theology is simply expressed in two phrases, "Humans bear divinity" and "Man is divine." The ethics of the sect emphasize respecting this universal divinity in others, as in the injunction, "Treat others as divine," a statement that seems tame today but was revolutionarily democratic in the status-conscious Korea of the nineteenth century. The group's goal is likewise this-worldly, seeking a heavenlike earthly existence marked by widespread social cooperation.

The Five Practices are the major rituals, indicating the effort that individuals actualize Ch'ondogyo communal ideals: (1) Incantation, chanted every evening and on special occasions, is designed to realize the mystical vision of the person as divine. It is simply: "Ultimate Energy being here and now, I yearn for its great descent." (2) Pure water, placed in a bowl centered on a table, is a subject of daily meditation, water symbolizing spiritual purity. (3) Service Day means attending a Sunday worship service. (4) Sincerity Rice refers to the member putting aside a bit of rice daily to donate as a tithe to the church. (5) Prayer, or "heart address," should be repeated silently at meals, bedtime, and upon rising.

The Older "New Religions" Arising in Pre-Meiji Japan

We have noted that by the end of the Tokugawa era, the feudal order in Japan had begun to break down and for some, the vitality of Buddhism and traditional Confucianism had waned. Spirit mediums and communal dances involving group possession rose in popularity; popular preachers also crossed the country drawing large audiences to hear their message of returning to simple Confucian morality. Several dozen new sects formed in this period, and among them three endured to become denominations among the postmodern "new religions" of the late twentieth century.

The arising of new ways of being religious in Japan began in each of these instances with a charismatic individual who experienced extraordinary revelations after a serious illness; having shared their discoveries with others, these leaders soon began building communities for whom the teachings helped individual followers reorder their own spiritual practice. Almost every "new religion" thus offered a singular path to salvation out of the maze of choices that had developed along the way of Japanese religious history: Buddhism, Neo-Confucianism, elements of Daoism, Shinto. All harmonized with the state's Neo-Shintoism, eventually becoming regarded as "Shinto sects."

Kurozumikyo Kurozumikyo ("Kurozumi's Religion") was founded by Kurozumi Munetada, a charismatic teacher who in 1814 was possessed by the central Shinto deity Amaterasu, the sun goddess, whom he identified as the single Lord of the universe. Although Kurozumi did not register his eponymous group until 1842, soon after his initial experience he began preaching and attracting disciples who spread the faith across Japan.

The doctrines include the belief that all humans are emanations of the kami and that they may become kami, or become one with them, securing eternal life, by adopted spiritual practices. Healthy living and "living cheerfully" are essential to reach this goal. The potential for all to realize the divine state made the Kurozumikyo emphasize the equality of all people, a radical idea when class completely determined individual destiny in pre-Meiji Japanese society. The group was among the first to articulate the common "new religion" theme that individuals have spiritual independence and should shape their own religious path. Kurozumikyo grew dramatically after winning Meiji recognition. Its leaders had a central shrine established in Okayama City, and the group numbered perhaps 700,000 by 1880; its membership dropped to about 200,000 at the end of the twentieth century.

Tenrikyo Tenrikyo ("Religion of Heavenly Wisdom") began with the trance-communicated messages experienced by its founder Nakayama Miki (1798–1887) from a spirit she called "God the Parent" (Oyagami). Regarded as the one true god of the universe, Oyagami commanded Nakayama to be his medium, to reject her role as wife and mother, and to further his mission through healing and preaching. Tenrikyo claimed that its new and universal doctrine of harmonious living would usher in a new world order, a divine kingdom in which humanity will enjoy blissful at-onement with God the Parent. Although in the sect's view the universe's "one, true kami" had created humanity to see them find harmonious life, and then entered pantheistically into creation in the form of ten other kami, he is thought to have made his new revelation to Nakayama to rectify growing human selfishness that has undermined the original divine intent.

The sect believes that this revelation also can be discerned in the place called the *jiba*, where (in the sect's view) humanity originated in Japan. Besides her preaching (whose collected sermons constitute the scripture of the sect), Nakayama taught an ecstatic salvation dance, the *kagura zutome*. While defying government prohibition against it at the jiba in 1887, she died there. Doctrine holds that she remains in a disembodied spiritual state, assisting followers who visit the site on pilgrimage.

The Tenrikyo dance ritual, an initiation ("receiving the holy grant"), and performance of daily social service for others are essential for salvation in a belief system that accepts reincarnation until the heart is purified of the "eight dusts" (grudges, covetousness, hatred, selfish love, enmity, fury, greed, arrogance). Tenrikyo became a recognized Shinto sect in 1888 and rapidly spread throughout Japan. Its members carried missions to the United States in 1896, Taiwan in 1897, Korea in 1898, and China in 1901. As with the other early Shinto-related sects, after the Second World War the group made efforts to "purify" Tenrikyo of its Shinto and nationalist accretions. By 1990, there were three million members, who had established over sixteen thousand centers in Japan, with an additional twenty thousand missions worldwide in twenty countries.

Konkokyo   The Konkokyo will be discussed later in the chapter.

Nichiren-related Sects of the Meiji Era

As the Meiji reforms opened and transformed Japanese society, and calls to modernize, change, and innovate to create a new Japan multiplied, this spirit of renewal found religious expression as well. In some cases, the sects arising passed beyond what the state found tolerable and thus followers suffered persecution and often pressures to modify their teachings. Other groups became vehicles of resistance to the state's militarism and nationalism. Numerous laity-led groups arose because the Buddhist "establishment" gave few openings for those wishing to reinterpret the doctrines or apply them in line with modern scientific discoveries from the West.

Many modern groups formed in association with Nichiren Buddhism, a Kamakura-era school created by a charismatic teacher in the thirteenth century, as discussed earlier. Directly stemming from this school (and so not really a "new religion" at all) is the largest new religion of Japan today, the lay organization called Soka Gakkai ("Value Creation Society"). It was established in 1937 by the Nichiren disciple and educator Makiguchi Tsunesaburo (1877–1944). But this newly created group was soon persecuted by the fascist government and Makiguchi was jailed, where he died. Reconstructed in the postwar era under the dynamic direction of Toda Josei (1900–1958) and Ikeda Daisaku (1928–), the Soka Gakkai aims to foster a "Third Civilization" based upon Nichiren's teachings, one in which the true faith would spread throughout the world. Its members believe that chanting the name of the great Buddhist text, the *Lotus Sutra*—rendered in Japanese honorifics as *Nam-Myoho-renge-kyo*—is "medicine for the soul" and a means for changing the world. The Soka Gakkai also considers its mission to work for world peace and human welfare, and after 1960 it established a political party (the Komeito) to implement specific programs to achieve this goal in Japan. It has also sent missionaries to every major country of the world. By 1990, the Soka Gakkai registered ten million Japanese members and claimed one million international adherents.

Also originated by and for Nichiren laity, Reiyukai Kyodan ("Spiritual Friends Association") was intended to support the school's regular practices and to exert beneficial influences upon Japanese society. Founded in 1925 by Kubo Kakutaro (1890–1944) and Kotani Kimi (1901–1971), the group stressed the need for ancestor worship by the laity, and attributed the upheavals of the era to ancestral distress over the ineffectiveness of the contemporary Buddhist clergy. Only when ancestors find peace and salvation through lay rituals utilizing the *Lotus Sutra* can the living really find spiritual grace. The Reiyukai also emphasizes conservative social values and expects its members to follow the

Confucian "three bonds" rigorously. Members are exhorted to develop their marriages as vessels of salvation and to live together in three-generation families. The Reiyukai are also strong supporters of imperial veneration and other conservative causes in Japanese society. One of the most active proselytizing new religions, the Reiyukai by 2000 had three million members and centers abroad in fourteen countries.

EAST ASIAN RELIGIONS AND POSTMODERN TRENDS IN A POSTCOLONIAL WORLD

Religious believers have pushed back at every barrier that the states of East Asia erected in the modern era. In Korea and Japan, this return to religious freedom opened the way for many reformers, both of ancient traditions as well as charismatic innovators founding "new religions." The coming of the Marxist state to mainland China in 1949 and the imposition of totalitarian rule by the officially atheistic Communist party brought the sustained repression of religious expression, the destruction of religious institutions, and concerted governmental attempts—unprecedented in world history—to exterminate from the enculturation of the young any vestige of traditional religious teaching or spiritual training. In China, this lasted for almost three generations.

But as we pointed out in Chapter 1, such repression and persecution have not led to the end of religion in China. Far from it. State-sponsored substitution of modernist Marxist ideologies, utopian mythology, and the orchestration of a personality cult centered on Mao Zedong represented attempts to substitute a communist Chinese civil religion for Confucianism, Daoism, and Buddhism. The effort failed, though it did succeed in separating the Chinese people from many of their cultural connections with the past. Now many are attempting to recover from the past what still means the most. Since the reform era ushered in by Deng Xiaoping (1910–1997) after the death of Mao in 1976, the restoration of religion in China, supervised loosely by the state, has been very gradual. A popular upsurge of practice at Daoist temples, family graves, Buddhist monasteries, Christian churches, and mosques is evident, however. Despite reverses, over the last decades, as the door has been cracked open, countless Chinese have rushed through to make pilgrimages, reopen shrines, and resume the ritual practices of their ancestors. We discuss here both the surviving traditions and new religions that have multiplied the pluralism characteristic of the postcolonial era.

Continuities and Transformations

The Reality of Gods and Spirits in China
Chinese myths dating back to the Chou era (700 BCE) mention deities of mountains, rivers, rain, and the earth that have remained part of the diffuse Chinese

religion. Interestingly, most deities appearing later in East Asia have human origins, as heroic ancestral spirits have become gods who have won renown beyond their own kin. We have noted this for the god of war (Guan Yu, in life the former Han general), for statesmen, for Confucius, and even in recent years (as we will see shortly), recently dead Communists such as Mao Zedong! Some spirits similarly have been adopted as gods by social groups as protectors of their localities, and by artisan guilds for their patron deities. The remaining important deities have been Buddhist in origin, the most prominent being Guanyin, Shakyamuni (the historical, human Buddha), and A-mi-to-fo (Amitabha, Jap.: Amida), the Buddha who resides in the western paradise.

In regional and local contexts, the East Asian pantheon has always been in flux as new heroes arise and the deities are obliged to continuously show their power (*ling*), perhaps through healing, or in the dramatic possessions of mediums, to prove their being worth the investment of further offerings. Those to whom such manifestations are attributed win devotees, patrons, new temples. Until the late modern era, the state would build shrines to recognize the most powerful new deities to ensure the performance of special propitiatory rituals aimed at inducing the gods to contribute to the stability of the realm. Alternatively, other deities have lost favor and efficacy, and so have faded from popularity. Thus, the East Asian understanding of and experience with divinities has not been based upon faith, but upon dramatic experiential encounters and proven long-term efficacy.

Who are the most common deities found on the typical altars in a Chinese community? One of the most ubiquitous icons seen in Chinese homes and temples are the *Triple Gods: Longevity* in the form of a vigorous old man, *Wealth* embodied by a Confucian official, and *Blessings* symbolized by the male god holding male progeny.

Another prominent deity, T'ien Shang Sheng-mu ("Holy Mother in Heaven"), is popularly known as Matsu ("Grandmother"). Her origins can be traced to a girl born in the ninth century in coastal Fukien, who saved her father and brothers at sea by exercising magical powers acquired via Daoist practice. She died young, and others began to experience apparitions and miracles. By the mid-12th century, the state had recognized her, and her cult and temples have spread along the southeastern coast of China, where Matsu remains popular still.

In every traditional Chinese and Korean home (but not in Japan) will be another deity, Zao Chun, the "Kitchen God." From the kitchen hearth, he records the household goings on and makes a yearly report to the Jade Emperor of Heaven right before New Year's Day. Zao Chun is also said to determine the length of every person's life living in the household. This popular notion led to more systematic understanding of the pantheon (reflecting the post-Song development of urban centers and government bureaucracy across the region), by which the Kitchen gods and Earth gods of each locality reported to the nearby City gods, who in turn informed the Jade Emperor and served as his heavenly officials. This notion of divine hierarchical officialdom was especially important in shaping the popular understanding of what happens at the death of an individual: the Earth God of the locality reports to the City God, who then escorts the soul to the underworld for judgment by ten judges who determine punishments and karmic destiny. It is to these divine "magistrates" that prayers are addressed and bribes are sent (via "hell money" burnt for delivery there) by the family to secure quick release for any punishments.

Ritual Practices

In many respects, what gives East Asia its unity as a religious and cultural area is less a common set of beliefs and more the shared ritualism within its temples and at family graves. The ideas underlying these core rituals are very straightforward, an extension of the human custom of feasting an honored guest, in these cases an ancestral spirit or a deity. Foods offered as "sacrifices" at temples are those humans consume, including alcoholic drinks, with the largest offerings (by prominent families or the imperial state) requiring the ritual slaughter of oxen, sheep, pigs, deer, or geese. These foods are not wasted: once the deities are thought to have consumed their essence, the humans eat up the material leavings. Other items presented in East Asian ritual include candles, flowers, oil lamps, and incense that are given to please the spirit(s), which is assumed to possess the human senses. In keeping with the idea that the deities are senior but essentially human is the practice of full prostration (kowtowing) before icons or tablets, a practice that junior kin also do before their living elders at festival times.

For most occasions in daily life, priests (be they Daoist, Buddhist, or shamans) are not needed, for senior householders and state officials, even at the highest level, have ritual tasks to perform according to their status. Such tasks are particularly well defined at the time of death. In particular, Confucian filial piety is shown at a parent's death through careful carrying out of the appropriate ritual performances. The reward is the spirit's blessings and the promise of an afterlife reunion with kin after the children's own demise. What must one do to meet one's obligation and live according to these beliefs?

Death is indeed a crisis and the funeral is a time to show one's loyalty and love to the departed. In East Asia, doing so traditionally takes a long period of time. Further, participation in the funeral is one of the key events binding families and transmitting family values, as all the relatives of the deceased set aside ornaments, wear sackcloth, and wail ritually during specific times until actual burial. Burial will be after two days in the more common households, longer in more well-to-do families, depending upon whether they also call Buddhist or (less commonly) Daoist priests, who have their own elaborate rituals involving text recitations and merit transfers to aid the deceased. (The full-blown Buddhist ritual sequence takes 7 weeks to complete.) The funeral itself involves the largest and most ostentatious procession that can be afforded, with musicians and large paper replicas of items the deceased will need carried along and burned for the initial "trial" by the judges in the afterlife.

Traditionally, children were thought to owe their parents three years of mourning, the three years being equal to the period when the children were infants and toddlers carried around by their parents. (This is a good example of the dual application of the Confucian notion of reciprocity and the Daoist norm of balance.) The mourning involved suspendion of all work, celebration, and the observance of dietary restrictions. Under imperial law, a three-year break from normal life was required to mourn one's parents. Even high ministers charged with important state tasks had to demonstrate their conformity to *li* (ritual propriety) and withdraw from this work. Today, of course, full mourning on this scale is regarded as impractical.

The death rituals end in establishing the soul in a place for future worship, one in common with those who long ago expired. Of essential importance is the yang soul: it is thought to be carried to the family's home with use of a sword-shaped paper brought from the graveside. It is then installed on the family altar in a permanent tablet inscribed with the person's name. Placed near other senior kin and the various images of the deities, this spirit receives all the offerings made to the gods. Any important event in the family is announced to the tablets as if the ancestors resided there. Families from influential clans also had a similar tablet installed in the clan temples.

Although not all families could afford family grave sites, all wished to have them, since with such a burial the family can most directly ensure the happiness of the yin souls. (So important was proper burial that traditionally once a person reached the age of 50, acquiring the proper coffin and grave clothes became a comforting task in preparation for the best possible burial.) For those possessing graveyards, on several occasions each year the families go to clean the premises, make sacrifices and eat among the tablets, and share in the communal meals and drinking. The cemeteries in East Asia are not dreaded locales, but places one can go to feel close to one's deceased parents and grandparents, as well as to conform to the basic Confucian requirement of caring for them after death.

The Reality of Spirit Possession

Given the widespread belief in deities inhabiting this earth and in the souls' afterlife destiny, it should not be surprising that East Asian religion everywhere has from its earliest history recognized the utility of spirit mediums who can communicate with the dead. Divination has provided answers to such problems as where grandmother's spirit might be residing, whether the ghost of a dead child was causing family troubles, or what might be done to please the god who could help end a drought. Unhappy spirits (*kuei*) were also thought to cause distress to the living, so here, too, the shaman had an important role in healing the sick.

Typically, a client approaches a healer to aid a person whose illness is suspected as related to ghost possession; the medium goes into trance in the sick one's presence and speaks or acts (sometimes writing on a slate or sand-covered board) after having made contact with the spirit(s) involved. (Most mediums acquire a tutelary deity via initiation who assists him or her in this working with other supernaturals.) The medium's communications are usually interpreted by an assistant, who acts as the intermediary for the family and community members present. For example, contemporary mediums in Taiwan, called *dangki*, continue the ancient Chinese tradition that shares much in common with Korean shamanism. (The Meiji state diminished the shamans' presence in Japan radically, although the possession experience has resurfaced in many "new religions," as we have seen.) Versed in the commonly "diffused teachings" of Daoism, Confucianism, and Buddhism, the dangkis become possessed and rapidly write divinely inspired characters in red ink on yellow papers, objects that become amulets for their patients either as written or, after being burned, when their ashes are mixed with water and drunk as medicine. The role of these spirit mediums has, if anything, grown with the modernization and rising prosperity of Taiwan, as has been the case in modern Korea as well.

The Religious Institutions: Monasteries, Temples, Shrines

The religious institutions that sustain the three traditions in East Asia vary widely. For their surrounding householder communities, Buddhist monasteries have temples with images of compassionate bodhisattvas and ritualists specializing in healing and death rituals. When literati Confucianism was the state religion and a career in the civil service for men was based on passing an examination measuring mastery of the classics, academies to teach the content and character-building imagined by this tradition dotted the country until the fall of imperial China, and were especially strong in urban areas.

Just as most deities were formerly human heroes and all are conceived of as if human in many respects, the temple is considered as simply a divine home. Temples can be modest small boxes where humble images or prints are kept by the roadside, or they can be massive palaces with a series of halls and side buildings, housing gilded images flanked by hosts of attending demigods. The greatest temples contain all the major deities of the pantheon, giving devotees "one-stop" access to the supernatural world.

Some deities, such as the Earth God found in most settlements, can be worshiped in a simple manner outdoors on a raised mound of decorated earth. Smaller temples are merely boxes made of wood or cement, often with a simple tablet with the name of the deity inscribed. Traditional communities are marked by a profusion of such shrines and larger temples, making it hard to understand the assertion that "Chinese have no religion!"

The larger temples share certain characteristics. The entrance always opens to the south, an auspicious direction, and is guarded by protectors in fierce poses that in larger establishments are lodged in a gatehouse through which all must pass. The building of multistory pagoda temples was in many cases related to geomancy calculations, introducing an artificial "mountain" to channel positive energy to the site. In larger compounds, the main deity will be in the last hall on the same axis as the entrance, with other halls containing lesser deities arrayed on the same line separated by courtyards and circumscribed by a wall. Before each icon there is an altar for receiving offerings, with ample provision for the most common presentation, the incense sticks that go into large braziers. Kneeling cushions are supplied and, usually to the side, some means of divination for posing questions to the deity: perhaps via two half-moon wooden blocks (that are thrown to derive a "yes" or "no" answer based on their resting alignment).

The aesthetic in contemporary Chinese temples can be described as highly baroque. The temples are full of bright colors, from roof beams to columns to the decorated vestments adorning the deities. Equipped and arrayed similarly, but in sharp decorative contrast, are the Japanese Shinto shrines, *jinja*. They are notable for their natural wood, plain roof tiles, and restrained aesthetic. Given the high emphasis upon purification in Shintoism, water sources for rinsing the face and mouth are always present at the entrance from which devotees approach the main shrine. Jinja are also marked by gateways called *toriis*. These distinctive features of Japan's indigenous religion delineate a transition from the ordinary world into a sacred space kept pure to please the local gods.

The larger Daoist temples are usually served by a resident priesthood that lives on the premises, and by spirit mediums who may simply use the premises to meet clients seeking their services. The latter, called *fa-shih*, serve in temples and specialize in exorcisms and in helping clients make simple offerings. The former, called *tao-shih*, also assist in such rites, but have also mastered complex Daoist liturgies and wear formal attire.

Chinese and Korean localities also support what can be referred to as "community temples" built through collective effort to enshrine a prominent deity along with the key members of the local pantheon. The community temple's space is also available for a school, playground, threshing floor after harvest, or community meetings; these institutions are important for their uniting of social groups beyond the circle of kin.

Prosperous clans have often found it convenient to erect lineage temples to consolidate their collective veneration of their kin, including sacrifices. In the clan temples, all the family branches array their kin lines in order of seniority, with the central place reserved for the "High Ancestor." The family genealogical records are also stored in the clan temple, as well as "instruction memorials" written by past notables in the family. These are powerful settings in which the younger generations encounter their forebears as "present" in their tablets and be inspired by their legacy. Records of distinguished service, scholarship, or heroism are also announced in the clan temple, with "trophies" displayed that reflect on the glory of the group and—adopting the believer's supernatural reference point—that share with the residing spirits of the clan's forebears the pleasures of their descendants' successes. The leaders of the clan also use the temple as a gathering place for meetings on business regarding the group. Here, too, the clan temple focuses awareness on the notion that the ancestors witness their living descendants and can either support or punish them.

Wen Miao: *Confucius Temples*

At various times since the Han, the state has supported the building of temples dedicated to Confucius in every major town and city, using the distinctive term *wen miao* ("Temple of Culture") to suggest their being different from deity shrines. For the literati, Master K'ung was the very human inspiration for their careers, the official guild deity of literati, just as other artisans have their own mythical ancestor whom they venerate for having established their trade or art. But even literati who view Confucius as their human exemplar of li still had the obligation to sacrifice to the deceased Master's ancestral spirit, a day that became a state holiday over a millennium ago. For the masses, however, Confucius is a deity known for miracles and blessings.

The architecture of the wen-miao was similar to that of other Chinese temples, with the main hall containing the central altar spirit tablets of the sage and his four attendants, the favored disciples Yen Hui, Tzu Ssu, Master Tseng, and Mencius. (Icons of the sage were used before 1530, but the Ming ordered them removed and allowed only inscribed tablets, except for the main Confucius temple in Qufu.) Master K'ung's tablets typically identify him as "Most Holy Former Master, the Philosopher K'ung." Side halls of major temples contain the tablets of twelve other disciples, the last being Zhu Xi, the Neo-Confucian master. Other literati recognized by the state, numbering over thirty-five, also had their tablets installed. These memorial halls were the scene of the twice-yearly sacrifices done in grand style.

The Religious Festivals of East Asia

In our collective discussion of the religious practices of China, Korea, and Japan, the treatment of festivals is constrained by each nation's having a number of solely national holidays in addition to those they have in common that originated in China.

By now, all East Asian nations have adopted Western calendar days and selected celebrations: China from its connections with international communism, Korea and Japan through Christian influences. Thus, the ancient Chinese system of twelve-year cycles, lunar days, and solar seasons, has been intermixed with the Western calendar as well. Since Japan shifted many of its holidays away from the Chinese calendar and to fixed "Western" days, the Meiji reformers expressed their intention to have Japan "leave Asia" in direct fashion; from New Year's Day to Ching Ming (see below), Japan's dates for festivals shared with the East Asian region are most often not on the same calendar day.

National holidays may be connected to a variety of origins: mythic events or deities indigenous to the particular nation; national days accentuating

ALL SOULS FESTIVAL

The ritual days observed in China and Korea fall on the fifteenth day of the seventh lunar month and in Japan from July 13 through 15. The former and Japan have come to emphasize different themes as central to the festival. In China, this festival is specifically for welcoming hungry ghosts and aiding them, as they are assumed to be "stuck" in this condition because their families have not looked after them. All sorts of offerings given on other festivals to one's own ancestors are now given freely to the ghosts to help them with the requisites and the infusion of merit needed to move on to another rebirth. Buddhist monks conduct elaborate liturgies and communities set bonfires, some on small boats floated down the rivers, to consign the offerings to their smoke-carried essence for transfer to the suffering ghosts. The textual story read is of the enlightened monk named Maudgalyayana who rescued his own mother from this state by following the Buddha's instruction to make offerings on this day to seven generations of ancestors, a tradition merging filial piety with Buddhist merit transfer.

Confucian values; or relatively recent phenomena that the nation's leaders still wish to mark in the country's "civil religion." For example, Japan celebrates the cherry blossom festival April 1 through 8 to thank the kami of the forests for the renewal of life seen in the blossoming of the trees. Modern states declare as national holidays (to cite several examples) the day(s) marking the mythological founding of the Japanese nation as "National Foundation Day" on February 5 through 7 and China's Revolution on October 1; Japan reserves September 15 as "Respect for the Aged Day" and consecrates "Heroes Festival" every December 14 to commemorate a group of forty-seven martyred samurai for their embodying sincerity and national loyalty. Japanese-Confucian values are inculcated in youth on Boy's Day (May 5), when samurai helmets are presented and carp flags flown (symbolizing bravery and longevity), and on Girl's Day (March 3), when imperial dolls are given for play and healing rituals.

Every major deity in every locality is thought to have a "birthday," either the day celebrated nationally or the day the more local deity's temple was first established. On these occasions that usually last two or three days each year, the priests and temple supporters arrange for extravagant ritual performances, local devotees come to make their most elaborate yearly offerings (and petitions), merchants and artisans set up their wares to create a temporary fair, and in the evenings theatrical performances are staged to entertain deity and devotees alike.

Most common festivals of East Asia have Chinese or Buddhist origins and can be mentioned only in passing. New Year's Day (by either calendar) is a time for gathering family and friends, settling debts, and seeking blessings and divine protection for the year ahead. In China and Korea (where the day changes yearly according to the lunar calendar), traditional rites before the day send off the Kitchen God (Zao Chun) to heaven and reinstall a new paper icon in the home, with other characters posted on home doorways to invite prosperity for the year ahead. The essentials of Confucian family life are marked in sacrifices offered to ancestors at their tablets and with the custom of junior family kow-towing to seniors, receiving gifts of money in special red envelopes given in re-turn. The day is called "Spring Festival" (although it falls usually near the mid-dle of winter!).

Ching-Ming ("Pure Brightness Festival") is the first of two dates over the year when families must visit the ancestral graves to maintain them, make sac-rifices, and feast together there with the departed spirits. In Japan, this festival has been fixed as the vernal equinox (March 21) and is called Higan ("Further Shore," with a second Higan on the autumnal equinox). On this day, families in the Chinese manner visit family graves, but with Buddhist priests also ex-pected to come to the home on a short visit in which they recite sacred scrip-tures, with the merit earned for this dedicated to the dead.

Japanese Buddhists mark the Buddha's Birthday on April 8, when people anoint images with flowers and scented water, just as the texts describe the local deities doing at the actual birth. Chinese and Korean Buddhists do the same on the eighth day of the fourth lunar month. Confucius' Birthday is cele-brated today only in Korea and on September 28 in Taiwan (as "Teacher's Day") with colorful rituals and elaborate sacrifices laid out before the Sage's temple tablets.

All Souls Festival (Chi.: *Chung Yuan*; Jap.: *O-bon*) occupies a month when the "gates of purgatory" are thought to be held open and families integrate practices from all three traditions to connect the living families with their de-parted kin.

The early fall Full Moon Festival (Chi.: *Chung Ch'iu*; Jap.: *Tsukimi*) is a time for women to worship the "harvest moon" with special sweet "moon cakes." The perception of the "Rabbit in the Moon" has both Buddhist and Daoist as-sociations: in the popular Buddhist scriptures, the future Buddha was born as a rabbit who rendered such extraordinary service to his fellow animals that the gods placed his image on the moon's surface; in the Daoist perception, a rab-bit can be seen on the moon who is pounding a pestle into a mortar that con-tains the herbs of immortality. Across East Asia, one should view the rising moon on this night, asking for blessings that in rural communities include a good rice harvest in the month ahead.

Religion in Contemporary East Asia: Case Studies

China

Just as we began the discussion of modern Hinduism with the comment that South Asia is a region of many subcultures and regional differences, so the same reminder needs to be made here, with one countervailing point on why China's breadth of variation is in certain respects much less now than in the past. The heavy hand of the Communist party–led government since 1949 through the era of the Cultural Revolution (1976) did succeed in disestablishing almost every public religious institution that anchored "the three faiths." It dispersed the religious specialists (monks, nuns, and priests) and destroyed much of the formal infrastructure of the organized religions of China, both Buddhist and Daoist buildings (monasteries and image shrines), as well as the nearly countless deity temples that before 1949 could be found in every urban or village locality. The party also pushed the devout underground, since any attempt to practice (be it prayer, meditation, even the reading of religious literature) was a serious offense, a sign of being "reactionary" or an "enemy of the revolution," a potentially capital crime. We now examine a few examples in pursuit of understanding the still-murky future of religion in the People's Republic of China.

Mao in the Rear View Mirror   Suppose you arrive in Beijing on your first visit to China and decide to go to the city's former imperial center, "The Forbidden City," the immense and walled inner city from where the Yuan, Ming, and Ching emperors ruled all of China. It was at the top of the palace's southern gateway, styled "The Gate of Heavenly Peace" (Tian'anmen), that Mao Zedong proclaimed the establishment of the People's Republic of China in 1949. Despite all the changes that have swept China since his death, you would easily see from your taxi window the immense painted portrait that hangs over that gateway to commemorate the "new beginning" of China then and Mao's heroic and determined role in leading the Communist party's triumphant success in coming to rule China.

The style of this portrait suggests that Mao is the ascetic servant of the people, a true Communist leader who bravely fought the Japanese, who in "The Long March" (1934) led troops in strategic retreat halfway across China, and who later exposed the internal enemies that had kept China backward, poor, and subjugated. Inspired by Marx, Engels, and Lenin, Mao found these enemies to be the landlords who oppressed the peasant masses as well as the ideas and institutions that kept them from rising up and forcing China to become a just society. For Mao and so for the early Communist Party leaders, religion and religious institutions were "enemies of the people." A rationalist who critiqued "superstitious" religious ideas that allegedly blocked the people's attempts to understand the world, Mao never ceased to highlight the classic modernist goal of setting the world free from the "superstitions" wrought by magical thought. Like Marx, Engels, and Lenin, Mao believed a true communist utopia was not obtainable in a society with strong religious traditions. Although officially sanctioned Chinese historians have admitted that Mao's own blind faith in communist mythology led to blunders causing the death of millions (in the 1958–1960 famine), the portrait still hangs as an icon of Communist China. (The occasional iconoclasts who have been caught defacing this portrait, even in recent incidents, have typically received multiyear prison terms.)

Even more than twenty years after his death, Mao's popularity endures. People who grew up since 1949 later painfully realized how full of "superstition" they had been in their regard for the Communist party and especially in their reverence for Chairman Mao. Yet for many Chinese, party members and nonparty members alike, he retains his standing as a sincere and uncorrupted champion of China's renewal who tried (however erringly) to seek justice and the common good. But regard for Mao endures in ways even he did not anticipate, either.

As your taxi driver turns the corner on the great square near the stolid mausoleum where Mao lies embalmed in a glass-enclosed tomb, you notice on the windshield mirror a gold-colored frame, decorated with red and yellow tassels, that contains back-to-back portraits of Mao, a youthful one and one from middle age (similar to that overlooking Tian'anmen Square). As this is a government-owned taxi, you ask your interpreter what the object is and what it means. The answer from the 30-something driver takes a few moments to register: "*Ta shi shen*" ("He is a deity"). The driver then adds with unconcealed sincerity that with so many more cars on the road it is quite dangerous and with the god's amulet there he feels safe. His income as a driver in fact has multiplied since he put it up, just as his fellow drivers in the work unit had promised. Upon subsequent questioning, and being alert to the presence of similar icons on later outings, you find others too who feel that the icon—and Mao's spirit—have helped them in their businesses. The transformations under way in China today and the restoration of religion among Chinese are embedded in this fully ironic turn of fate: the most powerful man in East Asia, while alive an atheist who suppressed religion, is in death a powerful spirit.

While his transformation to a revered protective spirit and god of wealth would doubtless have dismayed Mao, it does demonstrate the global pattern of religious traditions responding to the exigencies of local life. As the state and party have moved since the early 1990s away from collectivist policies to emphasize individual and private enterprise, leaders have exhorted the Chinese people that "to get rich is glorious." At the same time, leaders have retreated from promises of guaranteed state employment, pensions, and universal medical care. So is it surprising that an unassailable icon would be adopted as the very needed god of personal protection and wealth?

The Force of Feng Shui   Ideas about what constitute "religion" in China not only concern modern scholars but have been repeatedly debated by officials of the Communist party. In the reform era, as pressure has been exerted to reintroduce almost every sort of former spiritual practice, some traditions have been left largely unmolested. Others, particularly the "organized religions" such as Buddhism, Christianity, and Daoism, with their potential for reestablishing nationwide institutional networks, have had to deal with deliberate governmental attempts aimed at controlling and regulating them. In the former untouched category is *feng shui*, the school of applied religious Daoism that seeks to maximize human flourishing in natural and man-made environments. (Its literal title, "Wind-water" refers to the principal bearers of environmental energy used in geomancy analyses.)

Feng shui consultants have proliferated across mainland China as have books on the subject, with masters from overseas Chinese communities among those who have returned to advise those building the myriad new hotels, residences, and factories rising so quickly across China. The goal of feng shui is to determine the best sites, architectural designs, and living arrangements. Both private concerns and state ventures with party approval now take the "science" of mapping the *qi*, the inherent energy of a place, quite seriously before embarking on any construction project. Both success and disaster stories on the necessity of resorting to feng shui abound in the PRC today.

The state's support of feng shui's return to mainland Chinese life has given credence to the classical religious world view regarding humanity and the environment. It is based upon Daoist principles of balancing yin and yang, channeling the subterranean and atmospheric flow of their energy (*qi*), and pursuing health and prosperity through the conscious pursuit of harmonious design features. While the government's policy reflects the perennial Chinese emphasis on religion's practical, this-worldly benefits—one that gave doctors practicing acupuncture theory (itself based upon similar Daoist principles applied to the human body) unobstructed leeway to practice throughout the modern and postmodern eras—it has also lent credibility to some of the most basic concepts in China's traditional religious world view. Nor is mainland China the only area to see the effect of this revival: with the overseas migration of Chinese, modern real estate brokers from London to San Francisco are having to take account of feng shui analysis in the marketing of their properties. The micro ideas of house decorating have likewise entered into the ken of New Age religion where concern for "the wealth corner" of one's house, the situating of decorations recognized for their "harmonious vibrations," and the plotting of energy flow from front door to back have been borrowed from this Chinese system of thought.

Ancestor Veneration and the Return of Traditional Funerals   Chang-An was the greatest city in the world when it was the capital of T'ang-dynasty China (617–907), and the modern city (now called Xi'an) still bears the memory of that era with the remnants of its city walls, the imperial bell towers, many old temples, and the numerous imperial tombs set outside the modern urban precincts. Before 1949, the hills and vales surrounding this ancient city were also dotted with a great number of family ancestral shrines that were integral to the yearly family offerings and rituals prescribed in the common "diffuse religion."

In its zeal to end wasteful expenditures on death and ancestral ritualism, which for some traditional families meant going into nearly inescapable debt for extravagant funerals as survivors went all out in their attempts to demonstrate their extraordinary filial devotion, the Communist party issued strict regulations limiting funeral observances and—in the most radical break with the past—required secular cremation while also prohibiting rituals at ancestral graves. This attempt to break with the Confucian tradition went even further during the periods of greatest excess in the Cultural Revolution (1966–1976), when young revolutionaries ransacked and destroyed grave sites throughout China, including parts of the great imperial tombs, some of which had been in use for several thousand years. In doing so, the Communist zealots were trying to destroy the familial tradition that they saw as dividing "the people" and so undermining the party's quest to promote the collective good.

Beginning in the early 1990s, the practices of traditional funeral processions and burial of the dead in family graves slowly began to return, though largely in villages and smaller towns (although still not done around major cities such as Beijing). Graves are now increasingly visible and growing in elaborate design, including permanent brick structures with name plates affixed, across the rural areas, usually on sites unsuitable for agriculture.

When Li Shuxian, the widow of China's last emperor (Pu Yi) in 1995 was allowed to venerate the new grave site established for her husband on the traditional spring "tomb sweeping day" (*Ching Ming* festival), this was reported in the official press, signaling the government's renewed acceptance of the traditional burial rituals at least for influential families. Now a growing number of families, including those of party members, go openly to family graves for renewing the site and making offerings of wine, food, and other essentials. Shops specializing in funeral supplies in the cities carry the various garments needed to dress the corpse, as well as the customary two shrouds that bear printed or embroidered traditional symbols such as the phoenix. (These designs differ little from artifacts discovered in the Han tombs [c. 100 CE], indicating again the conservatism of Chinese "diffuse religion.") Official limits on death ritual have also been dropped in the case of the burning of paper money or paper gold ingots at gravesides: until 1996, road signs still threatened punishment for those engaging in this practice (one that is still exceedingly popular among Chinese living outside the mainland) that in traditional belief, conveys their essence to the dead. But by 1998, even government-owned shops were selling this ritual paper currency! Perhaps even more striking is the return of Confucius to an honored position in modern China.

Nationalism and Confucianism Revived   In the retreat from its socialist collectivism and having tacitly recognized the failure to convert the Chinese masses to the world view and ethos of Marxist-Maoist communism, the PRC government has been beset by the problem of corruption arising with its precipitously instituted market reforms. Many Chinese writers have pointed out the crisis in faith and values that has gripped China, as the profit-seeking motive has been unleashed over the last two decades. As one of China's first rock and roll stars Cui Jian sings in a popular album entitled *Eggs Under the Red Flag*, "Money is fluttering in the wind. We have no ideals."

The Communist party, in apparent recognition of this potential source of chaos, recently embarked on one of its greatest "reverse courses": it has turned back to Confucius in the attempt to help fill the society's normative vacuum. While the party ignores the failure to make communist ideology the common foundation of postwar China, the restoration of Confucius to respectability is part of its calculated co-opting of a more primordial Chinese tradition on which to base its future power: staunch nationalism.

Stoking nationalist flames draws out the still widely felt sense that the European-American world seeks superiority over China, a view rooted in the history of predatory colonialism (1820s onward), the legacy of America's early racist immigration laws, and incidents right up to the 1996 establishment of Radio Free Asia by the United States that beams continuously its own version of the news throughout the region. Regardless of whether they support the Communist government, Chinese widely share a certain pride in their civilization and its culture. Indeed, party ideologues see the future development of the world economy as eventually being dominated by China, and the party seems to have trimmed its demands on the people in the interest of guiding China to reach this pinnacle. The conviction that China occupies a place at the center of humanity has deep resonance with more ancient Chinese attitudes. It is expressed most directly in the two characters used since antiquity to represent China—*Zhong Guo*, "Middle Kingdom." This view was reflected in the traditionally imagined China-centric map of the globe that depicts all those living beyond the empire as inferior allies and ends with concentric rings of "barbarians" at the periphery.

Moreover, evoking nationalistic pride in the distinctness of China underlies the readmission of Confucianism to the PRC ideological stage, another ironic reversal by the Communist party leadership. During the Cultural Revolution, Mao required Red Guards to denounce Confucius and his sons specifically as "villainous slave owners," tarring the Master as an apologist for feudalism and exploitation, a symbol for all that the Communist party was out to replace.

Yet the hated excesses of this failed movement may have sparked renewed interest in Confucian thought in China. In October 1994, on the 2,545th birthday of the great sage, the party launched an initiative to revive Confucian thought. An international conference was convened, the Confucius temple in Beijing was restored and reopened to the public, and Confucius' home temple in Qufu was celebrated as a place to visit. By the year 2000, China's president Jiang Zemin frequently quoted from Confucius in his public speeches.

With this rather opportunistic attempt to use Confucian values to stabilize China (and hence its own political survival), the modern party leadership seems to reveal ignorance of Confucian teachings. In contrast to Deng Xiaoping's "to get rich is glorious," the *Analects* in strong language places merchants and commercial endeavors in very low esteem, especially if profit seeking outweighs moral uprightness in the state. And if party leaders had counted on the

Confucian emphasis on authority and social harmony to lessen popular support for China's dissidents, they failed to notice a central Confucian principle regarding political authority: only when the leaders are just and benevolent should the people submit to their authority. And finally, to reawaken remembrance of Mencius' doctrine of "Heaven's mandate" means that China's people will find that under circumstances of immoral leadership or misrule, the Confucian tradition insisted that Heaven's mandate can be withdrawn and shifted to favor reformers.

Qi Gong   Another area in which the spiritual has returned to mainland China in the guise of applied therapy is in the practice of *qi gong*. Like feng shui, this healing art draws upon Daoist theories of vital energy in the body (*chi'i* or *qi*) and upon techniques of awakening its force in practitioners, both of which have their origins in religious Daoism's ancient paths to achieve immortality. It is now quite common in major cities to see qi gong practitioners with open shops in the precincts of Buddhist or Daoist monasteries, with banners and posters unfurled outside their entranceways explaining the theory and practice along with testimonials on successful cures of various maladies. In most instances, this involves the qi gong master using his own body to concentrate the energy and project it outwardly (through the hands) to affect the flow of energy in the patient. In the famous Great Goose Pagoda in Xi'an, the Buddhist committee since 1993 has rented a side assembly hall to one master who now draws a steady stream of interested Chinese who can listen to an introductory lecture and for a modest fee take their first treatment.

In some governmental circles, there is ambivalence on such applied spirituality. Although the modern official press features an occasional article, often by a prominent scientist, that denounces "phony qi gong" as "harmful" and criticizes individual practitioners for "feudal and superstitious activities which use the flag of qi gong as a cover for swindling others," it continues to allow the practice to flourish, even in state-controlled temple precincts. Thus, while this medically oriented practice can be linked with other Chinese (and Western) therapies, qi gong now affirms in the personal experience of modern Chinese the credibility of the most elemental ideas of classical Daoism.

Shrines on Mountain Peaks, Village Squares, Shops, and Front Doors   Across mainland China since 1976, there has been the slow, hesitant, but unmistakable movement by devotees to reestablish shrines, temples, and the ritual practices destroyed or prohibited under government orders dating back to 1949. Exactly what has been the Communist Party's line of toleration has varied according to the region and its succession of officials; tensions exist still as to what is "superstition" (*mixin*), which is strongly discouraged by the government, and what is "religion" (*zongjiao*). Individuals have a constitutional right to practice a religion, but the state reserves the right to grant or withhold this designation from a given belief system.

Perhaps in recognition that "the people" really yearn to follow the older traditions, the Chinese government now supports the rehabilitation of selected older temples and is willing to invest in the infrastructure needed to make travel to important remote sites feasible. At the same time, it attempts to shape the various revival traditions at them in the content and form closest to the party's own tradition of Communist orthodoxy.

Even so, the return of temples to the public domain for ritual use is in evidence almost everywhere. Daoist and Buddhist shrines are now surrounded by flourishing votive markets (usually owned by or rented from the temple itself) that sell incense, candles, printed texts and scrolls with spiritual exhortations, souvenirs, amulets. Many devotional traditions are flourishing, and in forms that were popular centuries earlier.

Accounts of village life cite the near universal attempt of rural peasants to use part of their new earnings to build (or rebuild) the public temples that house the local and regional gods. None is more telling than the practice of making offerings to the local Earth gods (*t'u-ti*). In pre-PRC China, the humble Earth God shrines were found in every locality, possessing in fact a multiple presence according to the settlement: t'u-ti shrines were found in homes (under the altar boards), in neighborhoods, villages, government offices (where they received offerings from state officials), and even in Buddhist monasteries. All major events (deaths, births, troubles) were reported to them, and the simple icon or tablet was taken out of the temple to "inspect" sites where there were severe problems. If petitioned properly and sincerely, they would protect against locusts, mildew disease, and any obstacles to a rich harvest as well as solve any other difficulties in their domain. These shrines and cult have returned everywhere.

Even in the restaurant and home domains, the trend toward restoration of shrine and ritual has gone ahead. After several attempted crackdowns by the government, restaurants have succeeded in reinstalling small altars to the local gods of wealth and protection. Iconic guardians are also visible, even in Beijing, on the homes of government officials and party members. In private homes, the Chinese New Year has been increasingly observed with the traditional pasting of calligraphic good-luck icons, including the word for good fortune (*Fu*) placed upside down to indicate the sound of "Good Fortune's Arrival." Here again, by being sensitive to the importance and meaning of religion, we can comprehend the profundity of changes sweeping China: as the party expands economic opportunity but ends communal social safety-net programs, people feel that to prosper they need all the luck they can attract. Accordingly, the search for and perceived need of good fortune has surpassed the pull of communist doctrine and its representatives are correspondingly more reluctant to suppress "superstition."

Japan

Unlike in China, where the Cultural Revolution postponed the expression of religious awakening until after Mao's death in 1976, in Japan this era of innovation certainly commenced in 1945, with the literal necessity of rebuilding the war-ravaged country both physically and spiritually. For seven years occupied and ruled by the Allied powers (principally America), Japan had to reinvent a form of government, redesign its economic system, and rebuild its major cities and without reference to the emperor as their divine leader. For Japan's surrender was pronounced by Hirohito in his own voice, and during the occupation the emperor was compelled to explicitly renounce his divinity (as a Shinto kami) and underscore his purely ceremonial presence in Japan's political future. The state Neo-Shintoism system that was integral to the modernizations that began in 1868 was also discredited and discarded, as Shinto survived only in its myriad shrines (and their hereditary priests) dedicated to divinities of neighborhoods, villages, and regions. Establishment Buddhism, like the rest of Japan's cultural institutions, also had to rebuild its physical and social presence, overcoming the stigma of having supported the militaristic state. As the economic system flourished, the country's wealth eventually was used to rebuild these institutions, accelerating the traditional religion's material recovery and, in some cases, expansion.

The New Religions and the Old   Most striking in the present era is the rise of Japan's "new religions." Some of these were synthesized by charismatic founders from Japan's long-extant traditions along with (in different cases) aspects of modern nationalism, elements of Christianity, and science. Many of the new religions began in some measure as responses to the dislocations that Japanese society encountered through its sudden opening to the outside world in the mid-nineteenth century and the headlong modernization and Westernization during the Meiji era. Almost every older "new religion" splintered with the passing of its founder and the struggles of interpretation and succession that followed, adding to the number of such groups. But most of the "new religions" today are more recent in origin. They tend to draw on the extant (and themselves expanding) global traditions from every world area. They also attract followers who find themselves ever more disconnected from the melding of Shintoism and Buddhism that satisfied their ancestors.

As contemporary trends continue to change the lives of the Japanese people in many dimensions—through migration away from rural homesteads to burgeoning cities, with the concomitant separation from extended families and loss of community in newly built urban conclaves, and as travel and media have engendered an awareness of every portion of the world—many individuals have been drawn to the "new religions" to find original answers to life's perennial questions. Japanese spiritual leaders have likewise emerged to form groups independent from the older culture. Their successes, for a variety of reasons, indicate that many of these groups have met these new yearnings. Still, we must note that most Japanese today have not joined the new sects and instead find accommodation with the older traditions.

Educated Japanese, and oftentimes their friends in intellectual Western circles, are fond of proclaiming that the Japanese are "lacking in religion," an Enlightenment attitude found today among East Asian elites that did not participate in this European movement. They try to project an image of Japan as a modern society comparable to Europe or North America in its scientific sophistication and "secularization." While few Japanese care to learn much in depth about Shinto mythology or Buddhist doctrine, this indifference does not prove that Japan "lacks religion."

Beyond the unprecedented growth of the new religions (whose very presence and dynamism belie the assumption of some inherent nonreligiosity in Japan's "national character"!), one has only to know where and when to seek a wealth of examples that dispel this widespread stereotype about a Japanese people somehow different from everyone else. While it is foolish to ignore the force of skepticism, scientific theory, and cynicism in any modern society, it is also naïve to judge "religiousness" by formal institutional measures alone. Contemporary New Year's Day observances provide an example of the strength of "diffuse popular religion" in modern Japan.

During the Meiji era, Japan legislated a shift away from the Chinese lunar calendar determining the date of the "new year" festival and adopted the Western (or Gregorian) system that has the year begin on January 1. On this day and days around it, Japan shuts down its industrial economy. Families begin the process of renewal through a special cleaning of the house (*susaharai*, "soot and cobweb clearing"). A visit to any Shinto shrine on New Year's Eve or early New Year's morning—even in the most modern Tokyo urban neighborhood—would find long lines of family members coming for *hatsumode*, a formal visit to pay their respects to their neighborhood's deities (kami). They then consign to the carefully laid bonfires all the family amulets accumulated over the past year. (In Japan, unlike in every other Asian society, the power of amulets "runs down" after a set time, requiring replacement and so repurchase, a belief of considerable commercial importance for the votive retailers!) That evening or the next day, a family member will purchase new amulets from the local shrine (and perhaps from other temples) that will be carefully set up on the newly purified family altar. Many temples plan their annual festival for this period, when crowds throng to temple precincts to buy amulets and attend the priestly rituals empowering them. Nearly every shop and house bear decorations that are dedicated to the kami residing in the neighborhood. On New Year's morn, too, families gather to worship the Buddhas, Kannon, and local gods on their household altar. Thus, in the renewal of the family shrine at the year's turning, by "being careful" with local divinities, in sacralizing family ties, and by stopping the profane activities of markets and business activities, contemporary New Year's Day traditions in Japan fit perfectly into the "religion" framework we established in Chapter 1. In 2006, press reports in Tokyo noted that given the discomforts of joining the usual crowd of three million visitors who traditionally visit the Meiji Shrine on New Year's Day, this shrine like many across Japan has established a Web site. Without leaving home, a virtual visit can be made: Cyber-visitors can click onto the site, bow twice, clap their hands, and bow again, after which they can express their request to the shrine's *kami* and order auspicious amulets online. (For an online index, see for example: http://www.japan-guide.com/e/e2059.html.)

Continuing Support for Shinto Shrines   Most Japanese—housewives, salary-men, artisans—still widely believe that wherever one lives, and certainly wherever one's family still has an ancestral residence, one has loose ties to the shrine (*jinja*) that houses the deity of that locality, the *uji-kami*. We've seen that on New Year's Day at least, one should go to pay respects to that kami, and that this remains a very popular observance. It is almost equally popular in most parts of Japan for two important life-cycle rites to be held at this local Shinto shrine. The first is for wedding rituals that are conducted, at least in part, at the shrine with ministrations by the resident Shinto priests who petition the kami to aid in securing the new couple's health, success, and progeny. The second popular rite is after the birth of a child: it is still nearly universal for couples to bring their newborn babes to "meet" the kami and to pay their own respects, requesting protection.

As to how we can understand the typical individual today visiting a Shinto shrine, it is nearly impossible to separate the spiritual from the habitual or the recreational. In a recent survey on those who visited shrines, 65 percent of men and 75 percent of women reported feeling *aratamatta kimochi*, "a feeling of inner peace," afterward.[11] The observer at the shrine finds many ritual activities that ostensibly can be cited to indicate religious conviction there—clapping the hands together, bowing before an image, making an offering, buying the amulet.

A modern exponent of Shinto's relevance in contemporary Japan would certainly note that of the over 100,000 Shinto shrines, although some may be neglected, none of them is in ruins.

The Zen of Daruma-san   If any single religious icon could be said to embody all the mind-boggling complexities and paradoxes of religion in Japan today, it might be *Daruma-san*. The name and identity of this figure derives from Bodhidharma, the sage renowned as the transmitter of the Buddhist meditation tradition from India (around 500 CE) that became Ch'an in China and Zen in Japan. Daruma-san became an exemplary man of Zen and legends about him are part of the scriptural lore of this school. They celebrate his unbending commitment to meditation retreats and his terse, no-nonsense replies to students and patrons. From the Kamakura period in Japan when Zen schools were imported from China, Daruma-san became a favorite subject for painters and sculptors. Images of Daruma-san came to be popular in Japanese folk traditions as well: his visage adorns kites, toys, knock-down dolls, sake cups. Several dozen major Buddhist temples feature his icon and offer a full range of amulets. Today, the most widely used images of Daruma-san are limbless round paper-maché icons called *okiagari* that are employed for making vows or wishes, the most common of which is bought on New Year's Day. The standard ritual consists of making the wish, coloring in one eye of the statue, and placing it on the family altar. When there is success in the matter wished for, the other eye is colored in and the doll (like all other amulets) fuels the next New Year's bonfire. The Daruma-san icon is used in the same manner by businesspeople undertaking new ventures and politicians beginning election campaigns.

So with Daruma-san, then, we witness the domestication into popular Japanese ritual life of the founding saint of Zen Buddhism, whose fierce nature as an ascetic meditation master has become transmuted into an ostensibly comic figure, but one who nonetheless commands a considerable following among the hundreds of thousands who participate in this amulet cycle annually. The subtle meanings of Daruma-san stand in stark contrast to the extreme teachings of a recent Japanese cult, one that attempted to connect the Buddha's Four Noble Truths with a premeditated attack of nerve gas unleashed on innocent citizens.

The Rise and Fall of the Aum Cult   In March 1995, as government investigators were about to arrest its leaders, at least ten determined disciples of the Aum Shinrikyo sect executed a terrorist attack in the centrally located Kasumigaseki Station of the Tokyo subway that injured 5,500 people, twelve fatally. They were acting on the orders of the sect's guru, Shoko Asahara, a semiblind 40-year-old who claimed to be an incarnation of Jesus and a spiritual master who had distilled the final truths of tantric Buddhism, Hindu yoga, the LSD psychedelic experience, New Age astrology, and the figure Nostradamus. Since 1989, when he applied for and received registration as a tax-exempt religious organization called Aum Shinrikyo ("The True Teaching of Aum"), he built a religious organization around a core of commune-living disciples, many of whom were highly educated and successful and commanded considerable wealth.

In the aftermath, the Japanese cultural elite and the media engaged in a long period of self-reflection: What does this group's success say about the moral and cultural state of the nation? What did it say about Japan's educational system that among Aum's inner circle were some of the better minds of their generation, including standouts in law and science? How could the cult members be so brainwashed as to accept such an unlikely collection of ideas? How could they be induced to give up their families and all possessions to follow a pudgy dropout who claimed to be both Buddha and Jesus, and then to adopt his doomsday doctrine that led them into such murderous hatred?

Leading commentators saw in this group's rise a fault line within the generation born after World War II who are frustrated with the laborious old Japan of geriatric professors who block younger scholars' university careers, of business cartels that close off new competitors and market innovations, and of fathers who see no other avenue outside the Confucian code of work, hierarchy, and "waiting your turn."

The Aum tragedy also brought to attention the thousands of other "new religions" that claim the loyalty of an estimated 20 percent of modern Japanese; our survey of religion in Japan concludes with an overview and sampling of them.

THE BUSINESS OF THE AUM CULT: ENLIGHTENMENT AND MADNESS

By the time of their attack, the sect had set up a host of businesses (computer shops, health clubs, baby-sitting services) and made real estate transactions that had elevated its total assets to close to $1 billion. Roughly 20,000 Japanese were also on its membership roster, most of whom were first lured by Aum's disciples' adroit street come-on offering free yoga classes, then cultivated by sophisticated video productions that presented Asahara's teachings and invitations to live communally in inexpensive dormitories. Those advancing onward could aspire to rise through an intricate series of advanced spiritual stages, but they were intimidated with verbal threats and physical violence if they wanted to leave. (It turns out that several from the innermost circle who tried to resign were murdered by members.) On the basis of Asahara's interpretation of the Kobe earthquake that occurred several months before the attack, and on his reading of the New Testament's Book of Revelation, his inner circle of disciples followed him in his descent into paranoid madness and terrorism.

The New "New Religions" in Japan   In 1999 there were no less than 182,935 sects officially registered with the Japanese government, and most of them were formed over the last century. The great majority are exceedingly small in size, inconsequential, and for the most part inactive. Many are hard to distinguish from groups formed around health practitioners, interest groups, poetry circles, or philosophy clubs. The major sects are an important part of today's spiritual landscape, however; roughly 20 percent of Japanese people recently surveyed reported that their predominant religious affiliation is now with one of the "new religions."[12]

While Aum's mass murder attempt is completely atypical of the new religions, other aspects of the cult are not. Most form around a charismatic leader whose personal struggle to find the truth becomes paradigmatic for the movement; some sort of shamanic experience or performance is the most common ritual focus. There is also the frequent teaching that members reject the diffuse eclecticism of Shintoism or Buddhism and the proclamation of one practice and one singular revelation as definitive. Yet many of the elements are drawn from traditional sources such as Buddhist karma and reincarnation doctrines, Confucian moral teachings and ancestor rites, or Shinto styles of worship; some also import spiritual practices from the West in the form of Christianity (e.g., prayer) or Western psychology (e.g., 19th-century "new thought" or "the power of positive thinking"), or from India (e.g., Hindu yoga). Each new religion also tends to be this-worldly in its goals (especially in an emphasis on healing). The

most successful sects are built around a new "sacred center," a priestly administrative entity that both expresses and manages the sect's ushering in the new divine era. Membership in most is quite open, but a ritual of joining commonly
requires individuals to make a personal decision and commitment to the group.

Japan's new religions can be conveniently arranged according to their
chronological emergence. The earliest, which are "new" only in relation to Japan's
long history, are those that arose in the nineteenth century and were eventually
aligned with Shinto. The most popular among them, the Kurozumikyo, the
Tenrikyo, and the Konkokyo, mentioned earlier, have survived into the present.
The most prominent of the second-tier group, which arose during the Meiji,
remain among the largest new religions today: the Buddhist-derived Soka
Gakkai and Reiyukai Kyodan, and the Seicho no Ie, a group we have not mentioned that teaches the unity of all religions. Their influence to the present
has followed a standard pattern across an otherwise astonishingly diverse spiritual landscape: the new religions that began in prewar Japan have evolved
through tumultuous times, with those that survived abandoning their rebel-
lious stance toward the status quo. That those formerly angry denominations
have made their peace with Japanese society can be seen in a crucial change:
most new religions allow members to participate in the family worship of
Shinto gods and at the traditional Buddhist temple.

Many of the most successful new religions have built schools, colleges, hospitals, even residential communities and athletic facilities to sustain their
members from cradle to grave. These resources are also useful, as we saw in
the Aum case, for proselytizing purposes and for demonstrating the power and
success of the new path itself. The Tenrikyo, for example, one of the most successful new religions, now numbers 2.3 million persons, with chapters in every
area of Japan; its headquarters, called Tenri City (near Nara), is a center for pilgrimage comparable to Salt Lake City for Mormons.

Sociological surveys have shown that those who are devoted to the new religions are most commonly those excluded from dominant avenues to prestige in modern Japan, that is, members do not typically have employment in
the large corporations but run small family businesses. Within the group there
are characteristically hierarchies and internal ranks for which individuals aspire. This helps to explain why women typically outnumber men in membership
and serve as leaders, especially in their proselytizing in a style that represents
an extension of the mothering role.

The new religions assume a common outlook (and hence social posture) in
presenting themselves as expert at solving human problems. Whatever their
tenets, they hold that sickness, economic failure, and all interpersonal relations
are fully under individual control if persons will only discipline themselves in
actualizing the core values of Japanese culture: harmony, loyalty, filial piety,
selflessness, diligence, ritual service. Problems can be solved by making a concerted effort to practice these virtues, to perfect the self and harmonize it
with all levels of life (from personality integration to reconciliation with one's

family, society, nature, ancestors, and the supernatural). In how this is accomplished, the sects differ astoundingly, and we can give here only a sampling of representative groups formed in the postmodern era.

Among the most popular groups are the Perfect Liberty Kyodan ("P.L. Kyodan") whose primary slogan, "religion is art," indicates its emphasis on the spirituality of practicing the fine arts in everyday life. Unaffiliated with any major religion and claiming 2.6 million adherents worldwide, its focal practice is liturgical, that is, prayers choreographed with stylized prostrations, gestures, and offerings. The theology is monotheistic and explains that troubles are actually warnings from God, although their exact message can be correctly interpreted in a ritual manner only by a P.L. priest.

Another new religion that has become active all across Asia, with about a dozen international centers, is the Sekai Kyusei-kyo ("World Messianity"), a group that emphasizes faith healing, organic diet, and the creation of beautiful gardens in preparation for the coming paradise on earth. Its focal practice is called *jorei*: a trained priest moves a cupped upraised hand before a person or object, a practice believed to channel divine light that cleanses evil and anticipates the world's eventual transformation into a paradise through being suffused with the same divine light.

The Rissho Koseikai ("Society Establishing Righteousness and Harmony") was founded by a Reiyukai member Niwano Nikkyo (1906–), who retained the Nichiren Buddhist school's focus on the *Lotus Sutra*. After 1969, the group's focus shifted to the individual's personality development through special counseling sessions (*hoza*) led by trained lay "teachers" and the goal of world peace. The group does not insist that members refrain from joining other religious groups or participating in their rituals. International missionary movements have brought Rissho Koseikai to Korea, Brazil, and the United States. As of 2003, the Koseikai was Japan's second largest new religion, organized uniquely according to government unit lines, and claiming over six million members.

Agonshu, a new religion founded in 1971, also has a Buddhist identity. The group was founded by Kiriyama Seiyu (1921–), a charismatic spiritualist who declared that he has "cut off" his own karma and that through visits by Buddhas and deities, the true and original teachings of Shakyamuni Buddha were revealed to him. Kiriyama's distilled "essence of Buddhism" is that the ancestors must be properly "turned into realized Buddhas" through special rituals, a view that would be disputed by Buddhist monks and scholars almost everywhere. Agonshu teachings attribute the world's current troubles to the influence of the restless dead, who afflict the living due to neglect. In the group's view, Kiriyama has rescued for the good of the entire world esoteric practices to pacify and enlighten the dead, particularly through fire rituals kept secret for centuries by the tantric Buddhist school in Japan called Shingon. The greatest yearly practice of this Agonshu rite, called *hoshi matsuri*, "Star Festival," has become one of the most spectacular events in modern Japanese religion, attracting a half million viewers to the site while millions watch it on television.

Each year Agonshu priests set massive twin fires, one to benefit the ancestors, the other to promote the personal welfare of all participants, who contribute millions of wooden boards to fuel the fire.

The goal of world peace has also in the last decade been featured as part of the sect's mission; Kiriyama has been photographed with the Pope and with the Dalai Lama to highlight Agonshu's intention of acting on the world stage for that end. Even with its outward missionizing, like many other new religions the group does not neglect the individual benefits. Members are urged to chant the following five verses daily, the same words used to conclude Agonshu rallies:

> Let's do it!
> I will certainly succeed!
> I am blessed with very good luck!
> I will certainly do well!
> I will definitely win![13]

The group called Sukyo Mahikari, founded in 1963, provides an example of a more ethnocentric new religion that affirms fascistic prewar values and a more narrow, sectarian view of salvation: it teaches that the postwar occupation unnaturally imposed democracy and materialism on the Japanese people, causing them to be possessed by evil spirits angry over the corruption of the country. Then communism was sent by the gods to warn humanity of a coming ordeal, or "Baptism by Fire," that will claim all but the elect who must restore patriotic ties to the emperor and demonstrate their loyalty to other Confucian relationships (between parents-children, husbands-wives). Those who follow this vision set forth by the founder Okada Kotama will be the "Seed People" to restart the world in its proper order, as set forth in a cosmogonic myth adapted to require, today, the leadership of Okada. This group's social programs without subtlety evoke a religious expression of prewar fascism by military-style parades during which troops of disciples honor their founder with extended arms, a replica of the Nazi salute.

Korea
The Self-proclaimed Heart of Confucian Tradition in the Postmodern World   With the strong living tradition of Confucianism entrenched in family rituals, marriage arrangements, and the moral education programs in the public school curriculum, South Korea is by all accounts the "most Confucian" nation in East Asia. Institutions dedicated to Confucian studies thrive in Korea, and exponents preach Confucian values using mass media. A common message is that by being true to its Confucian identity, Korea has a key role to play in melding harmoniously the meeting of West and East.

Some among the Korean political elite (like many others in East Asia), seeking to jettison Confucianism as a millstone around the nation's neck, chose

Westernization, agnosticism, and/or Christianity as its antidote. However, Confucianism as the cultural center of Korea has endured even among Christian converts, most of whom continue to observe their family's venerable ancestor rituals. South Korea has likewise pursued modern economic development with the clear goal of strengthening Confucianism and adopting national economic goals in a Confucian framework: the central government takes responsibility for the citizenry's education and economic well-being; it supports the family as the basis for social stability; accepts the intelligentsia as the conscience of the nation; invests in education as the essential foundation for both material and cultural progress. The government has likewise supported major institutions dedicated to Confucian studies.

In the nation of North Korea, a strong if archaic emphasis on communist civil religion remains; much as in the Maoist era, citizens are expected to renounce the culture of the past, sacrifice themselves for the common good, and participate in the "cult of personality" centered on the modern nation's only ruling patriarch.

As with Japan, we highlight groups that are shaping the diverse religious environment in modern South Korea.

Confucian Revival: The T'oegyehak *Movement*   Since learning the lessons of history is a strong Confucian value, it is not surprising that one important South Korean group would emphasize a prominent figure in its own tradition, Yi T'oegye (1501–1570), a philosopher who developed the thought of the most famous Neo-Confucian Chinese thinker Zhu Xi, whom we have discussed already. Master T'oegye was responsible for making his system of thought prominent in Korea and wrote his own treatises on Zhu Xi's and others' writings. These works were especially influential in the realm of state law and in shaping strong allegiance to ancestor ritualism.

Due to the extraordinary leadership of a retired industrialist, Lee Dong-choon (1919–1989), the prolific writings of Master T'oegye were placed at the center of a traditionalist revivalist movement, the T'oegyehak, that has by now become international in its scope not only across East Asia but among East Asians living in the West as well. This group has tapped Lee's industrial fortune to promote detailed studies of the Confucian values as interpreted by Chinese and Korean masters, and it has published at low cost copies of their works and the Confucian classics, making them available across the globe.

Shamanism   Amidst the rising number of Christian converts and the modest revivals under way among the various Buddhist schools, old and new, one finds a steady and unmistakable reliance upon shamans, or *mudang*, in South Korea to deal with life's pragmatic problems. These practitioners tend to be women drawn into the role from one of two backgrounds: troubling personal experiences that led them to initiation or inheritance of the role through kinship lines. An estimated 100,000 Korean shamans still practice their healing arts today and their popularity endures.

The shamanic seances, called *kut,* are usually held to contact a deity to request economic blessings, healing, restoration of good marital relations, or help in becoming pregnant. Once the mudang is possessed, the deities speak through her. Typically they first complain of deficiencies in the offerings laid out or about impurity, which Korean deities dislike; once sponsors apologize and promise to do better next time the divinities entertain the patron's request(s). A second type of ritual has the mudang lead the soul of a recently dead individual to the next world or check on a recently departed soul's status.

Buddhist Revival   Despite many setbacks over the last century, the surviving Korean Buddhist institutions remain well endowed with landed income and have established an important niche in Korean society through the many schools their monasteries and lay institutions have started. The Son Buddhist school, the Korean version of Zen, has sent several prominent teachers to the West, winning international support and renown.

A new school calling itself Won Buddhism arose in 1924, founded by Soe-Tae San (1891–1943), a teacher who claimed to have been enlightened from his own independent ascetic practices. He and his disciples sought to revive Buddhism by simplifying its doctrines; their sole ritual involved the worship of a picture of a black circle in a white background that symbolizes the *dharmakaya,* the cosmic body of the Buddha. From this is derived the name of the group: "Won" is the Korean reading of the Chinese character "round," referring to this symbol.

Only after the death of San and the lifting of Japanese occupation did the group find popular acceptance across Korea. Typical of reformist "Protestant Buddhist" groups elsewhere in Asia (see Chapter 6), Won Buddhism has been especially popular in urban areas and emphasizes that Buddhist doctrines are compatible with modern thought. It also makes Buddhism attractive to the laity by translating classical texts into vernacular Korean publications and through weekly congregational worship involving chanting, simple rituals, and sermons. The group involves women as leaders and active participants. Won Buddhist monks, who lead the ritual services, can marry.

Another aspect of Won Buddhism that resembles reform Buddhism elsewhere is the attempt to cultivate both lay meditation and social service. For the former, members are encouraged to cultivate the "Buddha nature in all things" and bring this awareness to all work done in everyday life, an exercise called "Zen without time or place." For Won "social engagement," the Buddhist ideal of no self is sought through selfless service offered to the public, and this is also seen in classical terms as a means to address the universality of suffering. The primary form of service by Won Buddhists has been in building schools, from kindergartens to universities. Its moral emphasis is also quite Confucian, emphasizing filial relations as the proper Buddhist ethical aspiration.

By 2005, this school claimed 430 temples and 950,000 followers; it had built a grand central headquarters in Iri in southwest Korea and a convention center in Seoul. The group has also spread to California with immigrants settling there and a branch temple has been built. Won Buddhists have shown increasing interest in ecumenical relations with other faiths, both in Korea and with Japanese Buddhist groups.

Korean "New Religions" As in Japan, the collapse of the traditional order in the nineteenth century precipitated a host of religious responses, and one major avenue was syncretistic religious movements or "new religions" that sought to meet the challenge of rebuilding the nation, restoring its spiritual center, and supporting individuals in their coping with rapid and often traumatic changes.

Peak times of sociopolitical turmoil—for example, the years immediately following World War II—saw an especially great upsurge in these movements. Also conforming to the pattern seen in Japan's new religions, these groups have been founded around men who claim a new supernatural revelation, most often a reassemblage of traditional doctrines from Buddhism, Daoism, Confucianism, or Christianity. Most focus concern on this-world problems rather than the afterlife; some also imagine their playing a leading role in establishing Korea as humanity's global leader and/or creating a utopia on earth. Those sects that have survived have shown a tendency to develop their doctrinal teachings into a comprehensive world view and to create supportive social institutions. The total number of new religion adherents was last determined by the government to number about one million, or 5 percent of the South Korean population.

The Unification Church Known in Korea as the Tong Il Movement, the Unification Church, founded in 1954 by the Reverend Sun Myung Moon, is one of the most recognized if controversial religions in the world. The followers, colloquially known as "Moonies," seek to spread their belief that a messianic transformation of human life is imminent and that others should adopt their religion to establish a new heaven on earth.

Like many Japanese new religions, the Unification Church originated in an unprecedented mediumship attributed to its founder. Like the Chinese Taiping Movement's founder, Hong, however, Rev. Moon claims a distinctly Christian encounter: on Easter Day, 1936, Jesus appeared to him and requested that Moon establish Christ's kingdom on earth. The Unification scripture, called *Divine Principle*, recounts this and subsequent communications of the founder with Buddha, Moses, and God Almighty.

The theology of the Unification Church is based upon an elaborate variation on Christianity's doctrine of original sin. According to the church, human love arises from Eve's carnal relations with the archangel Lucifer, a fault passed down to subsequent generations. All of human history, then, is viewed as a series of attempts by a loving God to restore harmony with humanity. Moon teaches that Jesus failed at this mission, having been murdered before his marriage, an event alluded to only metaphorically in Christian scripture (e.g., Matthew 25:1). Moon further teaches that God's work will only finally succeed through the person of the messiah and his wife ("the Second Adam and Eve," also called "The True Parents"), whose children will usher in a new humanity.

The church proclaims that the prophetic signs of the current age are similar to those of Jesus' time and (less openly) avers that Rev. Moon is the long-awaited messiah. The work of the church is establishing the foundation for this transformation of humanity.

The movement grew only very slowly until 1972, when Moon moved to the United States. Converts among middle-class youth enthusiastically proselytized their peers in cities and on college campuses. The church gained financial security through having its core members live communally and work long hours in Unification Church–related businesses. Such funds and the wealth donated by wealthy converts enabled the church to purchase newspapers in Tokyo and Washington, buy prominent landmarks in Manhattan real estate, and sponsor conferences designed to attract leading intellectuals, in which Rev. Moon takes part. Publicity to the contrary, the church in 1987 had only around twenty thousand "pledging" collective-living members in Korea and around half that number in the West, although many times that number are supporters living as typical householders, a group referred to as "The Home Church." The church regards marriage sanctioned by Rev. Moon, known as "The Blessing," as its most important rite. There are few other rituals except for a pledge of loyalty made the first day of every week, month, and year, as well as on each of the church's holy days.

Christianity in Korea   An alert observer of religion living in North America will be aware that Koreans in significant numbers have converted to Christianity, as signs with Korean characters dot the landscape of many North American cities announcing that their congregations sometimes share churches with English-speaking co-religionists and sometimes possess their sanctuaries. As of 1985, approximately 30 percent of the South Korean population was Christian, with Protestants outnumbering Catholics by four to one. Similarities between the emotional Protestant rituals and the mudang tradition have been suggested, as well as several elements unique to the recent Korean historical experience such as the positive ties established at the turn of the century with the imperial court, the churches' prominent involvement in the struggle against Japanese occupation (1910–1945), and Korean Christians' subsequent leadership in human rights activism. With the exception of some churches tolerating shamanism and reinterpreting ancestor ritualism within a Christian framework, there has been little innovation outside the denominational frameworks.

CONCLUSION

Our study of the religions of East Asia, past and present, has shown conclusively that, contrary to the assertions of many among the modern elites of China and Japan, as well as numerous Western scholars who study them, religious belief and practices are central to the life and culture of the region. East Asians are by no means an exception to the common human conditions, namely, that in every known society there is a religious dimension at the center of social life! Moreover, only by understanding the religious dimensions of Shintoism and Confucianism can one comprehend the nationalism and economic success in Japan's recent history; likewise, only by recognizing the religious dimensions of Maoist communism is it possible to fathom how in China the party has sustained its place of power since 1949.

Nevertheless, Confucianism and Daoism present a challenge to the Western monotheistic model of "being religious," with some scholars of religion claiming that these belief systems are not "religions" at all. Of course, in no manner is either monotheistic. Rather, their diverse aspects, as illustrated here, suggest another way of humans being religious: not centering the sacred on a god above but in seeing as sacred this world "below" in which humans live in communities and amidst nature. Respect and reverence are the central religious emotions. Confucianism and the diffuse religions of East Asia have both cultural and supernatural dimensions. They create in the culture circles of reciprocal relatedness that sacralize, social relations, harmonize human existence with vital energies of nature, and respect the creative power of Heaven. Their supernatural dimension is directing belief to deities and to the survival of ancestors as spirits with whom relations can endure forever.

Both attributes of religion we outlined in Chapter 1—"being bound to others" and "being careful"—are abundantly highlighted across the diverse landscape of East Asian religions. The ethos promoted by East Asian religions, old and new, can be characterized as optimistic toward human life and human potential, seeing the improvement of the individual and society as sacred goals. Respect for others serves to uphold acceptance of pluralism and the tolerance of religious diversity. In that the "diffuse religion" supports family cohesion as the center of a moral society, the Confucian core of East Asia supports education for its role in cultivating character and the acquisition of practical knowledge. The resulting "pragmatic idealism" sees improving the world based on knowledge as a this-world orientation, not as the dictate of some transcendent deity. The success in the modern global marketplace of this complex of religion and culture has contradicted Western scholars who argued that East Asian religions were an obstacle to development.

Continued Religious Revival in China:
Problems and Possibilities

In the face of determined government efforts by the Chinese Communists to extirpate religion from the educational system, suppress religious institutions, and persecute individual practitioners, and despite three decades (1950–1980) of unchallenged propaganda, the reemergence of religion in China is a powerful disproof of Marx's consignment of religion to "the dustbin of history" even as modern science, technology, and nationalism advance.

If the Confucian system of family/ancestral devotion is regarded as the central pillar of Chinese tradition, then it is clear that it, too, has not only survived the criticisms and persecutions, but has done so strongly. What is remarkable is that this has happened largely independent of any formal institutions and simply through the family relations that continued even amidst fierce totalitarian blandishments and attempts to suppress or replace them.

Indeed, the revival of religion in China may threaten regional stability. The inherent problems that beset many large states trying to hold together diverse groups and disparate regions are found in the present relationship between the communist state and its principal minorities, and it is around religious issues that major fault lines affecting modern China are to be found.

For example, the Muslim minorities in western China (Xinjiang Province) have grown restive in the face of state attempts to regulate their religious communities, which have grown proportionally smaller as a result of an influx of Han immigrants who have achieved economic dominance. The same situation exists in the vast high-altitude region of Tibet that is claimed and controlled by the People's Republic. Tibetan Buddhists have retained their devotion to the Dalai Lama, the long-exiled political and spiritual head of pre-1949 Tibet. In addition, the Communist Party–sponsored attacks on religion that marked the early years of the PRC culminating in the Cultural Revolution (1966–1976) also served to stiffen resistance by the Taiwanese toward unification. Thus, minority adherence to religious traditions will likely contribute to separatist movements within China.

The East Asian Diaspora

The East Asian world in religious terms now extends to the Chinese (most from the southern provinces of Fujian, Chunking, and Kwangting) who have migrated throughout the modern era to rule Singapore and to become significant minorities with great economic importance in Vietnam, Cambodia, Malaysia, Thailand, and Indonesia. Smaller concentrations of Chinese immigrants are found in most every major city of the modern world. Like Chinese restaurants that now span the globe, the East Asian religious traditions have likewise been transported and can be found wherever Chinese have settled, from New York City and San Francisco to Honolulu, from Rome and Istanbul to Manila. Roughly 100 million Chinese have left the mainland, and in these communities the older Chinese traditions have been continued (typically in the variants carried by the immigrants from the home province of China). Both through their numbers and through their extraordinary wealth (estimated at $450 billion), transoceanic and entrepreneuring Chinese are playing a decisive role in shaping post-Communist China and underwriting the restoration of Chinese religious traditions there. The same pattern on a lesser scale can be discerned with Koreans, Japanese, and Vietnamese.

"New Religions" of East Asia: Japan and Korea

In the aftermath of war and cultural revolution in the years since 1945, all the peoples of the East Asian region—Chinese, Japanese, and the Koreans—have had to rebuild, and in so doing have restored many elements from older, often ancient, traditions. In every sphere, religion is returning to both private and public life, from Tian'anmen Square to Tokyo. Yet it is also true to say that while there has been reconstruction, there has also been an irreversible break of continuity with the past, as symbolized most dramatically by the awesome explosion of the atomic mushroom cloud over Hiroshima.

One characteristic of this period is the continuing formation of "new religions." In the Japanese media cliché, new religion groups proliferated after World War II "like bamboo sprouts after a fire," but in fact many groups there and in Korea probably would have emerged earlier absent the imperial Japanese government's policy of suppressing any group perceived as potentially weakening the citizenry's adherence to its nationalistic Neo-Shintoism. Still, the crisis of defeat in World War II, the discrediting of the older "establishment faiths" allied with the state, and the strong freedom of religion guaranteed in the new constitutions in Japan and South Korea all abetted religious leaders who wished to share their spiritual experiences and visions to rebuild their societies. The number of such movements, the diversity of perspectives, and the ambitions of the activists mark the East Asian region's thirst for spiritual experience in the aftermath of World War II.

Falun Gong

The role of governmental tolerance in encouraging this phenomenon can be highlighted simply by mentioning the lack of new religions in the People's Republic of China during the same period. But barely a quarter century after Mao's death, the Communist leadership discovered that its liberalizations had given space for the formation of a powerful new Chinese religion called Buddhist Law (*Falun Gong* or *Falun Dafa*). After it spread to millions across China—young and old, party members and poor migrating laborers—and built an organization across the nation, it began to attract government criticism and episodes of forceful intimidation. In late April of 1999, the group staged a successful protest against these actions, with ten thousand members surrounding the Community party leadership compound in central Beijing. Arriving undetected, they sat in silent, nonviolent protest throughout the day, and then dispersed without incident. This action baffled and unsettled the government, provoking first an official warning against future protest actions, then by summer an all-out propaganda offensive, with leaders arrested and charged with antigovernment subversion. By the fall, Falun Gong had been outlawed as pernicious superstition; the thousands of members in small groups who continued to stage protests against this persecution were imprisoned and tortured.

Falun Gong resembles the other new religions we have described in Korea and Japan: its doctrines comprise an original recombination of Buddhist and Daoist doctrines, and its founder, a charismatic leader named Li Hongzhi, claims supernormal status, "on a level the same as Buddha and Jesus." Its principal practice of qi gong exercises promises to promote individual health and spiritual transformation through the generation of extraordinary energy, connecting with Daoist traditions at least two millennia old. Claiming 100 million followers in China and thirty other countries, Master Li has written texts and used mass media (videos, audio tapes, and Internet Web sites) to spread disciples' connection with him and his teachings. Falun Gong is an apt example of religion in the age of media technology, when faiths are becoming global.

Christianity

Christianity, too, could be placed as a new religion in East Asia. It is difficult to gauge the size of the Christian community, since despite laws guaranteeing freedom of religion, China continues to persecute and repress groups that do not accept the Communist Party regulations. Reports describe the recent conversion rate as high, however. A number of prominent democracy activists who converted have described the faith's special appeal to those who see only a dramatic break with the past as the means of transforming China. One Chinese scholar estimated that in 2006, across China there is one new Daoist temple built every month and one new Buddhist monastery built every week, but there is one new church being built *every day*.

Buddhism and different Christian denominations today command loyalty in rough parity (30%) among South Korea's population. This is the largest percentage seen in any Asian country. This national response appears to be related in part to the disintegration of all indigenous religions during the chaotic first five decades of this century when the Japanese occupation (1910–1945) and the national war (1950–1953) inflicted widespread destruction. Yet here, shamanic healing and ancestor veneration are still integrated with Christian practices.

As economic development proceeds in China and Korea, and to the extent that the traditional sectarian religions Buddhism and Daoism fail to adapt their doctrinal presentations and institutions to meet the changes under way in their societies, the established new religions are likely to continue to make gains, and Christian groups likewise. New new religions will doubtless arise for this reason as well.

The Pull of Religious Nationalism: Japan's Yasukuni Shrine Controversy

As we note in the final chapter, every modern country has developed its own "civil religion" that seeks to legitimate its existence and policies. Civil religions draw upon each nation's historical traditions; find expression in flags, pledges of allegiance, anthems, and currency; and are embodied in the national monuments of the capital cities. In every nation, they seek to elicit the population's loyalty, especially its claim to tax income and require the service of its citizens, not least from the young who can, in wartime, be asked to give their lives for the "sacred motherland."

In Japan, this last element underlies the belief that a prime minister should express his gratitude to all who gave their lives for the county. Since 1869, the Yasukuni shrine in Tokyo has been one central place where this reverence is shown, where all the souls of the dead veterans have found an eternal presence by their names being enshrined collectively in a memorial ledger. Every August on the "All Souls Festival" (see "All Souls Festival"), this duty to the dead, whose souls in traditional belief are thought to assemble there, must be acted on. Out of Confucian respect and fear of supernatural reprisal, the millions of dead who sacrificed everything for the nation, and the well-being of their eternal souls, cannot be ignored. Yet what might at first be seen as a free expression of religion is no longer so simple: In the postmodern global world, the inward-directed national traditions of civil religion now have an international audience. Chinese, other Asians, and Americans are well aware that among the war dead at Yasukuni are notorious war criminals, and that displays there showing war memorabilia glorify war and treat the departed as heroes; a Prime Minister showing them reverence, as has been done every year through 2006, is taken as evidence that Japan has not really taken responsibility for its war atrocities. Here, a short civil religion ceremony and belief in ancestor ritual has become a crucial and divisive element in international relations.

A Third Confucian Epoch?

Although the analysis of East Asia's economic revival as due to the region's Confucian roots remains contested, there are signs of Confucian renewal in each country seeking to guide the respective societies, yet without abandoning the classical tradition. In the "Third Epoch" view, the traumas of the modern era did succeed in liberating the Confucian world view from the trappings of power that had developed in the imperial systems of China, Korea, and Japan. These had corrupted the application of the highest ideals, and turned the "mastery" of the classics into mere exercises in memorization needed for the imperial examinations.

Now the movement seeks to return to the basic teachings of the early sages (Confucius, Mencius, of the "First Epoch") and do what Master Zhu Xi and other reformers did in their time (Song Dynasty, 960–1276), when they revived, reinterpreted, and adapted the tradition to the challenges of their era posed by Daoism and Buddhism (the "Second Epoch" of Neo-Confucianism). The "Third Epoch" Confucian exponents, working in the states on the periphery of China and loosely aware of their separate initiatives, are now addressing their communities as each East Asian nation faces the challenges of globalization in economics and culture. Examples are found in Japan in the many private Confucian societies, especially among the Kyushu University professors who are active in training corporate executives; in Korea (now the most Confucian of the region's nations) in the official school curriculum, in the rites performed in the Confucius temple in Seoul, and in the T'oegyehak movement; in Taiwan, as propagated by the Friends Association of Oriental Humanism and in the outreach programs of the Confucius-Mencius Scholarly

Society of Chen Lifu; and in the People's Republic of China through the post-1989 sanctioning of Confucian study. Also in this direction is an initiative by the Chinese government begun in 2004, establishing "Confucius Institutes" at (as of 2007) forty universities in twenty-five U.S. cities and in twenty other countries, including Australia, Sweden, Japan, and Great Britain. Although their first priority is to teach Chinese language, these institutes are also tasked with promoting a greater understanding of Chinese culture and history.

Such efforts to revive the spiritual tradition has made Third Epoch exponents critical of the global modernizing process, especially when it has resulted in the extreme fragmenting of society, promoted the vulgarization of social life, disregarded the public good, or overglorified the value of wealth. The vast majority of modernist Confucians adopt this critical stance while also being committed to modern Euro-American values such as empirical science, democratic politics, and the economic development in their own countries.

Yet the global vision of Third Epoch exponents is also to bring the Confucian tradition into the debate about how the twenty-first century's international order should be conceived, bringing its world view into dialog with the ideologies of sociopolitical modernization and consumerism prominent in the Euro-American world. One exponent summarized this goal as follows:

Copernicus de-centered the earth, Darwin relativized the godlike image of man, Marx exploded the ideology of social harmony, and Freud complicated our conscious life. They have redefined humanity for the modern age. Yet they have also empowered us with communal, critical self-awareness, to renew our faith in the ancient Confucian wisdom that the globe is the center of our universe and the only home for us and that we are the guardians of the good earth, the trustees of the Mandate of Heaven that enjoins us to make our bodies healthy, our hearts sensitive, our minds alert, our souls refined, and our spirits brilliant....We are Heaven's partners, indeed co-creators....Since we help Heaven to realize itself through our self-discovery and self-understanding in day-to-day living, the ultimate meaning of life is found in our ordinary human existence.[14]

Informed by very different notions of religious truth and by their own ethnocentric notions of their own central place in the cosmos, will the world's people outside East Asia be interested in such a dialog?

DISCUSSION QUESTIONS

1. What beliefs from each of the three traditions of the region might explain the East Asian peoples' unique capacity for sustaining the three without choosing just one?

2. How is the ancestral cult related to the norms of Confucian family morality?

3. A Chinese novelist in the colonial period described the Chinese family as "a prison

ward" that denies basic rights to the individual, exploits women, and wastes the energy of the young. How would you defend Confucian ideals against these criticisms?

4. What Daoist teachings would explain the Chinese capacity to embrace Buddhism despite strong teachings about the inferiority of non-Chinese?

5. How could Neo-Confucianism be seen as an attempt to harmonize Buddhism, Daoism, and early Confucianism?

6. Why, from the Daoist perspective, would disasters in the natural world be taken so seriously by politicians in East Asia?

7. In the modernization of Japan, how might the influences of Buddhism have been mediated by the samurai class that was so influenced by Zen culture?

8. Why do purity and brightness sum up the ethos of Shintoism?

9. Is the fate of Daruma-san a reflection of how irrelevant Zen ideals have become in the popular imagination, or is this an apt cultural reminder embedded in the "diffuse popular religion" of Zen Buddhism's embracing a spirituality that connects the transcendent with the comic?

10. Critique the following proposition: China's religious revival was postponed by the Chinese Communists who imposed a "forced conversion" of the nation to the "new religion" it imported from Europe, Marxism-Leninism.

11. For all the nations of East Asia, the colonial era was very destructive. But there are also examples of individuals fusing ideas from global culture with older beliefs, creating new and original religious understandings. Cite an example of this process in China, Korea, and Japan.

12. What influences from the West might have influenced elites in East Asia to claim that "Chinese (or Japanese) are "not religious"?

KEY TERMS

Amaterasu	diffuse religion	Master K'ung
Analects	Five Classics	Mencius
ancestor veneration	Guan Yu	mudang
Ching Ming festival	Hong Xiuquan	nembutsu
Ch'ondogyo	hsaio	Neo-Confucianism
City God	Huang-di	Neo-Shintoism
Confucius	kami	"new religions"
Confucianism	Kitchen God	Nichiren
Cultural Revolution	Lao Zi	qi
Dao	li	qi gong
Daoism	ling	ren
Daruma	mappo	shamanism

Shang-di	*te*	*wu-wei*
shen	"Three Faiths"	*yin-yang* theory
Shinto	T'oegyehak	Zhu Xi
Soka Gakkai	T'u-ti	Zhuang Zi
Taiping Rebellion	Unification Church	

SUGGESTED READING

H. Byron Earhart, *Japanese Religion: Unity and Diversity* (Belmont, Calif.:
 Wadsworth, 1983)

Laurel Kendall, *Shamans, Housewives, and Other Restless Spirits: Women in Korean
 Ritual Life* (Honolulu: University of Hawaii Press, 1985)

Lewis R. Lancaster, ed., *Contemporary Korean Religion* (Berkeley, Calif.: Institute for
 East Asian Studies, 1992)

Peter H. Lee, ed., *Sources of Korean Tradition: From Early Times to the 16th Century*
 (New York: Columbia University Press, 1996)

Donald S. Lopez, Jr., ed., *Religions of China in Practice* (Princeton, N.J.: Princeton
 University Press, 1996)

Donald E. MacInnis, *Religion in China Today* (New York: Orbis, 1989)

John K. Nelson, *A Year in the Life of a Shinto Shrine* (Seattle: University of
 Washington Press, 1996)

S. D. B. Picken, *Shinto: Japan's Spiritual Roots* (Tokyo: Kodansha International, 1980)

Ian Reader, *Religion in Contemporary Japan* (Honolulu: University of Hawaii Press,
 1991)

_____ and George J. Tanabe, Jr., *Practically Religious: Worldly Benefits and the
 Common Religion of Japan* (Honolulu: University of Hawaii Press, 1998)

T. R. Reid, *Confucius Lives Next Door: What Living in the East Teaches Us About Living
 in the West* (New York: Vintage Books, 1999)

Laurence G. Thompson, *Chinese Religion: An Introduction*, 5th ed. (Belmont, Calif.:
 Wadsworth Publishing, 1996)

Holmes Welch, *The Practice of Chinese Buddhism, 1900–1950* (Cambridge, Mass.:
 Harvard University Press, 1973)

NOTES

1. In D. C. Lau, *Confucius: The Analects* (New York: Penguin, 1979), p. 63.

2. In D. C. Lau, *Mencius* (New York: Penguin, 1970), p. 191.

3. Quoted in Stephen Teiser, "Popular Religion," *Journal of Asian Studies* 54(2),
1995, 378.

4. In Wing-sit Chan, *A Source book of Chinese Philosophy* (Princeton, N.J. Princeton University Press, 1973), 86–87.

5. Ibid., pp. 497–498.

6. Timothy Brook, "Rethinking Syncretism: The Unity of the Three Teachings and Their Joint Worship in Late-Imperial China," *Journal of Chinese Religions*, 21, 1993, 17.

7. Ibid., 18.

8. Ibid., 22.

9. Quoted in Wing-tsit Chan, *Instructions for Practical Living and Other Neo-Confucian Writings by Wang Yang-ming.* (New York: Columbia University Press, 1962), p. 272.

10. In Donald E. MacInnis, *Religion in China Today* (New York: Orbis, 1989), p. 206.

11. S. D. B. Picken, *Shinto: Japan's Spiritual Roots* (Tokyo: Kodansha International, 1980), p. 56.

12. Ian Reader, *Religion in Contemporary Japan* (Honolulu: University of Hawaii Press, 1991), p. 100.

13. Ian Reader, "The Rise of a Japanese 'New New Religion,'" *Japanese Journal of Religious Studies* 15(4), 1988, 244.

14. Tu Wei-ming, *Life Magazine*, December 1988, 76.

CHAPTER EIGHT

GLOBALIZATION FROM NEW TO NEW AGE RELIGIONS

Overview

Marie belongs to an Episcopal parish in Minneapolis, but she has other religious interests as well. Indeed, she regularly checks her astrological chart, and tonight she and her friend Allison are going to an introductory lecture on Transcendental Meditation. Last week, Marie's friend Jack talked her into going on a weekend retreat led by a psychic medium who offered to put people in touch with their dead relatives. In addition, Marie has been reading *Dianetics*, by Scientology founder L. Ron Hubbard, and she is thinking about responding to a questionnaire entitled, "Are You Curious About Yourself?" Distributed by the local Church of Scientology, the flyer had come with the morning newspaper.

All these activities mark Marie as one of countless individuals who are on a personal quest that is typical of new age religion: they are eager to explore the mystery of the "self" and its perfection. Marie has another friend, Mark, who thinks she is too self-absorbed and needs to pay more attention to issues of social justice in a global society that is shaped by mass media and multinational corporations and marred by racial and economic exploitation. Mark is trying to get her involved in a small interracial activist group inspired by the life and teachings of Martin Luther King Jr. All these approaches to life, and many more, as we shall see, could be grouped together under the heading of "new age religions."

In this chapter we will first explore what we mean by "new" religions and then focus primarily on "new age religions"—the distinctive forms that new religions and new ways of being religious have taken in response to globalization. New religions represent the integration of influences from multiple religions   523 and cultures, resulting in the creation of new variations and expressions of known religious practices. In one familiar pattern, a new prophet or sage reveals new understandings of an existing tradition, given to him or her in religious experiences or revelations.

In the past the message of prophets and sages reflected primarily local situations—typically the incursion of elements imported from nearby religions and cultures. Today, however, many new religious movements reflect not just a response to local diversity—to this or that movement that has entered the environment of a relatively stable culture. Rather, they are indicative of an awareness of global religious diversity as a whole, past and present. This awareness is fostered by mass communications and widespread access to transportation, introduced by modern science and technology.

It is in this new environment of the awareness of the diversity of human religious experience that the "new age" religions are emerging, both accommodating and integrating diverse elements of varying, often quite dissimilar, existing traditions. Some movements, however, represent the attempt to reassert particular forms of religious expression that adherents believe have been neglected but should be operative in the new age of global interdependence. Contemporary interest in shamanism and goddess worship would be examples of this. What these movements typically have in common is the belief that humanity is indeed entering a "new age" in which global harmony must be achieved, not only with other religions and cultures but also with the natural environment.

NEW RELIGIONS

Old Religions and New Religions in the History of Religions

From a historical perspective, as this book has amply indicated, no religion has ever managed to remain unchanged. Indeed, while every chapter in this book began with an "overview" description of the religious beliefs and practices of the tradition, in every case we went on to say that such a snapshot was no more than a broad generalization that did not accurately reflect the tremendous diversity found among practitioners, yesterday or today. There is not one Judaism but many, not one Buddhism but many—likewise there are many Christianities, many Islams and Hinduisms, many Daoisms and Confucianisms.

Every tradition tolerates a tremendous amount of diversity. An emerging movement that at first is treated as a form of error may finally be accepted into the fold, or at least tolerated as a distant cousin. It may, for example, be seen as a reform within the tradition to bring it back to its original purity. But then there are other movements, perhaps brought about by new religious experiences and extraordinary revelations, whose "errors" seem too great. Changes that had started out as reforms may present such a dramatic break with past beliefs and practices that they come to be perceived not as a continuation of the old tradition but as a fatal error—a deviation from the true path. The new tradition, of course, sees the error lying not in itself but in the old tradition, which had somehow lost its way.

Although before the Common Era there was more than one form of Judaism, Christianity, which began as a Jewish sect called the Nazarenes, came to be seen and, to see itself, as crossing a boundary that made it no longer a Jewish alternative but a "new religion." And while Christianity also encompasses tremendous diversity, when Islam emerged in Arabia in the seventh century it was seen by Christians as a new and heretical religion, even though Muslims recounted many of the same biblical stories and saw their faith as the continuation and culmination of God's revelations handed down through Moses and Jesus. Moreover, Islam developed two major branches, Sunni and Shiah, as well as many schools of theology and law. Later, in nineteenth-century Persia, when the Baha'i movement claimed to bring a final revelation that included all the religions, East and West, it too came to be viewed as "not true Islam," hence as a new belief system.

When we look at Asian religions we find the same pattern. Hinduism encompasses great diversity, and yet as Buddhism grew and developed, it was seen, and came to see itself, as a "new religion." Buddhism too splintered into many Buddhisms, some claiming to be more advanced than others.

Some movements emerged and then disappeared in every tradition. Even so, in century after century, many of "today's" new religions become tomorrow's old and established religions. We can illustrate the character of new religions with a few examples before turning to our primary concern, examples of "new age" religions that have appeared in our emerging global civilization. The relatively recent history of Christianity in North American culture presents an interesting illustration of how a new religion comes to be.

In the 1800s, Christian denominationalism began to emerge as a way of moving beyond the hostile sectarianism that had divided Christians, and by the late twentieth century there was a broad spectrum of religious diversity in America. Nevertheless, a number of very distinctive religious movements that originated in the nineteenth century tested the limits of denominationalism. As a rule, contemporary mainline Christian denominations (i.e., those representing widely established, long-accepted church traditions in America, such as the Methodists, Presbyterians, and Episcopalians) regard these unique movements as having strayed beyond the boundaries of Christianity. Mormonism provides us with a good example.

The Church of Jesus Christ of Latter-day Saints: A New American Christianity

The Church of Jesus Christ of Latter-day Saints, or Mormonism, was established on April 6, 1830, by Joseph Smith Jr. It appears to have arisen in response to the confusion created by the incredible sectarian diversity of nineteenth-century Christianity. Joseph Smith believed he had been led by angels to discover a revelation that would overcome this confusion. The new revelation, contained in the Book of Mormon, was understood by Smith and his followers as a continuation of the revelation given in the Bible. It was a revelation that had been given first to Native Americans, as descendants of the lost tribes of ancient Israel. Mormons believe that these tribes had migrated to the North American continent, where the risen Christ visited them and gave them new revelations. Eventually the book containing these pronouncements was buried by a Native American named Mormon, who was killed by tribesmen who rejected the new message and wanted to suppress it. It was these "pagan" natives who met Columbus in 1492. But the revelation could not be suppressed forever, and so Joseph Smith was guided by angels to find the Book of Mormon so that it could flourish once more.

Earlier we noted the incorporation into Christianity of traditions specific to Africa and Asia. Similarly, Mormonism links biblical religion to the history of an indigenous population—in this case producing a distinctively American Christianity, one that includes visits of the risen Christ and several of the risen apostles to a new land, to guarantee the purity of Mormon revelation and so set it apart from existing human interpretations of Christianity. The capstone of the message was the promise that at the end of the "latter days," Christ would return to establish a "New Jerusalem" in America. Mormonism, with its emphasis on family, community, and healthy, wholesome living, has flourished, with well over 10 million members worldwide.

Ahmadiyyat: A New Islamic Religion

The Ahmadiyyat is an example of a new religious movement in modern Islam. From its inception in 1899 in British India, it has been one of the most active, progressive, and controversial movements in Islam, rejected by many Muslims as heretical. Mirza Ghulam Ahmad, the founder, was born in Qadian, a village in the Punjab. He wrote prolifically, built and expanded the organization, and engaged in sometimes heated debates with many Sunni ulama and Christian missionaries.

Ghulam Ahmad described his spiritual status and mission in both messianic and prophetic terminology. His claim to be a renewer of Islam, a mujaddid, fell within the boundaries of official Islam or orthodoxy. When he assumed the titles of Mahdi and prophet, however, he was roundly condemned by the ulama and by prominent Muslim groups like the Jamaat-i-Islami. Ahmad answered criticisms by saying that unlike legislative prophets, like Jesus and Muhammad, who bring God's revelation and divine law to the people, he had a divine mandate to renew and reform the Islamic community. Thus, as a nonlegislative prophet, Ahmad affirmed the finality of the prophethood of Muhammad while maintaining that God continued to send religious reformers like himself to provide prophetic guidance to the Islamic community.

The Ahmadis are great supporters of modern education and Islamic reform. As a global missionary movement they have established a large network of mosques and centers and peacefully propagated their faith in Asia, Africa, Europe, and America.

Civil Religion in China and the United States

Civil religions represent yet another form in which new religious movements can accomplish very traditional roles in a society. In most times and most places throughout the history of civilization, religion and politics permeated all of culture and were like two sides of the same coin. It was, as we have seen, modernity that introduced secular nation-states and the idea that government should not impose on citizens the obligation to join or practice any religion. But having removed religion as a legitimizer of their own authority, these modern states faced a new problem—winning loyalty from their citizens without the traditional appeal to religion. The result has been the creation of a distinct entity we shall call "civil religion," which reintroduces religion under the disguise of "indigenous cultural history and tradition" to reinforce the authority of new and more secular socio-political orders.

Thus a civil religion is based on a sacred narrative of the state's founding, in which the development of the state is portrayed as a just moral enterprise, in harmony with ideals of the religious traditions shared by most citizens. Typically, the state's leaders developed a set of national rituals and yearly holidays (holy days) that celebrate and allow the regular, solemn reliving of key events the nation's history. Such civil religions come to expression in national anthems and patriotic songs, school textbooks that emphasize the righteousness of the country's founders, and war memorials honoring those who sacrificed their lives for the nation.

In many cases, the cultural pattern from one tradition (Christianity, Islam, Confucianism etc.) clearly comes to underlie the nation's civil religion, though seldom to the extent of specific endorsement. What is striking is how nearly all the great ideas in the history of religions (e.g., sacrifice, sage, prophet, martyrdom, sacred center, "chosen people," rebirth, millennialism) have been adopted across the world in the service of creating and sustaining the civil religions that support modern nations. Two examples will illustrate this: Chinese Communist civil religion and civil religion in the United States.

Chinese Communist Civil Religion   When the Red Army gained control of the mainland of China in 1949, Communist party leader Mao Zedong ascended the southern gateway to the emperor's old palace in Beijing (the Forbidden City) to proclaim the creation of the People's Republic of China. This moment was later pictured on currency and in popular prints, and soon thereafter an immense portrait of Chairman Mao was mounted over the ancient gateway, where it hangs to this day. Over the next 25 years, the Communist party drew upon a variety of religious conceptions to legitimate its position in China and to wield power. The Communist millennial doctrine, imported from Russian revolutionaries but rooted in the prophetic biblical understanding, insisted that a paradise on earth was inevitable if the people changed their ways and lived in thoroughgoing cooperation. Citizens who sacrificed themselves for the common good were immortalized as "heroes of the people," their dying was said to hasten the arrival of the new age.

Early on, the government adapted ancient Confucian imperial doctrine to promote the cult of Mao himself as the sage–philosopher leader of the nation, whose words and teachings were pivotal for national salvation, whose character radiated the morality of communist truth. Statues of Mao were put up in public spaces around the nation, his portrait replaced images of family ancestors in home shrines, and during the Cultural Revolution (1966–1976) his "Little Red Book" became a sacred text to be memorized, followed, and always possessed. Officially, the Communist party disavowed religion as superstition and railed at long-dead Chinese emperors as feudal exploiters of the masses. Nevertheless, it is not hard to see how party strategists adapted powerful religious ideas from both European and Chinese traditions to create a civil religion to confirm the legitimacy of the dictatorship.

American Civil Religion   American civil religion as found in the United States develops from European colonization, justifying the history of American ancestors claiming the land "from sea to shining sea" as being part of a divine plan unfolding its "manifest destiny." God is said to have given America as a "promised land," to those who are his "chosen people" to foster the sacred values of freedom and democracy. Thus the narrative of American civil religion presents the United States as a "city on a hill," called by God to be a model for all nations.

Although founded by those who consciously avoided the establishment of any state religion, American civil religion, according to sociologist Robert Bellah, appeals to George Washington as the "Father" of the country while Abraham Lincoln is its "Savior" who led the nation from the sin of slavery through the crisis of civil war, dying in the service of the sacred land and leading to its moral and spiritual renewal. National holidays such as Presidents' Day, the Fourth of July, Memorial Day, and Thanksgiving celebrate American civil religion. The rituals of these celebrations connect patriotism to the sacredness of the American way of life and God's special blessings on the United States.

As the record of the recent past makes clear, civil religion has had the effect of assimilating individuals and diverse ethnic groups into the world's new nations. But the rise of civil religions has also led to excesses, fueling genocidal campaigns by states on four continents against those who are not part of their sacred history.

NEW AGE RELIGIONS

The New Age: Modern and Postmodern

The collapse of colonialism was followed by the emergence of globalization—the development of international corporations, global mass transportation, and global mass media under the impact of science and technology. Logically enough, then, since the 1960s and 1970s new patterns of religion have appeared that reflect a global consciousness. The religions shaped by science and technology as well as by the traditional considerations, although incredibly diverse, are often grouped together under the title "new age religions." Not all new age religions are postmodern as we have defined that term. Indeed, many are content to continue the modernist pattern of privatization rather than seek a new public role for religion. But global consciousness has been a significant factor in the emergence of all new age religions. In this section and the next, we will look at examples of modernist and postmodernist new age religions.

In the first chapter we cited Jean-François Lyotard's definition of postmodernism as the collapse of metanarratives, the grand stories or myths that gave each civilization a sense of meaning, purpose, and identity. The great metanarratives crafted a relationship of identity between religion and culture, giving us Hindu civilization, Christian civilization, Islamic civilization, and so on. Each civilization was centered in its own grand stories and the social practices that came from the vision of life the stories promoted. Modernism and its myth of scientific progress was a relatively recent addition.

The problem with a secular understanding of time, history, and society is that the significance and drama provided by the grand narratives of religions are missing. The resurgence of religions since the 1970s may well represent the need to fill the vacuum created by the tendency of secularization to purge events of meaning. Pluralism may have collapsed the grand metanarratives into smaller stories, but there is still a great hunger for such stories, and new age religions help people discover the meaning and significance of time and their place in it. New age religions provide a rich feast for the religious imagination as seekers attempt to penetrate the mysteries of their time and to explore the wonders it offers.

Postmodern culture represents the loss of a normative center in every culture that has been touched by global mass media, international corporations, and global mass transportation. Postmodern culture is pluralistic, relativistic, and eclectic—seemingly without any public norms or standards. The choice between "truths" is said to be intellectually undecidable and so is decided pragmatically, in terms of "what works for me." Truth, goodness, and beauty are in the eye of the beholder. People mix and match beliefs, practices, and aesthetic choices to their own taste in all areas of life—whether music, clothing, architecture, intellectual beliefs, or religion.

Globalization provides the social context of postmodernism. Globalization "marbelizes" all cultures so that the world's religions are accessible in everyone's hometown. Today, much more than in the past, in the same community you will find Jews, Christians, Muslims, Hindus, Buddhists, and many others. Such pluralism is a powerful social force inducing the collapse of the metanarrative, whereby a story that was once embraced by almost all people in a given culture is now simply one of many stories. In this situation religions are challenged first to relinquish their position of being identical with the culture and then to accommodate an existing cultural pluralism. In this context, almost all religious communities have had to embrace denominational identities, accepting the existence of other beliefs and practices, although fundamentalist communities strive mightily to resist such an accommodation. This, we said, was what sociologist Peter Berger meant by saying that all religions have become "Protestant." But for most new age groups their religious practices have gone a step further, moving from organizational pluralism (denominationalism) to eclecticism.

Many of the "new age" religions, like older "new religions," represent the integration of the diverse influences from different traditions. The new age religions are not based solely on the great world religions; often they incorporate elements of primal religions, exhibiting a special interest in shamanism. Moreover, today these eclectic belief systems typically reflect not only global religious diversity but the global influence of science and technology as well.

New age religious movements can be divided into modernist forms, which continue to privatize religion, and postmodernist public forms of religious practice, which seek an active role, socially and politically, in transforming society. Most modernist new age religions are highly diverse in their practices and beliefs, with minimal organizational structure. Nevertheless, there are some very important instances of highly structured new age movements; as we shall see, Scientology is one. What unites new age seekers, despite their diversity, however, is the quest for the perfection of the self. Their goal is to realize a "higher self" through intense personal experiences of transformation.

Many new age seekers are not interested in joining religious organizations. They typically integrate a variety of interests into their personal style of spiritual practice. Many read "spiritual" books and go to workshops and seminars intended to guide them to self-realization. Modernist "new agers" are interested in such shamanistic practices as channeling information from other-worldly spiritual beings, contacting the dead through mediums, spiritual healing, and the cultivation of ecstatic out-of-body experiences (sometimes referred to as "astral projection"). They are also interested in the mystical traditions and meditation practices of all religions, as well as the ancient divination practice of astrology. Some combine these interests with the teachings and practices of transpersonal psychologists such as Abraham Maslow (1908–1970) and Fritz Perls (1894–1970); others embrace speculative visions that combine the "new physics" with religion, believing that science itself is finally coming to discover and affirm ancient religious and metaphysical insights. The final test of each seeker's synthesis is personal experience and pragmatically evaluated usefulness.

Modernity, we learned in the chapter on Christianity, emerged out of the splitting of the medieval unity of faith and reason into *via moderna* of empirical rationality and the *devotio moderna* of personal emotional experiences of transformation (mysticism, pietism, and the experience of being "born again"). The first path became dominant in the Enlightenment and the second in the Romantic movement, as a reaction to the Enlightenment. The growth of new age religiousness is deeply rooted in this Romantic reaction to the rationalism of the Enlightenment.

The Enlightenment emphasized universal rationality, science, progress, and the sameness of human nature. Its philosophers rejected the ancient, the archaic, the traditional, the idiosyncratic, and the nonrational. The Romantic reaction did just the opposite, embracing in all their diversity the emotional, the experientially transformational, the historically unique and particular, and the "primitive" and traditional.

Like fundamentalist evangelical Christianity, modernist forms of new age religions are expressions of the human need for transformative experience, a need as old as shamanism and as recent as the Romantic reaction to Enlightenment rationalism. Both de-emphasize rationality and focus on the experiential transformation and perfection of the self through deeply emotional experiences of the kind we have called religious. And both share the conviction that all social change begins by changing the self.

The Age of Apocalypse or the Age of Aquarius?

Two new age models of religious meaning are playing a role in our emerging global civilization—the apocalyptic and the astrological. These models share a vision of the conflict and discord of the past and present giving way to a future era of global peace and harmony. Among Christian evangelicals the popularity of the belief that the end of time is near is evidenced by sales of tens of millions of books like Hal Lindsey's *The Late Great Planet Earth* and the *Left Behind* series of novels. As indicated by the popularity of biblical prophecies of the end times among evangelical Christians, there are still many heirs to the apocalyptic religious vision of the medieval monk Joachim of Fiore, who anticipated a "third age" (the age of the Spirit) as a time of global peace and harmony. However, the third age will be preceded by the biblical apocalypse, which in turn will bring the cataclysmic end of time. The belief that there will be a cataclysmic end to time followed by a new age of peace and harmony is also illustrated in such late-twentieth-century movements as the Unification Church and Aum Shinrikyo, to be reviewed shortly. But first we will turn to the alternative vision—the astrological vision of the age of Aquarius.

A gentler vision of the new age, the age of Aquarius, has been offered by some astrologers in recent decades: "We are passing out of 2,000 years of Piscean astrological influence into the influence of Aquarius, which will affect all aspects of our culture as we move from Piscean structures of hierarchical devotion to more fluid and spontaneous relationships that dance to an Aquarian rhythm."[1] Predictions of the coming of a new age by others not of the apocalyptic tradition include the writings of Jose Arguelles. In his book *The Mayan*

Factor, this new age author used ancient Mayan and Aztec astrology to calculate that the age of Aquarius would begin in 1987, on August 16 or 17.[2]

In these Aquarian times, many forms of new age religion tap into a very ancient type of religious experience found in primal animistic and early urban polytheistic religious practices—that of the shaman. As we saw in Chapter 2, in his or her ecstatic or out-of-body experiences, the shaman explores the spirit world, the realm of contact with spiritual beings and dead ancestors.

Everywhere in the world, shamanism appears to be the earliest form of religious experience. And everywhere, the great world religions emerge with the discovery that the shaman's realm is really an intermediate spiritual realm between the earthly physical world and a higher unitary reality. For example, in the Vedas of Hinduism the highest realities are the many gods and goddesses of nature, but in the Upanishads the discovery is made that the gods are part of the order of this world of samsara and that there is a higher power beyond their realm, the reality of Brahman.

The emergence of monotheism out of polytheism in the Mediterranean world (in Judaism, Christianity, and Islam) provides another example. The polytheistic realm of the gods was not denied. It could not be denied because many people continued to have shamanistic-type experiences of another realm, inhabited by spiritual beings. So this realm of the deities was reassigned to a different kind of spiritual being and renamed the realm of angels and demons. Like the devas or gods of Hinduism, angels were recognized as spiritual beings, yet they were part of the cosmic order created by a higher reality, God. In China this concept of a higher unitary reality was given the impersonal name of Dao.

For all the differences between ancient urban religious cultures and religions in postmodern society, there is at least one profound similarity between them: both premodern urban society, as typified by the polytheistic culture of ancient Rome, and postmodern society, with its myriad eclectic religious practices, lack an integrating center. In both, being religious is not so much about belonging to "a religion" as it is about selecting from the chaotic variety of available beliefs and practices, a mix that will serve the pragmatic purposes of finding health, happiness, and meaning, that is, of having the unseen powers that govern your destiny on your side.

Wicca and the Resurgence of Goddess Worship

Determining how many people "practice new age religion" is next to impossible. This is because it is quite common for nominal adherents to one of these belief systems to practice several different forms in their private life, while perhaps also belonging to a traditional church or synagogue. One form this eclectic spirituality can take is sometimes called "neopaganism," which is vividly exemplified in a return to the practice of witchcraft, or attunement to the sacred powers of nature, a pattern found in all premodern societies. The most prominent such practice today is Wicca, which appears to be a self-conscious reconstruction of ancient pagan religious practices. The Wiccan movement can be traced back to England in the 1940s and the writings of Gerald Gardener, who claimed to be an initiate of a Wiccan coven, authorized to reveal its teachings and practices to the public. Two students of Gardener's brought the practice to America in the 1960s. By 1965 a church of Wicca was established in Mississippi, and by 1978 the handbook for U.S. military chaplains included Wicca in its list of religions.

Wiccans see the world ordered by sacred forces that can be accessed through ritual magic. These powers are personified as gods and goddesses. Wiccan rituals involve the elaborate use of chant, dance, drumming, and meditation. By following the ancient Celtic agricultural cycle of festivals for the seasons of the year, these rituals enable Wiccans to reconnect with the rhythms of nature and to experience its hidden unity. Many tend to see their ritual practice as an outward expression of the fundamental truth of the interconnectivity of all things, a view that they believe modern science also affirms. One strand of Wicca, Dianic Wicca, presents itself as a feminist religion that rejects references to gods in favor of goddess worship and has radicalized its practice by banning male membership.

The Convergence of Science, Technology, and Religion: The Path to Scientology

The precedents for Wicca and many other forms of new age religion go back to the interest in esoteric religious beliefs and practices that flourished in the nineteenth century, when historical and ethnographic researchers were just beginning to catalog the diverse practices of primal (tribal) and archaic (early urban) religions. From Europe, the teachings of Emanuel Swedenborg (1688–1772) and Franz Anton Mesmer (1734–1815) spread belief in the validity of the shamanistic experience of other worlds and in the animistic unity of all things, which made spiritual healing possible. In America, Ralph Waldo Emerson (1803–1882) and others popularized a school of thought called transcendentalism, which integrated certain Asian religious beliefs (especially Hinduism) with American philosophy, affirming the existence of a "world soul" that all beings shared. In this context the practice of spiritualism also flourished, with psychic mediums performing in private séances the ancient shamanistic rituals for contacting spirit beings and dead relatives.

One of the most important movements to emerge at this time was Theosophy, founded in New York by Helena Petrovna Blavatsky (1831–1891) in 1875. Like the transcendentalists, theosophists found great spiritual wisdom in esoteric teachings, especially in the ancient teachings of Hinduism, with their focus on the interconnectedness of all beings through the universal Brahman. In the theosophical view, all world religions have a hidden unity of message and metaphysical reality, which could be sought through the truths of esoteric texts, as well as through the help of leaders who claimed to receive guidance from "living masters," residing in the Himalayas. As we saw in Chapter Seven,

Theosophists had considerable influence among Asian reformers who were trying to modernize Buddhism. The growing interest in global religious wisdom was evident in the first Parliament of World Religions in Chicago in 1893, at which representatives of all the world's religions convened to share their views.

This historical milieu gave birth to two important nineteenth-century precursors of new age religion, both with roots in the nineteenth century "mind cure" movement: The Church of Christ, Scientist (Christian Science) and the New Thought movement. Women were leaders in both movements. Mary Baker Eddy was the founder of the Christian Science movement, and Emma Curtis Hopkins, a former disciple, broke with Eddy to form what would become the New Thought movement. The two movements drew on popular forms of philosophical idealism, and New Thought, while affirming a Christian orientation, included or adapted teachings from a number of religious traditions, including Hinduism, Buddhism, and the Western esoteric tradition. Both Christian Science and New Thought presented themselves as offering "scientific" practices that, when properly followed, allowed individuals to experience God or Divine Mind, leading to spiritual and physical healing and spiritual control over events and experiences in their lives.

As the new age religions began to appear in the twentieth century, the religious fascination with the authority of "science" broke free of its earlier linkage to Christianity in movements of the "Christian Science" type. One result was the emergence of Scientology, founded by L. Ron Hubbard (1911–1986). In 1950 Hubbard published *Dianetics: The Modern Science of Mental Healing*, in which he claimed to have discovered a cure for all human psychological and psychosomatic ills through the realization of a state of mind he called "Clear." Hubbard went on to establish the Hubbard Dianetic Research Foundation in Elizabeth, New Jersey. Later he moved the organization to Phoenix, Arizona, where the Hubbard Association of Scientologists was founded in 1952.

Scientology goes beyond the psychological orientation of Dianetics to develop an elaborate mythology according to which all humans were once advanced beings Hubbard called Thetans: all-powerful, eternal, and omniscient. The first Thetans relieved their boredom by playing mind games in which they used imagination to create different physical worlds. However, they soon forgot their true identity as creators and found themselves trapped in these worlds, living as mortals who died, only to be reincarnated again and again. At each reincarnation, people accumulated more psychological baggage, which Hubbard called engrams. To be liberated from this pattern and realize one's true identity, it is necessary to gain insight into one's engrams. Upon finally achieving the "Clear" state of mind, a person gains control over both mind and life. The auditing process that leads to this liberation came to involve the use of a machine that works somewhat like a lie detector. This device, the E-meter, it is believed, measures reactions of resistance to words and other symbols that

L. RON HUBBARD

Scientology was founded by L. Ron Hubbard (1911–1986). Although born in Tilden, Nebraska, Ron Hubbard was exposed to Asian religion and culture as a child because his father was in the navy. As a young man with an adventurous spirit Hubbard was involved in three Central American ethnological expeditions. He received a commission in the navy during World War II, during which service he was pronounced dead twice. In one instance he apparently had something like a shamanistic out-of-body experience in which he acquired spiritual knowledge that gave him his life's mission.

In 1950 Hubbard published *Dianetics: The Modern Science of Mental Healing*, which became the foundation for Scientology. According to *Dianetics*, the mind is made up of two parts, the analytic and the reactive. Traumatic experiences in early life, or even in the womb, are said to imprint themselves on the reactive mind as "engrams," which cause psychological and psychosomatic problems if they are not dissolved. The way to dissolve these traumatic impressions is to work with a counselor called an auditor, who leads the individual into reenacting the events that caused the trauma, thus releasing or liberating the individual from the engrams' negative effects. Hubbard called this state of release "Clear", and devotees of Scientology work hard to attain it.

reveal undissolved engrams. After achieving Clear, one can go on to higher states that involve out-of-body experiences.

In 1954 Hubbard established the first Church of Scientology in Washington, D.C., and in 1959 he started the Hubbard College of Scientology in England. Whereas many new age religious movements stress individualism and are quite loosely organized, Scientology has an elaborate global organization; bureaucratically and hierarchically, it is not unlike Roman Catholicism and Mormonism. Perhaps an even better analogy is to the modern international business corporation, with its penchant for technical language, efficient organization, and the dissemination of polished communications to interface with the world. And yet all this organization and efficiency is focused on bringing about a powerful experience of enlightenment or rebirth that perfects the self and opens it to the spiritual world that shamans have traversed throughout the ages.

Scientologists have also shown a keen interest in Buddhist teachings, and of course, the parallels of the auditing practices to depth psychology are obvious. The description of Clear by one Scientologist shows the movement's affinity with both Western experiences of being "born again" and Eastern experiences of enlightenment:

> There is no name to describe the way I feel. At last I am at cause. I am Clear—I can do anything I want to do. I feel like a child with a new life— everything is so wonderful and beautiful. Clear is Clear! It's unlike anything I could have imagined. The colors, the clarity, the brightness of everything is beyond belief. Everything is so new, I feel new born. I am filled with the wonder of everything.[3]

Scientology is, in many ways, the perfect illustration of the global eclectic integration of the elements that make up new age religions: science (especially psychology), technology (corporate and technical structure), Asian religions (reincarnation and the quest for liberation), and shamanism (out-of-body spiritual explorations). A Thetan, according to Hubbard, goes "through walls, barriers, vanishes space, appears anywhere at will and does other remarkable things."[4]

East Goes West: Transcendental Meditation

Transcendental Meditation (TM) is an example of an Asian religion moving West, yet another manifestation of the globalization process inherent in new age religion. The mantra system known by its trademarked name, Transcendental Meditation, first came to global public attention in the 1960s when its founder, Maharishi Mahesh Yogi, became the guru of the Beatles, then at the height of their popularity.

The Maharishi taught a kind of spiritual hedonism, according to which our desire to enjoy life is natural, holding that TM offers the most efficient path to this joy. One need not become an ascetic, fasting and meditating for endless hours: twenty minutes, twice a day, could suffice to bring spiritual transformation. Drawing on traditional teachings from Vedantic Hinduism, the Maharishi taught that happiness could be achieved by tapping into one's naturally serene self, a fragment of the universal Brahman self that all beings share. This is accomplished by stopping all distracting thoughts so that one's consciousness can reach its true center.

Becoming a practitioner was made fairly easy. There is an introductory lecture on the philosophy and scientific benefits of TM. Then in a second meeting, more advanced information is provided and the seeker is initiated. A short period of fasting precedes the initiation, and an offering of fruit, flowers, and money is brought to the event. Then the seeker is given a personal mantra, a secret Sanskrit phrase attuned to the individual's unique needs and temperament, that is to be chanted silently in daily meditation. This mantra must never be revealed to anyone. The initiation rites are followed by three days of supervised meditation and small-group discussions. After ten days the initiate returns for checking by his or her teacher and after that returns once a month.

MAHARISHI MAHESH YOGI

The Maharishi Mahesh Yogi, who had once studied physics in India, abandoned his academic courses to learn yoga from a master known as Guru Dev. Urged by his guru to take the teachings of yoga to the West, Maharishi journeyed to the United States, where he was able to tap the growing interest in Asian religions that was part of the cultural scene of the 1960s. He gave lectures to crowds all across America, hired a PR firm, made the TV talk shows, and drew a following among prominent actors and rock musicians. In the 1970s he founded the Maharishi International University in Fairfield, Iowa. In addition to the more conventional curriculum, the school offers a doctorate in the neuroscience of human consciousness, and all students and faculty meet twice a day to practice Transcendental Meditation.

Initially a countercultural protest against the commercial technobureaucracy ("the system") of modern society, TM soon adapted itself to this bureaucracy. In the 1970s the movement began to market itself to a corporate clientele, presenting workshops to upper-level personnel as a way of creating more efficient and happier professionals on and off the job. To achieve scientific legitimacy the movement attempted to accumulate hard evidence that twenty minutes of meditation twice a day improved sleep, greater oxygen consumption, and made one more creative and happier in life as a result of lower metabolism.

Like many of the new age movements, and perhaps more than most, TM offered a new "Methodism" for a new age. It provided a minimal set of required beliefs, and a simple methodical set of practices aimed at self perfection, all attuned to the needs of busy individuals in a modern scientificly and technologically oriented culture.

West Goes East: The Unification Church of Sun Myung Moon and Aum Shinrikyo

The new age religions we have looked at so far have been more Aquarian than apocalyptic. They have been rooted in the nature-oriented religions deeply attuned to the cycles of nature, like the astrological tradition that posits the Aquarian age. But other new age religions reflect the pattern of the eastward migration of biblical apocalyptic traditions, leading to some interesting integrations of West and East. The Unification Church, originating in Korea, is one such example.

Unification Church

The Unification Church reflects the impact of globalization, for it is the product of colonialism and the very successful impact of Christian missions in

Korea, as noted in Chapter 2 on Christianity and Chapter 7 on East Asian religions. But, even more, it is an example of the transformation of Christianity in a new cultural environment, followed by the exportation of this new form of Christianity back to the West, especially to the United States.

The founder of the Unification Church, Sun Myung Moon, established a religion of divine principle called Tong Il. Eventually, Tong Il became known in the West as the Unification Church. In its earliest form this movement drew heavily on Korean shamanism, emphasizing out-of-body travels, healing, communication with spirits, and so on. As the religion moved from East to West, these elements have been downplayed. The church's global outreach really began with the emigration of Sun Myung Moon to the United States in 1971. Like Scientology (and to a lesser degree like TM), the movement showed a penchant for organization and public relations. Just as Scientology developed a reputation for attracting famous entertainers, the Unification Church courted political and academic figures with some success.

Unification's teachings are based on Moon's book, *Divine Principle*, which is really a kind of Asian or Daoist interpretation of the Bible in terms of polarities, or opposites (divine–human, male–female, etc.), beginning with the polarity of male and female in God. As in the Confucian traditions, these polarities are arranged hierarchically. The proper fourfold foundation of social order puts God at the top, then male and female as equals, with children at the bottom. The lowest order shows deference to the next higher, and all defer to God.

According to Moon's teachings, the "original sin" was Lucifer's spiritual seduction of Eve, leading her to rebel against God, after which she seduced Adam, who had intercourse with her before the time God intended, undermining the proper order of love and deference. To restore the sacred order, says Moon, God has repeatedly sent great prophets—Abraham, Moses—Jesus—but none were able to succeed. If Jesus, for instance, had not been destroyed by his enemies, he (as the second Adam) would have married a second Eve and reinstituted the right order of family and society.

Moon teaches that God has sent three "Israel's" to attempt to redeem the world. First he chose the Jews, then the Gentiles. In the twentieth century he chose the Koreans as the people of salvation, and a Korean (Moon himself) is the third Adam. Just as the early Hebrews, the first Israel, suffered persecution at the hands of the Babylonians, and the second Israel, in the days of the second Temple, at the hands of the Romans, so Korea, the third Israel, suffered at the hands of the Japanese during World War II. Finally, in Korea Satan is making his last stand. For in Korea the forces of God and Satan (democracy and communism) are engaged in the final apocalyptic conflict. But God has chosen as the divine center for the salvation of the world Korea, where East and West have met. Confucianism, Buddhism, and Christianity have come together, and now God has sent Rev. and Mrs. Moon, a third Adam and Eve, to restore the human race and complete the unification mission.

SUN MYUNG MOON

Sun Myung Moon, the founder of the Unification Church, was born in 1920 in northern Korea, where his family joined the Presbyterian church. Moon's experience presents striking parallels to that of Joseph Smith and the emergence of the Church of Latter-day Saints (Mormonism) in the United States. In both cases, the risen Christ visits a country far from the Middle East to establish it as the new center of salvation history.

Sun Myung Moon says that when he was 16 years old, Jesus appeared to him on Easter Sunday and told him to "complete my mission." Over time, Moon says, he also was visited by other great religious figures, including Abraham, Moses, and Buddha. For nine years he struggled against "satanic forces," and as he began to draw a small following, he was arrested, imprisoned, and tortured by the Communists—an ordeal his followers see as divinely ordained suffering that will lead to the redemption of the human race from the sin of the first parents, Adam and Eve.

Moon was liberated from his imprisonment during the Korean War and took refuge in the southern part of the penninsula. There he established a "religion of divine principle" called Tong Il. It soon became known in the West as the Holy Spirit Association for the Unification of World Christianity, or the United Family, and finally as the "Unification Church."

Moon's followers generally believe that Moon is the new Messiah and that he and his wife are the new and true parents who are regenerating the human race. To effect this regeneration, Sun Myung Moon chooses marriage partners for his followers and then, with his wife, officiates at mass wedding ceremonies, which have attracted considerable media attention. For the movement, every new crop of married couples furthers the struggle against the Communists, Satan's representatives on earth, who Moon depicts as arrayed against himself as demonic agents in a lifelong cosmic battle. Though famous globally, the Unification Church claims only a modest number of adherents in Korea.

Aum Shinrikyo

An apocalyptic new age vision has also taken root in Japan, and members of one cult, Aum Shinrikyo, achieved global notoriety and terrorist status when they released deadly sarin gas into the Tokyo subway system in 1995.

The Aum Shinrikyo ("Supreme Truth") movement is the creation of Chizuo Matsumoto, who in 1986 changed his name to Shoko Asahara and registered his two-year-old group as a religion with the Japanese government. Having done this, he attracted additional followers by writing extensively in his country's

new age religious publications, promising to teach seekers out-of-body shamanistic skills such as clairvoyance and teleportation. He had a charismatic personality, and his movement, which has had an extraordinary appeal to the
university-educated professional class, quickly became one of the fastest growing new religions in Japan.

Through a well-developed bureaucracy with Asahara at the top, Aum
Shinrikyo established monastic-like separatist communities throughout Japan,
where the most devoted followers congregated, having left their families and
given all their earthly belongings to the movement. Descriptions of the initiation rituals have mentioned the heavy use of hallucinogens, the drinking of vials
of Asahara's blood, and a total surrender to Asahara as the spiritual master.

In the beginning Asahara taught that the world would end soon and that it
was the task of his followers to save humanity through their hard work in Aum
business ventures and through purification by personal spiritual practices.
After Asahara and some his hand-picked leaders were decisively defeated in an
attempt to win seats in Japan's parliament in 1990, Asahara's teachings took a
darker turn, seeking to destroy what he believed were the demonic forces that
opposed his movement.

By 1993 Aum Shinrikyo had plants producing automatic weapons, as well as
chemical and biological weapons, ostensibly to protect Japan against its enemies. Believing that the United States was about to trigger an apocalyptic nuclear war, Aum scientists traveled to Russia and Africa in search of biological
and nuclear weapons. Aum Shinrikyo's following in Russia by 1995 was estimated at 30,000, roughly three times its membership in Japan. The group's terrorist plans, however, were known only to a small, mostly Japanese, elite.

Asahara came under legal scrutiny for his varied activities, especially after
authorities learned that the worth of Aum's assets exceeded 1 billion dollars. In
1994, convinced that the Japanese government's special police force had set out
to destroy him, Asahara ordered the assassination of three judges by releasing
poison gas in their neighborhoods. The judges survived, but some innocent
bystanders were killed. The next year, after the Tokyo subway gassing, he was
arrested.

Asahara integrated Japanese Shinto beliefs with Hinduism and Tibetan
Buddhism in a way that appealed to many young Japanese professionals (including scientists) by calling into question modern materialism as well as the
stress and decadence of modern life. Indeed, influenced by the science fiction
of Isaac Asimov, Asahara developed a vision of the role of scientists as building an elite secret society that would save civilization from cataclysmic wars.
To this he added a strong dose of Christian apocalyptic expectations (mixed
with the predictions of Nostradamus) about the imminent end of the world in
a battle between good and evil. He justified his murderous assaults on his fellow citizens by pronouncing that killing those who are creating bad karma was
actually doing them a spiritual favor, since it stopped them before they produced even more negative karma.

SHOKO ASAHARA (CHIZUO MATSUMOTO)

As a child in a school for the blind, Aum Shinrikyo founder Chizuo Matsumoto boasted that he would one day be prime minister of Japan. Yet the early years of the severely sight-impaired youth were not promising. After two failures to enter the Japanese university system, he joined a new religious movement called Agonshu, which mixed Buddhist, Daoist, and Hindu teachings. In 1984 he broke with Agonshu and developed a personal religious vision, integrating elements of Hindu yoga, Buddhist meditation, and Christian apocalyptic beliefs. He visited India in 1986 and had what he believed to be a powerful enlightenment experience. Convinced that he was destined to be a great spiritual master, Chizuo Matasumoto, then the leader of his own small movement, took on the name of Shoko Asahara and changed the name of his group to Aum Shinrikyo.

To his followers, Asahara declared himself to be Jesus Christ, come to bring judgment upon the world. In preparation for the global nuclear war he believed the United States to be plotting, he bought land in Australia. There his followers could start to build a new civilization as they waited out the years of lethal radiation in a devasted Northern Hemisphere. Ultimately, Asahara was convicted for having masterminded the Tokyo sarin gas attack. He was sentenced to death in 2004, and the movement, which regrouped under the name Aleph ("the beginning") still reveres him as its spiritual leader.

Like Scientology, Aum Shinrikyo illustrates the integration of shamanism and Eastern mysticism with scientific research and technological applications organized by a highly efficient globally oriented bureaucratic organization. The difference between them is equally important, for Asahara's eclectic religious vision adds elements of Western apocalyptic thought colored by his own paranoid vision of himself as the rejected prophet and spiritual master. The result was dangerously violent.

RELIGIOUS POSTMODERNISM AND GLOBAL ETHICS

The Challenge of Postmodern Secular Relativism

As explained in the chapter on Christianity, the difference between fundamentalists and modernists stems from an argument about the impact of science on traditional religious beliefs. Fundamentalists often seem to believe they must oppose science to reaffirm traditional religious beliefs, whereas modernists seem to embrace science, preferring to adapt religious beliefs to the changing understanding science brings.

Fundamentalists generally had no objection to the use of science to invent things like the automobile or for the creation of better medications. When science impinged on religious beliefs concerning the origins of humanity and the right way to order society, however, many drew a line. If the human self and society do not have sacred origins but are the result of biological evolution and human decisions, then the human self and society seem to be set adrift in a world without meaning, purpose, or ethical norms.

As modern science and technology—and the worldview they foster—were carried around the world by colonialism, the impact of modernity was felt in different ways in different societies and cultures. Not every religious tradition emphasizes orthodoxy ("right beliefs") the way Christianity does. For example, Hinduism, Judaism, and Islam place far more emphasis on orthopraxy ("right actions"), the maintenance of a sacred way of life. Thus the most common feature of the fundamentalist reaction to modernity across religions and cultures is the desire to preserve the premodern sacred way of life against the threat of secularization and the normless relativism it seems to engender.

The social sciences of the nineteenth century promoted a technological viewpoint according to which society itself could be redesigned, just as engineers periodically redesign cars. The use of scientific and technological inventions per se was relatively uncontroversial. Many, however, rejected treating the social order in a secular and technological fashion, as if society could or should be shaped and reshaped by human choices, without regard to the sacred ways of one's ancestors. In our chapter on Christianity, we pointed to the emergence of existentialism as a watershed moment in the history of modernization, opening the door to postmodern relativism by calling into question the idea of "human nature" and arguing that both self and society were the products of human choices.

For many, this seeming disappearance of human nature is terrifying, suggesting that we as human beings know neither who we are nor what we ought to do. This is the mindset Nietzsche was addressing when he said that "modern man" had murdered God and so now wandered the universe without a sense of direction. For many today, it seems that the secular "technologized" understandings of self and society can only lead to moral decadence—a decadence in which the family and the fabric of society will be destroyed. Those who believe that secularization is robbing humanity of an understanding of its sacred origins and destiny reject technologized understandings of self and society. As an antidote, they favor a return to the fundamental truths about human nature as understood in premodern times.

Modernization is often presented in terms of a story about the secularization of society, that is, the liberation of the various dimensions of cultural life from the authority of religion. Since religion in premodern societies preserves the sacred by governing every aspect of life, modernization and secularization are threats to traditional societies everywhere.

Nevertheless, sacralizing society to protect a divinely ordered way of life is not the only role religion has played in history. The great sociologist Max Weber pointed out that religion not only sacralizes and reinforces the unchanging "routine" order of society, sometimes it also "charismatically" desacralizes and transforms society. Brahmanic Hinduism sacralized caste society in ancient India, but Buddhism began as a movement to desacralize the priestly elite and see all persons in the caste system as capable of achieving spiritual deliverance. Sacralization is total and readily accommodates hierarchies (e.g., a caste system, a multitiered priesthood), whereas desacralizing breaks with caste, inviting pluralism and equality.

Because religions (even the same traditions) often manifest dramatically opposing values and orientations, the sociologist Jacques Ellul has argued that it is helpful in understanding the role of religion in society to distinguish between two terms that are typically used interchangeably: "sacred" and "holy." In his view, the experience of the sacred leads to a view of society as an order that is itself sacred and must be protected from all profane attempts to change it. The experience of the holy, on the other hand, calls into question the very idea of a sacred order. It desacralizes (or secularizes) society and seeks to introduce change in the name of a higher truth and/or justice. According to this view, the same religious tradition can express itself in opposite ways in different times and places. In Asia, early Buddhism called into question the sacred order of Hindu caste society, but later Buddhist societies developed their own sacred orders. Early Daoists in China called into question the sacred hierarchical order of Confucianism but later also integrated themselves into the sacred order of Confucian society by means of the neo-Confucian synthesis.

In the West, early Christianity, sharing a common ethos with Judaism, called the sacred order of Roman civilization into question, but medieval Christianity resacralized Europe. Then later, Protestantism desacralized the medieval European social order and unleashed the dynamics of modernism. From this perspective, the struggle between fundamentalism and modernism in the modern world that we have surveyed in this textbook is an example of the conflict between the sacralizing and desacralizing (secularizing) roles of religion.

Religious fundamentalists express the desire to preserve the sacredness of human identity in a rightly ordered society against what they perceive as the chaos of today's decadent, normless secular relativism. To restore the sacred normative order, therefore, they tend to affirm the desirability of achieving the premodern ideal of one society, one religion. They remain uncomfortable with the religious diversity that thrives in a secular society.

Religious modernism as it emerged in the West rejected the fundamentalist ideal, adopted from premodern societies, of identity between religion and society. Instead of dangerous absolutism, modernists looked for an accommodation between religion and modern secular society. They argued that it is possible to desacralize one way of life and identity to create a new identity that preserves the essential values or norms of the past tradition, but in harmony with a new modern way of life. Modernists secularize society and privatize their religious practices, hoping by their encouragement of denominational forms of religion to ensure an environment that supports religious diversity.

What we are calling religious postmodernism, like religious modernism, accepts secularization and religious pluralism. But religious postmodernism, like fundamentalism, rejects the modernist solution of privatization and seeks a public role for religion. It differs from fundamentalism, however, in that it rejects the domination of society by a single religion. Religious postmodernists insist that there is a way for religious communities in all their diversity to shape the public order and so rescue society from secular relativism. The chief example of this option is the model established by Mohandas K. Gandhi. Because his disciples rejected the privatization of religion while affirming religious diversity, Gandhi's movement is a postmodern new age religious movement rather than a modern one.

Exploring Religious Diversity by "Passing Over": A Postmodern Spiritual Adventure for a New Age of Globalization

All the great world religions date back a millennium or more, and each provided a grand metanarrative for the premodern civilization in which it emerged—in the Middle East, in India, and in China. In the past these world religions were relatively isolated from one another. There were many histories in the world, each shaped by a great metanarrative, but no global history.

The perspective of religious postmodernism arises from a dramatically different situation. We are at the beginning of a new millennium, which is marked by the development of a global civilization. The diverse spiritual heritages of the human race have become the common inheritance of all. Modern changes have ended the isolation of the past, and people following one great tradition are now very likely to live in proximity to adherents of other faiths. New age religion has tapped this condition of globalism, but in two different ways. In its modernist forms it has privatized the religious quest as a quest for the perfection of the self. In its postmodern forms, without rejecting self-transformation, it has turned that goal outward in forms of social organization committed to bettering society, with a balance between personal and social transformation.

The time when a new world religion could be founded has passed, argues John Dunne in his book, *The Way of All the Earth*. What is required today is not the conquest of the world by any one religion or culture but a meeting and sharing of religious and cultural insight. The postmodern spiritual adventure occurs when we engage in what Dunne calls "passing over" into another's religion and culture and come to see the world through another's eyes. When we do this, we "come back" to our own religion and culture enriched with new insight not only into the other's but also our own religion and culture—insight that builds bridges of understanding, a unity in diversity between people of diverse religions and cultures. The model for this spiritual adventure is found in the lives of Leo Tolstoy (1828–1910), Mohandas K. Gandhi (1869–1948), and Martin Luther King Jr. (1929–1968).

Two of the most inspiring religious figures of the twentieth century were Mahatma Gandhi and Dr. King. They are the great champions of the fight for the dignity and rights of all human beings, from all religions and cultures. Moreover, they are models for a different kind of new age religious practice, one that absorbs the global wisdom of diverse religions, but does so without indiscriminately mixing elements to create a new religion, as is typical of the eclectic syncretism of most new age religions. Yet clearly these religious leaders initiated a new way of being religious that could occur only in an age of globalization.

Martin Luther King Jr. stated repeatedly that his commitment to nonviolent resistance, or civil disobedience, as a strategy for protecting human dignity had its roots in two sources: Jesus' Sermon on the Mount and Gandhi's teachings of nonviolence derived from his interpretation of the Hindu sacred story called the *Bhagavad Gita*. Gandhi died when King was a teenager, but the American clergyman did travel to India to study the effects of Gandhi's teachings of nonviolence on Indian society. In this he showed a remarkable openness to the insights of another religion and culture. In Gandhi and his spiritual heirs, King found kindred spirits, and he came back to his own religion and culture enriched by the new insights that came to him in the process of passing over and coming back. Martin Luther King Jr. never considered becoming a Hindu, but his Christianity was profoundly transformed by his encounter with Gandhi's Hinduism.

Just as important, however, is the spiritual passing over of Gandhi himself. As a young man, Gandhi went to England to study law. His journey led him not away from Hinduism but more deeply into it. For it was in England that Gandhi discovered the *Bhagavad Gita* and began to appreciate the spiritual and ethical power of Hinduism.

Having promised his mother that he would remain vegetarian, Gandhi took to eating his meals with British citizens who had developed similar commitments to vegetarianism through their fascination with India and its religions. It is in this context that Gandhi was brought into direct contact with the nineteenth-century Theosophy. In these circles of new age globalization he met Madam Blavatsky and her disciple Annie Besant, both of whom had a profound influence upon him. His associates also included Christian followers of the Russian novelist Leo Tolstoy, who, after his midlife conversion, had embraced an ethic of nonviolence based on the Sermon on the Mount (Matthew 5–7).

At the invitation of his Theosophist friends, Gandhi read the *Bhagavad Gita* for the first time, in an English translation by Sir Edwin Arnold, entitled *The Song Celestial*. It was only much later that he took to a serious study of the

Hindu text in Sanskrit. He was also deeply impressed by Arnold's *The Light of Asia*, recounting the life of the Buddha. Thus, through the eyes of Western friends, he was first moved to discover the spiritual riches of his own Hindu heritage. The seeds were planted in England, nourished by more serious study during his years in South Africa, and brought to fruition upon his return to India in 1915.

From his Theosophist friends, Gandhi not only learned to appreciate his own religious tradition but came to see Christianity in a new way. For unlike the evangelical missionaries he had met in his childhood, the theosophists had a deeply allegorical way of reading the Christian scriptures. This approach to Bible study allowed people to find in the teachings of Jesus a universal path toward spiritual truth that was in harmony with the wisdom of Asia. The power of allegory lay in opening the literal stories of the scripture to reveal a deeper symbolic meaning based on what the theosophists believed was profound universal religious experience and wisdom. From the Theosophists, Gandhi took an interpretive principle that has its roots in the New Testament writings of St. Paul: "the letter killeth, but the spirit giveth life" (2 Corinthians 3:6). This insight would enable him to read the *Bhagavad Gita* in the light of his own deep religious experience and find in it the justification for nonviolent civil disobedience.

Gandhi was likewise profoundly influenced by Tolstoy's understanding of the Sermon on the Mount. The message of nonviolence—love your enemy, turn the other cheek—took hold of Gandhi. And yet Gandhi did not become a Christian. Rather, he returned to his parents' religion and culture, finding parallels to Jesus' teachings in the Hindu tradition. And so he read Hindu scriptures with new insight, interpreting the *Bhagavad Gita* allegorically, as an enjoinder to resist evil by nonviolent means. And just as King would later use the ideas of Gandhi in the nonviolent struggle for the dignity of blacks in America, so Gandhi was inspired by Tolstoy as he led the fight for the dignity of the lower castes and outcasts within Hindu society, and for the liberation of India from British colonial rule.

Gandhi never seriously considered becoming a Christian any more than King ever seriously considered becoming a Hindu. Nevertheless, Gandhi's Hindu faith was profoundly transformed by his encounter with the Christianity of Tolstoy, just as King's Christian faith was profoundly transformed by his encounter with Gandhi's Hinduism. In the lives of these two twentieth-century religious activists we have examples of "passing over" as a transformative postmodern spiritual adventure.

Whereas in the secular forms of postmodernism all knowledge is relative, and therefore the choice between interpretations of any claim to truth is undecidable, Gandhi and King opened up an alternate path. While agreeing that in matters of religion, truth is undecidable, they showed that acceptance of diversity does not have to lead to the kind of ethical relativism that so deeply troubles fundamentalists. For in the cases of Gandhi and King, passing over led to a sharing of wisdom among traditions that gave birth to an ethical coalition in defense of human dignity across religions and cultures—a global ethic for a new age.

By their lives, Gandhi and King demonstrated that the sharing of a common ethic and of spiritual wisdom across traditions does not require any practitioners to abandon their religious identity—another worrisome issue for fundamentalists. Instead, Gandhi and King offered the model of unity in diversity. Finally, both Gandhi and King rejected the privatization of religion, insisting that religion in all its diversity plays a decisive role in shaping the public order. And both were convinced that only a firm commitment to nonviolence on the part of religious communities would allow society to avoid a return to the kind of religious wars that accompanied the Protestant Reformation and the emergence of modernity.

The spiritual adventure initiated by Gandhi and King involves passing over (through imagination, through travel and cultural exchange, through a common commitment to social action to promote social justice, etc.) into the life and stories and traditions of others, sharing in them and, in the process, coming to see one's own tradition through them. Such encounters enlarge our sense of human identity to include the other. The religious metanarratives of the world's civilizations may have become "smaller narratives" in an age of global diversity, but they have not lost their power. Indeed, in this Gandhian model, it is the sharing of the wisdom from another tradition's metanarratives that gives the stories of a seeker's own tradition their power. Each seeker remains on familiar religious and cultural ground, yet each is profoundly influenced by the other.

Tolstoy, Jesus, and "Saint Buddha": An Ancient Tale with a Thousand Faces

Although at first glance, the religious worlds of humankind seem to have grown up largely independent of one another, a closer look will reveal that hidden threads from different religions and cultures have, for centuries, been woven together to form a new tapestry, one that contributes to the sharing of religious insight in an age of globalization. In *Toward a World Theology*, Wilfred Cantwell Smith traces the threads of this new tapestry, and the story he tells is quite amazing.[5] Smith notes, for example, that to fully appreciate the influence on Gandhi of Tolstoy's understanding of the Sermon on the Mount, it is important to know that Tolstoy's own conversion to Christianity, which occurred in a period of midlife crisis, was deeply influenced not only by the Sermon on the Mount but also by the life of the Buddha.

Tolstoy was a member of the Russian nobility, rich and famous because of his novels, which included *War and Peace* and *Anna Karenina*. Yet in his fifties, Tolstoy went through a period of great depression that resolved itself in a powerful religious conversion experience. Although nominally a member of the (Russian) Orthodox Church, Tolstoy had not taken his faith seriously until he came to the point of making the Sermon on the Mount a blueprint for his life. After his conversion, Tolstoy freed his serfs, gave away all his wealth, and spent the rest of his life serving the poor.

As Wilfred Cantwell Smith tells it, a key factor in Tolstoy's conversion was his reading of a story from the lives of the saints. The story was that of Barlaam and Josaphat. It is the story of a wealthy young Indian prince by the name of Josaphat who gave up all his wealth and power, and abandoned his family, to embark on an urgent quest for an answer to the problems of old age, sickness, and death. During his search, the prince comes across a Christian monk by the name of Barlaam, who told him a story. It seems that once there was a man who fell into a very deep well and was hanging onto two vines for dear life. As he was trapped in this precarious situation, two mice, one white and one black, came along and began to chew on the vines. The man knew that in short order the vines would be severed and he would plunge to his death.

The story was a parable of the prince's spiritual situation. Barlaam points out that the two mice represent the cycle of day and night, the passing of time that brings us ever closer to death. The paradox is that like the man in the well, Josaphat cannot save his life by clinging to it. He must let go of the vines, so to speak. He can save his life only by losing it. That is, if he lets go of his life now, no longer clinging to it but surrendering himself completely to the divine will, this spiritual death will lead to a new life that transcends death. This story and its parable touched the deeply depressed writer and led him first to a spiritual surrender that brought about his rebirth. Out of this rebirth came a new Tolstoy, the author of *The Kingdom of God Is Within You*, which advocates a life of nonviolent resistance to evil based on the Sermon on the Mount.

The story of the Indian prince who abandons a life of wealth and power and responds to a parable of a man about to fall into an abyss is of course a thinly disguised version of the life story of the Buddha. Versions of the story and the parable can be found in almost all the world's great religions, recorded in a variety of languages (Greek, Latin, Czech, Polish, Italian, Spanish, French, German, Swedish, Norwegian, Arabic, Hebrew, Yiddish, Persian, Sanskrit, Chinese, Japanese, etc.). The Greek version came into Christianity from an Islamic Arabic version, which was passed on to Judaism as well. The Muslims apparently got it from members of a gnostic cult in Persia, who got it from Buddhists in India. The Latinate name *Josaphat* is a translation of the Greek *Loasaf*, which is translated from the Arabic *Yudasaf*, which comes from the Persian *Bodisaf*, which is a translation of *Bodhisattva*, a Sanskrit title for the future Buddha.

The parable of the man clinging to the vine may be even older than the story of the prince (Buddha) who renounces his wealth. It may well go back to early sources at the beginnings of Indic civilization. It is one of the oldest and most universal stories in the history of religions and civilizations. Tolstoy's conversion was brought about in large part by the story of a Christian saint, Josaphat, who was, so to speak, really the Buddha in disguise.

The history of the story of a great sage's first steps toward enlightenment suggests that the process leading to globalization may have started much earlier than we had thought. Therefore the line between new religions and new age (globalized) religions may not be as sharp as previously assumed. We can see that the practice of passing over and coming back, of being open to the stories of others, and of coming to understand one's own tradition through these stories is in fact very ancient. Therefore, when Martin Luther King Jr. embraced the teachings of Gandhi, he embraced not only Gandhi but also Tolstoy, and through Tolstoy two of the greatest religious teachers of nonviolence: Jesus of Nazareth, whose committed follower King already was, and Siddhartha the Buddha. Thus from the teachings of Gandhi, King actually assimilated important teachings from at least four religious traditions—Hinduism, Buddhism, Judaism, and Christianity. This rich spiritual debt to other religions and cultures never in any way diminished Martin Luther King Jr.'s faith. On the contrary, the Baptist pastor's Christian beliefs were deeply enriched, in turn enriching the world in which we live. The same could be said about Gandhi and Hinduism.

Gandhi's transformation of the *Bhagavad Gita*—a Hindu story that literally advocates the duty of going to war and killing one's enemies—into a story of nonviolence is instructive of the transforming power of the allegorical method that he learned from his Theosophist friends. The *Bhagavad Gita* is a story about a warrior named Arjuna, who argues with his chariot driver, Krishna, over whether it is right to go to war if it means having to kill one's own relatives. Krishna's answer is Yes—Arjuna must do his duty as a warrior in the cause of justice, but he is morally obliged to do it selflessly, with no thought of personal loss or gain. Gandhi, however, reinterpreted the story of Arjuna and Krishna as a story of hate conquered by love, untruth conquered by the truth of civil disobedience.

If the message of spiritual realization in the *Gita* is that all beings share the same self (as Brahman or Purusha), how could the *Gita* be literally advocating violence? For to do violence against another would be to do violence against oneself. The self-contradiction of a literal interpretation, in Gandhi's way of thinking, forces the mind into an allegorical mode, where it can grasp the Gita's true spiritual meaning. Reading the *Gita* allegorically, Gandhi insisted that the impending battle described in the Hindu classic is really about the battle between good and evil going on within every self.

Krishna's command to Arjuna to stand up and fight is thus a "spiritual" command. But for Gandhi this does not mean, as it usually does in "modern" terms, that the struggle is purely inner (private) and personal. On the contrary, the spiritual person will see the need to practice nonviolent civil disobedience: that is, to replace "body force" (i.e., violence) with "soul force." As the *Gita* suggests, there really is injustice in the world, and therefore there really is an obligation to fight, even to go to war, to reestablish justice. One must be prepared to exert Gandhian soul force, to put one's body on the line, but in a nonviolent way.

In so doing, one leaves open the opportunity to gain the respect, understanding, and perhaps transformation of one's enemy.

The lesson Gandhi derived from the *Gita* is that the encounter with the other need not lead to conquest. It can lead, instead, to mutual understanding and mutual respect. King's relationship to Gandhi and Gandhi's relationship to Tolstoy are models of a postmodern spirituality and ethics that transform postmodern relativism and eclecticism into the opportunity to follow a new spiritual and ethical path—"the way of all the earth"—the sharing of spiritual insight and ethical wisdom across religions and cultures in an age of globalization.

On this path, people of diverse religions and cultures find themselves sharing an ethical commitment to protect human dignity beyond the postmodern interest in personal transformation the modernist ideal of privatization. Gandhi and King were not engaged in a private quest to perfect the self (although neither neglected the need for personal transformation). Rather, each man embarked on a public quest to transform human communities socially and politically by invoking a global ethical commitment to protect the dignity of all persons. The religious movements associated with both men fit the pattern of the holy that affirms the secularization of society and religious pluralism. Gandhi and King recovered the premodern ideal of religion shaping the public order but now in a postmodern mode, committed to religious pluralism.

The Children of Gandhi: An Experiment in Postmodern Global Ethics

In April 1968, Martin Luther King Jr., sometimes referred to as "the American Gandhi," went to Memphis to support black municipal workers in the midst of a strike. The Baptist minister was looking forward to spending the approaching Passover with Rabbi Abraham Joshua Heschel. Heschel, who had marched with King during the voter registration drive in Selma, Alabama, three years earlier, had become a close friend and supporter. Unfortunately, King was not able to keep that engagement. On April 4, 1968, like Gandhi before him, Martin Luther King Jr., a man of nonviolence, was shot to death by an assassin.

The Buddhist monk and anti–Vietnam War activist Thich Nhat Hanh, whom King had nominated for a Nobel Peace Prize, received the news of his friend's death while at an interreligious conference in New York City. Only the previous spring, King had expressed his opposition to the Vietnam War, largely at the urging of Thich Nhat Hanh and Rabbi Heschel. King spoke out at an event sponsored by Clergy and Laymen Concerned about Vietnam, a group founded by Heschel, Protestant cleric John Bennett, and Richard Neuhaus, then a Lutheran minister. Now another champion in the struggle against hatred, violence, and war was dead. But the spiritual and ethical vision he shared with his friends, across religions and cultures, has continued to inspire followers throughout the world.

These religious activists—a Baptist minister who for his leadership in the American civil rights movement won the Noble Peace Prize, a Hasidic rabbi and scholar who narrowly escaped the death camps of the Holocaust, and a Buddhist monk who had been targeted for death in Vietnam but survived to lead the Buddhist peace delegation to the Paris peace negotiations in 1973—are the spiritual children of Gandhi. By working together to protest racial injustice and the violence of war, they demonstrated that religious and cultural pluralism do not have to end in ethical relativism and, given a commitment to nonviolence, can play a role in shaping public life in an age of globalization. The goal, Martin Luther King Jr. insisted, is not to humiliate and defeat your enemy but to win him or her over, bringing about not only justice but also reconciliation. The goal, he said, was to attack the evil in systems, not to attack persons. The goal was to love one's enemy, not in the sense of sentimental affection, nor in the reciprocal sense of friendship, but in the constructive sense of seeking the opponent's well-being.

Nonviolence, King argued, is more than just a remedy for this or that social injustice. It is, he was convinced, essential to the survival of humanity in an age of nuclear weapons. The choice, he said, was "no longer between violence and nonviolence. It is either nonviolence or nonexistence."

Truth is to be found in all religions, King said many times, and "injustice anywhere is a threat to justice everywhere. We are caught in an inescapable network of mutuality, tied in a single garment of destiny. Whatever affects one directly affects all indirectly."[6] The scandal of our age, said Abraham Joshua Heschel, is that in a world of diplomacy "only religions are not on speaking terms." He also said, no religion is an island, and all must realize that "holiness is not the monopoly of any particular religion or tradition."[7]

"Buddhism today," writes Thich Nhat Hanh, "is made up of non-Buddhist elements, including Jewish and Christian ones." And likewise with every tradition. "We have to allow what is good, beautiful, and meaningful in the other's tradition to transform us," the Vietnamese monk continues. The purpose of such passing over into the other's tradition is to allow each to return to his or her own place transformed. What is astonishing, says Thich Nhat Hanh, is that we will find kindred spirits in other traditions with whom we share more than we do with many in our own tradition.[8]

The Future of Religion in an Age of Globalization

Will the global future of religion and civilization be shaped by this Gandhian model of new age spiritual practice? It clearly offers an alternative to both traditional denominational modernist religions and the more privatistic modernist forms of new age religion. The Gandhian model also offers an alternative to the fundamentalist rejection of modernization, secularization, and the privatization of religion, which they fear can only lead to the moral decadence of ethical relativism. But the sharing of spiritual wisdom does require seeing the religions and cultures of others as having wisdom to share, and not all will accept this presupposition. Nevertheless, the emergence of religious postmodernism means that in the future, the struggle among religions will most likely be not between fundamentalism and modernism, as a conflict between the sacred and the secular (public and private religion), but between the sacred and the holy—religious exclusivism and religious pluralism as alternative forms of public religion.

DISCUSSION QUESTIONS

1. What is the difference between a "new religion" and a "new age religion"?

2. How do modernist new age religious belief and practice differ from postmodernist new age religious belief and practice? Give an example of each.

3. How does new age religion relate to the split between faith and reason (the *via moderna* and the *devotio moderna*) that shaped the emergence of the modern

world through the Enlightenment and the Romantic reaction it provoked?

4. In what sense is "civil religion" a new way of being religious, and in what sense is it a very old way of being religious?

5. In what way is the postmodern path of religious ethics opened up by M.K. Gandhi and Martin Luther King Jr. similar to fundamentalist ideals for society, and in what way is it different?

KEY TERMS

civil religions	new religions	passing over
millennialism	new age religions	shamanism
neopaganism	non-violence	

SUGGESTED READINGS

Steve Bruce, *Religion in the Modern World* (Oxford: Oxford University Press, 1996).
Harold Coward, *Pluralism in the World Religions: A Short Introduction* (Oxford: Oneworld, 2000).
John S. Dunne, *The Way of All the Earth* (New York: Macmillan, 1972).
Robert S. Ellwood and Harry B. Partin, eds., *Religious and Spiritual Groups in Modern America*, 2nd ed. (Upper Saddle River, N.J.: Prentice Hall, 1973, 1988).
Darrell J. Fasching, *The Coming of the Millennium* (San Jose, Calif.: Authors Choice Press, 1996, 2000).
———, "Stories of War and Peace: Sacred, Secular and Holy," Sarah Deets and Merry Kerry, eds., *War and Word*, (Lanham, MD: Rowman and Littlefield, 2004).

————, and Dell deChant, *Comparative Religious Ethics* (Oxford: Blackwell Publishers, 2001).

Mark Juergensmeyer, *Terror in the Mind of God* (Berkeley: University of California Press, 2000).

————, ed. *Global Religions: An Introduction* (New York: Oxford University Press, 2003).

Gary Laderman, and Luis Leon, eds., *Religion and American Cultures*, Vol. 1 (Santa Barbara, CA: ABC Clio, 2003).

James R. Lewis, ed., *The Oxford Handbook of New Religious Movements* (Oxford: Oxford University Press, 2004).

Mikael Rothstein, ed., *New Age Religion and Globalization*, (Aarhus, Denmark: Aarhus University Press, 2001).

Kronerborg Reender, *New Religions in a Postmodern World*—, (Aarhus, Denmark: Aarhus University Press, 2003).

Bryan S. Turner, *Orientalism, Postmodernism and Globalism* (London: Routledge, 1994).

NOTES

1. William Bloom, *The New Age: An Anthology of Essential Writings* (London: Rider/Channel 4, 1991), p. xviii. Quoted in Steve Bruce, *Religion in the Modern World* (Oxford: Oxford University Press, 1996).

2. Sarah Pike, "New Age," quoted in Robert S. Ellwood and Harry B. Partin, eds., *Religious and Spiritual Groups in America*, 2nd ed. (Upper Saddle River, N.J.: Prentice Hall, 1988), p. 140.

3. Quoted in Ellwood and Partin, eds. *Religious and Spiritual Groups in America*, 2nd ed. (Upper Saddle River, N.J.: Prentice Hall, 1988), p. 140, citing a publication of the Church of Scientology of California dated 1970.

4. L. Ron Hubbard, *Scientology: The Fundamentals of Thought* (Edinburgh: Publications Organization Worldwide, 1968); originally published 1950. Quoted in Ellwood and Partin, eds., *Religious and Spiritual Groups in America*, 2nd ed. (Upper Saddle River, N.J.: Prentice Hall, 1988), p. 147.

5. Wilfred Contrell Smith, *Toward a World Theology* (Philadelphia: Westminster Press, 1981), Chap. 1.

6. Martin Luther King Jr., "Letter from Birmingham Jail," in King, *I Have a Dream: Writings and Speeches That Changed the World*, James M. Washington, ed. (San Francisco: HarperSanFrancisco, 1992), p. 85.

7. Abraham Joshua Heschel, *Moral Grandeur and Spiritual Audacity: Essays [of] Abraham Joshua Heschel*, Susannah Heschel, ed. (New York: Farrar, Straus & Giroux, 1996), pp 241, 247.

8. Thich Nhat Hanh, *Living Buddha, Living Christ* (New York: G. P. Putnam and Sons, Riverhead Books, 1995), pp. 9, 11.

GLOSSARY

INTRODUCTION

Metanarrative: a grand cosmic and/or historical story accepted by the majority of a society as expressing its beliefs about origin, destiny, and identity

Modern: a civilization that separates its citizen's lives into public and private spheres, assigning politics to public life while restricting religion to personal and family life. A dominant scientific metanarrative provides the most certain public truths people believe they know. Society and politics are governed by secular, rational, and scientific norms rather than religion

Postmodern: a society typified by diversity in both beliefs and social practices that has no single dominant metanarrative (other than the narrative of diversity) and is skeptical of finding either certain knowledge or norms in any public form of truth, whether religious or scientific

Premodern: a civilization in which there is no separation between religion and society. A dominant religious metanarrative provides the most certain truths people believe they know. By being a member of that culture, one automatically participates in its religious vision and lives by its religious norms

via analogia: a way of knowing spiritual reality through the use of analogy, for example, "God is my shepherd"

via negativa: the mystical way of knowing the highest spiritual reality (God, Brahman, etc.) by negating all finite qualities and characteristics; Hindus, for instance, say Brahman is "neti...neti"—not this and not that (i.e., Brahman is not a thing, Brahman is no-thing and therefore is pure nothingness, Brahman is beyond imagination and cannot be imaged, Brahman can only be known by a mystical experience of unknowing)

CHRISTIANITY

Augustinian: refers to views of St. Augustine, for example, his view of the separation of church and state, in which the state is answerable to the church in religious matters while the church is answerable to the state in secular matters—yet both exist to promote the spread of the Gospel

Catholic: those churches that define their Christian authenticity through apostolic succession

Christ: from Greek translation of the Hebrew word meaning "messiah" or "anointed one," title Christians apply to Jesus of Nazareth

Constantinianism: view of the unity of church and state, in which the state exists to rule over and protect the church as the official religion of the empire

Deism: Enlightenment view that God created the world the way a watchmaker creates a clock and leaves it to run on its own without interference

evangelical: refers to pietistic Christian movements that arose in response to the Enlightenment and also dogmatic divisions within Protestantism; emphasizes the unifying power of conversion as an emotional transformation rather than a rational/dogmatic one

Fundamentalist: term first emerged to refer to evangelical Protestants who believed that certain fundamental truths of the Gospel were threatened by modern interpreters; in general, fundamentalist movements in all religions see modernity as corrupting the fundamental truths and practices as they were expressed in the premodern stage of their respective traditions

Gospel: literally, "good news"; usually refers to the four Gospels of the New Testament, which retell the words and deeds of Jesus of Nazareth; can also refer to other similar ancient writings not included in the Christian scriptures

grace: expresses the idea of unmerited divine love and assistance given to humans

heresy: comes from Greek term that means "choice"; came to be used as a negative term for choosing to believe doctrines viewed as erroneous by those who considered themselves to be "more orthodox"

homoousios/homoiousios: first term used to assert that the Word of God through which all things were created is "the same as" God; second term was used to assert that this Word was "like God"; Council of Nicaea (325 CE) affirmed the first and rejected the second

incarnation: the eternal word of God became flesh in Jesus during his earthly life

justification by faith: Protestant Reformation doctrine formulated by Martin Luther, asserting that humans are saved by faith as a gift rather than through works of obedience to the law

Kingdom of God: the kingdom occurs whenever humans live in accord with the will of God and especially at the end of time when God will be all in all

original sin: the sin of Adam and Eve, who disobeyed the command of God not to eat the fruit of the tree of knowledge of good and evil; said to have affected all human beings by corrupting their will so that they are often unable to do the good they intend

Pentecostal: refers to churches that emphasize possession by the Holy Spirit and speaking in tongues

Protestant: the churches, beginning at time of Martin Luther, that reject mediation of the church through apostolic succession as necessary for salvation in favor of a direct personal relationship with God in Christ

Protestant ethic: term coined by sociologist Max Weber, who noted that the Calvinist branch of the Reformation fostered a belief in working hard and living simply for the glory of God, and as proof that one was among those destined to be saved; such as an attitude, Weber said, contributed to the accumulation of wealth needed for investment and fueled the Industrial Revolution and the flourishing of capitalist societies

redemption: root meaning is "to be rescued or freed," especially from slavery; used in both a literal and metaphorical sense: God redeemed Israel from slavery in Egypt and exile in Babylonia; God redeems sinners from punishment and death due to sin

sacraments: ritual actions, such as baptism and Holy Communion, said to impart the grace of God to Christians, usually through the mediation of ordained clergy

Second Coming: belief that Jesus, who died on the cross, arose from the dead, and ascended into heaven will return at the end of time to raise the dead and establish a new heaven and a new earth

Son of God: title applied to Jesus of Nazareth

Trinity: God as Father, Son, and Holy Spirit; meant to suggest that the transcendent God can be immanent in the world without losing his transcendence—when God acts in the world (as Son or Spirit), God does not cease to be father and Creator of the universe; therefore God is not many gods but one God in three persons

two natures, one person: doctrine affirmed by Council of Chalcedon (451 CE); in the one person of Jesus are two natures (divine and human) said to coexist in unity but without confusion or mixture, so that Jesus is fully human in everything except sin, and yet the fullness of God is also present in him and united to him

JUDAISM

Aggadah: the stories of the *Tanak* and *Talmud* that communicate spiritual truths

amoriam: the generation of sages that created the Gemara

Ashkenazi: Jews whose traditions originated in central and Eastern Europe

bar/bat mitzvah: the rite of passage for boys (bar mitzvah) whereby they become full members of Israel who are able to read and interpret Torah; in modern times a parallel rite for girls (bat mitzvah) has been established in some forms of Judaism

circumcision: the cutting of the foreskin of the penis as a sign of the covenant of Abraham

covenant: the agreement between God and the people Israel whereby they are chosen to be God's people; God agrees to guide and protect them; the people agree to follow God's commandments (*halakhah*)

diaspora: the dispersion of a religious people outside their geographic homeland, where they must live as a minority among others

dual Torah: the scriptures of Rabbinic Judaism, composed of the written Torah (*Tanak*) and the oral Torah (*Talmud*)

Gemara: see *Talmud*

Gentile: anyone not Jewish

Halakhah: the commandments of God revealed in the *Tanak* and commented on in the *Talmud;* the word means to walk in the way of God by obeying his commands or laws

haredim: Jewish ultra-Orthodox movements that reject all modernist forms of Judaism

Hasidism: a form of Judaism emerging in the eighteenth century, focused on piety and joy, with strong roots in Jewish mysticism

Israel: either Jews as a religious people or the land and state of Israel, depending on the context

Kabbalah: Jewish mysticism; the most important Kabbalistic work is the *Zohar;* for Kabbalists, God is the *En Sof,* the limitless or infinite, who manifests himself in the world through his *Shekinah,* or "divine presence" in all things; the reunion of all with the infinite through mystical contemplation will bring about nothing less than the messianic kingdom

kosher: what is suitable or fit, used especially in reference to foods permitted by Jewish dietary laws

Marrano: the Jews of Spain who were forced to convert to Christianity during the Inquisition but secretly continued to practice their Jewish faith

Mishnah: see *Talmud*

mitzvot: the commandments of God requiring deeds of loving kindness

Rabbinic: a rabbi is a teacher; the name came to designate the Judaism of the *dual Torah* created by the Pharisees, which came to be normative in the premodern period

Sephardi: Jews whose traditions originated in Spain and Portugal

Shema: the fundamental creed of Judaism: "Hear O Israel, the Lord our God, the Lord is One"

synagogue: a community centered on the study of Torah and prayer to God; the buildings used to house these activities also came to be known as synagogues

Talmud: the oral Torah, recorded in the *Mishnah,* and the commentary on the *Mishnah* called the *Gemara.* There are two Talmuds: the Bavli (Talmud of Babylonia) and the Yerushalmi (the Jerusalem Talmud); the former is considered the more comprehensive and authoritative

Tanak: the written Torah or Hebrew Bible, made up of Torah (the first five books from Genesis to Deuteronomy), Nevi'im (the prophets and historical writings such as Jeremiah and I and II Kings), and Ketuvim (the wisdom writings, such as Proverbs, Job, etc.)

tannaim: the generation of sages, beginning with Hillel and Shammai, that created the *Mishnah*

temple: a place to worship God or the gods in diverse religions; in Judaism only one temple was allowed for the worship of God in Jerusalem, whereas each Jewish community would have a synagogue for study and prayers

Zionism: the desire to return to the land of Israel as a homeland; in modern times, the secular movement started by Theodor Herzl that led to the formation of the state of Israel

Zohar: major book of Jewish kabbalism: *The Book of Splendor*

ISLAM

Allah: God

ayatollah: literally, "sign of God"; title used by certain Shiah religious leaders who are widely reputed for their learning and piety

bida: innovation or deviation in religious belief or practice

caliph (*khalifah*): successor of Muhammad as the political and military head of the Muslim community

dar al-Islam: the house or abode of Islam, as opposed to the house of war; territory controlled and ruled by Muslims

dawah: call, missionary work, proselytization

dhimmi: literally, protected non-Muslim peoples; refers to Jews and Christians (later extended to others) who were granted "protected" status and religious freedom under Muslim rule in exchange for payment of a special tax

fana: in Sufi usage, annihilation of the ego-centered self

faqih (pl. *fuqaha*): jurist, legal scholar; one who elaborates *fiqh*

faqir: ascetic mendicant mystic ideal; Sufi *shaykh*

fatwa: legal opinion or interpretation issued upon request by legal expert (mufti) to either judges or private individuals

fiqh: understanding; science of Islamic law; jurisprudence; human interpretation and application of divine law

hadith: narrative report of Muhammad's sayings and actions

hajj: annual pilgrimage to Mecca; all Muslims should make the hajj at least once in their lifetime, but it is recognized that individual circumstances may make compliance impossible

halal: permitted, allowed; when referring to food, indicates meat that has been slaughtered in religiously prescribed manner

al-haram al-sharif: the noble sanctuary

hijab: Arabic word for veil or external covering; can consist of headscarf alone or full body covering; also known as *chador* (in Iran) or *burqa* (in Afghanistan)

hijrah: migration; Muhammad's hijrah from Mecca to Medina in 622 marks the first year of the Muslim lunar calendar

hudud: quranically prescribed crimes and punishments for consumption of alcohol, theft, fornication, adultery, and false witnessing; some countries have adopted these punishments as evidence of the "Islamic" nature of their political rule and law

ibadat: worship, ritual obligations

ijma: consensus; in Islamic law, refers to agreement of scholars on interpretation of legal questions; some have reinterpreted this principle to justify the right of a parliament to enact legislation

ijtihad: human interpretation or independent reasoning in Islamic law

imam: in Sunni Islam, the prayer leader and the one who delivers the Friday sermon; in Shiah Islam, refers to Muhammad's descendants as legitimate successors, not prophets, but divinely inspired, sinless, infallible, and the final authoritative interpreter of God's will as formulated in Islamic law

Islam: submission or surrender to God

jahiliyyah: unbelief, ignorance; used to describe the pre-Islamic era

jihad: to strive or struggle; exerting oneself to realize God's will, lead a virtuous life, fulfill the universal mission of Islam, and spread Islam through preaching and/or writing; defense of Islam and Muslim community; currently often used to refer to the struggle for educational and social reform and social justice as well as armed struggle, holy war

khatam: seal or last of the prophets; Muhammad

khutbah: sermon delivered at Friday prayer session in the mosque

Mahdi: expected or awaited one; divinely guided one who is expected to appear at the end of time to vindicate and restore the faithful Muslim community and usher in the perfect Islamic society of truth and justice

majlis al-shura: consultative assembly

masjid: mosque; Muslim place of worship and prayer

minbar: pulpit in the mosque from which the Friday sermon (*khutbah*) is preached

muamalat: social interactions

muezzin: one who issues the call to prayer from the top of the minaret

mufti: legal expert, adviser, or consultant; one who issues *fatwas* to judges and litigants

mujaddid: renewer; one who comes to restore and revitalize the Islamic community; one who purifies and restores true Islamic practice; one mujaddid is to be sent at the beginning of each century

mujtahid: expert in Islamic law; one who exercises *ijtihad,* or independent reasoning, in legal matters; one capable of interpreting Islamic law

Muslim: one who submits or surrenders himself or herself to God and his will; one who follows Islam

People of the Book (*Ahl al-Kitab*): those possessing a revelation or scripture from God; typically refers to Jews and Christians, sometimes includes Zoroastrians

purdah: seclusion of women from men who are not relatives; segregation of the sexes

qiyas: legal term for analogical reasoning

al-Quds: the holy city (i.e., Jerusalem)

Quran: revelation, recitation, message; Muslim scripture

Ramadan: month of fasting; ninth month of the Muslim calendar

salat: official prayer or worship performed five times each day

shahadah: declaration of faith, witness, testimony; refers to the declaration of Muslim faith: "There is no god but God and Muhammad is His Messenger"

shariah: Islamic law; straight path

shaykh: master, teacher, leader; head of a *Sufi* order, also known as *pir*

Shi or Shiah: follower(s), partisan(s); refers to those who followed the leadership of Ali, the nephew and son-in-law of Muhammad, as Muhammad's successor, those who believe that leadership of the Muslim community should belong to Muhammad's descendants

shirk: polytheism, idolatry, association of anyone or anything with God; the biggest sin in Islam

shura: consultation; today some have interpreted this concept as prescribing democracy

Sufi: literally "one who wears wool"; Muslim mystic or ascetic

Sufism: Islamic mysticism or asceticism

Sunnah: example; typically refers to Muhammad's example, which is believed by Muslims to be the living out of the principles of the *Quran;* "Sunni" is derived from this word

Sunni: those who accept the *sunna* and the historic succession of the Caliphs; the majority of the Muslim community

surah: chapter, particularly of the *Quran*

tajdid: revival, renewal

tariqah: path, way; used by Sufis to designate order to which they belong

tawhid: oneness, unity and uniqueness of God; absolute monotheism

ulama (sing. *alim*): religious scholars

ummah: Muslim community of believers

wali: friend or protege of God; *Sufi* term referring to saint; one reputed to have the power to bilocate, cure the sick, multiply food, and read minds

zakat: almsgiving, one of the Five Pillars of Islam: 2.5 percent tithe on one's net worth to help the poor is required of all Muslims

HINDUISM

ahimsa: nonviolence, the ideal of doing no killing, especially for its karmic effects

atman: in Hindu thought, the soul that resides in the heart, is the source of both life energy and spiritual awareness, and transmigrates after death

avatara: "incarnation" of the gods that descends to earth; avataras assume life-forms that aid creation, usually to defeat demons and overcome evil

Bhagavad Gita: Hindu scripture inserted into the great epic, the *Mahabharata*, extolling the divinity of Krishna as the ultimately real deity

bhakti: devotionalism to a divinity, a means to reach salvation from the world of rebirth

BJP *(Bharatiya Janata party)*: Hindu nationalism party that rose meteorically in popularity in the 1990s and assumed national rule in 1998

Brahman: world spirit that arises at creation, which Hindus hold is either in impersonal form, *nirguna Brahman*, or human form, *saguna Brahman*

brahmin: member of the highest caste, innately possessing the highest natural purity; the men traditionally specialize in ritual performance, textual memorization and study, and theology

dharma: "duty" determined by one's caste and gender

guru: a teacher in matters spiritual and cultural, whom disciples regard as semi-divine

Kali Yuga: the dark age the world has now entered, when human spiritual capacity is thought to be diminished; a view shared by some Hindus and Buddhists

karma: literally "action," but also meaning the effects of actions that, through a hidden natural causality, condition a being's future; Hindus fix karma as acting on the inborn soul, Buddhists define its effects on the consciousness and habits

moksha: "release" from *samsara*, freedom from future rebirth and redeath (i.e., salvation)

nirguna Brahman: see *Brahman*

puja: a ritual offering to a Hindu or bodhisattva deity, Buddha or bodhisattva

puranas: texts extolling the histories, theologies, and necessary rituals for expressing the *bhakti* faith for the different Hindu deities

Ramakrishna Mission: founded by Swami Vivekananda to further the teachings of his guru, Ramakrishna; an influential Hindu missionary and reform organization that today runs hospitals, schools, and temples and has centers in over a dozen countries

Ramanuja: an influential theologian (1025–1137) who argued that the ultimate reality humans could relate to was *saguna Brahman*

RSS (Rashtriya Svayamsevak Sangh): "National Union of [Hindu] Volunteers," a group that since 1923 has proposed a nativist definition of "Hinduism" as devotion to "Mother India"

saguna Brahman: see *Brahman*

samsara: "the world" of rebirth subject to the law of karma and the inevitable reality of death, a religious understanding shared by Hinduism, Buddhism, Jainism, and Sikhism

Shaivite: devotee of Shiva

Shankara: Hindu philosopher (788–820) and monastic organizer, whose monistic interpretation of the *Upanishads* became the most influential expression of *nirguna Brahman* doctrine

tantra: the esoteric tradition common to both Hinduism and Buddhism that employs practices that defy caste and gender orthopraxy to lead individuals to *moksha/nirvana* quickly

Upanishads: appendices to the Vedas that record early Hindu speculations on *Brahman, atman,* the means to realize their identity, and *moksha*

Vaishnavite: devotee of Vishnu or his incarnations

Veda: the collection of the earliest Hindu hymns directed to the pantheon of deities, including ritual directions and chanting notations for their use

yoga: a term meaning "union" that refers to the various means of realizing union with the divine; earliest use of yoga refers to ascetic practices but expands to include the path of philosophical inquiry, *bhakti,* and *tantra*

Yoga sutras: codification of yoga practices, attributed to Patanjali

BUDDHISM

anatman: "no soul," the doctrine denying the reality of a permanent, immortal soul as the spiritual center of the human being

arhat: an enlightened disciple, according to the Theravada school; an advanced disciple, according to the Mahayana

Bodh Gaya: the site of Shakyamuni Buddha's enlightenment, under a tree

bodhisattva: a Buddha to be, either in the present life or in a future life; in the Mahayana tradition, all individuals should aspire to be Buddhas, hence the bodhisattva is the highest human role; some future Buddhas can be reborn as deities, hence in Mahayana Buddhism there are also bodhisattvas who can assist humans

Buddha: literally, one who has "awakened," ended karmic bondage, and will no longer be reborn; one who will enter *nirvana*

dependent coarising/origination: a twelve-part formula explaining how individuals are bound to future rebirth until they extirpate desire and ignorance

Dharma: the Buddha's teaching, one of the three refuges; more broadly, the truth at the center of Buddhism, the basis for realizing enlightenment

Eightfold Path: the eight qualities needed to reach nirvana, concerning morality, meditation, and salvific wisdom

engaged Buddhism: a reformist movement among global Buddhists seeking to relate the teachings to contemporary suffering

Enlightenment: see *nirvana*

Four Good Deeds: a doctrinal formula guiding the laity on the uses of wealth, advising the pursuit of happiness, security, philanthropy, and ritual

Four Noble Truths: a doctrinal formula focusing on diagnosing the human condition as marked by suffering and distorted by desire, then prescribing the Eightfold Path as a solution

karuna: compassion, the quality that motivated the Buddha to preach and the principal Buddhist social virtue

koan: a Buddhist spiritual riddle desgined to foster spiritual growth, posed by monastic teacher to junior monks, such as "What is the sound of one hand clapping?" or "Does a dog have a Buddhist nature?"

Lotus Sutra: one of the earliest and most influential *Mahayana* Buddhist texts, which reveals the cosmological nature of a Buddha and the universal character of Buddhist truth

Madhyamaka: a *Mahayana* philosophical school that posits the provisional and incomplete nature of all assertions; its goal is to clear away attachment even for words, making realization possible

Mahayana: the "Great Vehicle" that was the dominant school of Buddhism in Tibet and East Asia; the Mahayana philosophical schools developed cosmological theories of Buddhahood and envisioned the universe permeated by bodhisattvas, some of whom were like deities and the focus of ritual veneration

maitri: loving-kindness, a Buddhist ethical virtue and topic of meditation

merit: (see *punya*)

nirvana: a blissful state achieved by individuals who have cut off their karma by ending desire, attachment, and ignorance; after death, they enter the final trans-personal state for eternity, free from future rebirth

Pali canon: the only complete canon among the early collection of Buddha's teachings, in this case in the Pali language derived from Sanskrit; it is divided into three divisions: *Vinaya* (monastic code), *Sutras* (sermons), and *Abhidhamma* (advanced teaching formula)

prajna: the "insight" or "wisdom" necessary for enlightenment in Buddhism, comprising the ability to "see clearly" into the nature of existence as marked by suffering, impermanence, and absence of a soul

"Protestant Buddhism": a term signifying a pattern of reform in which Buddhists protested colonial rule yet adopted perspectives and missionary techniques of Protestant Christianity

punya: merit, or the good karma that enters into the content of an individual's life earned in Buddhist doctrine by moral practices, learning, and meditation

Pure Land: in *Mahayana* Buddhism, the belief that Buddhas and advanced bodhi-sattvas can through their inexhaustible merit create rebirth realms where humans can easily engage in Buddhist practices conducive to enlightenment

sangha: the Buddhist monastic community of monks and nuns

shramana: wandering ascetics known at the time of the Buddha

skandha: an aggregate, used in Buddhist thought to identify each of the five components that define a human being: the physical body (*rupa*), feelings (*vedana*), perceptions (*samjna*), habitual mental dispositions (*samskaras*), and consciousness (*vijnana*)

Sthaviravadins: the traditionalists among the early Buddhist monastic schools, the only surviving school today being the Theravadins

stupa: the distinctive Buddhist shrine, a raised mound surmounted by a ceremonial pole and umbrella; contains the relics of a Buddha or enlightened saint, either the literal bodily relics or other items left behind such as words in textual form or clothing items worn

Theravada: traditionalists, the last surviving Buddhist school of elders (Sthaviravadins) that is now dominant in South and Southeast Asia

Three Marks of Existence: the Buddhist terms for analyzing human reality as marked by impermanence, suffering, and no soul

Three Refuges: see *Triratna*

Thunder Vehicle: see *Vajrayana*

Triratna: the "Three Jewels" that every Buddhist takes refuge in for all rituals: the Buddha, the Dharma, and the Sangha

Vajrayana: the Mahayana-derived Buddhist tantric "vehicle" of belief and practice that uses unorthodox means, including sexual experience, to propel individuals quickly toward enlightenment

Vipasyana (Vipassana): the widespread Buddhist meditation practice focusing on calming the mind and discerning the truly real

vihara: a Buddhist monastery

Zen: the Japanese *Mahayana* Buddhist school focused on meditation practice, as transmitted from and organized in China as the Chan

EAST ASIAN RELIGIONS

Amaterasu: the *kami* of the sun and progenitor of the Japanese imperial line

Analects: collection of sayings attributed to *Confucius*

ancestor veneration: worship, feeding, and petitioning of the souls of dead ancestors at family graves, temples, or home altars

Ch'ondogyo: Korean movement reaffirming the truth of human dignity and the vitality of *Daoism* and *Confucianism*

city god: Chinese deity with influence on spirits living within city precincts, to whom every family's *kitchen god* reported at year's end

Confucianism: culture of the literate elite (*rujia*) informed by *Confucius* and his disciples, who mastered the classics and rituals; the moral tradition upholding the "three bonds" and the "three principles" as the basis of social life; the spiritual tradition of revering ancestors as part of the family bond

Confucius: see *Master K'ung*

Cultural Revolution: period from 1966 to 1976 when China's Communist party, under leadership of Mao Zedong, attacked religious traditions and practitioners

Dao: mysterious power that moves the universe and all beings

Daoism, philosophical: Chinese tradition advocating the way to harmony for individual and society based on understanding natural forces and flowing with life naturally

Daoism, religious: Chinese tradition that cultivates individual immortality through either alchemical infusions or meditative practices

Daruma-san: Japanese name for the monk Bodhidharma, who brought a meditative-centered Buddhist tradition to China, which would be called Zen in Japan

de: mysterious and spontaneous energy of the universe

diffuse religion: spiritual tradition centered on family and locality, informed by common ideas from *Confucianism, Daoism,* and Buddhism

Five Classics: Confucian canon attributed to Master K'ung: *Book of Changes (Yi-Jhing), Book of Documents (Shu Jing), Book of Poetry (Shi Jing), Book of Rites(Li Jing),* and a historical work that uses events in the early Chinese state to show how to assess praise and blame

Guan Yu: Chinese god of war, regarded as protector of merchants

Hong Xiuquan (1814–1864): charismatic instigator of the *Taiping Rebellion,* whose trance experiences led him to believe that he was the "younger brother" of Jesus; charged with establishing a new state in China

Huang-di: "Yellow Emperor," first immortal in *religious Daoism*

jun-zi: a Confucian gentleman who has cultivated character and learning

kami: deity of Japan associated with places, certain animals, and the emperor

kitchen god (Zao Wangye): deity residing in every household, thought to observe and report on family events to his celestial superiors yearly

Lao Zi (Lao Tzu): "Old Sage," reputed author of *Daodejing* and founder of *Daoism*

li: in Confucian thought, individual performances needed for personal development, including manners, service to others, and rituals

ling: spiritual force possessed by geographic places such as rivers, mountains, caves, as well as by deities and charismatic sages

literati tradition: see *Confucianism*

mappo: Buddhist doctrine of the world in decline, especially in that humans cannot practice meditation as well as in the time of the Buddha

Master K'ung: sage (551–479 BCE) given Latin name to whom Catholic missionaries later gave the Latinate name, *Confucius*

Mencius: first major disciple of *Master K'ung,* a systematizer of Confucian ideals who lived 371–289 BCE

***Mizuko* cult:** the newly popularized Japanese tradition of ritual apology and merit transfer to the spirits of aborted fetuses

mudang: Korean shaman

nembutsu: repetition of the name of the Buddha Amitabha, for the purpose of making merit and gaining rebirth in the Pure Land

neo-Confucianism: tradition originating in Song dynasty and developed subsequently by masters such as Zhu Xi who sought to harmonize early Confucian humanism with more cosmological theories of *Daoism* and *karma* doctrine of Buddhism, adopting meditation techniques from both

neo-Shintoism (or state Shinto): Meiji state's adoption of *Shinto* as state religion, with emperor as focal divinity, that lasted from 1868 to 1945

"new religions": sects arising in Japan from the early nineteenth century combining elements of Buddhism, *Daoism,* and *Confucianism* with ideas imported from abroad; term may be applied outside Japan

Nichiren: thirteenth-century Buddhist monk who taught that the *Lotus Sutra* was sole true Buddhist text and that chanting its title was an essential salvation practice; founded new school based on these ideas

qi: vital force of life within individuals and in nature

qi gong: discipline of cultivating the vital individual life force that can be used for worldly goals such as healing or to reach immortality

Qing-Ming festival: yearly spring festival when Chinese visit and clean family graves, then feast after making offerings to the ancestors

ren: Confucian ideal of being "fully human" in ethics, manners, cultivation

shamanism: tradition by which human mediums are possessed by spirits and communicate with the living; called in China, *wu/xi or fa-shih;* in Korea, *mudang*

Shang-di: Heavenly Lord, thought to preside over early Chinese pantheon; term Christians used to translate "God"

shen: usual term in Chinese for a kindly god or goddess

Shinto: indigenous religion of Japan that reveres the deities of the islands including the emperor

Soka Gakkai: *Nichiren* Buddhist offshoot, now global religion seeking world peace through Mahayana Buddhist teachings

Taiping Rebellion: nineteenth-century revolt in China led by converts to Christianity, who established a separate state in city of Nanjing; resulting civil war was bloodiest in world history

Three Faiths: Chinese grouping of the three great traditions: *Confucianism, Daoism,* and Buddhism

t'i: affection for siblings, in Confucianism a marker of character

Tian: "heaven" understood as impersonal yet responsive to human actions

T'oegyehak: modern Korean Confucian group based on teachings of master Yi T'oegye (1501–1570)

Tu-di (or Tu Chu): "Earth Ruler," local god who controls earth's fertility

Unification Church: Korean *"new religion"* founded by Rev. Sun Myung Moon, who claims to be completing the work of Jesus as a messiah by establishing a global community

wu-wei: "noninterference" or "non-[forced] action," an ideal in *Daoism*

xiao: Confucian ideal of children honoring their parents, attitude that extends to the ruler

yin-yang theory: twin forces by which the Dao is known, each complementing the other (female–male, valley–mountain, etc.)

Zhu Xi: great Chinese master of neo-Confucian thought who integrated into _Confucianism_ elements of Buddhism and _Daoism_ and established core rituals of subsequent tradition

Zhuang Zi: second great s

CHRISTIANITY

31 CE	Crucifixion of Jesus of Nazareth
48–60	Letters of Paul of Tarsus
70	Fall of the Jewish temple in Jerusalem to the Romans Gospel of Mark written
80–100	Gospels of Matthew and Luke and John written
313	Edict of Milan by Constantine permitting Christianity in Roman Empire
325	Council of Nicaea declares Word of God to be same as (*homoousios*) God
380	Christianity declared the official religion of the Roman Empire by Emperor Theodosius
451	Council of Chalcedon, doctrine of two natures and one substance in Christ
500s	Development of Benedictine monasticism in the West
590–604	Pontificate of Gregory the Great, first great pope of Middle Ages
732	Muslim invasion of Europe stopped at Tours by Charles Martel
800	Coronation of Charlemagne
1095	First Crusade against Muslims and mass violence against Jews
1184	Inauguration of church inquisitions by Pope Lucius III
1198–1216	Pontificate of Innocent III, most powerful pope in history
1224–1274	St. Thomas Aquinas, greatest theologian of Middle Ages
1414	Council of Constance—papal decadence and the declaration of conciliar rule in the church
1517	Luther's Ninety-five Theses posted on church door at Wittenberg, beginning of Protestant Reformation
1545–1563	Council of Trent, Catholic Counter-Reformation

1555	Peace of Augsburg—first attempt to end religious wars of the Reformation
1648	Peace of Westphalia—end of religious wars, quest for religious tolerance
1703–1791	John Wesley, founder of Methodism
1768–1834	Friedrich Schleiermacher, father of modern theology
1791	1st Amendment to US Constitution
1813–1855	Søren Kierkegaard, Christian existentialism
1851	Karl Marx publishes *Communist Manifesto*
1859	Charles Darwin publishes *On the Origin of Species*
1869–1870	First Vatican Council
1910–1915	Publication of *The Fundamentals* begins fundamentalist/modernist controversy
1939–1945	World War II and the Holocaust
August 6, 1945	Atomic bomb dropped on Hiroshima, Japan, leading to end of World War II
1947	India achieves independence; Church of South India is formed
1950s, 1960s	Emergence of civil rights movement under Martin Luther King Jr. Pope John XXIII and the 2nd Vatican Council
1970s–1990s	Religious resurgence of evangelical fundamentalism and emergence of liberation theology movements
2005	Death of Pope John Paul II

JUDAISM

2000 BCE	Abraham
1280	Moses, Exodus, and covenant
1240	Conquest of land of Canaan under Joshua
1004–965	King David
721	Fall of northern kingdom of Israel to Assyrians
586	Fall of southern kingdom of Judah to Babylonians
538	Return from Exile
198–167	Maccabean revolt against enforced Hellenization
63	Beginning of rule by Rome
c. 30 CE	Hillel and Shammai—first of the Tannaim
70	Destruction of the second temple
73	Fall of Zealot fortress at Masada
90	Emergence of Academy at Yavneh

90–200	Formation of the Mishnah
200–500	Formation of the Gemara
1070	Founding of Talmudic academy by Rashi in Troyes, France
1095	First Crusade—beginnings of pogroms—mass slaughter of Europe's Jews
1306	Jews expelled from France, beginning of pattern repeated throughout Europe
1700–1760	Hasidic leader Israel ben Eliezer, the Ba'al Shem Tov
1729–1786	Moses Mendelssohn, leading figure in Jewish *Haskalah* (Enlightenment) movement/Reform Judaism
1808–1888	Samson Raphael Hirsch, leading figure in emergence of Orthodox Judaism
1860–1904	Theodor Herzl, founder of modern Zionism
1917	Balfour Declaration—proposal for Jewish homeland in Palestine endorsed by British government
1933–1945	Rise and fall of Nazi party; the Holocaust, 6 million Jews murdered
1939–1945	World War II
May 14, 1948	Birth of state of Israel
May 11, 1949	Israel admitted to United Nations
1967	Six-Day War, followed by emergence of Judaism of Holocaust and Redemption
1973	Yom Kippur War, followed by growth of ultra-Orthodox movements
1979	Camp David peace treaty between Egypt and Israel
1980s	*Intifada*: Palestinian uprising and escalation of conflict between Palestinians and Israelis
1993	*Oslo Accord*, developing increased autonomy for Palestinians and the framework for negotiating peace with Israel, followed by continued violence on the part of radicals on both sides who view compromise as betrayal. Also continued tension between secular Israeli Jews and ultra-Orthodox Haredim and also between Israeli Haredim and Conservative and Reformed Jews of the Diaspora

ISLAM

c. 570	Birth of Muhammad
610	Muhammad receives first revelation, commemorated as "Night of Power and Excellence"
620	Muhammad's Night Journey to Jerusalem

622	Emigration (hijrah) of the Muslim community from Mecca to Medina; first year of the Muslim lunar calendar
632	Muhammad's final pilgrimage to Mecca, farewell sermon, and death
632–661	Rule of the Four Rightly Guided Caliphs, formative period for Sunnis
638	Muslim conquest of Jerusalem
661–750	Umayyad Empire
680	Martyrdom of Husayn and his followers at Karbala, Iraq
750–1258	Abbasid Empire: height of Islamic civilization, patronage of art and culture, development of Islamic law, and rising trade, agriculture, industry and commerce
756–1492	Andalusia (Muslim Spain): period of interfaith coexistence of Muslims, Christians, and Jews
765	Death of sixth Shii imam, Jafar al-Sadiq; succession disputed, causing split between Sevener and Twelver Shiis
8th–9th centuries	Formation of major Sunni law schools
1000–1492	Christian reconquest of Muslim-ruled territories in Spain, Sicily, and Italy
1095–1453	Crusades
12th century	Rise of Sufi orders
1187	Saladin and Muslim forces reconquer Jerusalem
1281–1924	Ottoman Empire (Middle East, North Africa, and portions of Eastern Europe)
1453	Fall of Constantinople/Istanbul, capital of former Byzantine Empire, to Ottomans
1483–1857	Mughal Empire (South Asia)
1501–1722	Safavid Empire (Iran)
1876–1938	Muhammad Iqbal, Islamic modernist and ideologue for foundation of Pakistan
1897–1975	Elijah Muhammad, leader of the Nation of Islam in the United States
1903–1979	Mawlana Abu Ala Mawdudi, founder of the Jamaat-i Islami in India/Pakistan
1906–1949	Hassan al-Banna, founder of the Muslim Brotherhood in Egypt
1906–1966	Sayyid Qutb, radical, militant ideologue of the Muslim Brotherhood in 1950s and 1960s
1975	Wallace D. Muhammad (name later changed to Warith Deen Muhammad) succeeds his father Elijah Muhammad and progressively brings his followers into conformity with mainstream Sunni Islam
1979	Iranian Revolution and foundation of Iranian Islamic Republic under leadership of Ayatollah Khomeini; seizure of the Grand Mosque in Mecca by Muslim militants; Soviet Union invades Afghanistan

1989	FIS (Islamic Salvation Front) sweeps municipal elections in Algeria; Tunisia bars Renaissance Party (formerly MTI) from participation in elections; death of Ayatollah Khomeini in Iran
1990	FIS wins Algerian municipal and regional elections
1993	Bombing of World Trade Center in New York City by Muslim militants
1995	Welfare (Refah) party wins parliamentary; Dr. Necmettin Erbakan becomes Turkey's first Islamist prime minister
1998	US Embassies in Tanzania and Kenya bombed by Muslim militants
September 11, 2001	Terrorist attacks against the World Trade Center in New York City and the Pentagon in Washington, D.C. sparks U.S. led war against global terrorism and the hunt for Osama bin Laden and al-Qaeda
2004	French Parliament bans Muslim headscarf in schools and public places

HINDUISM

ca. 3500–1800 BCE	Indus Valley civilization in northwestern South Asia
1500 BCE	Decline of major Indus cities; populations migrate east to Gangetic plain
1500–500 BCE	Period of Vedic civilization
900–400 BCE	Shramana period of wandering ascetics and composition of the Upaniṣads
300–100 BCE	Texts of brahmanical orthodoxy formulated (e.g., *Laws of Manu*)
100 BCE–400 CE	Composition of devotional texts and epics *Ramayana* and *Mahabharata*
50 BCE–300 CE	Composition of the *Bhagavad Gita* and Patanjali's *Yoga Sutras*
100 CE–700 CE	Hinduism established along rim of Indian Ocean in Southeast Asia
320–647	Classical temple Hinduism established
500–ff	Development of Advaita *Vedanta* school; textual expressions of Hindu tantrism as counterculture
788–820	Life of Shankara, *Vedanta* school exponent of Advaita Vedanta and creator of Hindu monasticism
800–1200	Six brahmanical schools established as divisions in elite philosophical Hinduism
1025–1137	Life of Ramanuja, philosophical defender of *bhakti* faith
1200–1757	Muslim rule of North India; Buddhism virtually extinguished in South Asia

1420–1550	Era of great devotional saints (e.g., Mirabai, Ravidas, Kabir, Chaitanya, Surdas)
1469–1539	Life of Nanak, the founder of the Sikh faith
1526–1707	Mughal dynasty; Muslim rulers alternate between anti-Hindu and ecumenical policies
1708	Death of tenth guru, Gobind Singh; Sikh text *Adi Grantha* declared guru of the community
1757–1857	British East India Company dominates Indian political life
1815	Christian missionaries present in most cities and towns of British India
1828	Founding of the Brahmo Sabha (later Brahmo Samaj) by Rammohan Roy
1834–1886	Life of Ramakrishna, charismatic guru with ecumenical teaching
1858–1947	After uprising, British crown assumes direct rule over India; South Asian ethnic groups recruited for government service spread Hinduism globally
1863–1902	Life of Swami Vivekananda, Ramakrishna's disciple, who led global Ramakrishna Mission
1875	Foundation of the Arya Samaj by Swami Dayananda Saraswati
1893	Speeches by Swami Vivekananda inspire interest at Parliament of World Religions in Chicago
1920–1948	M.K. Gandhi (1869–1948) leads civil disobedience campaigns, articulating ecumenical Hindu reformism influenced by Western culture
1923	Founding of the Rastriya Svayamsevak Sangh (RSS), Hindu nationalist group
1940	Ashram established by Sathya Sai Baba, beginning of large global movement
1947	Independence of India from Britain; prime minister, J. Nehru, declares India a secular state
1948	Gandhi assassinated by Hindu extremist
1964	Vishva Hindu Parishad (VHP) founded to unite Hindu leaders and devotees worldwide
1964	International Society for Krishna Consciousness (ISKON) established by Bhaktivedanta (1896–1977)
1984	Sikh extremists occupy Golden Temple in Amritsar; armed removal by Indian army; assassination of the prime minister, Indira Gandhi
1987	Weekly Indian television series *Ramayana* inspires rising sentiments of Hindu nationalism
1992	Hindu agitation in Ayodhya culminates in destruction of Babri Mosque; Hindu–Muslim riots across South Asia
1998	The Bharatiya Janta party (BJP), a Hindu nationalist political party, wins parliamentary majority for the first time; rules until 2004

BUDDHISM

563 BCE	Birth of Siddhartha [some traditions give 483 BCE]
528	Enlightenment of Shakyamuni, the Buddha; creation of the *sangha*, the monastic order
c. 510	Establishment of nuns' order
483	Death of the Buddha [some traditions give 360 BCE]
482	First Council collects and organizes oral accounts
383	Council of Vaishali leads to the first split in the sangha
273–232	Reign of Ashoka, convert to Buddhism, who spread Buddhism throughout India and beyond (Afghanistan, Burma, Ceylon)
250	Council of Pataliputra leads to division in "18 schools"
240	Sanchi *stupa* and other *stupas* built across India; relic cult at *stupas* central to community
c. 100	Origins of the Mahayana school, beginning with *Prajnaparamita* literature
80	First collections of written canon begun, beginning with the Vinaya, the monastic code; Pali Canon collection begun in Ceylon
c. 85 CE	Composition of the *Lotus Sutra*
50–180	Spread of Buddhism into central Asia via the Silk Road
124	Buddhist monks in western China
c. 200	Writings of Nagarjuna, the most influential Mahayana philosopher; Madhyamaka school formed
220–589	Buddhist missions reach Southeast Asia, Java, Sumatra, Korea, Japan, Vietnam; Buddhist monasteries established throughout China in era of weak central state
c. 300	Rituals and visualization meditations dedicated to bodhisattvas developed by Mahayana monks
c. 300	Origins of Pure Land school in India
320ff	Development of Yogacara school, led by monastic brothers Asanga and Vasubandhu
c. 425	Writings of a monk who shaped the Theravada school, Buddhaghosa, in Ceylon
c. 500	Rise of the Vajrayana Thunderbolt school in India, which eventually dominates Buddhist communities in Northeastern India, Nepal, and Tibet
c. 600	Formation of the Ch'an school in China inspired by teachings of the Indian monk Bodhidharma
700–1270	Buddhism dominates Sri Vijaya kingdom on Sumatra–Java; rulers build Borobodur *stupa*
749	First Buddhist monastery in Tibet

760–1142	Pala Dynasty rules North India, patronizes Buddhist monasteries and promotes Mahayana traditions; tradition in decline elsewhere in India
841–845	Extensive destruction of monasteries in China and defrocking of Buddhist monks and nuns
900ff	Restoration of Chinese Buddhism, principally the Pure Land and Ch'an schools
c. 1000	Second introduction of monastic Mahayana Buddhism into Tibet from India
1192	Muslim rule established across northern India; final destruction of Indian monasteries and decline of Bodh Gaya as center of Buddhist pilgrimage
1193–1227	In Japan, formation of new schools: Zen brought from China by Eisei (1141–1215) and Dogen (1200–1253); Pure Land by Honen (1133–1212) and Shinran (1173–1262), and school founded by Nichiren (1222–1282)
1000–1400	Era of Pagan Kingdom in Burma, establishing one of the great centers of Buddhism
1642–1959	Tibet dominated by Gelugpa monastic school under the Dalai and Panchen lamas
1815–1948	Era of British colonial rule. Conflicts in Ceylon lead to reformist movement styled "Protestant Buddhism" that influences Buddhists across Asia
1851–1868	Rule of King Monghut in Siam, who revived the sangha and placed it under state control
1864–1933	Anagarika Dharmapala, Ceylonese reformist, founder of the Mahabodhi Society who spread reformism across Asia
1871–1876	Heavy Meiji persecution of Buddhism; 70% of monasteries lost as 75% of monks defrocked
1871	Fifth Buddhist Council held in Burma
1877–1945	Buddhist establishment in Japan supports nationalism, militarism, and seizures of Korea, Taiwan, and northern China
1893	Parliament of World Religions in Chicago; speeches by Zen monk and Dharmapala stir interest
1944	Buddhist Churches of America, a Pure Land organization, founded in California
1945	Soka Gokkai established in Japan, a branch of Nichiren school until 1991
1949–1976	Chinese Communist government persecutes Buddhists and seizes 250,000 monasteries and temples, with the Cultural Revolution (1966–1969) a period of intense destruction
1954–1956	Sixth Buddhist Council in Rangoon, Burma, culminating in the marking of the 2,500-year anniversary of Shakyamuni's death

1956	Foundation of the Mahasangha Sahayaka Gana in central India, a Buddhist organization
1959–present	Exile of the fourteenth Dalai Lama from Tibet and the era of the globalization of Tibetan Buddhism
1976–present	Slow restoration of Buddhist institutions in China
1982–present	Civil war against Tamil minority in Sri Lanka polarizes Buddhist community
1987	Founding of Shakyaditya, a worldwide organization of Buddhist women
1989	Foundation of the International Network of Engaged Buddhists by Thai activist Sulak Sivaraksha
1990	Revival of Buddhism in Mongolia after 88 years of suppression
1991	Founding of *Tricycle,* a Buddhist mass market magazine in America
1998–present	Full ordination taken by Theravada nuns in Chinese monasteries, reviving a lost tradition

EAST ASIAN RELIGIONS

1766–1122 BCE	Shang dynasty in China; cult of departed ancestors and oracle bone divination practiced
1122–221	Zhou dynasty in China; yin-yang theory develops; era of intermittent civil disorder
c. 551–479	Life of Master K'ung (Confucius)
c. 520–286	Era of first Daoist sages, philosophers Lao Zi (d. 500 BCE?) and Zhuang Zi (365–290 BCE)
450–223	Era of Confucian sage scholars, Master Meng (Mencius, 371–289 BCE), Master Xun (298–238 BCE); origins of Confucian *Analects* and compilation of the *Five Classics*
221–206	Qin dynasty, the first to unify China; Great Wall completed
200 BCE–220 CE	Han dynasty in China; civil service based upon Confucian teachings
220–588 CE	Period of weak central state and the growth of Daoism and Buddhism
c. 450	"Three Caves" of Daoist scriptures collected
618–907	T'ang dynasty in China; period of Confucian revival; translations of Indian Buddhist texts
668–918	Silla dynasty in Korea, centered on Buddhism as state religion
710–784	Nara period in Japan; Shinto tradition organized; Buddhism made state religion

794–1185	Heian period in Japan, ends with emperor removed from rulership
918–1392	Koryo dynasty in Korea, with ecumenical development of Mahâyâna Buddhism
960–1279	Song dynasty in China; period of neo-Confucianism (the "Second Epoch")
c. 1150	Goddess Mazu becomes popular in China, recognized by the state
1130–1200	Life of Zhu Xi, leading neo-Confucian exponent, who reestablished the tradition as preeminent among the Chinese literati
1185–1333	Kamakura era in Japan, era of civil disorder and the rise of new Buddhist schools
1279–1368	Yuan dynasty in China, era of Mongol rule
1336–1600	Ashikaga period in Japan; era of Shinto–Buddhist syncretism, popularity of Pure Land Buddhism adoption of Zen among the literati
1368–1644	Ming dynasty in China, the last era of Han Chinese rule; doctrine of harmonizing the "three faiths"
1380ff	In China, *The Canonization of the Gods* fixes folk pantheon in hierarchy mirroring state bureaucracy
1392–1910	Yi dynasty in Korea, an era marked by state-favored Confucianism
1472–1529	Life of Wang Yangming, a neo-Confucian who promoted mind cultivation and character development
1501–1570	Life of Yi T'oegye, important Korean neo-Confucian
1534–1582	Life of Nobunaga, Japanese shogun who persecuted Buddhism and gave support to Christianity
1592	Publication of *Journey the West* written by Wu Cheng-en
1600–1867	Tokugawa era in Japan, with capital in Tokyo; Buddhism under strong state support
1644–1911	Qing (Manchu) dynasty in China; era promoting Confucianism
1815–1888	Oldest new religions in Japan: Kurozumikyo (1814), Tenrikyo (1838)
1850–1864	Taiping Rebellion in China, led by Hong Xiuquan (1814–1864)
1860	Ch'ondogyo movement founded in Korea by Ch'oe Suun (1824–1864)
1868–1945	Return of emperor's rule in Japan and the rise of state Shinto; Japan adopts Western calendar, technology, imperialist political views
1871–1945	Japanese Buddhist establishment joins Shinto nationalists and Christians in support of militarism
1880–present	Best and brightest individuals across the East Asia region studying Western learning, technology to seek rapid modernization
1889–1890	New constitution and Japanese government initiatives draw heavily on Confucian doctrines
1912	Fall of Qing dynasty in China, ending state patronage of Confucianism

1900–1945	Founding of "new religions" in pre-War Japan: P.L. Kyodan in 1924; Reikukai Kyodan in 1925, Soka Gakkai in 1930, Rissho Koseikai in 1938
1946–present	Founding of "new 'new religions'" in post-War Japan: Sukyo Mahikari in 1963, Agonshu in 1971, Aum Shinrikyo in 1989
1949–1976	People's Republic of China established; Communist party persecutes monks, priests, institutions
1966–1976	Cultural Revolution brings renewed persecution of religions and adherents in China
1984–present	Buddhist monasteries and Daoist temples reopen, many with newly trained monks and nuns in residence; pilgrims visit major sites to perform traditional rites
1994	Study of Confucianism officially supported by Chinese state
1995	Aum Shinrikyo sect in Japan launches poison gas attack in Tokyo
1996–present	Return of traditional ancestor veneration to China; images of Mao Zedong and other deceased Communist party leaders found on popular religious amulets
1999	Falun Gong, a syncretistic Buddhist–Daoist group founded by Li Hongzhu claiming 100 million followers in 30 countries, protests in Beijing; within months, Chinese government bans the group and begins persecution of practitioners

INDEX

Abbasid Dynasty, 208, 210, 211, 212, 214, 226, 228, 229, 239
Abbots, 66, 345
Abd Allah, 198
Abd al-Raziq, Ali, 239
Abduh, Muhammad, 240, 241–42, 276
Abhissheka, 404
Abraham, 20, 538, 539
   in Christianity, 52, 54, 69, 70, 71
   in Islam, 188, 197, 200, 201, 202, 203, 204, 218, 219, 271
   in Judaism, 120, 121, 122, 125, 128, 140, 173
Abu Bakr, 204, 208, 209, 210
Abu Hanifa, 214
Abu Talib, 198
Acupuncture, 446, 496
Adam, 20, 38, 61, 110, 121, 140, 150, 154, 168, 202, 253, 511, 538, 539
Adam's Peak, 408
Adi Granth, 320, 321
Advaita Vedanta, 312
Advent, 64
Afghanistan, 250, 252, 255, 257, 258, 259, 260, 264, 275, 277, 279, 380
Africa, 30, 109
   American embassy attacked in, 257
   Christianity in, 37, 92, 94–95, 98
   Islam in, 192, 212, 230, 235, 260, 266, 267
   liberation theology in, 94, 95
African Americans, 94, 104, 267, 268–71
Afterlife. *See also* Death rituals; Heaven; Hell
   in early Chinese religions, 449–50, 456
   in Hinduism, 295
Age of Aquarius, 531–32, 537
Aggadah, 132, 142, 143
Aggiornamento, 42, 43
Agha Khan, 211, 212
Agni, 295
Agonshu, 507–8, 541
Agudat Yisrael, 113, 118
Ahimsa, 327–28
Ahmad, Khurshid, 274
Ahmad, Mirza Ghulam, 526
Ahmad, Muhammad, 236–37
Ahmad Ibn Hanbal, 214
Ahmadiyyat, 526–27
AIDS/HIV, 308, 421
Aisha, 209
Ajima, 307
Akal Takht, 356
Akbar, Emperor, 320
Akshaya Tritaya, 339
Alberuni, 288
Albigensians, 68

Alchemy, 453, 454, 459, 473
Aleph, 541
Alexander the Great, 125, 380
Alexandria, 55
Alexius I, Emperor, 231–32
Alfred P. Murrah Federal Building (bombing of), 102
Algeria, 187, 194, 210, 250, 256, 263, 279
Ali, 198, 204, 209, 210, 212, 228
Ali, Muhammad (boxer), 269
Ali, Muhammad (Egyptian ruler), 237–38
Ali, Noble Drew, 268
Aligarh University, 242
Allah, 25, 196, 197, 199, 200, 202, 268
Allahabad River, 343
All-Buddhist Network Television, 424
All-India Action Committee, 415
All India Adi Dharma Mission, 316
All Souls Festival, 492, 493, 517
Almsgiving, 216, 217–18
Alpert, Richard, 333
Altneuland (Herzl), 166
Amar Citra Katha comic book series, 348
Amaterasu, 461–62, 483
Ambedkar, Bhimrao, 300–301, 429
Ambika, 307
American Methodist Church, 480
American Muslim Journal, 270
American Muslim Mission, 270–71
American University of Beirut, 238
Amida Buddha, 393, 466, 468, 486
Amish people, 77
Amitabha Buddha, 393, 400, 404, 466, 486
A-mi-to-fo, 393, 468, 486
Amoraim, 132, 133
Amos, 123, 198
Amritaanandamayi, 355
Amritsar, 320, 325, 356
Amulets, 228, 337, 489, 502, 503–4
Anabaptism, 77
Analects, 451, 472, 498
Analogical reasoning (qiyas), 214, 215
Anaology, way of. *See* Via analogia
Anatman, 385, 386, 404
Anatolia, 205, 231
Ancestor veneration, 447, 448, 449, 450, 456–57, 458, 496–97
   Christian view of, 479
   in Korea, 440, 509, 516
   Reiyukai Kyodan on, 484
Angels, 64–66, 532
Anglicanism, 77–78, 96, 99
Animal sacrifice, 219, 287, 342, 487
Anitya, 404
Anna Karenina (Tolstoy), 547